Archie®

THE MARRIED LIFE

TWO WORLDS. TWO LOVES. TWO DESTINIES.

ook Three

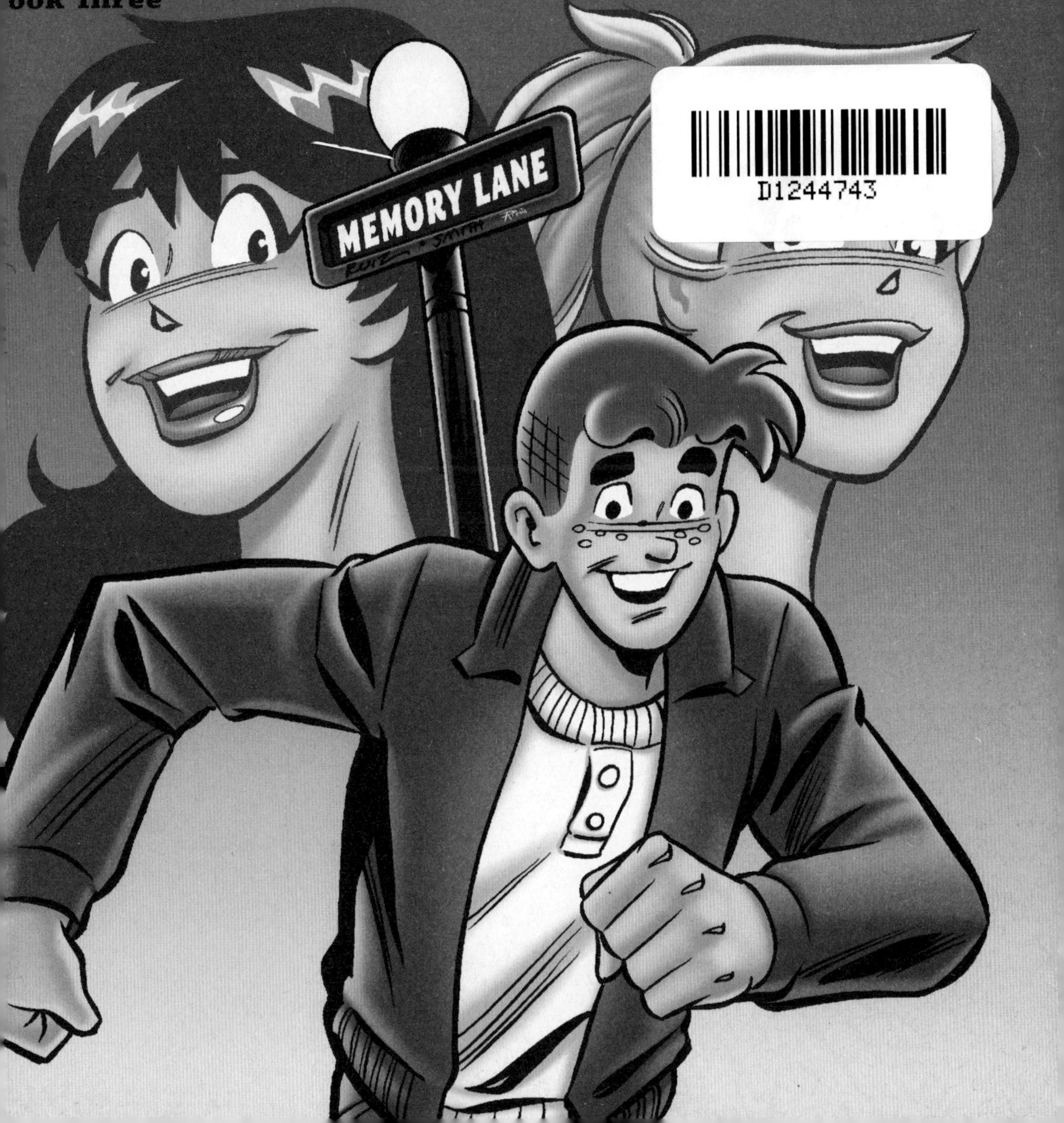
MEMORY LANE

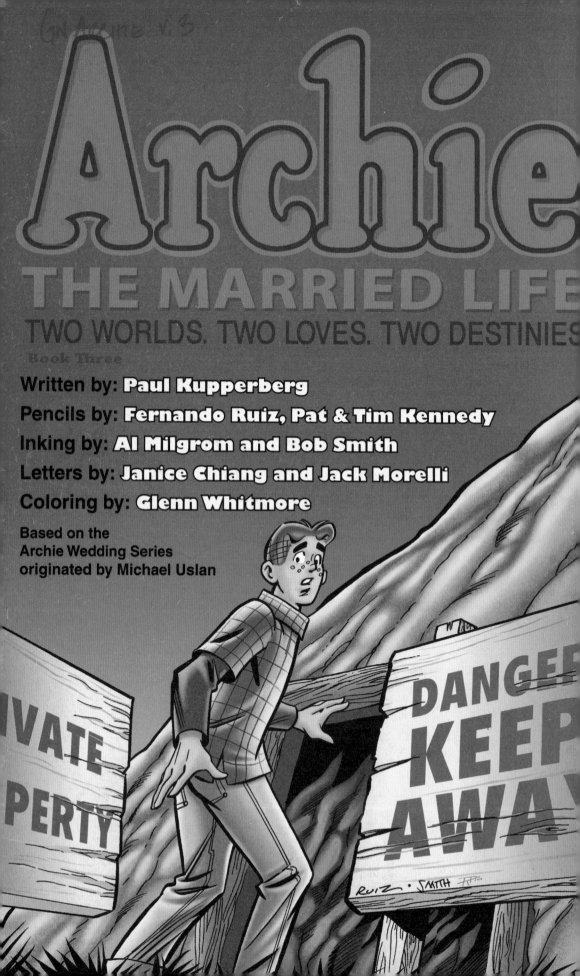

Archie

THE MARRIED LIFE

TWO WORLDS. TWO LOVES. TWO DESTINIES

Book Three

Written by: **Paul Kupperberg**

Pencils by: **Fernando Ruiz, Pat & Tim Kennedy**

Inking by: **Al Milgrom and Bob Smith**

Letters by: **Janice Chiang and Jack Morelli**

Coloring by: **Glenn Whitmore**

Based on the
Archie Wedding Series
originated by Michael Uslan

VATE
PERTY
DANGE
KEEP
AWA
RUIZ · SMITH

Archie®

THE MARRIED LIFE

TWO WORLDS. TWO LOVES. TWO DESTINIES.

Book Three

ARCHIE: THE MARRIED LIFE. BOOK THREE
Published by Archie Comic Publications, Inc.
325 Fayette Avenue, Mamaroneck, New York 10543-2318.

 ISBN: 978-1-936975-35-8
SECOND PRINTING. Printed in USA.

Publisher/Co-CEO: Jon Goldwater
Co-CEO: Nancy Silberkleit
President: Mike Pellerito
Co-President/Editor-In-Chief: Victor Gorelick
Chief Creative Officer: Roberto Aguirre-Sacasa
Senior Vice President - Sales & Business Development: Jim Sokolowski
Senior Vice President - Publishing & Operations: Harold Buchholz
Senior Vice President - Publicity & Marketing: Alex Segura
Executive Director of Editorial: Paul Kaminski
Production Manager: Stephen Oswald
Project Coordinator & Book Design: Joe Morciglio
Editorial Assistant / Proofreader: Jamie Lee Rotante
Production: Tito Peña, Jon Gray

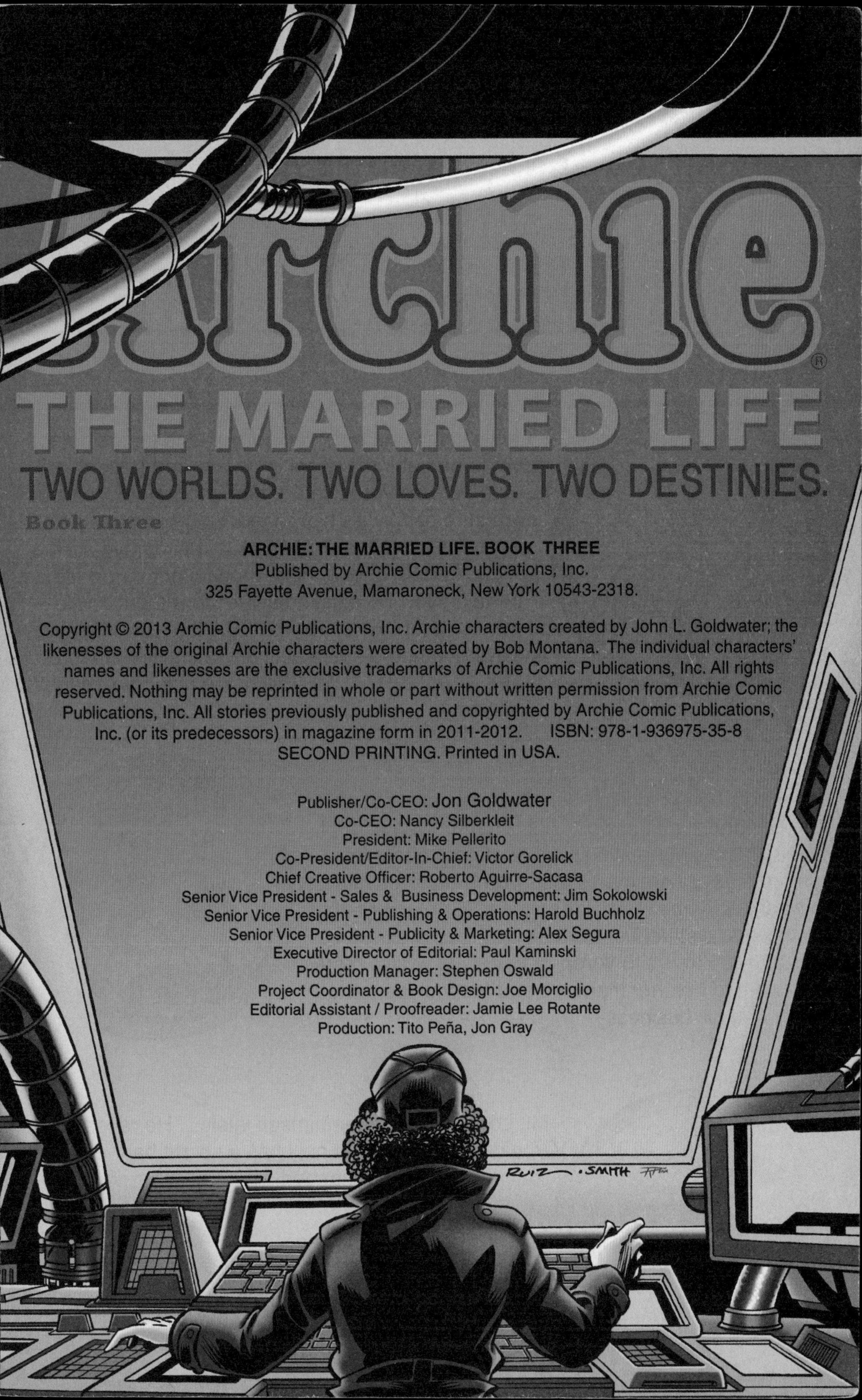

Two Worlds. Two Loves. Two Destinies.
In an alternate universe where anything can happen and what you think is familiar is anything but...

Archie Marries Veronica

Previously...

Archie's had a bumpy ride so far—and things do not seem to be getting any easier for our red-headed pal. He and his wife Veronica are now separated! He's not even sure of why it's happened, but he suspects foul play from someone very close to their family. Archie is certain of one thing, though: nothing in life is certain! Now he must adjust to life without a wife—and without a job! He's also realizing that the single life and living at home again ain't all it's cracked up to be. Will he be able to manage?

Veronica's been handling her situation well—but could she be handling it too well? She's been given a lot of damaging misinformation from her father about her marriage, and it seems as though she believes him more than she believes her husband. Could her father be trying to distract her from his own secret business maneuvers? It's up to Veronica to decide what's more important to her: her marriage and friendships or her father and his business?

Mr. Lodge hasn't been himself lately... He recently told Veronica that Archie not only has a secret bank account, but that he also demanded a million dollar dowry prior to their wedding! What would drive him to deceive his own daughter in such a cruel way? He's also framed Reggie to cover up his own illegal business dealings, and has been engaging in secret, shady meetings with Dilton Doiley. Now someone has made a move against Lodge Industries! What is he going to do?

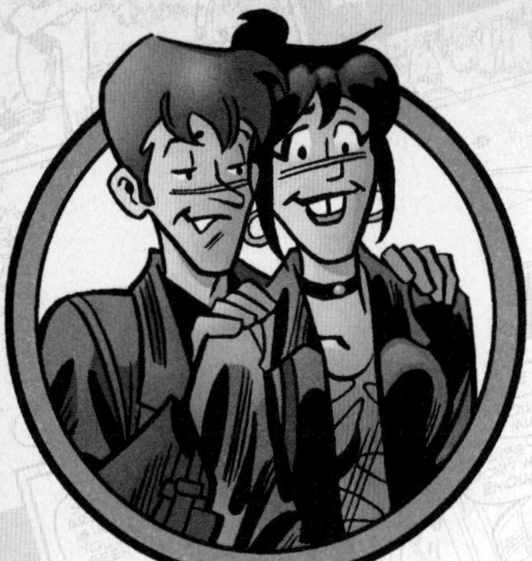

Ethel has gotten back together with her ex-fiancé, millionaire business mogul Fred Mirth—and she couldn't be happier! However, she may be the only person happy about Fred's return. Once an employee of Lodge Industries, Fred is now trying to bring the whole company down, and Ethel is none the wiser! Will she finally see who he really is and what he's up to?

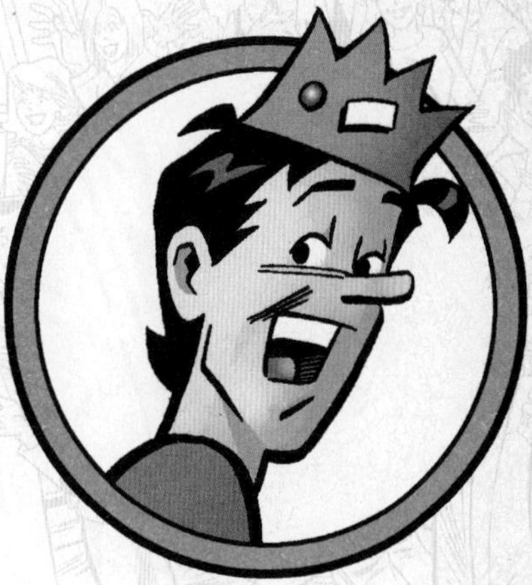

Archie's not the only one running out of luck in the romance department! The last time we saw Jughead, he went AWOL due to the stresses of the Chocklit Shoppe franchise, leaving Midge to handle it all on her own! Now she's fed up and has called it quits—on both the Chocklit Shoppe and her fiancé! But as co-owner, what does this mean for the couple, and for the business?

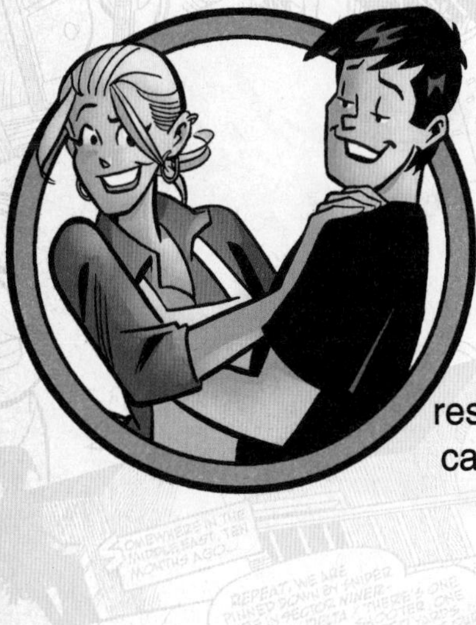

Not every relationship in Riverdale is on the rocks! While others are puttering out, Betty and Reggie are rolling on, full steam ahead! Now that Reggie's trial has been cancelled because the prosecution didn't have a case, he and Betty can finally spend some much-needed time together! That is, when they're not busy with their own careers! Reggie's gone back to work restoring classic cars, while Betty's been busy running her catering business and helping out at the Chocklit Shoppe.

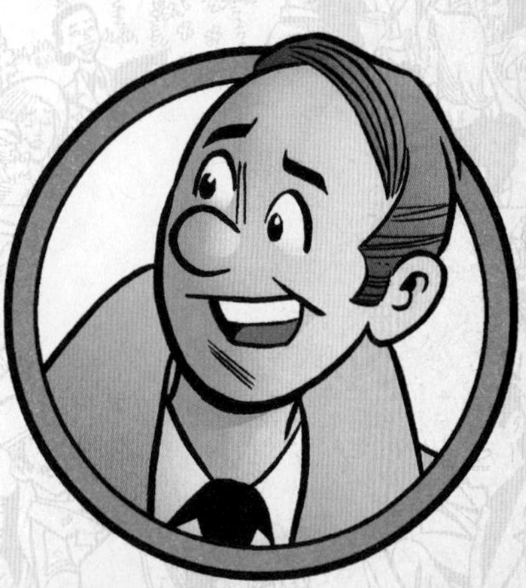

Archie hasn't seen his childhood friend Ambrose in over twenty years! Ambrose is now the owner of a diner in New York, where Betty stopped in on chance to grab a burger. Neither of them knew who the other was, but they both were reminded of their hometown. That encounter prompted Betty to come back—will Ambrose pay Riverdale a visit as well?

"MY DEAR...

YOU WOULD BE *ASTONISHED*..."

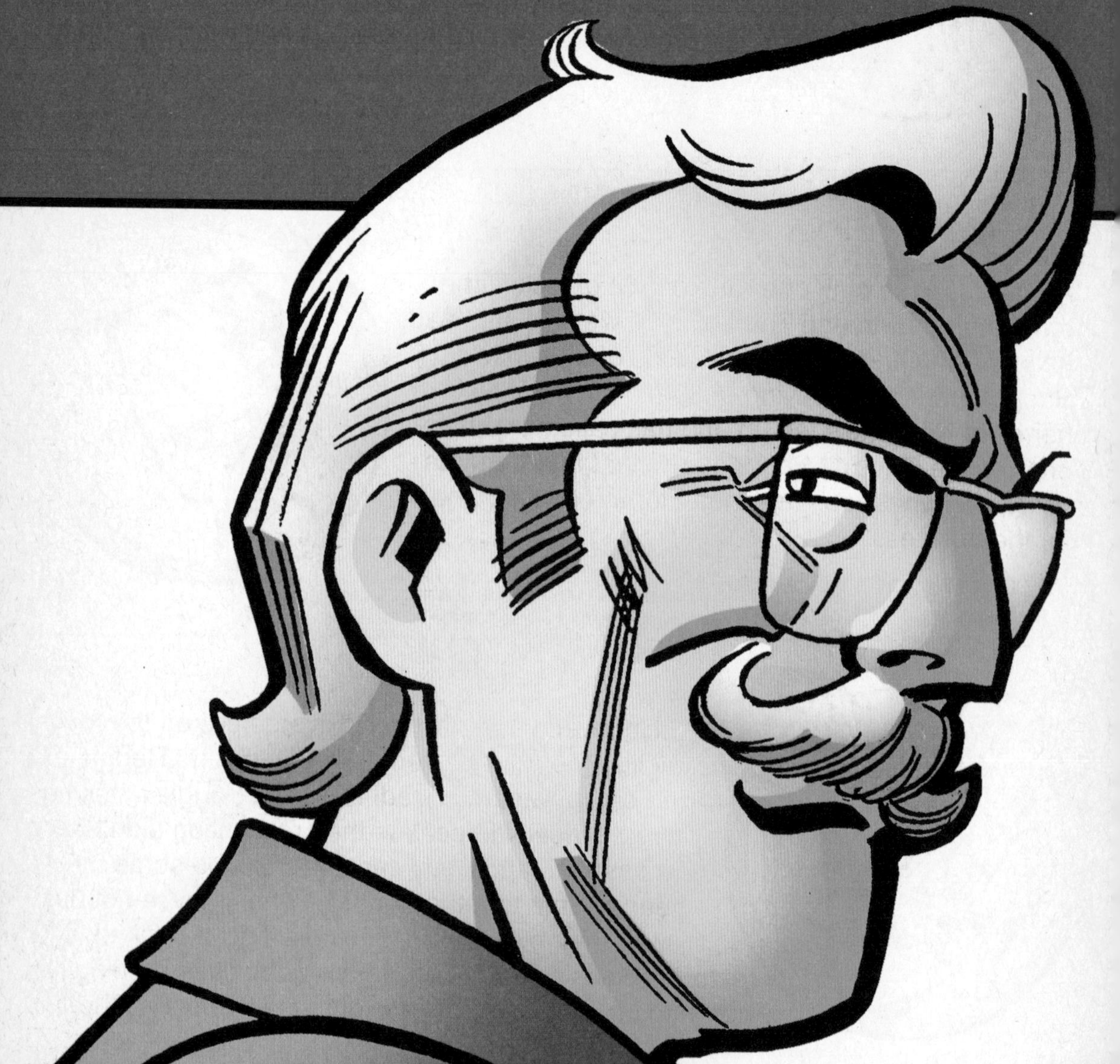

"...AT THE *WORLDS* OF RESOURCES AT MY COMMAND!"

- HIRAM LODGE

Archie Marries Veronica

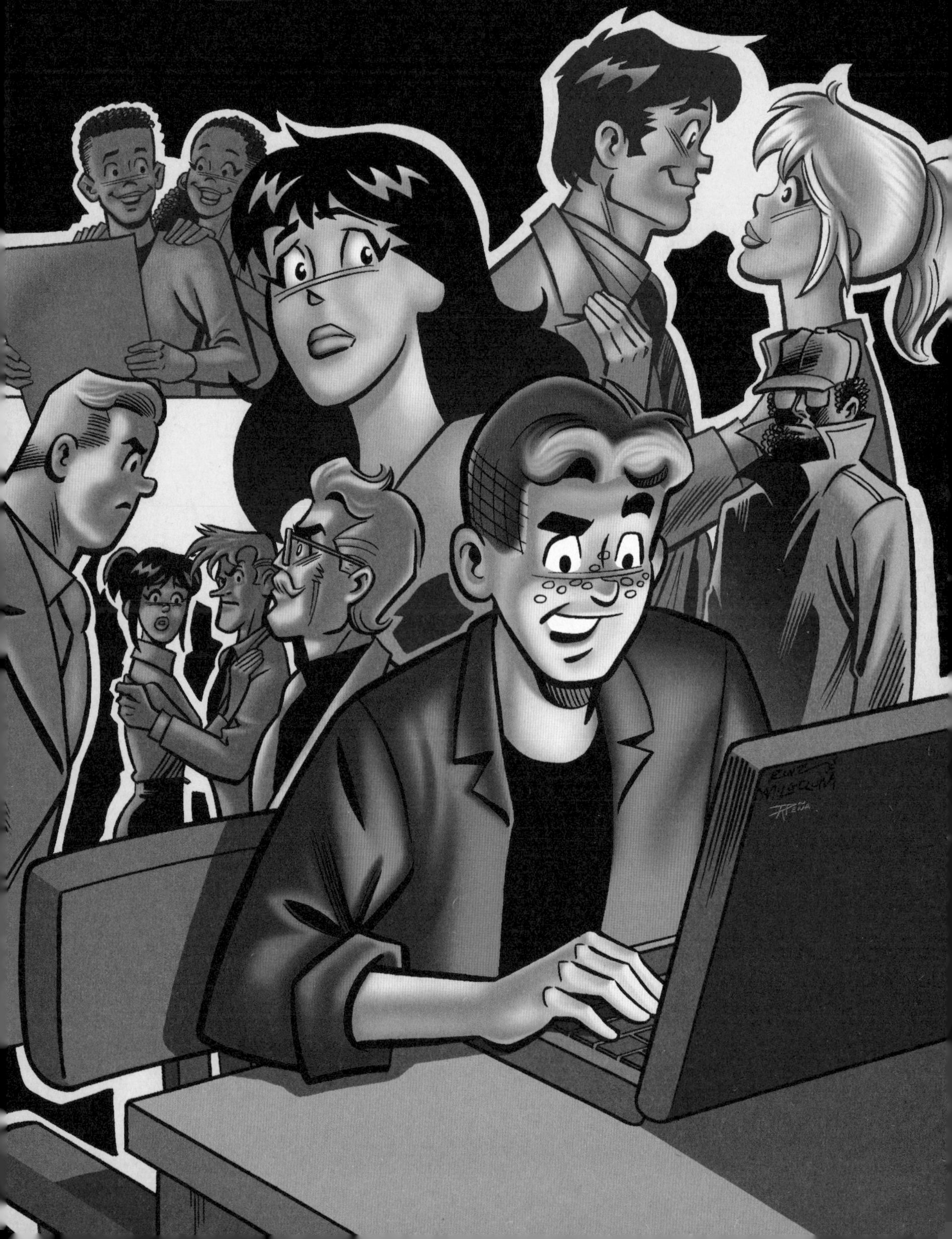

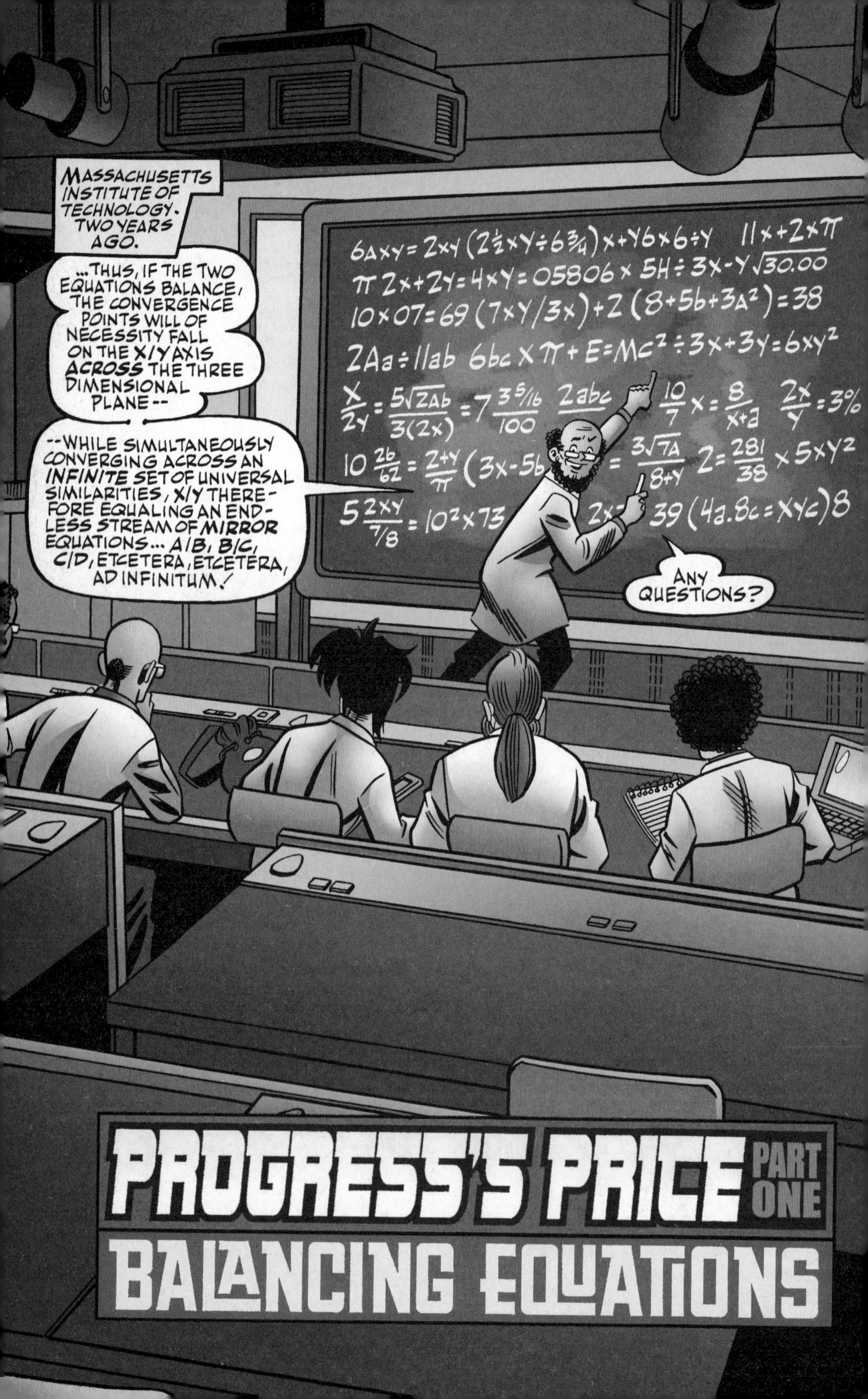
MASSACHUSETTS INSTITUTE OF TECHNOLOGY. TWO YEARS AGO.
...THUS, IF THE TWO EQUATIONS BALANCE, THE CONVERGENCE POINTS WILL OF NECESSITY FALL ON THE X/Y AXIS ACROSS THE THREE DIMENSIONAL PLANE--
--WHILE SIMULTANEOUSLY CONVERGING ACROSS AN INFINITE SET OF UNIVERSAL SIMILARITIES, X/Y THEREFORE EQUALING AN ENDLESS STREAM OF MIRROR EQUATIONS... A/B, B/C, C/D, ETCETERA, ETCETERA, AD INFINITUM!
ANY QUESTIONS?
PROGRESS'S PRICE PART ONE
BALANCING EQUATIONS

QUESTIONS?

I-- I WOULDN'T KNOW WHERE TO *BEGIN!*

ANYONE?

I'M NOT EMBARRASSED TO ADMIT THAT MR. DOILEY'S UNDERSTANDING OF THE PHYSICS OF THIS MATTER FAR SURPASSES MY OWN!

INDEED, IT SURPASSES THAT OF ANYONE ALIVE...

...AND WILL REQUIRE *YEARS* OF STUDY TO *VERIFY* BEFORE...

EXCUSE ME, MA'AM, BUT IT'S ALREADY *VERIFIED!* I ASSURE YOU, MY WORK IS *FAULTLESS!*

$$\frac{2}{x} = \sqrt{AXY}\ 8.9$$
$$10/700\,\pi \times (6$$
$$4 \quad 2 \times y\,(4a$$
$$x = \frac{3}{5}x$$
$$10\tfrac{1}{2} = 5b$$
$$12\%$$
$$0\sqrt{xy}$$

HOW EXACTLY DID YOU CALCULATE YOUR CONVERGENCE POINT, MR. DOILEY?

IN TRUTH, SIR, THE CONVERGENCE POINT CAME *FIRST*--

--LEAVING ME JUST THE MATH TO WORK OUT... ALL THANKS TO AN UNLIKELY INSPIRATION NAMED *JUGHEAD!*

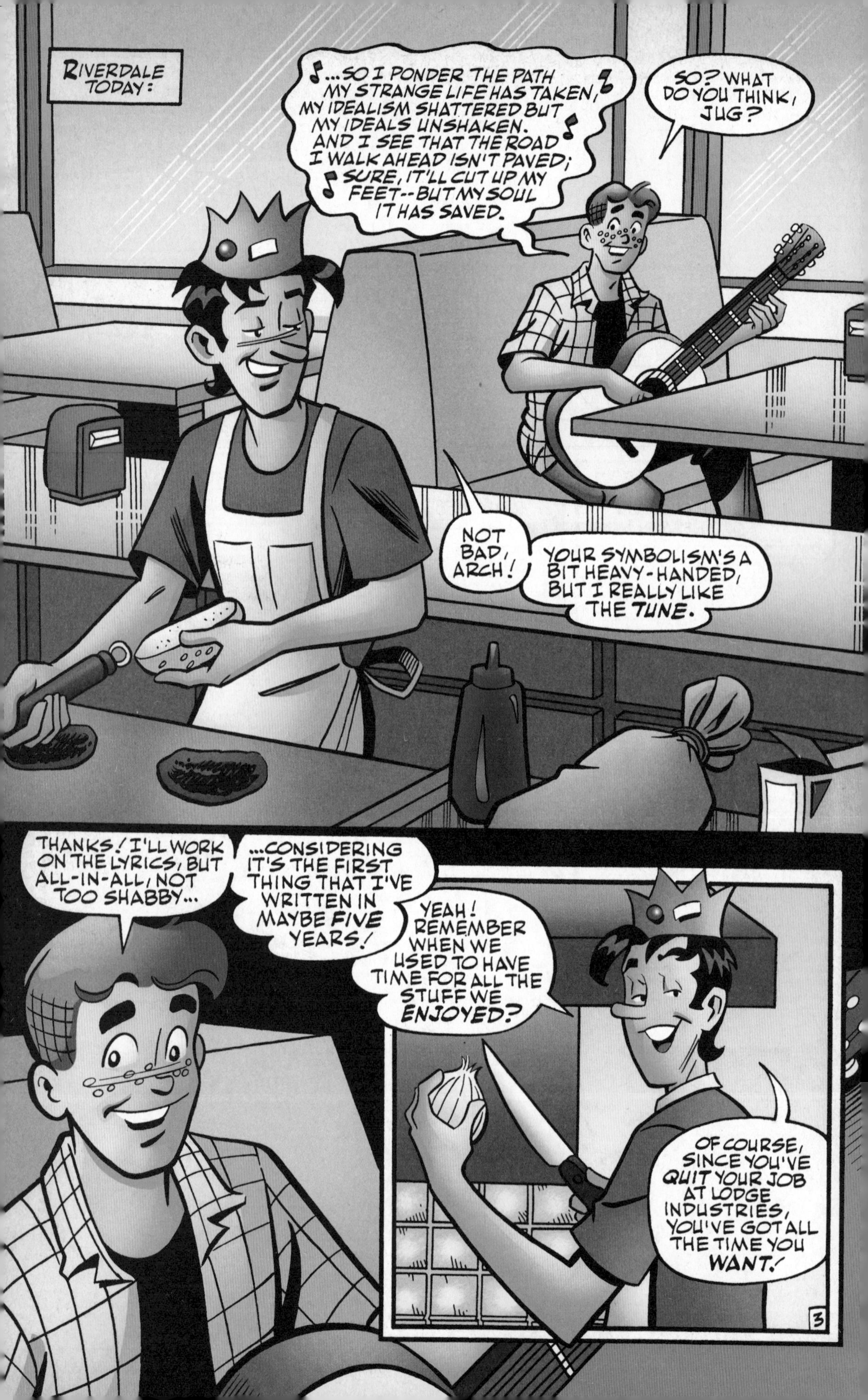
RIVERDALE TODAY:
...SO I PONDER THE PATH MY STRANGE LIFE HAS TAKEN, MY IDEALISM SHATTERED BUT MY IDEALS UNSHAKEN. AND I SEE THAT THE ROAD I WALK AHEAD ISN'T PAVED; SURE, IT'LL CUT UP MY FEET--BUT MY SOUL IT HAS SAVED.
SO? WHAT DO YOU THINK, JUG?
NOT BAD, ARCH!
YOUR SYMBOLISM'S A BIT HEAVY-HANDED, BUT I REALLY LIKE THE TUNE.
THANKS! I'LL WORK ON THE LYRICS, BUT ALL-IN-ALL, NOT TOO SHABBY...
...CONSIDERING IT'S THE FIRST THING THAT I'VE WRITTEN IN MAYBE FIVE YEARS!
YEAH! REMEMBER WHEN WE USED TO HAVE TIME FOR ALL THE STUFF WE ENJOYED?
OF COURSE, SINCE YOU'VE QUIT YOUR JOB AT LODGE INDUSTRIES, YOU'VE GOT ALL THE TIME YOU WANT!
3

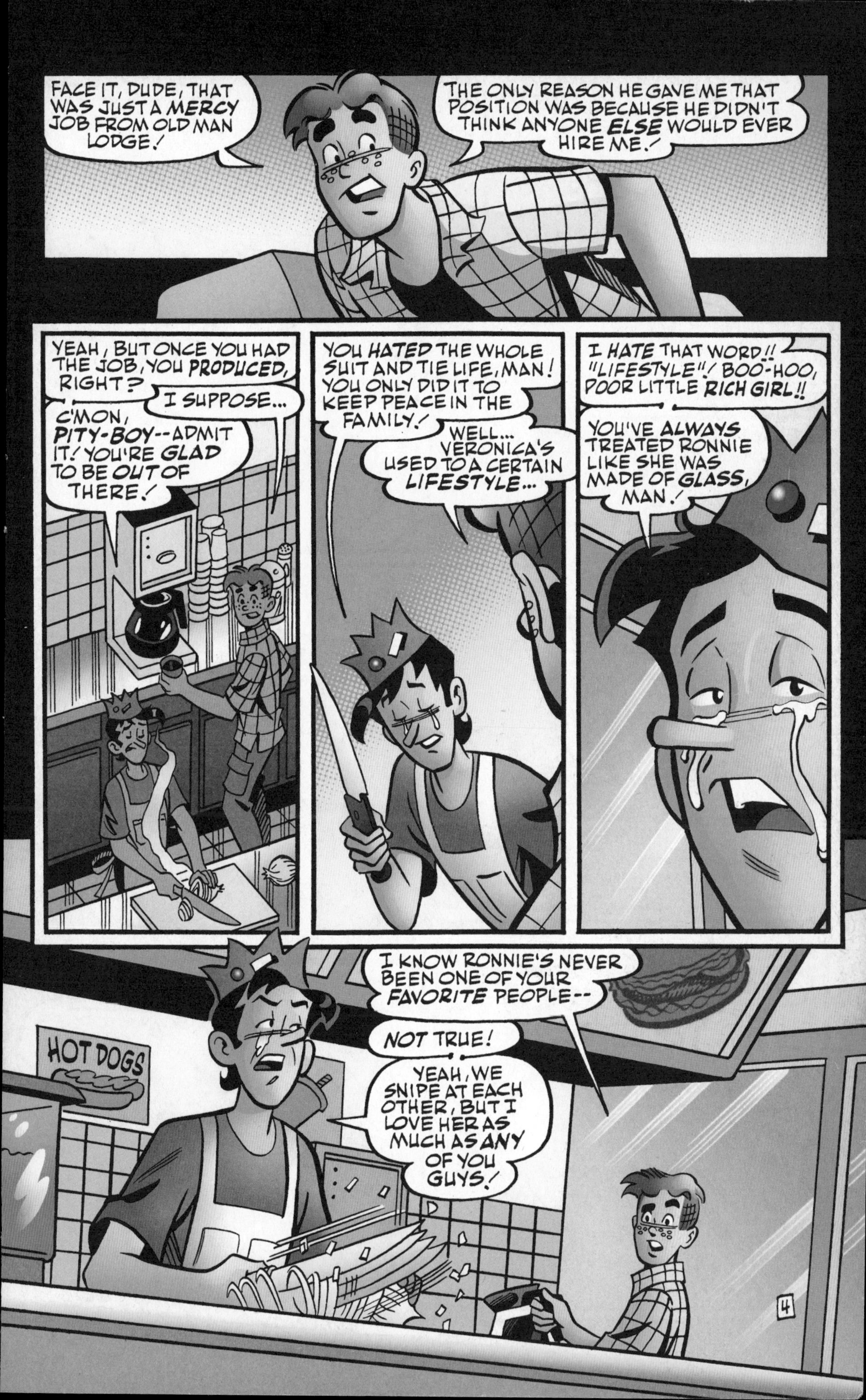

FACE IT, DUDE, THAT WAS JUST A MERCY JOB FROM OLD MAN LODGE!
THE ONLY REASON HE GAVE ME THAT POSITION WAS BECAUSE HE DIDN'T THINK ANYONE ELSE WOULD EVER HIRE ME.!
YEAH, BUT ONCE YOU HAD THE JOB, YOU PRODUCED, RIGHT?
I SUPPOSE...
C'MON, PITY-BOY--ADMIT IT! YOU'RE GLAD TO BE OUT OF THERE!
YOU HATED THE WHOLE SUIT AND TIE LIFE, MAN! YOU ONLY DID IT TO KEEP PEACE IN THE FAMILY!
WELL... VERONICA'S USED TO A CERTAIN LIFESTYLE...
I HATE THAT WORD!! "LIFESTYLE"! BOO-HOO, POOR LITTLE RICH GIRL!!
YOU'VE ALWAYS TREATED RONNIE LIKE SHE WAS MADE OF GLASS, MAN!
I KNOW RONNIE'S NEVER BEEN ONE OF YOUR FAVORITE PEOPLE--
NOT TRUE!
YEAH, WE SNIPE AT EACH OTHER, BUT I LOVE HER AS MUCH AS ANY OF YOU GUYS!
HOT DOGS

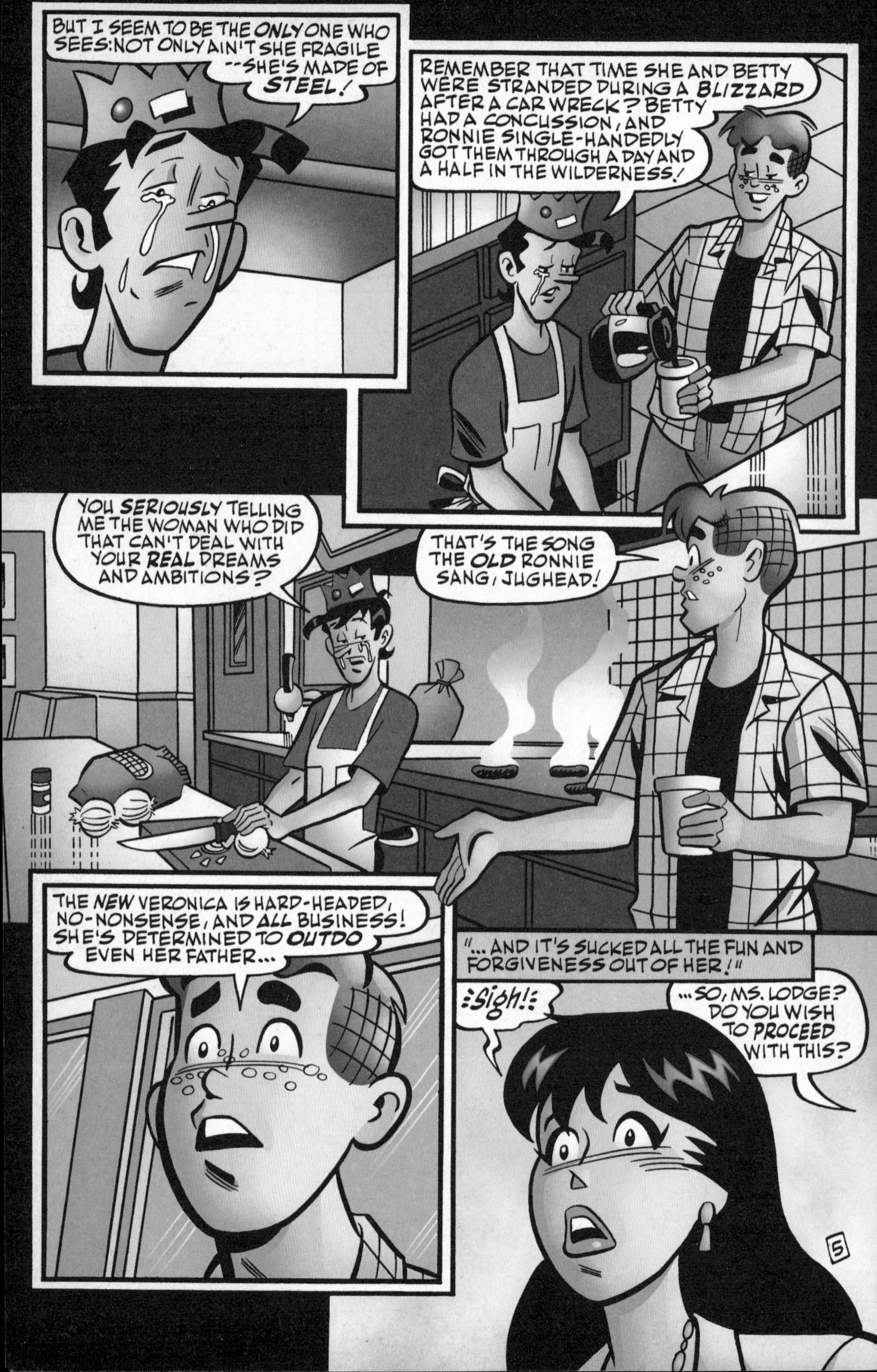
BUT I SEEM TO BE THE ONLY ONE WHO SEES: NOT ONLY AIN'T SHE FRAGILE --SHE'S MADE OF STEEL!
REMEMBER THAT TIME SHE AND BETTY WERE STRANDED DURING A BLIZZARD AFTER A CAR WRECK? BETTY HAD A CONCUSSION, AND RONNIE SINGLE-HANDEDLY GOT THEM THROUGH A DAY AND A HALF IN THE WILDERNESS!
YOU SERIOUSLY TELLING ME THE WOMAN WHO DID THAT CAN'T DEAL WITH YOUR REAL DREAMS AND AMBITIONS?
THAT'S THE SONG THE OLD RONNIE SANG, JUGHEAD!
THE NEW VERONICA IS HARD-HEADED, NO-NONSENSE, AND ALL BUSINESS! SHE'S DETERMINED TO OUTDO EVEN HER FATHER...
"...AND IT'S SUCKED ALL THE FUN AND FORGIVENESS OUT OF HER!"
:Sigh!:
...SO, MS. LODGE? DO YOU WISH TO PROCEED WITH THIS?
5

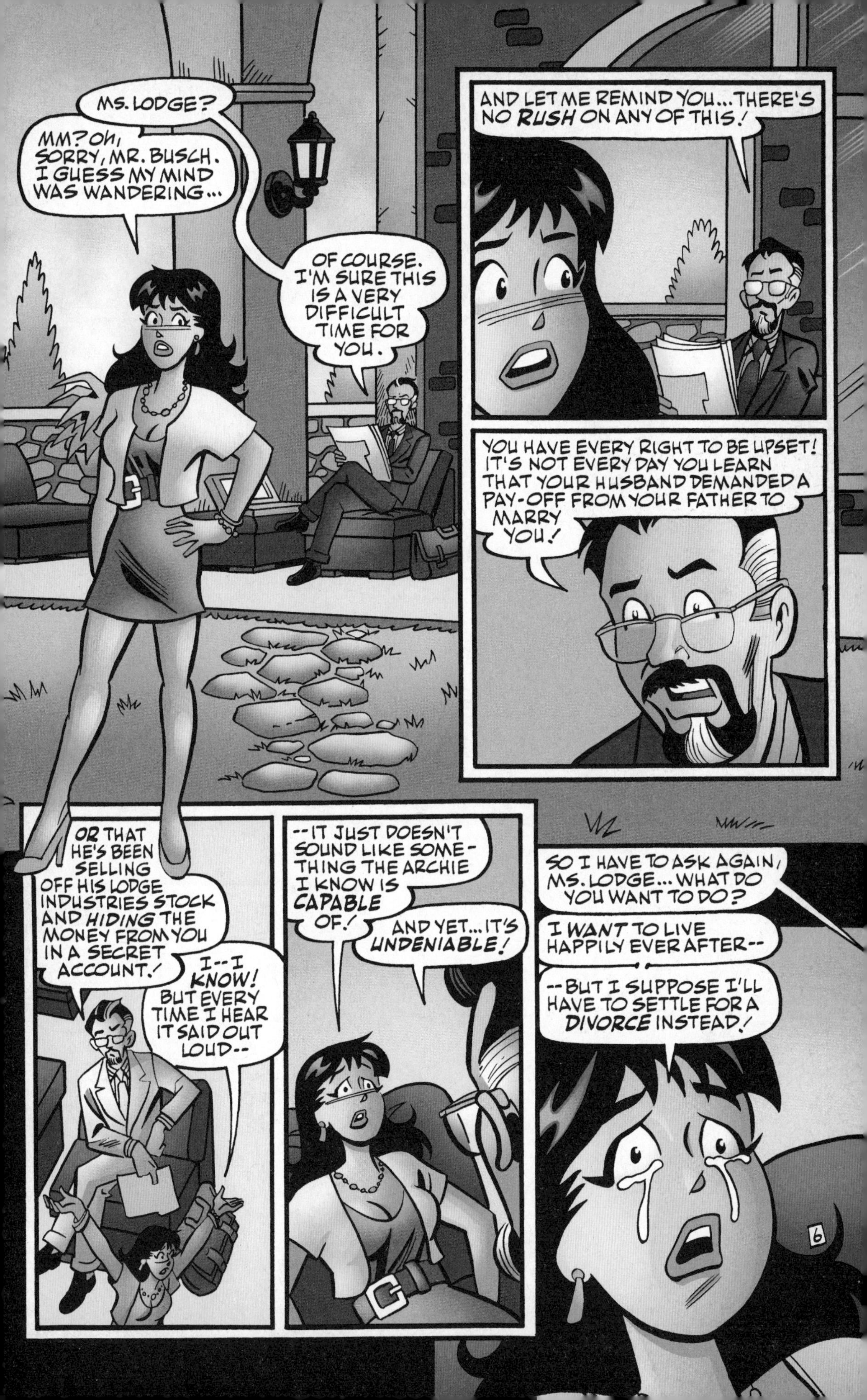
MS. LODGE?
MM? Oh, SORRY, MR. BUSCH. I GUESS MY MIND WAS WANDERING...
OF COURSE. I'M SURE THIS IS A VERY DIFFICULT TIME FOR YOU.
AND LET ME REMIND YOU... THERE'S NO RUSH ON ANY OF THIS!
YOU HAVE EVERY RIGHT TO BE UPSET! IT'S NOT EVERY DAY YOU LEARN THAT YOUR HUSBAND DEMANDED A PAY-OFF FROM YOUR FATHER TO MARRY YOU!
OR THAT HE'S BEEN SELLING OFF HIS LODGE INDUSTRIES STOCK AND HIDING THE MONEY FROM YOU IN A SECRET ACCOUNT!
I--I KNOW! BUT EVERY TIME I HEAR IT SAID OUT LOUD--
--IT JUST DOESN'T SOUND LIKE SOME-THING THE ARCHIE I KNOW IS CAPABLE OF!
AND YET... IT'S UNDENIABLE!
SO I HAVE TO ASK AGAIN, MS. LODGE... WHAT DO YOU WANT TO DO?
I WANT TO LIVE HAPPILY EVER AFTER--
--BUT I SUPPOSE I'LL HAVE TO SETTLE FOR A DIVORCE INSTEAD!
6

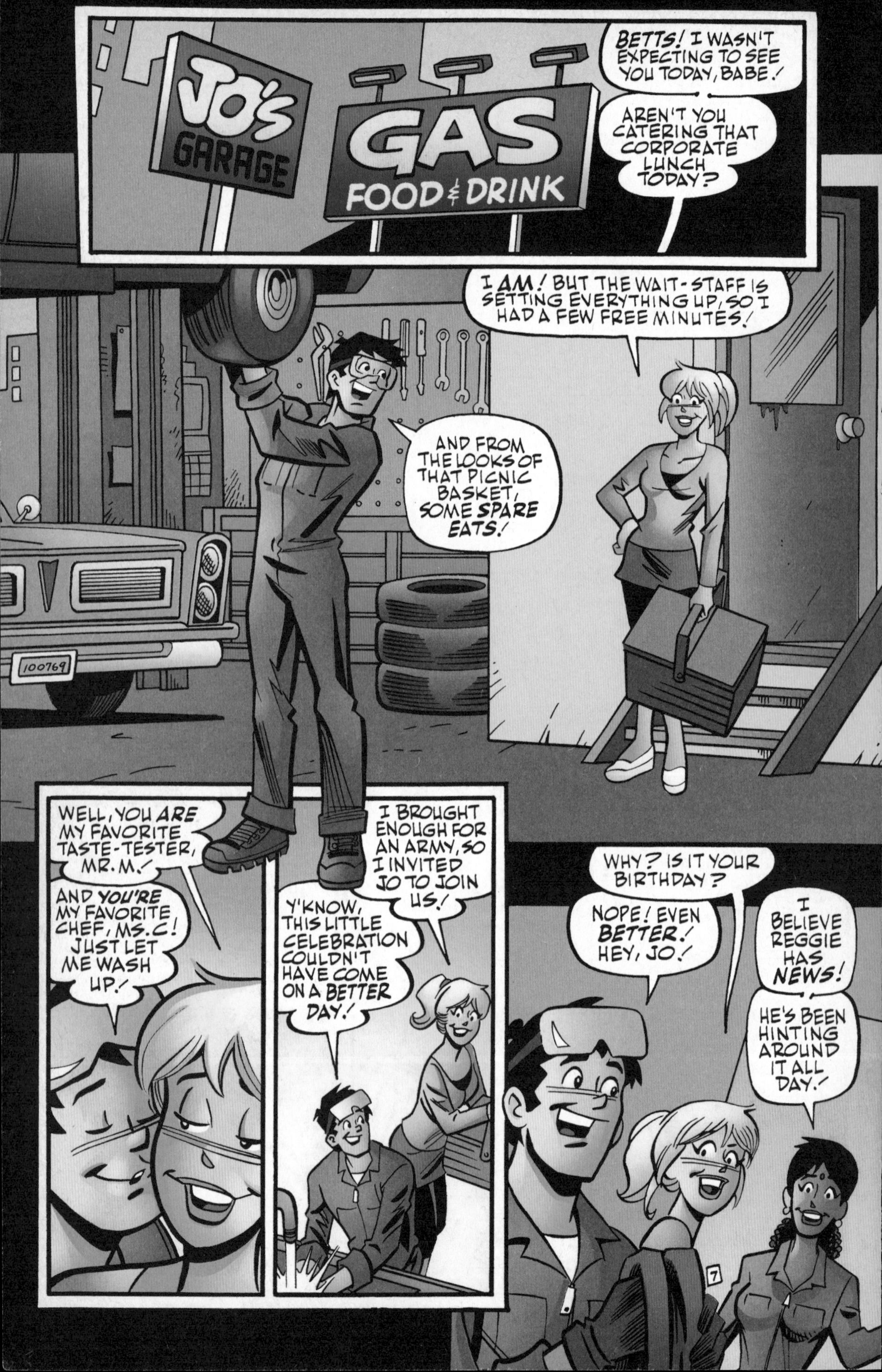
JO'S GARAGE
GAS FOOD & DRINK
BETTS! I WASN'T EXPECTING TO SEE YOU TODAY, BABE!
AREN'T YOU CATERING THAT CORPORATE LUNCH TODAY?
I AM! BUT THE WAIT-STAFF IS SETTING EVERYTHING UP, SO I HAD A FEW FREE MINUTES!
AND FROM THE LOOKS OF THAT PICNIC BASKET, SOME SPARE EATS!
100769
WELL, YOU ARE MY FAVORITE TASTE-TESTER, MR. M.!
AND YOU'RE MY FAVORITE CHEF, MS. C! JUST LET ME WASH UP!
I BROUGHT ENOUGH FOR AN ARMY, SO I INVITED JO TO JOIN US!
Y'KNOW, THIS LITTLE CELEBRATION COULDN'T HAVE COME ON A BETTER DAY!
WHY? IS IT YOUR BIRTHDAY?
NOPE! EVEN BETTER! HEY, JO!
I BELIEVE REGGIE HAS NEWS!
HE'S BEEN HINTING AROUND IT ALL DAY!
7

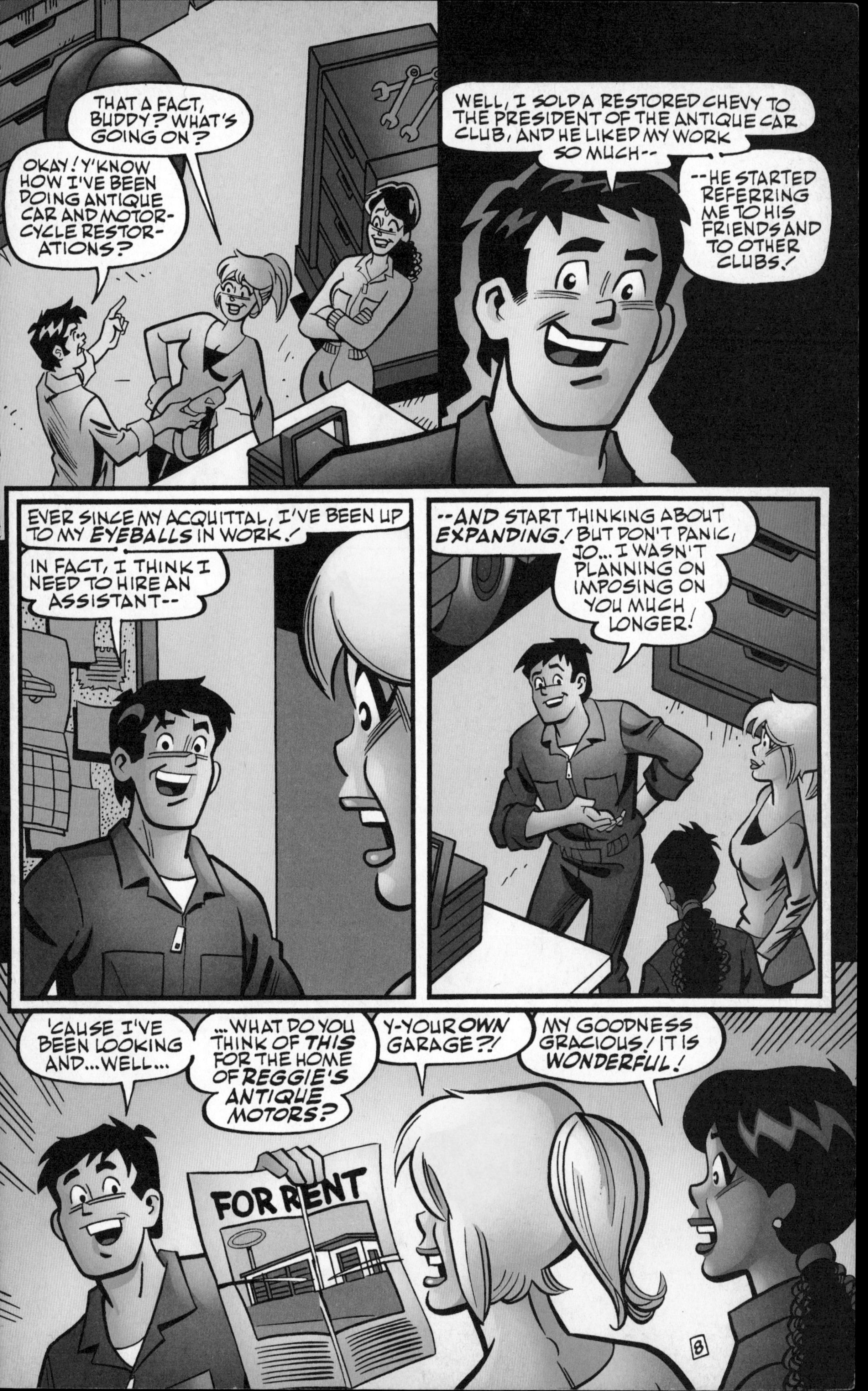
THAT A FACT, BUDDY? WHAT'S GOING ON?
OKAY! Y'KNOW HOW I'VE BEEN DOING ANTIQUE CAR AND MOTOR-CYCLE RESTOR-ATIONS?
WELL, I SOLD A RESTORED CHEVY TO THE PRESIDENT OF THE ANTIQUE CAR CLUB, AND HE LIKED MY WORK SO MUCH--
--HE STARTED REFERRING ME TO HIS FRIENDS AND TO OTHER CLUBS!
EVER SINCE MY ACQUITTAL, I'VE BEEN UP TO MY EYEBALLS IN WORK!
IN FACT, I THINK I NEED TO HIRE AN ASSISTANT--
--AND START THINKING ABOUT EXPANDING! BUT DON'T PANIC, JO... I WASN'T PLANNING ON IMPOSING ON YOU MUCH LONGER!
'CAUSE I'VE BEEN LOOKING AND... WELL...
...WHAT DO YOU THINK OF THIS FOR THE HOME OF REGGIE'S ANTIQUE MOTORS?
Y-YOUR OWN GARAGE?!
MY GOODNESS GRACIOUS! IT IS WONDERFUL!
FOR RENT

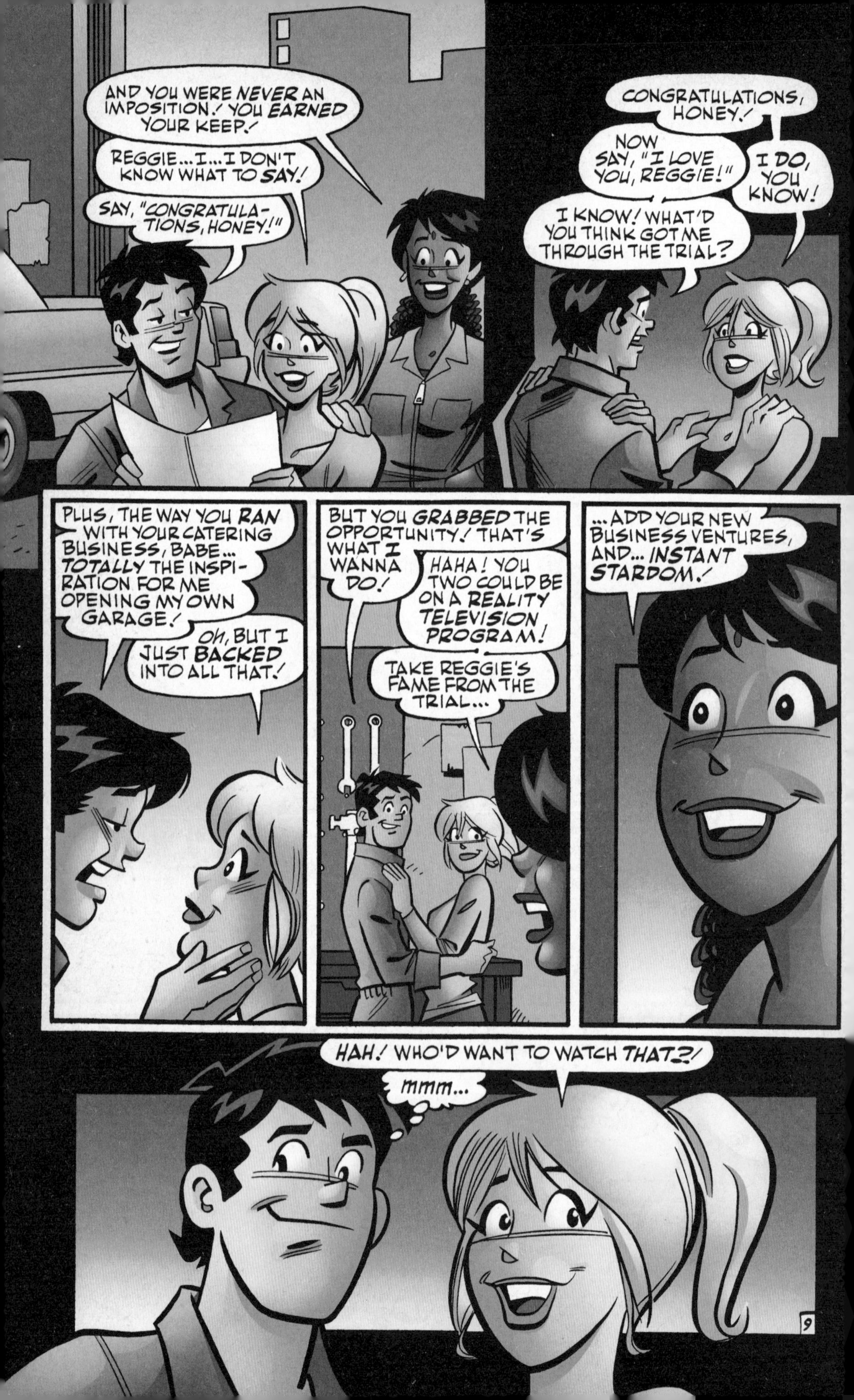
AND YOU WERE NEVER AN IMPOSITION! YOU EARNED YOUR KEEP!
REGGIE... I... I DON'T KNOW WHAT TO SAY!
SAY, "CONGRATULATIONS, HONEY!"
CONGRATULATIONS, HONEY!
NOW SAY, "I LOVE YOU, REGGIE!"
I DO, YOU KNOW!
I KNOW! WHAT'D YOU THINK GOT ME THROUGH THE TRIAL?
PLUS, THE WAY YOU RAN WITH YOUR CATERING BUSINESS, BABE... TOTALLY THE INSPIRATION FOR ME OPENING MY OWN GARAGE!
OH, BUT I JUST BACKED INTO ALL THAT!
BUT YOU GRABBED THE OPPORTUNITY! THAT'S WHAT I WANNA DO!
HAHA! YOU TWO COULD BE ON A REALITY TELEVISION PROGRAM!
TAKE REGGIE'S FAME FROM THE TRIAL...
...ADD YOUR NEW BUSINESS VENTURES, AND... INSTANT STARDOM!
HAH! WHO'D WANT TO WATCH THAT?!
mmm...
9

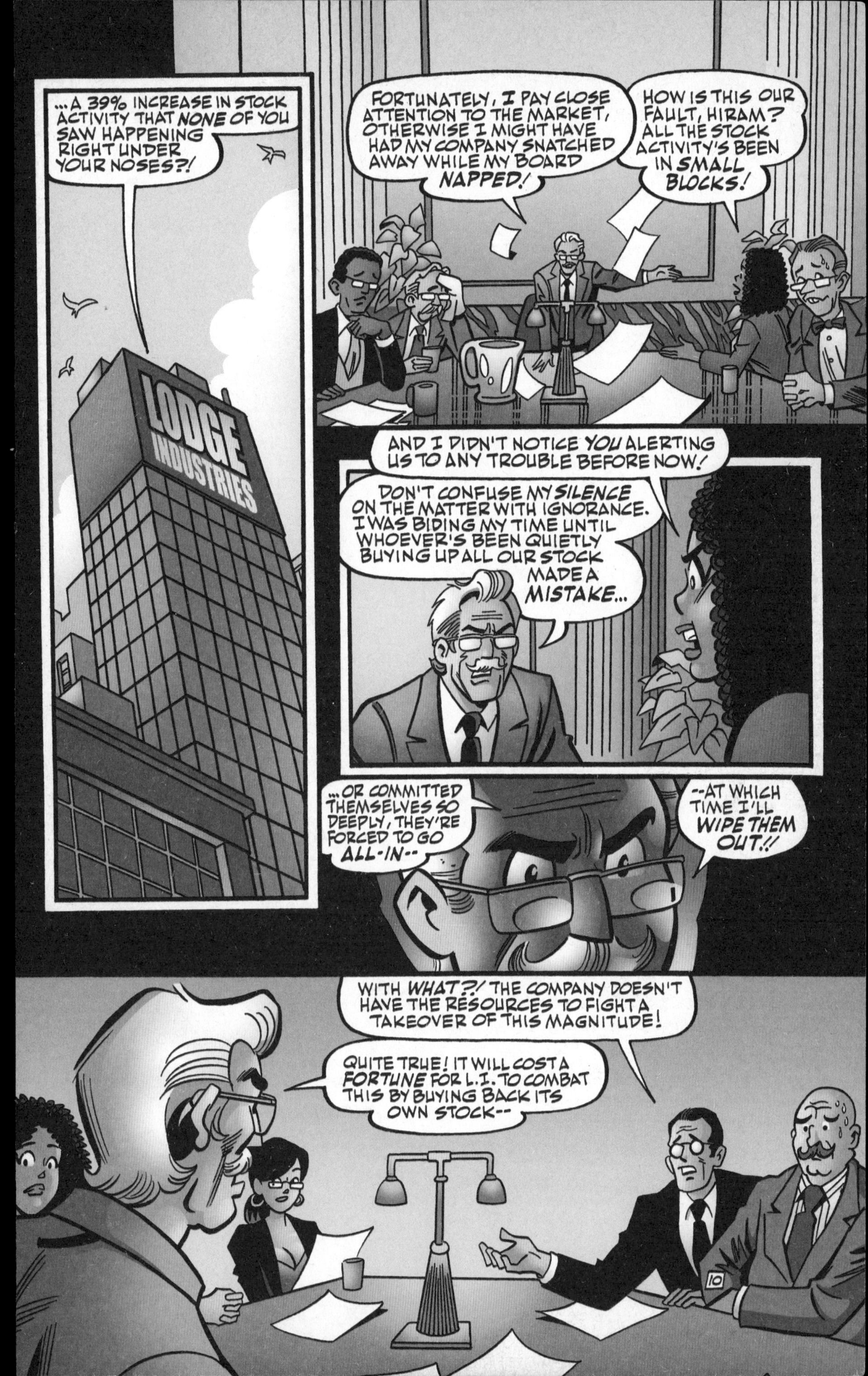
...A 39% INCREASE IN STOCK ACTIVITY THAT NONE OF YOU SAW HAPPENING RIGHT UNDER YOUR NOSES?!
LODGE INDUSTRIES
FORTUNATELY, I PAY CLOSE ATTENTION TO THE MARKET, OTHERWISE I MIGHT HAVE HAD MY COMPANY SNATCHED AWAY WHILE MY BOARD NAPPED!
HOW IS THIS OUR FAULT, HIRAM? ALL THE STOCK ACTIVITY'S BEEN IN SMALL BLOCKS!
AND I DIDN'T NOTICE YOU ALERTING US TO ANY TROUBLE BEFORE NOW!
DON'T CONFUSE MY SILENCE ON THE MATTER WITH IGNORANCE. I WAS BIDING MY TIME UNTIL WHOEVER'S BEEN QUIETLY BUYING UP ALL OUR STOCK MADE A MISTAKE...
...OR COMMITTED THEMSELVES SO DEEPLY, THEY'RE FORCED TO GO ALL-IN--
--AT WHICH TIME I'LL WIPE THEM OUT!!
WITH WHAT?! THE COMPANY DOESN'T HAVE THE RESOURCES TO FIGHT A TAKEOVER OF THIS MAGNITUDE!
QUITE TRUE! IT WILL COST A FORTUNE FOR L.I. TO COMBAT THIS BY BUYING BACK ITS OWN STOCK--

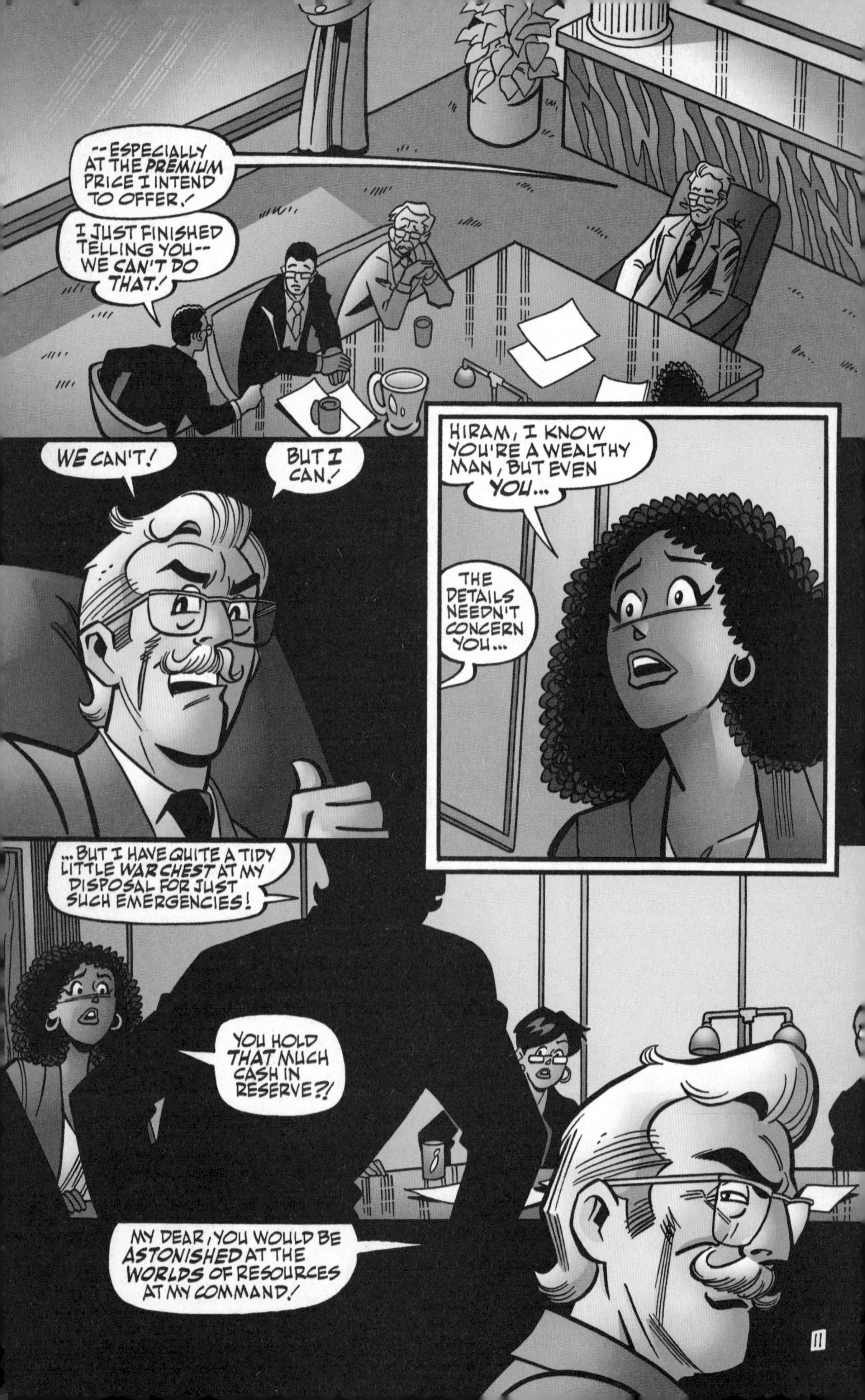
-- ESPECIALLY AT THE PREMIUM PRICE I INTEND TO OFFER!
I JUST FINISHED TELLING YOU-- WE CAN'T DO THAT!
WE CAN'T!
BUT I CAN!
HIRAM, I KNOW YOU'RE A WEALTHY MAN, BUT EVEN YOU...
THE DETAILS NEEDN'T CONCERN YOU...
...BUT I HAVE QUITE A TIDY LITTLE WAR CHEST AT MY DISPOSAL FOR JUST SUCH EMERGENCIES!
YOU HOLD THAT MUCH CASH IN RESERVE?!
MY DEAR, YOU WOULD BE ASTONISHED AT THE WORLDS OF RESOURCES AT MY COMMAND!

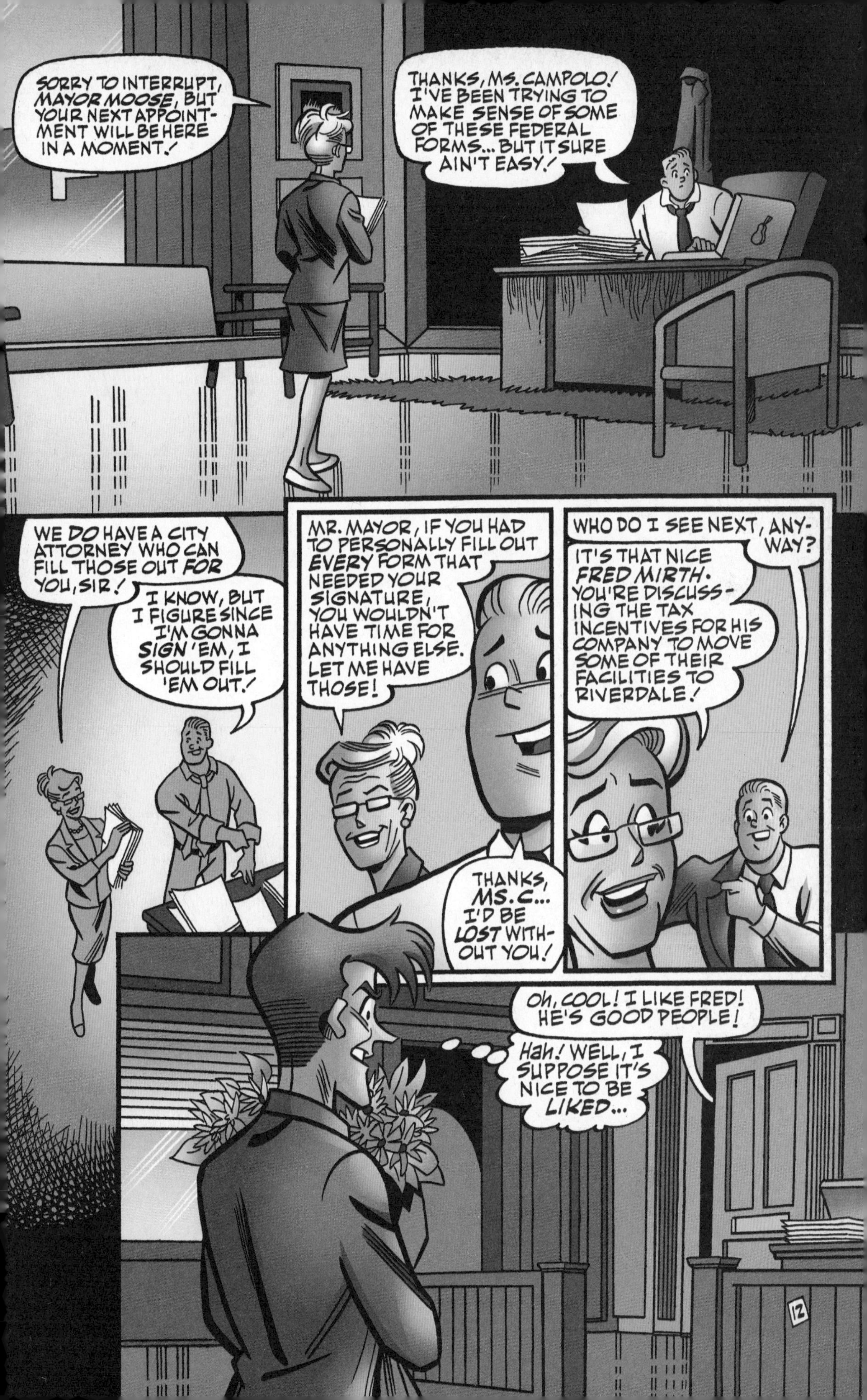

SORRY TO INTERRUPT, MAYOR MOOSE, BUT YOUR NEXT APPOINTMENT WILL BE HERE IN A MOMENT!
THANKS, MS. CAMPOLO! I'VE BEEN TRYING TO MAKE SENSE OF SOME OF THESE FEDERAL FORMS... BUT IT SURE AIN'T EASY!
WE DO HAVE A CITY ATTORNEY WHO CAN FILL THOSE OUT FOR YOU, SIR!
I KNOW, BUT I FIGURE SINCE I'M GONNA SIGN 'EM, I SHOULD FILL 'EM OUT!
MR. MAYOR, IF YOU HAD TO PERSONALLY FILL OUT EVERY FORM THAT NEEDED YOUR SIGNATURE, YOU WOULDN'T HAVE TIME FOR ANYTHING ELSE. LET ME HAVE THOSE!
THANKS, MS. C... I'D BE LOST WITHOUT YOU!
WHO DO I SEE NEXT, ANYWAY?
IT'S THAT NICE FRED MIRTH. YOU'RE DISCUSSING THE TAX INCENTIVES FOR HIS COMPANY TO MOVE SOME OF THEIR FACILITIES TO RIVERDALE!
OH, COOL! I LIKE FRED! HE'S GOOD PEOPLE!
HAH! WELL, I SUPPOSE IT'S NICE TO BE LIKED...
12

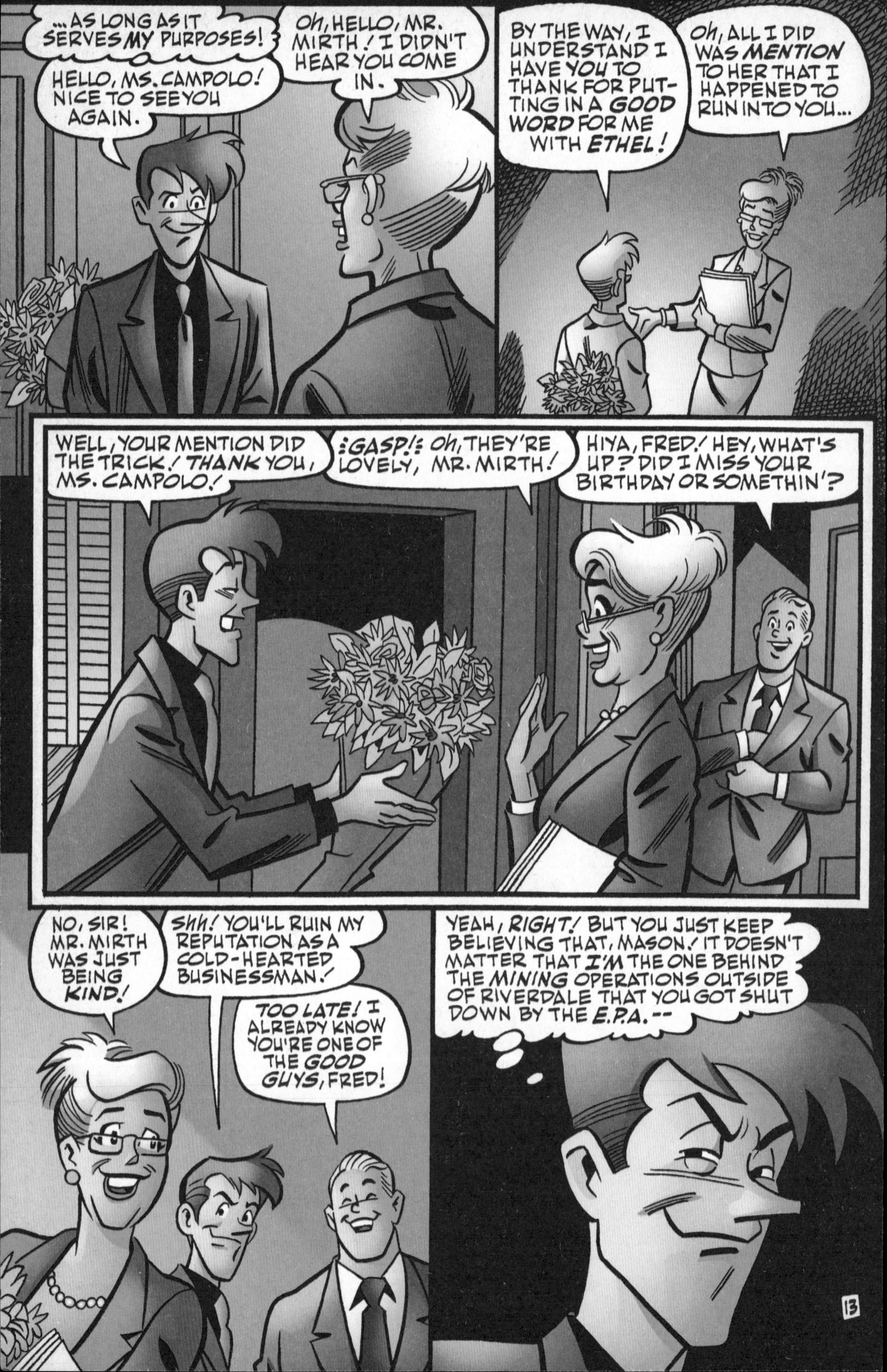
...AS LONG AS IT SERVES MY PURPOSES!
HELLO, MS. CAMPOLO! NICE TO SEE YOU AGAIN.
OH, HELLO, MR. MIRTH! I DIDN'T HEAR YOU COME IN.
BY THE WAY, I UNDERSTAND I HAVE YOU TO THANK FOR PUTTING IN A GOOD WORD FOR ME WITH ETHEL!
OH, ALL I DID WAS MENTION TO HER THAT I HAPPENED TO RUN INTO YOU...
WELL, YOUR MENTION DID THE TRICK! THANK YOU, MS. CAMPOLO!
:GASP!: OH, THEY'RE LOVELY, MR. MIRTH!
HIYA, FRED! HEY, WHAT'S UP? DID I MISS YOUR BIRTHDAY OR SOMETHIN'?
NO, SIR! MR. MIRTH WAS JUST BEING KIND!
SHH! YOU'LL RUIN MY REPUTATION AS A COLD-HEARTED BUSINESSMAN!
TOO LATE! I ALREADY KNOW YOU'RE ONE OF THE GOOD GUYS, FRED!
YEAH, RIGHT! BUT YOU JUST KEEP BELIEVING THAT, MASON! IT DOESN'T MATTER THAT I'M THE ONE BEHIND THE MINING OPERATIONS OUTSIDE OF RIVERDALE THAT YOU GOT SHUT DOWN BY THE E.P.A.--
13

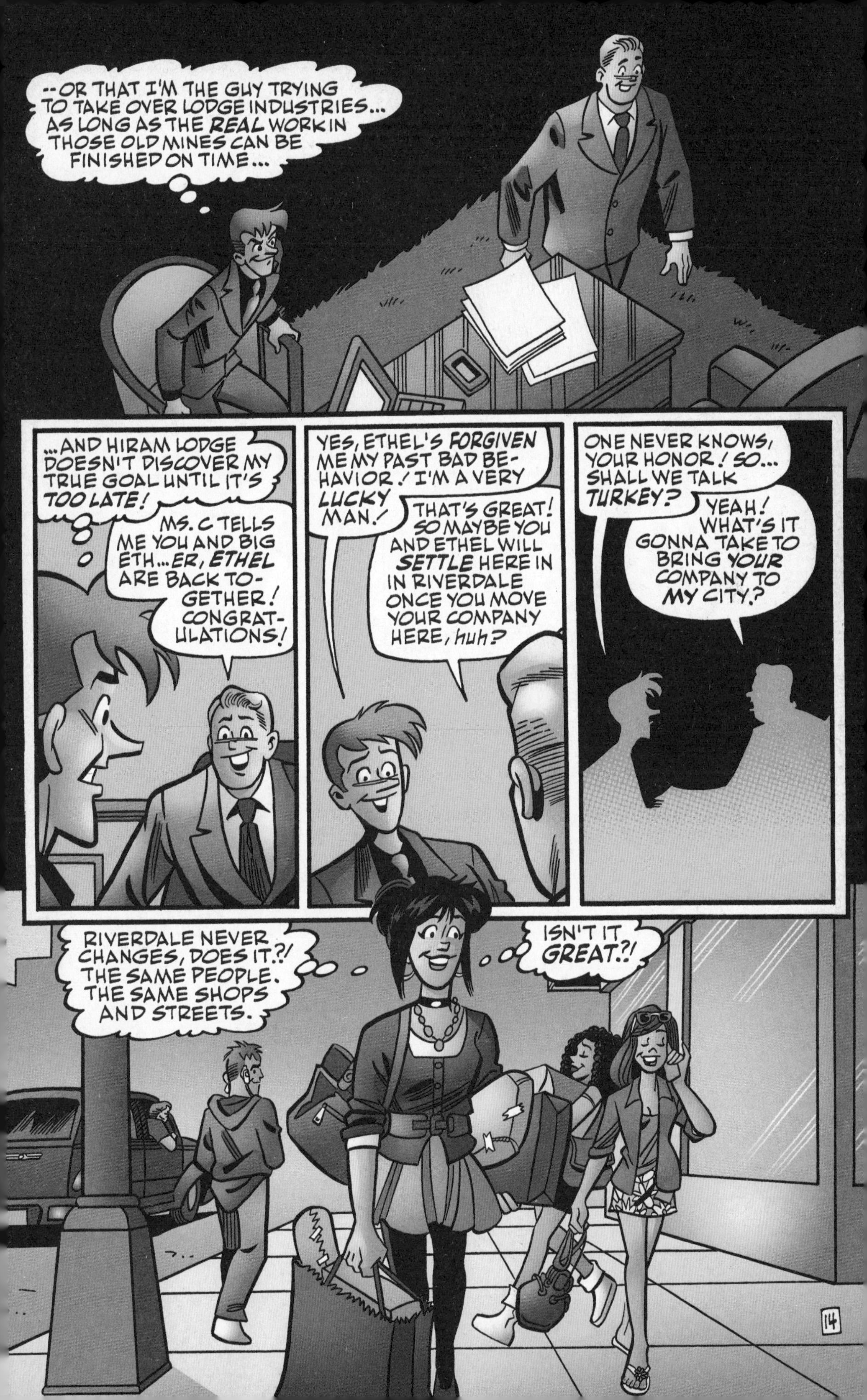
--OR THAT I'M THE GUY TRYING TO TAKE OVER LODGE INDUSTRIES... AS LONG AS THE REAL WORK IN THOSE OLD MINES CAN BE FINISHED ON TIME...
...AND HIRAM LODGE DOESN'T DISCOVER MY TRUE GOAL UNTIL IT'S TOO LATE!
MS. C TELLS ME YOU AND BIG ETH...ER, ETHEL ARE BACK TOGETHER! CONGRATULATIONS!
YES, ETHEL'S FORGIVEN ME MY PAST BAD BEHAVIOR! I'M A VERY LUCKY MAN!
THAT'S GREAT! SO MAYBE YOU AND ETHEL WILL SETTLE HERE IN IN RIVERDALE ONCE YOU MOVE YOUR COMPANY HERE, huh?
ONE NEVER KNOWS, YOUR HONOR! SO... SHALL WE TALK TURKEY?
YEAH! WHAT'S IT GONNA TAKE TO BRING YOUR COMPANY TO MY CITY?
RIVERDALE NEVER CHANGES, DOES IT?! THE SAME PEOPLE. THE SAME SHOPS AND STREETS.
ISN'T IT GREAT?!

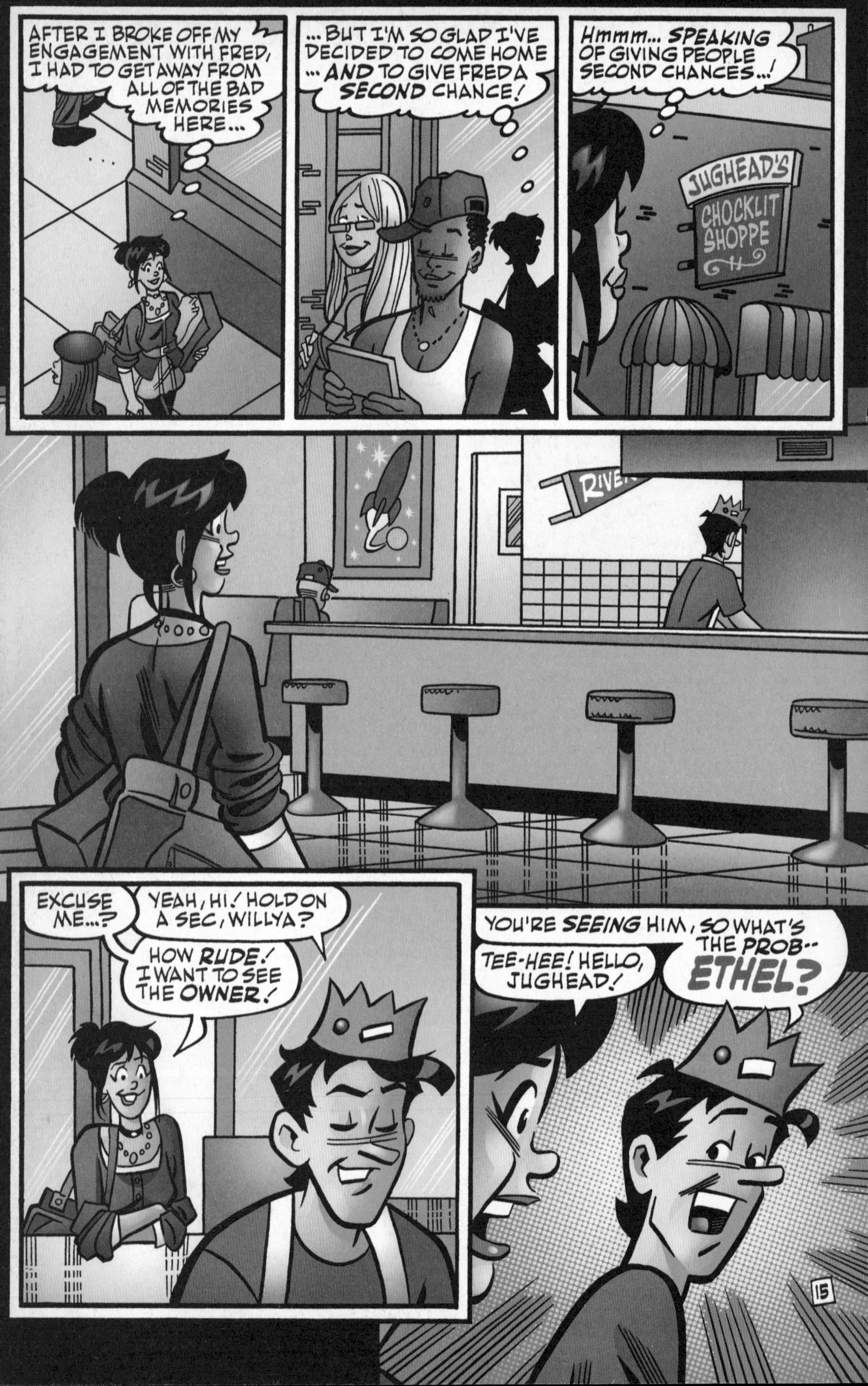
AFTER I BROKE OFF MY ENGAGEMENT WITH FRED, I HAD TO GET AWAY FROM ALL OF THE BAD MEMORIES HERE...
...BUT I'M SO GLAD I'VE DECIDED TO COME HOME ...AND TO GIVE FRED A SECOND CHANCE!
Hmmm... SPEAKING OF GIVING PEOPLE SECOND CHANCES...!
JUGHEAD'S CHOCKLIT SHOPPE
EXCUSE ME...?
YEAH, HI! HOLD ON A SEC, WILLYA?
HOW RUDE! I WANT TO SEE THE OWNER!
YOU'RE SEEING HIM, SO WHAT'S THE PROB-- ETHEL?
TEE-HEE! HELLO, JUGHEAD!
15

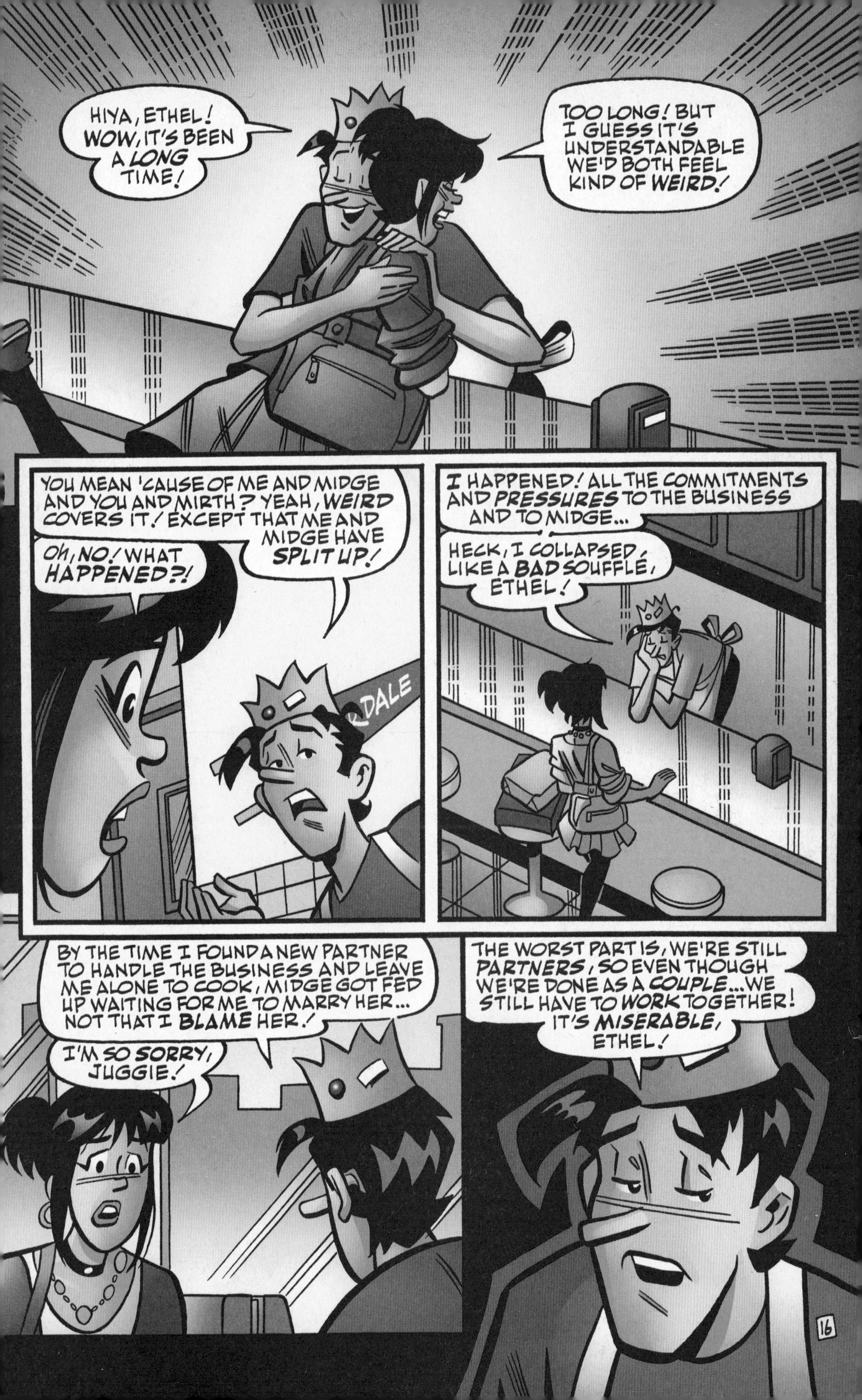
HIYA, ETHEL! WOW, IT'S BEEN A LONG TIME!
TOO LONG! BUT I GUESS IT'S UNDERSTANDABLE WE'D BOTH FEEL KIND OF WEIRD!
YOU MEAN 'CAUSE OF ME AND MIDGE AND YOU AND MIRTH? YEAH, WEIRD COVERS IT! EXCEPT THAT ME AND MIDGE HAVE SPLIT UP!
OH, NO! WHAT HAPPENED?!
DALE
I HAPPENED! ALL THE COMMITMENTS AND PRESSURES TO THE BUSINESS AND TO MIDGE...
HECK, I COLLAPSED, LIKE A BAD SOUFFLÉ, ETHEL!
BY THE TIME I FOUND A NEW PARTNER TO HANDLE THE BUSINESS AND LEAVE ME ALONE TO COOK, MIDGE GOT FED UP WAITING FOR ME TO MARRY HER... NOT THAT I BLAME HER!
I'M SO SORRY, JUGGIE!
THE WORST PART IS, WE'RE STILL PARTNERS, SO EVEN THOUGH WE'RE DONE AS A COUPLE... WE STILL HAVE TO WORK TOGETHER! IT'S MISERABLE, ETHEL!
16

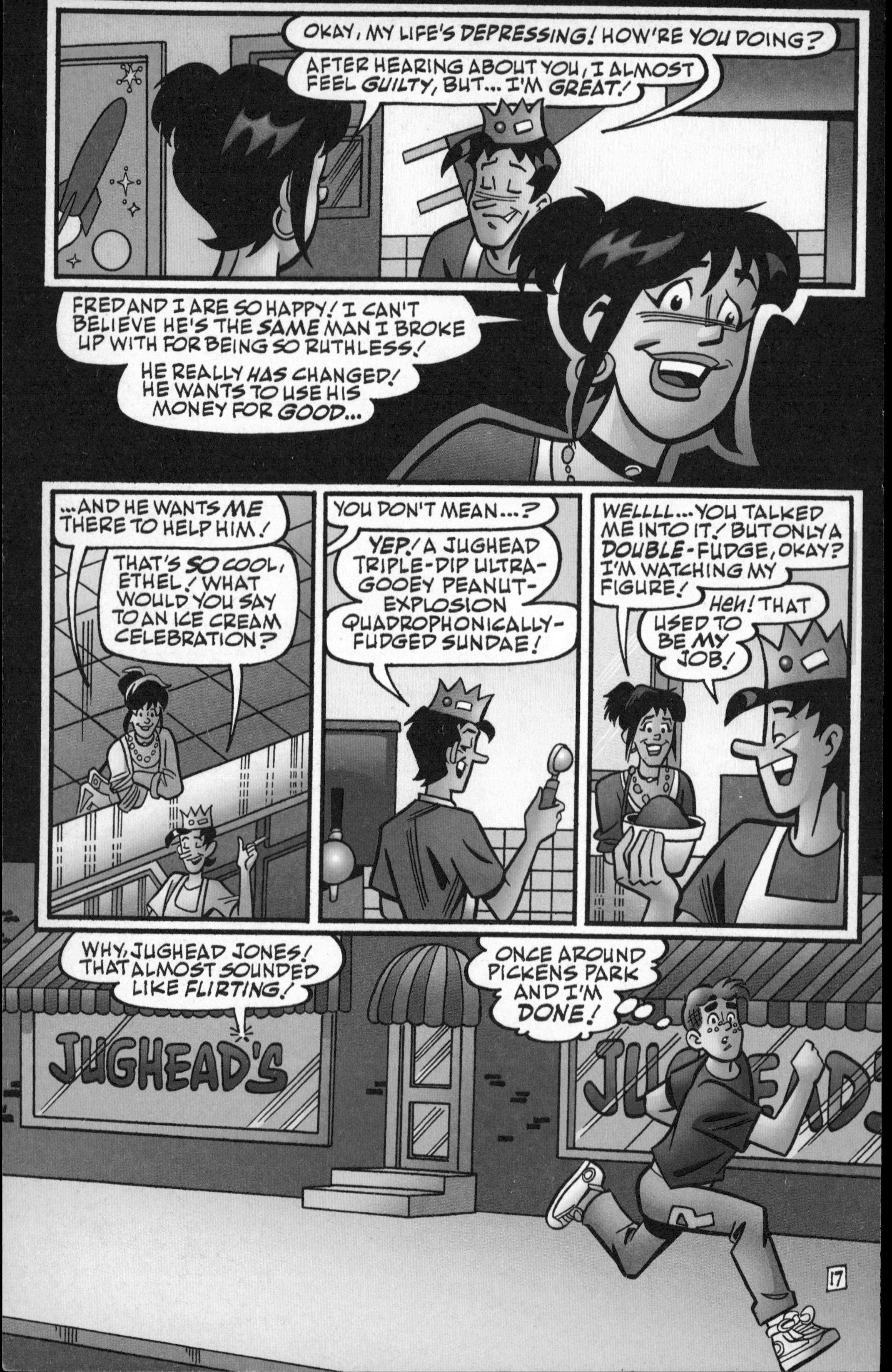
OKAY, MY LIFE'S DEPRESSING! HOW'RE YOU DOING?
AFTER HEARING ABOUT YOU, I ALMOST FEEL GUILTY, BUT... I'M GREAT!
FRED AND I ARE SO HAPPY! I CAN'T BELIEVE HE'S THE SAME MAN I BROKE UP WITH FOR BEING SO RUTHLESS!
HE REALLY HAS CHANGED! HE WANTS TO USE HIS MONEY FOR GOOD...
...AND HE WANTS ME THERE TO HELP HIM!
THAT'S SO COOL, ETHEL! WHAT WOULD YOU SAY TO AN ICE CREAM CELEBRATION?
YOU DON'T MEAN...?
YEP! A JUGHEAD TRIPLE-DIP ULTRA-GOOEY PEANUT-EXPLOSION QUADROPHONICALLY-FUDGED SUNDAE!
WELLLL... YOU TALKED ME INTO IT! BUT ONLY A DOUBLE-FUDGE, OKAY? I'M WATCHING MY FIGURE!
Heh! THAT USED TO BE MY JOB!
WHY, JUGHEAD JONES! THAT ALMOST SOUNDED LIKE FLIRTING!
ONCE AROUND PICKENS PARK AND I'M DONE!
JUGHEAD'S

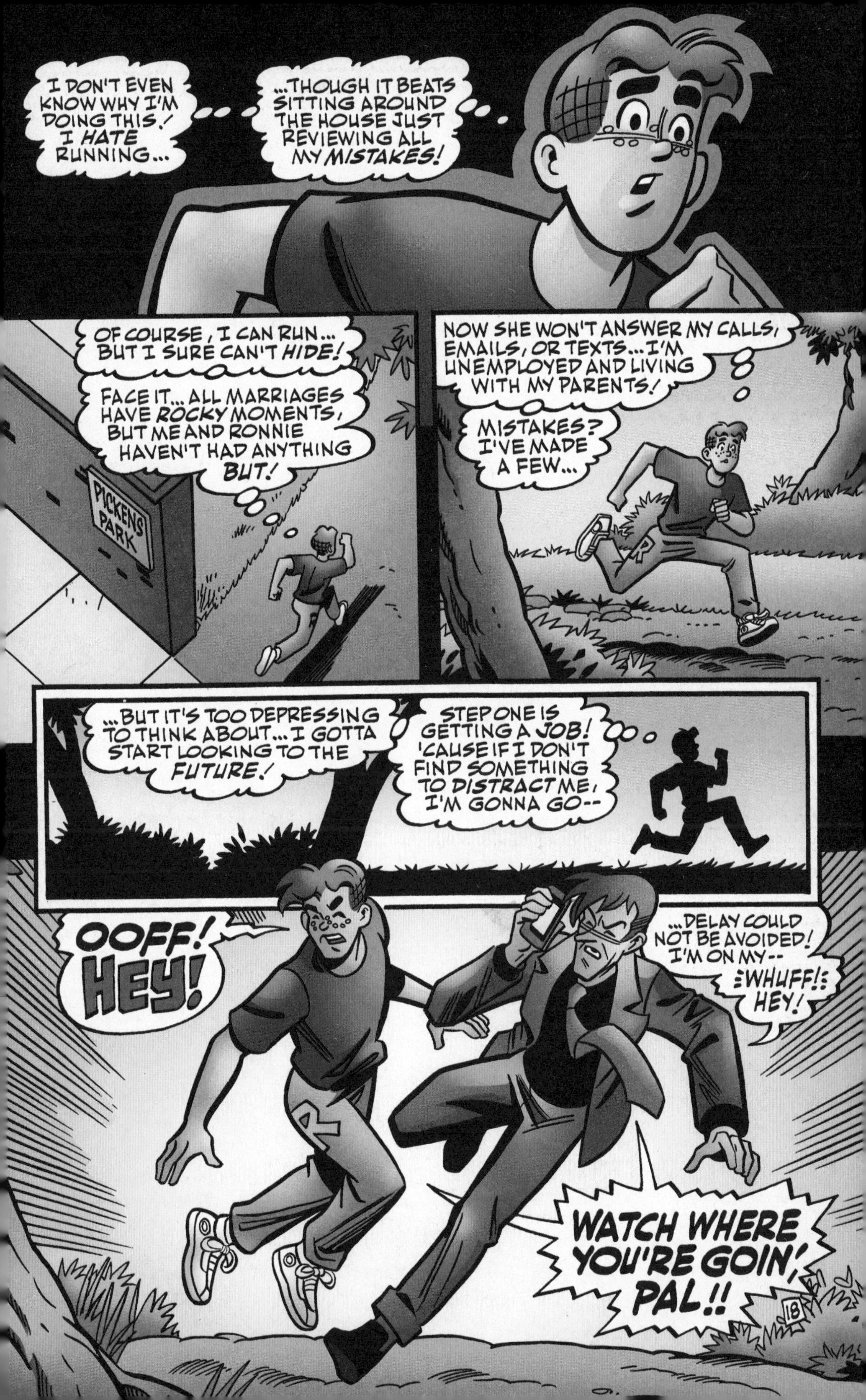
I DON'T EVEN KNOW WHY I'M DOING THIS! I HATE RUNNING...
...THOUGH IT BEATS SITTING AROUND THE HOUSE JUST REVIEWING ALL MY MISTAKES!
OF COURSE, I CAN RUN... BUT I SURE CAN'T HIDE!
FACE IT... ALL MARRIAGES HAVE ROCKY MOMENTS, BUT ME AND RONNIE HAVEN'T HAD ANYTHING BUT!
PICKENS PARK
NOW SHE WON'T ANSWER MY CALLS, EMAILS, OR TEXTS... I'M UNEMPLOYED AND LIVING WITH MY PARENTS!
MISTAKES? I'VE MADE A FEW...
...BUT IT'S TOO DEPRESSING TO THINK ABOUT... I GOTTA START LOOKING TO THE FUTURE!
STEP ONE IS GETTING A JOB! 'CAUSE IF I DON'T FIND SOMETHING TO DISTRACT ME, I'M GONNA GO--
OOFF! HEY!
...DELAY COULD NOT BE AVOIDED! I'M ON MY-- WHUFF! HEY!
WATCH WHERE YOU'RE GOIN', PAL!!
18

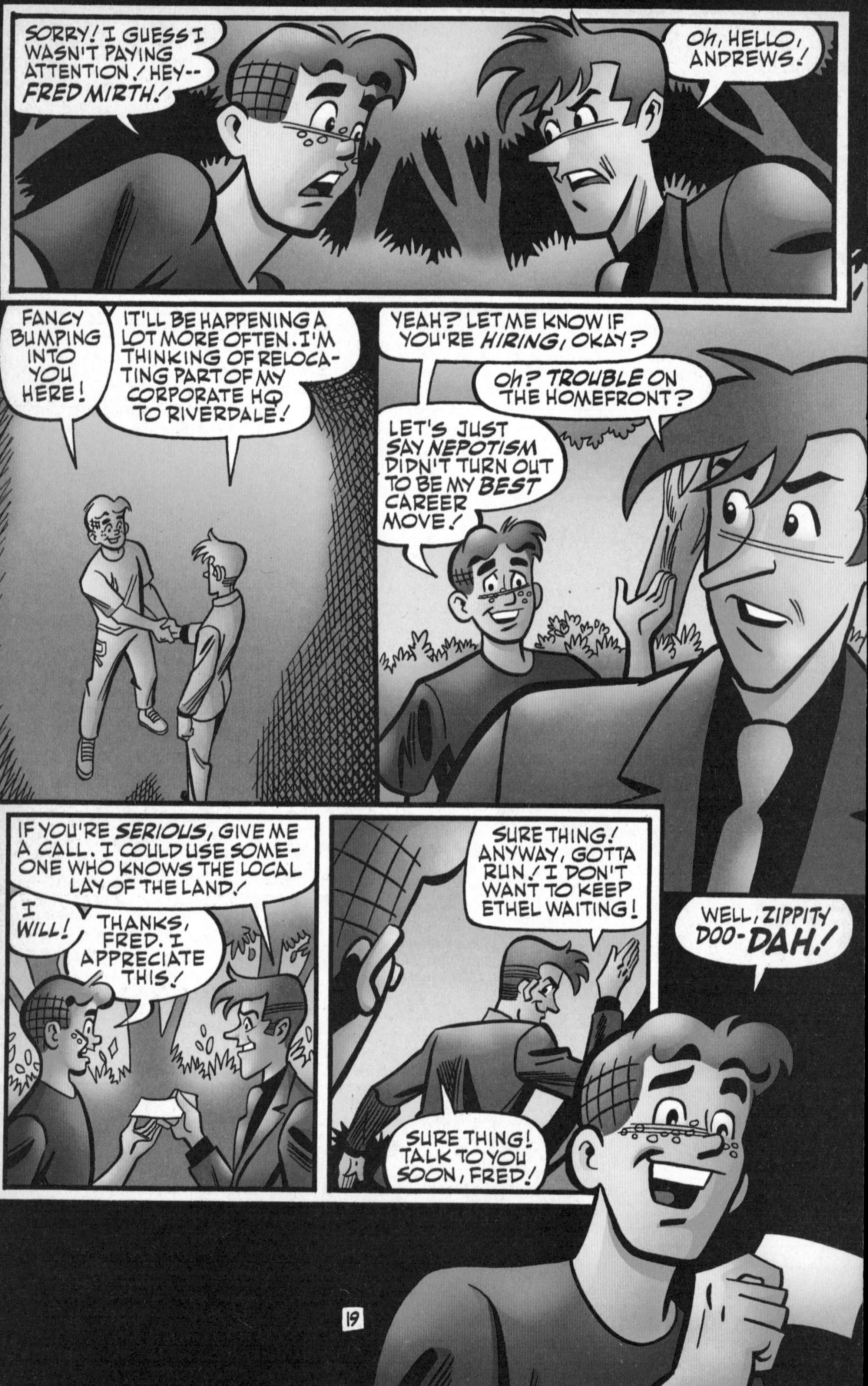
SORRY! I GUESS I WASN'T PAYING ATTENTION! HEY-- FRED MIRTH!
Oh, HELLO, ANDREWS!
FANCY BUMPING INTO YOU HERE!
IT'LL BE HAPPENING A LOT MORE OFTEN. I'M THINKING OF RELOCATING PART OF MY CORPORATE HQ TO RIVERDALE!
YEAH? LET ME KNOW IF YOU'RE HIRING, OKAY?
Oh? TROUBLE ON THE HOMEFRONT?
LET'S JUST SAY NEPOTISM DIDN'T TURN OUT TO BE MY BEST CAREER MOVE!
IF YOU'RE SERIOUS, GIVE ME A CALL. I COULD USE SOMEONE WHO KNOWS THE LOCAL LAY OF THE LAND!
I WILL!
THANKS, FRED. I APPRECIATE THIS!
SURE THING! ANYWAY, GOTTA RUN! I DON'T WANT TO KEEP ETHEL WAITING!
SURE THING! TALK TO YOU SOON, FRED!
WELL, ZIPPITY DOO-DAH!

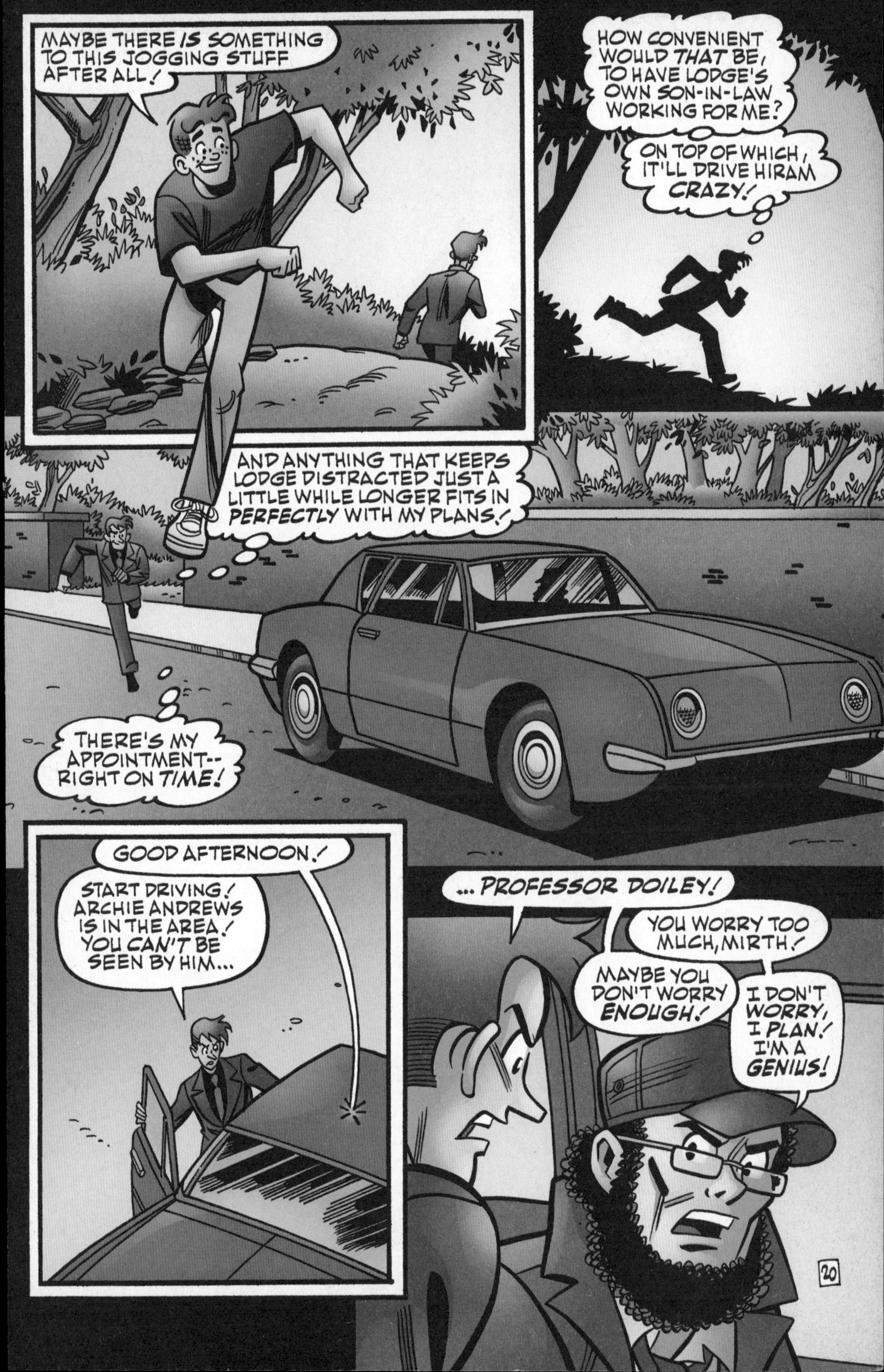
MAYBE THERE IS SOMETHING TO THIS JOGGING STUFF AFTER ALL!
HOW CONVENIENT WOULD THAT BE, TO HAVE LODGE'S OWN SON-IN-LAW WORKING FOR ME?
ON TOP OF WHICH, IT'LL DRIVE HIRAM CRAZY!
AND ANYTHING THAT KEEPS LODGE DISTRACTED JUST A LITTLE WHILE LONGER FITS IN PERFECTLY WITH MY PLANS!
THERE'S MY APPOINTMENT-- RIGHT ON TIME!
GOOD AFTERNOON!
...PROFESSOR DOILEY!
START DRIVING! ARCHIE ANDREWS IS IN THE AREA! YOU CAN'T BE SEEN BY HIM...
YOU WORRY TOO MUCH, MIRTH!
MAYBE YOU DON'T WORRY ENOUGH!
I DON'T WORRY, I PLAN! I'M A GENIUS!
20

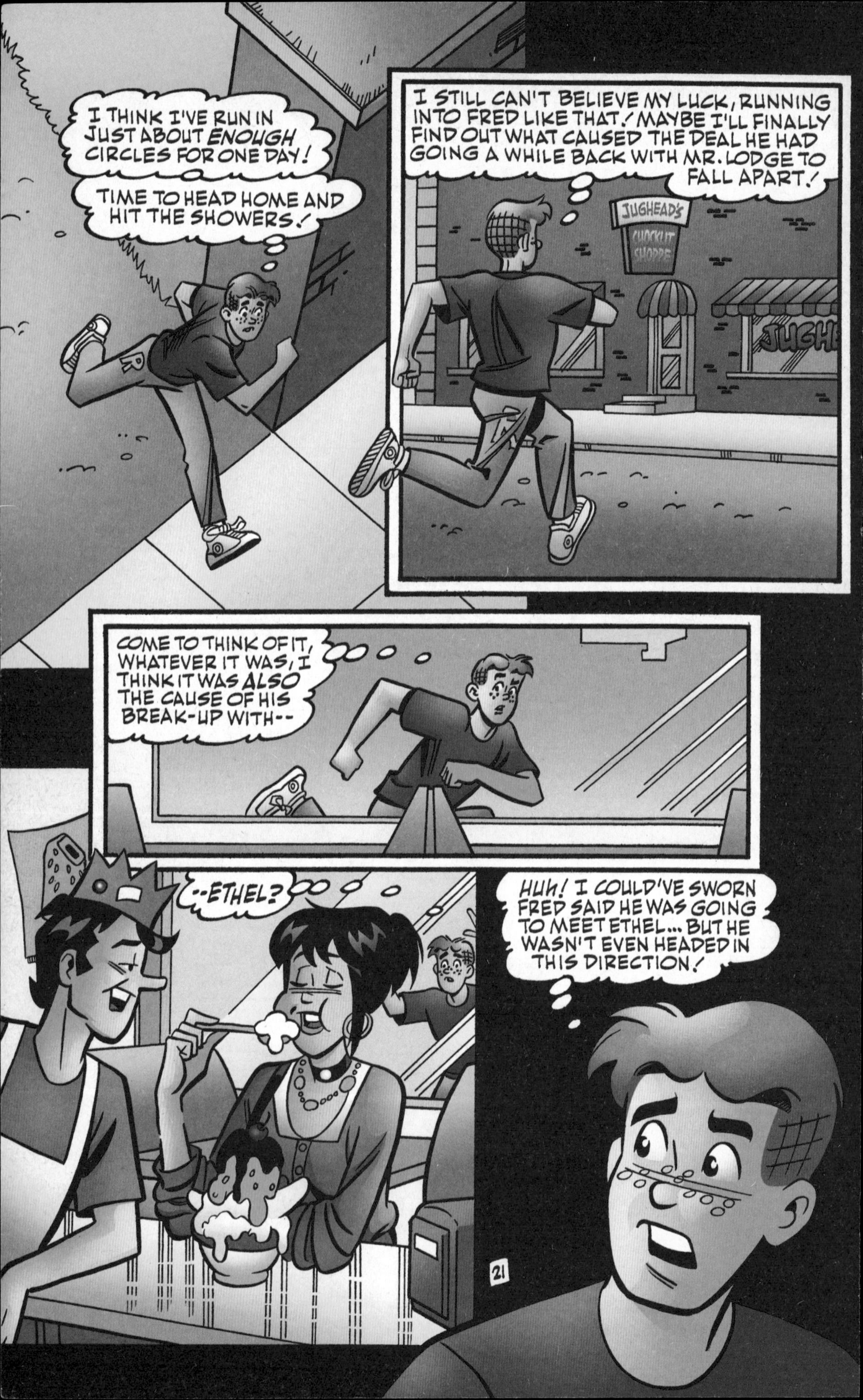
I THINK I'VE RUN IN JUST ABOUT ENOUGH CIRCLES FOR ONE DAY!
TIME TO HEAD HOME AND HIT THE SHOWERS!
I STILL CAN'T BELIEVE MY LUCK, RUNNING INTO FRED LIKE THAT! MAYBE I'LL FINALLY FIND OUT WHAT CAUSED THE DEAL HE HAD GOING A WHILE BACK WITH MR. LODGE TO FALL APART!
JUGHEAD'S CHOCKLIT SHOPPE
COME TO THINK OF IT, WHATEVER IT WAS, I THINK IT WAS ALSO THE CAUSE OF HIS BREAK-UP WITH--
--ETHEL?
HUH! I COULD'VE SWORN FRED SAID HE WAS GOING TO MEET ETHEL... BUT HE WASN'T EVEN HEADED IN THIS DIRECTION!
21

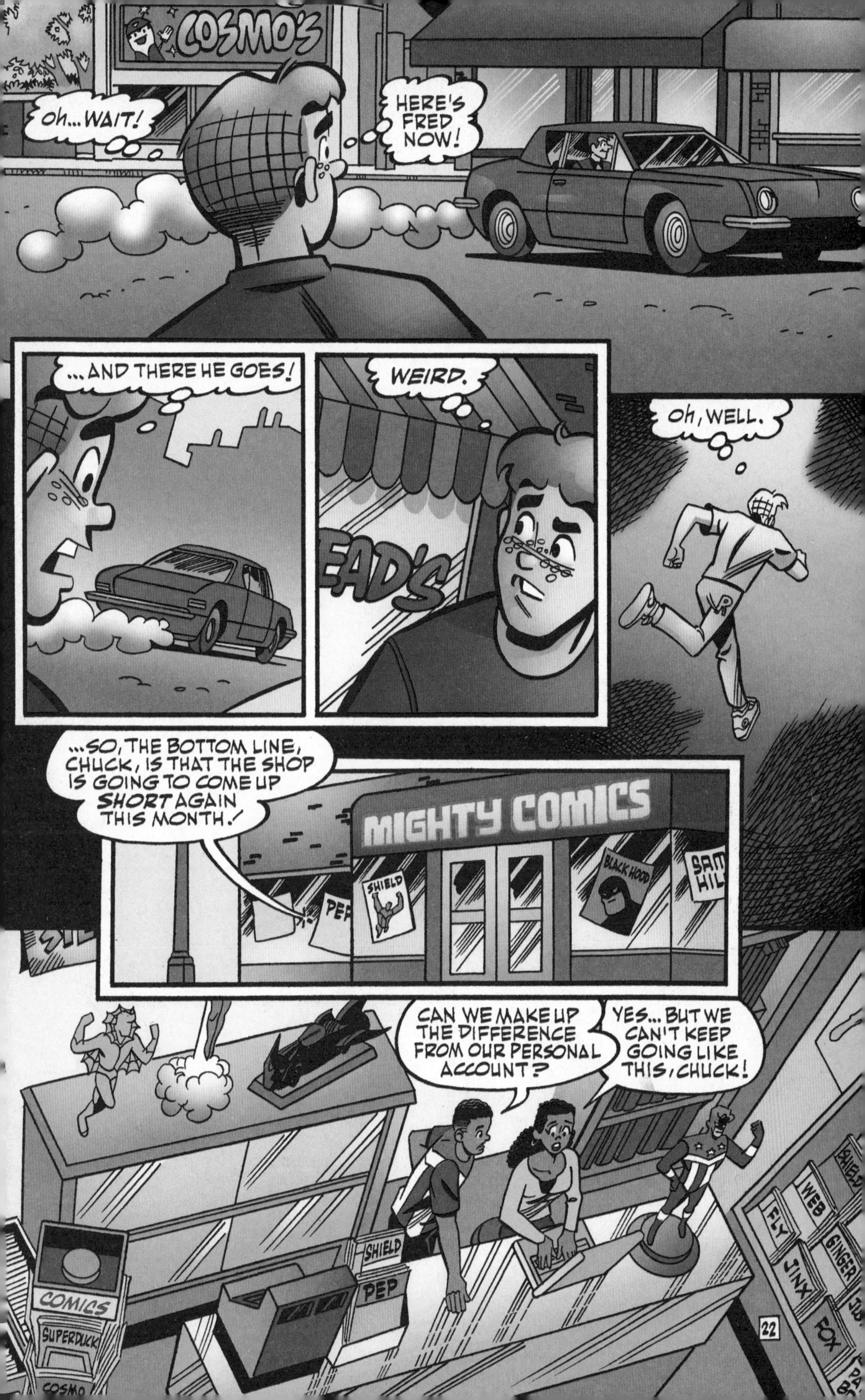
COSMO'S
Oh... WAIT!
HERE'S FRED NOW!
...AND THERE HE GOES!
WEIRD.
EAD'S
Oh, WELL.
...SO, THE BOTTOM LINE, CHUCK, IS THAT THE SHOP IS GOING TO COME UP SHORT AGAIN THIS MONTH.!
MIGHTY COMICS
SHIELD
BLACK HOOD
SAM HILL
PEP
CAN WE MAKE UP THE DIFFERENCE FROM OUR PERSONAL ACCOUNT?
YES... BUT WE CAN'T KEEP GOING LIKE THIS, CHUCK!
SHIELD
PEP
COMICS
SUPERDUCK
COSMO
WEB
FLY
GINGER
JINX
FOX

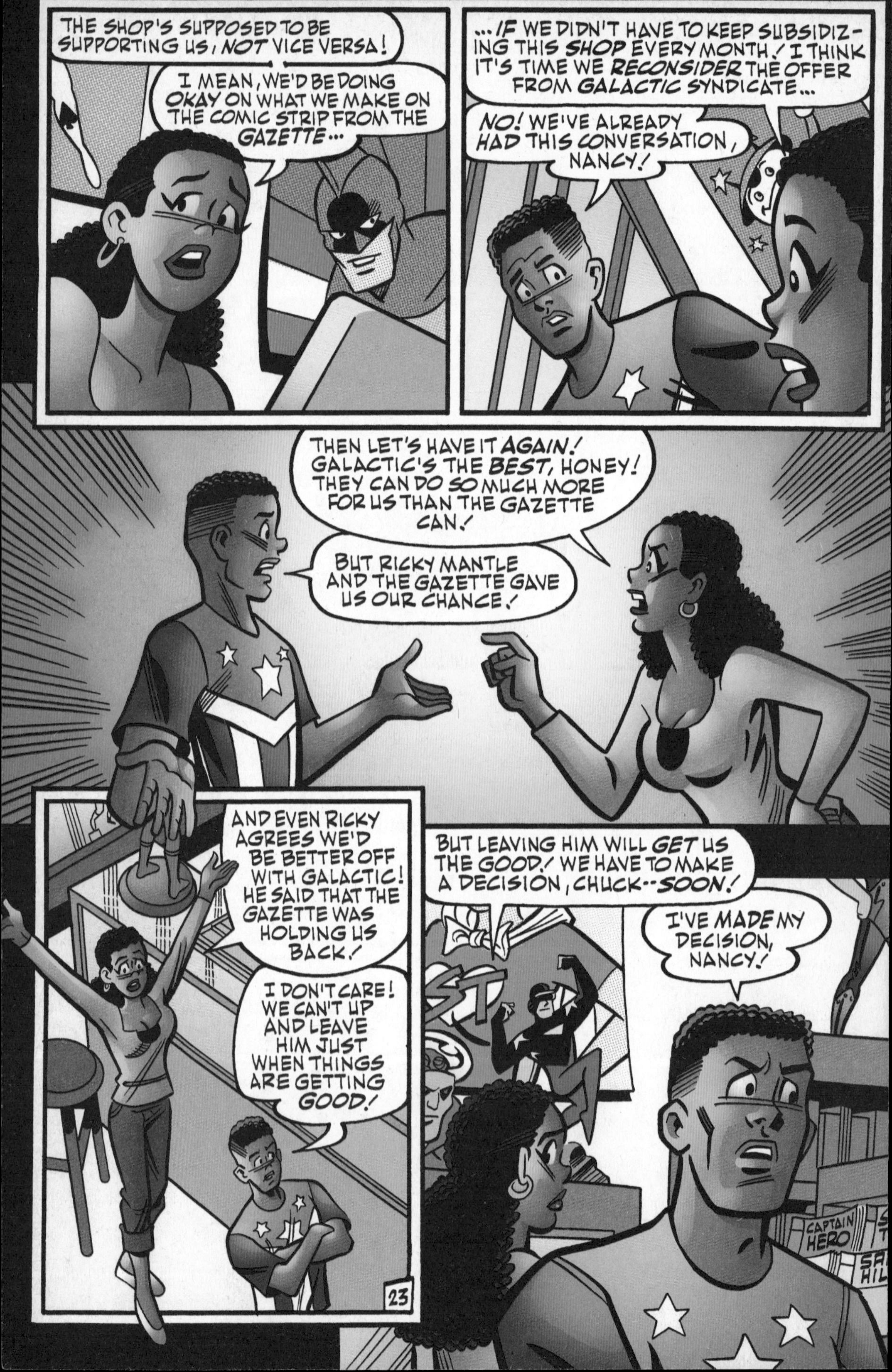
THE SHOP'S SUPPOSED TO BE SUPPORTING US, NOT VICE VERSA!
I MEAN, WE'D BE DOING OKAY ON WHAT WE MAKE ON THE COMIC STRIP FROM THE GAZETTE...
...IF WE DIDN'T HAVE TO KEEP SUBSIDIZING THIS SHOP EVERY MONTH! I THINK IT'S TIME WE RECONSIDER THE OFFER FROM GALACTIC SYNDICATE...
NO! WE'VE ALREADY HAD THIS CONVERSATION, NANCY!
THEN LET'S HAVE IT AGAIN! GALACTIC'S THE BEST, HONEY! THEY CAN DO SO MUCH MORE FOR US THAN THE GAZETTE CAN!
BUT RICKY MANTLE AND THE GAZETTE GAVE US OUR CHANCE!
AND EVEN RICKY AGREES WE'D BE BETTER OFF WITH GALACTIC! HE SAID THAT THE GAZETTE WAS HOLDING US BACK!
I DON'T CARE! WE CAN'T UP AND LEAVE HIM JUST WHEN THINGS ARE GETTING GOOD!
BUT LEAVING HIM WILL GET US THE GOOD! WE HAVE TO MAKE A DECISION, CHUCK--SOON!
I'VE MADE MY DECISION, NANCY!
CAPTAIN HERO
23

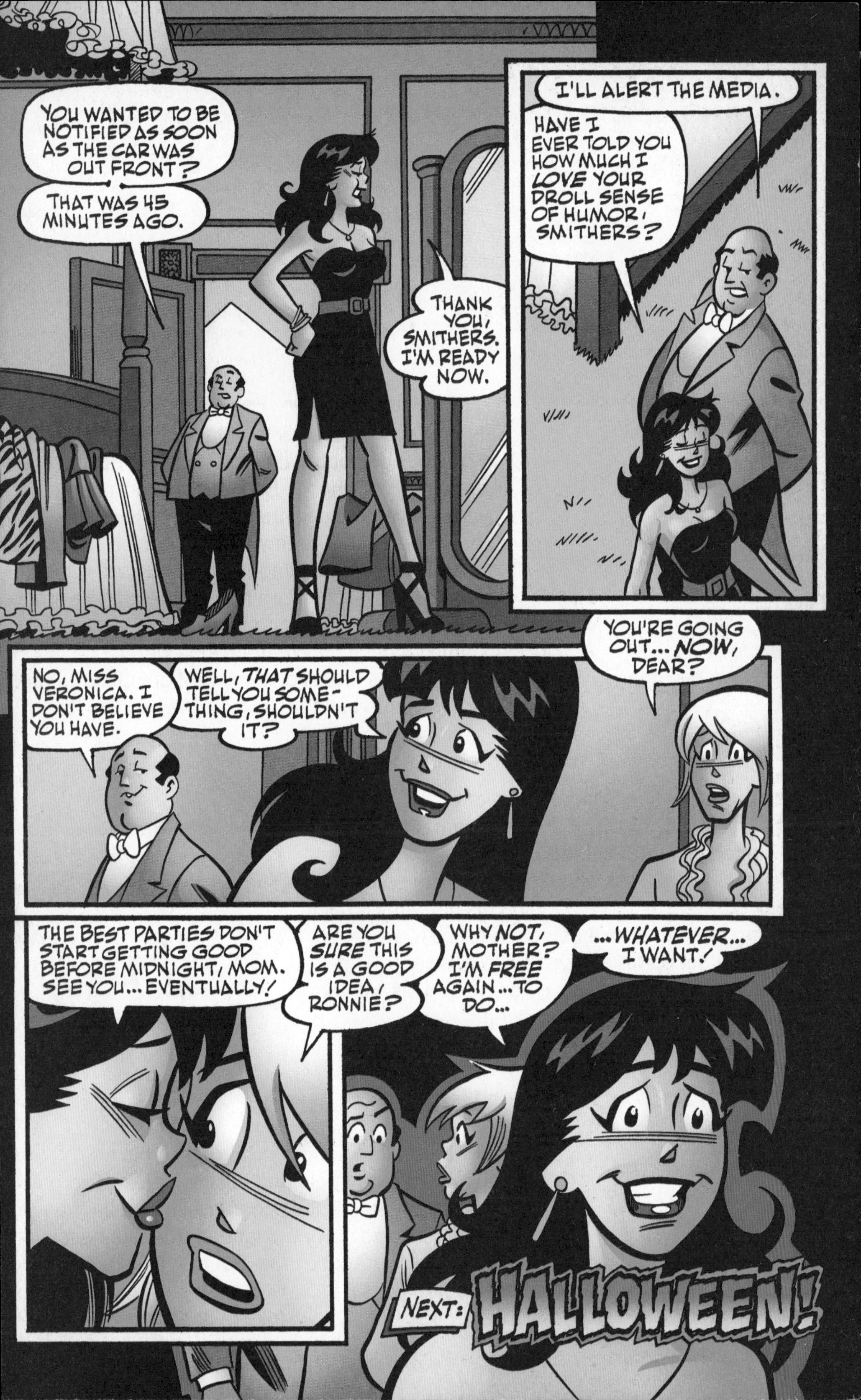

YOU WANTED TO BE NOTIFIED AS SOON AS THE CAR WAS OUT FRONT?
THAT WAS 45 MINUTES AGO.
THANK YOU, SMITHERS. I'M READY NOW.
I'LL ALERT THE MEDIA.
HAVE I EVER TOLD YOU HOW MUCH I LOVE YOUR DROLL SENSE OF HUMOR, SMITHERS?
NO, MISS VERONICA. I DON'T BELIEVE YOU HAVE.
WELL, THAT SHOULD TELL YOU SOME-THING, SHOULDN'T IT?
YOU'RE GOING OUT... NOW, DEAR?
THE BEST PARTIES DON'T START GETTING GOOD BEFORE MIDNIGHT, MOM. SEE YOU... EVENTUALLY!
ARE YOU SURE THIS IS A GOOD IDEA, RONNIE?
WHY NOT, MOTHER? I'M FREE AGAIN... TO DO...
...WHATEVER... I WANT!
NEXT: HALLOWEEN!

Two Worlds. Two Loves. Two Destinies.
In an alternate universe where anything can happen and what you think is familiar is anything but...

Archie Marries BETTY

Previously...

The heat is on in the Archie Marries Betty universe! The couple have both taken on teaching positions at Riverdale High School—Betty as an English teacher and Archie as a music instructor. Betty's loved by both staff and students, but Archie hasn't been so lucky. His students first took advantage of his laid back attitude, and now they've turned on him for trying to be strict. They may have gone too far with their pranks—by locking him in a cabinet! What the kids weren't counting on, however, was a fire! Archie made it out okay, but the same can't be said for the building itself...

The Riverdale High School fire might not have been just a freak accident! The school may have been sabotaged—on Mr. Lodge's orders! Why would he do such a thing? He's also been planning some shady business ventures behind his daughter's back, insisting on her instead going to France to work! What's he got up his sleeves? The answer to that question may have to wait, since he and his wife have just found out some very shocking news...

Outsider Fred Mirth seems to be getting his hands into a lot of lucrative deals and businesses in Riverdale. He just became a silent partner/investor for Jughead's Chocklit Shoppe, saving Jughead from the hassle of franchising and negotiations. But are his intentions all that noble? Or is it just another step in his attempt to take over Lodge Industries?

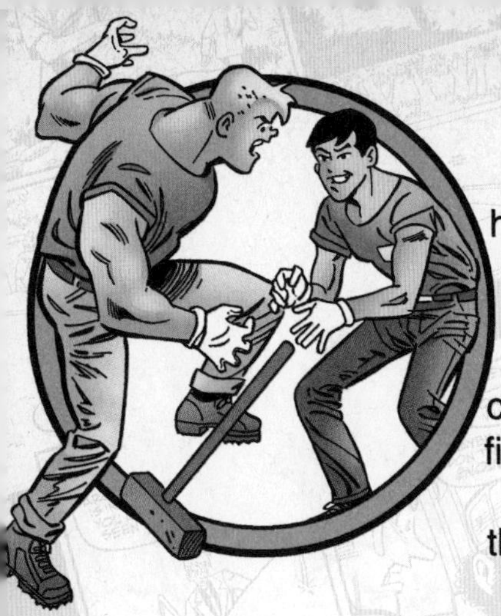

Archie and Betty aren't the only alumni working at Riverdale High School. Moose has taken a position as head janitor, and it hasn't been easy! He's been running around trying to handle all of the numerous repairs that keep mysteriously cropping up. His assistant Mikio Sasaki has only been making the situation worse by constantly ignoring his orders and arguing with him! The final straw came when Moose discovered Mikio messing with the pipe that ultimately started the fire that burnt the school down. But Mikio wasn't working alone— what exactly does Mr. Lodge have to do with all of this?

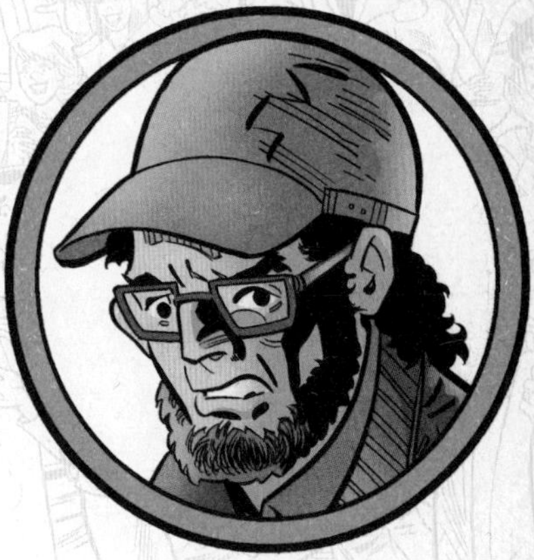

Dilton seems to be lurking in the shadows these days, only ever communicating with Fred Mirth or Mr. Lodge. He seems to be helping out the two rivals— but how can that be? Whose side is he really on? And why has he been incommunicado with all of his friends in Riverdale?

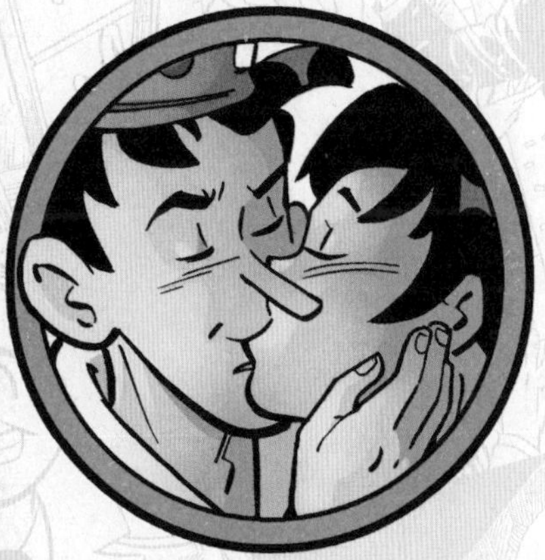

Midge was shocked to find out that Jughead quit the Chocklit Shoppe, almost leaving them in financial limbo! Fortunately, he found an investor willing to take over all of the financial aspects of the business—and back them entirely! Now Jughead and Midge can focus on their marriage instead of the Chocklit Shoppe, except of course, for the fact that they both work there all day long!

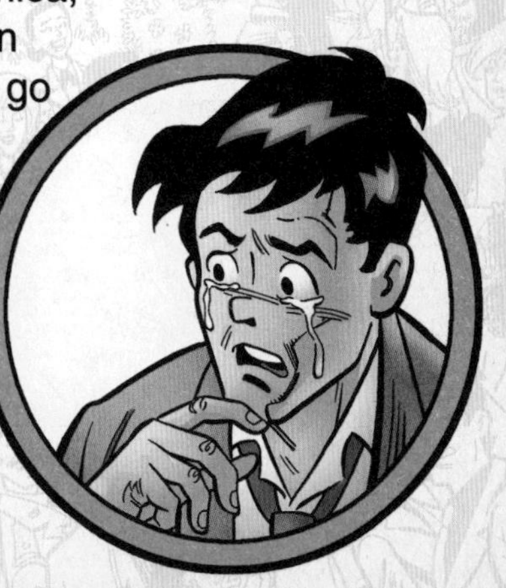

Reggie's had a lot on his mind as of late. He loves Veronica, but doesn't trust either her father or her co-worker Jason Blossom. He's also less-than-thrilled about her plans to go to France for business. He's been keeping himself busy at his father's paper, the Gazette, getting the scoop on some mysterious construction set to take place by Lodge Industries. He's ready to crack this case along with the help of Veronica, and Veronica's been willing to give him a hand and talk to her father about it! But duty calls and Veronica had to leave. Things only get worse when Reggie finds out that her plane never touched down in Paris, and has instead disappeared…

"EVERYTHING'S STARTED *GOING* SO GOOD LATELY."

"IT SURE LOOKED LIKE WE'D *ALL* FOUND WHAT WE *WANTED...*"

- JUGHEAD JONES

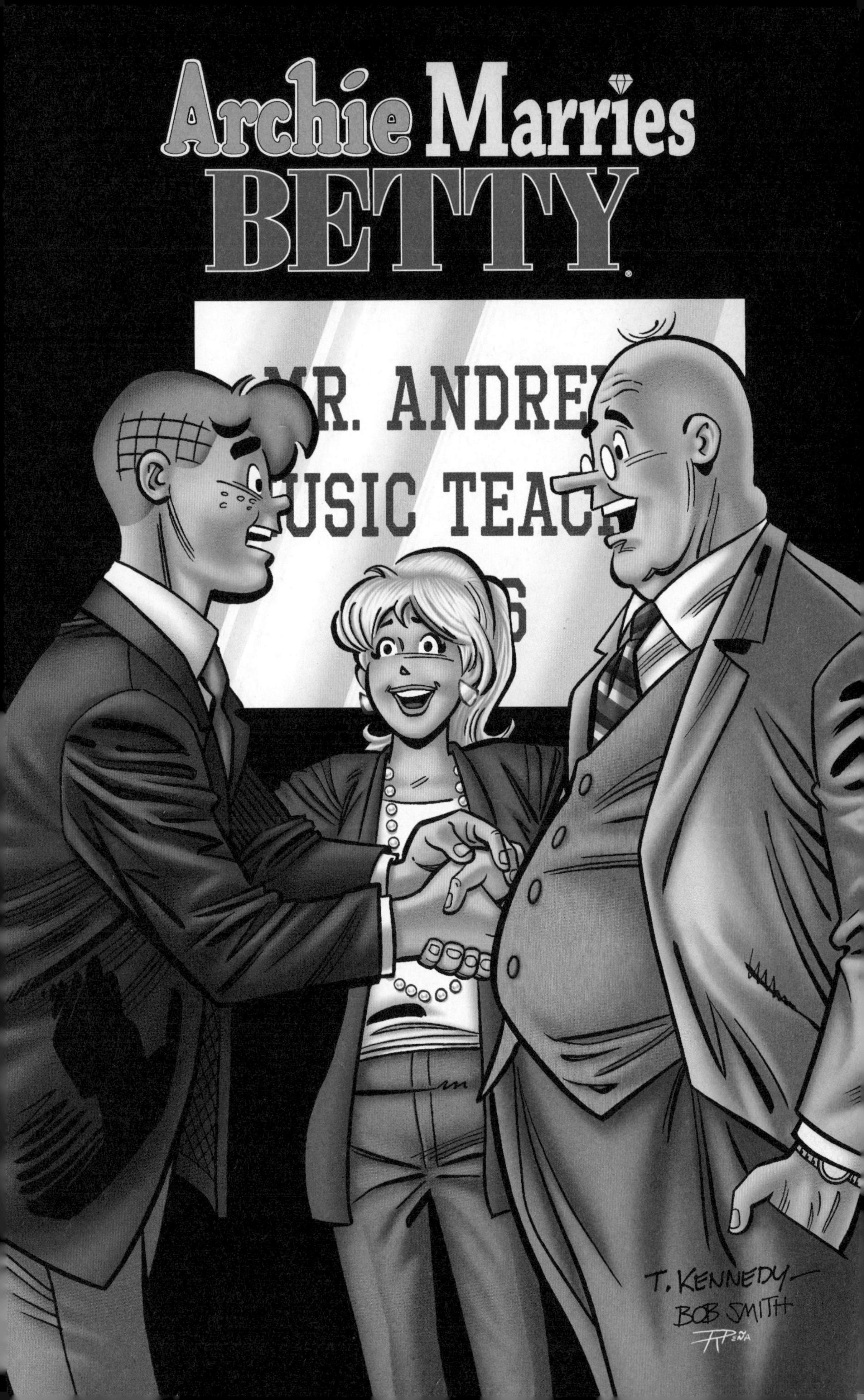
Archie Marries
BETTY
T. KENNEDY
BOB SMITH

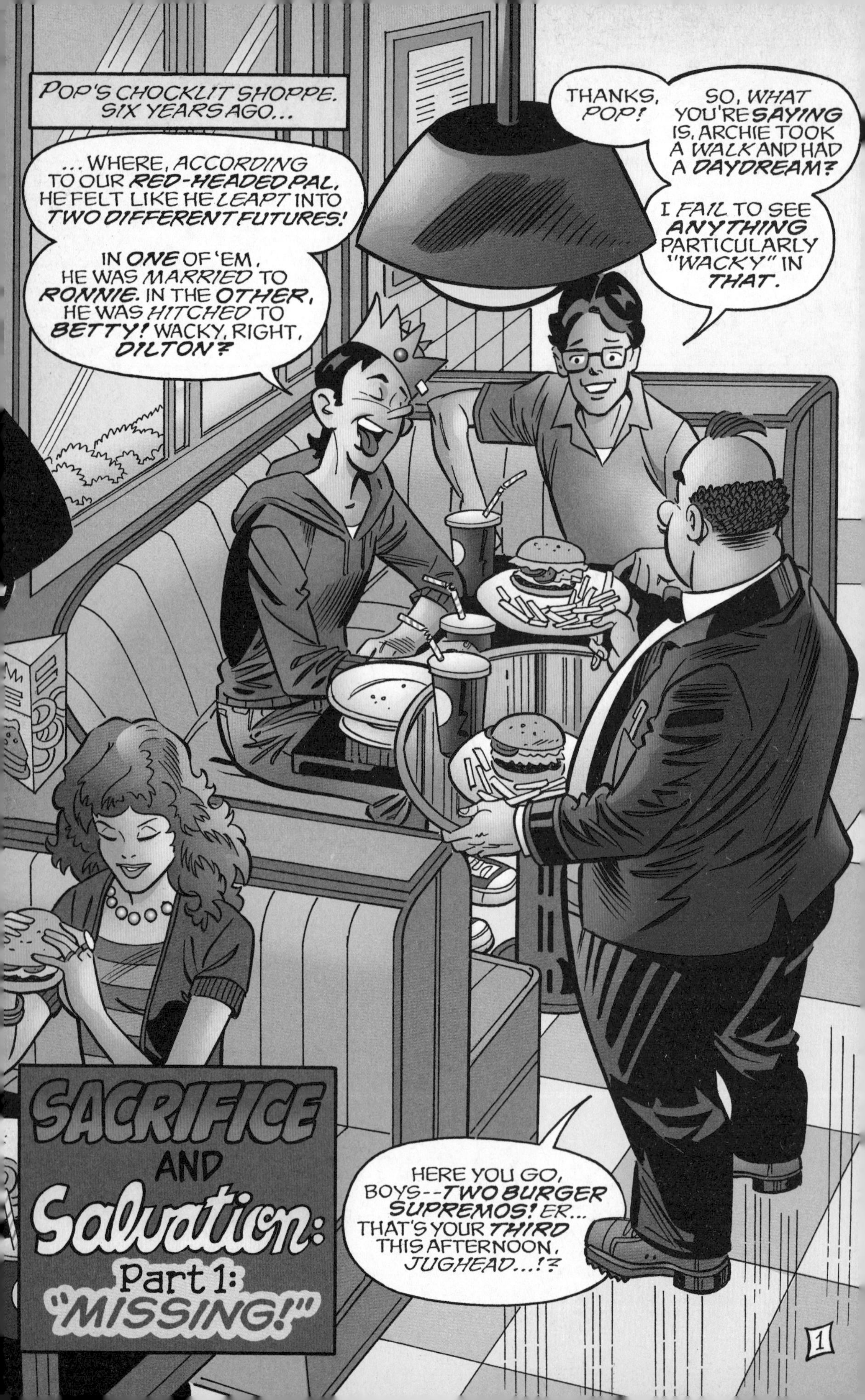
POP'S CHOCKLIT SHOPPE. SIX YEARS AGO...
...WHERE, ACCORDING TO OUR RED-HEADED PAL, HE FELT LIKE HE LEAPT INTO TWO DIFFERENT FUTURES!
IN ONE OF 'EM, HE WAS MARRIED TO RONNIE. IN THE OTHER, HE WAS HITCHED TO BETTY! WACKY, RIGHT, DILTON?
THANKS, POP!
SO, WHAT YOU'RE SAYING IS, ARCHIE TOOK A WALK AND HAD A DAYDREAM?
I FAIL TO SEE ANYTHING PARTICULARLY "WACKY" IN THAT.
SACRIFICE AND Salvation: Part 1: "MISSING!"
HERE YOU GO, BOYS--TWO BURGER SUPREMOS! ER... THAT'S YOUR THIRD THIS AFTERNOON, JUGHEAD...!?
1

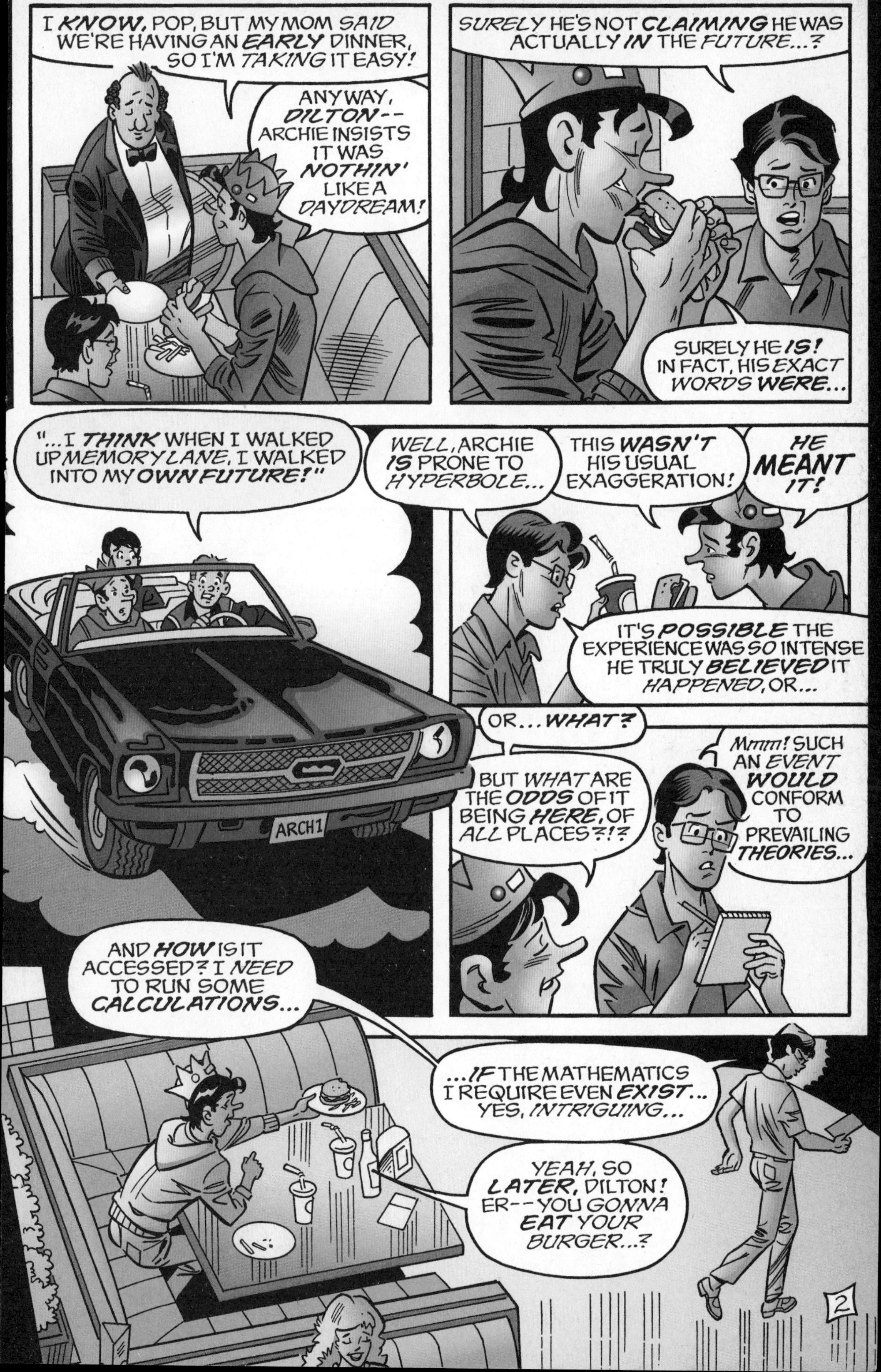
I KNOW, POP, BUT MY MOM SAID WE'RE HAVING AN EARLY DINNER, SO I'M TAKING IT EASY!
ANYWAY, DILTON-- ARCHIE INSISTS IT WAS NOTHIN' LIKE A DAYDREAM!
SURELY HE'S NOT CLAIMING HE WAS ACTUALLY IN THE FUTURE...?
SURELY HE IS! IN FACT, HIS EXACT WORDS WERE...
"...I THINK WHEN I WALKED UP MEMORY LANE, I WALKED INTO MY OWN FUTURE!"
ARCH1
WELL, ARCHIE IS PRONE TO HYPERBOLE...
THIS WASN'T HIS USUAL EXAGGERATION!
HE MEANT IT!
IT'S POSSIBLE THE EXPERIENCE WAS SO INTENSE HE TRULY BELIEVED IT HAPPENED, OR...
OR... WHAT?
Mmm! SUCH AN EVENT WOULD CONFORM TO PREVAILING THEORIES...
BUT WHAT ARE THE ODDS OF IT BEING HERE, OF ALL PLACES?!?
AND HOW IS IT ACCESSED? I NEED TO RUN SOME CALCULATIONS...
...IF THE MATHEMATICS I REQUIRE EVEN EXIST... YES, INTRIGUING...
YEAH, SO LATER, DILTON! ER--YOU GONNA EAT YOUR BURGER...?
2

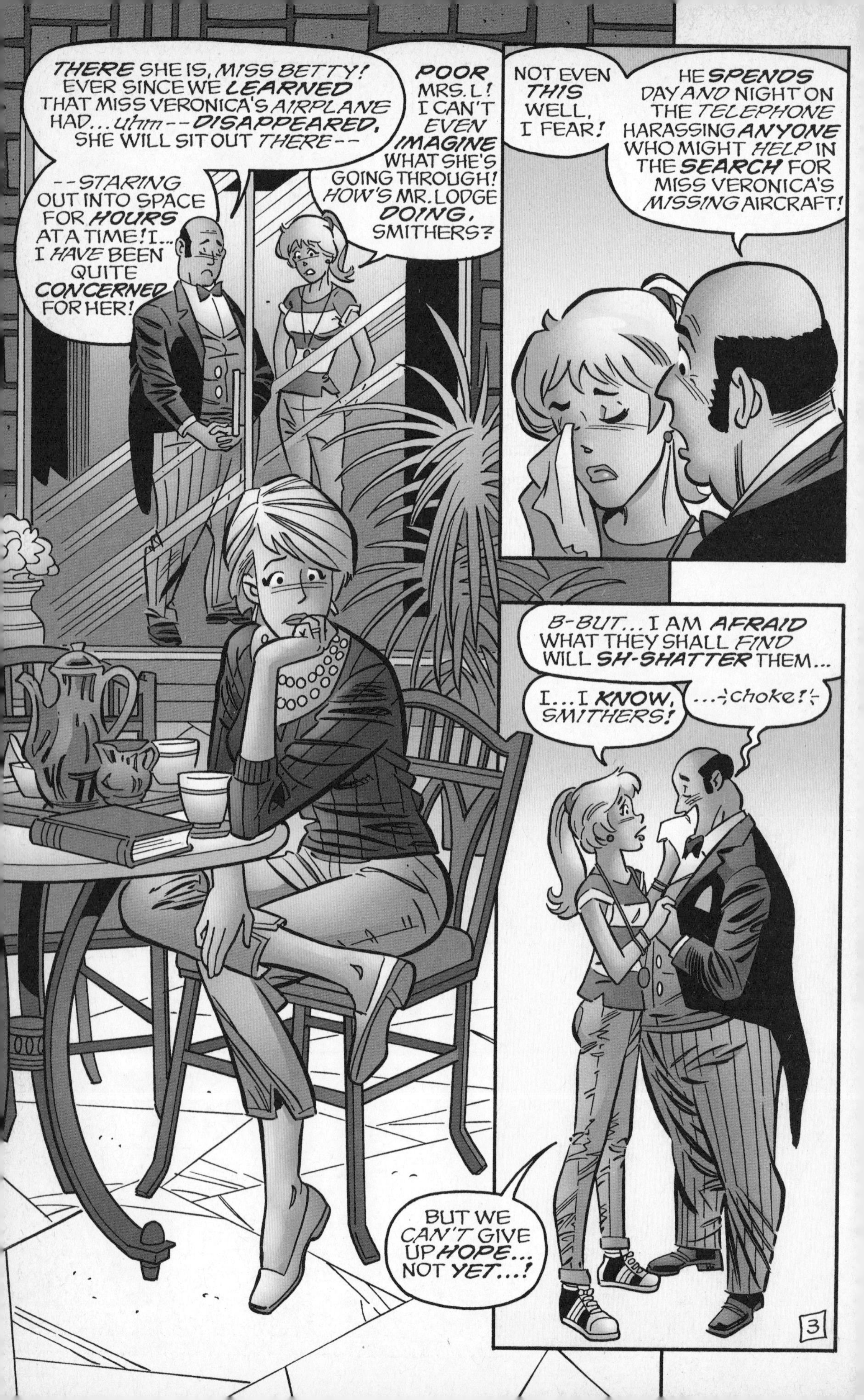
THERE SHE IS, MISS BETTY! EVER SINCE WE LEARNED THAT MISS VERONICA'S AIRPLANE HAD... uhm -- DISAPPEARED, SHE WILL SIT OUT THERE --
-- STARING OUT INTO SPACE FOR HOURS AT A TIME! I... I HAVE BEEN QUITE CONCERNED FOR HER!
POOR MRS. L! I CAN'T EVEN IMAGINE WHAT SHE'S GOING THROUGH! HOW'S MR. LODGE DOING, SMITHERS?
NOT EVEN THIS WELL, I FEAR!
HE SPENDS DAY AND NIGHT ON THE TELEPHONE HARASSING ANYONE WHO MIGHT HELP IN THE SEARCH FOR MISS VERONICA'S MISSING AIRCRAFT!
B-BUT... I AM AFRAID WHAT THEY SHALL FIND WILL SH-SHATTER THEM...
I... I KNOW, SMITHERS!
...choke!
BUT WE CAN'T GIVE UP HOPE... NOT YET...!
3

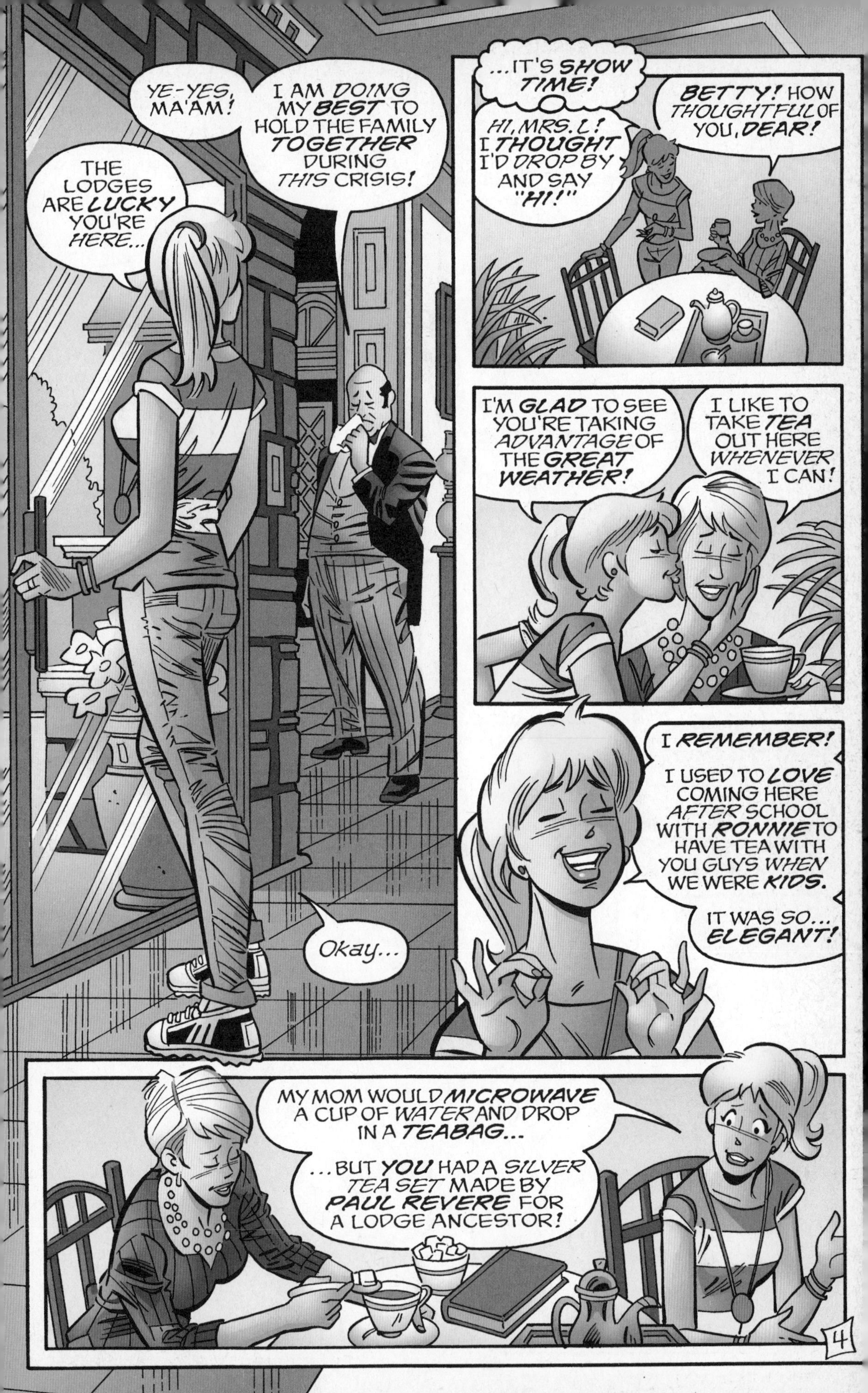
YE-YES, MA'AM!
I AM DOING MY BEST TO HOLD THE FAMILY TOGETHER DURING THIS CRISIS!
THE LODGES ARE LUCKY YOU'RE HERE...
Okay...
...IT'S SHOW TIME!
HI, MRS. L! I THOUGHT I'D DROP BY AND SAY "HI!"
BETTY! HOW THOUGHTFUL OF YOU, DEAR!
I'M GLAD TO SEE YOU'RE TAKING ADVANTAGE OF THE GREAT WEATHER!
I LIKE TO TAKE TEA OUT HERE WHENEVER I CAN!
I REMEMBER!
I USED TO LOVE COMING HERE AFTER SCHOOL WITH RONNIE TO HAVE TEA WITH YOU GUYS WHEN WE WERE KIDS.
IT WAS SO... ELEGANT!
MY MOM WOULD MICROWAVE A CUP OF WATER AND DROP IN A TEABAG...
...BUT YOU HAD A SILVER TEA SET MADE BY PAUL REVERE FOR A LODGE ANCESTOR!

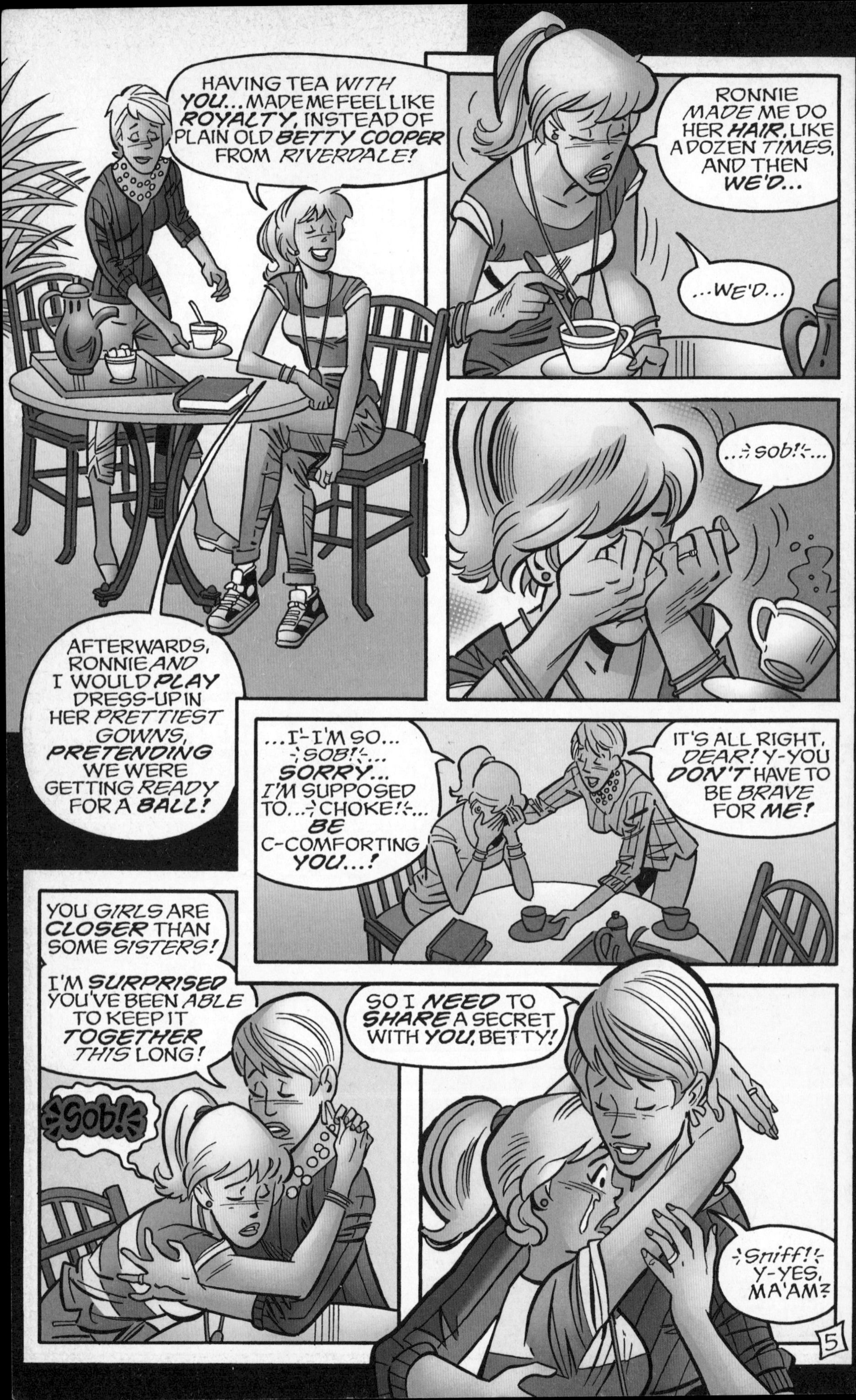

HAVING TEA WITH YOU... MADE ME FEEL LIKE ROYALTY, INSTEAD OF PLAIN OLD BETTY COOPER FROM RIVERDALE!
AFTERWARDS, RONNIE AND I WOULD PLAY DRESS-UP IN HER PRETTIEST GOWNS, PRETENDING WE WERE GETTING READY FOR A BALL!
RONNIE MADE ME DO HER HAIR, LIKE A DOZEN TIMES, AND THEN WE'D...
...WE'D...
...SOB!...
...I-I'M SO... SOB!... SORRY... I'M SUPPOSED TO... CHOKE!... BE C-COMFORTING YOU...!
IT'S ALL RIGHT, DEAR! Y-YOU DON'T HAVE TO BE BRAVE FOR ME!
YOU GIRLS ARE CLOSER THAN SOME SISTERS!
I'M SURPRISED YOU'VE BEEN ABLE TO KEEP IT TOGETHER THIS LONG!
SOB!
SO I NEED TO SHARE A SECRET WITH YOU, BETTY!
SNIFF! Y-YES, MA'AM?

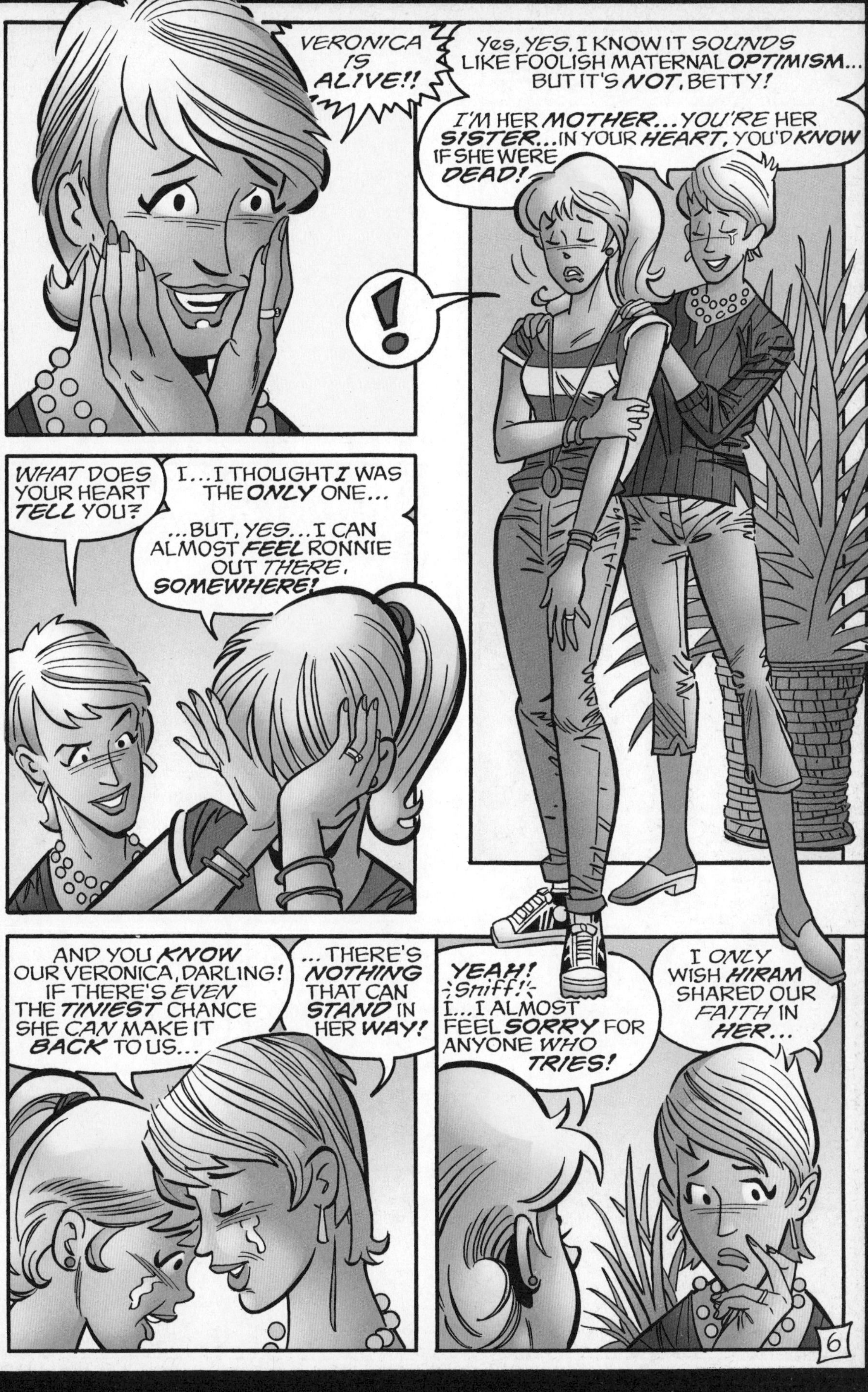
VERONICA IS ALIVE!!
Yes, YES. I KNOW IT SOUNDS LIKE FOOLISH MATERNAL OPTIMISM... BUT IT'S NOT, BETTY!
I'M HER MOTHER... YOU'RE HER SISTER... IN YOUR HEART, YOU'D KNOW IF SHE WERE DEAD!
!
WHAT DOES YOUR HEART TELL YOU?
I... I THOUGHT I WAS THE ONLY ONE...
...BUT, YES... I CAN ALMOST FEEL RONNIE OUT THERE, SOMEWHERE!
AND YOU KNOW OUR VERONICA, DARLING! IF THERE'S EVEN THE TINIEST CHANCE SHE CAN MAKE IT BACK TO US...
...THERE'S NOTHING THAT CAN STAND IN HER WAY!
YEAH! -Sniff!- I... I ALMOST FEEL SORRY FOR ANYONE WHO TRIES!
I ONLY WISH HIRAM SHARED OUR FAITH IN HER...
6

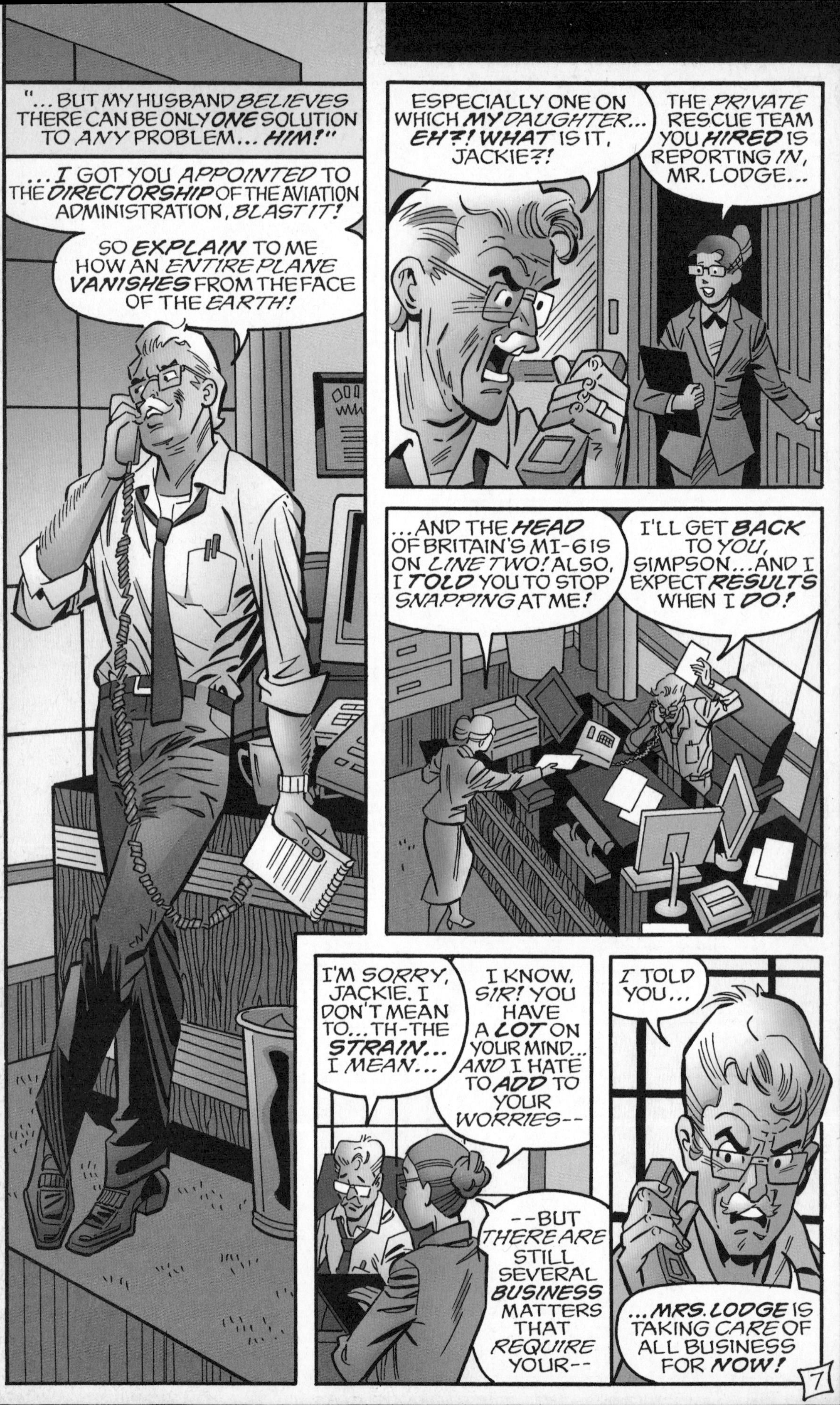

"... BUT MY HUSBAND BELIEVES THERE CAN BE ONLY ONE SOLUTION TO ANY PROBLEM... HIM!"
... I GOT YOU APPOINTED TO THE DIRECTORSHIP OF THE AVIATION ADMINISTRATION, BLAST IT!
SO EXPLAIN TO ME HOW AN ENTIRE PLANE VANISHES FROM THE FACE OF THE EARTH!
ESPECIALLY ONE ON WHICH MY DAUGHTER... EH?! WHAT IS IT, JACKIE?!
THE PRIVATE RESCUE TEAM YOU HIRED IS REPORTING IN, MR. LODGE...
...AND THE HEAD OF BRITAIN'S MI-6 IS ON LINE TWO! ALSO, I TOLD YOU TO STOP SNAPPING AT ME!
I'LL GET BACK TO YOU, SIMPSON... AND I EXPECT RESULTS WHEN I DO!
I'M SORRY, JACKIE. I DON'T MEAN TO... TH-THE STRAIN... I MEAN...
I KNOW, SIR! YOU HAVE A LOT ON YOUR MIND... AND I HATE TO ADD TO YOUR WORRIES--
--BUT THERE ARE STILL SEVERAL BUSINESS MATTERS THAT REQUIRE YOUR--
I TOLD YOU...
...MRS. LODGE IS TAKING CARE OF ALL BUSINESS FOR NOW!

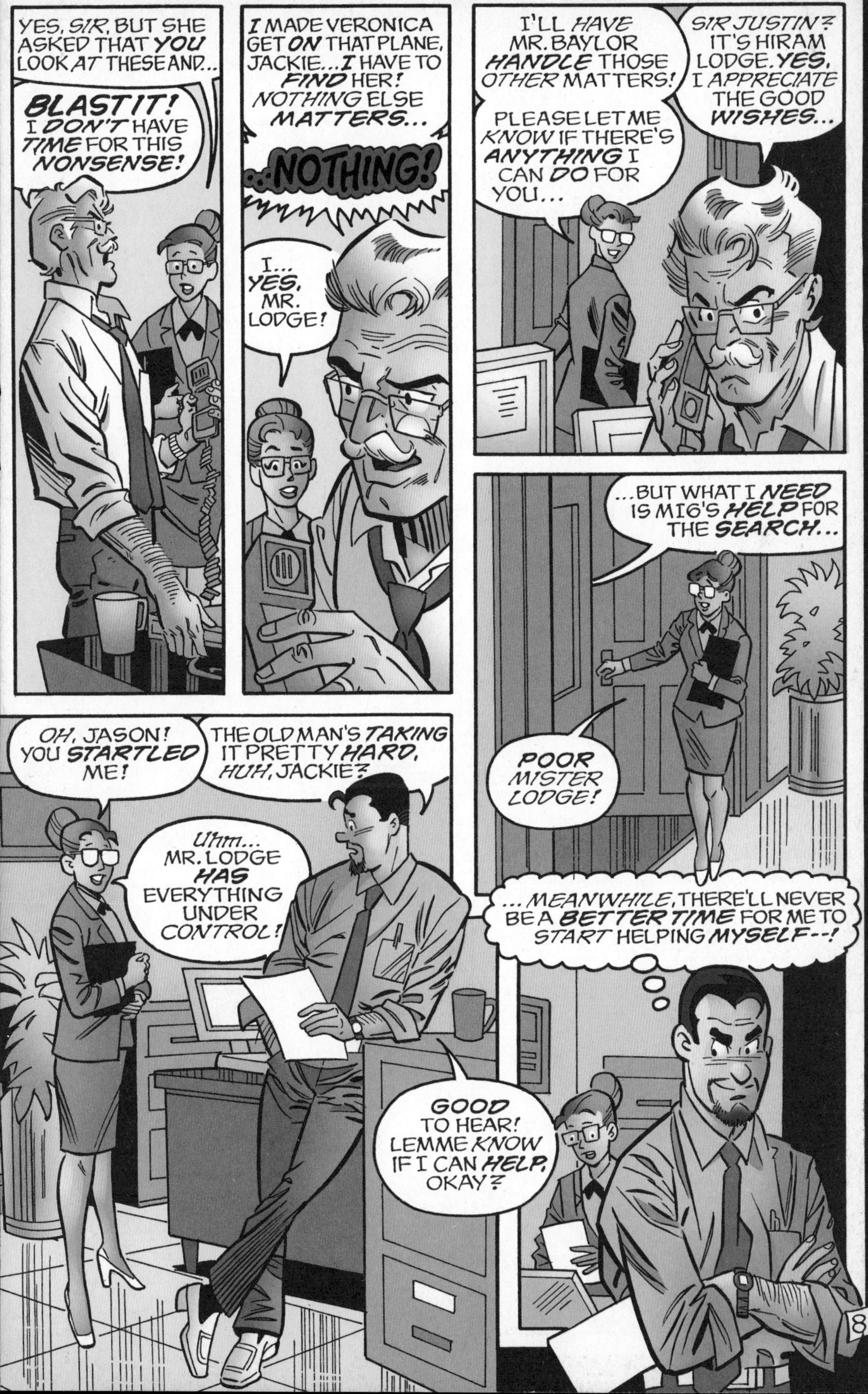

YES, SIR, BUT SHE ASKED THAT YOU LOOK AT THESE AND...
BLAST IT! I DON'T HAVE TIME FOR THIS NONSENSE!
I MADE VERONICA GET ON THAT PLANE, JACKIE... I HAVE TO FIND HER! NOTHING ELSE MATTERS...
...NOTHING!
I... YES, MR. LODGE!
I'LL HAVE MR. BAYLOR HANDLE THOSE OTHER MATTERS!
PLEASE LET ME KNOW IF THERE'S ANYTHING I CAN DO FOR YOU...
SIR JUSTIN? IT'S HIRAM LODGE. YES, I APPRECIATE THE GOOD WISHES...
...BUT WHAT I NEED IS MI6'S HELP FOR THE SEARCH...
POOR MISTER LODGE!
OH, JASON! YOU STARTLED ME!
THE OLD MAN'S TAKING IT PRETTY HARD, HUH, JACKIE?
Uhm... MR. LODGE HAS EVERYTHING UNDER CONTROL!
GOOD TO HEAR! LEMME KNOW IF I CAN HELP, OKAY?
...MEANWHILE, THERE'LL NEVER BE A BETTER TIME FOR ME TO START HELPING MYSELF--!

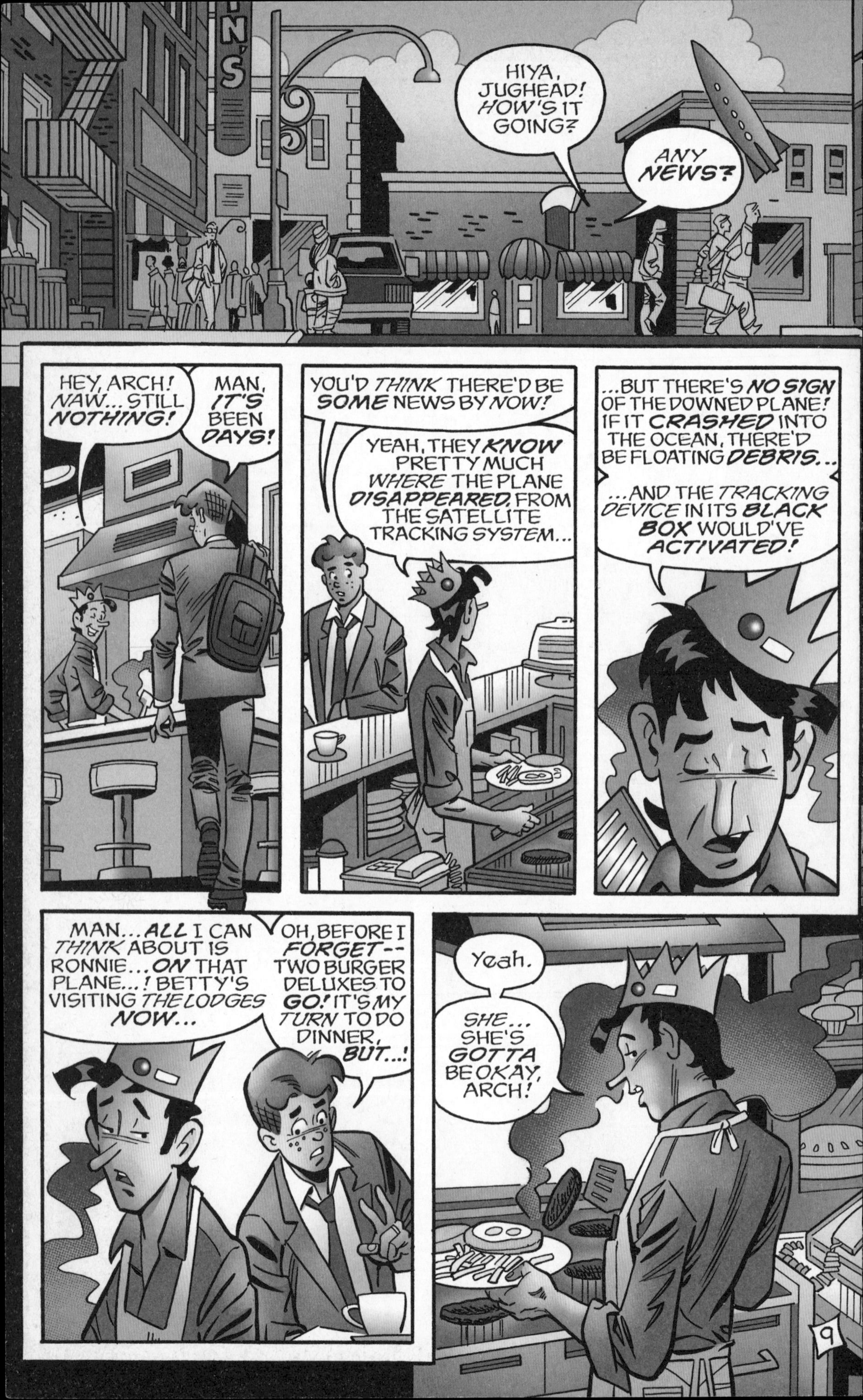
HIYA, JUGHEAD! HOW'S IT GOING?
ANY NEWS?
HEY, ARCH! NAW... STILL NOTHING!
MAN, IT'S BEEN DAYS!
YOU'D THINK THERE'D BE SOME NEWS BY NOW!
YEAH, THEY KNOW PRETTY MUCH WHERE THE PLANE DISAPPEARED, FROM THE SATELLITE TRACKING SYSTEM...
...BUT THERE'S NO SIGN OF THE DOWNED PLANE! IF IT CRASHED INTO THE OCEAN, THERE'D BE FLOATING DEBRIS...
...AND THE TRACKING DEVICE IN ITS BLACK BOX WOULD'VE ACTIVATED!
MAN... ALL I CAN THINK ABOUT IS RONNIE... ON THAT PLANE...! BETTY'S VISITING THE LODGES NOW...
OH, BEFORE I FORGET -- TWO BURGER DELUXES TO GO! IT'S MY TURN TO DO DINNER, BUT...!
Yeah.
SHE... SHE'S GOTTA BE OKAY, ARCH!
9

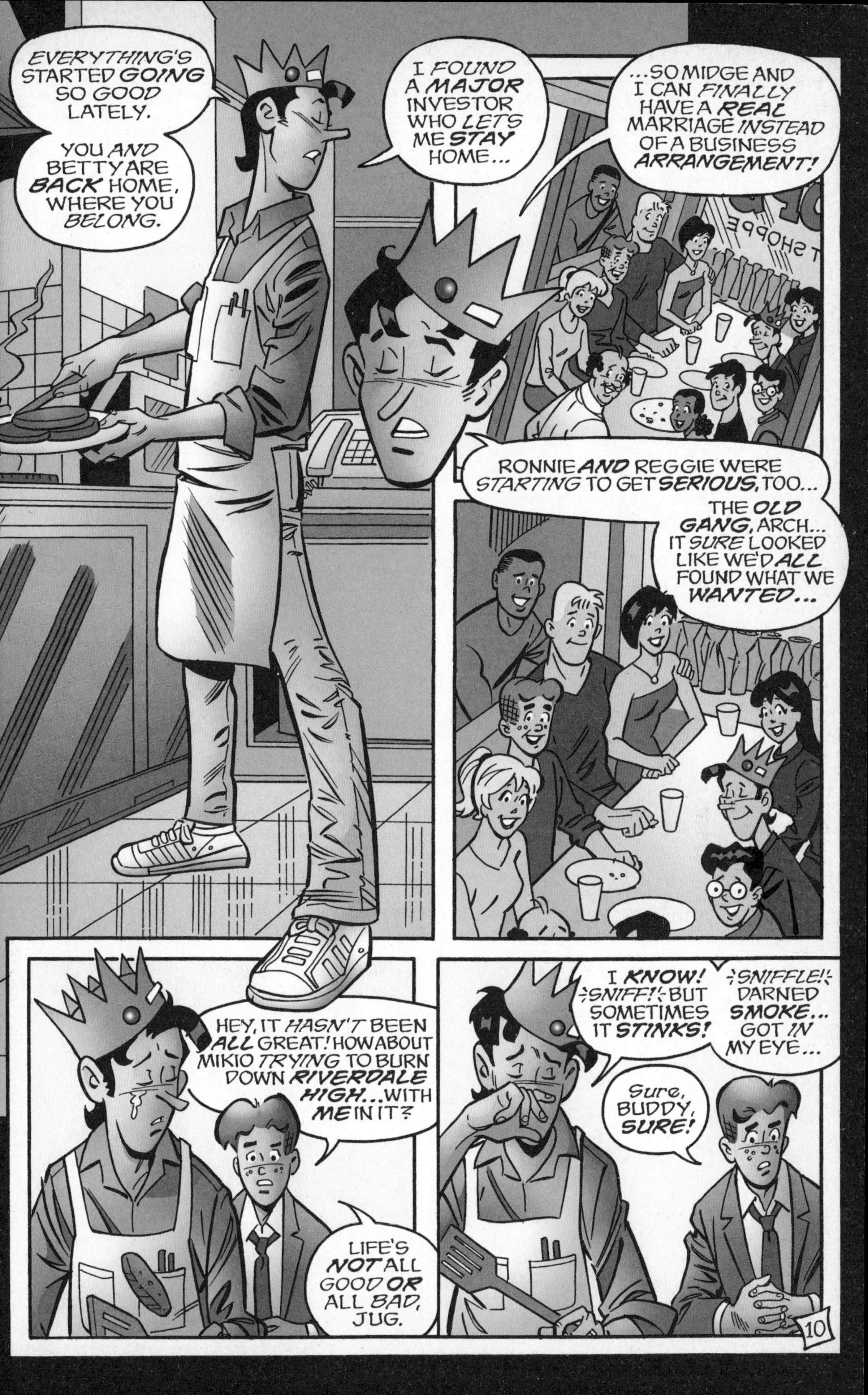
EVERYTHING'S STARTED GOING SO GOOD LATELY.
YOU AND BETTY ARE BACK HOME, WHERE YOU BELONG.
I FOUND A MAJOR INVESTOR WHO LETS ME STAY HOME...
...SO MIDGE AND I CAN FINALLY HAVE A REAL MARRIAGE INSTEAD OF A BUSINESS ARRANGEMENT!
RONNIE AND REGGIE WERE STARTING TO GET SERIOUS, TOO...
THE OLD GANG, ARCH... IT SURE LOOKED LIKE WE'D ALL FOUND WHAT WE WANTED...
HEY, IT HASN'T BEEN ALL GREAT! HOW ABOUT MIKIO TRYING TO BURN DOWN RIVERDALE HIGH... WITH ME IN IT?
LIFE'S NOT ALL GOOD OR ALL BAD, JUG.
I KNOW! -SNIFF!- BUT SOMETIMES IT STINKS!
-SNIFFLE!- DARNED SMOKE... GOT IN MY EYE...
Sure, BUDDY, SURE!

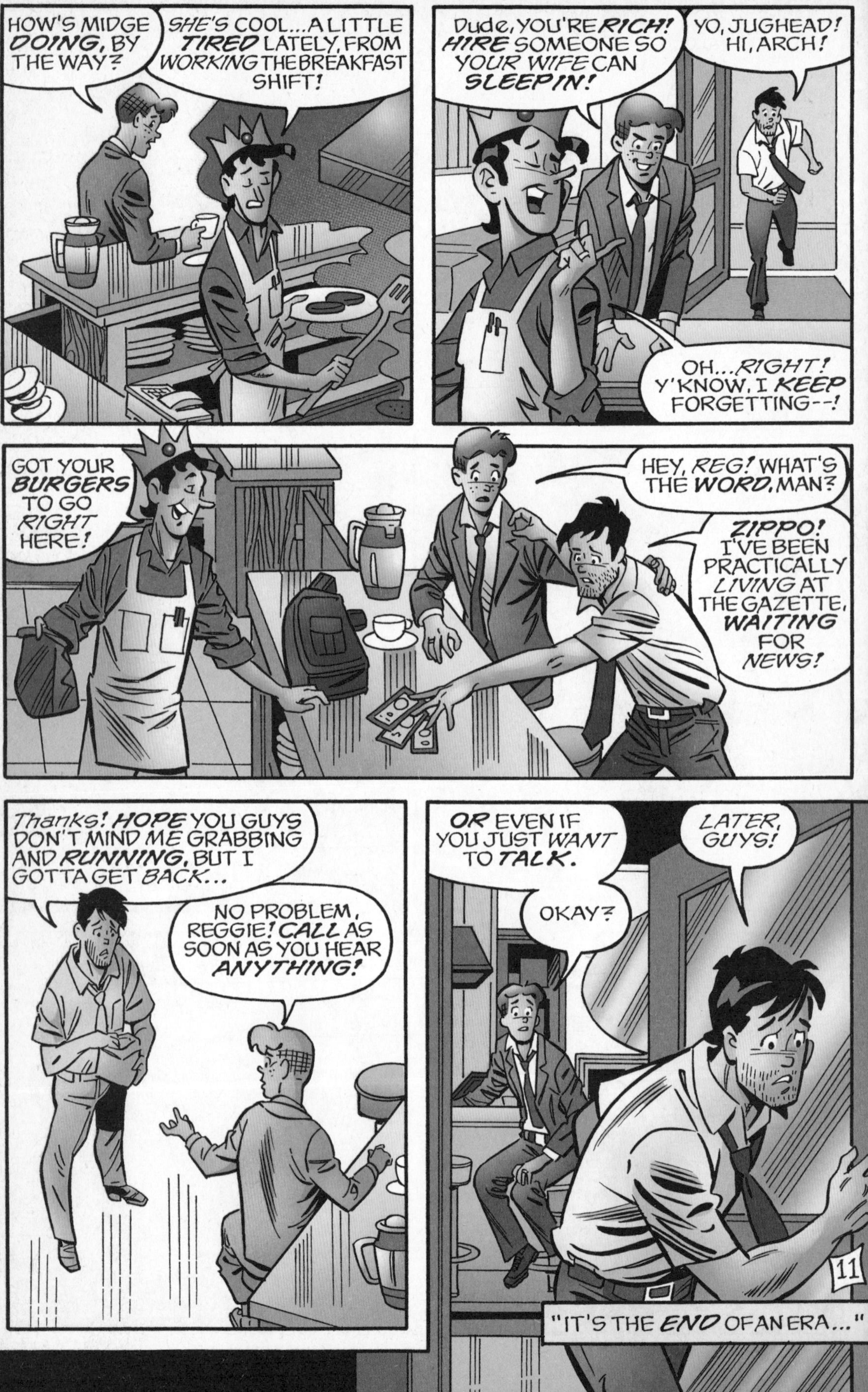
HOW'S MIDGE DOING, BY THE WAY?
SHE'S COOL...A LITTLE TIRED LATELY, FROM WORKING THE BREAKFAST SHIFT!
Dude, YOU'RE RICH! HIRE SOMEONE SO YOUR WIFE CAN SLEEP IN!
YO, JUGHEAD! HI, ARCH!
OH...RIGHT! Y'KNOW, I KEEP FORGETTING--!
GOT YOUR BURGERS TO GO RIGHT HERE!
HEY, REG! WHAT'S THE WORD, MAN?
ZIPPO! I'VE BEEN PRACTICALLY LIVING AT THE GAZETTE, WAITING FOR NEWS!
Thanks! HOPE YOU GUYS DON'T MIND ME GRABBING AND RUNNING, BUT I GOTTA GET BACK...
NO PROBLEM, REGGIE! CALL AS SOON AS YOU HEAR ANYTHING!
OR EVEN IF YOU JUST WANT TO TALK.
OKAY?
LATER, GUYS!
"IT'S THE END OF AN ERA..."

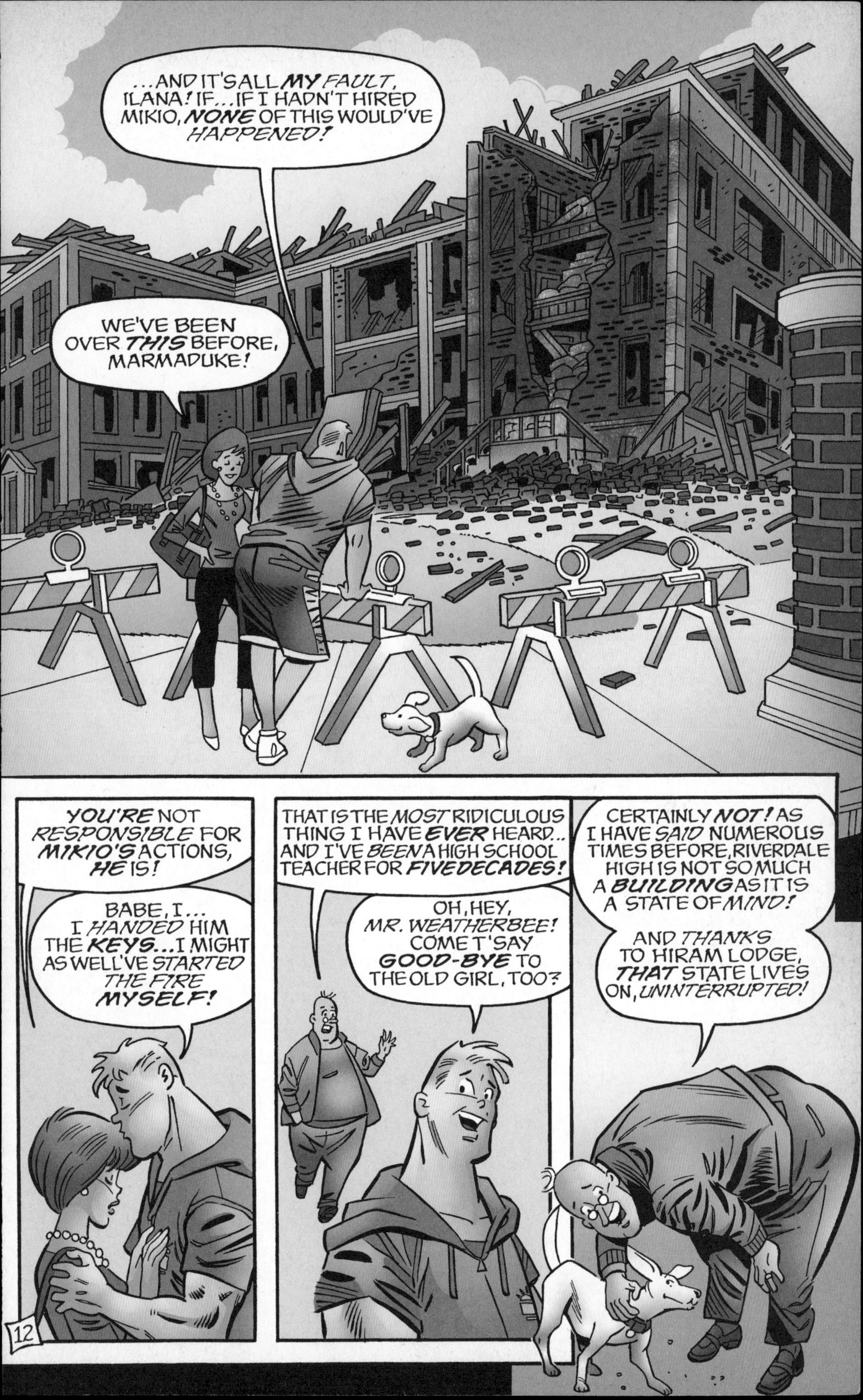
...AND IT'S ALL MY FAULT, ILANA! IF...IF I HADN'T HIRED MIKIO, NONE OF THIS WOULD'VE HAPPENED!
WE'VE BEEN OVER THIS BEFORE, MARMADUKE!
YOU'RE NOT RESPONSIBLE FOR MIKIO'S ACTIONS, HE IS!
BABE, I... I HANDED HIM THE KEYS...I MIGHT AS WELL'VE STARTED THE FIRE MYSELF!
OH, HEY, MR. WEATHERBEE! COME T'SAY GOOD-BYE TO THE OLD GIRL, TOO?
THAT IS THE MOST RIDICULOUS THING I HAVE EVER HEARD... AND I'VE BEEN A HIGH SCHOOL TEACHER FOR FIVE DECADES!
CERTAINLY NOT! AS I HAVE SAID NUMEROUS TIMES BEFORE, RIVERDALE HIGH IS NOT SO MUCH A BUILDING AS IT IS A STATE OF MIND!
AND THANKS TO HIRAM LODGE, THAT STATE LIVES ON, UNINTERRUPTED!

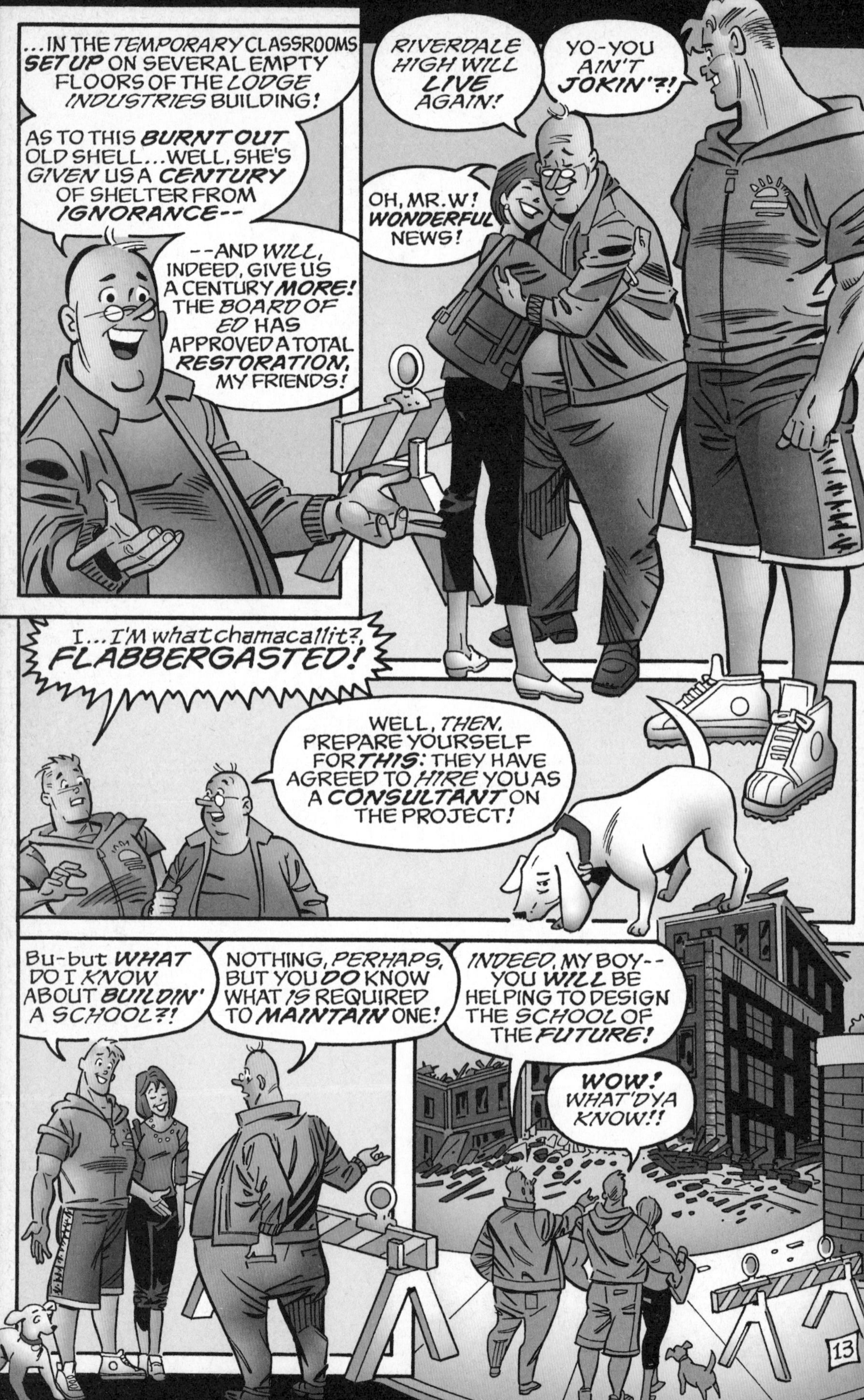

...IN THE TEMPORARY CLASSROOMS SET UP ON SEVERAL EMPTY FLOORS OF THE LODGE INDUSTRIES BUILDING!
AS TO THIS BURNT OUT OLD SHELL...WELL, SHE'S GIVEN US A CENTURY OF SHELTER FROM IGNORANCE--
--AND WILL, INDEED, GIVE US A CENTURY MORE! THE BOARD OF ED HAS APPROVED A TOTAL RESTORATION, MY FRIENDS!
RIVERDALE HIGH WILL LIVE AGAIN!
YO-YOU AIN'T JOKIN'?!
OH, MR. W! WONDERFUL NEWS!
I...I'M whatchamacallit?, FLABBERGASTED!
WELL, THEN, PREPARE YOURSELF FOR THIS: THEY HAVE AGREED TO HIRE YOU AS A CONSULTANT ON THE PROJECT!
Bu-but WHAT DO I KNOW ABOUT BUILDIN' A SCHOOL?!
NOTHING, PERHAPS, BUT YOU DO KNOW WHAT IS REQUIRED TO MAINTAIN ONE!
INDEED, MY BOY--YOU WILL BE HELPING TO DESIGN THE SCHOOL OF THE FUTURE!
WOW! WHAT'DYA KNOW!!

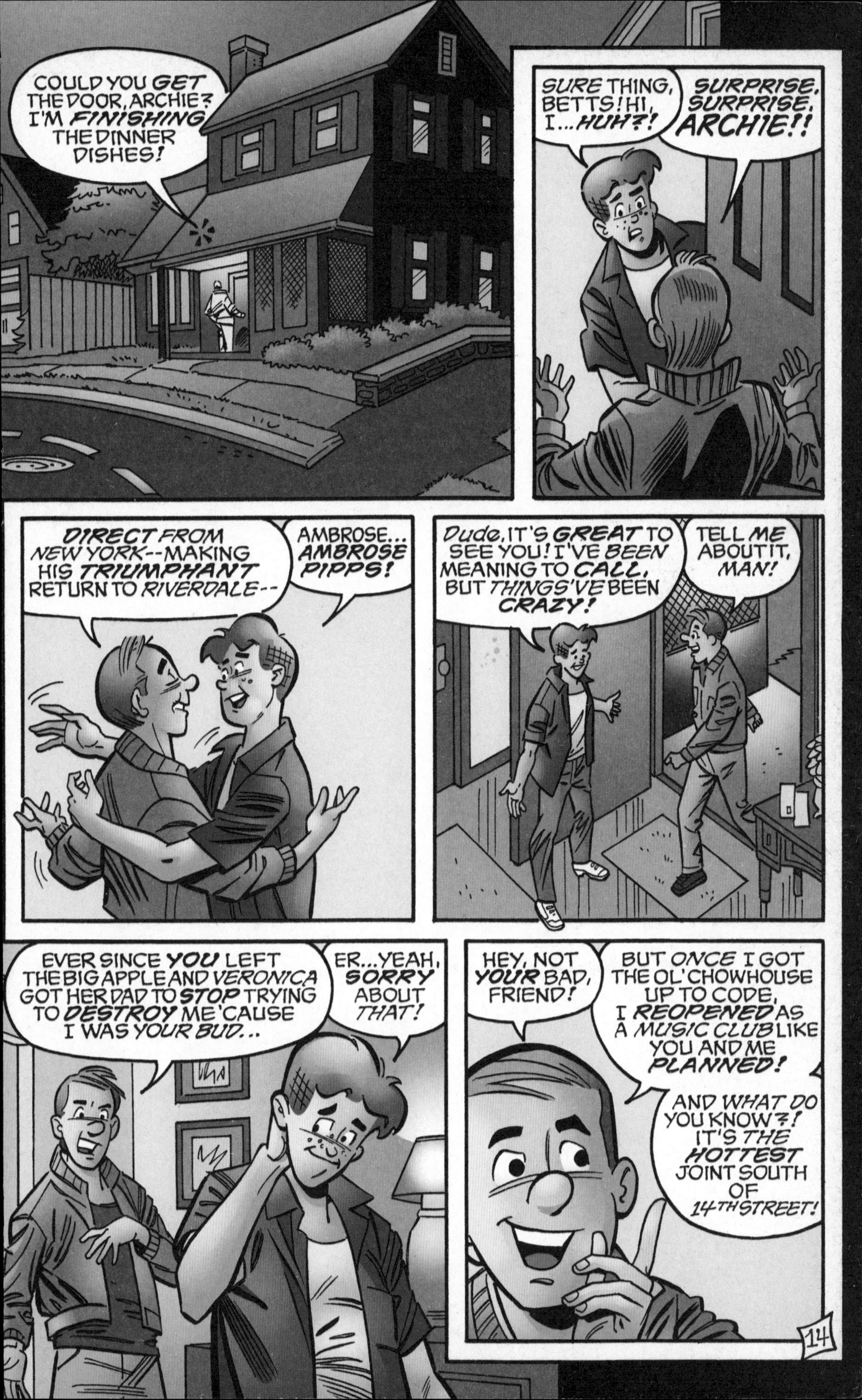
COULD YOU GET THE DOOR, ARCHIE?
I'M FINISHING THE DINNER DISHES!
SURE THING, BETTS! HI, I... HUH?!
SURPRISE, SURPRISE, ARCHIE!!
DIRECT FROM NEW YORK--MAKING HIS TRIUMPHANT RETURN TO RIVERDALE--
AMBROSE... AMBROSE PIPPS!
Dude, IT'S GREAT TO SEE YOU! I'VE BEEN MEANING TO CALL, BUT THINGS'VE BEEN CRAZY!
TELL ME ABOUT IT, MAN!
EVER SINCE YOU LEFT THE BIG APPLE AND VERONICA GOT HER DAD TO STOP TRYING TO DESTROY ME 'CAUSE I WAS YOUR BUD...
ER... YEAH, SORRY ABOUT THAT!
HEY, NOT YOUR BAD, FRIEND!
BUT ONCE I GOT THE OL' CHOWHOUSE UP TO CODE, I REOPENED AS A MUSIC CLUB LIKE YOU AND ME PLANNED!
AND WHAT DO YOU KNOW?! IT'S THE HOTTEST JOINT SOUTH OF 14TH STREET!
14

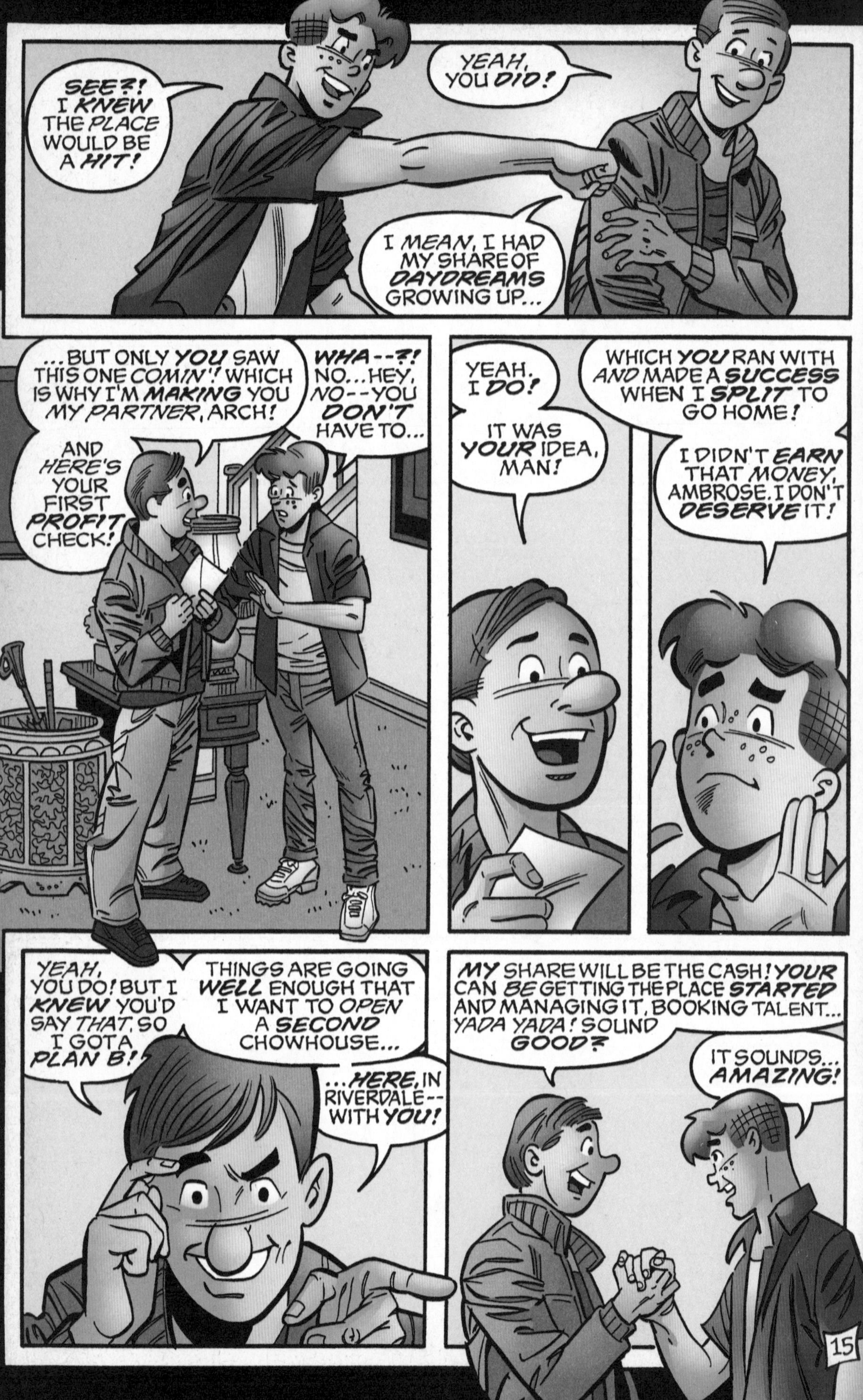
SEE?! I KNEW THE PLACE WOULD BE A HIT!
YEAH, YOU DID!
I MEAN, I HAD MY SHARE OF DAYDREAMS GROWING UP...
...BUT ONLY YOU SAW THIS ONE COMIN'! WHICH IS WHY I'M MAKING YOU MY PARTNER, ARCH!
AND HERE'S YOUR FIRST PROFIT CHECK!
WHA--?! NO...HEY, NO--YOU DON'T HAVE TO...
YEAH, I DO!
IT WAS YOUR IDEA, MAN!
WHICH YOU RAN WITH AND MADE A SUCCESS WHEN I SPLIT TO GO HOME!
I DIDN'T EARN THAT MONEY, AMBROSE. I DON'T DESERVE IT!
YEAH, YOU DO! BUT I KNEW YOU'D SAY THAT, SO I GOT A PLAN B!
THINGS ARE GOING WELL ENOUGH THAT I WANT TO OPEN A SECOND CHOWHOUSE...
...HERE, IN RIVERDALE--WITH YOU!
MY SHARE WILL BE THE CASH! YOUR CAN BE GETTING THE PLACE STARTED AND MANAGING IT, BOOKING TALENT... YADA YADA! SOUND GOOD?
IT SOUNDS... AMAZING!

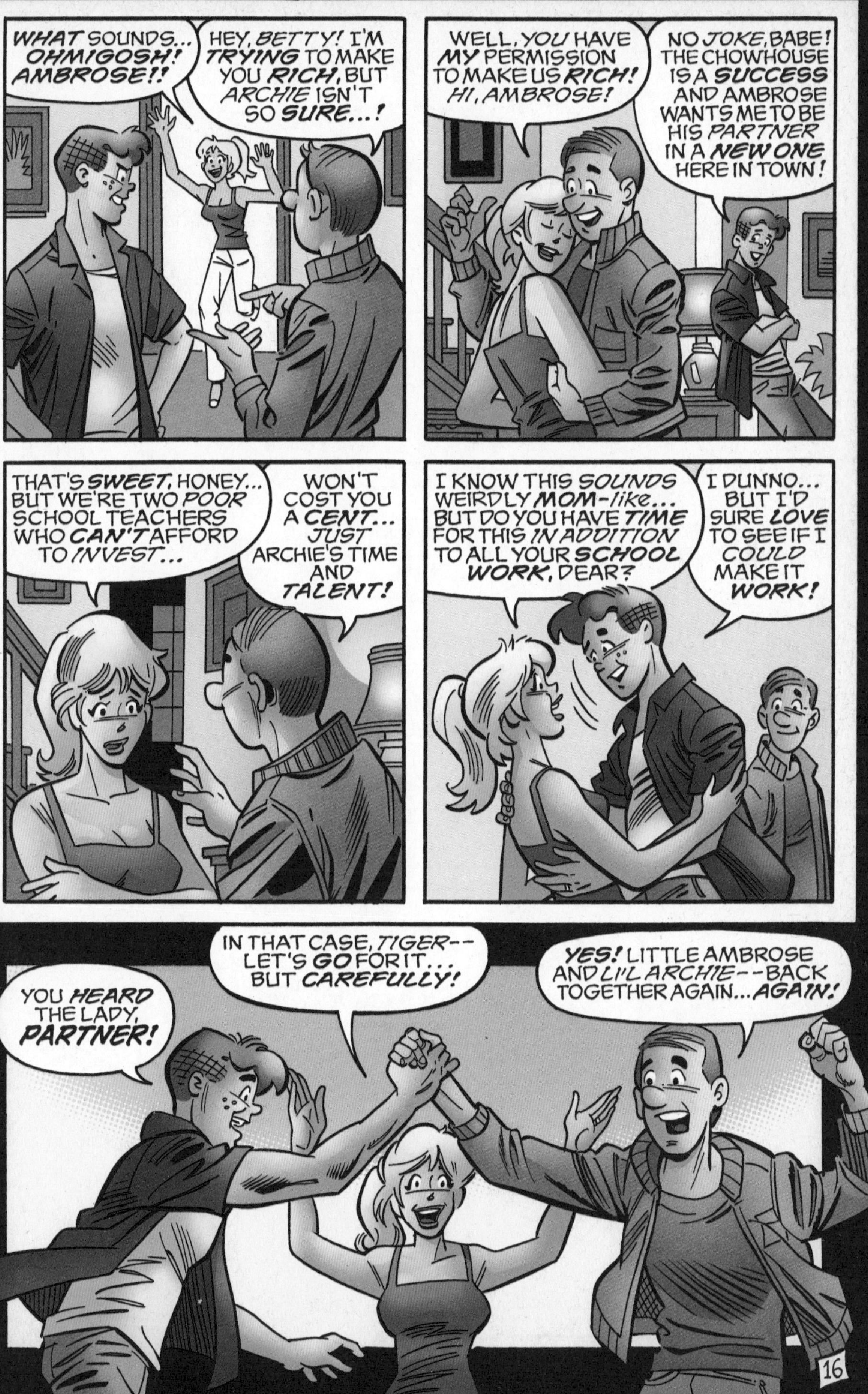
WHAT SOUNDS... OHMIGOSH! AMBROSE!!
HEY, BETTY! I'M TRYING TO MAKE YOU RICH, BUT ARCHIE ISN'T SO SURE...!
WELL, YOU HAVE MY PERMISSION TO MAKE US RICH! HI, AMBROSE!
NO JOKE, BABE! THE CHOWHOUSE IS A SUCCESS AND AMBROSE WANTS ME TO BE HIS PARTNER IN A NEW ONE HERE IN TOWN!
THAT'S SWEET, HONEY... BUT WE'RE TWO POOR SCHOOL TEACHERS WHO CAN'T AFFORD TO INVEST...
WON'T COST YOU A CENT... JUST ARCHIE'S TIME AND TALENT!
I KNOW THIS SOUNDS WEIRDLY MOM-like... BUT DO YOU HAVE TIME FOR THIS IN ADDITION TO ALL YOUR SCHOOL WORK, DEAR?
I DUNNO... BUT I'D SURE LOVE TO SEE IF I COULD MAKE IT WORK!
YOU HEARD THE LADY, PARTNER!
IN THAT CASE, TIGER-- LET'S GO FOR IT... BUT CAREFULLY!
YES! LITTLE AMBROSE AND LI'L ARCHIE--BACK TOGETHER AGAIN...AGAIN!
16

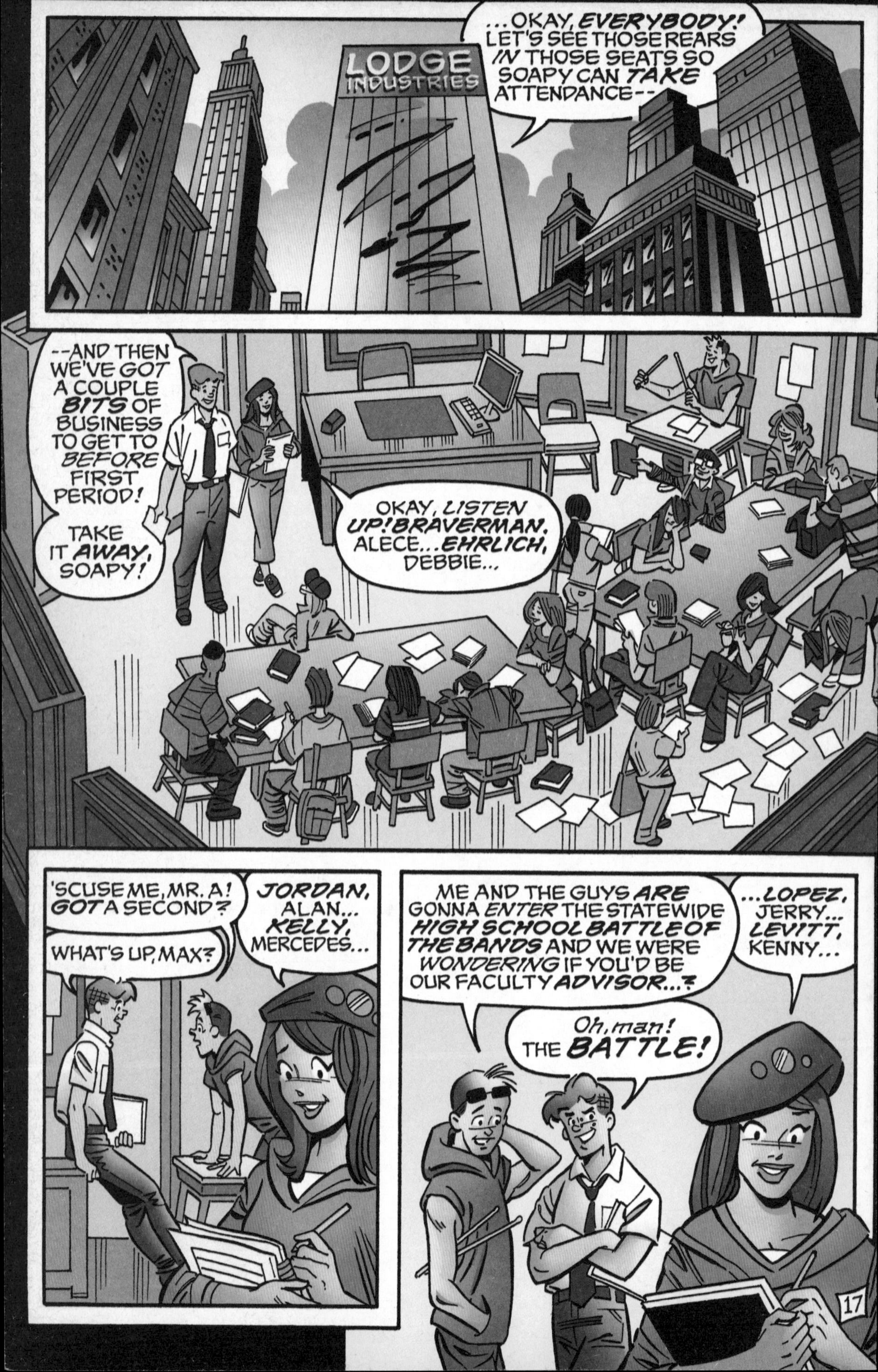
LODGE INDUSTRIES
...OKAY, EVERYBODY! LET'S SEE THOSE REARS IN THOSE SEATS SO SOAPY CAN TAKE ATTENDANCE--
--AND THEN WE'VE GOT A COUPLE BITS OF BUSINESS TO GET TO BEFORE FIRST PERIOD!
TAKE IT AWAY, SOAPY!
OKAY, LISTEN UP! BRAVERMAN, ALECE... EHRLICH, DEBBIE...
'SCUSE ME, MR. A! GOT A SECOND?
WHAT'S UP, MAX?
JORDAN, ALAN... KELLY, MERCEDES...
ME AND THE GUYS ARE GONNA ENTER THE STATEWIDE HIGH SCHOOL BATTLE OF THE BANDS AND WE WERE WONDERING IF YOU'D BE OUR FACULTY ADVISOR...?
...LOPEZ, JERRY... LEVITT, KENNY...
Oh, man! THE BATTLE!

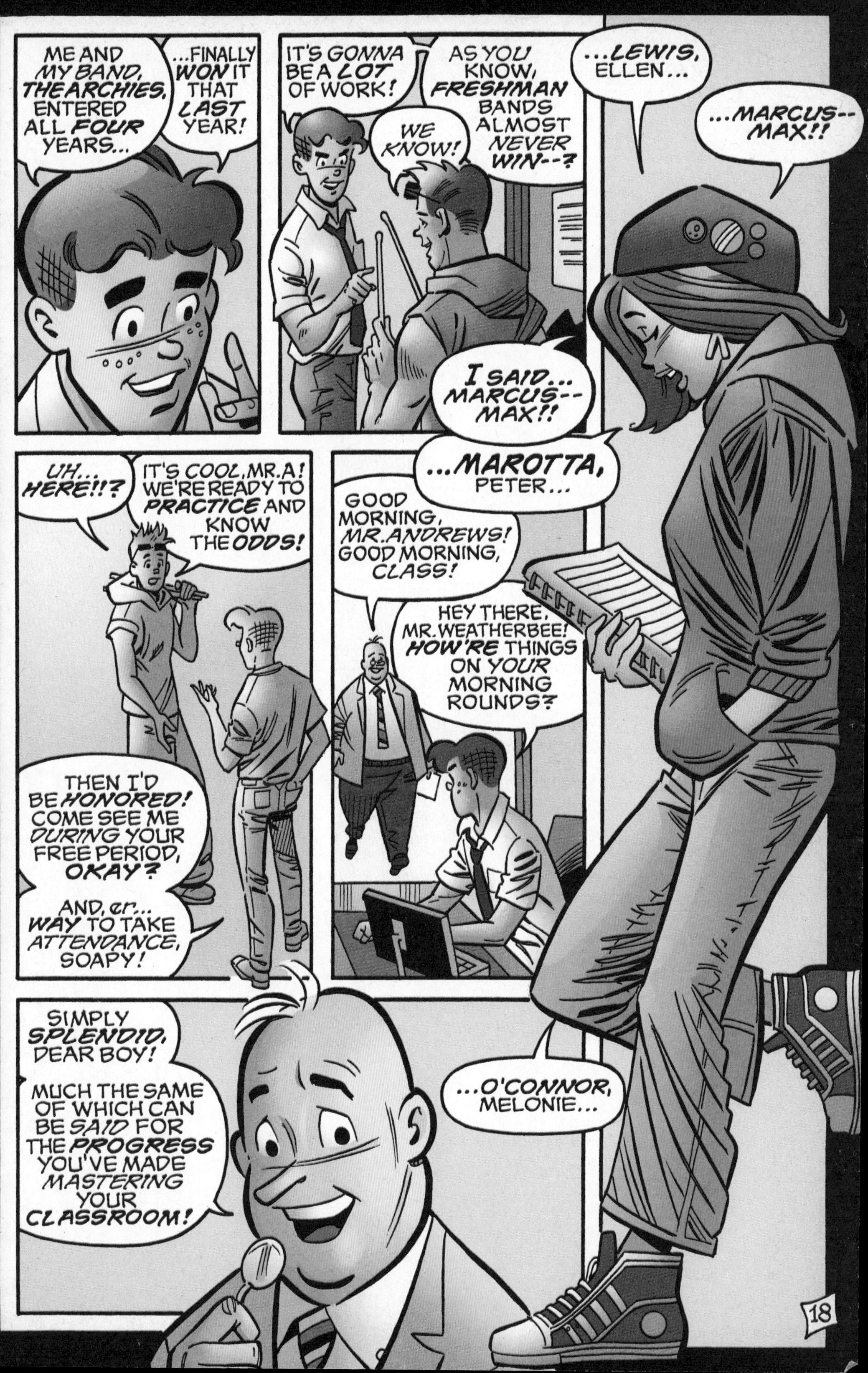

ME AND MY BAND, THE ARCHIES, ENTERED ALL FOUR YEARS...
...FINALLY WON IT THAT LAST YEAR!
IT'S GONNA BE A LOT OF WORK!
AS YOU KNOW, FRESHMAN BANDS ALMOST NEVER WIN--?
WE KNOW!
...LEWIS, ELLEN...
...MARCUS--MAX!!
I SAID... MARCUS--MAX!!
UH... HERE!!?
IT'S COOL, MR. A! WE'RE READY TO PRACTICE AND KNOW THE ODDS!
THEN I'D BE HONORED! COME SEE ME DURING YOUR FREE PERIOD, OKAY?
AND, er... WAY TO TAKE ATTENDANCE, SOAPY!
...MAROTTA, PETER...
GOOD MORNING, MR. ANDREWS! GOOD MORNING, CLASS!
HEY THERE, MR. WEATHERBEE! HOW'RE THINGS ON YOUR MORNING ROUNDS?
SIMPLY SPLENDID, DEAR BOY!
MUCH THE SAME OF WHICH CAN BE SAID FOR THE PROGRESS YOU'VE MADE MASTERING YOUR CLASSROOM!
...O'CONNOR, MELONIE...

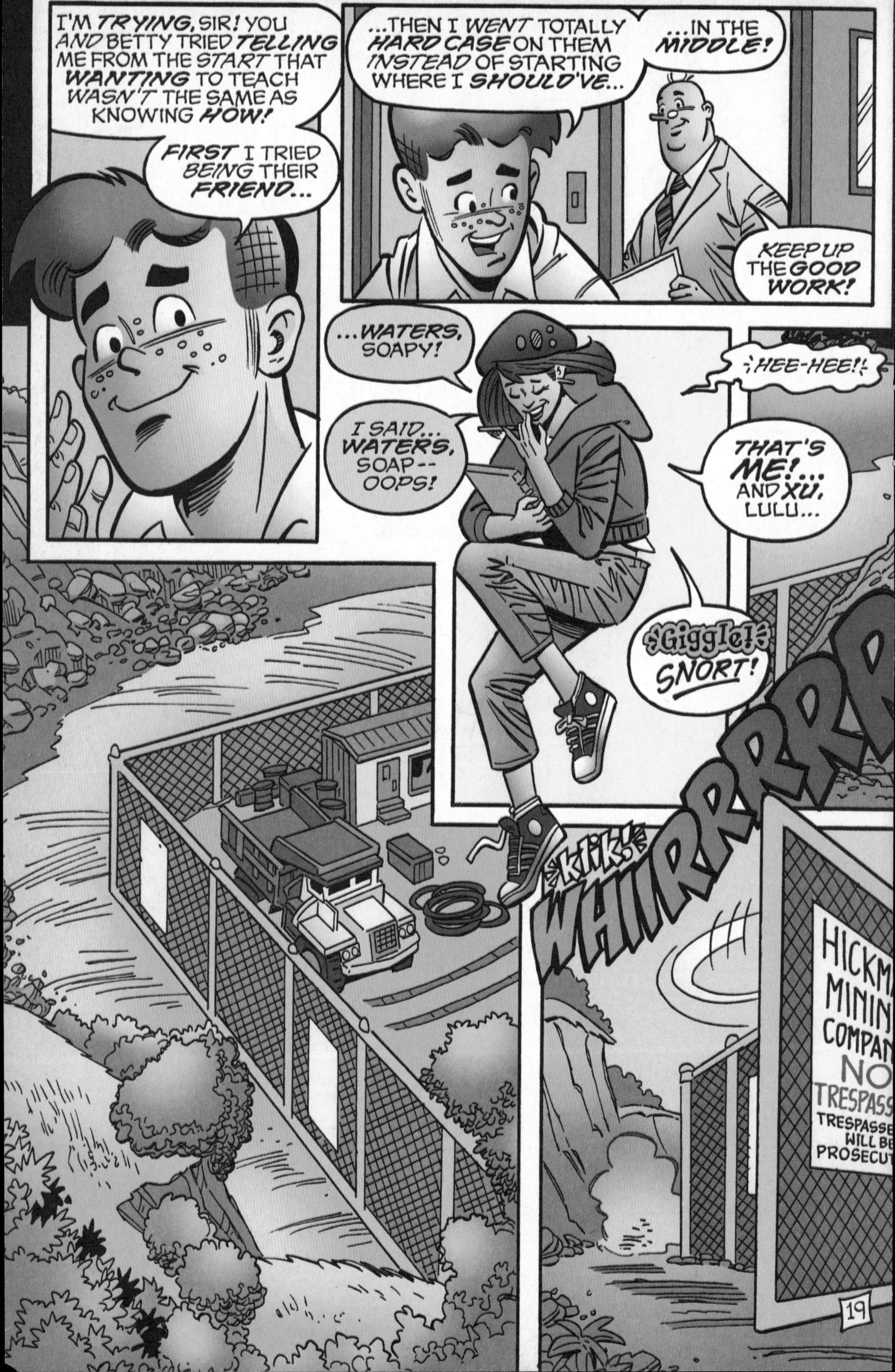
I'M TRYING, SIR! YOU AND BETTY TRIED TELLING ME FROM THE START THAT WANTING TO TEACH WASN'T THE SAME AS KNOWING HOW!
FIRST I TRIED BEING THEIR FRIEND...
...THEN I WENT TOTALLY HARD CASE ON THEM INSTEAD OF STARTING WHERE I SHOULD'VE...
...IN THE MIDDLE!
KEEP UP THE GOOD WORK!
...WATERS, SOAPY!
I SAID... WATERS, SOAP-- OOPS!
HEE-HEE!!
THAT'S ME!... AND XU, LULU...
Giggle! SNORT!
klik!
WHIIRRRRR
HICKM
MININ
COMPAN
NO
TRESPASS
TRESPASSE
WILL BE
PROSECUT

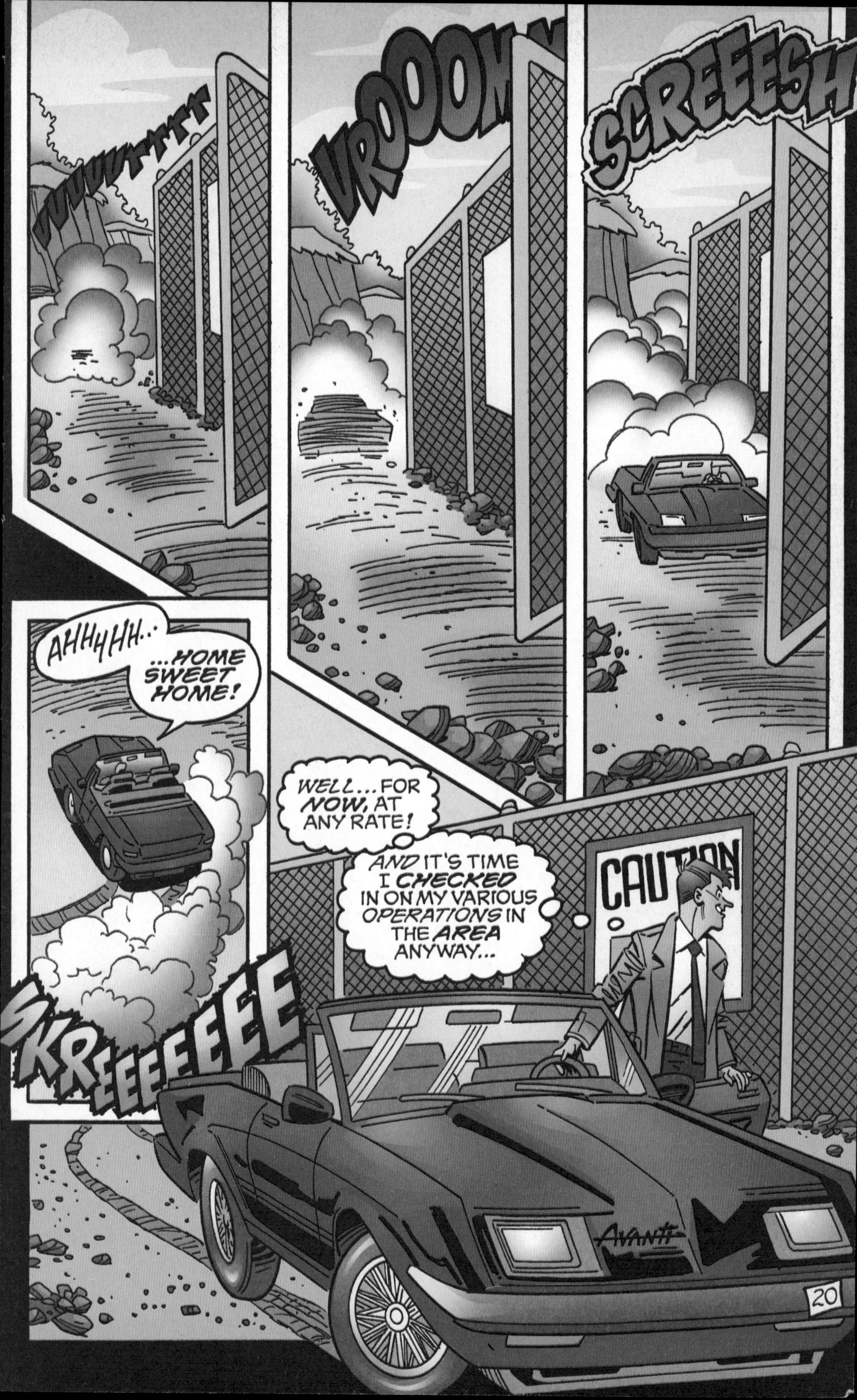
VVVVVVVTTTT
VROOOOM
SCREEESH
AHHHHH...
...HOME SWEET HOME!
WELL... FOR NOW, AT ANY RATE!
AND IT'S TIME I CHECKED IN ON MY VARIOUS OPERATIONS IN THE AREA ANYWAY...
CAUTION
SKREEEEEEE
AVANTI
20

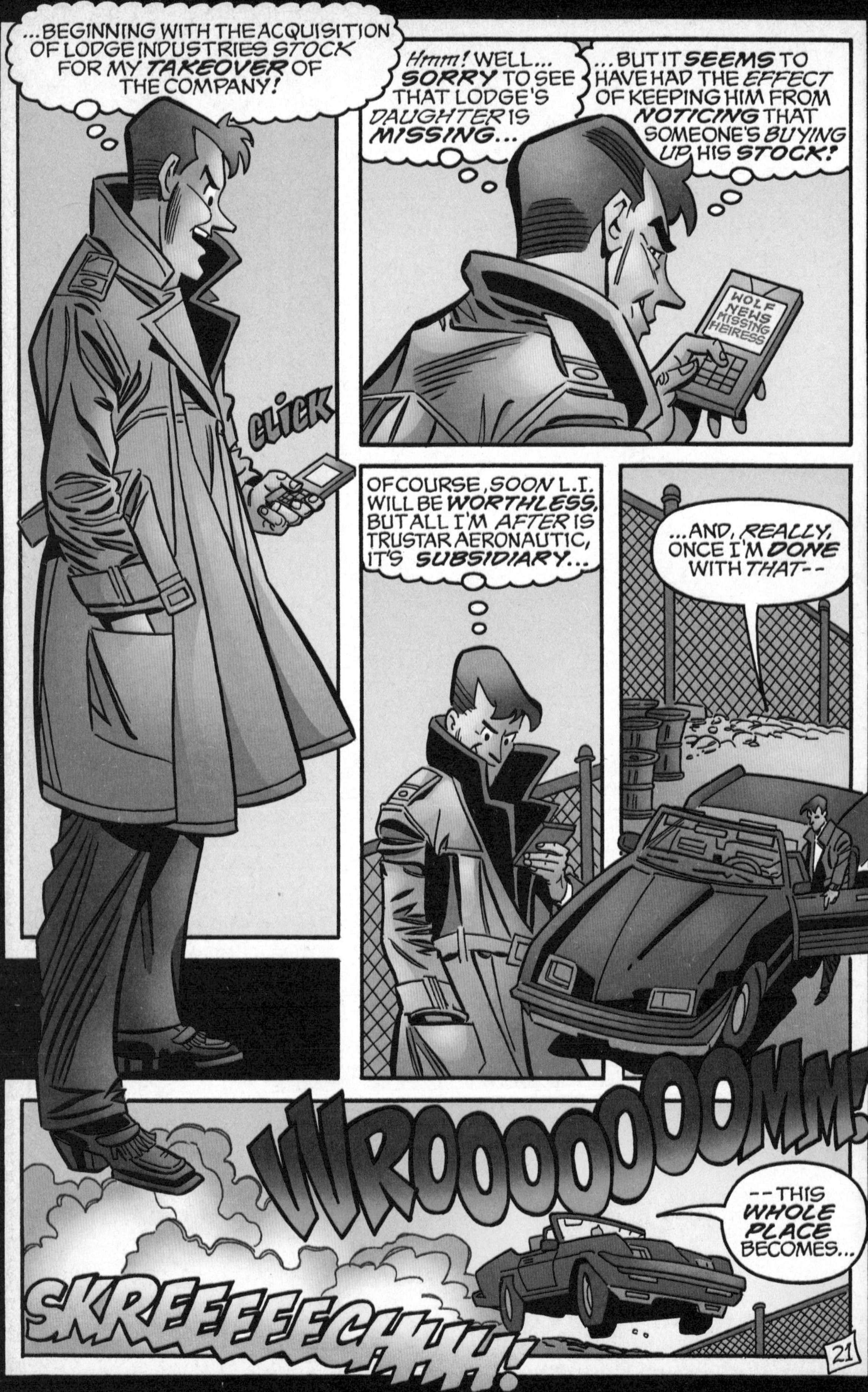
...BEGINNING WITH THE ACQUISITION OF LODGE INDUSTRIES STOCK FOR MY TAKEOVER OF THE COMPANY!
CLICK
Hmm! WELL... SORRY TO SEE THAT LODGE'S DAUGHTER IS MISSING...
...BUT IT SEEMS TO HAVE HAD THE EFFECT OF KEEPING HIM FROM NOTICING THAT SOMEONE'S BUYING UP HIS STOCK!
WOLF NEWS MISSING HEIRESS
OF COURSE, SOON L.I. WILL BE WORTHLESS, BUT ALL I'M AFTER IS TRUSTAR AERONAUTIC, IT'S SUBSIDIARY...
...AND, REALLY, ONCE I'M DONE WITH THAT--
VVROOOOOOOOMM!
--THIS WHOLE PLACE BECOMES...
SKREEEEEECHHH!

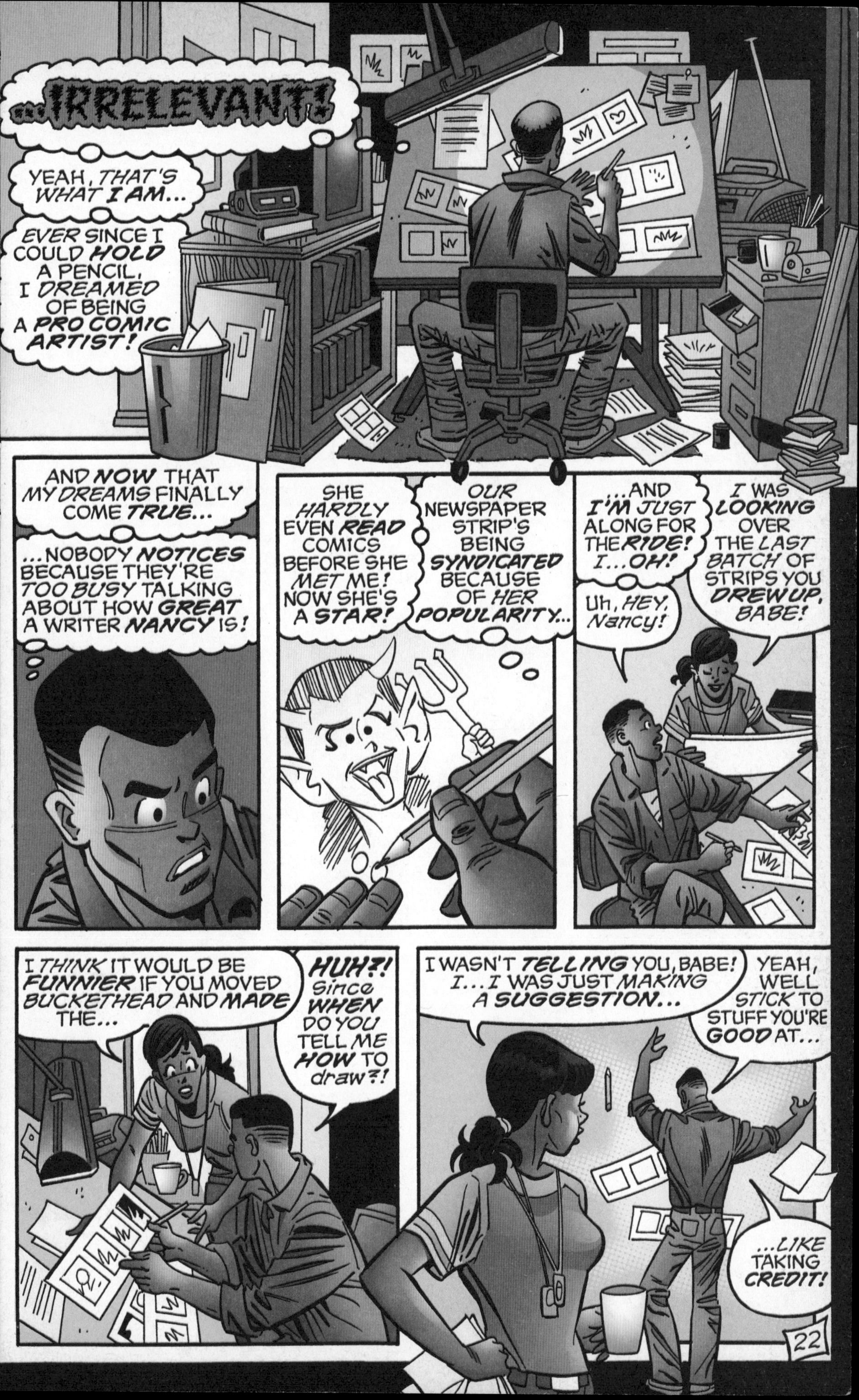
...IRRELEVANT!
YEAH, THAT'S WHAT I AM...
EVER SINCE I COULD HOLD A PENCIL, I DREAMED OF BEING A PRO COMIC ARTIST!
AND NOW THAT MY DREAMS FINALLY COME TRUE...
...NOBODY NOTICES BECAUSE THEY'RE TOO BUSY TALKING ABOUT HOW GREAT A WRITER NANCY IS!
SHE HARDLY EVEN READ COMICS BEFORE SHE MET ME! NOW SHE'S A STAR!
OUR NEWSPAPER STRIP'S BEING SYNDICATED BECAUSE OF HER POPULARITY...
...AND I'M JUST ALONG FOR THE RIDE! I...OH!
I WAS LOOKING OVER THE LAST BATCH OF STRIPS YOU DREW UP, BABE!
Uh, HEY, Nancy!
I THINK IT WOULD BE FUNNIER IF YOU MOVED BUCKETHEAD AND MADE THE...
HUH?! Since WHEN DO YOU TELL ME HOW TO draw?!
I WASN'T TELLING YOU, BABE! I...I WAS JUST MAKING A SUGGESTION...
YEAH, WELL STICK TO STUFF YOU'RE GOOD AT...
...LIKE TAKING CREDIT!

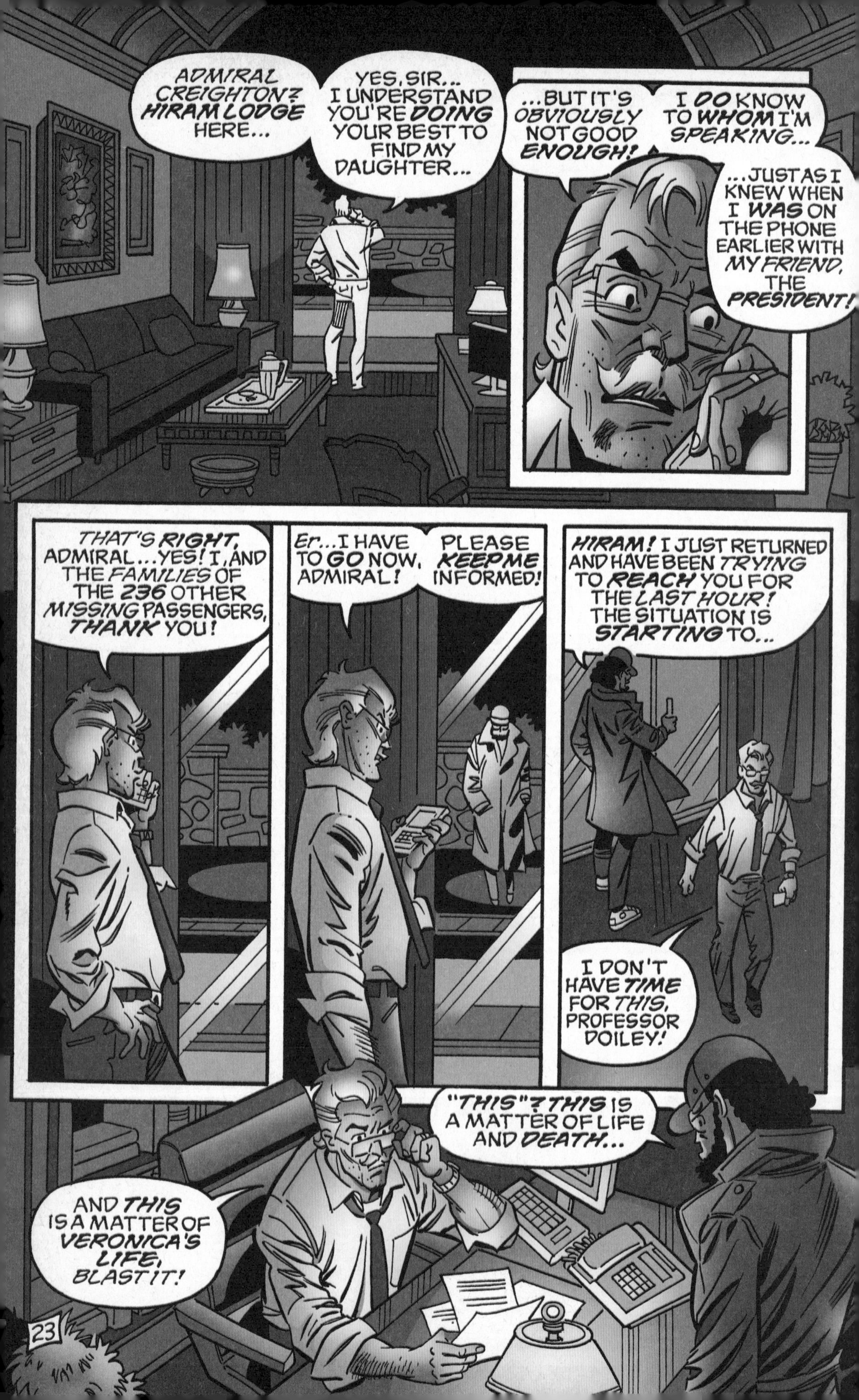
ADMIRAL CREIGHTON? HIRAM LODGE HERE...
YES, SIR... I UNDERSTAND YOU'RE DOING YOUR BEST TO FIND MY DAUGHTER...
...BUT IT'S OBVIOUSLY NOT GOOD ENOUGH!
I DO KNOW TO WHOM I'M SPEAKING...
...JUST AS I KNEW WHEN I WAS ON THE PHONE EARLIER WITH MY FRIEND, THE PRESIDENT!
THAT'S RIGHT, ADMIRAL... YES! I, AND THE FAMILIES OF THE 236 OTHER MISSING PASSENGERS, THANK YOU!
Er... I HAVE TO GO NOW, ADMIRAL!
PLEASE KEEP ME INFORMED!
HIRAM! I JUST RETURNED AND HAVE BEEN TRYING TO REACH YOU FOR THE LAST HOUR! THE SITUATION IS STARTING TO...
I DON'T HAVE TIME FOR THIS, PROFESSOR DOILEY!
"THIS"? THIS IS A MATTER OF LIFE AND DEATH...
AND THIS IS A MATTER OF VERONICA'S LIFE, BLAST IT!

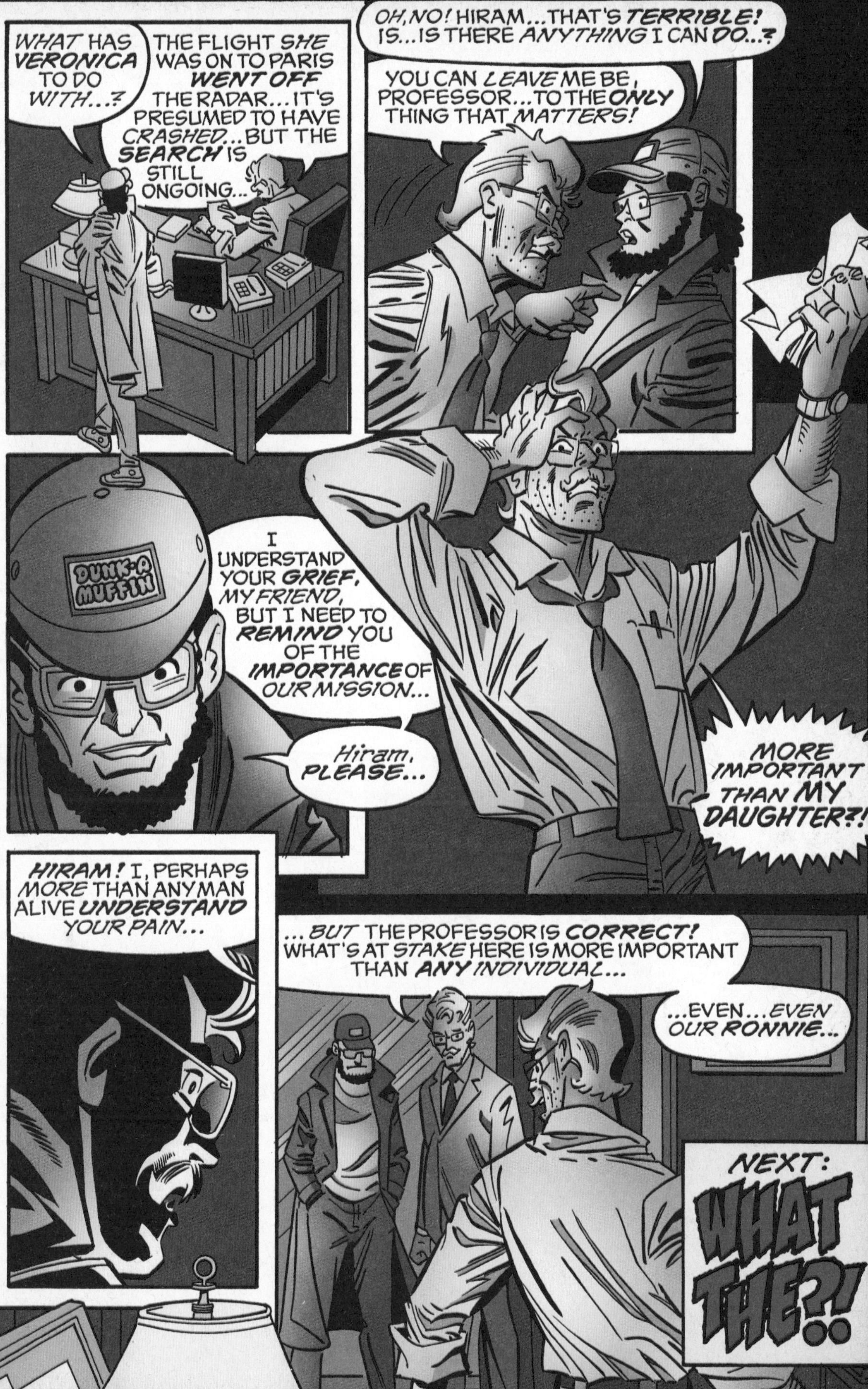

WHAT HAS VERONICA TO DO WITH...?
THE FLIGHT SHE WAS ON TO PARIS WENT OFF THE RADAR... IT'S PRESUMED TO HAVE CRASHED... BUT THE SEARCH IS STILL ONGOING...
OH, NO! HIRAM... THAT'S TERRIBLE! IS... IS THERE ANYTHING I CAN DO...?
YOU CAN LEAVE ME BE, PROFESSOR... TO THE ONLY THING THAT MATTERS!
DUNK-A MUFFIN
I UNDERSTAND YOUR GRIEF, MY FRIEND, BUT I NEED TO REMIND YOU OF THE IMPORTANCE OF OUR MISSION...
Hiram, PLEASE...
MORE IMPORTANT THAN MY DAUGHTER?!
HIRAM! I, PERHAPS MORE THAN ANY MAN ALIVE UNDERSTAND YOUR PAIN...
...BUT THE PROFESSOR IS CORRECT! WHAT'S AT STAKE HERE IS MORE IMPORTANT THAN ANY INDIVIDUAL...
...EVEN... EVEN OUR RONNIE...
NEXT: WHAT THE?!

"YOU NEVER WANTED
THE RESPONSIBILITY
OF BEING A LODGE..."

"AND I WON'T SETTLE
FOR ANYTHING *LESS!*"

- *VERONICA LODGE ANDREWS*

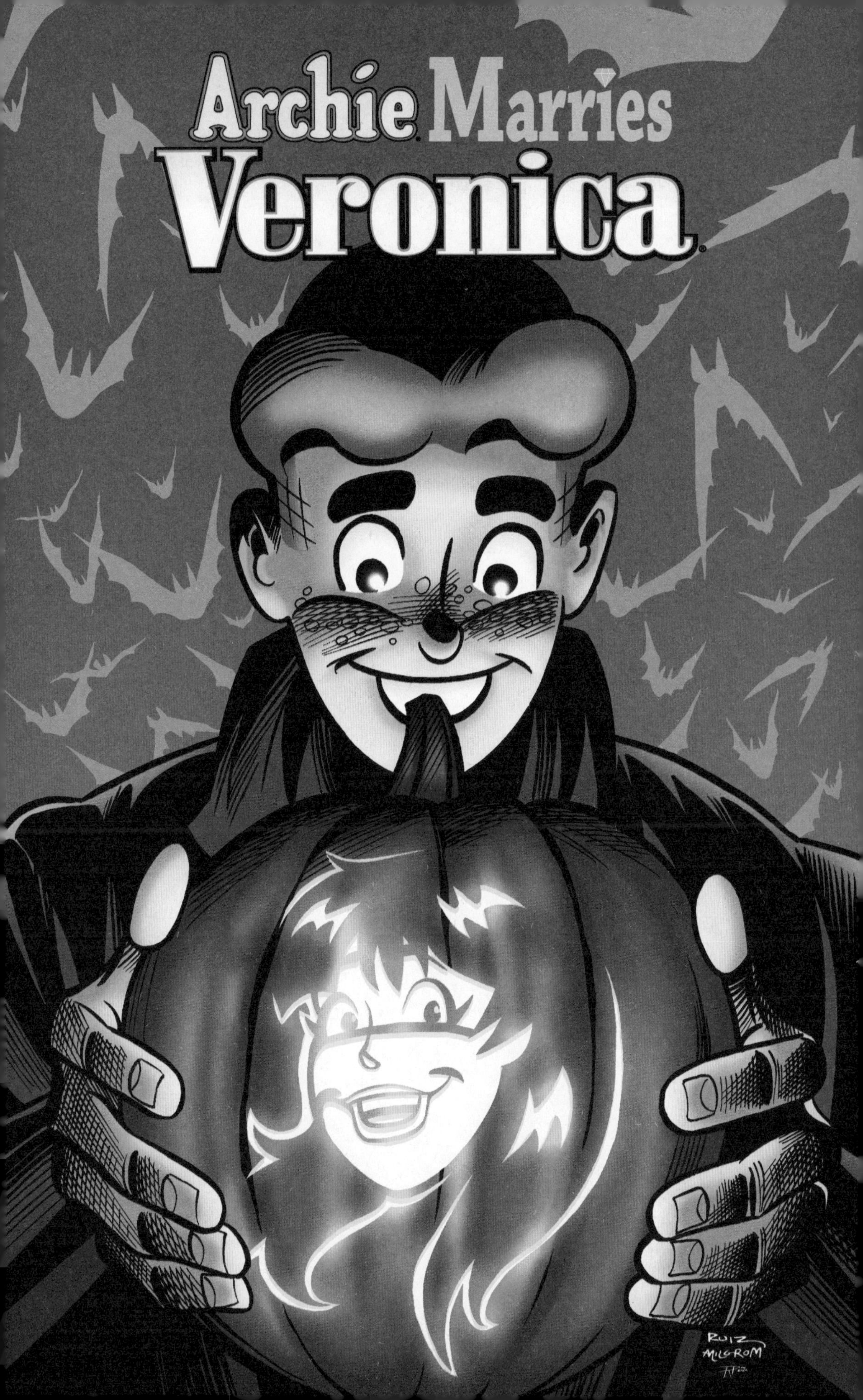
Archie Marries
Veronica
RUIZ
MILGROM

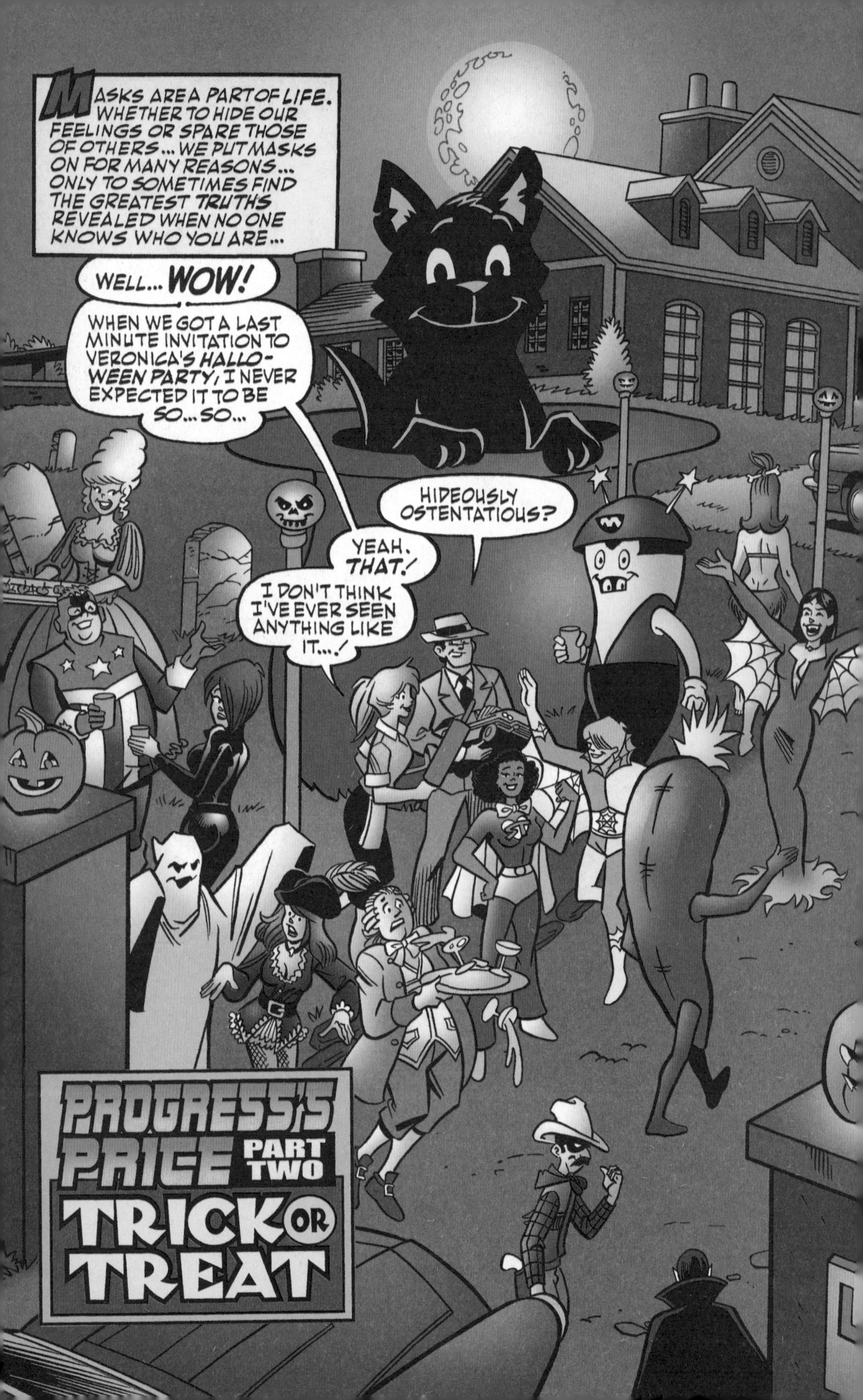
MASKS ARE A PART OF LIFE. WHETHER TO HIDE OUR FEELINGS OR SPARE THOSE OF OTHERS... WE PUT MASKS ON FOR MANY REASONS... ONLY TO SOMETIMES FIND THE GREATEST TRUTHS REVEALED WHEN NO ONE KNOWS WHO YOU ARE...
WELL... WOW!
WHEN WE GOT A LAST MINUTE INVITATION TO VERONICA'S HALLOWEEN PARTY, I NEVER EXPECTED IT TO BE SO... SO...
HIDEOUSLY OSTENTATIOUS?
YEAH. THAT.!
I DON'T THINK I'VE EVER SEEN ANYTHING LIKE IT...!
PROGRESS'S PRICE PART TWO
TRICK OR TREAT

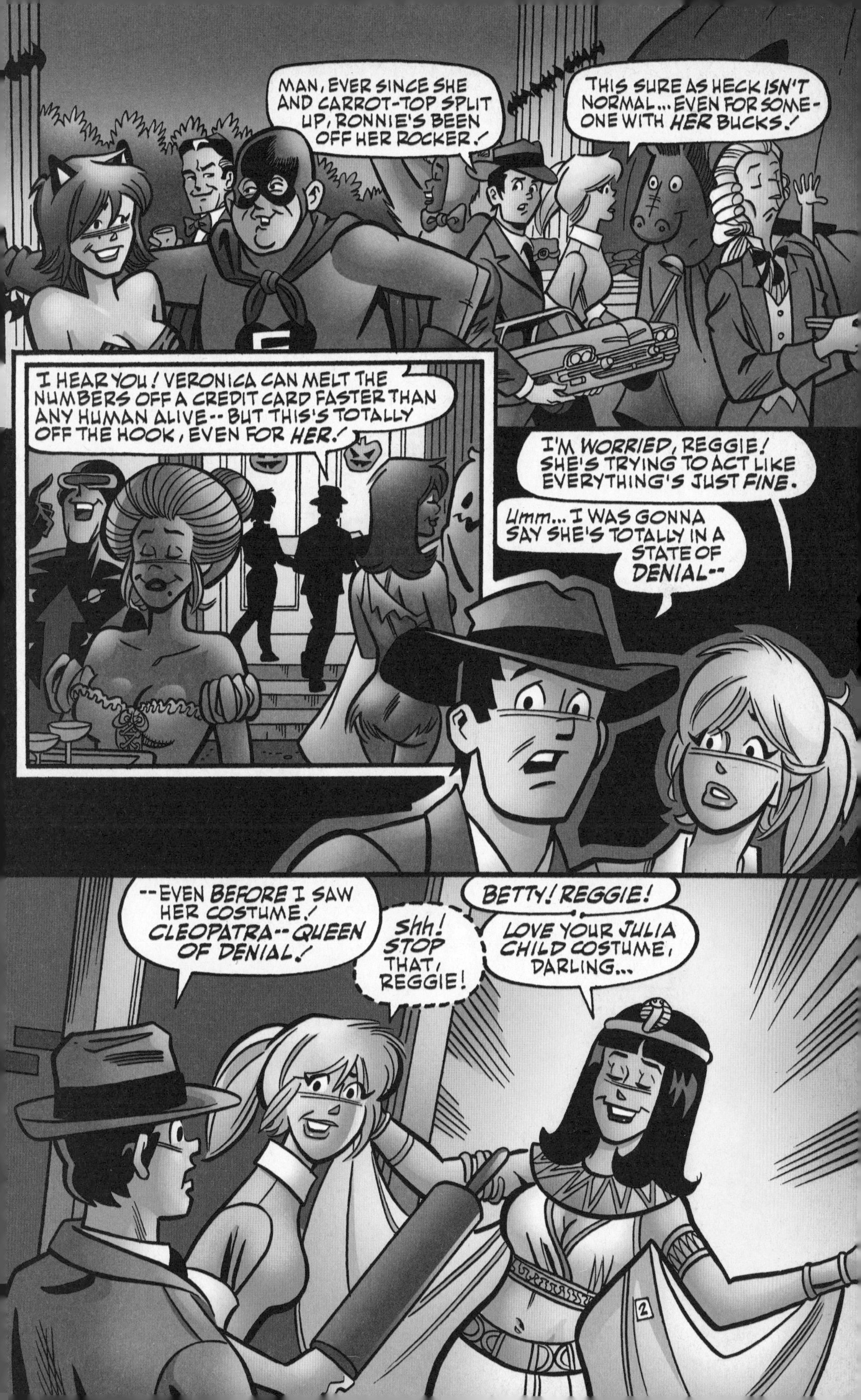

MAN, EVER SINCE SHE AND CARROT-TOP SPLIT UP, RONNIE'S BEEN OFF HER ROCKER!
THIS SURE AS HECK ISN'T NORMAL... EVEN FOR SOME-ONE WITH HER BUCKS!
I HEAR YOU! VERONICA CAN MELT THE NUMBERS OFF A CREDIT CARD FASTER THAN ANY HUMAN ALIVE-- BUT THIS'S TOTALLY OFF THE HOOK, EVEN FOR HER!
I'M WORRIED, REGGIE! SHE'S TRYING TO ACT LIKE EVERYTHING'S JUST FINE.
Umm... I WAS GONNA SAY SHE'S TOTALLY IN A STATE OF DENIAL--
--EVEN BEFORE I SAW HER COSTUME! CLEOPATRA-- QUEEN OF DENIAL!
Shh! STOP THAT, REGGIE!
BETTY! REGGIE!
LOVE YOUR JULIA CHILD COSTUME, DARLING...
2

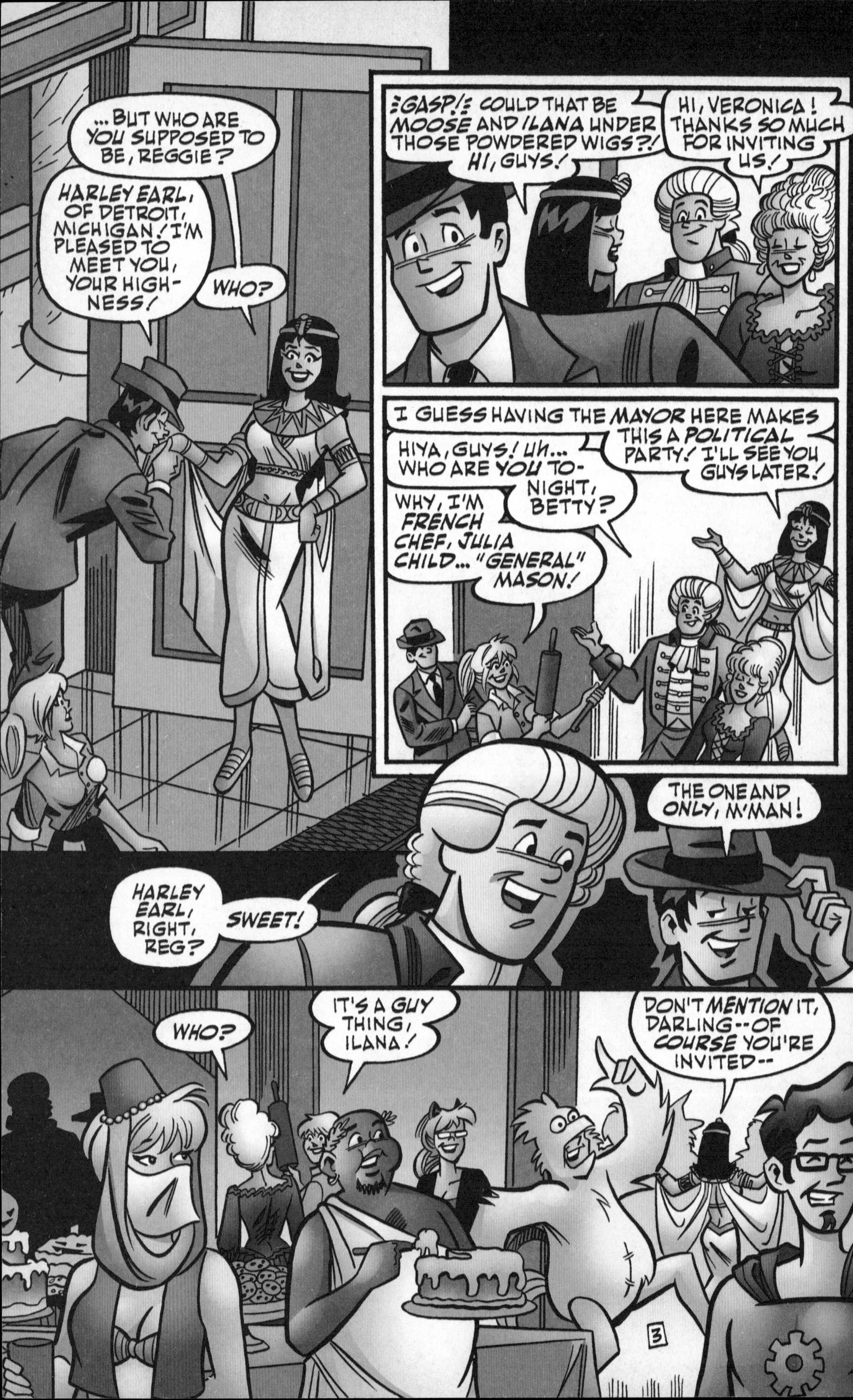
...BUT WHO ARE YOU SUPPOSED TO BE, REGGIE?
HARLEY EARL, OF DETROIT, MICHIGAN! I'M PLEASED TO MEET YOU, YOUR HIGHNESS!
WHO?
:GASP!: COULD THAT BE MOOSE AND ILANA UNDER THOSE POWDERED WIGS?! HI, GUYS!
HI, VERONICA! THANKS SO MUCH FOR INVITING US!
I GUESS HAVING THE MAYOR HERE MAKES THIS A POLITICAL PARTY! I'LL SEE YOU GUYS LATER!
HIYA, GUYS! UH... WHO ARE YOU TONIGHT, BETTY?
WHY, I'M FRENCH CHEF, JULIA CHILD... "GENERAL" MASON!
THE ONE AND ONLY, M'MAN!
HARLEY EARL, RIGHT, REG?
SWEET!
WHO?
IT'S A GUY THING, ILANA!
DON'T MENTION IT, DARLING--OF COURSE YOU'RE INVITED--
3

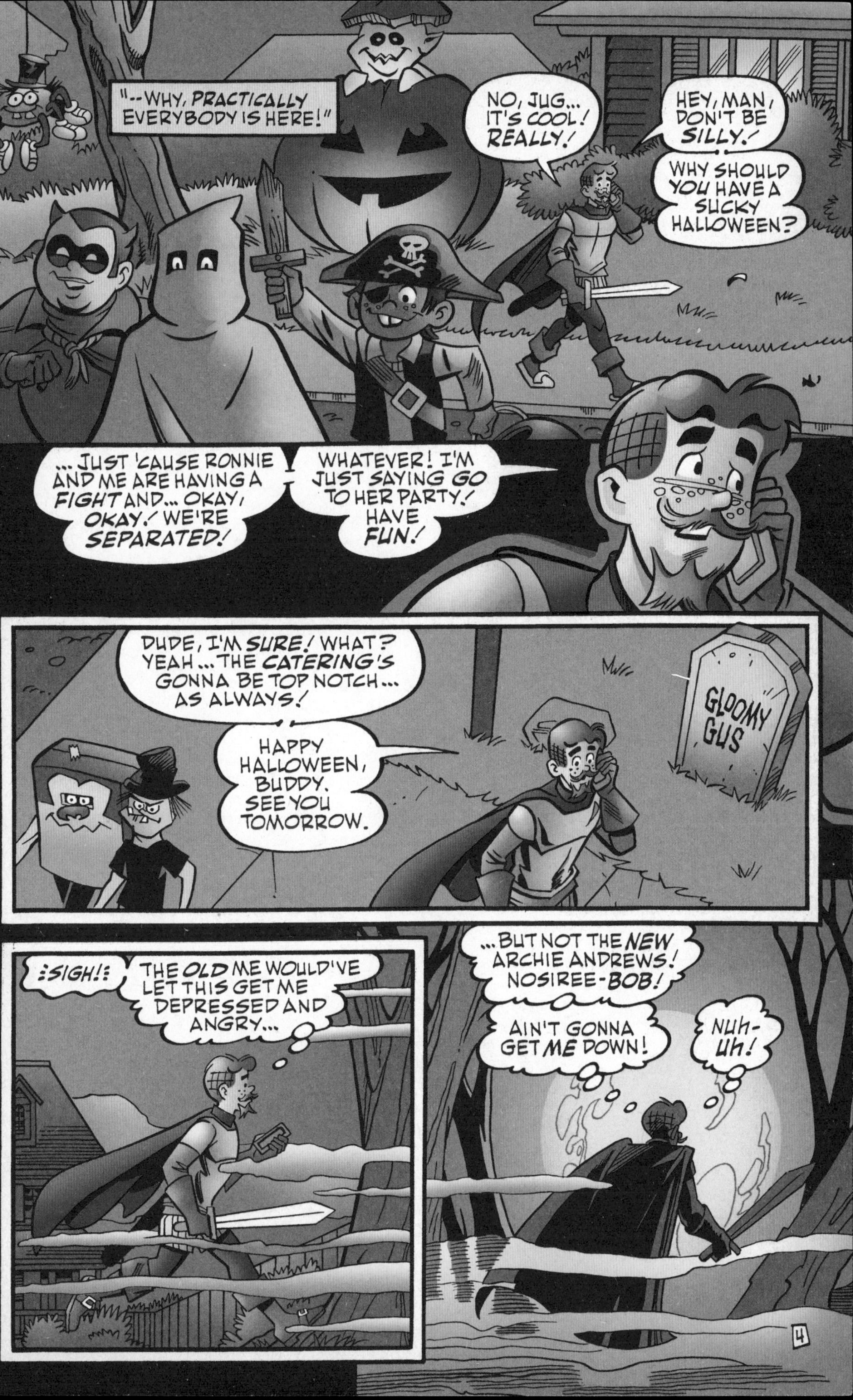
"--WHY, PRACTICALLY EVERYBODY IS HERE!"
NO, JUG... IT'S COOL! REALLY!
HEY, MAN, DON'T BE SILLY!
WHY SHOULD YOU HAVE A SUCKY HALLOWEEN?
...JUST 'CAUSE RONNIE AND ME ARE HAVING A FIGHT AND... OKAY, OKAY! WE'RE SEPARATED!
WHATEVER! I'M JUST SAYING GO TO HER PARTY! HAVE FUN!
DUDE, I'M SURE! WHAT? YEAH... THE CATERING'S GONNA BE TOP NOTCH... AS ALWAYS!
HAPPY HALLOWEEN, BUDDY. SEE YOU TOMORROW.
GLOOMY GUS
SIGH!
THE OLD ME WOULD'VE LET THIS GET ME DEPRESSED AND ANGRY...
...BUT NOT THE NEW ARCHIE ANDREWS! NOSIREE-BOB!
AIN'T GONNA GET ME DOWN!
NUH-UH!

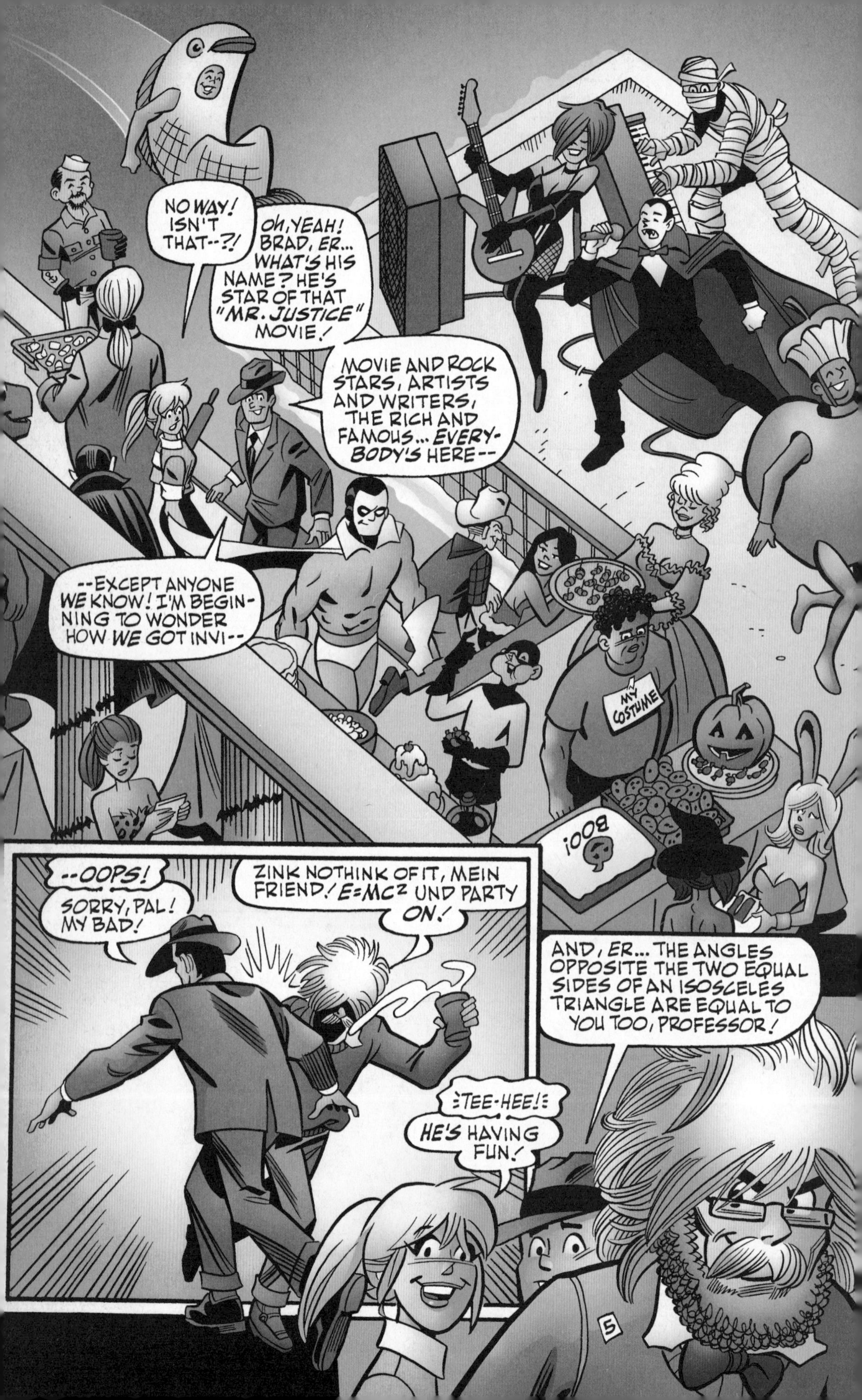
NO WAY! ISN'T THAT--?!
Oh, YEAH! BRAD, ER... WHAT'S HIS NAME? HE'S STAR OF THAT "MR. JUSTICE" MOVIE!
MOVIE AND ROCK STARS, ARTISTS AND WRITERS, THE RICH AND FAMOUS... EVERY-BODY'S HERE--
--EXCEPT ANYONE WE KNOW! I'M BEGIN-NING TO WONDER HOW WE GOT INVI--
MY COSTUME
BOO!
--OOPS!
SORRY, PAL! MY BAD!
ZINK NOTHINK OF IT, MEIN FRIEND! E=MC2 UND PARTY ON!
AND, ER... THE ANGLES OPPOSITE THE TWO EQUAL SIDES OF AN ISOSCELES TRIANGLE ARE EQUAL TO YOU TOO, PROFESSOR!
TEE-HEE!
HE'S HAVING FUN!
5

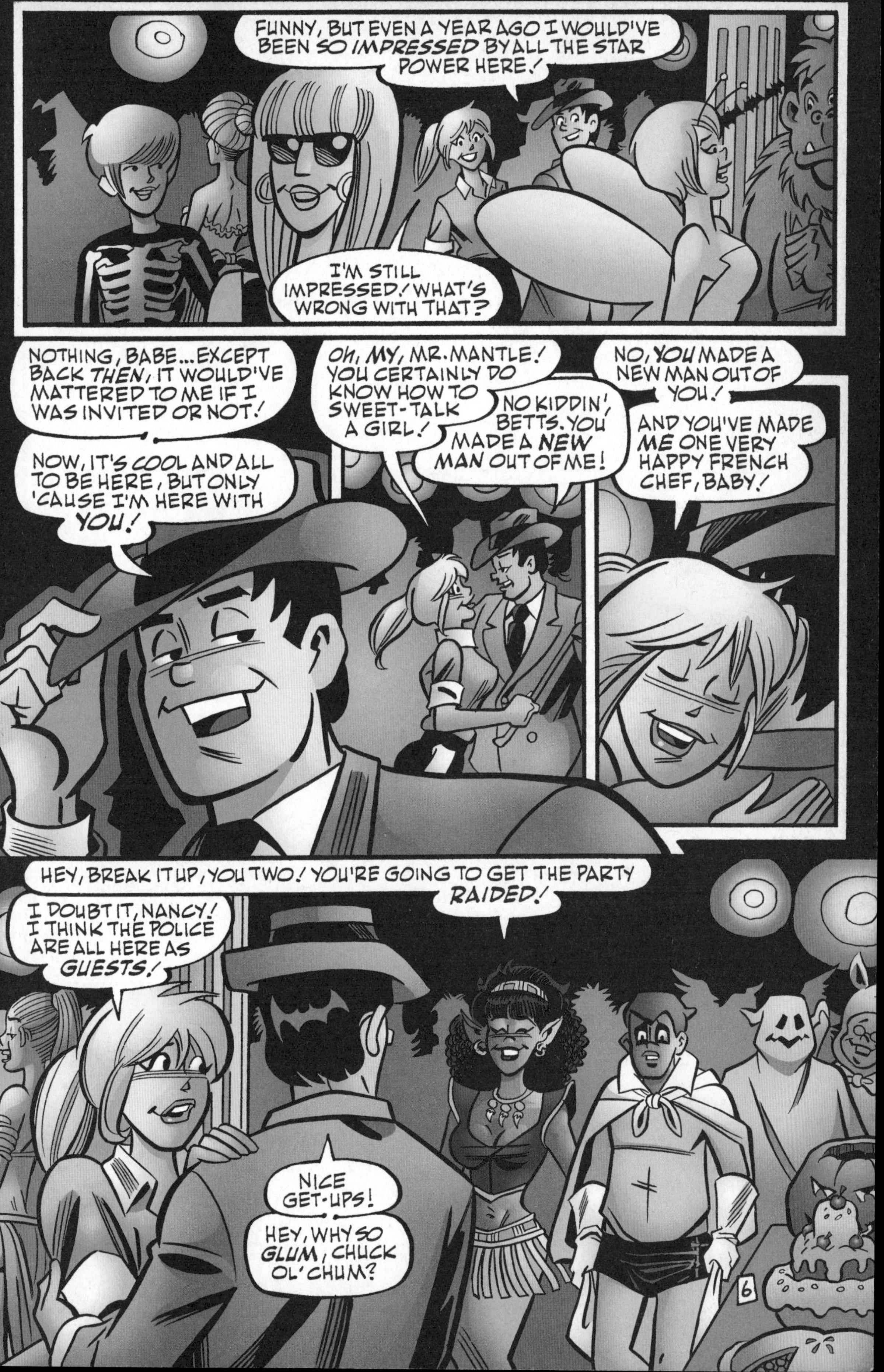
FUNNY, BUT EVEN A YEAR AGO I WOULD'VE BEEN SO *IMPRESSED* BY ALL THE STAR POWER HERE!
I'M STILL IMPRESSED! WHAT'S WRONG WITH THAT?
NOTHING, BABE... EXCEPT BACK *THEN*, IT WOULD'VE MATTERED TO ME IF I WAS INVITED OR NOT!
NOW, IT'S *COOL* AND ALL TO BE HERE, BUT ONLY 'CAUSE I'M HERE WITH *YOU*!
OH, *MY*, MR. MANTLE! YOU CERTAINLY DO KNOW HOW TO SWEET-TALK A GIRL!
NO KIDDIN', BETTS. YOU MADE A *NEW MAN* OUT OF ME!
NO, *YOU* MADE A NEW MAN OUT OF YOU!
AND YOU'VE MADE *ME* ONE VERY HAPPY FRENCH CHEF, BABY!
HEY, BREAK IT UP, YOU TWO! YOU'RE GOING TO GET THE PARTY *RAIDED*!
I DOUBT IT, NANCY! I THINK THE POLICE ARE ALL HERE AS *GUESTS*!
NICE GET-UPS!
HEY, WHY SO *GLUM*, CHUCK OL' CHUM?

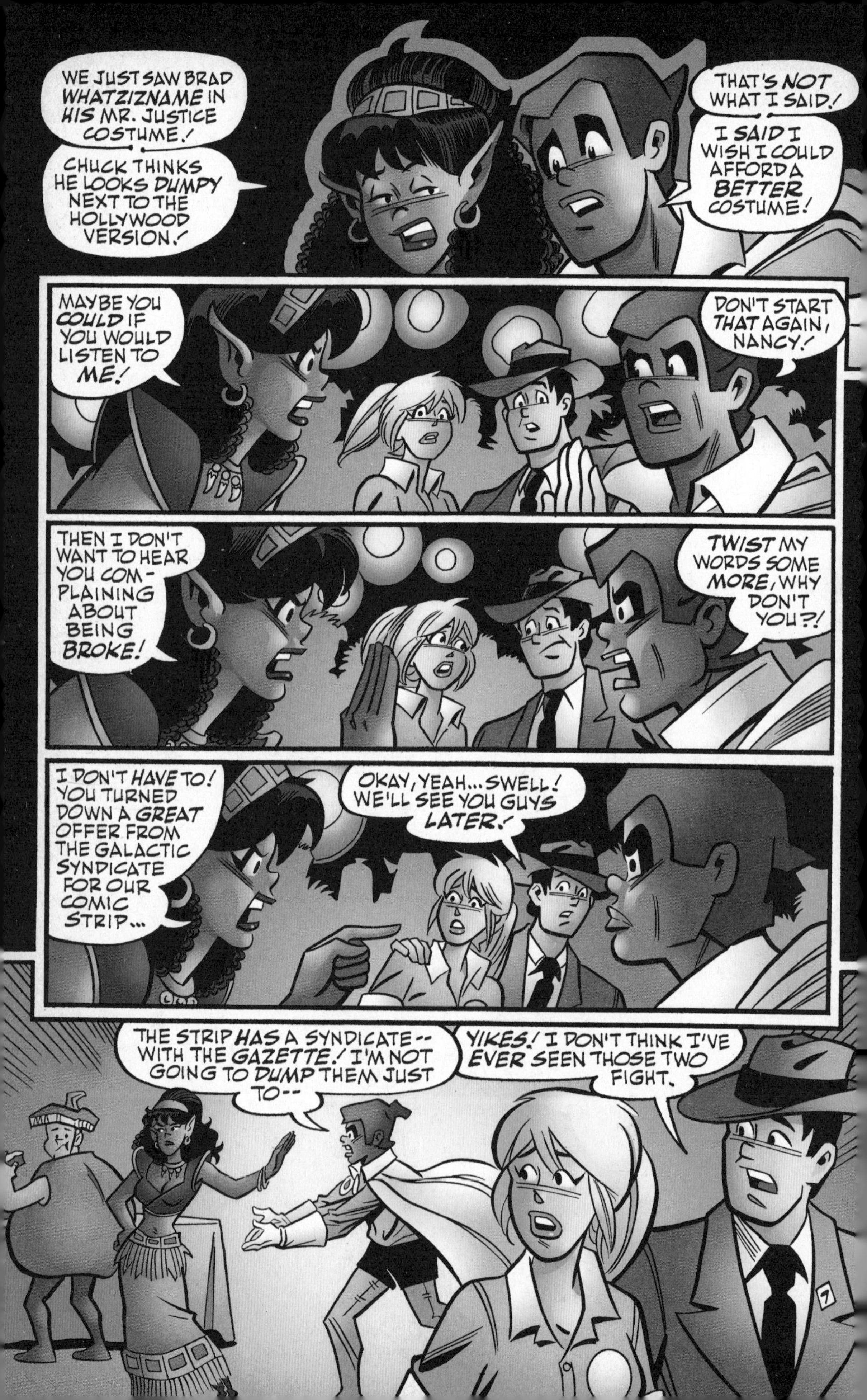

WE JUST SAW BRAD WHATZIZNAME IN HIS MR. JUSTICE COSTUME!
CHUCK THINKS HE LOOKS DUMPY NEXT TO THE HOLLYWOOD VERSION!
THAT'S NOT WHAT I SAID!
I SAID I WISH I COULD AFFORD A BETTER COSTUME!
MAYBE YOU COULD IF YOU WOULD LISTEN TO ME!
DON'T START THAT AGAIN, NANCY!
THEN I DON'T WANT TO HEAR YOU COM-PLAINING ABOUT BEING BROKE!
TWIST MY WORDS SOME MORE, WHY DON'T YOU?!
I DON'T HAVE TO! YOU TURNED DOWN A GREAT OFFER FROM THE GALACTIC SYNDICATE FOR OUR COMIC STRIP...
OKAY, YEAH... SWELL! WE'LL SEE YOU GUYS LATER!
THE STRIP HAS A SYNDICATE -- WITH THE GAZETTE! I'M NOT GOING TO DUMP THEM JUST TO--
YIKES! I DON'T THINK I'VE EVER SEEN THOSE TWO FIGHT.
7

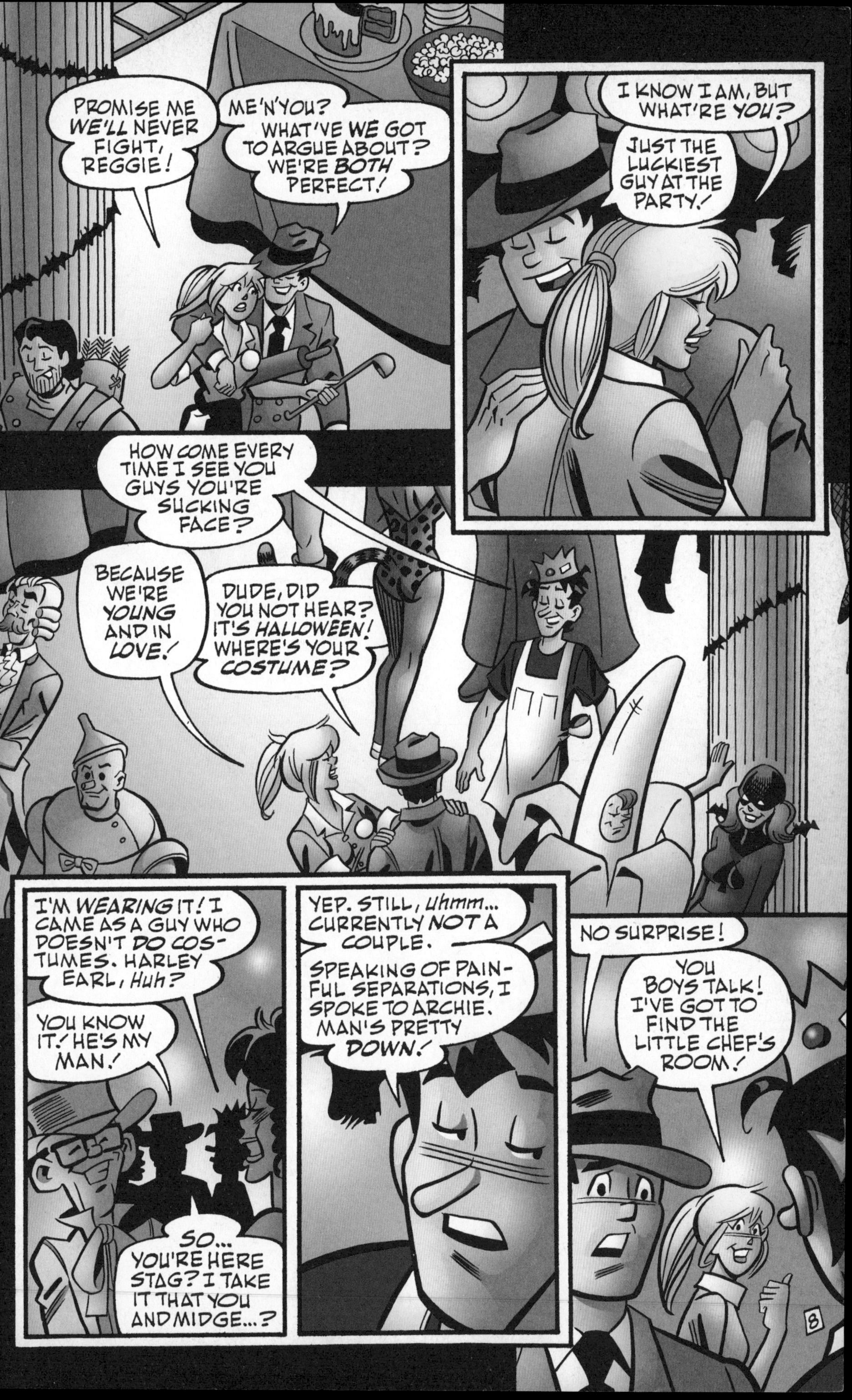
PROMISE ME WE'LL NEVER FIGHT, REGGIE!
ME'N'YOU?
WHAT'VE WE GOT TO ARGUE ABOUT? WE'RE BOTH PERFECT!
I KNOW I AM, BUT WHAT'RE YOU?
JUST THE LUCKIEST GUY AT THE PARTY!
HOW COME EVERY TIME I SEE YOU GUYS YOU'RE SUCKING FACE?
BECAUSE WE'RE YOUNG AND IN LOVE!
DUDE, DID YOU NOT HEAR? IT'S HALLOWEEN! WHERE'S YOUR COSTUME?
I'M WEARING IT! I CAME AS A GUY WHO DOESN'T DO COSTUMES. HARLEY EARL, HUH?
YOU KNOW IT! HE'S MY MAN!
SO... YOU'RE HERE STAG? I TAKE IT THAT YOU AND MIDGE...?
YEP. STILL, UHMM... CURRENTLY NOT A COUPLE.
SPEAKING OF PAINFUL SEPARATIONS, I SPOKE TO ARCHIE. MAN'S PRETTY DOWN!
NO SURPRISE!
YOU BOYS TALK! I'VE GOT TO FIND THE LITTLE CHEF'S ROOM!
8

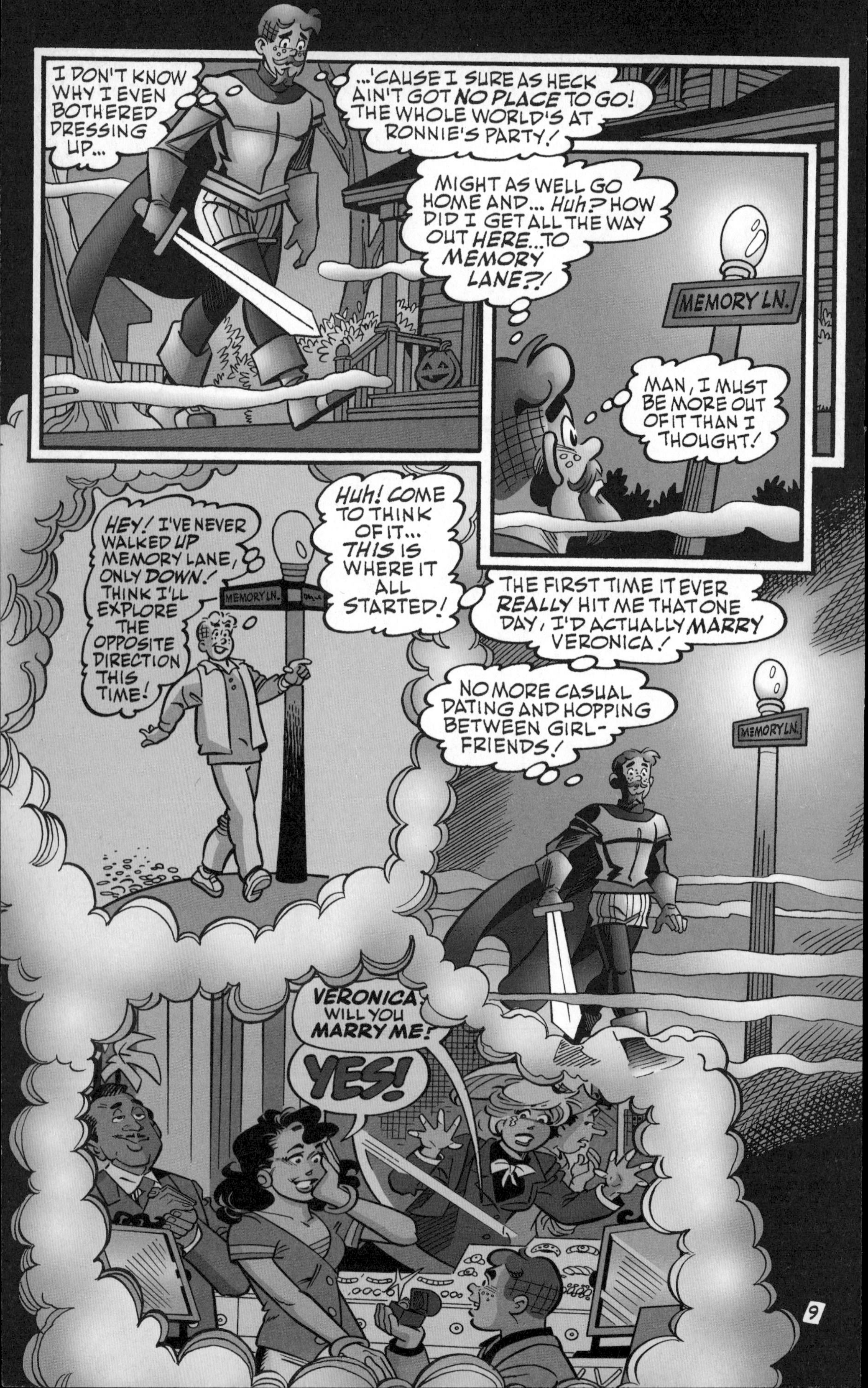
I DON'T KNOW WHY I EVEN BOTHERED DRESSING UP...
...'CAUSE I SURE AS HECK AIN'T GOT NO PLACE TO GO! THE WHOLE WORLD'S AT RONNIE'S PARTY!
MIGHT AS WELL GO HOME AND... Huh? HOW DID I GET ALL THE WAY OUT HERE...TO MEMORY LANE?!
MEMORY LN.
MAN, I MUST BE MORE OUT OF IT THAN I THOUGHT!
HEY! I'VE NEVER WALKED UP MEMORY LANE, ONLY DOWN! THINK I'LL EXPLORE THE OPPOSITE DIRECTION THIS TIME!
MEMORY LN.
Huh! COME TO THINK OF IT... THIS IS WHERE IT ALL STARTED!
THE FIRST TIME IT EVER REALLY HIT ME THAT ONE DAY, I'D ACTUALLY MARRY VERONICA!
NO MORE CASUAL DATING AND HOPPING BETWEEN GIRL-FRIENDS!
MEMORY LN.
VERONICA, WILL YOU MARRY ME!
YES!

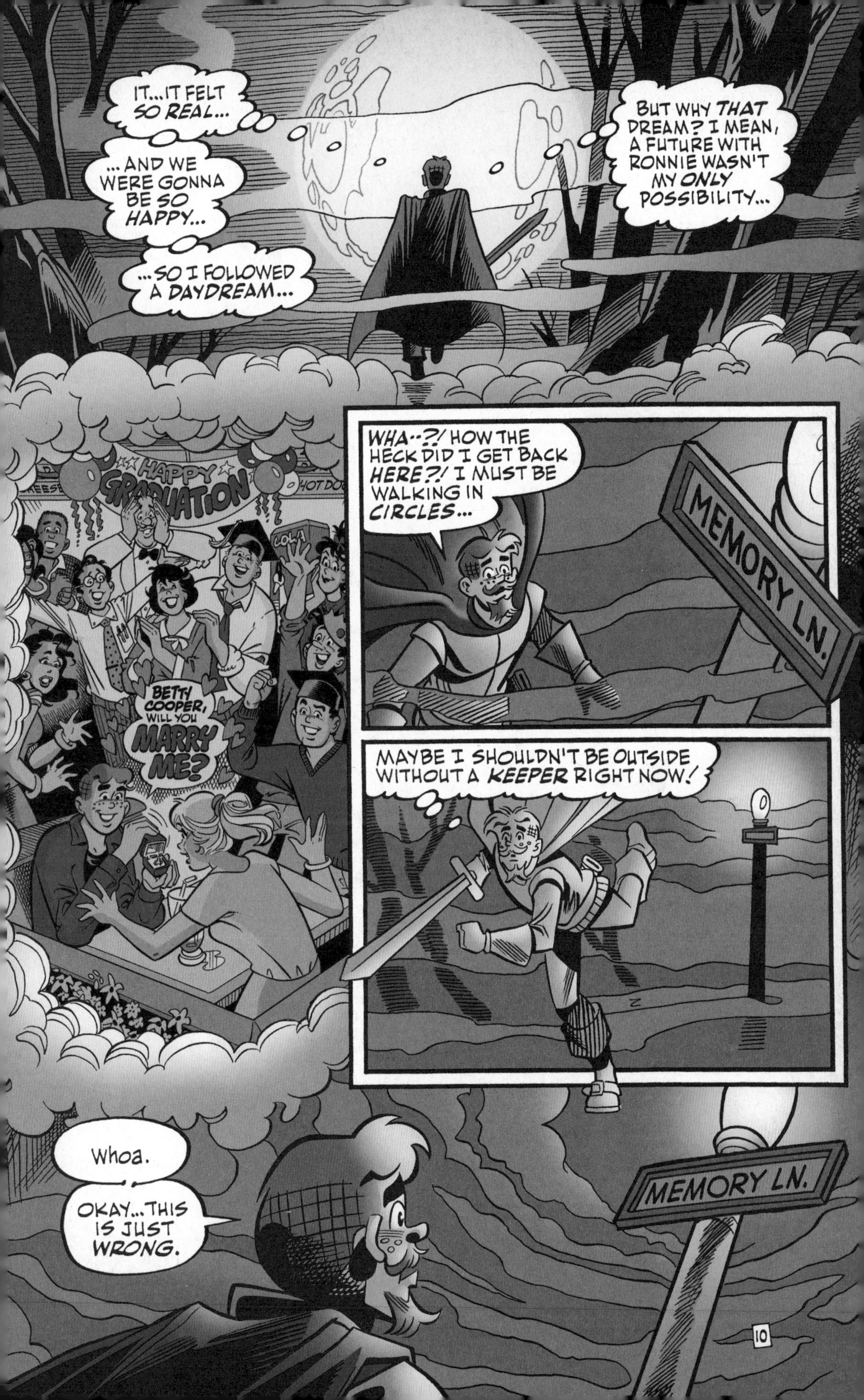
IT...IT FELT SO REAL...
...AND WE WERE GONNA BE SO HAPPY...
...SO I FOLLOWED A DAYDREAM...
BUT WHY THAT DREAM? I MEAN, A FUTURE WITH RONNIE WASN'T MY ONLY POSSIBILITY...
HAPPY GRADUATION
HOT DOG
COLA
BETTY COOPER, WILL YOU MARRY ME?
WHA--?! HOW THE HECK DID I GET BACK HERE?! I MUST BE WALKING IN CIRCLES...
MEMORY LN.
MAYBE I SHOULDN'T BE OUTSIDE WITHOUT A KEEPER RIGHT NOW!
Whoa.
OKAY...THIS IS JUST WRONG.
MEMORY LN.

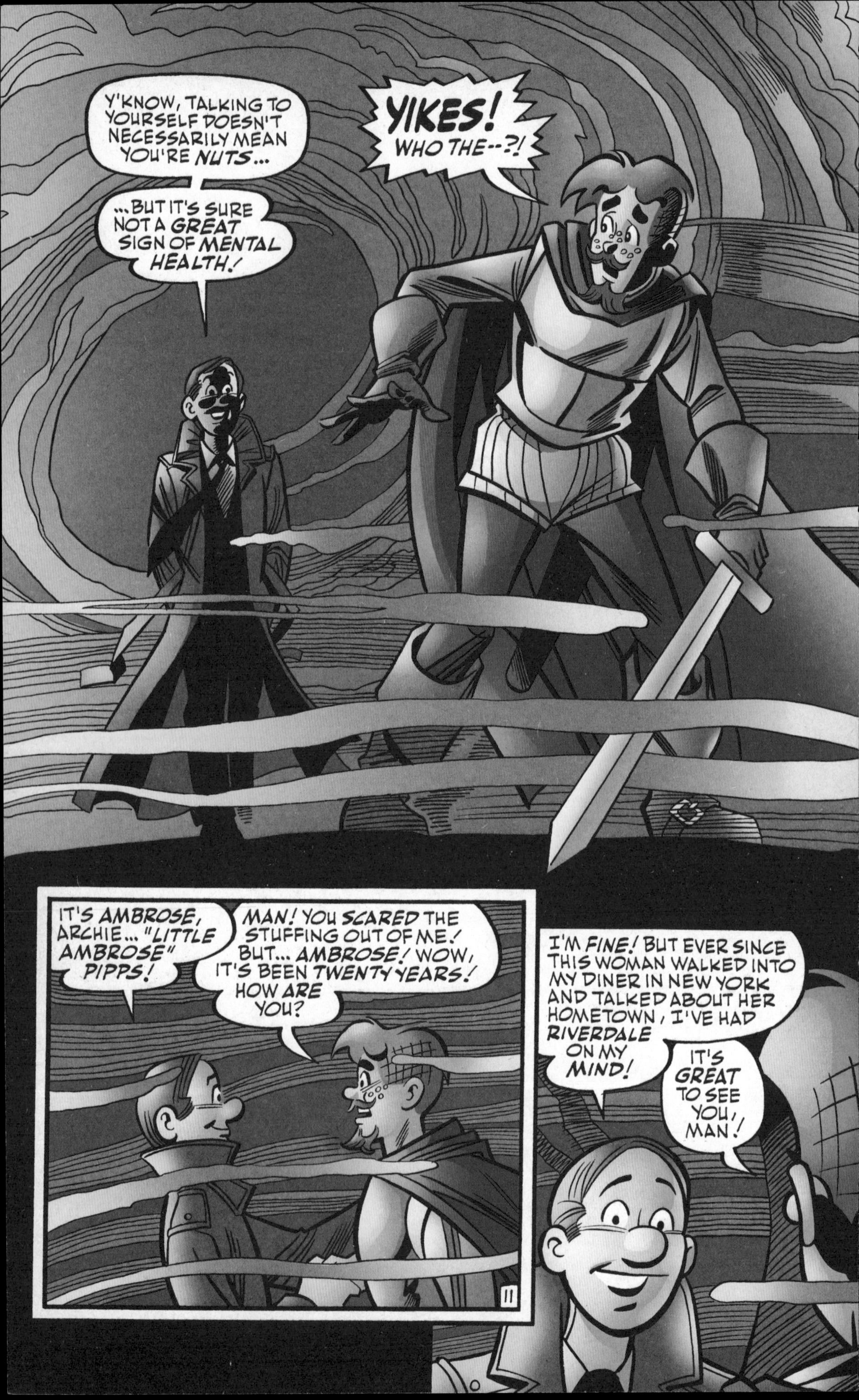
Y'KNOW, TALKING TO YOURSELF DOESN'T NECESSARILY MEAN YOU'RE NUTS...
...BUT IT'S SURE NOT A GREAT SIGN OF MENTAL HEALTH!
YIKES! WHO THE--?!
IT'S AMBROSE, ARCHIE... "LITTLE AMBROSE" PIPPS!
MAN! YOU SCARED THE STUFFING OUT OF ME! BUT... AMBROSE! WOW, IT'S BEEN TWENTY YEARS! HOW ARE YOU?
I'M FINE! BUT EVER SINCE THIS WOMAN WALKED INTO MY DINER IN NEW YORK AND TALKED ABOUT HER HOMETOWN, I'VE HAD RIVERDALE ON MY MIND!
IT'S GREAT TO SEE YOU, MAN!
11

I CAN'T BELIEVE IT! THE OLD TOWN LOOKS *EXACTLY* THE SAME!

MEMORY LN.

WHAT YOU CAN STILL SEE OF IT THROUGH THIS *FOG*!

SO YOU WOUND UP IN *NEW YORK*, HUH?

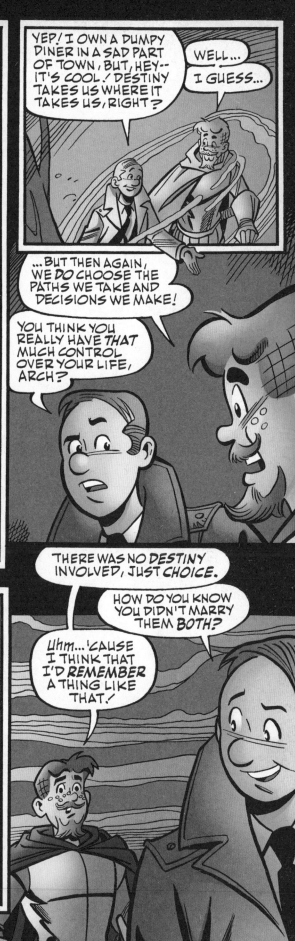

YEP! I OWN A DUMPY DINER IN A SAD PART OF TOWN, BUT, HEY-- IT'S *COOL*! DESTINY TAKES US WHERE IT TAKES US, RIGHT?

WELL... I GUESS...

...BUT THEN AGAIN, WE *DO* CHOOSE THE PATHS WE TAKE AND DECISIONS WE MAKE!

YOU THINK YOU REALLY HAVE *THAT* MUCH CONTROL OVER YOUR LIFE, ARCH?

THERE WAS NO *DESTINY* INVOLVED, JUST *CHOICE*.

HOW DO YOU KNOW YOU DIDN'T MARRY THEM *BOTH*?

UHM...'CAUSE I THINK THAT I'D *REMEMBER* A THING LIKE THAT!

YEAH, I DO! I CAN SHOW YOU THE *EXACT SPOT* BACK THERE WHERE I DECIDED TO ASK VERONICA LODGE TO MARRY ME!

YOU AND RONNIE? *CONGRATS*, MAN!

YEAH, WELL...IT DIDN'T WORK OUT EXACTLY THE WAY THAT I *THOUGHT*!

POINT IS, I MARRIED RONNIE, *NOT* BETTY!

12

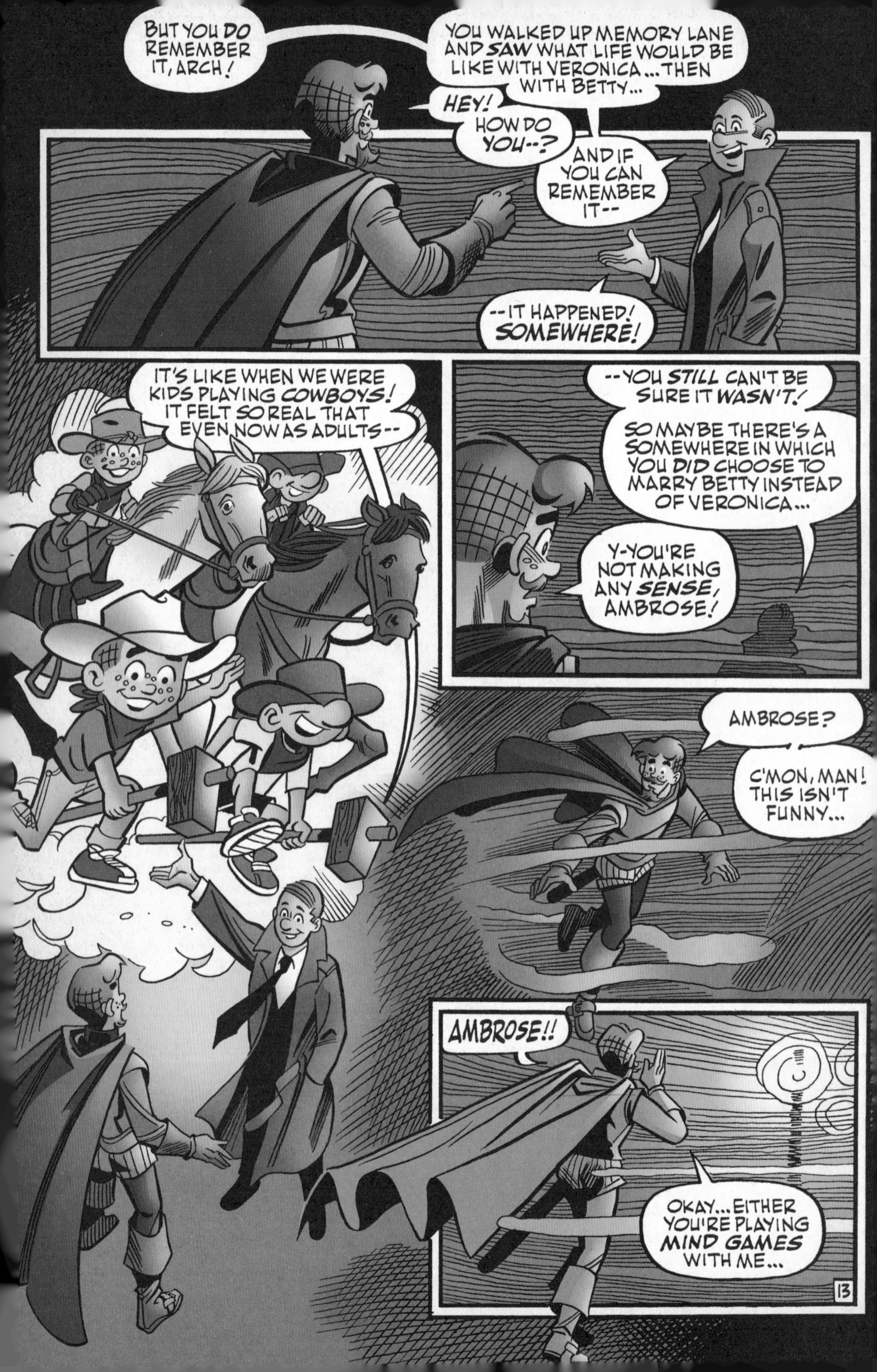
BUT YOU DO REMEMBER IT, ARCH!
YOU WALKED UP MEMORY LANE AND SAW WHAT LIFE WOULD BE LIKE WITH VERONICA... THEN WITH BETTY...
HEY! HOW DO YOU--?
AND IF YOU CAN REMEMBER IT--
--IT HAPPENED! SOMEWHERE!
IT'S LIKE WHEN WE WERE KIDS PLAYING COWBOYS! IT FELT SO REAL THAT EVEN NOW AS ADULTS--
--YOU STILL CAN'T BE SURE IT WASN'T!
SO MAYBE THERE'S A SOMEWHERE IN WHICH YOU DID CHOOSE TO MARRY BETTY INSTEAD OF VERONICA...
Y-YOU'RE NOT MAKING ANY SENSE, AMBROSE!
AMBROSE?
C'MON, MAN! THIS ISN'T FUNNY...
AMBROSE!!
OKAY... EITHER YOU'RE PLAYING MIND GAMES WITH ME...
13

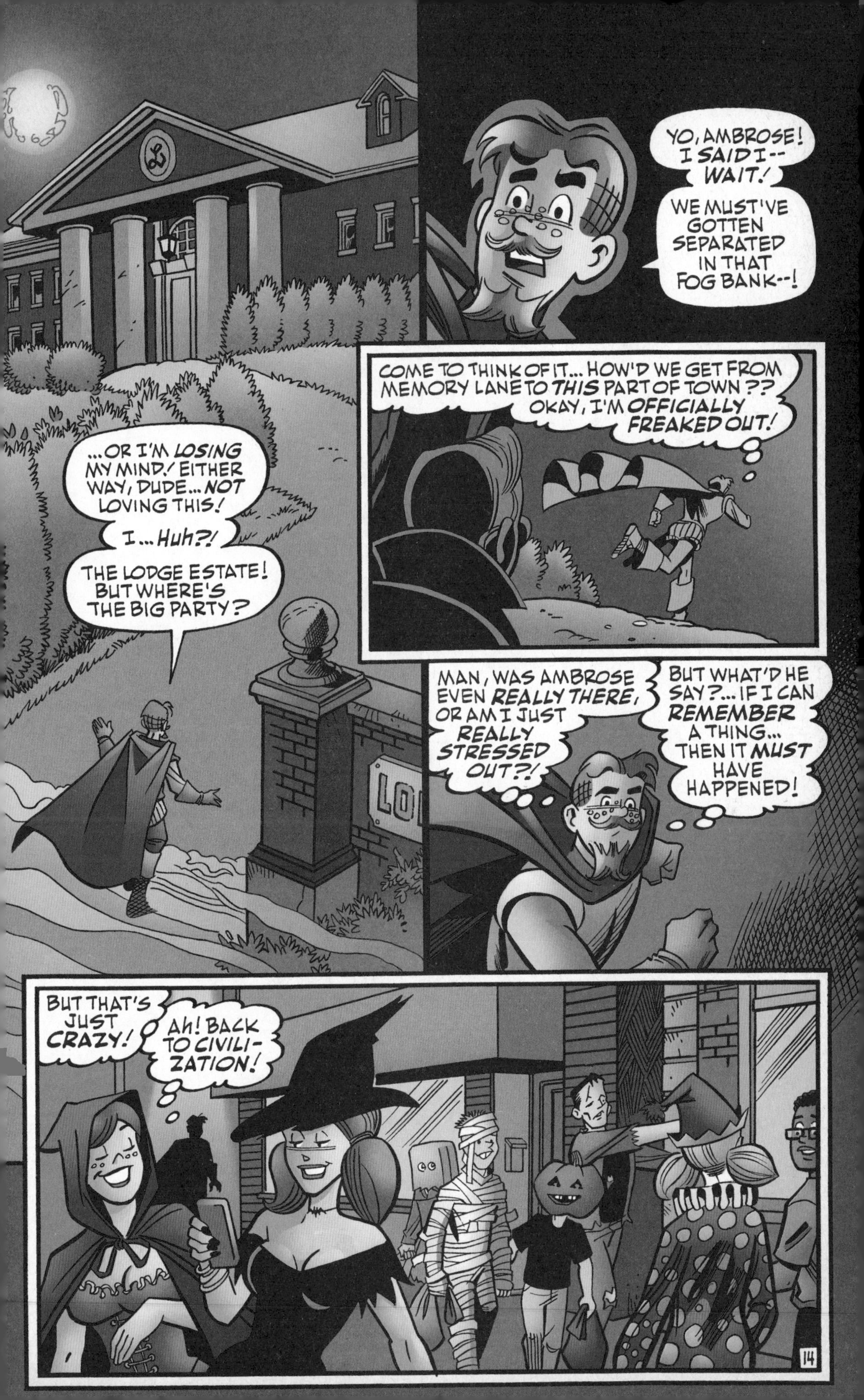
YO, AMBROSE! I SAID I-- WAIT!
WE MUST'VE GOTTEN SEPARATED IN THAT FOG BANK--!
...OR I'M LOSING MY MIND! EITHER WAY, DUDE... NOT LOVING THIS!
I... Huh?!
THE LODGE ESTATE! BUT WHERE'S THE BIG PARTY?
LO
COME TO THINK OF IT... HOW'D WE GET FROM MEMORY LANE TO THIS PART OF TOWN?? OKAY, I'M OFFICIALLY FREAKED OUT!
MAN, WAS AMBROSE EVEN REALLY THERE, OR AM I JUST REALLY STRESSED OUT?!
BUT WHAT'D HE SAY?... IF I CAN REMEMBER A THING... THEN IT MUST HAVE HAPPENED!
BUT THAT'S JUST CRAZY!
Ah! BACK TO CIVILI-ZATION!
14

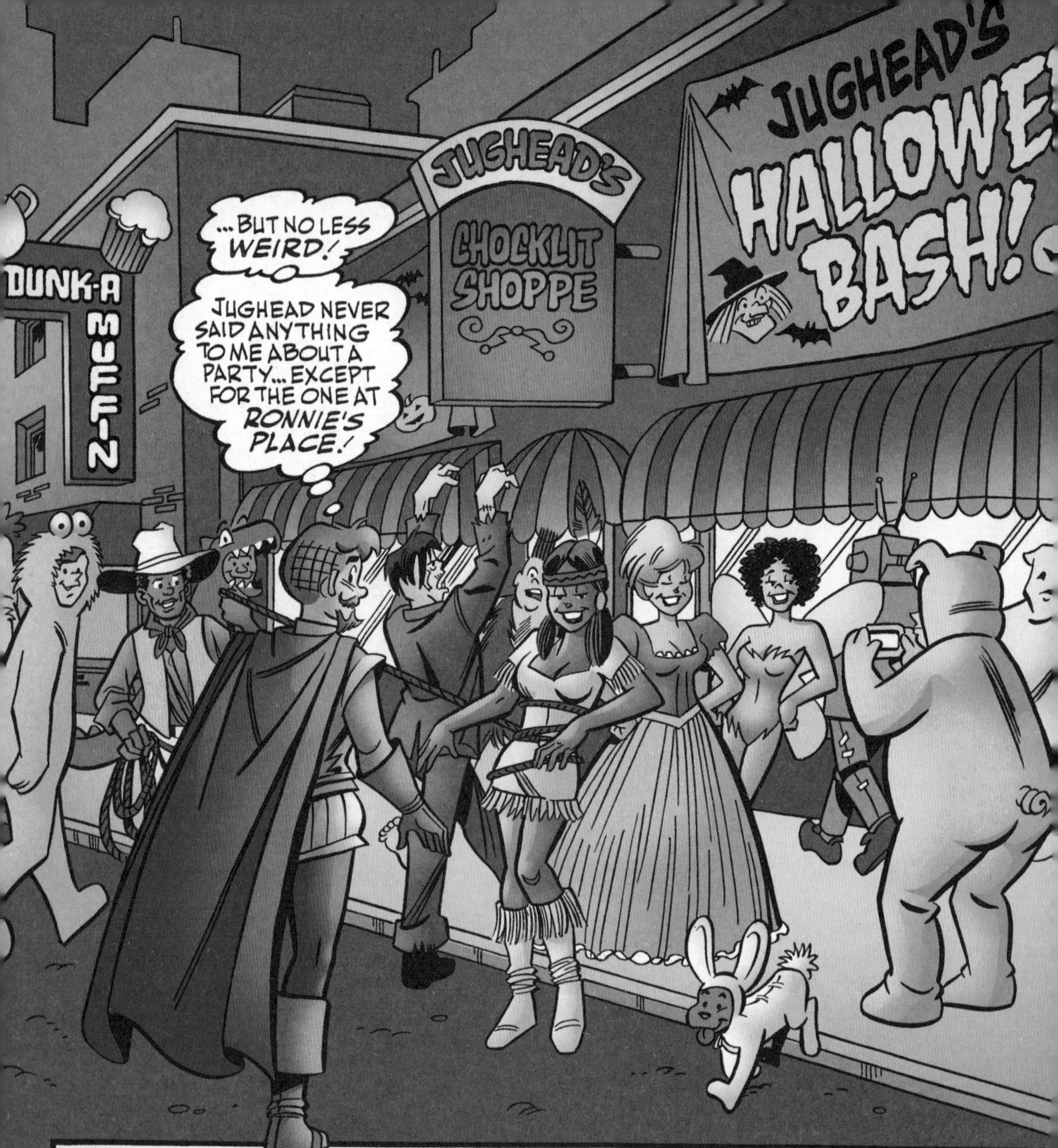
JUGHEAD'S HALLOWE
BASH!
DUNK-A MUFFIN
JUGHEAD'S
CHOCKLIT SHOPPE
...BUT NO LESS WEIRD!
JUGHEAD NEVER SAID ANYTHING TO ME ABOUT A PARTY... EXCEPT FOR THE ONE AT RONNIE'S PLACE!

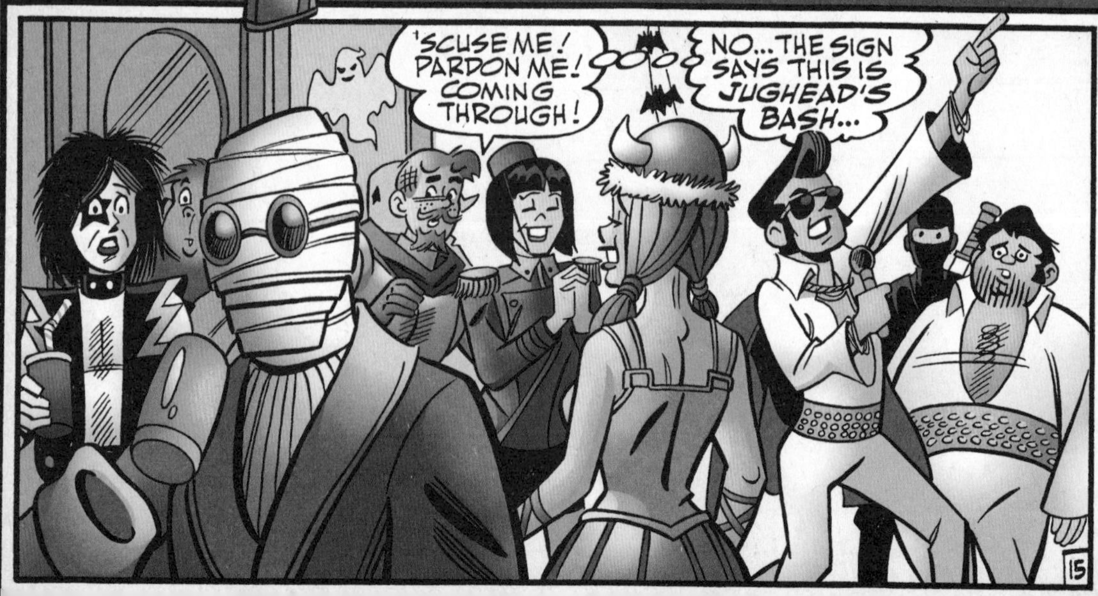
'SCUSE ME! PARDON ME! COMING THROUGH!
NO... THE SIGN SAYS THIS IS JUGHEAD'S BASH...

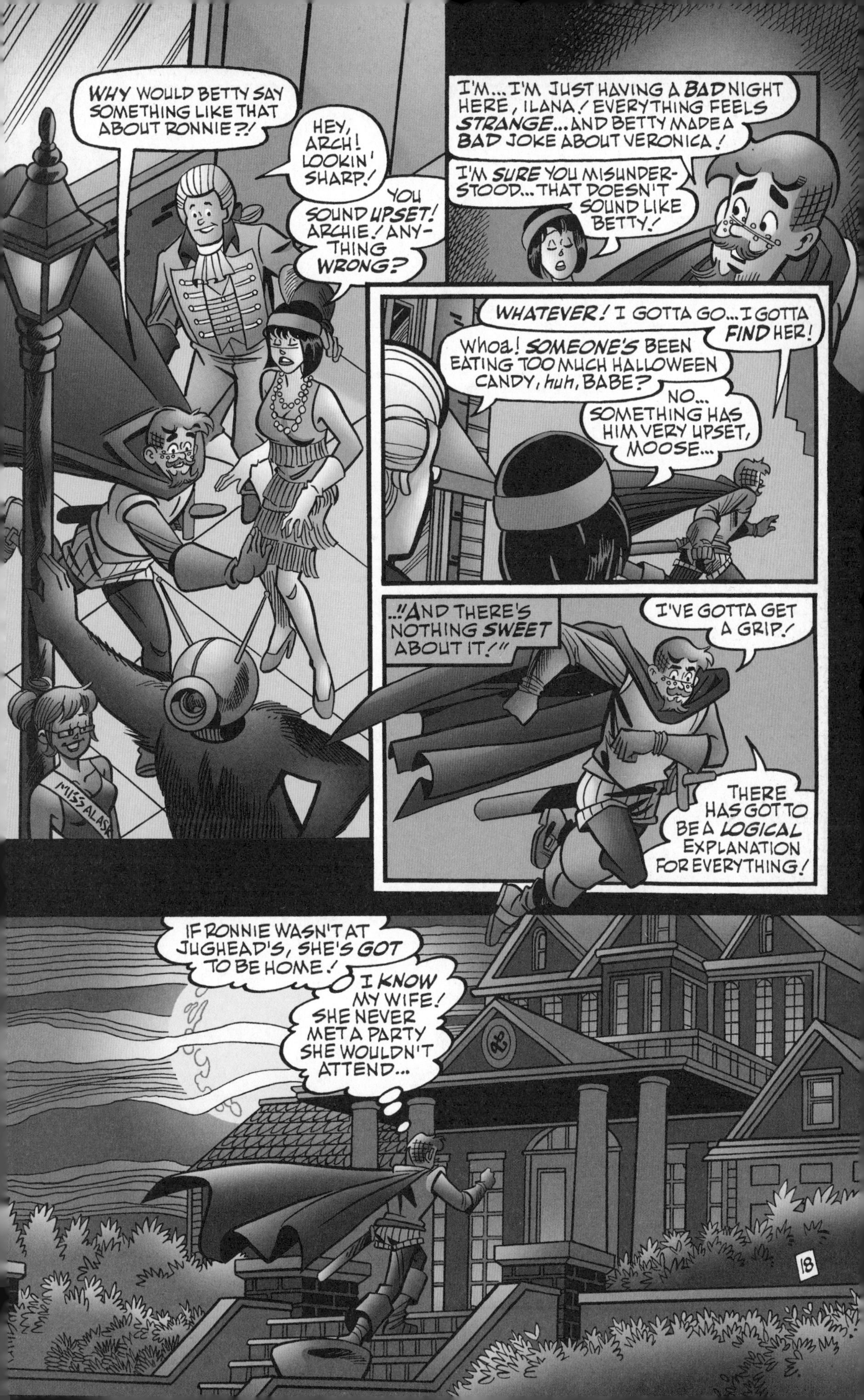
WHY WOULD BETTY SAY SOMETHING LIKE THAT ABOUT RONNIE?!
HEY, ARCH! LOOKIN' SHARP!
YOU SOUND UPSET! ARCHIE! ANY-THING WRONG?
I'M... I'M JUST HAVING A BAD NIGHT HERE, ILANA! EVERYTHING FEELS STRANGE... AND BETTY MADE A BAD JOKE ABOUT VERONICA!
I'M SURE YOU MISUNDER-STOOD... THAT DOESN'T SOUND LIKE BETTY!
MISS ALASKA
WHATEVER! I GOTTA GO... I GOTTA FIND HER!
Whoa! SOMEONE'S BEEN EATING TOO MUCH HALLOWEEN CANDY, huh, BABE?
NO... SOMETHING HAS HIM VERY UPSET, MOOSE...
..."AND THERE'S NOTHING SWEET ABOUT IT!"
I'VE GOTTA GET A GRIP!
THERE HAS GOT TO BE A LOGICAL EXPLANATION FOR EVERYTHING!
IF RONNIE WASN'T AT JUGHEAD'S, SHE'S GOT TO BE HOME!
I KNOW MY WIFE! SHE NEVER MET A PARTY SHE WOULDN'T ATTEND...
18

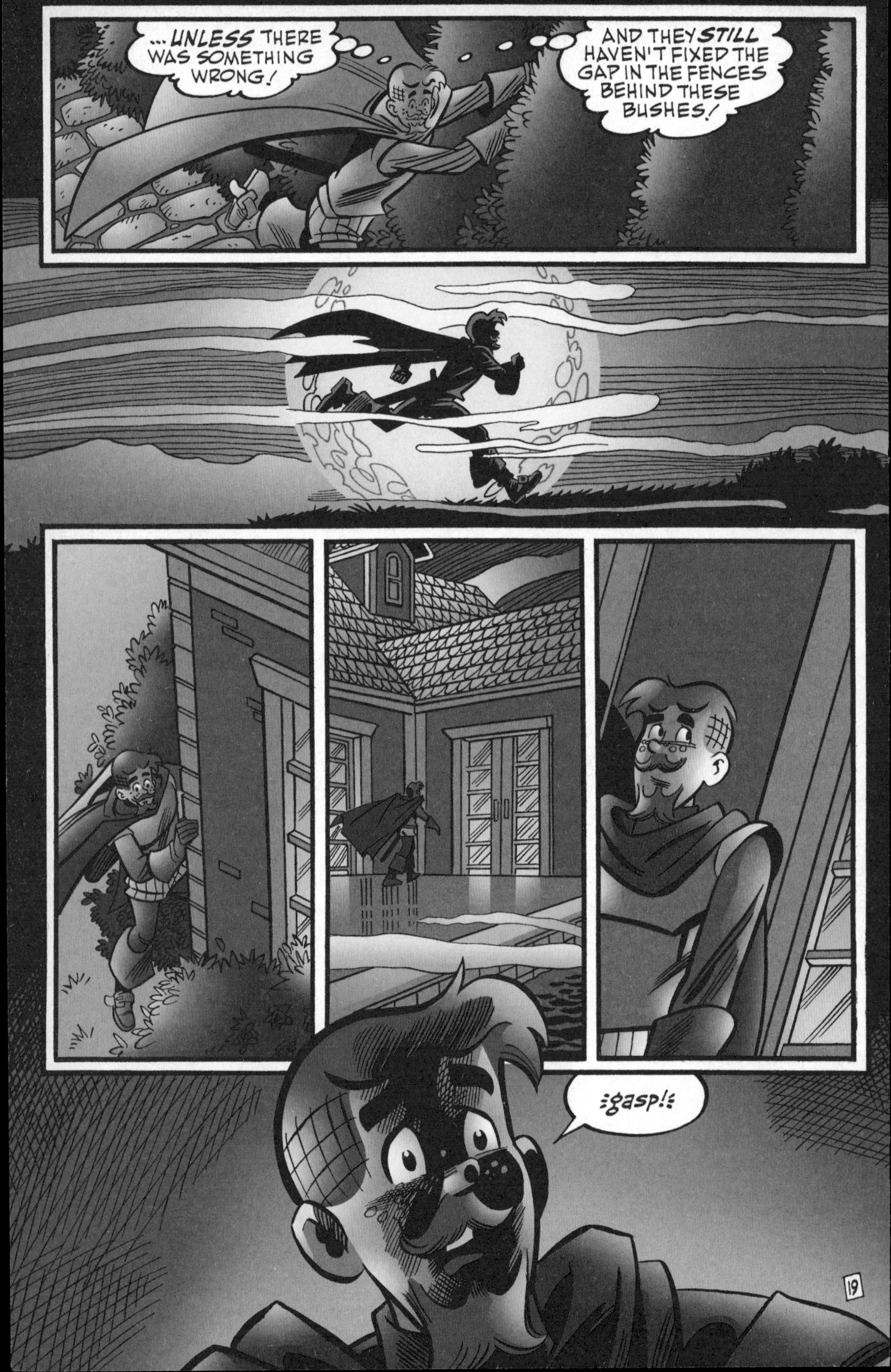
...UNLESS THERE WAS SOMETHING WRONG!
AND THEY STILL HAVEN'T FIXED THE GAP IN THE FENCES BEHIND THESE BUSHES!
:gasp!:

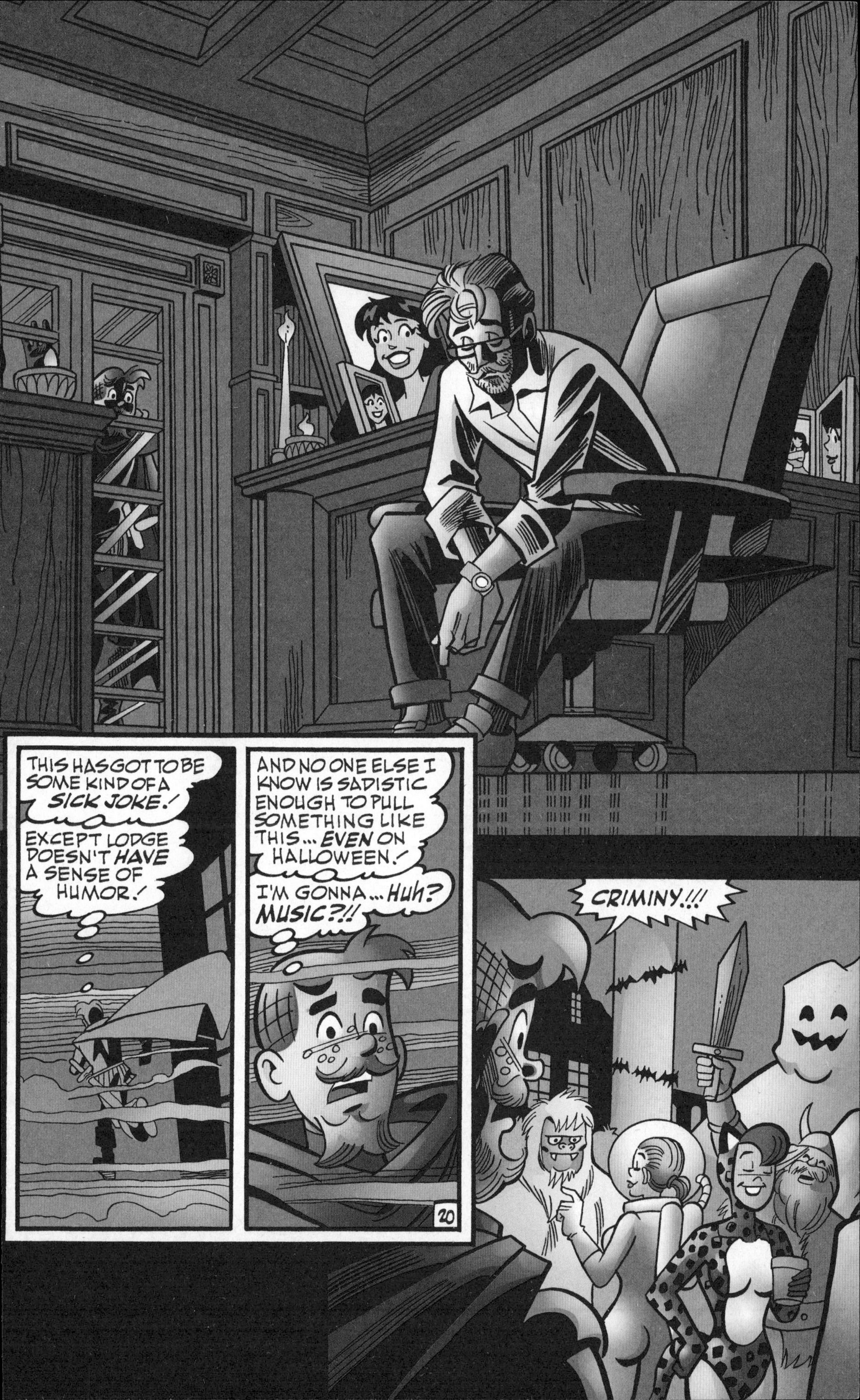

THIS HAS GOT TO BE SOME KIND OF A SICK JOKE.!
EXCEPT LODGE DOESN'T HAVE A SENSE OF HUMOR.!
AND NO ONE ELSE I KNOW IS SADISTIC ENOUGH TO PULL SOMETHING LIKE THIS... EVEN ON HALLOWEEN.!
I'M GONNA... Huh? MUSIC?!!
CRIMINY.!!!
20

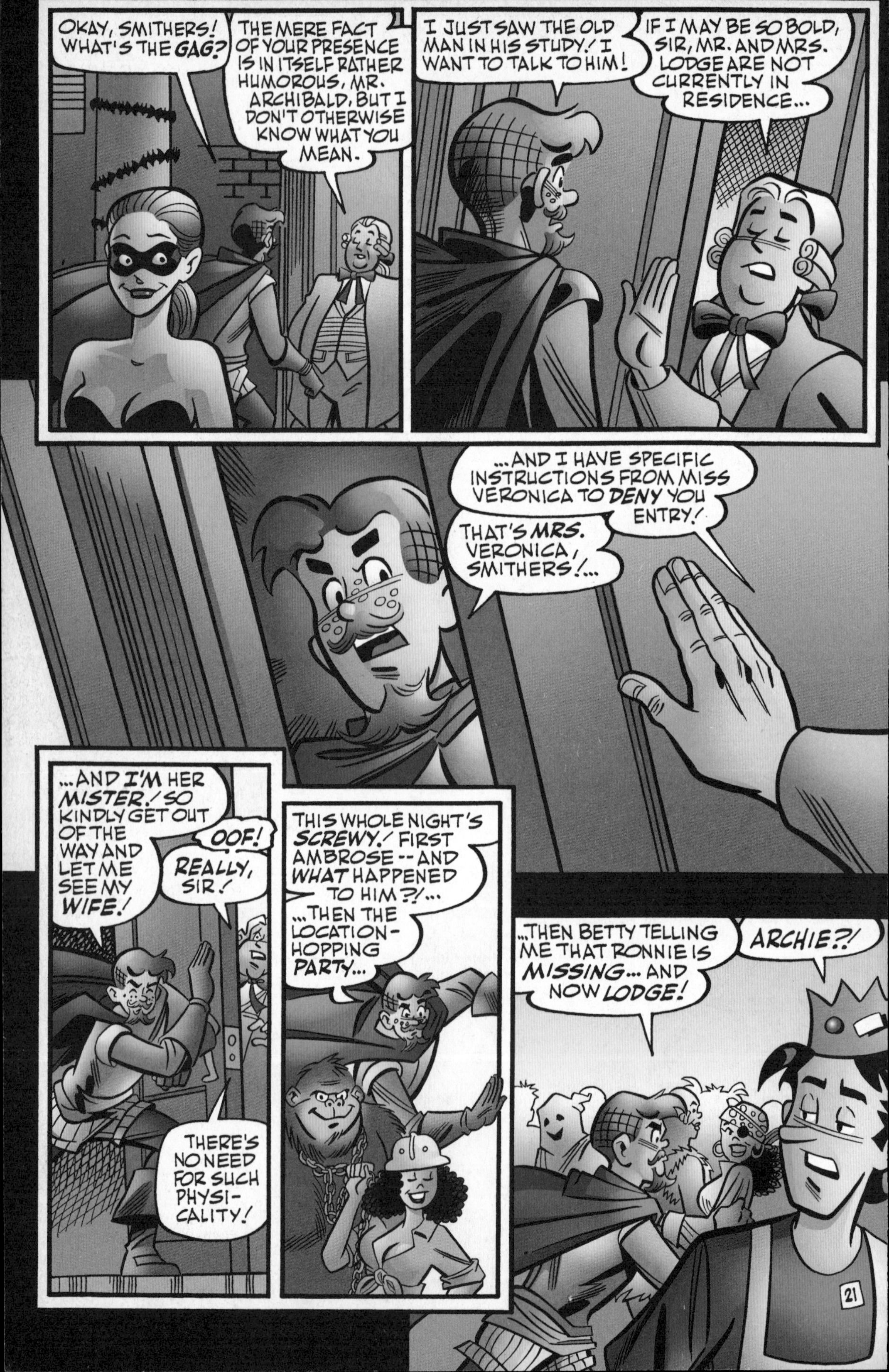
OKAY, SMITHERS! WHAT'S THE GAG?
THE MERE FACT OF YOUR PRESENCE IS IN ITSELF RATHER HUMOROUS, MR. ARCHIBALD, BUT I DON'T OTHERWISE KNOW WHAT YOU MEAN.
I JUST SAW THE OLD MAN IN HIS STUDY! I WANT TO TALK TO HIM!
IF I MAY BE SO BOLD, SIR, MR. AND MRS. LODGE ARE NOT CURRENTLY IN RESIDENCE...
...AND I HAVE SPECIFIC INSTRUCTIONS FROM MISS VERONICA TO DENY YOU ENTRY!
THAT'S MRS. VERONICA, SMITHERS!...
...AND I'M HER MISTER! SO KINDLY GET OUT OF THE WAY AND LET ME SEE MY WIFE!
OOF!
REALLY, SIR!
THERE'S NO NEED FOR SUCH PHYSICALITY!
THIS WHOLE NIGHT'S SCREWY! FIRST AMBROSE -- AND WHAT HAPPENED TO HIM?!...
...THEN THE LOCATION-HOPPING PARTY...
...THEN BETTY TELLING ME THAT RONNIE IS MISSING... AND NOW LODGE!
ARCHIE?!
21

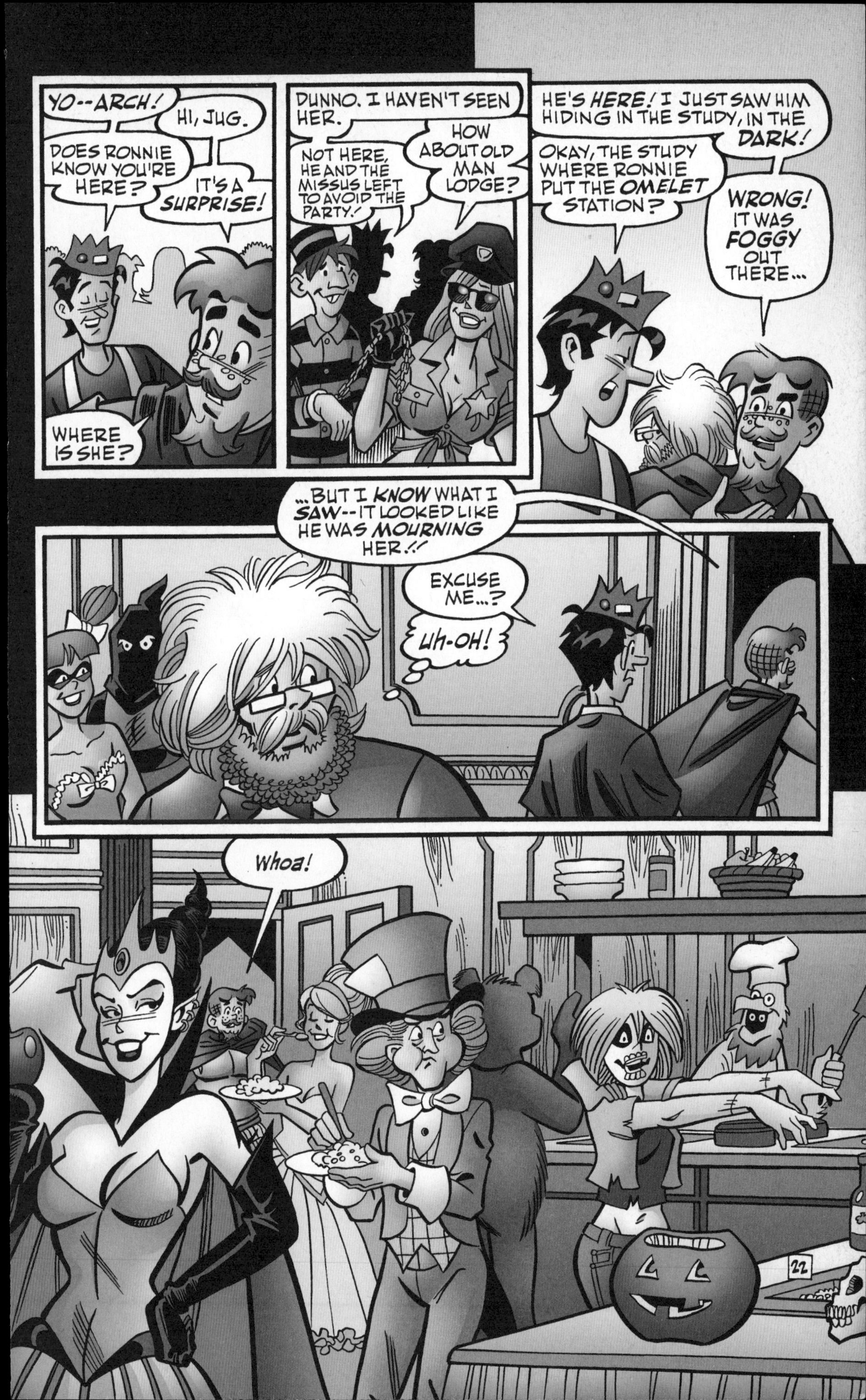
YO--ARCH!
HI, JUG.
DOES RONNIE KNOW YOU'RE HERE?
IT'S A SURPRISE!
WHERE IS SHE?
DUNNO. I HAVEN'T SEEN HER.
HOW ABOUT OLD MAN LODGE?
NOT HERE, HE AND THE MISSUS LEFT TO AVOID THE PARTY.!
HE'S HERE! I JUST SAW HIM HIDING IN THE STUDY, IN THE DARK!
OKAY, THE STUDY WHERE RONNIE PUT THE OMELET STATION?
WRONG! IT WAS FOGGY OUT THERE...
...BUT I KNOW WHAT I SAW--IT LOOKED LIKE HE WAS MOURNING HER.!!
EXCUSE ME...?
uh-OH!
Whoa!
22

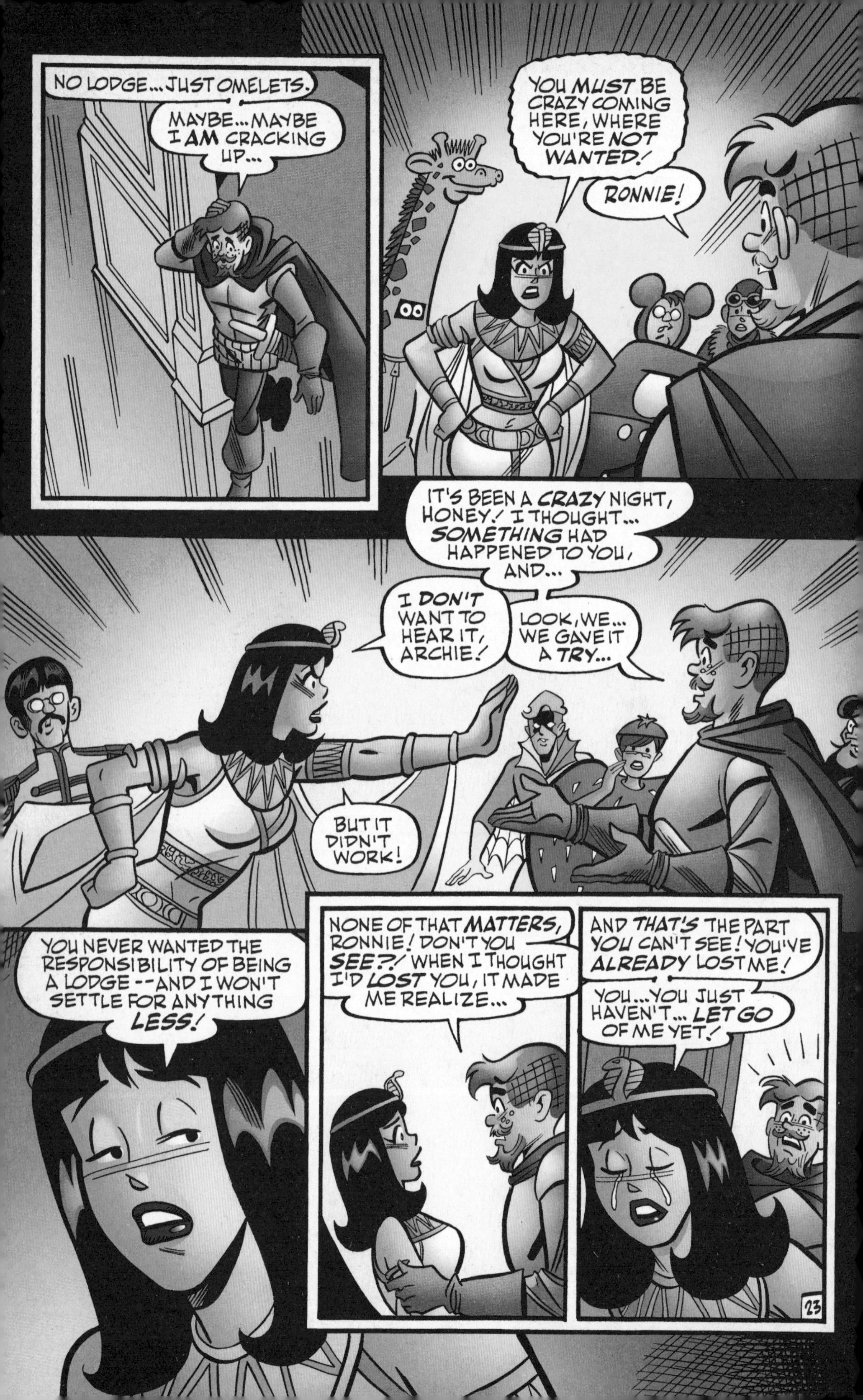

NO LODGE... JUST OMELETS.
MAYBE... MAYBE I AM CRACKING UP...
YOU MUST BE CRAZY COMING HERE, WHERE YOU'RE NOT WANTED!
RONNIE!
IT'S BEEN A CRAZY NIGHT, HONEY! I THOUGHT... SOMETHING HAD HAPPENED TO YOU, AND...
I DON'T WANT TO HEAR IT, ARCHIE!
LOOK, WE... WE GAVE IT A TRY...
BUT IT DIDN'T WORK!
YOU NEVER WANTED THE RESPONSIBILITY OF BEING A LODGE -- AND I WON'T SETTLE FOR ANYTHING LESS!
NONE OF THAT MATTERS, RONNIE! DON'T YOU SEE?! WHEN I THOUGHT I'D LOST YOU, IT MADE ME REALIZE...
AND THAT'S THE PART YOU CAN'T SEE! YOU'VE ALREADY LOST ME!
YOU... YOU JUST HAVEN'T... LET GO OF ME YET!
23

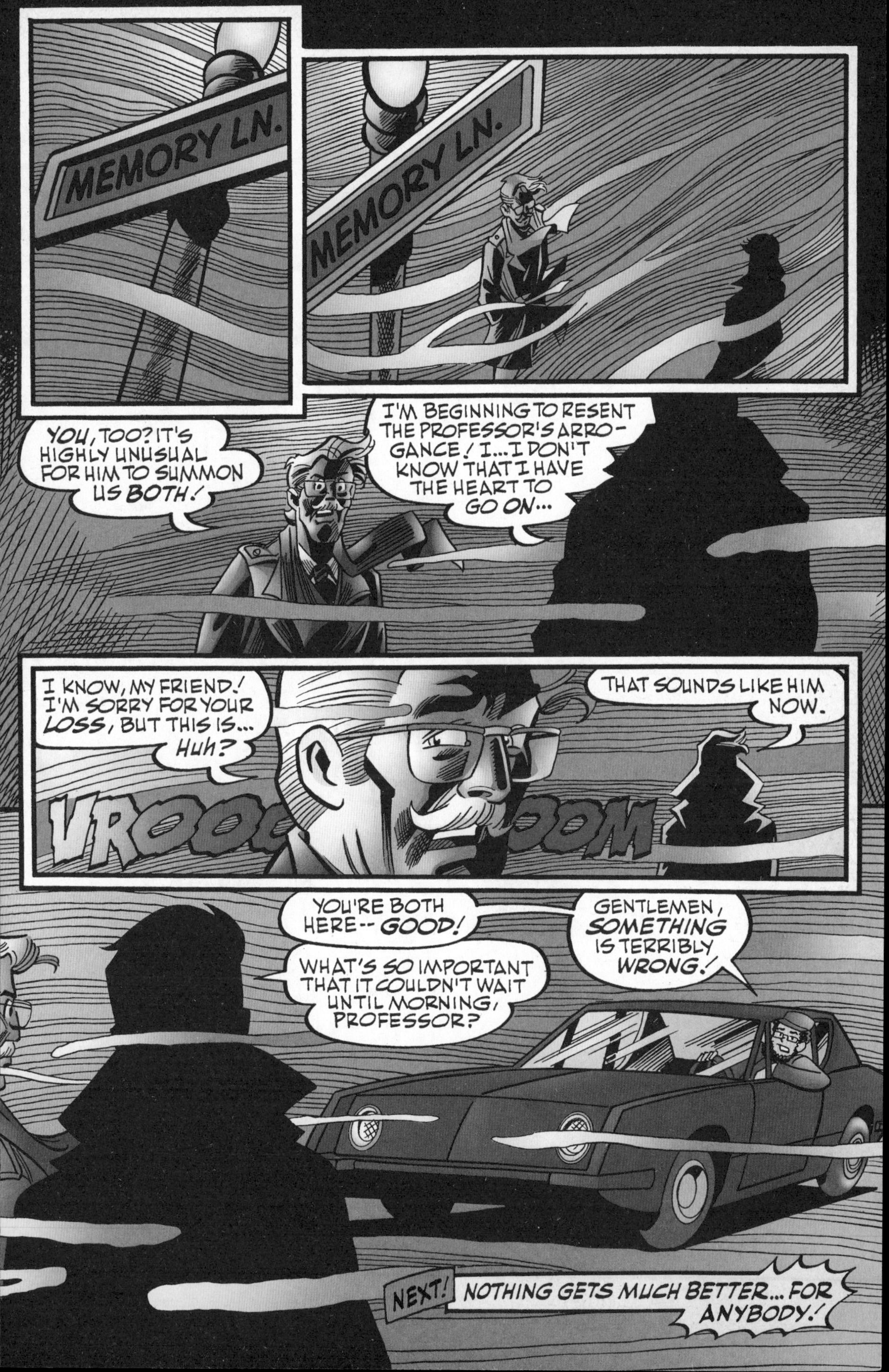
MEMORY LN.
MEMORY LN.
YOU, TOO? IT'S HIGHLY UNUSUAL FOR HIM TO SUMMON US BOTH!
I'M BEGINNING TO RESENT THE PROFESSOR'S ARROGANCE! I... I DON'T KNOW THAT I HAVE THE HEART TO GO ON...
I KNOW, MY FRIEND! I'M SORRY FOR YOUR LOSS, BUT THIS IS... Huh?
THAT SOUNDS LIKE HIM NOW.
VROOO OOM
YOU'RE BOTH HERE-- GOOD!
GENTLEMEN, SOMETHING IS TERRIBLY WRONG!
WHAT'S SO IMPORTANT THAT IT COULDN'T WAIT UNTIL MORNING, PROFESSOR?
NEXT! NOTHING GETS MUCH BETTER... FOR ANYBODY!

"THE HIRAM LODGE *I* MARRIED COULD ***NEVER*** HAVE GIVEN UP HOPE... "

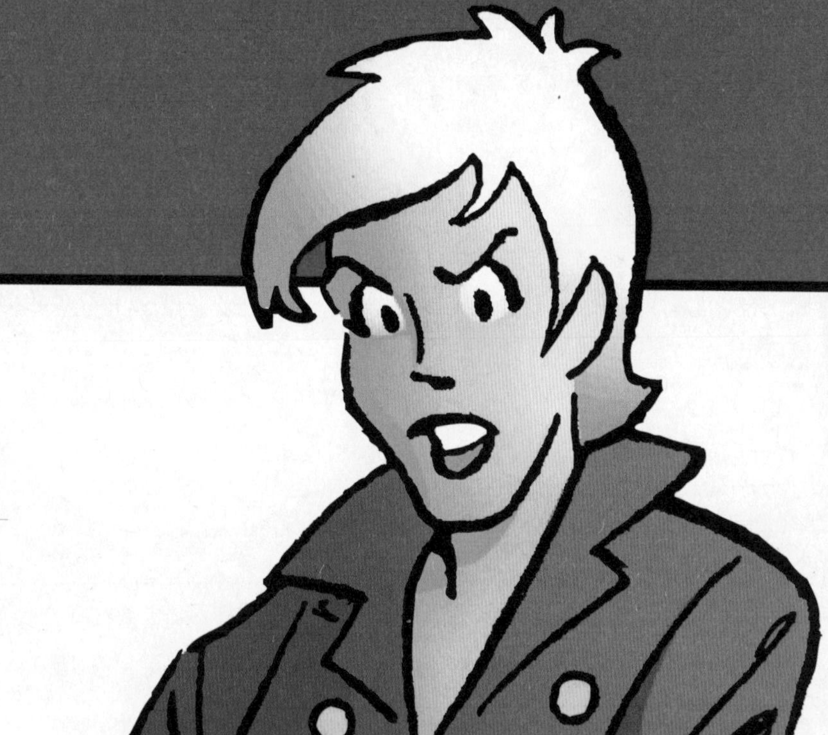

"...OR FORGOTTEN THE PEOPLE DEPENDING ON HIM! HIS EMPLOYEES ***AND*** HIS *WIFE!*"

- MRS. HERMIONE LODGE

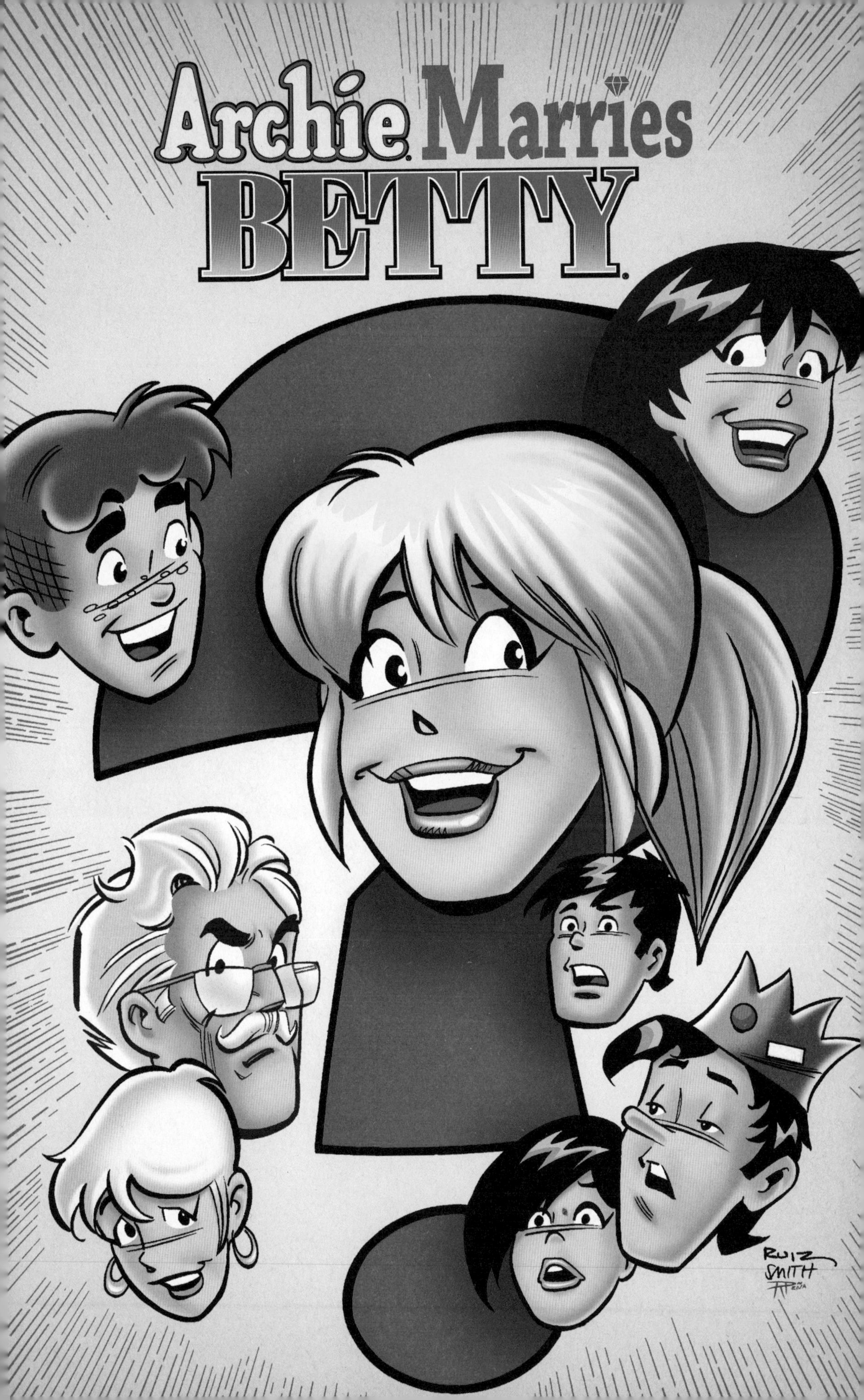
Archie Marries
BETTY
RUIZ
SMITH

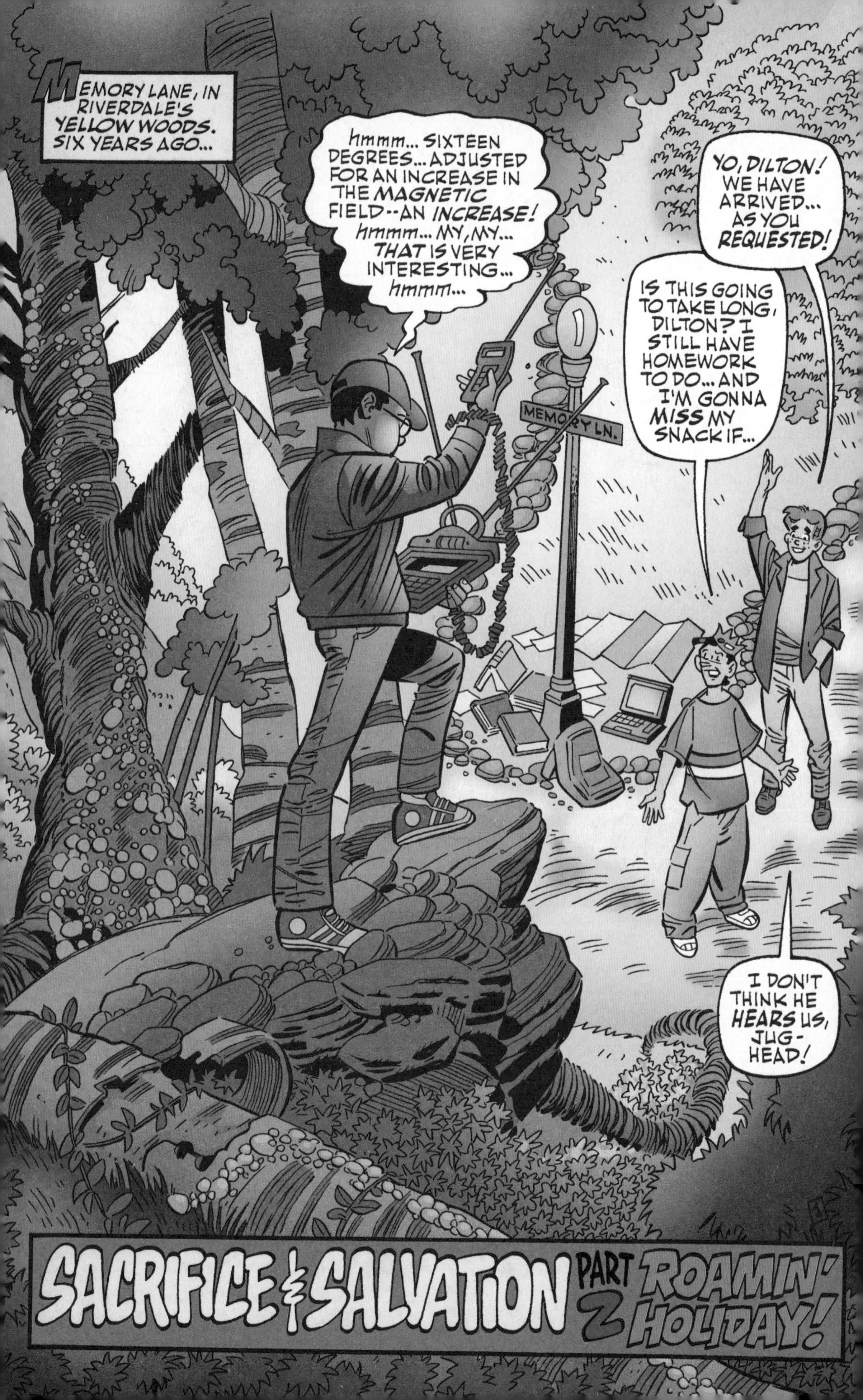
MEMORY LANE, IN RIVERDALE'S YELLOW WOODS. SIX YEARS AGO...
hmmm... SIXTEEN DEGREES... ADJUSTED FOR AN INCREASE IN THE MAGNETIC FIELD--AN INCREASE! hmmm... MY, MY... THAT IS VERY INTERESTING... hmmm...
MEMORY LN.
YO, DILTON! WE HAVE ARRIVED... AS YOU REQUESTED!
IS THIS GOING TO TAKE LONG, DILTON? I STILL HAVE HOMEWORK TO DO... AND I'M GONNA MISS MY SNACK IF...
I DON'T THINK HE HEARS US, JUG-HEAD!
SACRIFICE & SALVATION PART 2 ROAMIN' HOLIDAY!

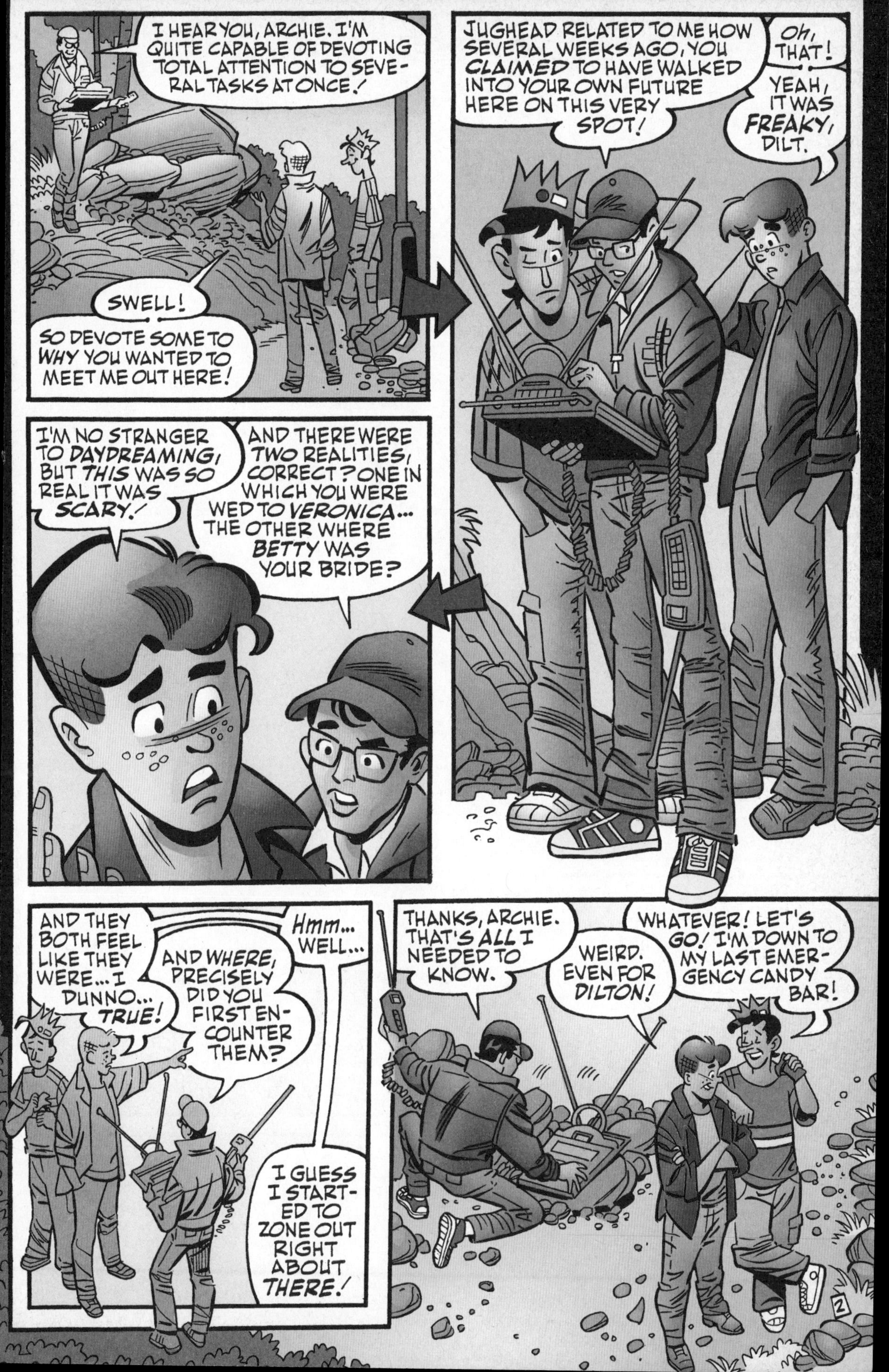
I HEAR YOU, ARCHIE. I'M QUITE CAPABLE OF DEVOTING TOTAL ATTENTION TO SEVERAL TASKS AT ONCE!
SWELL!
SO DEVOTE SOME TO WHY YOU WANTED TO MEET ME OUT HERE!
JUGHEAD RELATED TO ME HOW SEVERAL WEEKS AGO, YOU CLAIMED TO HAVE WALKED INTO YOUR OWN FUTURE HERE ON THIS VERY SPOT!
Oh, THAT!
YEAH, IT WAS FREAKY, DILT.
I'M NO STRANGER TO DAYDREAMING, BUT THIS WAS SO REAL IT WAS SCARY!
AND THERE WERE TWO REALITIES, CORRECT? ONE IN WHICH YOU WERE WED TO VERONICA... THE OTHER WHERE BETTY WAS YOUR BRIDE?
AND THEY BOTH FEEL LIKE THEY WERE... I DUNNO... TRUE!
AND WHERE, PRECISELY DID YOU FIRST ENCOUNTER THEM?
Hmm... WELL...
I GUESS I STARTED TO ZONE OUT RIGHT ABOUT THERE!
THANKS, ARCHIE. THAT'S ALL I NEEDED TO KNOW.
WEIRD. EVEN FOR DILTON!
WHATEVER! LET'S GO! I'M DOWN TO MY LAST EMERGENCY CANDY BAR!
2

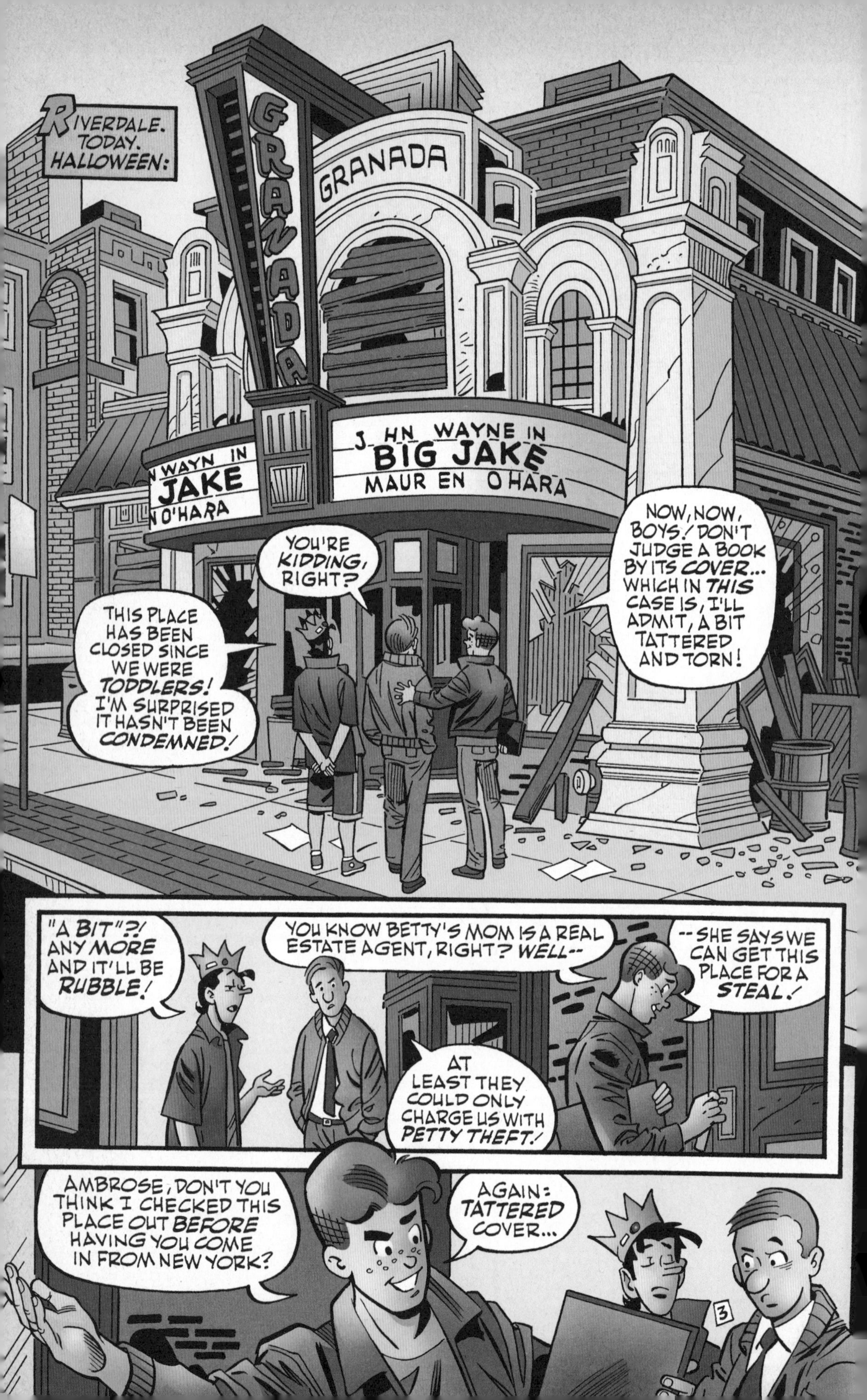
RIVERDALE. TODAY. HALLOWEEN:
GRANADA
GRANADA
J_HN WAYNE IN BIG JAKE MAUR EN O'HARA
N WAYN IN JAKE N O'HARA
YOU'RE KIDDING, RIGHT?
THIS PLACE HAS BEEN CLOSED SINCE WE WERE TODDLERS! I'M SURPRISED IT HASN'T BEEN CONDEMNED!
NOW, NOW, BOYS! DON'T JUDGE A BOOK BY ITS COVER... WHICH IN THIS CASE IS, I'LL ADMIT, A BIT TATTERED AND TORN!
"A BIT"?! ANY MORE AND IT'LL BE RUBBLE!
YOU KNOW BETTY'S MOM IS A REAL ESTATE AGENT, RIGHT? WELL--
--SHE SAYS WE CAN GET THIS PLACE FOR A STEAL!
AT LEAST THEY COULD ONLY CHARGE US WITH PETTY THEFT!
AMBROSE, DON'T YOU THINK I CHECKED THIS PLACE OUT BEFORE HAVING YOU COME IN FROM NEW YORK?
AGAIN: TATTERED COVER...
3

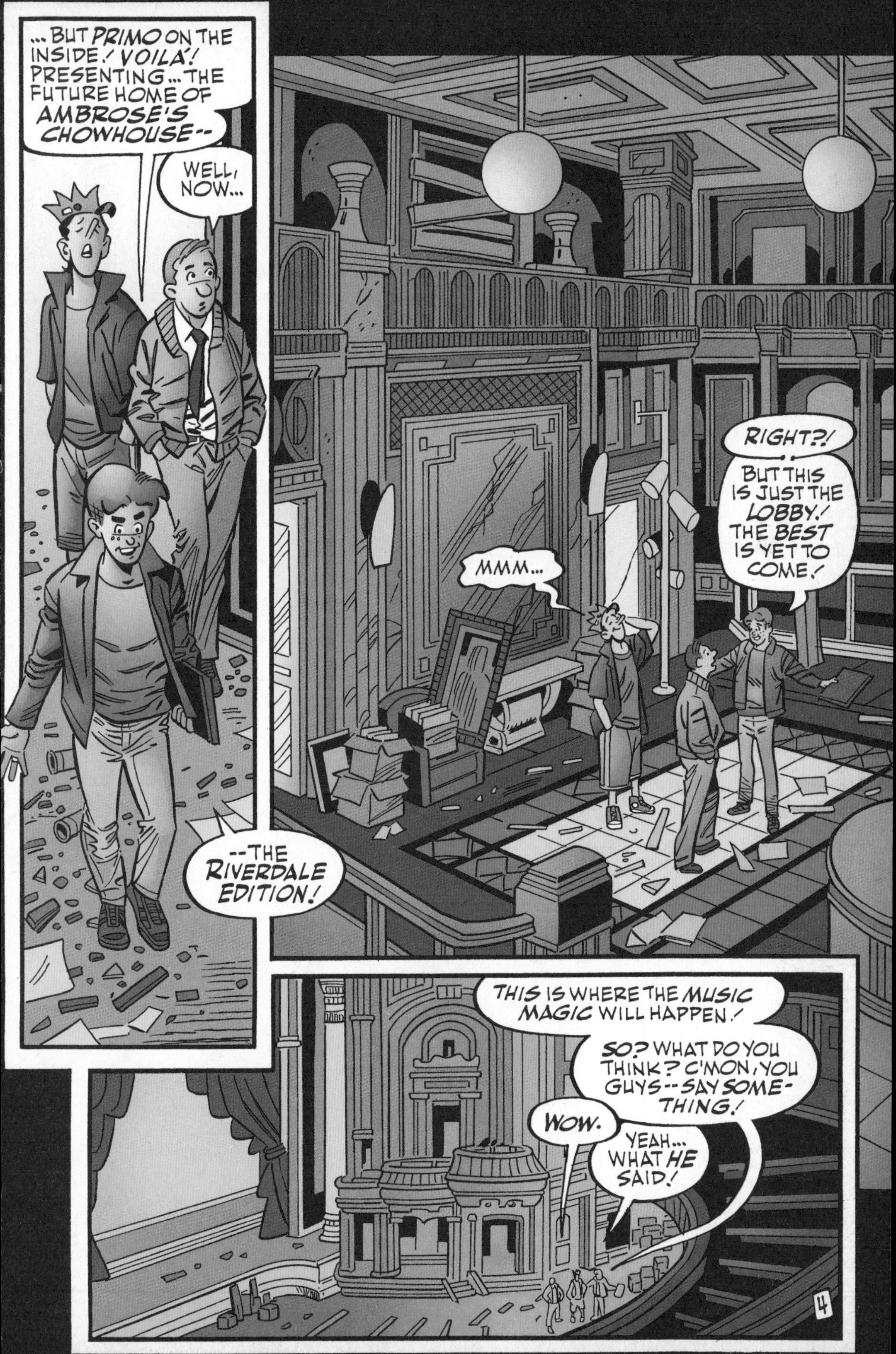

...BUT PRIMO ON THE INSIDE! VOILÀ! PRESENTING...THE FUTURE HOME OF AMBROSE'S CHOWHOUSE--
WELL, NOW...
--THE RIVERDALE EDITION!
MMM...
RIGHT?!
BUT THIS IS JUST THE LOBBY! THE BEST IS YET TO COME!
THIS IS WHERE THE MUSIC MAGIC WILL HAPPEN!
SO? WHAT DO YOU THINK? C'MON, YOU GUYS--SAY SOME-THING!
WOW.
YEAH... WHAT HE SAID!
4

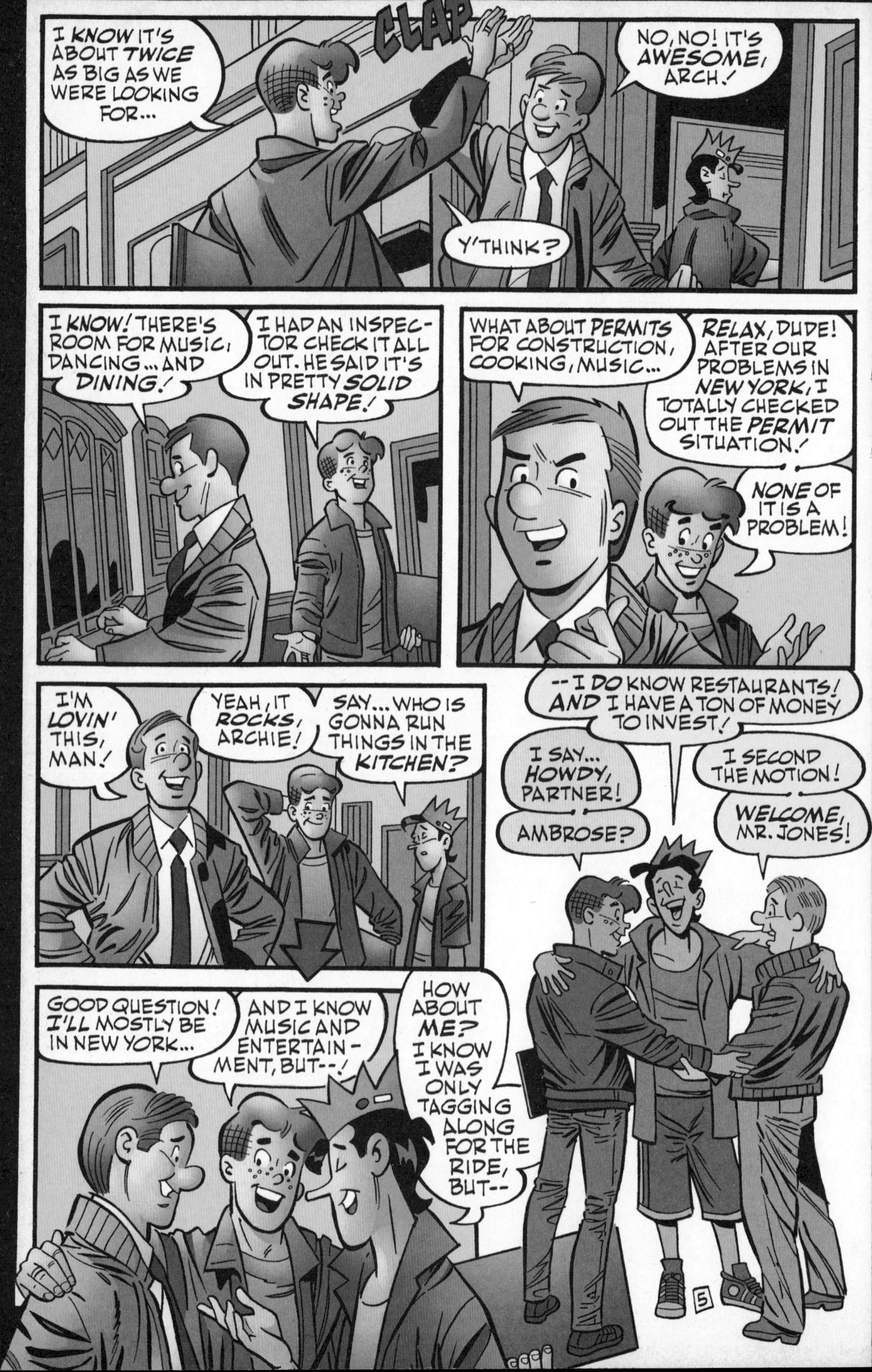
CLAP
I KNOW IT'S ABOUT TWICE AS BIG AS WE WERE LOOKING FOR...
NO, NO! IT'S AWESOME, ARCH!
Y'THINK?
I KNOW! THERE'S ROOM FOR MUSIC, DANCING... AND DINING!
I HAD AN INSPECTOR CHECK IT ALL OUT. HE SAID IT'S IN PRETTY SOLID SHAPE!
WHAT ABOUT PERMITS FOR CONSTRUCTION, COOKING, MUSIC...
RELAX, DUDE! AFTER OUR PROBLEMS IN NEW YORK, I TOTALLY CHECKED OUT THE PERMIT SITUATION!
NONE OF IT IS A PROBLEM!
I'M LOVIN' THIS, MAN!
YEAH, IT ROCKS, ARCHIE!
SAY... WHO IS GONNA RUN THINGS IN THE KITCHEN?
GOOD QUESTION! I'LL MOSTLY BE IN NEW YORK...
AND I KNOW MUSIC AND ENTERTAINMENT, BUT--!
HOW ABOUT ME? I KNOW I WAS ONLY TAGGING ALONG FOR THE RIDE, BUT--
--I DO KNOW RESTAURANTS! AND I HAVE A TON OF MONEY TO INVEST!
I SAY... HOWDY, PARTNER!
AMBROSE?
I SECOND THE MOTION!
WELCOME, MR. JONES!
5

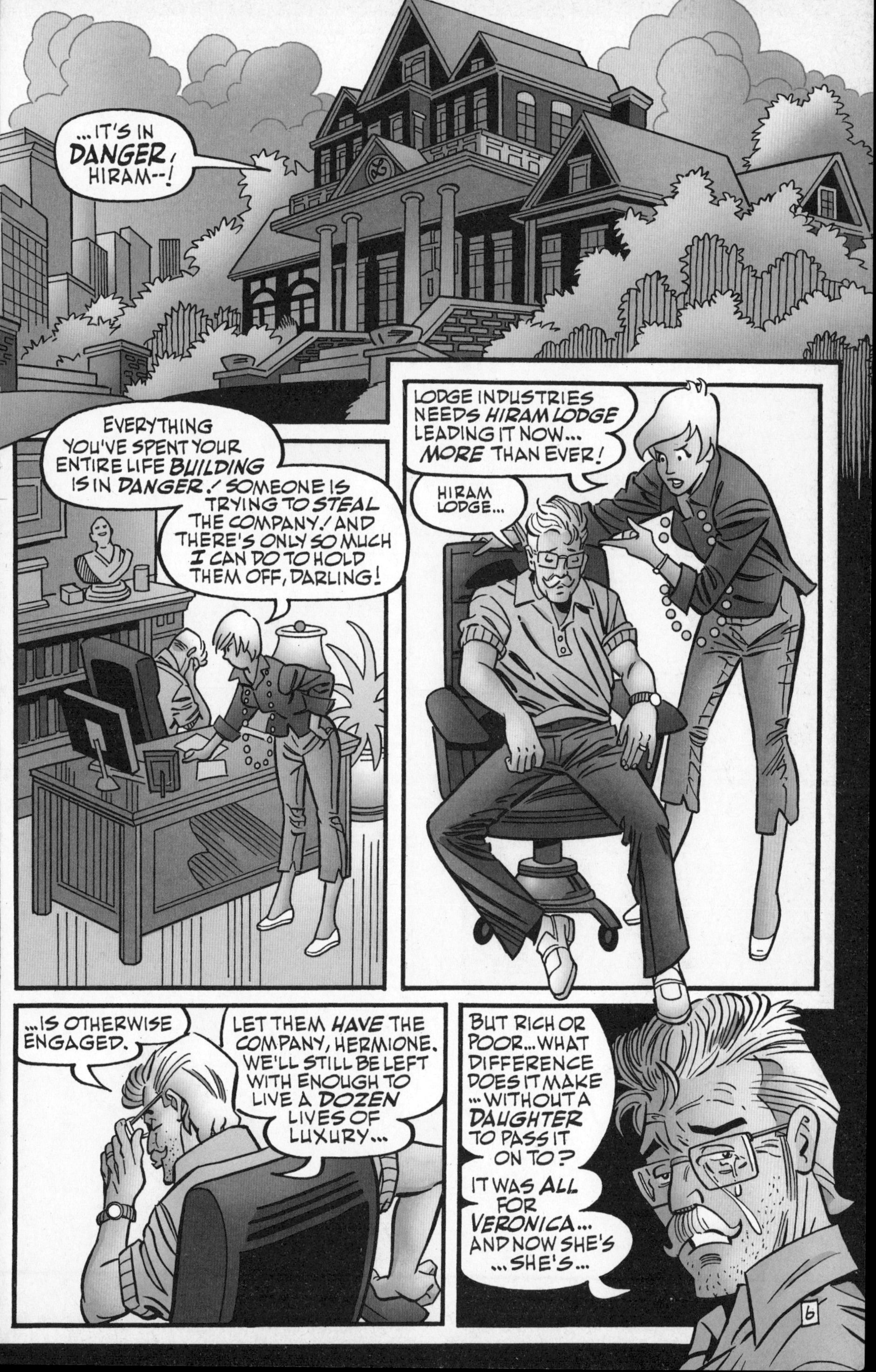
...IT'S IN DANGER, HIRAM--!
EVERYTHING YOU'VE SPENT YOUR ENTIRE LIFE BUILDING IS IN DANGER! SOMEONE IS TRYING TO STEAL THE COMPANY! AND THERE'S ONLY SO MUCH I CAN DO TO HOLD THEM OFF, DARLING!
LODGE INDUSTRIES NEEDS HIRAM LODGE LEADING IT NOW... MORE THAN EVER!
HIRAM LODGE...
...IS OTHERWISE ENGAGED.
LET THEM HAVE THE COMPANY, HERMIONE. WE'LL STILL BE LEFT WITH ENOUGH TO LIVE A DOZEN LIVES OF LUXURY...
BUT RICH OR POOR... WHAT DIFFERENCE DOES IT MAKE ...WITHOUT A DAUGHTER TO PASS IT ON TO?
IT WAS ALL FOR VERONICA... AND NOW SHE'S ...SHE'S...
6

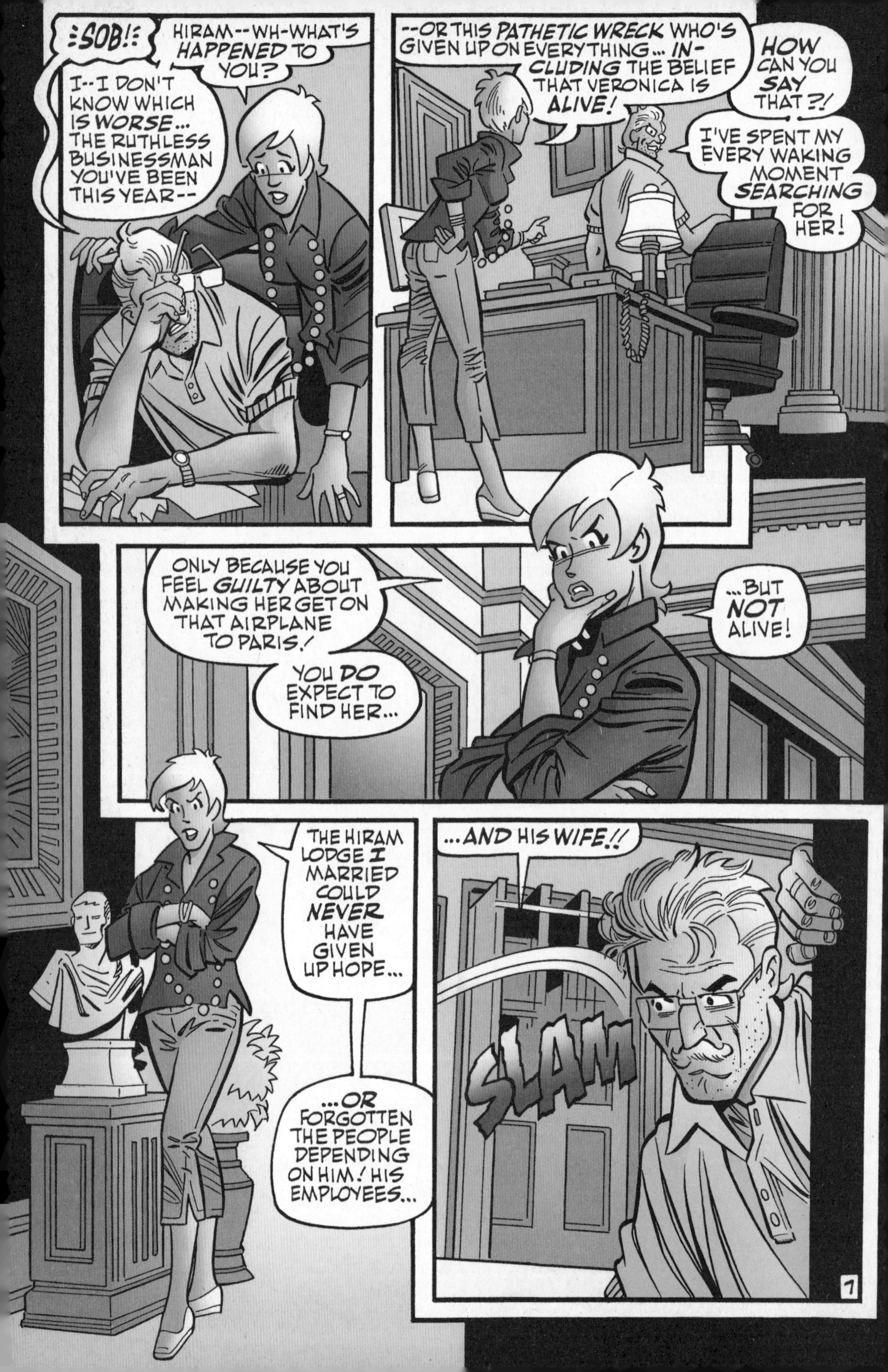

:SOB!:
HIRAM--WH-WHAT'S HAPPENED TO YOU?
I--I DON'T KNOW WHICH IS WORSE... THE RUTHLESS BUSINESSMAN YOU'VE BEEN THIS YEAR--
--OR THIS PATHETIC WRECK WHO'S GIVEN UP ON EVERYTHING... IN-CLUDING THE BELIEF THAT VERONICA IS ALIVE!
HOW CAN YOU SAY THAT?!
I'VE SPENT MY EVERY WAKING MOMENT SEARCHING FOR HER!
ONLY BECAUSE YOU FEEL GUILTY ABOUT MAKING HER GET ON THAT AIRPLANE TO PARIS!
YOU DO EXPECT TO FIND HER...
...BUT NOT ALIVE!
THE HIRAM LODGE I MARRIED COULD NEVER HAVE GIVEN UP HOPE...
...OR FORGOTTEN THE PEOPLE DEPENDING ON HIM! HIS EMPLOYEES...
...AND HIS WIFE!!
SLAM

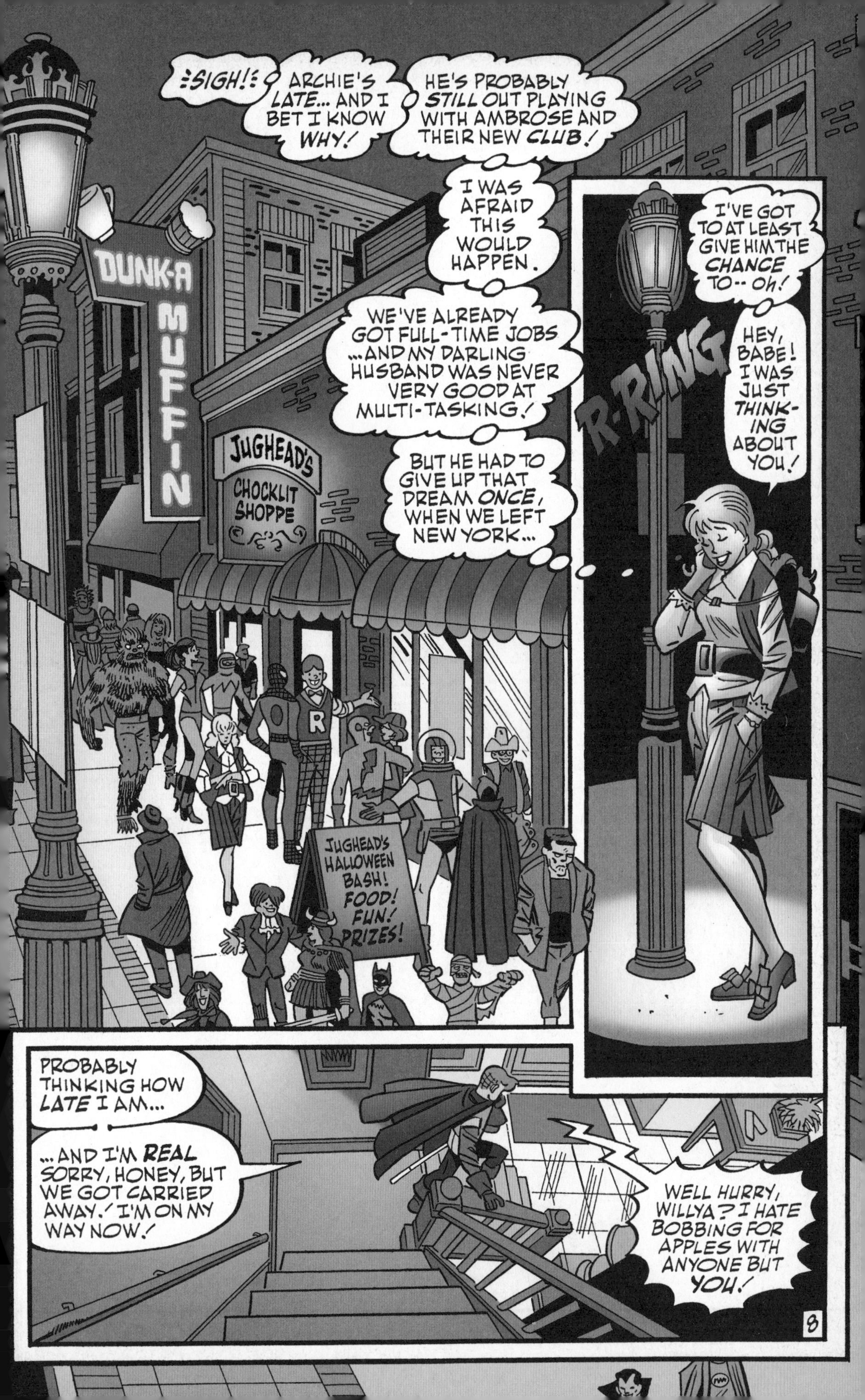
:SIGH!:
ARCHIE'S LATE... AND I BET I KNOW WHY!
HE'S PROBABLY STILL OUT PLAYING WITH AMBROSE AND THEIR NEW CLUB!
I WAS AFRAID THIS WOULD HAPPEN.
WE'VE ALREADY GOT FULL-TIME JOBS ...AND MY DARLING HUSBAND WAS NEVER VERY GOOD AT MULTI-TASKING!
BUT HE HAD TO GIVE UP THAT DREAM ONCE, WHEN WE LEFT NEW YORK...
DUNK-A MUFFIN
JUGHEAD'S CHOCKLIT SHOPPE
JUGHEAD'S HALLOWEEN BASH! FOOD! FUN! PRIZES!
I'VE GOT TO AT LEAST GIVE HIM THE CHANCE TO-- OH!
R-RING
HEY, BABE! I WAS JUST THINKING ABOUT YOU!
PROBABLY THINKING HOW LATE I AM...
...AND I'M REAL SORRY, HONEY, BUT WE GOT CARRIED AWAY! I'M ON MY WAY NOW!
WELL HURRY, WILLYA? I HATE BOBBING FOR APPLES WITH ANYONE BUT YOU!
8

YOU *SURE* YOU CAN'T STAY FOR JUGHEAD'S PARTY?

I WISH I COULD, BUT I'VE GOTTA GET BACK TO THE BIG APPLE. MY CAR'S PARKED IN TOWN...

I'M HEADED THAT WAY MY-SELF! MAN, I *SO* CAN'T BELIEVE WE'RE GETTING THIS *RE-DO*, AMBROSE!

YEAH, LIFE'S *SURPRISING* THAT WAY!

IT'S FUNNY-- OF *ALL* OUR CHILDHOOD ADVENTURES, WE *NEVER* DREAMED OF BEING BUSINESSMEN!

WHAT KID WANTS TO GROW UP TO WRITE BUSINESS PROPOSALS AND DO PROFIT AND LOSS PROJEC-TIONS?

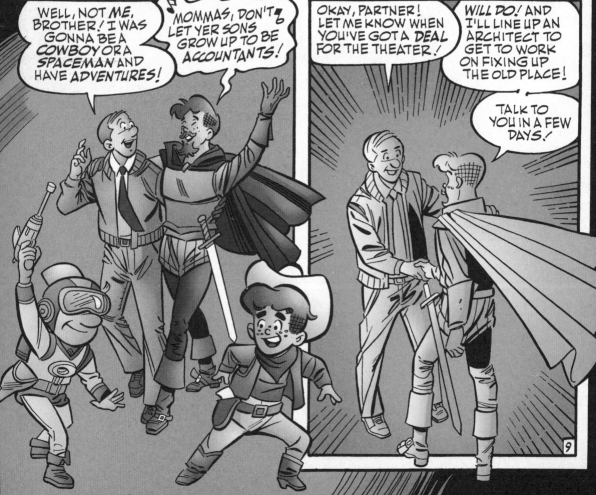

WELL, NOT *ME*, BROTHER! I WAS GONNA BE A *COWBOY* OR A *SPACEMAN* AND HAVE *ADVENTURES!*

♪ MOMMAS, DON'T LET YER SONS GROW UP TO BE ACCOUNTANTS! ♪

OKAY, PARTNER! LET ME KNOW WHEN YOU'VE GOT A *DEAL* FOR THE THEATER!

WILL DO! AND I'LL LINE UP AN ARCHITECT TO GET TO WORK ON FIXING UP THE OLD PLACE!

TALK TO YOU IN A FEW DAYS!

9

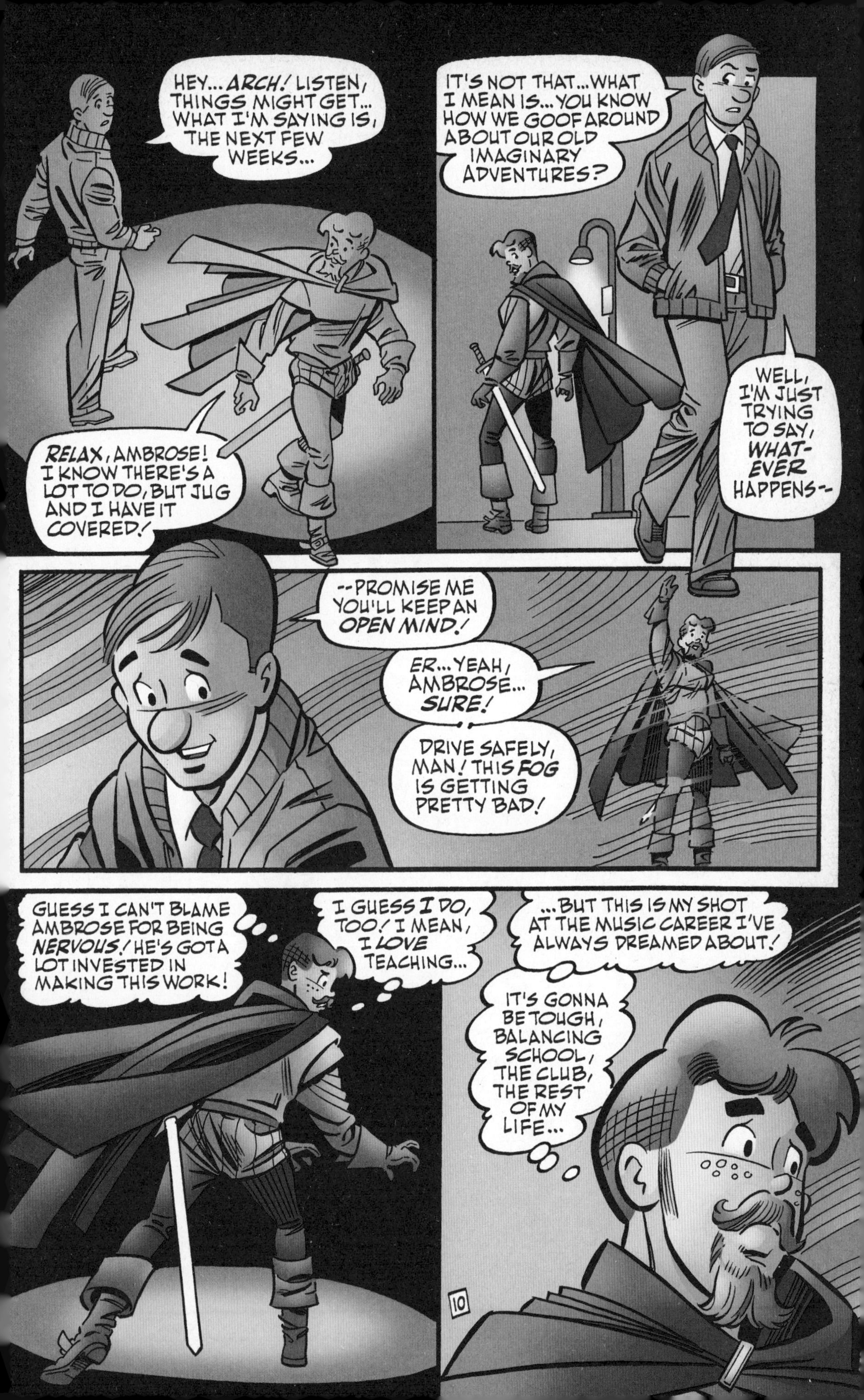
HEY... ARCH! LISTEN, THINGS MIGHT GET... WHAT I'M SAYING IS, THE NEXT FEW WEEKS...
RELAX, AMBROSE! I KNOW THERE'S A LOT TO DO, BUT JUG AND I HAVE IT COVERED!
IT'S NOT THAT... WHAT I MEAN IS... YOU KNOW HOW WE GOOF AROUND ABOUT OUR OLD IMAGINARY ADVENTURES?
WELL, I'M JUST TRYING TO SAY, WHAT-EVER HAPPENS--
--PROMISE ME YOU'LL KEEP AN OPEN MIND!
ER... YEAH, AMBROSE... SURE!
DRIVE SAFELY, MAN! THIS FOG IS GETTING PRETTY BAD!
GUESS I CAN'T BLAME AMBROSE FOR BEING NERVOUS! HE'S GOT A LOT INVESTED IN MAKING THIS WORK!
I GUESS I DO, TOO! I MEAN, I LOVE TEACHING...
...BUT THIS IS MY SHOT AT THE MUSIC CAREER I'VE ALWAYS DREAMED ABOUT!
IT'S GONNA BE TOUGH, BALANCING SCHOOL, THE CLUB, THE REST OF MY LIFE...
10

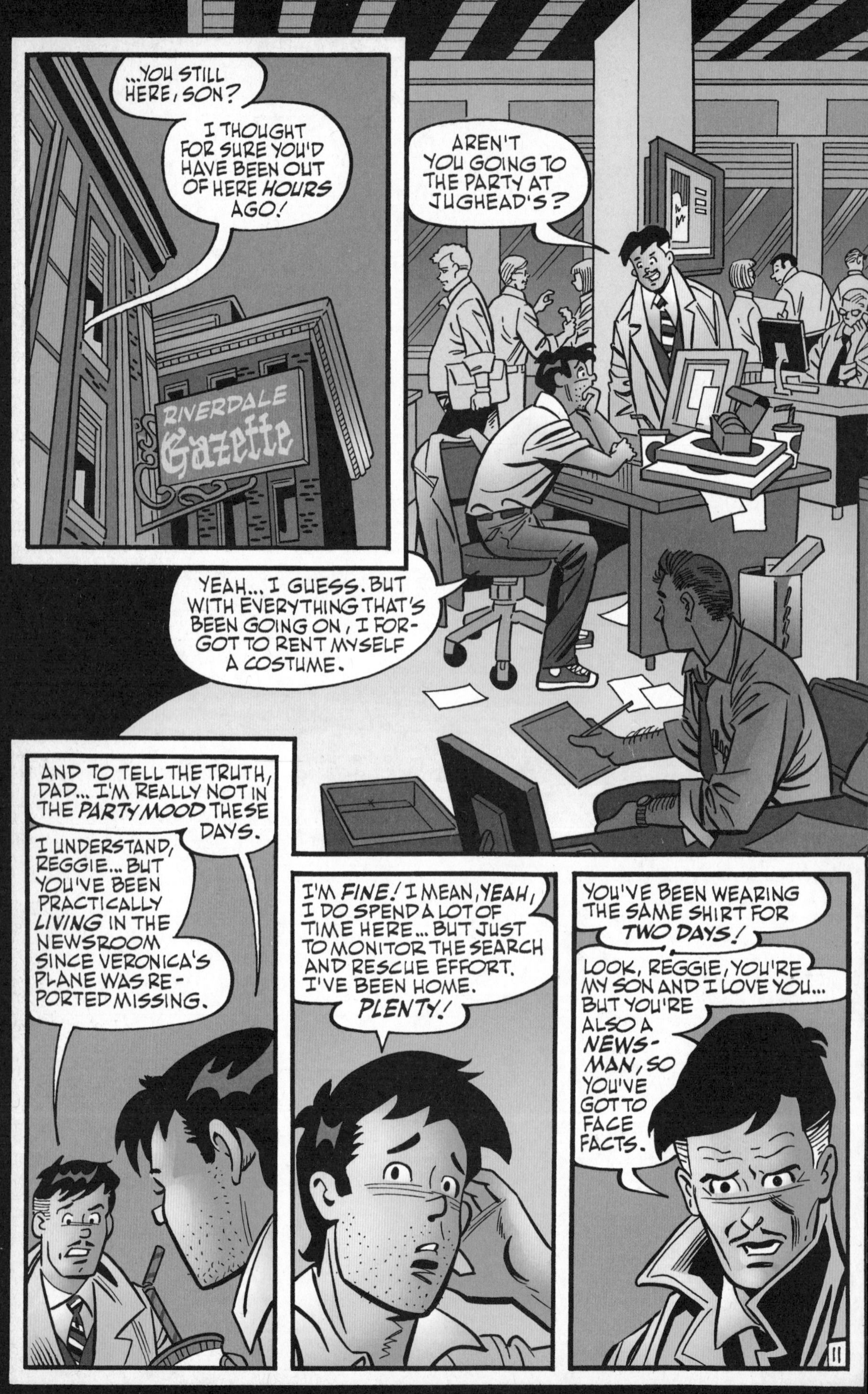
...YOU STILL HERE, SON?
I THOUGHT FOR SURE YOU'D HAVE BEEN OUT OF HERE HOURS AGO!
RIVERDALE Gazette
AREN'T YOU GOING TO THE PARTY AT JUGHEAD'S?
YEAH... I GUESS. BUT WITH EVERYTHING THAT'S BEEN GOING ON, I FORGOT TO RENT MYSELF A COSTUME.
AND TO TELL THE TRUTH, DAD... I'M REALLY NOT IN THE PARTY MOOD THESE DAYS.
I UNDERSTAND, REGGIE... BUT YOU'VE BEEN PRACTICALLY LIVING IN THE NEWSROOM SINCE VERONICA'S PLANE WAS REPORTED MISSING.
I'M FINE! I MEAN, YEAH, I DO SPEND A LOT OF TIME HERE... BUT JUST TO MONITOR THE SEARCH AND RESCUE EFFORT. I'VE BEEN HOME. PLENTY!
YOU'VE BEEN WEARING THE SAME SHIRT FOR TWO DAYS!
LOOK, REGGIE, YOU'RE MY SON AND I LOVE YOU... BUT YOU'RE ALSO A NEWSMAN, SO YOU'VE GOT TO FACE FACTS.

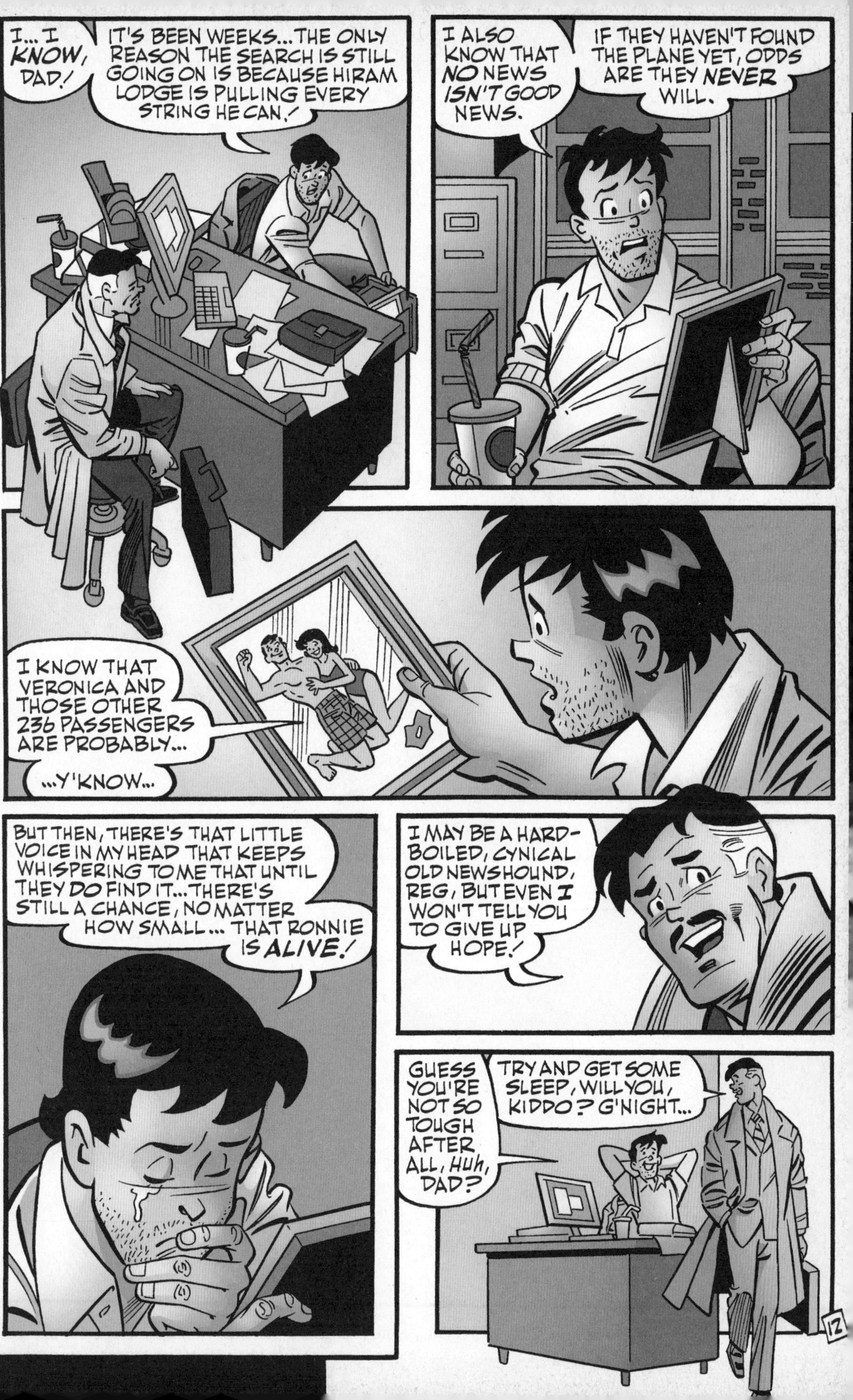
I... I KNOW, DAD!
IT'S BEEN WEEKS... THE ONLY REASON THE SEARCH IS STILL GOING ON IS BECAUSE HIRAM LODGE IS PULLING EVERY STRING HE CAN!
I ALSO KNOW THAT NO NEWS ISN'T GOOD NEWS.
IF THEY HAVEN'T FOUND THE PLANE YET, ODDS ARE THEY NEVER WILL.
I KNOW THAT VERONICA AND THOSE OTHER 236 PASSENGERS ARE PROBABLY...
...Y'KNOW...
BUT THEN, THERE'S THAT LITTLE VOICE IN MY HEAD THAT KEEPS WHISPERING TO ME THAT UNTIL THEY DO FIND IT... THERE'S STILL A CHANCE, NO MATTER HOW SMALL... THAT RONNIE IS ALIVE!
I MAY BE A HARD-BOILED, CYNICAL OLD NEWSHOUND, REG, BUT EVEN I WON'T TELL YOU TO GIVE UP HOPE!
GUESS YOU'RE NOT SO TOUGH AFTER ALL, HUH, DAD?
TRY AND GET SOME SLEEP, WILL YOU, KIDDO? G'NIGHT...
12

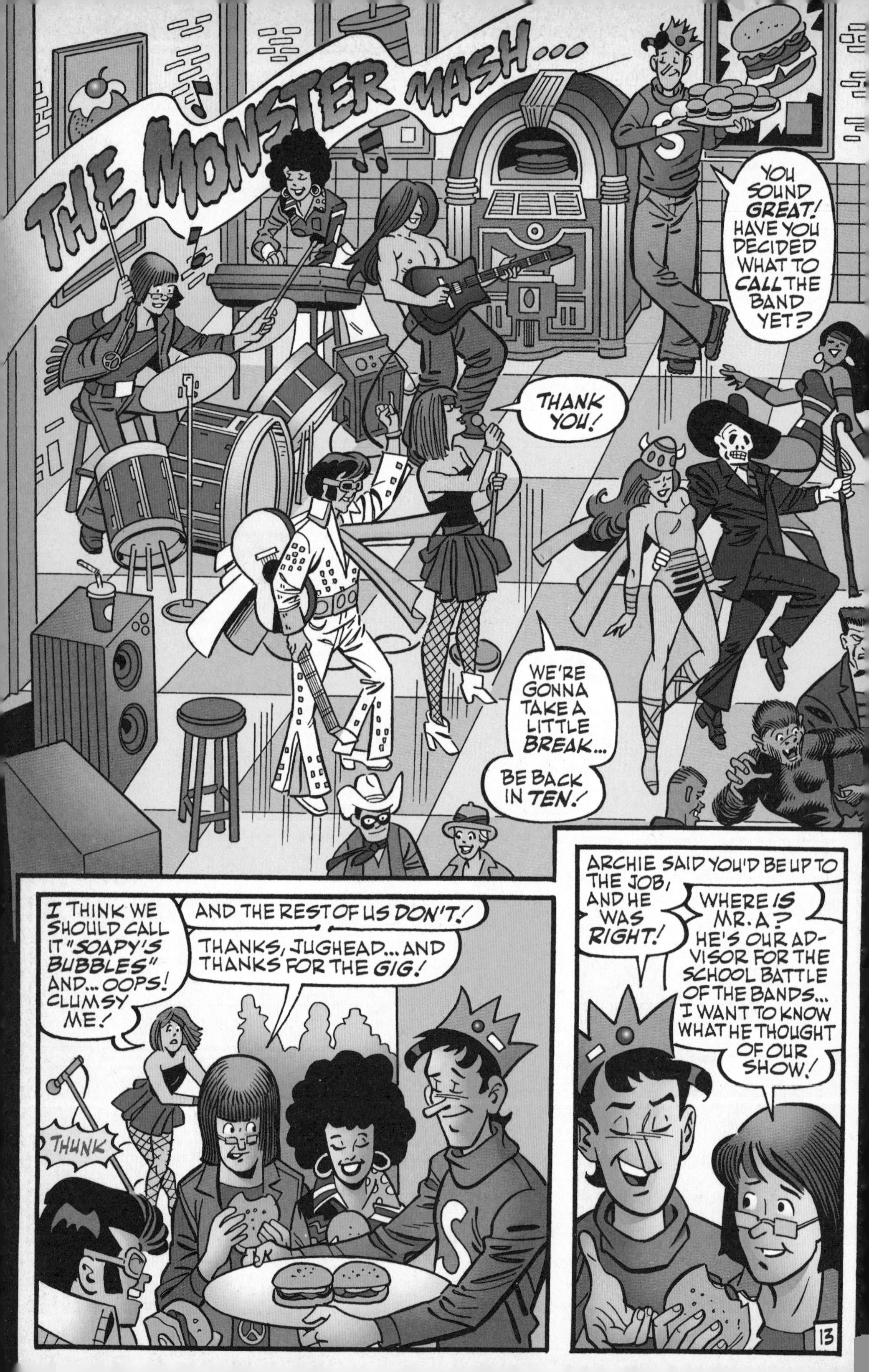
THE MONSTER MASH...
YOU SOUND GREAT! HAVE YOU DECIDED WHAT TO CALL THE BAND YET?
THANK YOU!
WE'RE GONNA TAKE A LITTLE BREAK...
BE BACK IN TEN!
I THINK WE SHOULD CALL IT "SOAPY'S BUBBLES" AND... OOPS! CLUMSY ME!
AND THE REST OF US DON'T!
THANKS, JUGHEAD... AND THANKS FOR THE GIG!
THUNK
ARCHIE SAID YOU'D BE UP TO THE JOB,
AND HE WAS RIGHT!
WHERE IS MR. A? HE'S OUR AD-VISOR FOR THE SCHOOL BATTLE OF THE BANDS... I WANT TO KNOW WHAT HE THOUGHT OF OUR SHOW!
13

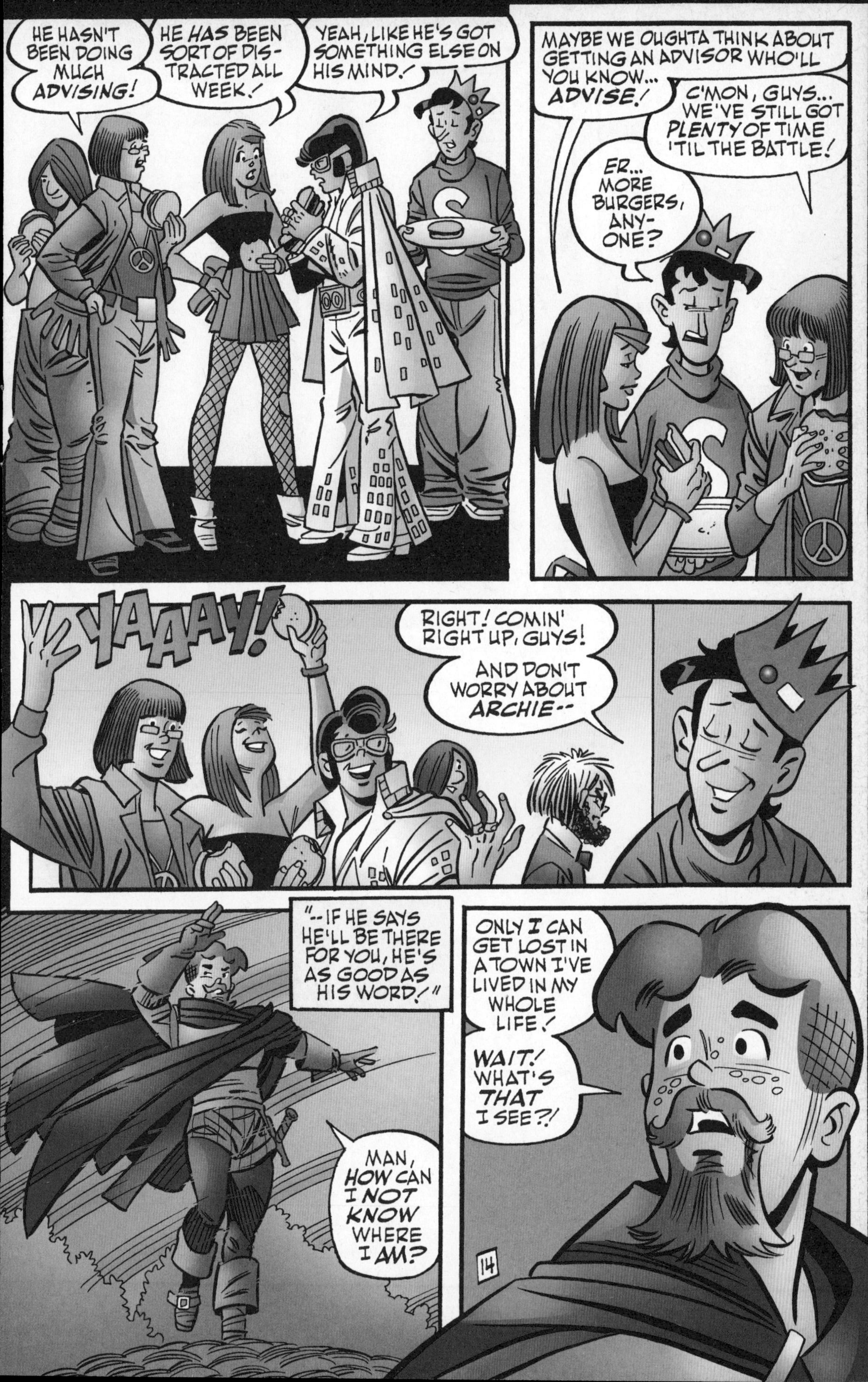
HE HASN'T BEEN DOING MUCH ADVISING!
HE HAS BEEN SORT OF DIS-TRACTED ALL WEEK!
YEAH, LIKE HE'S GOT SOMETHING ELSE ON HIS MIND!
MAYBE WE OUGHTA THINK ABOUT GETTING AN ADVISOR WHO'LL YOU KNOW... ADVISE!
C'MON, GUYS... WE'VE STILL GOT PLENTY OF TIME 'TIL THE BATTLE!
ER... MORE BURGERS, ANY-ONE?
YAAAY!
RIGHT! COMIN' RIGHT UP, GUYS!
AND DON'T WORRY ABOUT ARCHIE--
"--IF HE SAYS HE'LL BE THERE FOR YOU, HE'S AS GOOD AS HIS WORD!"
MAN, HOW CAN I NOT KNOW WHERE I AM?
ONLY I CAN GET LOST IN A TOWN I'VE LIVED IN MY WHOLE LIFE!
WAIT! WHAT'S THAT I SEE?!

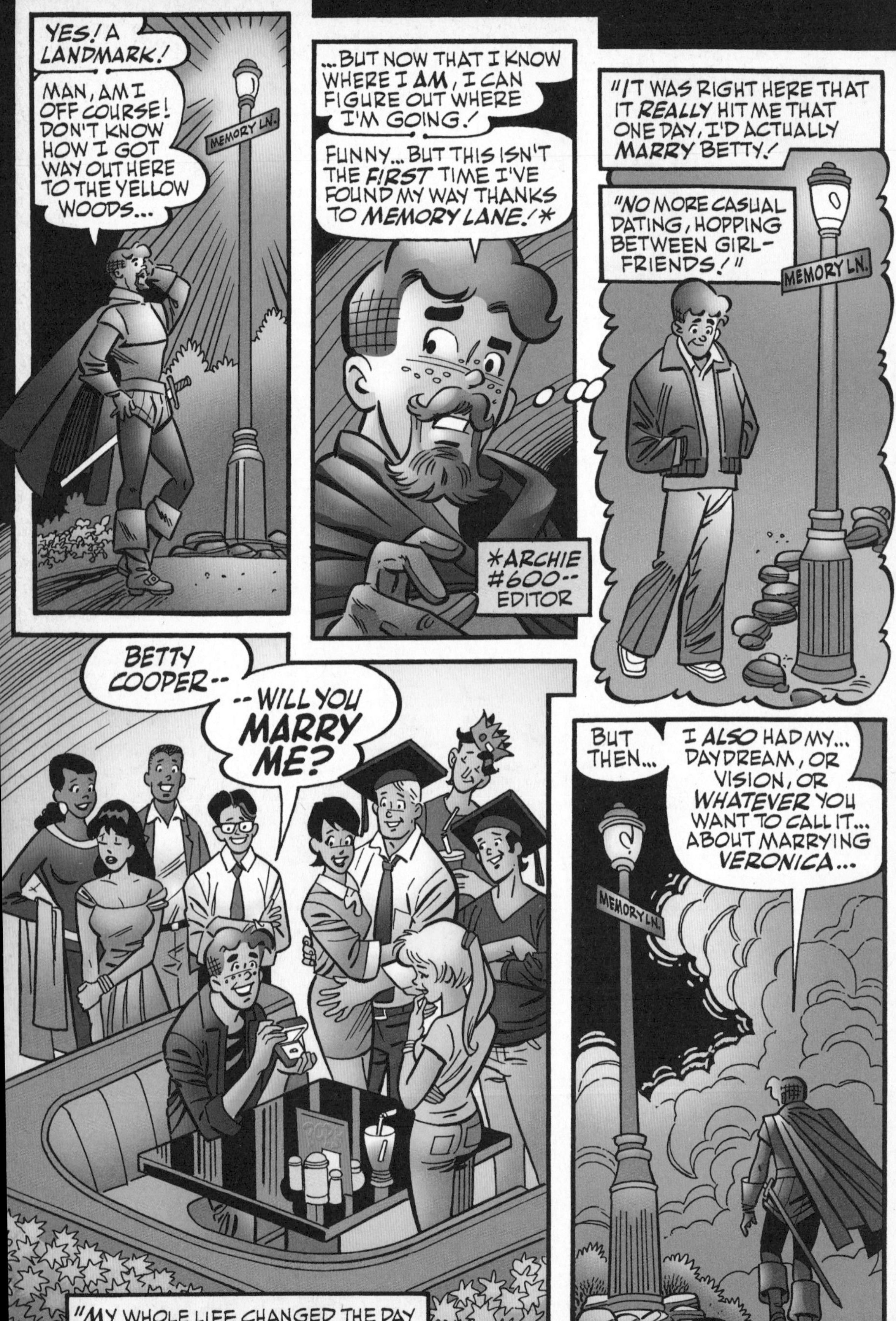

YES! A LANDMARK!
MAN, AM I OFF COURSE! DON'T KNOW HOW I GOT WAY OUT HERE TO THE YELLOW WOODS...
MEMORY LN.
...BUT NOW THAT I KNOW WHERE I AM, I CAN FIGURE OUT WHERE I'M GOING!
FUNNY... BUT THIS ISN'T THE FIRST TIME I'VE FOUND MY WAY THANKS TO MEMORY LANE! *
*ARCHIE #600-- EDITOR
"IT WAS RIGHT HERE THAT IT REALLY HIT ME THAT ONE DAY, I'D ACTUALLY MARRY BETTY!
"NO MORE CASUAL DATING, HOPPING BETWEEN GIRL-FRIENDS!"
MEMORY LN.
BETTY COOPER--
--WILL YOU MARRY ME?
"MY WHOLE LIFE CHANGED THE DAY BETTY SAID "YES"!
BUT THEN...
I ALSO HAD MY... DAYDREAM, OR VISION, OR WHATEVER YOU WANT TO CALL IT... ABOUT MARRYING VERONICA...
MEMORY LN.
15

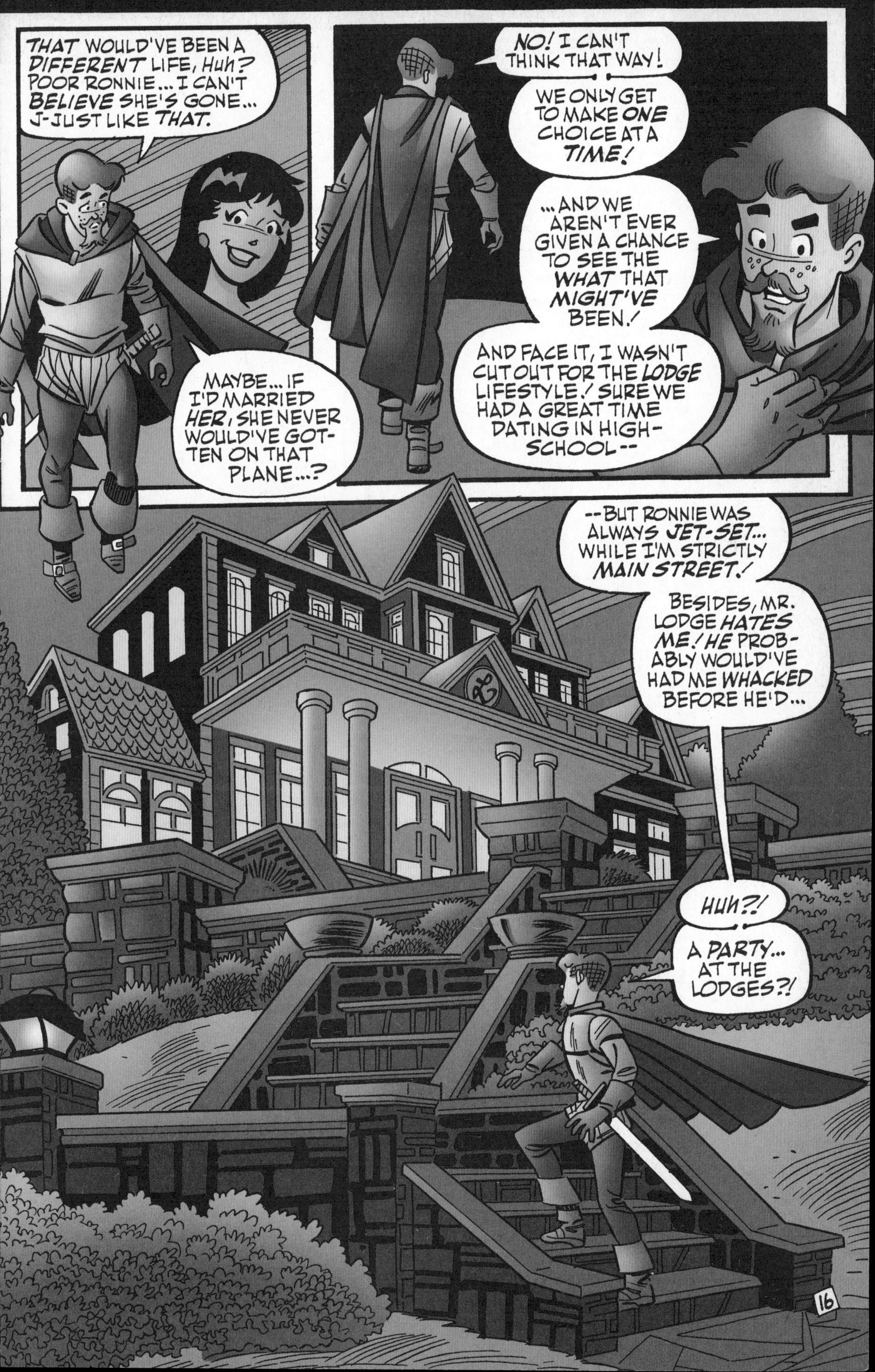
THAT WOULD'VE BEEN A DIFFERENT LIFE, HUH? POOR RONNIE... I CAN'T BELIEVE SHE'S GONE... J-JUST LIKE THAT.
MAYBE... IF I'D MARRIED HER, SHE NEVER WOULD'VE GOTTEN ON THAT PLANE...?
NO! I CAN'T THINK THAT WAY!
WE ONLY GET TO MAKE ONE CHOICE AT A TIME!
...AND WE AREN'T EVER GIVEN A CHANCE TO SEE THE WHAT THAT MIGHT'VE BEEN.!
AND FACE IT, I WASN'T CUT OUT FOR THE LODGE LIFESTYLE.! SURE WE HAD A GREAT TIME DATING IN HIGH-SCHOOL --
--BUT RONNIE WAS ALWAYS JET-SET... WHILE I'M STRICTLY MAIN STREET.!
BESIDES, MR. LODGE HATES ME.! HE PROBABLY WOULD'VE HAD ME WHACKED BEFORE HE'D...
HUH?!
A PARTY... AT THE LODGES?!
16

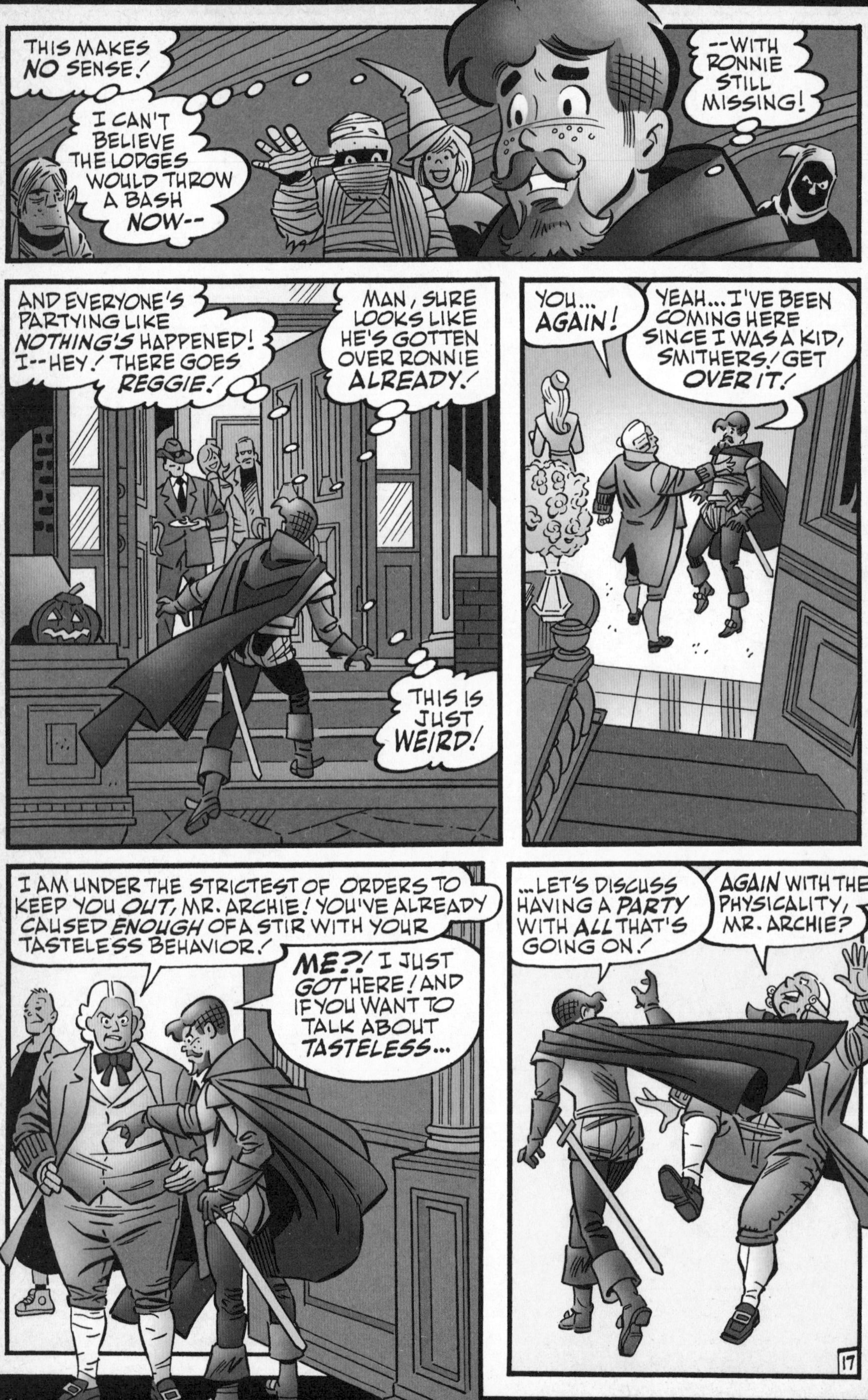
THIS MAKES NO SENSE!
I CAN'T BELIEVE THE LODGES WOULD THROW A BASH NOW--
--WITH RONNIE STILL MISSING!
AND EVERYONE'S PARTYING LIKE NOTHING'S HAPPENED! I--HEY! THERE GOES REGGIE!
MAN, SURE LOOKS LIKE HE'S GOTTEN OVER RONNIE ALREADY!
THIS IS JUST WEIRD!
YOU... AGAIN!
YEAH... I'VE BEEN COMING HERE SINCE I WAS A KID, SMITHERS! GET OVER IT!
I AM UNDER THE STRICTEST OF ORDERS TO KEEP YOU OUT, MR. ARCHIE! YOU'VE ALREADY CAUSED ENOUGH OF A STIR WITH YOUR TASTELESS BEHAVIOR!
ME?! I JUST GOT HERE! AND IF YOU WANT TO TALK ABOUT TASTELESS...
...LET'S DISCUSS HAVING A PARTY WITH ALL THAT'S GOING ON!
AGAIN WITH THE PHYSICALITY, MR. ARCHIE?
17

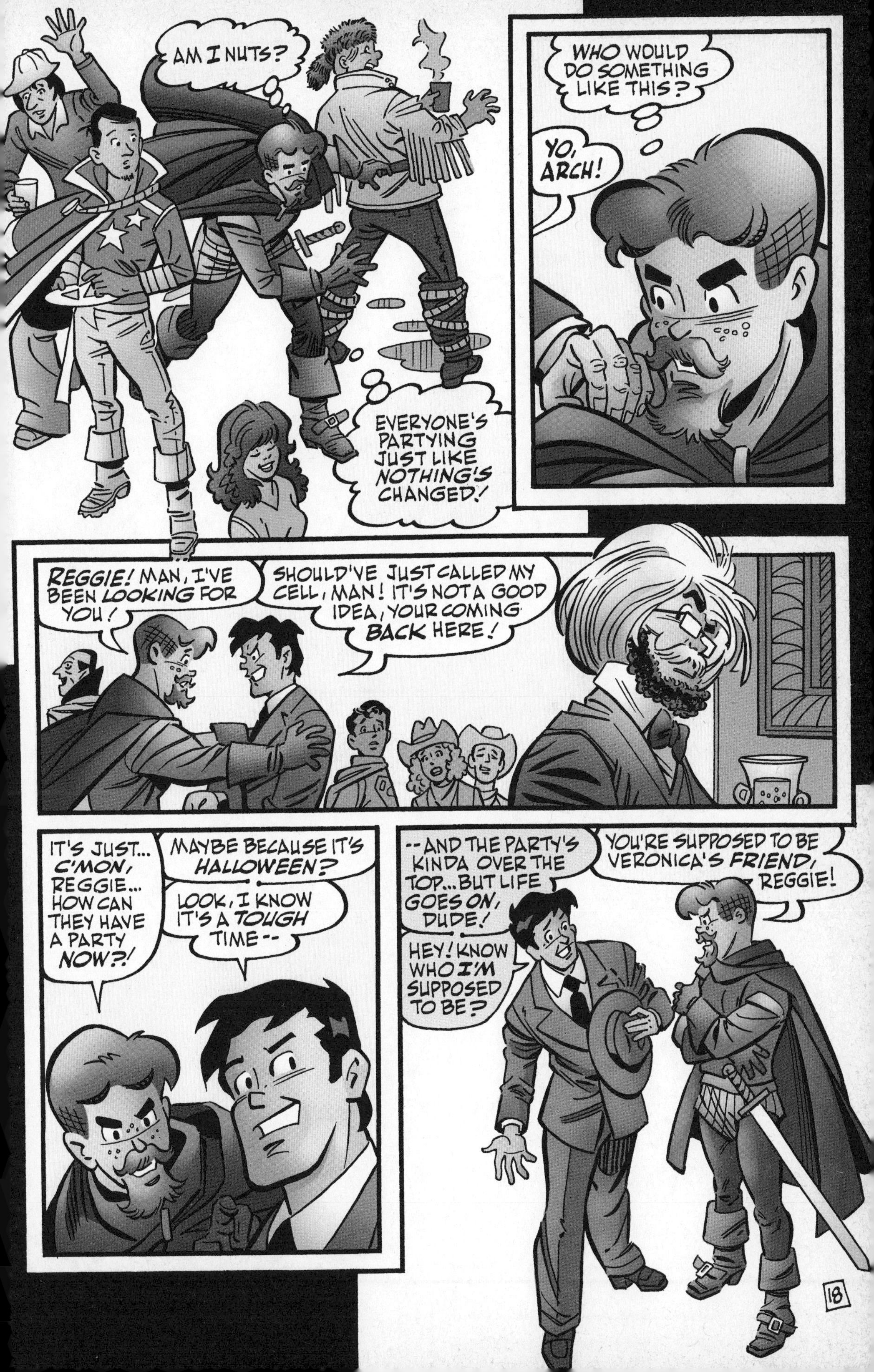
AM I NUTS?
EVERYONE'S PARTYING JUST LIKE NOTHING'S CHANGED!
WHO WOULD DO SOMETHING LIKE THIS?
YO, ARCH!
REGGIE! MAN, I'VE BEEN LOOKING FOR YOU!
SHOULD'VE JUST CALLED MY CELL, MAN! IT'S NOT A GOOD IDEA, YOUR COMING BACK HERE!
IT'S JUST... C'MON, REGGIE... HOW CAN THEY HAVE A PARTY NOW?!
MAYBE BECAUSE IT'S HALLOWEEN?
LOOK, I KNOW IT'S A TOUGH TIME --
-- AND THE PARTY'S KINDA OVER THE TOP... BUT LIFE GOES ON, DUDE!
HEY! KNOW WHO I'M SUPPOSED TO BE?
YOU'RE SUPPOSED TO BE VERONICA'S FRIEND, REGGIE!
18

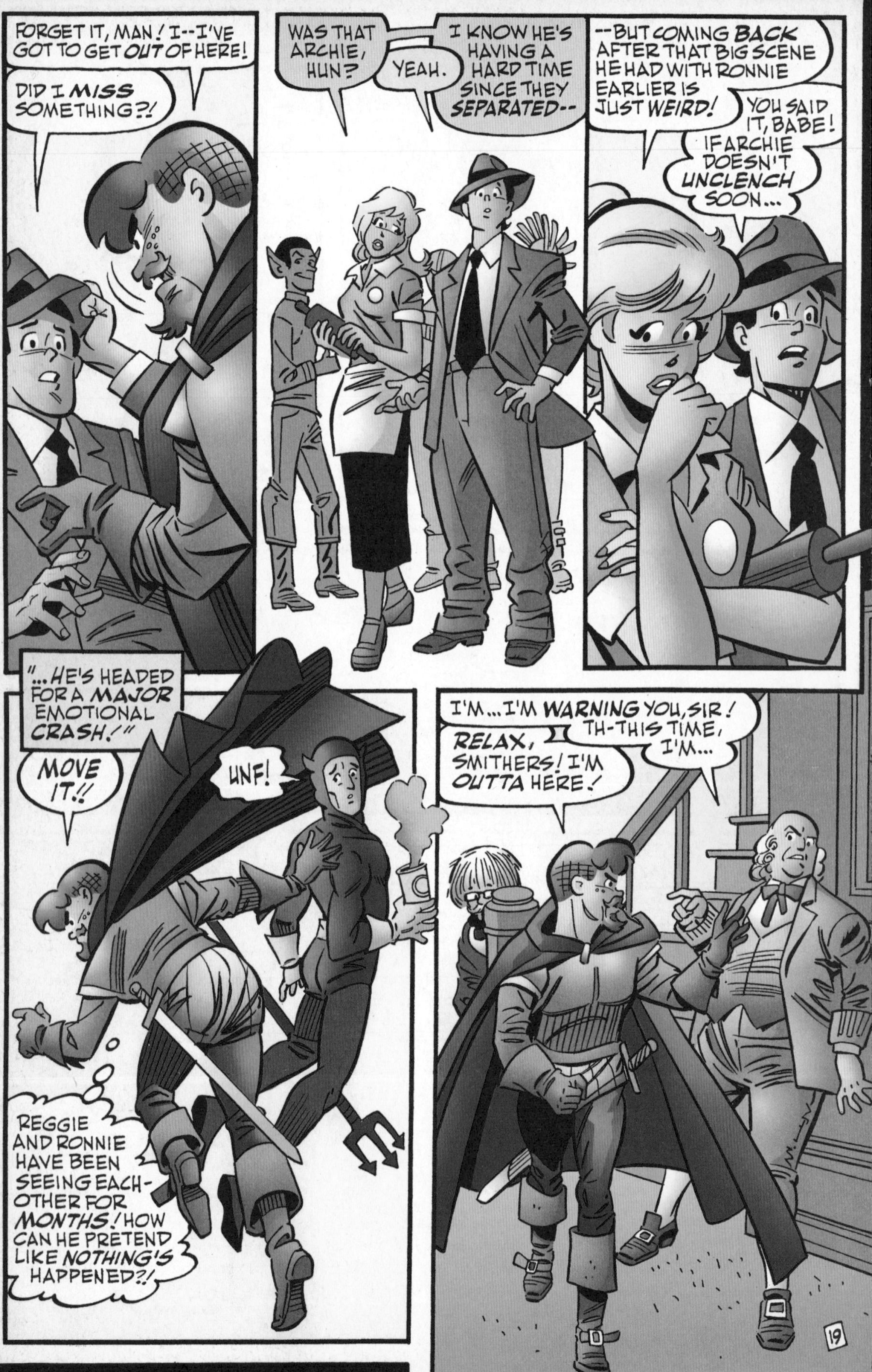
FORGET IT, MAN! I--I'VE GOT TO GET OUT OF HERE!
DID I MISS SOMETHING?!
WAS THAT ARCHIE, HUN?
YEAH.
I KNOW HE'S HAVING A HARD TIME SINCE THEY SEPARATED--
--BUT COMING BACK AFTER THAT BIG SCENE HE HAD WITH RONNIE EARLIER IS JUST WEIRD!
YOU SAID IT, BABE! IF ARCHIE DOESN'T UNCLENCH SOON...
"...HE'S HEADED FOR A MAJOR EMOTIONAL CRASH!"
MOVE IT!!
UNF!
REGGIE AND RONNIE HAVE BEEN SEEING EACH-OTHER FOR MONTHS! HOW CAN HE PRETEND LIKE NOTHING'S HAPPENED?!
I'M... I'M WARNING YOU, SIR! TH-THIS TIME, I'M...
RELAX, SMITHERS! I'M OUTTA HERE!

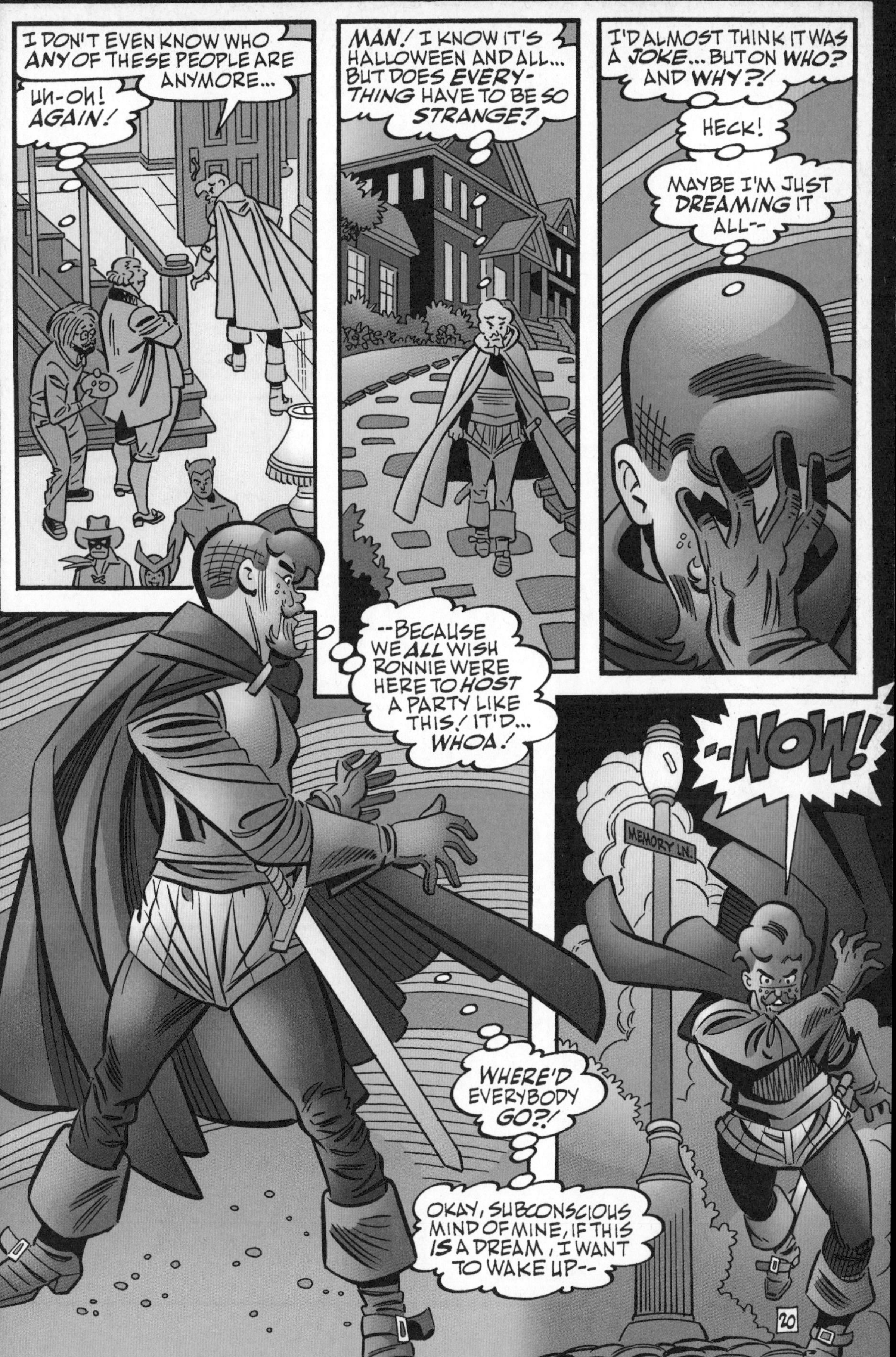
I DON'T EVEN KNOW WHO ANY OF THESE PEOPLE ARE ANYMORE...
UH-OH! AGAIN!
MAN! I KNOW IT'S HALLOWEEN AND ALL... BUT DOES EVERY-THING HAVE TO BE SO STRANGE?
I'D ALMOST THINK IT WAS A JOKE... BUT ON WHO? AND WHY?!
HECK!
MAYBE I'M JUST DREAMING IT ALL--
--BECAUSE WE ALL WISH RONNIE WERE HERE TO HOST A PARTY LIKE THIS! IT'D... WHOA!
WHERE'D EVERYBODY GO?!
OKAY, SUBCONSCIOUS MIND OF MINE, IF THIS IS A DREAM, I WANT TO WAKE UP--
--NOW!
MEMORY LN.
20

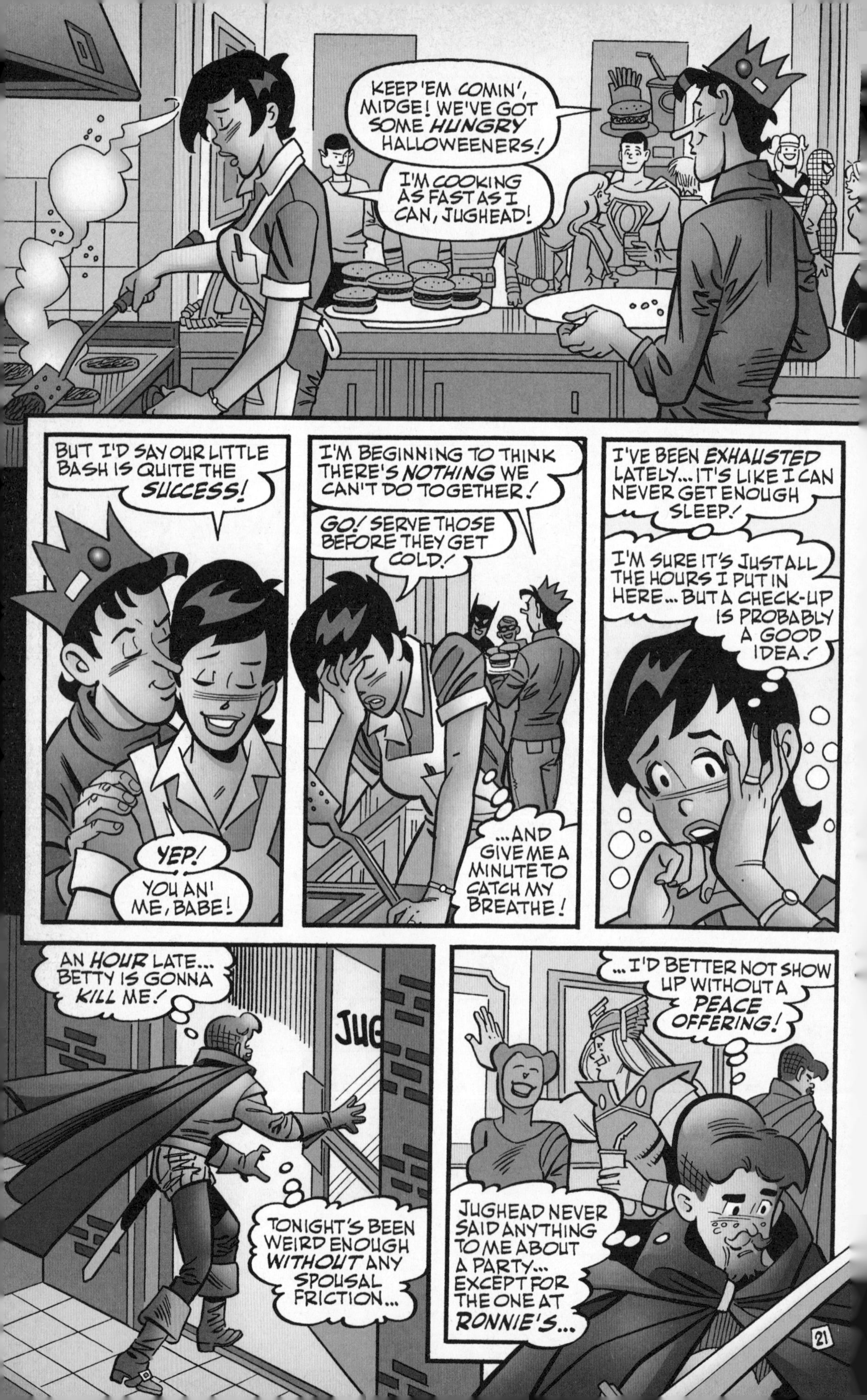
KEEP 'EM COMIN', MIDGE! WE'VE GOT SOME HUNGRY HALLOWEENERS!
I'M COOKING AS FAST AS I CAN, JUGHEAD!
BUT I'D SAY OUR LITTLE BASH IS QUITE THE SUCCESS!
YEP!
YOU AN' ME, BABE!
I'M BEGINNING TO THINK THERE'S NOTHING WE CAN'T DO TOGETHER!
GO! SERVE THOSE BEFORE THEY GET COLD!
...AND GIVE ME A MINUTE TO CATCH MY BREATHE!
I'VE BEEN EXHAUSTED LATELY... IT'S LIKE I CAN NEVER GET ENOUGH SLEEP!
I'M SURE IT'S JUST ALL THE HOURS I PUT IN HERE... BUT A CHECK-UP IS PROBABLY A GOOD IDEA!
AN HOUR LATE... BETTY IS GONNA KILL ME!
JUG
TONIGHT'S BEEN WEIRD ENOUGH WITHOUT ANY SPOUSAL FRICTION...
...I'D BETTER NOT SHOW UP WITHOUT A PEACE OFFERING!
JUGHEAD NEVER SAID ANYTHING TO ME ABOUT A PARTY... EXCEPT FOR THE ONE AT RONNIE'S...

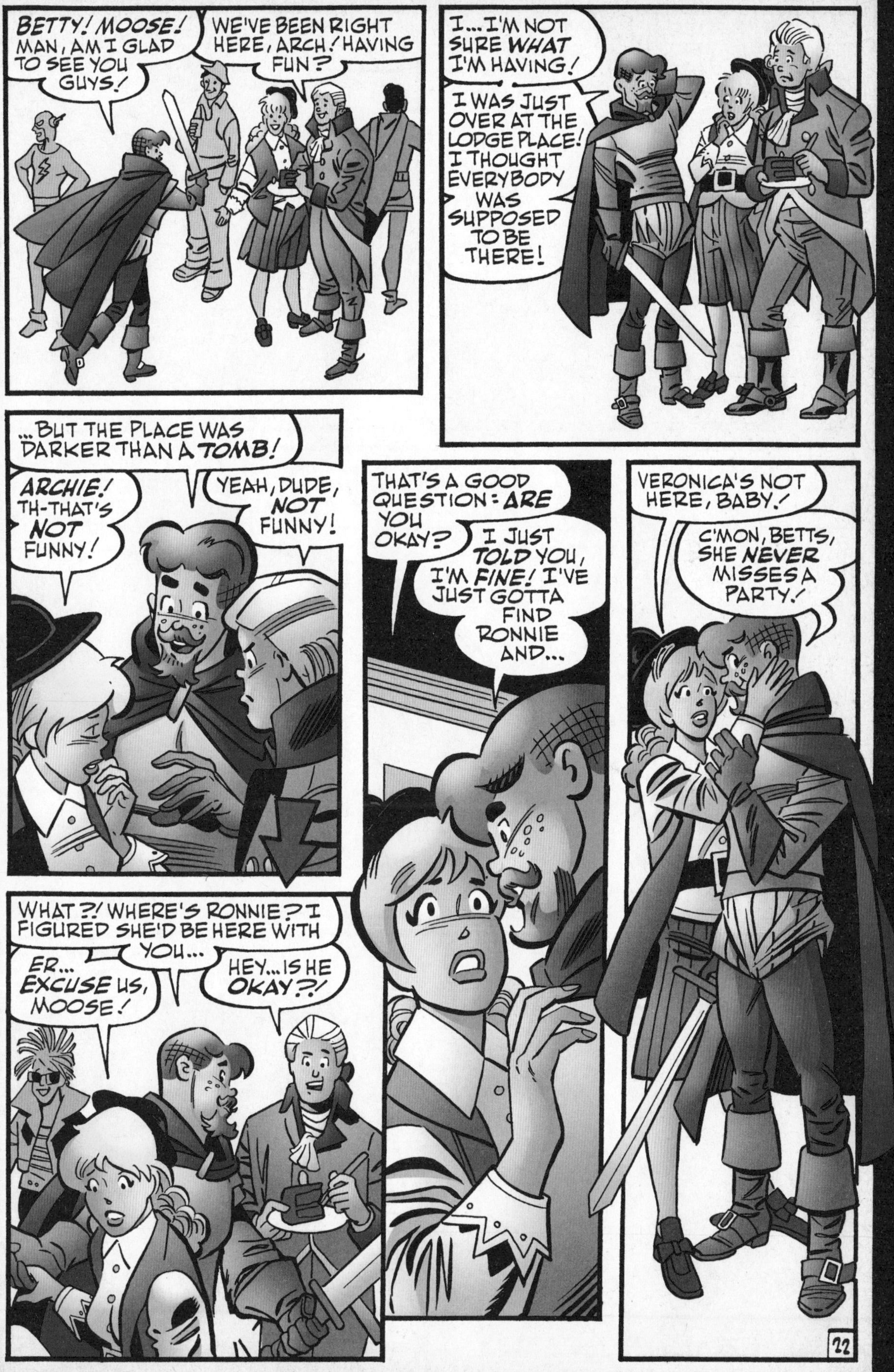

BETTY! MOOSE! MAN, AM I GLAD TO SEE YOU GUYS!
WE'VE BEEN RIGHT HERE, ARCH! HAVING FUN?
I... I'M NOT SURE WHAT I'M HAVING!
I WAS JUST OVER AT THE LODGE PLACE! I THOUGHT EVERYBODY WAS SUPPOSED TO BE THERE!
...BUT THE PLACE WAS DARKER THAN A TOMB!
ARCHIE! TH-THAT'S NOT FUNNY!
YEAH, DUDE, NOT FUNNY!
WHAT?! WHERE'S RONNIE? I FIGURED SHE'D BE HERE WITH YOU...
ER... EXCUSE US, MOOSE!
HEY... IS HE OKAY?!
THAT'S A GOOD QUESTION: ARE YOU OKAY?
I JUST TOLD YOU, I'M FINE! I'VE JUST GOTTA FIND RONNIE AND...
VERONICA'S NOT HERE, BABY!
C'MON, BETTS, SHE NEVER MISSES A PARTY!
22

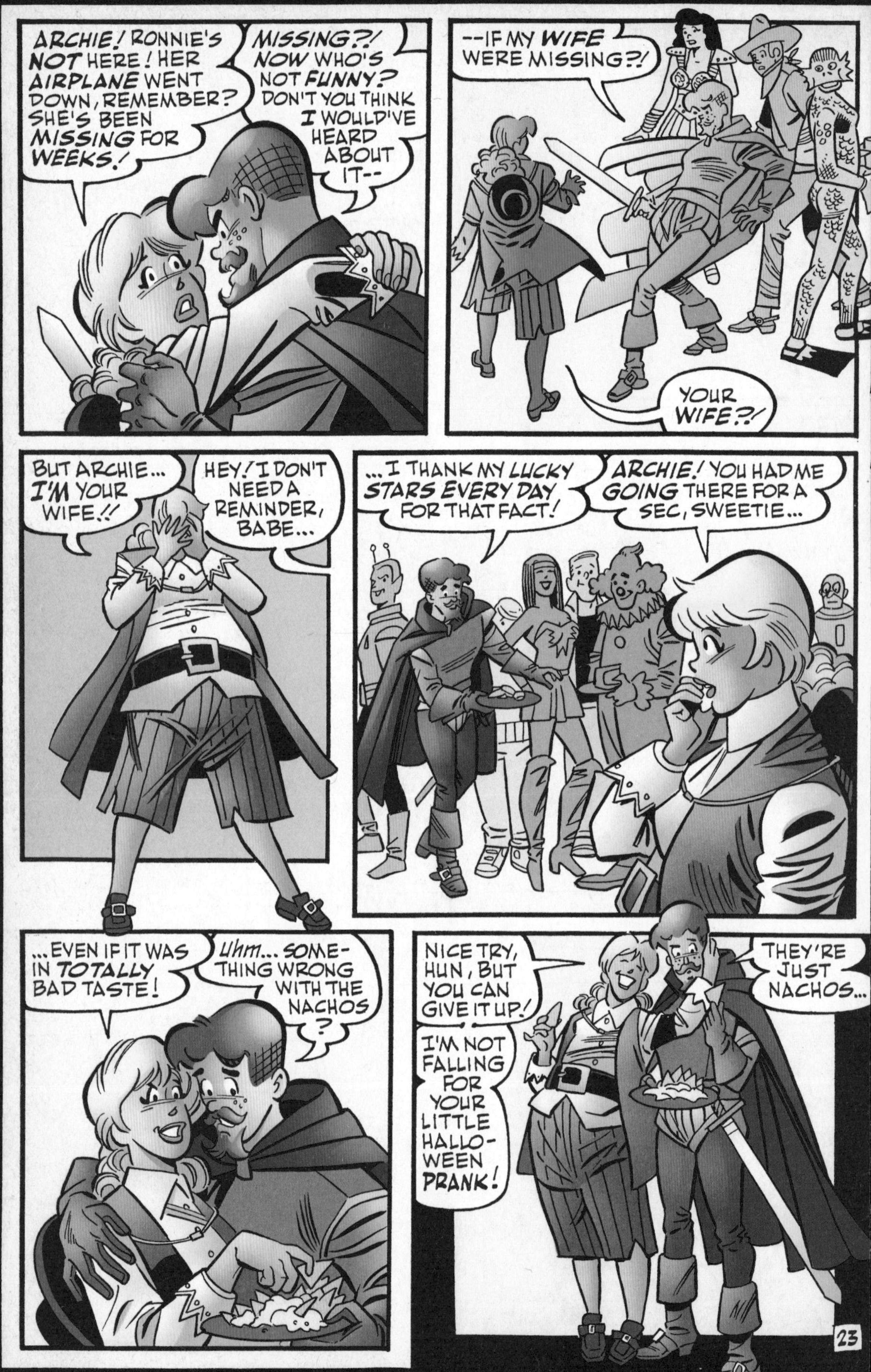
ARCHIE! RONNIE'S NOT HERE! HER AIRPLANE WENT DOWN, REMEMBER? SHE'S BEEN MISSING FOR WEEKS!
MISSING?! NOW WHO'S NOT FUNNY? DON'T YOU THINK I WOULD'VE HEARD ABOUT IT--
--IF MY WIFE WERE MISSING?!
YOUR WIFE?!
BUT ARCHIE... I'M YOUR WIFE!!
HEY! I DON'T NEED A REMINDER, BABE...
...I THANK MY LUCKY STARS EVERY DAY FOR THAT FACT!
ARCHIE! YOU HAD ME GOING THERE FOR A SEC, SWEETIE...
...EVEN IF IT WAS IN TOTALLY BAD TASTE!
Uhm... SOMETHING WRONG WITH THE NACHOS?
NICE TRY, HUN, BUT YOU CAN GIVE IT UP!
I'M NOT FALLING FOR YOUR LITTLE HALLOWEEN PRANK!
THEY'RE JUST NACHOS...
23

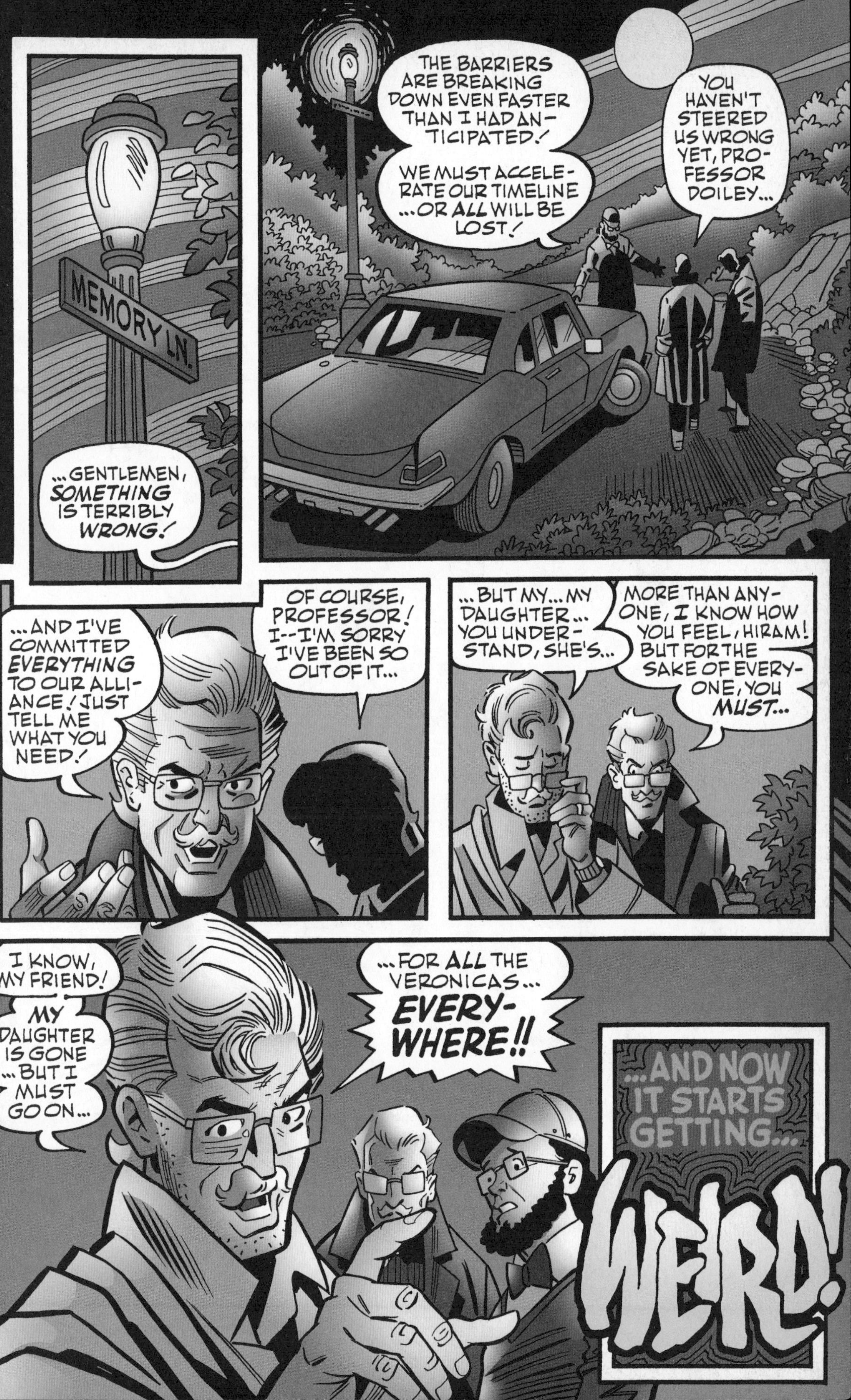
MEMORY LN.
...GENTLEMEN, SOMETHING IS TERRIBLY WRONG!
THE BARRIERS ARE BREAKING DOWN EVEN FASTER THAN I HAD AN-TICIPATED!
WE MUST ACCELE-RATE OUR TIMELINE ...OR ALL WILL BE LOST!
YOU HAVEN'T STEERED US WRONG YET, PRO-FESSOR DOILEY...
...AND I'VE COMMITTED EVERYTHING TO OUR ALLI-ANCE! JUST TELL ME WHAT YOU NEED!
OF COURSE, PROFESSOR! I--I'M SORRY I'VE BEEN SO OUT OF IT...
...BUT MY... MY DAUGHTER... YOU UNDER-STAND, SHE'S...
MORE THAN ANY-ONE, I KNOW HOW YOU FEEL, HIRAM! BUT FOR THE SAKE OF EVERY-ONE, YOU MUST...
I KNOW, MY FRIEND!
MY DAUGHTER IS GONE ...BUT I MUST GO ON...
...FOR ALL THE VERONICAS... EVERY-WHERE!!
...AND NOW IT STARTS GETTING...
WEIRD!

“...SHE’S REALLY ONLY SENDING A MESSAGE TO *ONE* PERSON,”

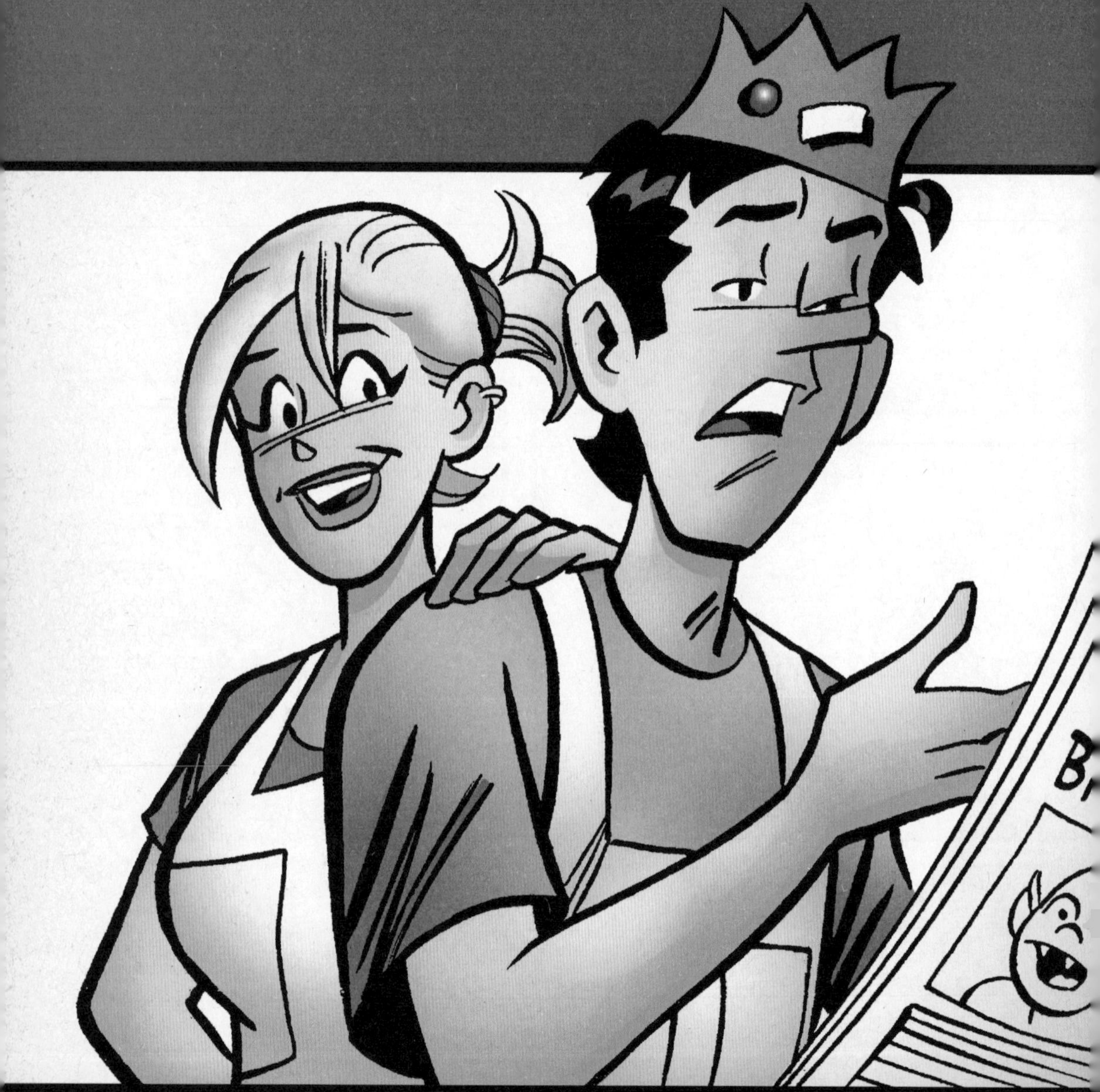

“...THE **ONE** SHE WANTS TO KNOW SHE CAN LIVE *WITHOUT*, AND THAT’S ***ARCHIE!***”

- BETTY COOPER

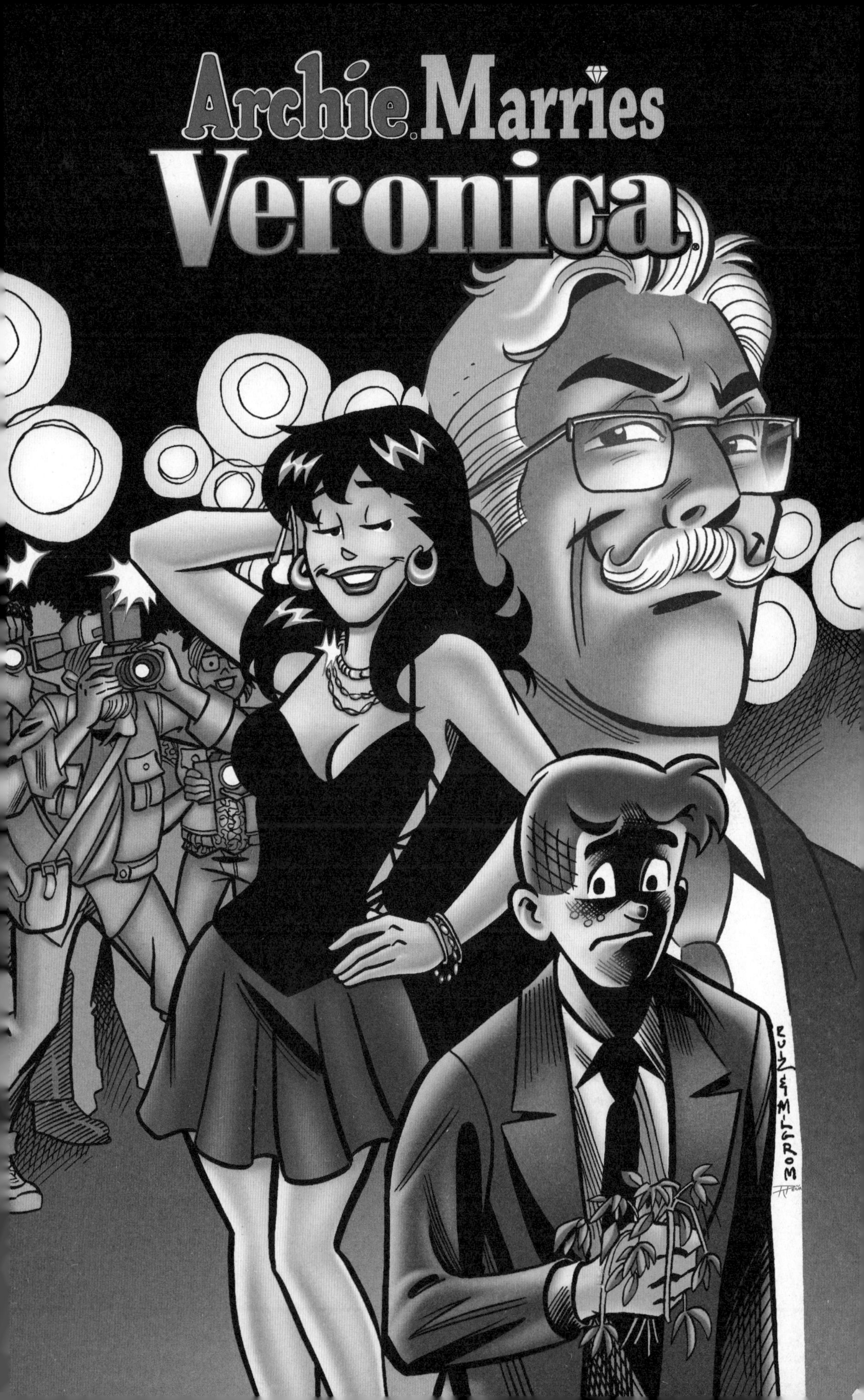
Archie Marries
Veronica
RUIZ & MILGROM

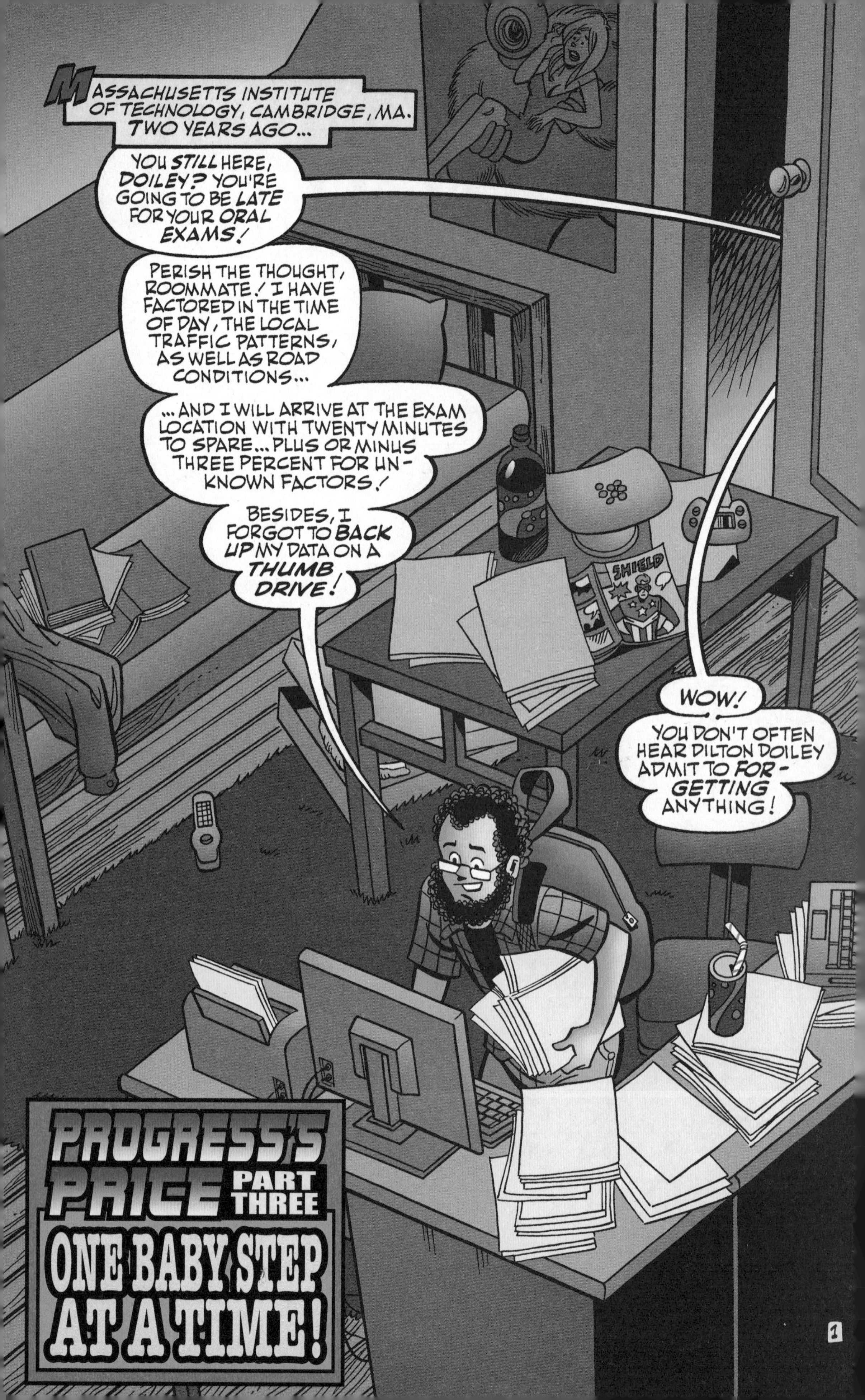
MASSACHUSETTS INSTITUTE OF TECHNOLOGY, CAMBRIDGE, MA. TWO YEARS AGO...
YOU STILL HERE, DOILEY? YOU'RE GOING TO BE LATE FOR YOUR ORAL EXAMS!
PERISH THE THOUGHT, ROOMMATE! I HAVE FACTORED IN THE TIME OF DAY, THE LOCAL TRAFFIC PATTERNS, AS WELL AS ROAD CONDITIONS...
...AND I WILL ARRIVE AT THE EXAM LOCATION WITH TWENTY MINUTES TO SPARE... PLUS OR MINUS THREE PERCENT FOR UN-KNOWN FACTORS!
BESIDES, I FORGOT TO BACK UP MY DATA ON A THUMB DRIVE!
SHIELD
WOW!
YOU DON'T OFTEN HEAR DILTON DOILEY ADMIT TO FOR-GETTING ANYTHING!
PROGRESS'S PRICE PART THREE
ONE BABY STEP AT A TIME!

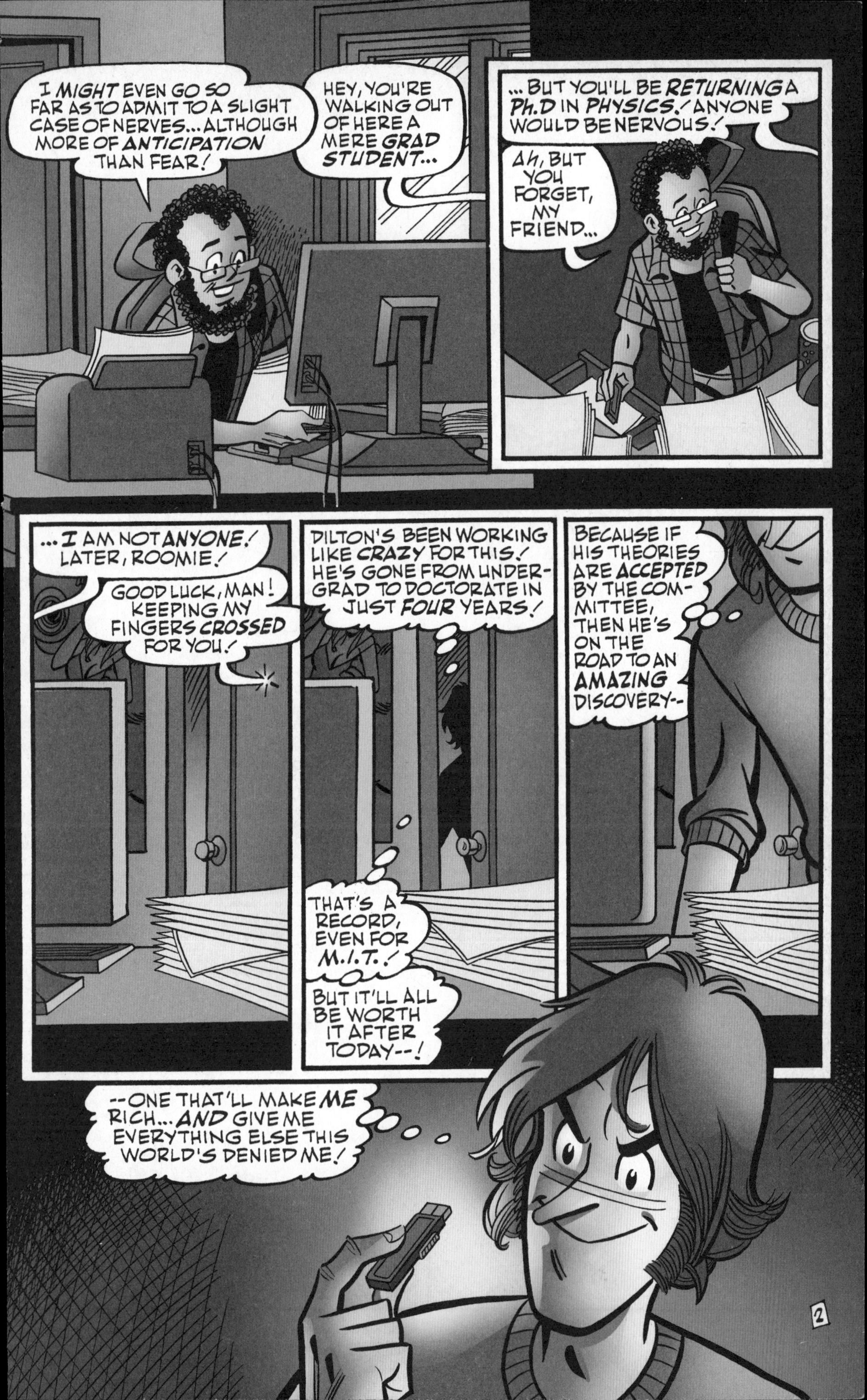
I MIGHT EVEN GO SO FAR AS TO ADMIT TO A SLIGHT CASE OF NERVES... ALTHOUGH MORE OF ANTICIPATION THAN FEAR!
HEY, YOU'RE WALKING OUT OF HERE A MERE GRAD STUDENT...
... BUT YOU'LL BE RETURNING A Ph.D IN PHYSICS! ANYONE WOULD BE NERVOUS!
Ah, BUT YOU FORGET, MY FRIEND...
... I AM NOT ANYONE! LATER, ROOMIE!
GOOD LUCK, MAN! KEEPING MY FINGERS CROSSED FOR YOU!
DILTON'S BEEN WORKING LIKE CRAZY FOR THIS! HE'S GONE FROM UNDER-GRAD TO DOCTORATE IN JUST FOUR YEARS!
THAT'S A RECORD, EVEN FOR M.I.T.!
BUT IT'LL ALL BE WORTH IT AFTER TODAY--!
BECAUSE IF HIS THEORIES ARE ACCEPTED BY THE COM-MITTEE, THEN HE'S ON THE ROAD TO AN AMAZING DISCOVERY--
--ONE THAT'LL MAKE ME RICH... AND GIVE ME EVERYTHING ELSE THIS WORLD'S DENIED ME!
2

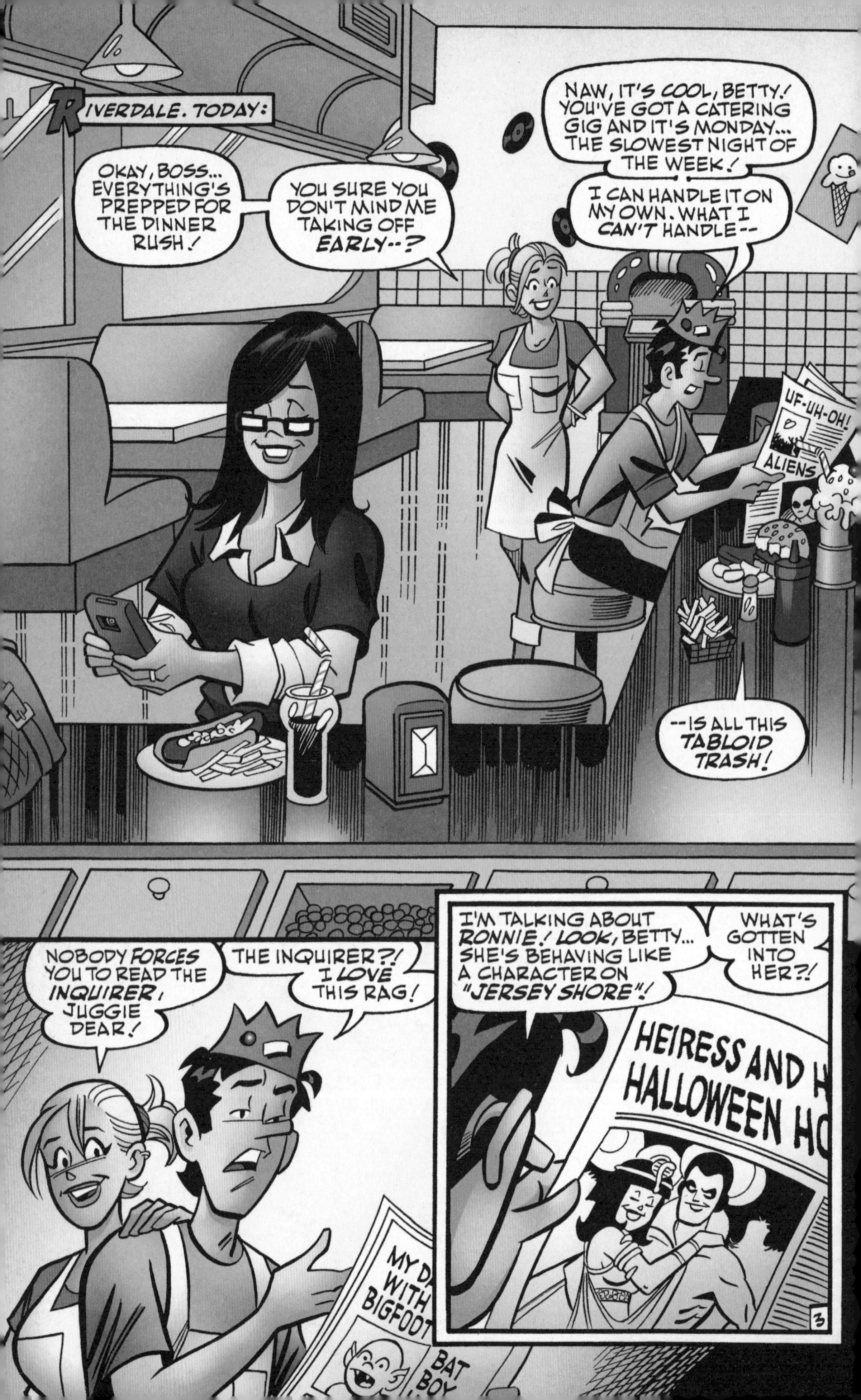
RIVERDALE. TODAY:
OKAY, BOSS... EVERYTHING'S PREPPED FOR THE DINNER RUSH!
YOU SURE YOU DON'T MIND ME TAKING OFF EARLY--?
NAW, IT'S COOL, BETTY! YOU'VE GOT A CATERING GIG AND IT'S MONDAY... THE SLOWEST NIGHT OF THE WEEK!
I CAN HANDLE IT ON MY OWN. WHAT I CAN'T HANDLE--
--IS ALL THIS TABLOID TRASH!
UF-UH-OH!
ALIENS
NOBODY FORCES YOU TO READ THE INQUIRER, JUGGIE DEAR!
THE INQUIRER?! I LOVE THIS RAG!
MY D WITH BIGFOOT
BAT BOY
I'M TALKING ABOUT RONNIE! LOOK, BETTY... SHE'S BEHAVING LIKE A CHARACTER ON "JERSEY SHORE"!
WHAT'S GOTTEN INTO HER?!
HEIRESS AND H
HALLOWEEN H
3

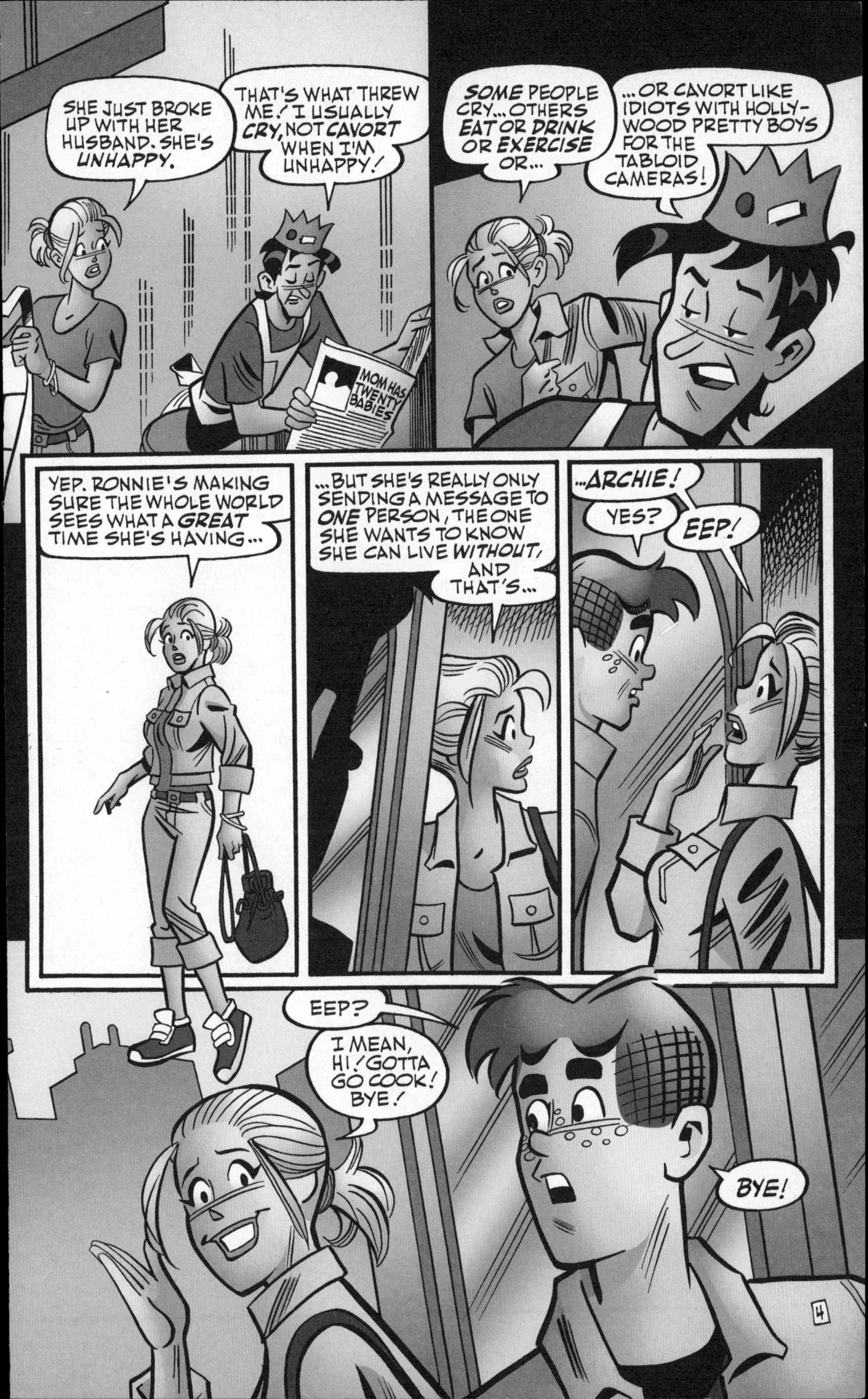
SHE JUST BROKE UP WITH HER HUSBAND. SHE'S UNHAPPY.
THAT'S WHAT THREW ME! I USUALLY CRY, NOT CAVORT WHEN I'M UNHAPPY!
MOM HAS TWENTY BABIES
SOME PEOPLE CRY... OTHERS EAT OR DRINK OR EXERCISE OR...
...OR CAVORT LIKE IDIOTS WITH HOLLY-WOOD PRETTY BOYS FOR THE TABLOID CAMERAS!
YEP. RONNIE'S MAKING SURE THE WHOLE WORLD SEES WHAT A GREAT TIME SHE'S HAVING...
...BUT SHE'S REALLY ONLY SENDING A MESSAGE TO ONE PERSON, THE ONE SHE WANTS TO KNOW SHE CAN LIVE WITHOUT, AND THAT'S...
...ARCHIE!
YES?
EEP!
EEP?
I MEAN, HI! GOTTA GO COOK! BYE!
BYE!
4

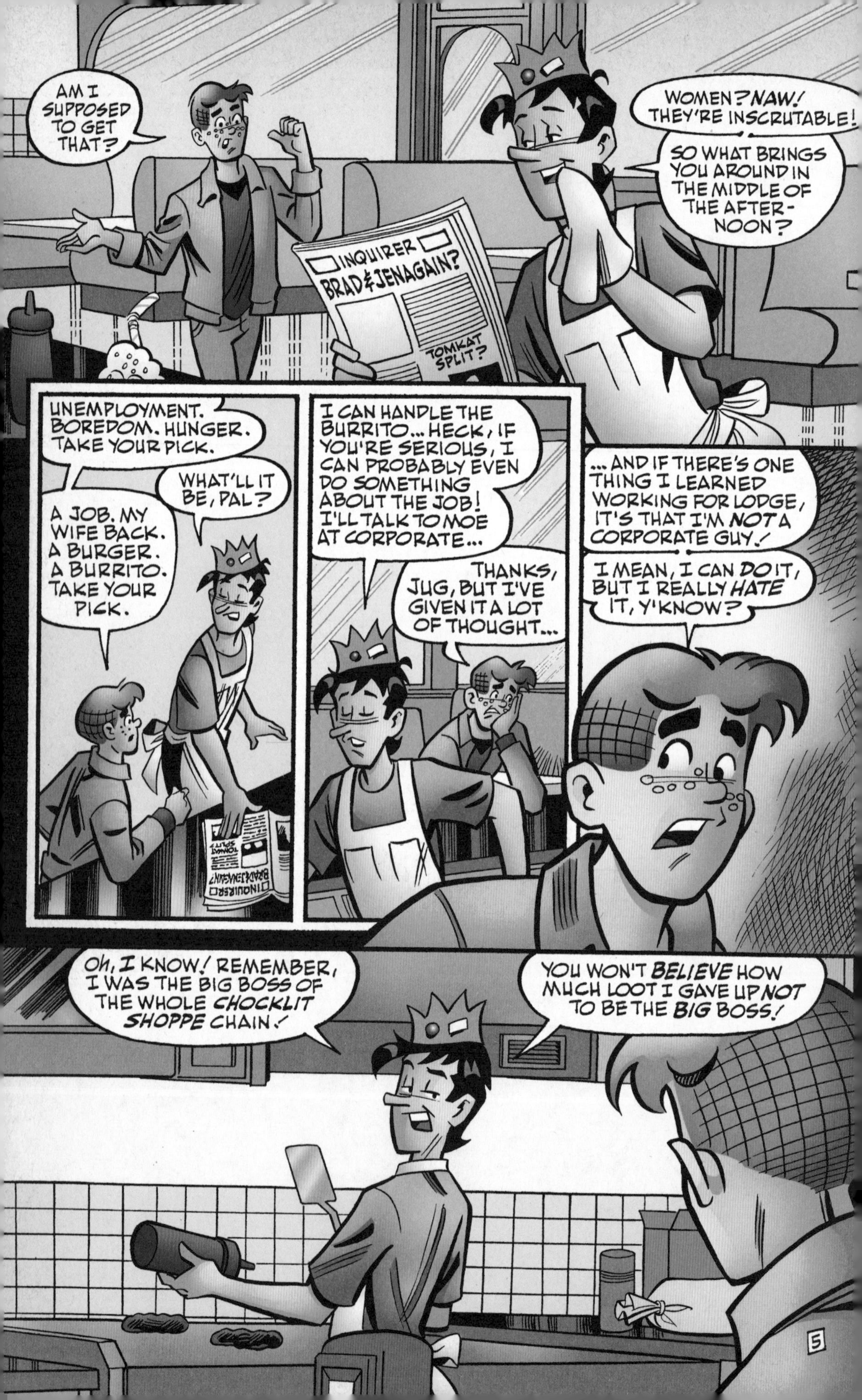
AM I SUPPOSED TO GET THAT?
WOMEN? NAW! THEY'RE INSCRUTABLE!
SO WHAT BRINGS YOU AROUND IN THE MIDDLE OF THE AFTER-NOON?
INQUIRER
BRAD & JEN AGAIN?
TOMKAT SPLIT?
UNEMPLOYMENT. BOREDOM. HUNGER. TAKE YOUR PICK.
WHAT'LL IT BE, PAL?
A JOB. MY WIFE BACK. A BURGER. A BURRITO. TAKE YOUR PICK.
I CAN HANDLE THE BURRITO... HECK, IF YOU'RE SERIOUS, I CAN PROBABLY EVEN DO SOMETHING ABOUT THE JOB! I'LL TALK TO MOE AT CORPORATE...
THANKS, JUG, BUT I'VE GIVEN IT A LOT OF THOUGHT...
...AND IF THERE'S ONE THING I LEARNED WORKING FOR LODGE, IT'S THAT I'M NOT A CORPORATE GUY!
I MEAN, I CAN DO IT, BUT I REALLY HATE IT, Y'KNOW?
Oh, I KNOW! REMEMBER, I WAS THE BIG BOSS OF THE WHOLE CHOCKLIT SHOPPE CHAIN!
YOU WON'T BELIEVE HOW MUCH LOOT I GAVE UP NOT TO BE THE BIG BOSS!

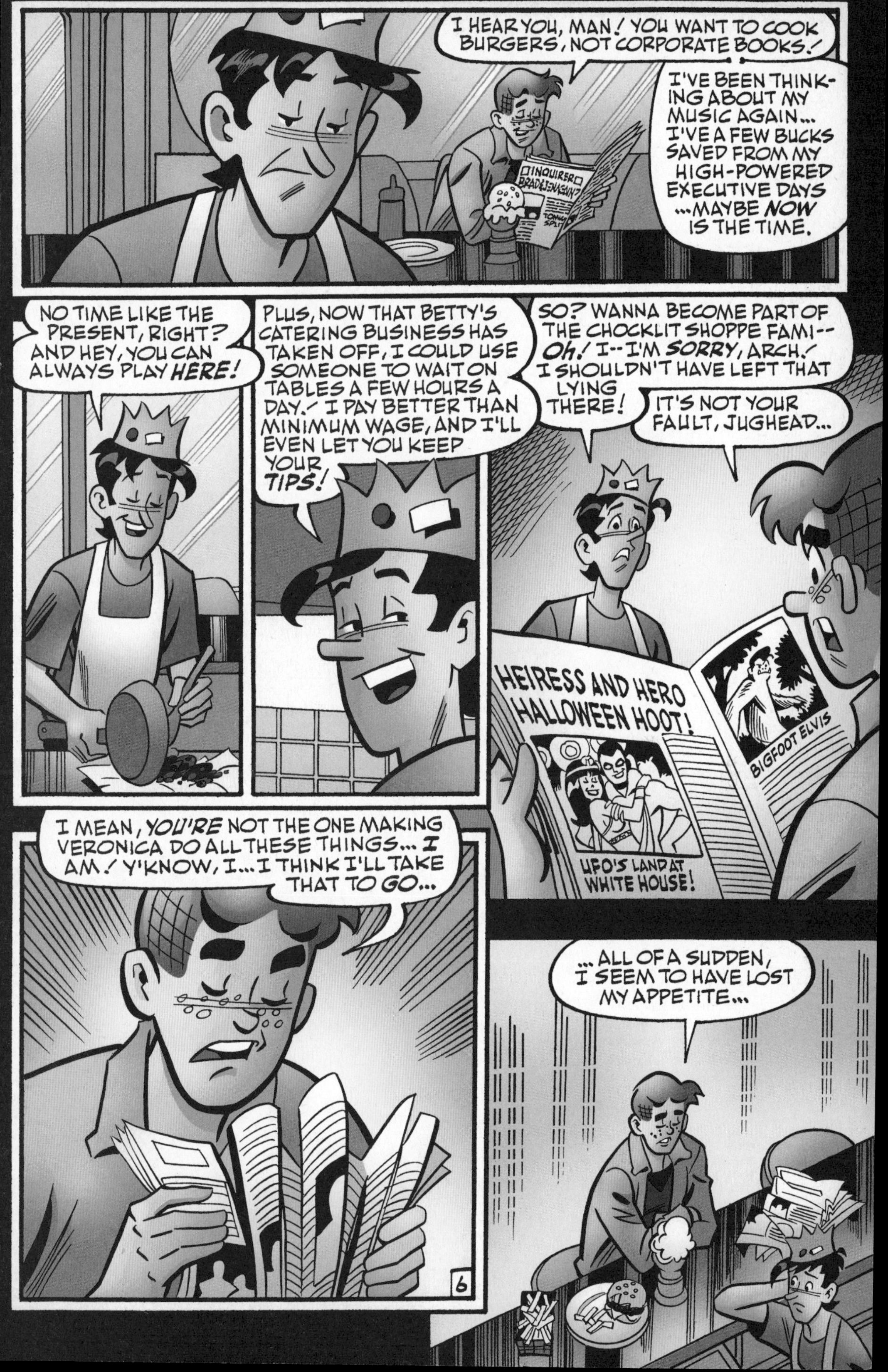
I HEAR YOU, MAN! YOU WANT TO COOK BURGERS, NOT CORPORATE BOOKS!
I'VE BEEN THINKING ABOUT MY MUSIC AGAIN... I'VE A FEW BUCKS SAVED FROM MY HIGH-POWERED EXECUTIVE DAYS ...MAYBE NOW IS THE TIME.
INQUIRER
NO TIME LIKE THE PRESENT, RIGHT? AND HEY, YOU CAN ALWAYS PLAY HERE!
PLUS, NOW THAT BETTY'S CATERING BUSINESS HAS TAKEN OFF, I COULD USE SOMEONE TO WAIT ON TABLES A FEW HOURS A DAY! I PAY BETTER THAN MINIMUM WAGE, AND I'LL EVEN LET YOU KEEP YOUR TIPS!
SO? WANNA BECOME PART OF THE CHOCKLIT SHOPPE FAMI-- OH! I--I'M SORRY, ARCH! I SHOULDN'T HAVE LEFT THAT LYING THERE!
IT'S NOT YOUR FAULT, JUGHEAD...
HEIRESS AND HERO HALLOWEEN HOOT!
BIGFOOT ELVIS
UFO'S LAND AT WHITE HOUSE!
I MEAN, YOU'RE NOT THE ONE MAKING VERONICA DO ALL THESE THINGS... I AM! Y'KNOW, I... I THINK I'LL TAKE THAT TO GO...
...ALL OF A SUDDEN, I SEEM TO HAVE LOST MY APPETITE...
6

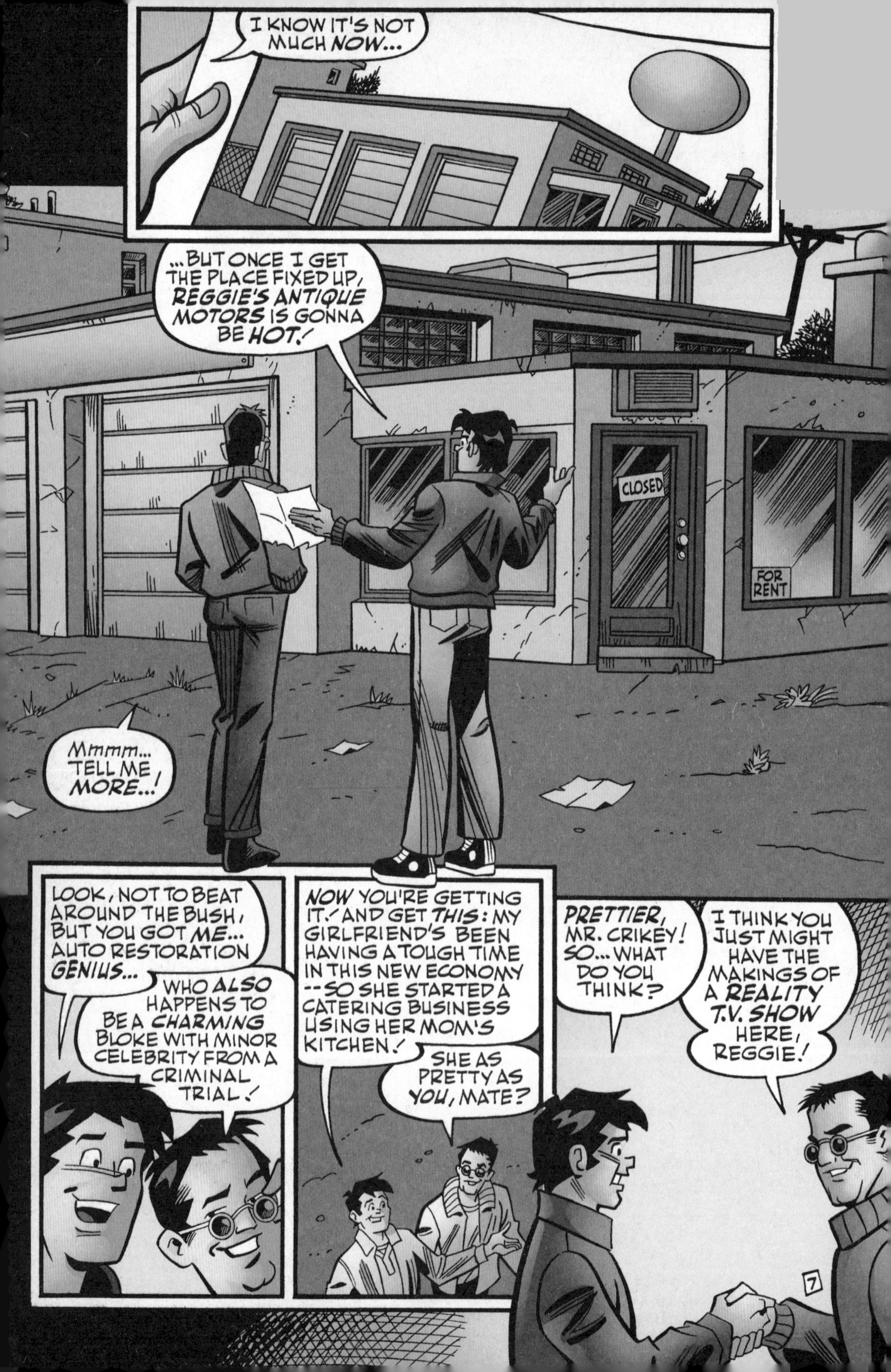
I KNOW IT'S NOT MUCH NOW...
...BUT ONCE I GET THE PLACE FIXED UP, REGGIE'S ANTIQUE MOTORS IS GONNA BE HOT!
CLOSED
FOR RENT
Mmmm... TELL ME MORE...!
LOOK, NOT TO BEAT AROUND THE BUSH, BUT YOU GOT ME... AUTO RESTORATION GENIUS...
WHO ALSO HAPPENS TO BE A CHARMING BLOKE WITH MINOR CELEBRITY FROM A CRIMINAL TRIAL!
NOW YOU'RE GETTING IT! AND GET THIS: MY GIRLFRIEND'S BEEN HAVING A TOUGH TIME IN THIS NEW ECONOMY --SO SHE STARTED A CATERING BUSINESS USING HER MOM'S KITCHEN!
SHE AS PRETTY AS YOU, MATE?
PRETTIER, MR. CRIKEY! SO... WHAT DO YOU THINK?
I THINK YOU JUST MIGHT HAVE THE MAKINGS OF A REALITY T.V. SHOW HERE, REGGIE!
7

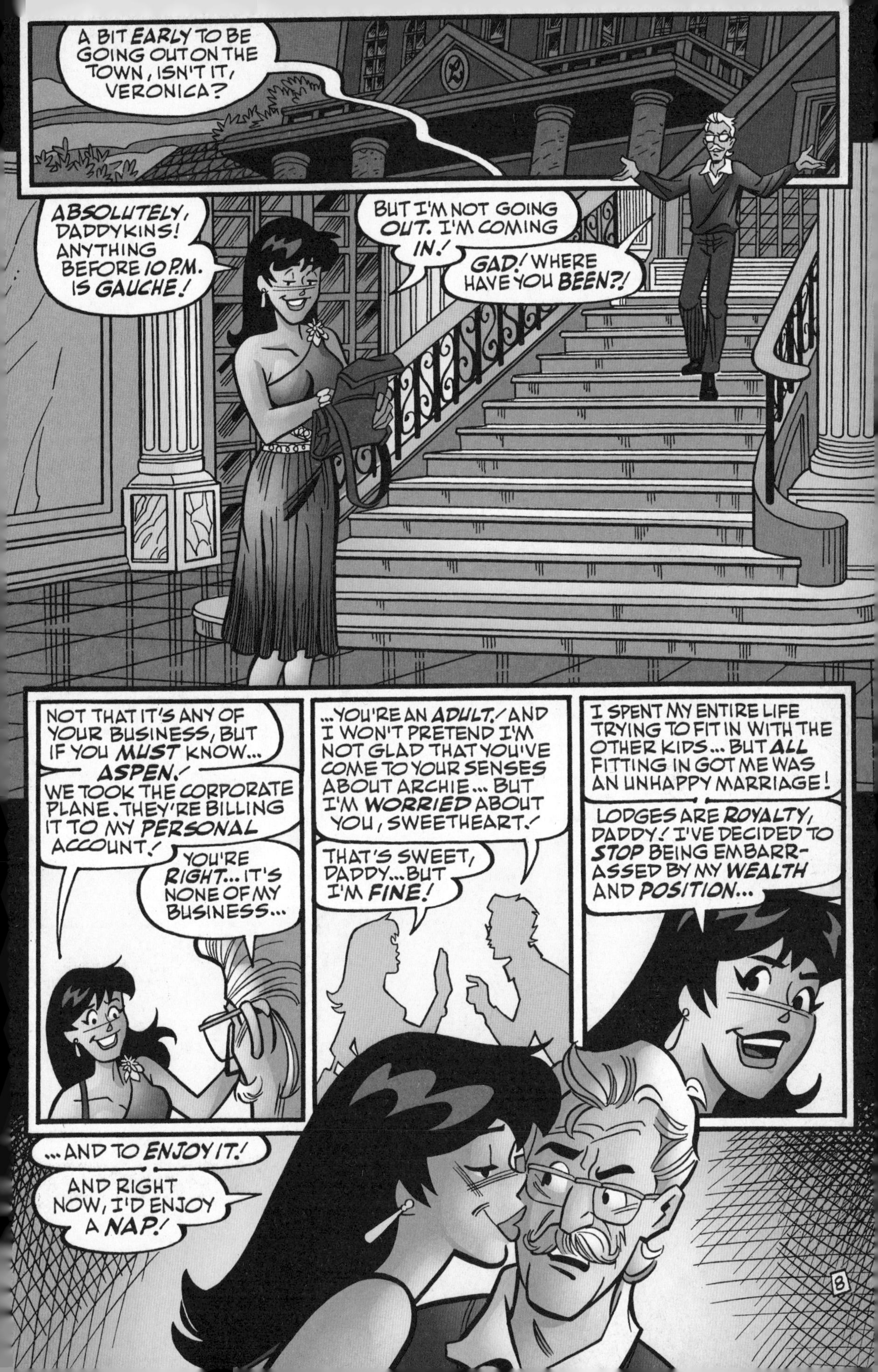
A BIT EARLY TO BE GOING OUT ON THE TOWN, ISN'T IT, VERONICA?
ABSOLUTELY, DADDYKINS! ANYTHING BEFORE 10 P.M. IS GAUCHE!
BUT I'M NOT GOING OUT. I'M COMING IN!
GAD! WHERE HAVE YOU BEEN?!
NOT THAT IT'S ANY OF YOUR BUSINESS, BUT IF YOU MUST KNOW... ASPEN!
WE TOOK THE CORPORATE PLANE. THEY'RE BILLING IT TO MY PERSONAL ACCOUNT!
YOU'RE RIGHT... IT'S NONE OF MY BUSINESS...
...YOU'RE AN ADULT! AND I WON'T PRETEND I'M NOT GLAD THAT YOU'VE COME TO YOUR SENSES ABOUT ARCHIE... BUT I'M WORRIED ABOUT YOU, SWEETHEART!
THAT'S SWEET, DADDY... BUT I'M FINE!
I SPENT MY ENTIRE LIFE TRYING TO FIT IN WITH THE OTHER KIDS... BUT ALL FITTING IN GOT ME WAS AN UNHAPPY MARRIAGE!
LODGES ARE ROYALTY, DADDY! I'VE DECIDED TO STOP BEING EMBARR-ASSED BY MY WEALTH AND POSITION...
...AND TO ENJOY IT!
AND RIGHT NOW, I'D ENJOY A NAP!
8

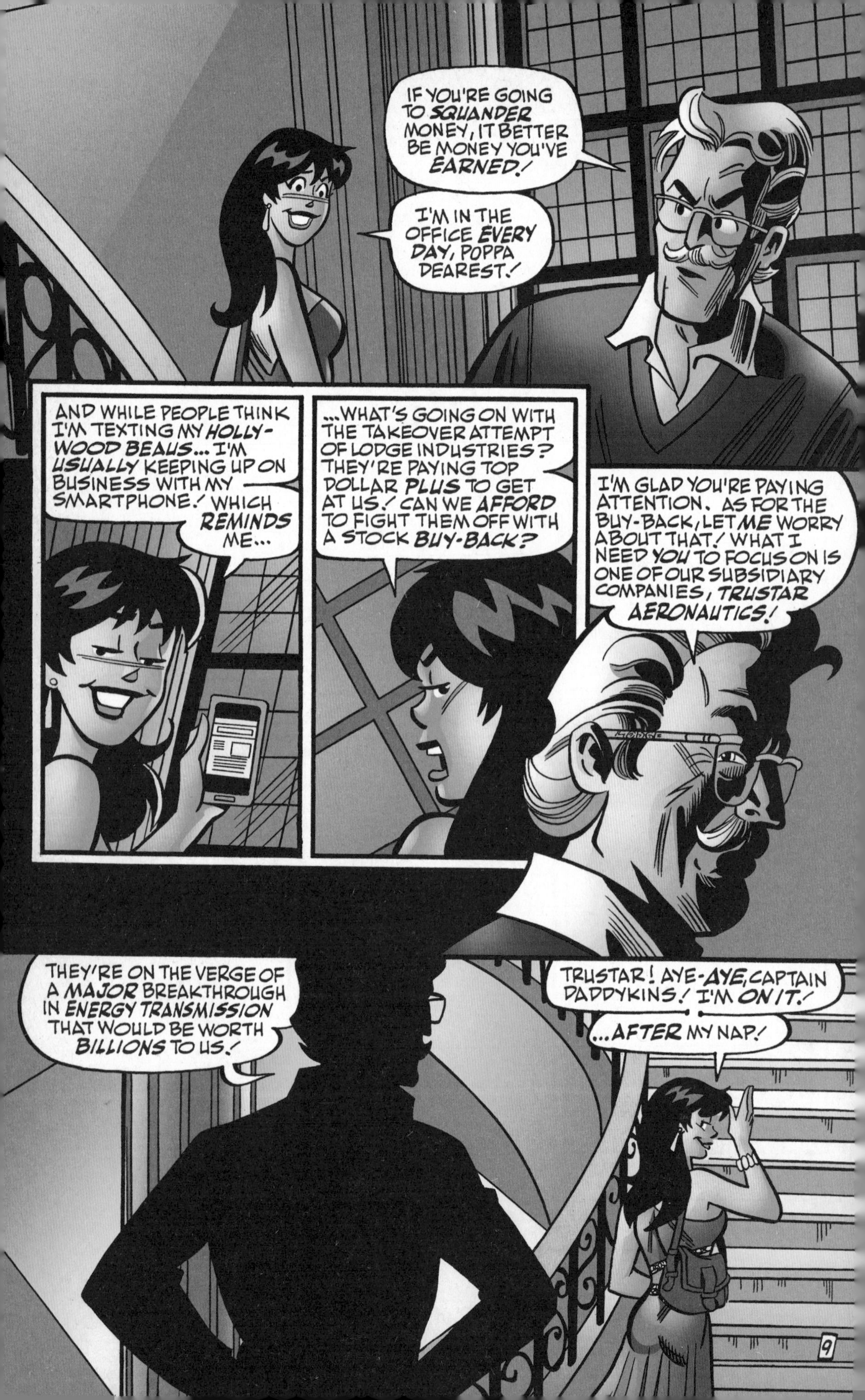
IF YOU'RE GOING TO SQUANDER MONEY, IT BETTER BE MONEY YOU'VE EARNED!
I'M IN THE OFFICE EVERY DAY, POPPA DEAREST!
AND WHILE PEOPLE THINK I'M TEXTING MY HOLLYWOOD BEAUS... I'M USUALLY KEEPING UP ON BUSINESS WITH MY SMARTPHONE! WHICH REMINDS ME...
...WHAT'S GOING ON WITH THE TAKEOVER ATTEMPT OF LODGE INDUSTRIES? THEY'RE PAYING TOP DOLLAR PLUS TO GET AT US! CAN WE AFFORD TO FIGHT THEM OFF WITH A STOCK BUY-BACK?
I'M GLAD YOU'RE PAYING ATTENTION. AS FOR THE BUY-BACK, LET ME WORRY ABOUT THAT! WHAT I NEED YOU TO FOCUS ON IS ONE OF OUR SUBSIDIARY COMPANIES, TRUSTAR AERONAUTICS!
THEY'RE ON THE VERGE OF A MAJOR BREAKTHROUGH IN ENERGY TRANSMISSION THAT WOULD BE WORTH BILLIONS TO US!
TRUSTAR! AYE-AYE, CAPTAIN DADDYKINS! I'M ON IT!
...AFTER MY NAP!
9

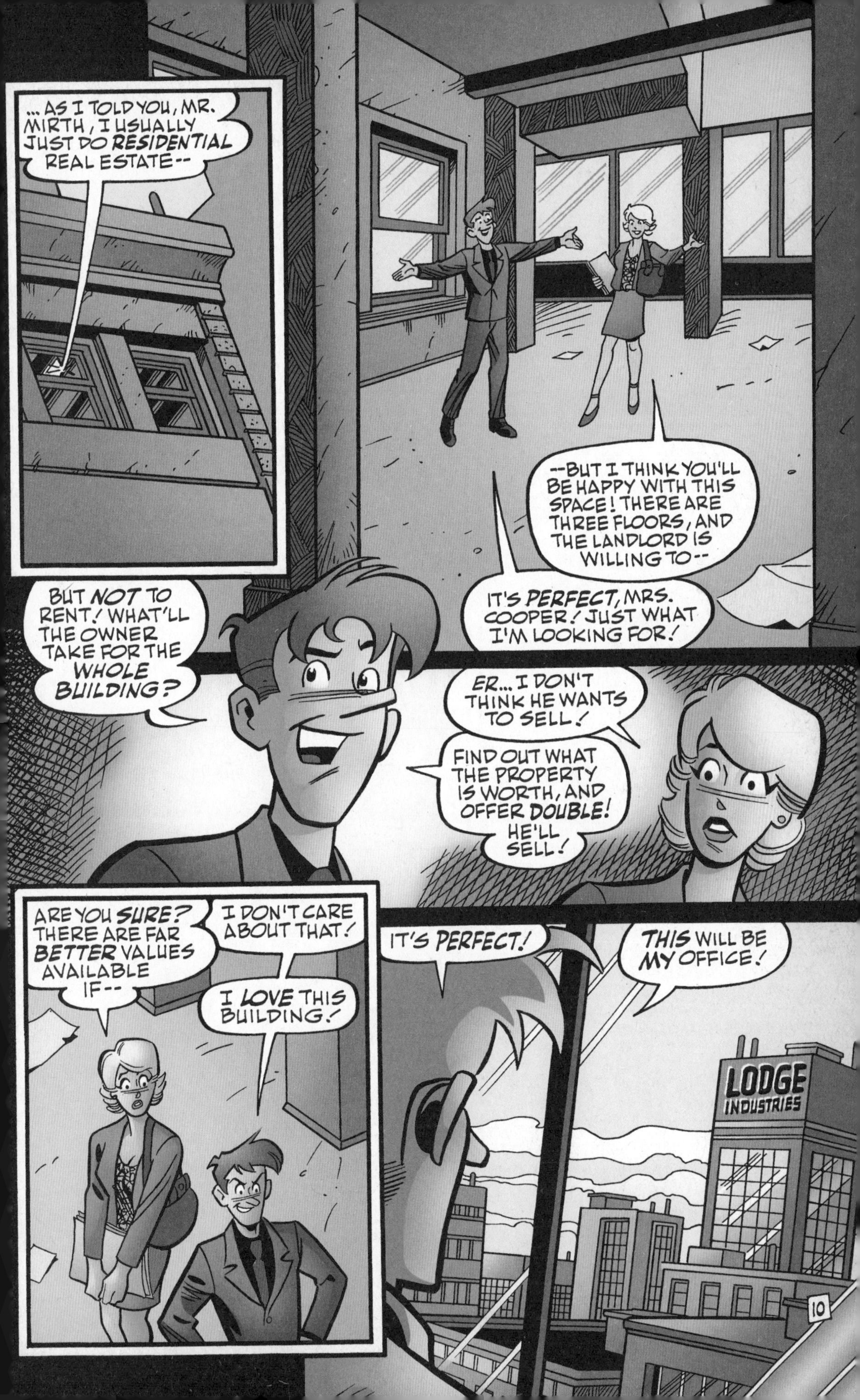
...AS I TOLD YOU, MR. MIRTH, I USUALLY JUST DO RESIDENTIAL REAL ESTATE--
--BUT I THINK YOU'LL BE HAPPY WITH THIS SPACE! THERE ARE THREE FLOORS, AND THE LANDLORD IS WILLING TO--
IT'S PERFECT, MRS. COOPER! JUST WHAT I'M LOOKING FOR!
BUT NOT TO RENT! WHAT'LL THE OWNER TAKE FOR THE WHOLE BUILDING?
ER... I DON'T THINK HE WANTS TO SELL!
FIND OUT WHAT THE PROPERTY IS WORTH, AND OFFER DOUBLE! HE'LL SELL!
ARE YOU SURE? THERE ARE FAR BETTER VALUES AVAILABLE IF--
I DON'T CARE ABOUT THAT!
I LOVE THIS BUILDING!
IT'S PERFECT!
THIS WILL BE MY OFFICE!
LODGE INDUSTRIES
10

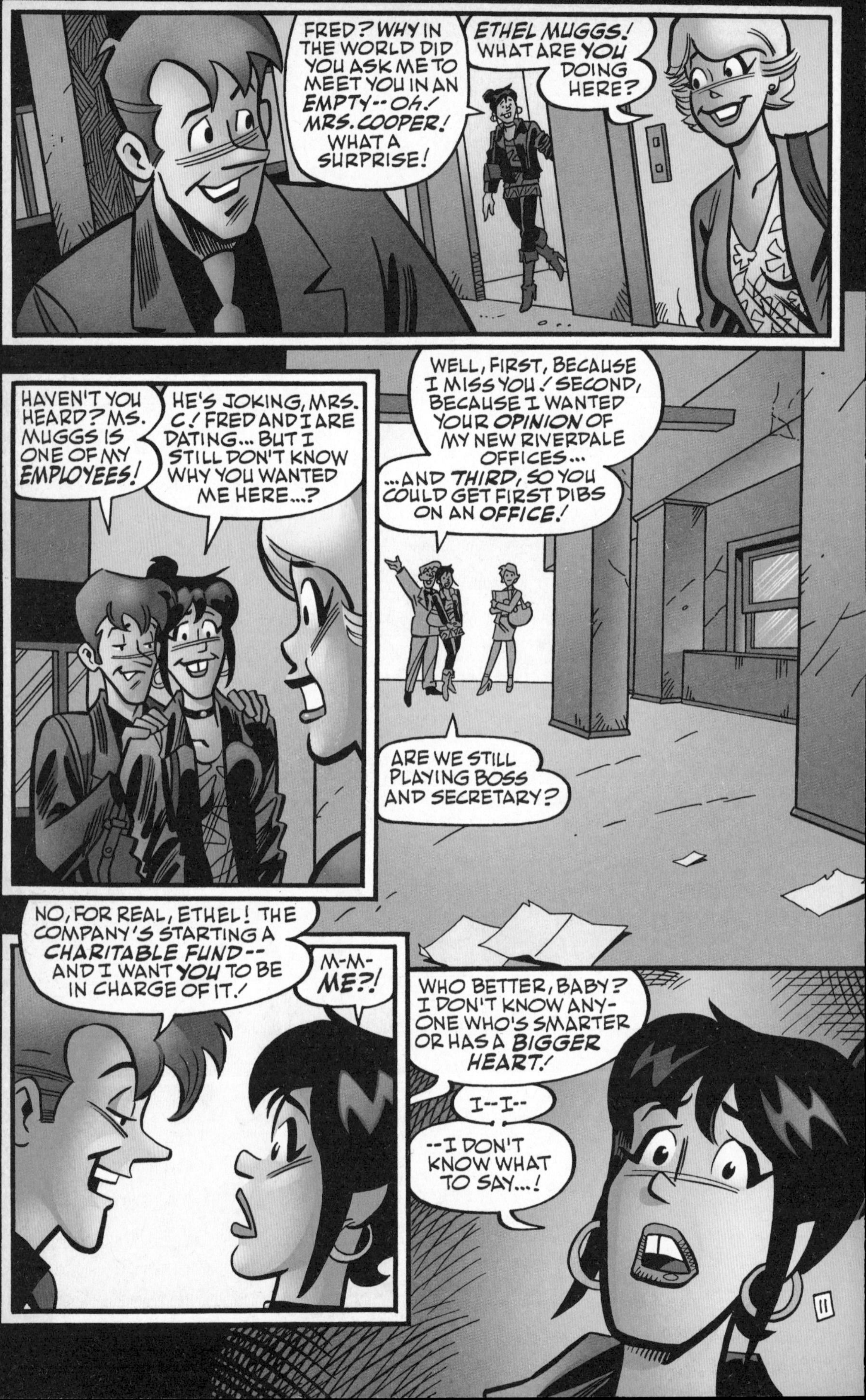

FRED? WHY IN THE WORLD DID YOU ASK ME TO MEET YOU IN AN EMPTY-- OH! MRS. COOPER! WHAT A SURPRISE!
ETHEL MUGGS! WHAT ARE YOU DOING HERE?
HAVEN'T YOU HEARD? MS. MUGGS IS ONE OF MY EMPLOYEES!
HE'S JOKING, MRS. C! FRED AND I ARE DATING... BUT I STILL DON'T KNOW WHY YOU WANTED ME HERE...?
WELL, FIRST, BECAUSE I MISS YOU! SECOND, BECAUSE I WANTED YOUR OPINION OF MY NEW RIVERDALE OFFICES...
...AND THIRD, SO YOU COULD GET FIRST DIBS ON AN OFFICE!
ARE WE STILL PLAYING BOSS AND SECRETARY?
NO, FOR REAL, ETHEL! THE COMPANY'S STARTING A CHARITABLE FUND-- AND I WANT YOU TO BE IN CHARGE OF IT!
M-M-ME?!
WHO BETTER, BABY? I DON'T KNOW ANY-ONE WHO'S SMARTER OR HAS A BIGGER HEART!
I--I--
--I DON'T KNOW WHAT TO SAY...!
11

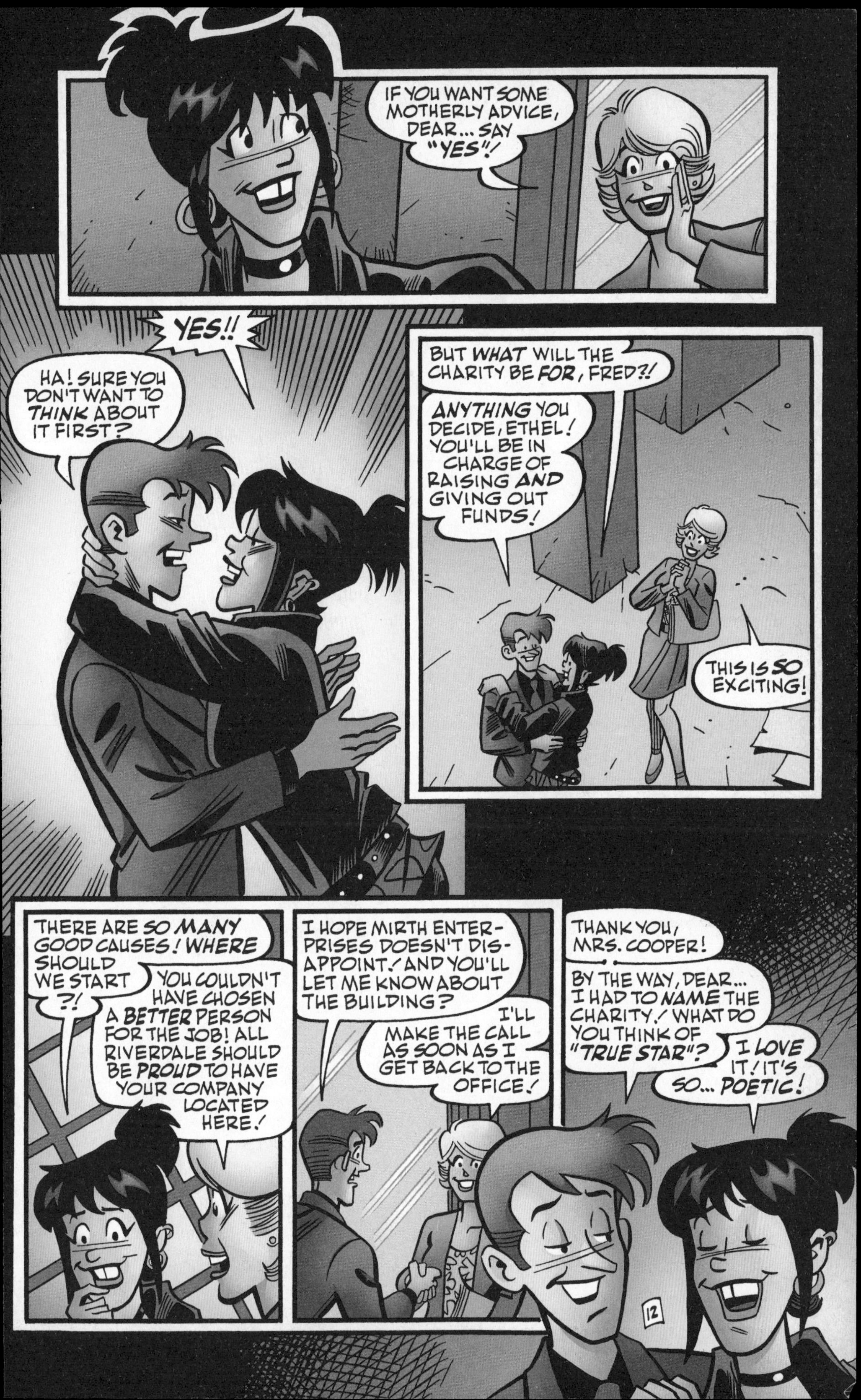
IF YOU WANT SOME MOTHERLY ADVICE, DEAR... SAY "YES"!!
YES!!
HA! SURE YOU DON'T WANT TO THINK ABOUT IT FIRST?
BUT WHAT WILL THE CHARITY BE FOR, FRED?!
ANYTHING YOU DECIDE, ETHEL! YOU'LL BE IN CHARGE OF RAISING AND GIVING OUT FUNDS!
THIS IS SO EXCITING!
THERE ARE SO MANY GOOD CAUSES! WHERE SHOULD WE START?!
YOU COULDN'T HAVE CHOSEN A BETTER PERSON FOR THE JOB! ALL RIVERDALE SHOULD BE PROUD TO HAVE YOUR COMPANY LOCATED HERE!
I HOPE MIRTH ENTERPRISES DOESN'T DISAPPOINT! AND YOU'LL LET ME KNOW ABOUT THE BUILDING?
I'LL MAKE THE CALL AS SOON AS I GET BACK TO THE OFFICE!
THANK YOU, MRS. COOPER!
BY THE WAY, DEAR... I HAD TO NAME THE CHARITY! WHAT DO YOU THINK OF "TRUE STAR"?
I LOVE IT! IT'S SO... POETIC!
12

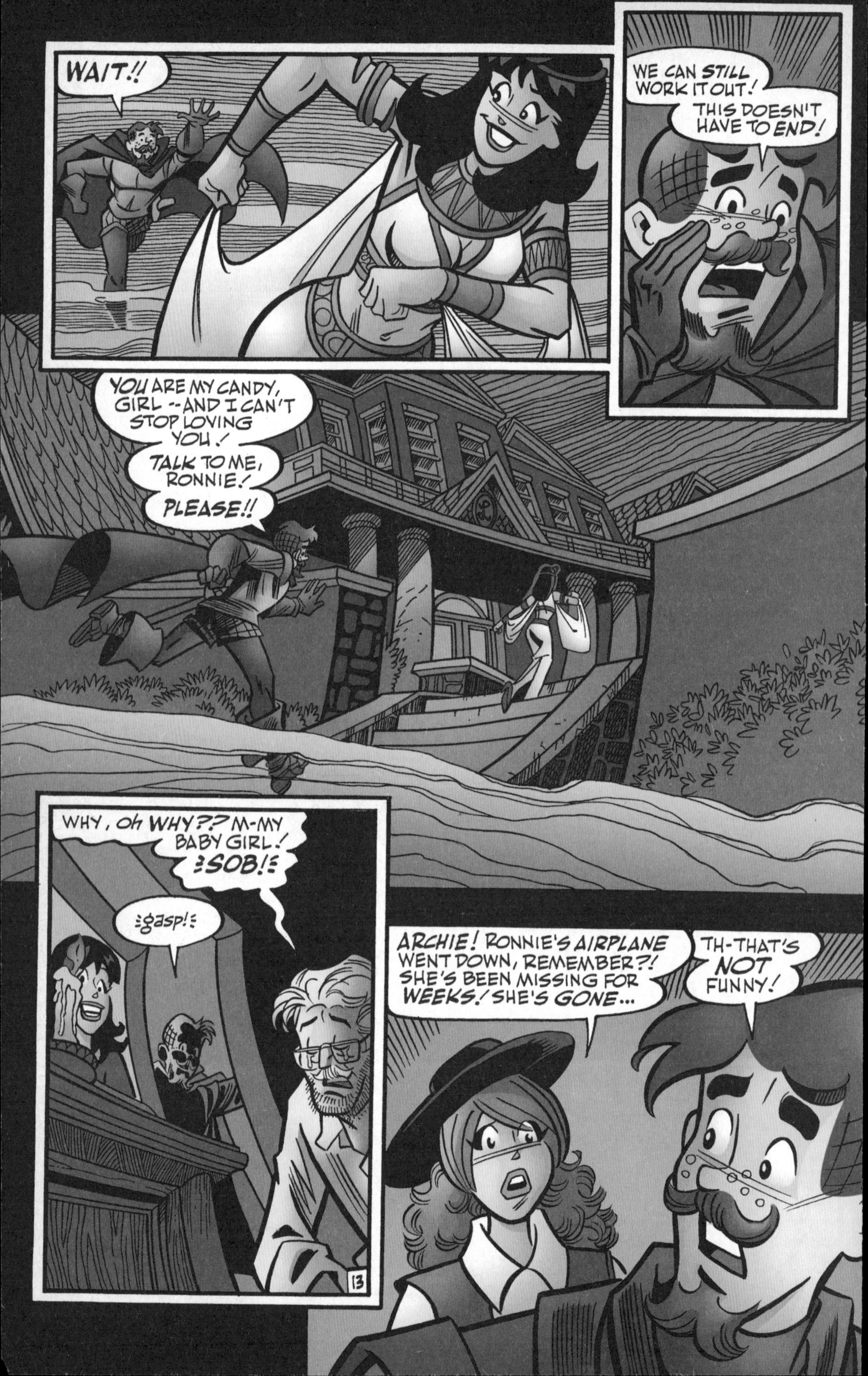
WAIT!!
WE CAN STILL WORK IT OUT!
THIS DOESN'T HAVE TO END!
YOU ARE MY CANDY, GIRL --AND I CAN'T STOP LOVING YOU!
TALK TO ME, RONNIE!
PLEASE!!
WHY, oh WHY?? M-MY BABY GIRL!
SOB!
gasp!
ARCHIE! RONNIE'S AIRPLANE WENT DOWN, REMEMBER?! SHE'S BEEN MISSING FOR WEEKS! SHE'S GONE...
TH-THAT'S NOT FUNNY!
13

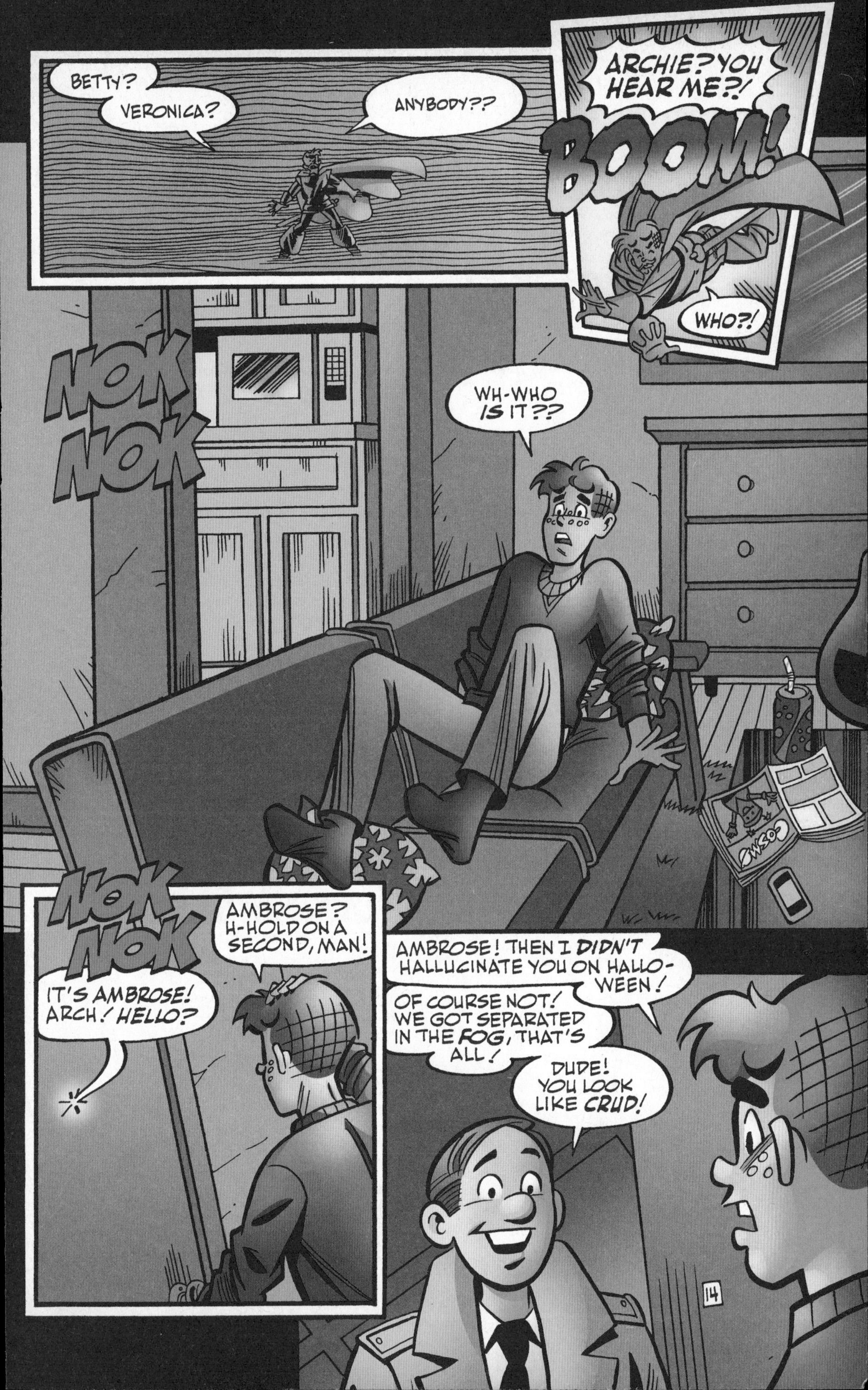
BETTY?
VERONICA?
ANYBODY??
ARCHIE? YOU HEAR ME?!
BOOM!
WHO?!
NOK NOK
WH-WHO IS IT??
NOK NOK
IT'S AMBROSE! ARCH! HELLO?
AMBROSE? H-HOLD ON A SECOND, MAN!
AMBROSE! THEN I DIDN'T HALLUCINATE YOU ON HALLO-WEEN!
OF COURSE NOT! WE GOT SEPARATED IN THE FOG, THAT'S ALL!
DUDE! YOU LOOK LIKE CRUD!
14

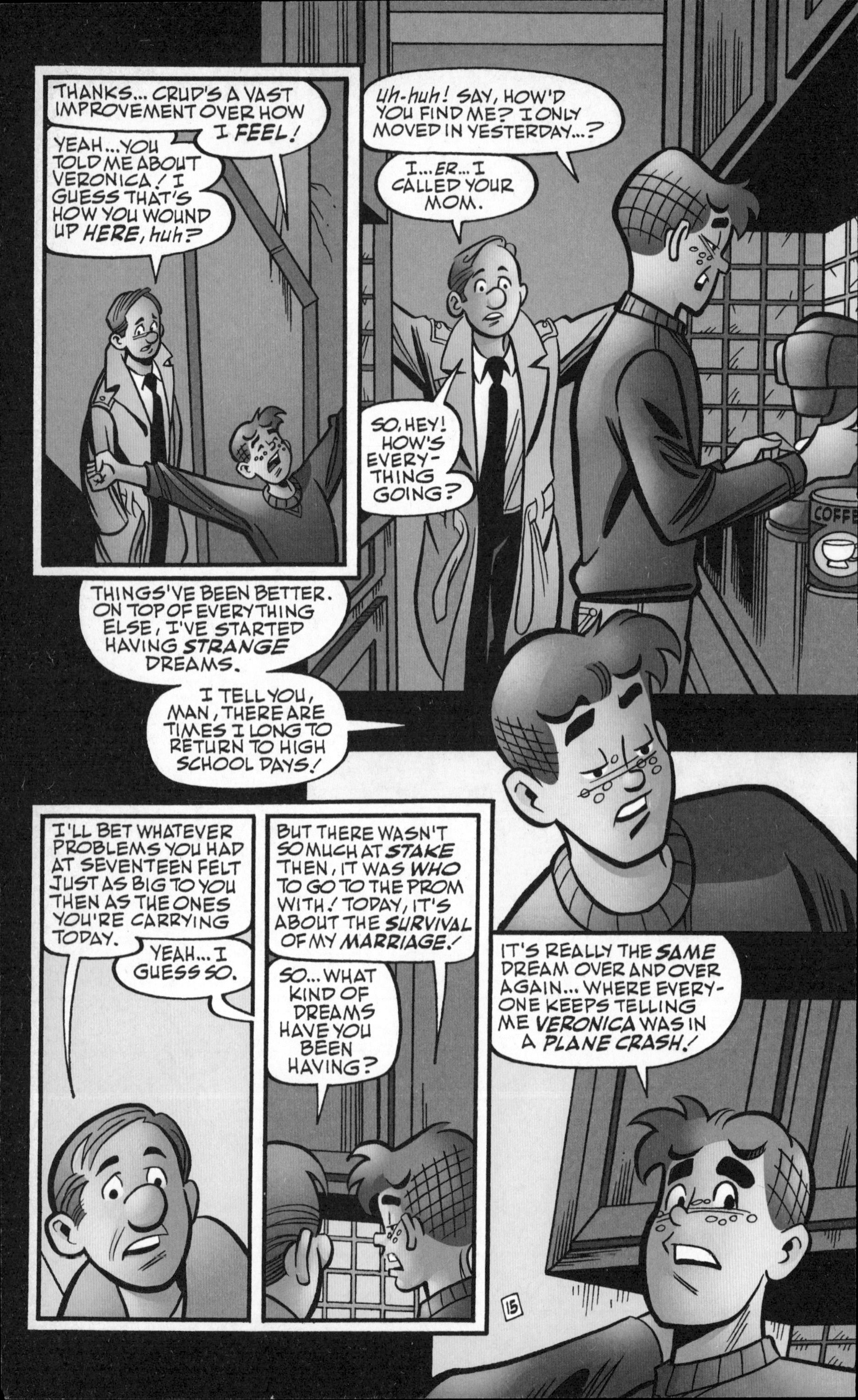

THANKS... CRUD'S A VAST IMPROVEMENT OVER HOW I FEEL!
YEAH... YOU TOLD ME ABOUT VERONICA! I GUESS THAT'S HOW YOU WOUND UP HERE, huh?
uh-huh! SAY, HOW'D YOU FIND ME? I ONLY MOVED IN YESTERDAY...?
I... ER... I CALLED YOUR MOM.
SO, HEY! HOW'S EVERYTHING GOING?
COFFEE
THINGS'VE BEEN BETTER. ON TOP OF EVERYTHING ELSE, I'VE STARTED HAVING STRANGE DREAMS.
I TELL YOU, MAN, THERE ARE TIMES I LONG TO RETURN TO HIGH SCHOOL DAYS!
I'LL BET WHATEVER PROBLEMS YOU HAD AT SEVENTEEN FELT JUST AS BIG TO YOU THEN AS THE ONES YOU'RE CARRYING TODAY.
YEAH... I GUESS SO.
BUT THERE WASN'T SO MUCH AT STAKE THEN, IT WAS WHO TO GO TO THE PROM WITH! TODAY, IT'S ABOUT THE SURVIVAL OF MY MARRIAGE!
SO... WHAT KIND OF DREAMS HAVE YOU BEEN HAVING?
IT'S REALLY THE SAME DREAM OVER AND OVER AGAIN... WHERE EVERYONE KEEPS TELLING ME VERONICA WAS IN A PLANE CRASH!

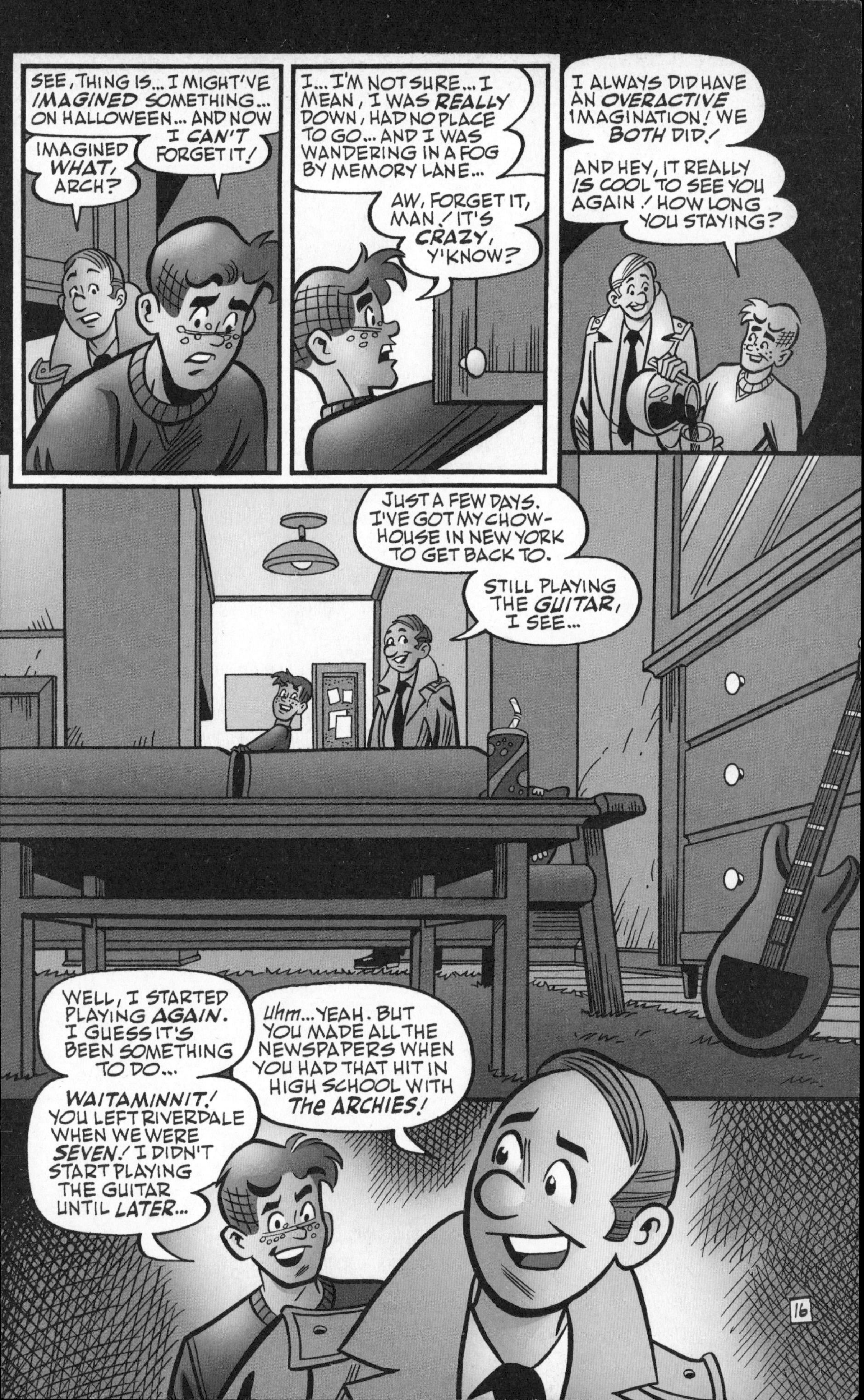
SEE, THING IS... I MIGHT'VE IMAGINED SOMETHING... ON HALLOWEEN... AND NOW I CAN'T FORGET IT!
IMAGINED WHAT, ARCH?
I... I'M NOT SURE... I MEAN, I WAS REALLY DOWN, HAD NO PLACE TO GO... AND I WAS WANDERING IN A FOG BY MEMORY LANE...
AW, FORGET IT, MAN! IT'S CRAZY, Y'KNOW?
I ALWAYS DID HAVE AN OVERACTIVE IMAGINATION! WE BOTH DID!
AND HEY, IT REALLY IS COOL TO SEE YOU AGAIN! HOW LONG YOU STAYING?
JUST A FEW DAYS. I'VE GOT MY CHOW-HOUSE IN NEW YORK TO GET BACK TO.
STILL PLAYING THE GUITAR, I SEE...
WELL, I STARTED PLAYING AGAIN. I GUESS IT'S BEEN SOMETHING TO DO...
UHM... YEAH. BUT YOU MADE ALL THE NEWSPAPERS WHEN YOU HAD THAT HIT IN HIGH SCHOOL WITH The ARCHIES!
WAITAMINNIT! YOU LEFT RIVERDALE WHEN WE WERE SEVEN! I DIDN'T START PLAYING THE GUITAR UNTIL LATER...
16

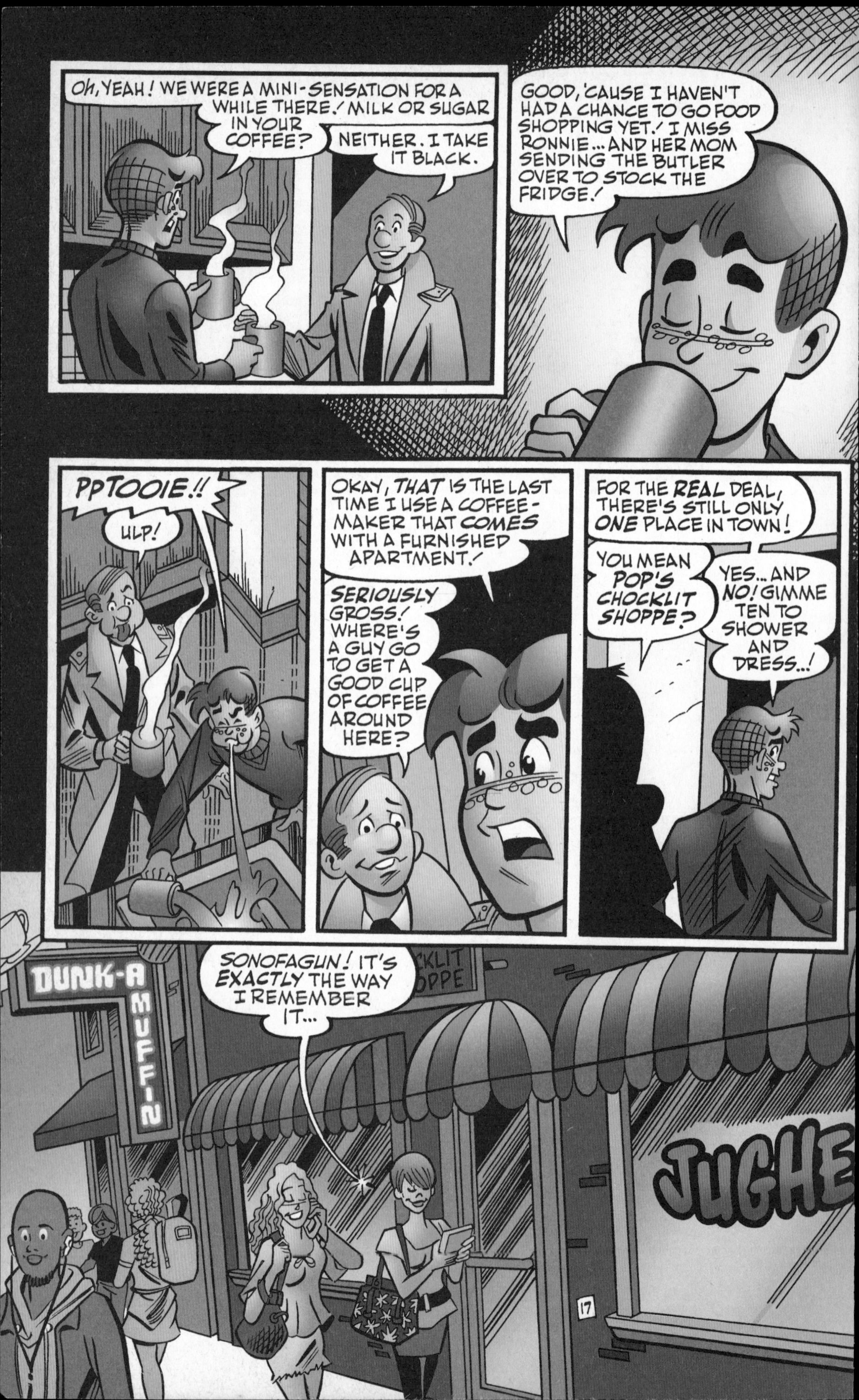

Oh, YEAH! WE WERE A MINI-SENSATION FOR A WHILE THERE! MILK OR SUGAR IN YOUR COFFEE?
NEITHER. I TAKE IT BLACK.
GOOD, 'CAUSE I HAVEN'T HAD A CHANCE TO GO FOOD SHOPPING YET! I MISS RONNIE... AND HER MOM SENDING THE BUTLER OVER TO STOCK THE FRIDGE!
PPTOOIE!!
ULP!
OKAY, THAT IS THE LAST TIME I USE A COFFEE-MAKER THAT COMES WITH A FURNISHED APARTMENT!
SERIOUSLY GROSS! WHERE'S A GUY GO TO GET A GOOD CUP OF COFFEE AROUND HERE?
FOR THE REAL DEAL, THERE'S STILL ONLY ONE PLACE IN TOWN!
YOU MEAN POP'S CHOCKLIT SHOPPE?
YES... AND NO! GIMME TEN TO SHOWER AND DRESS...!
DUNK-A MUFFIN
SONOFAGUN! IT'S EXACTLY THE WAY I REMEMBER IT...
JUGHE
17

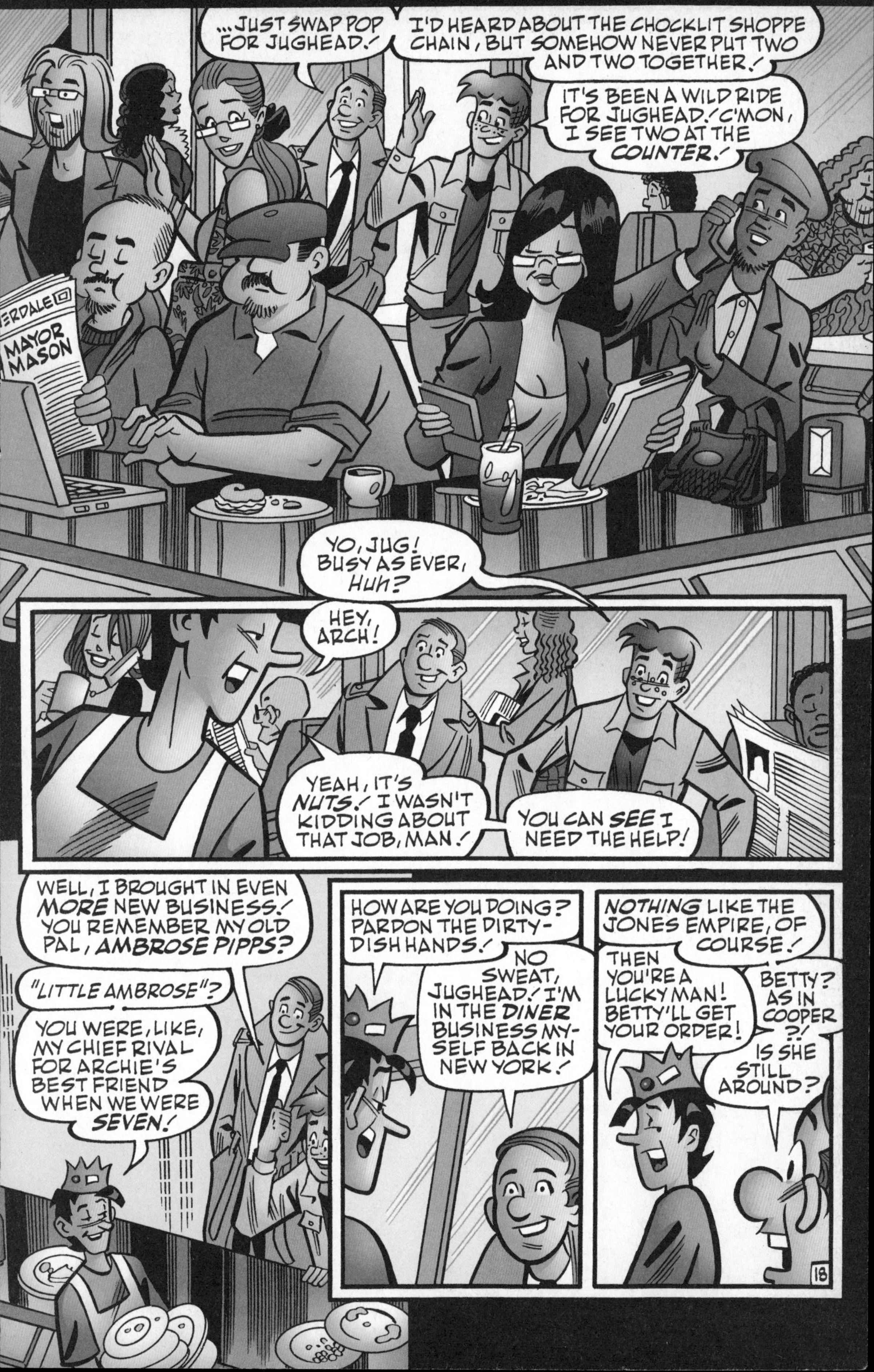
...JUST SWAP POP FOR JUGHEAD!
I'D HEARD ABOUT THE CHOCKLIT SHOPPE CHAIN, BUT SOMEHOW NEVER PUT TWO AND TWO TOGETHER!
IT'S BEEN A WILD RIDE FOR JUGHEAD! C'MON, I SEE TWO AT THE COUNTER!
RDALE
MAYOR MASON
YO, JUG! BUSY AS EVER, HUH?
HEY, ARCH!
YEAH, IT'S NUTS! I WASN'T KIDDING ABOUT THAT JOB, MAN!
YOU CAN SEE I NEED THE HELP!
WELL, I BROUGHT IN EVEN MORE NEW BUSINESS! YOU REMEMBER MY OLD PAL, AMBROSE PIPPS?
"LITTLE AMBROSE"?
YOU WERE, LIKE, MY CHIEF RIVAL FOR ARCHIE'S BEST FRIEND WHEN WE WERE SEVEN!
HOW ARE YOU DOING? PARDON THE DIRTY-DISH HANDS!
NO SWEAT, JUGHEAD! I'M IN THE DINER BUSINESS MY-SELF BACK IN NEW YORK!
NOTHING LIKE THE JONES EMPIRE, OF COURSE!
THEN YOU'RE A LUCKY MAN! BETTY'LL GET YOUR ORDER!
BETTY? AS IN COOPER?! IS SHE STILL AROUND?
18

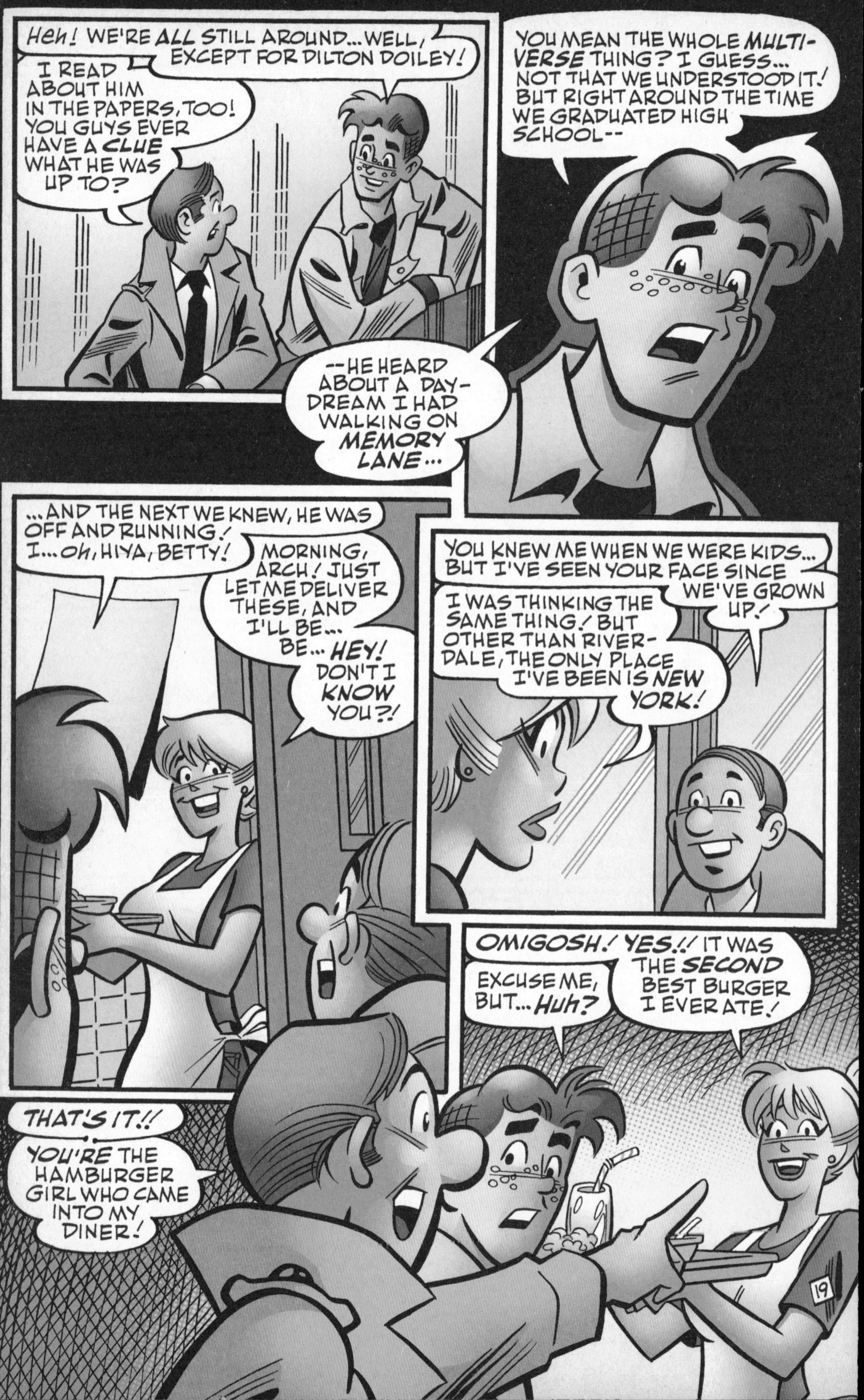
Heh! WE'RE ALL STILL AROUND...WELL, EXCEPT FOR DILTON DOILEY!
I READ ABOUT HIM IN THE PAPERS, TOO! YOU GUYS EVER HAVE A CLUE WHAT HE WAS UP TO?
YOU MEAN THE WHOLE MULTI-VERSE THING? I GUESS... NOT THAT WE UNDERSTOOD IT! BUT RIGHT AROUND THE TIME WE GRADUATED HIGH SCHOOL--
--HE HEARD ABOUT A DAY-DREAM I HAD WALKING ON MEMORY LANE...
...AND THE NEXT WE KNEW, HE WAS OFF AND RUNNING! I...oh, HIYA, BETTY!
MORNING, ARCH! JUST LET ME DELIVER THESE, AND I'LL BE... BE... HEY! DON'T I KNOW YOU?!
YOU KNEW ME WHEN WE WERE KIDS... BUT I'VE SEEN YOUR FACE SINCE WE'VE GROWN UP!
I WAS THINKING THE SAME THING! BUT OTHER THAN RIVER-DALE, THE ONLY PLACE I'VE BEEN IS NEW YORK!
OMIGOSH! YES!! IT WAS THE SECOND BEST BURGER I EVER ATE!
EXCUSE ME, BUT... Huh?
THAT'S IT!!
YOU'RE THE HAMBURGER GIRL WHO CAME INTO MY DINER!
19

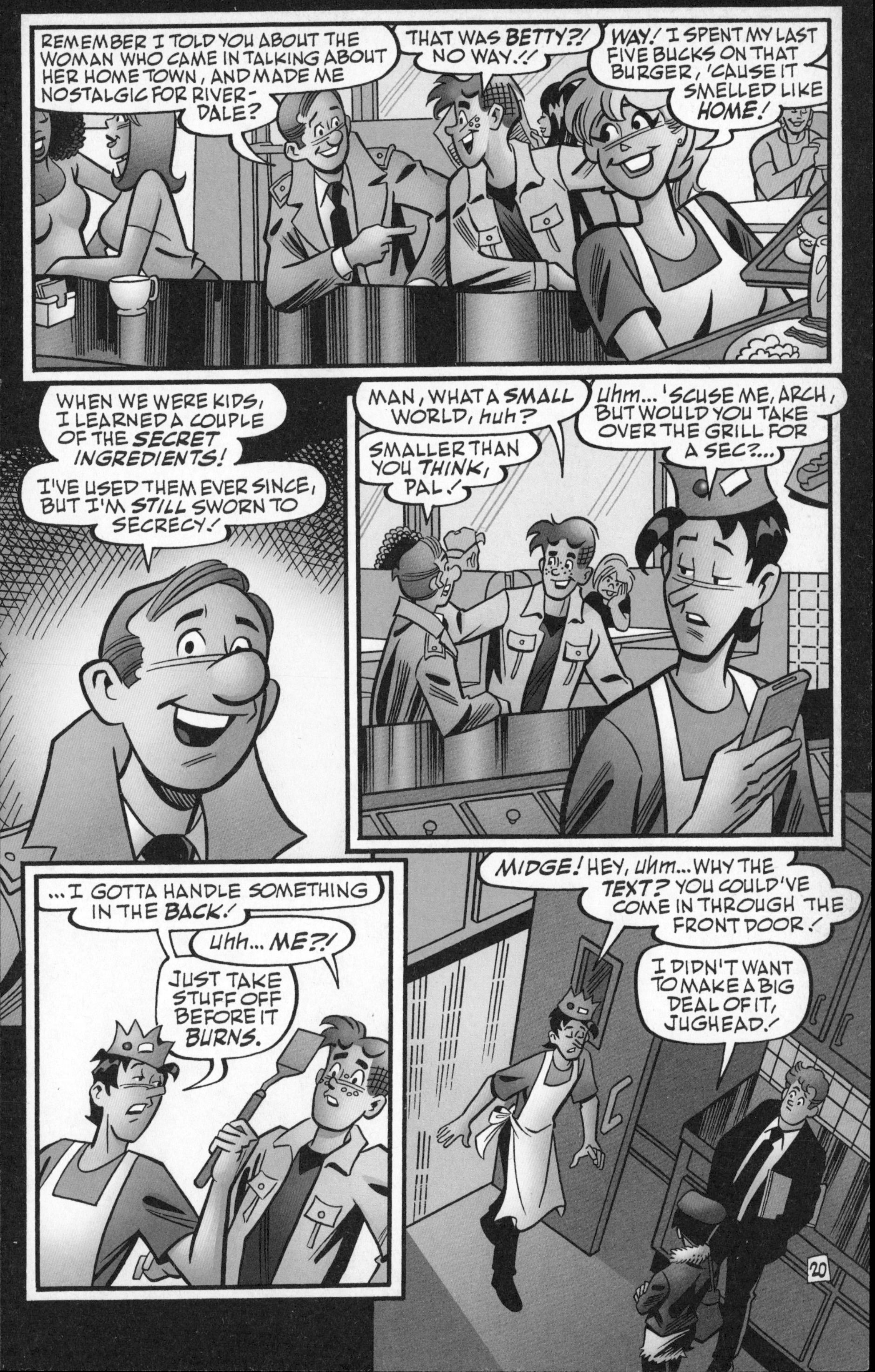
REMEMBER I TOLD YOU ABOUT THE WOMAN WHO CAME IN TALKING ABOUT HER HOME TOWN, AND MADE ME NOSTALGIC FOR RIVER-DALE?
THAT WAS BETTY?! NO WAY.!!
WAY! I SPENT MY LAST FIVE BUCKS ON THAT BURGER, 'CAUSE IT SMELLED LIKE HOME!
WHEN WE WERE KIDS, I LEARNED A COUPLE OF THE SECRET INGREDIENTS!
I'VE USED THEM EVER SINCE, BUT I'M STILL SWORN TO SECRECY!
MAN, WHAT A SMALL WORLD, huh?
SMALLER THAN YOU THINK, PAL!
uhm... 'SCUSE ME, ARCH, BUT WOULD YOU TAKE OVER THE GRILL FOR A SEC?...
...I GOTTA HANDLE SOMETHING IN THE BACK!
uhh... ME?!
JUST TAKE STUFF OFF BEFORE IT BURNS.
MIDGE! HEY, uhm... WHY THE TEXT? YOU COULD'VE COME IN THROUGH THE FRONT DOOR!
I DIDN'T WANT TO MAKE A BIG DEAL OF IT, JUGHEAD!
20

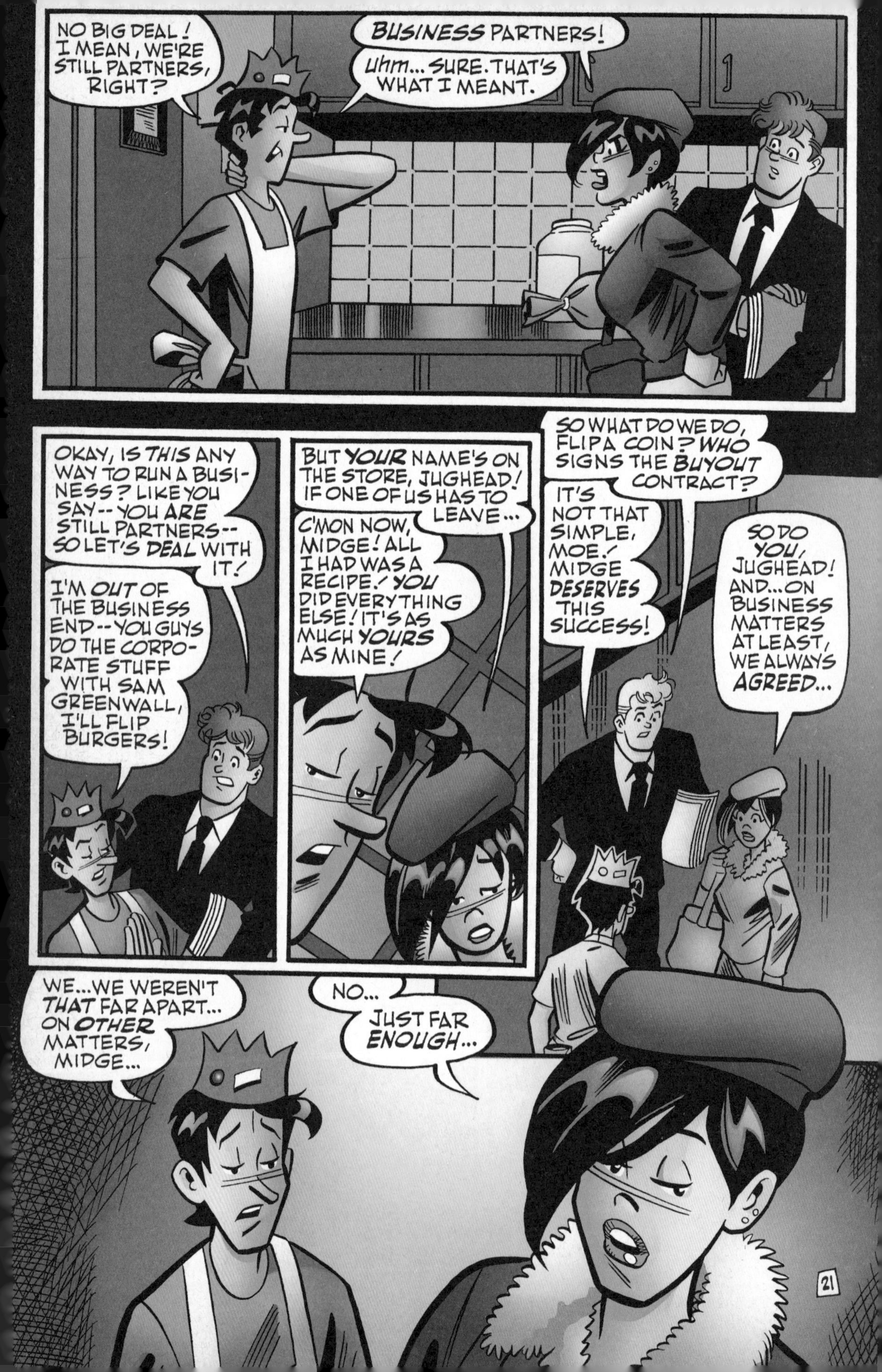
NO BIG DEAL! I MEAN, WE'RE STILL PARTNERS, RIGHT?
BUSINESS PARTNERS!
UHM... SURE. THAT'S WHAT I MEANT.
OKAY, IS THIS ANY WAY TO RUN A BUSINESS? LIKE YOU SAY-- YOU ARE STILL PARTNERS-- SO LET'S DEAL WITH IT!
I'M OUT OF THE BUSINESS END-- YOU GUYS DO THE CORPORATE STUFF WITH SAM GREENWALL, I'LL FLIP BURGERS!
BUT YOUR NAME'S ON THE STORE, JUGHEAD! IF ONE OF US HAS TO LEAVE...
C'MON NOW, MIDGE! ALL I HAD WAS A RECIPE! YOU DID EVERYTHING ELSE! IT'S AS MUCH YOURS AS MINE!
SO WHAT DO WE DO, FLIP A COIN? WHO SIGNS THE BUYOUT CONTRACT?
IT'S NOT THAT SIMPLE, MOE! MIDGE DESERVES THIS SUCCESS!
SO DO YOU, JUGHEAD! AND... ON BUSINESS MATTERS AT LEAST, WE ALWAYS AGREED...
WE... WE WEREN'T THAT FAR APART... ON OTHER MATTERS, MIDGE...
NO...
JUST FAR ENOUGH...

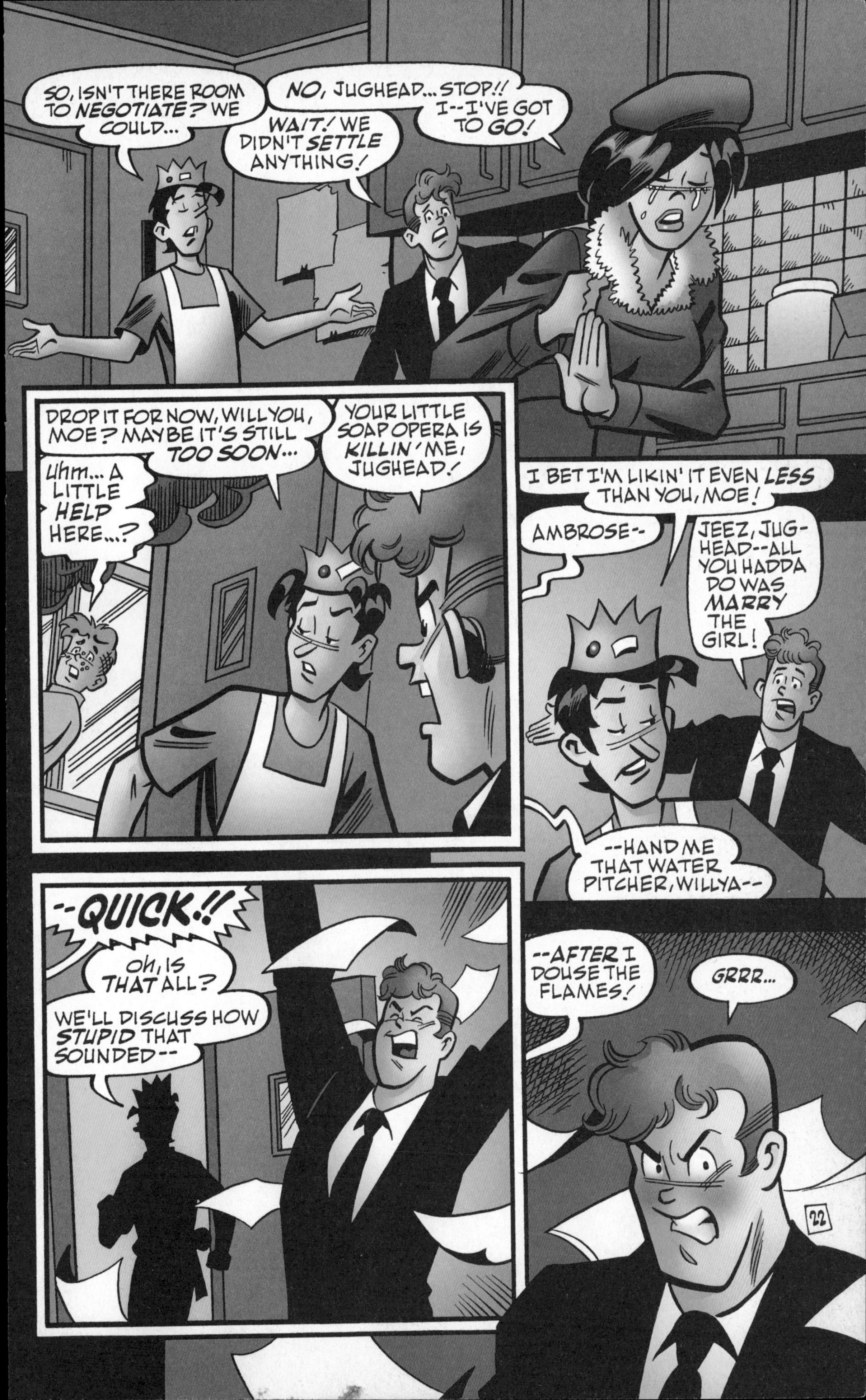
SO, ISN'T THERE ROOM TO NEGOTIATE? WE COULD...
NO, JUGHEAD... STOP!! I--I'VE GOT TO GO!
WAIT! WE DIDN'T SETTLE ANYTHING!
DROP IT FOR NOW, WILL YOU, MOE? MAYBE IT'S STILL TOO SOON...
YOUR LITTLE SOAP OPERA IS KILLIN' ME, JUGHEAD!
Uhm... A LITTLE HELP HERE...?
I BET I'M LIKIN' IT EVEN LESS THAN YOU, MOE!
AMBROSE--
JEEZ, JUG-HEAD--ALL YOU HADDA DO WAS MARRY THE GIRL!
--HAND ME THAT WATER PITCHER, WILLYA--
--QUICK!!
Oh, IS THAT ALL?
WE'LL DISCUSS HOW STUPID THAT SOUNDED--
--AFTER I DOUSE THE FLAMES!
GRRR...
22

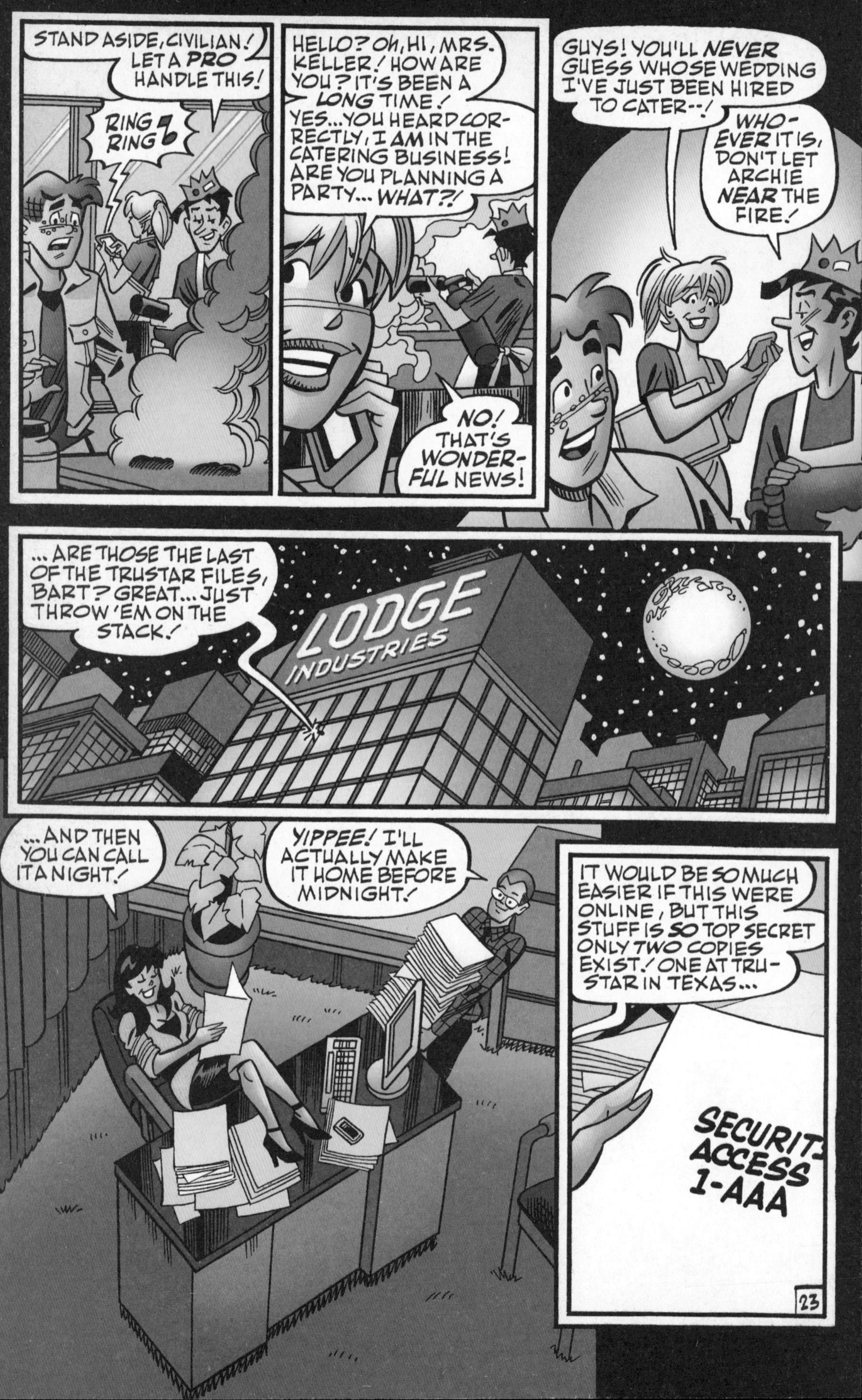
STAND ASIDE, CIVILIAN! LET A PRO HANDLE THIS!
RING RING
HELLO? OH, HI, MRS. KELLER! HOW ARE YOU? IT'S BEEN A LONG TIME! YES...YOU HEARD CORRECTLY, I AM IN THE CATERING BUSINESS! ARE YOU PLANNING A PARTY... WHAT?!
NO! THAT'S WONDERFUL NEWS!
GUYS! YOU'LL NEVER GUESS WHOSE WEDDING I'VE JUST BEEN HIRED TO CATER--!
WHOEVER IT IS, DON'T LET ARCHIE NEAR THE FIRE!
... ARE THOSE THE LAST OF THE TRUSTAR FILES, BART? GREAT... JUST THROW 'EM ON THE STACK!
LODGE INDUSTRIES
... AND THEN YOU CAN CALL IT A NIGHT!
YIPPEE! I'LL ACTUALLY MAKE IT HOME BEFORE MIDNIGHT!
IT WOULD BE SO MUCH EASIER IF THIS WERE ONLINE, BUT THIS STUFF IS SO TOP SECRET ONLY TWO COPIES EXIST! ONE AT TRUSTAR IN TEXAS...
SECURIT- ACCESS 1-AAA

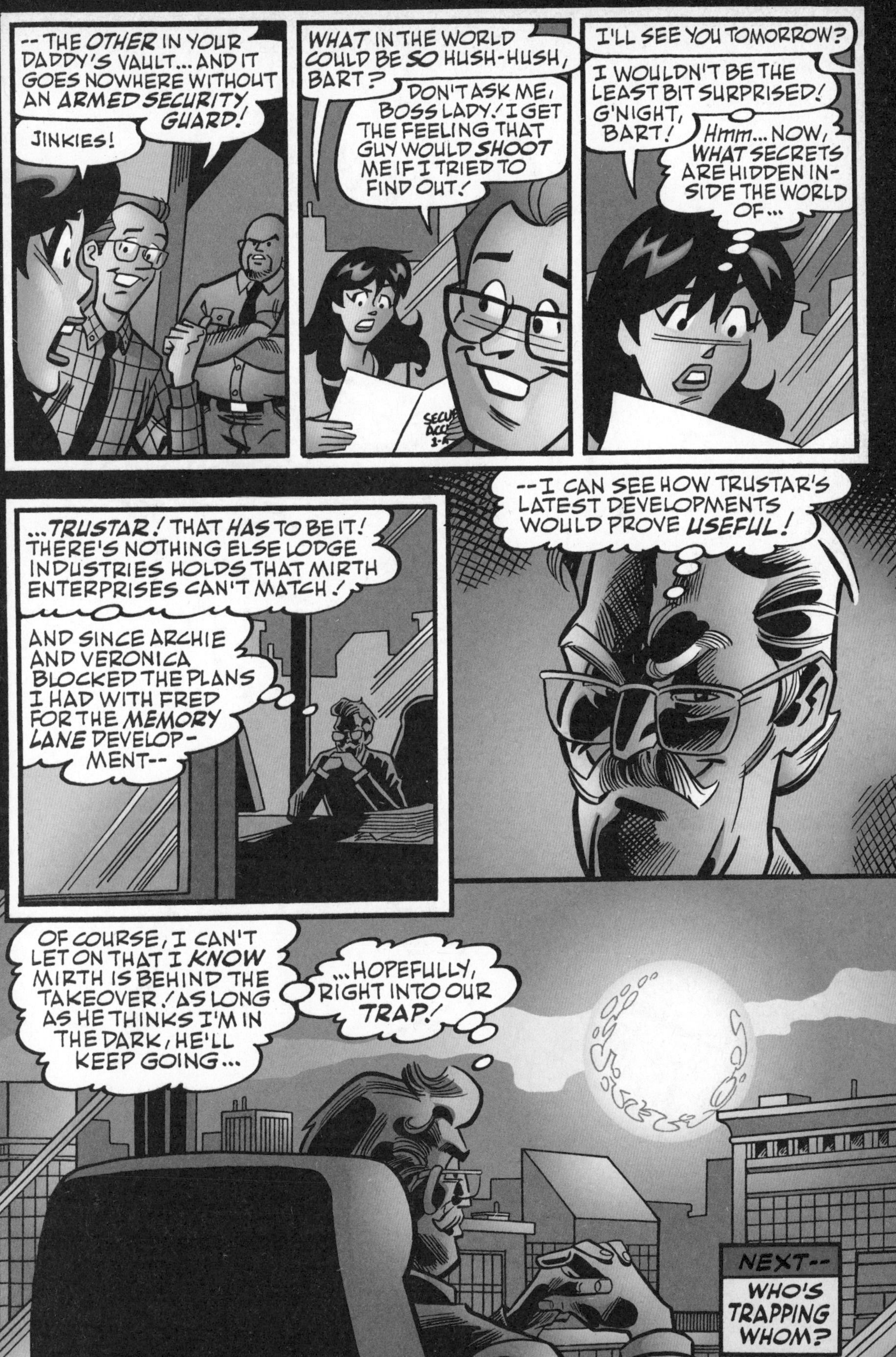
-- THE OTHER IN YOUR DADDY'S VAULT... AND IT GOES NOWHERE WITHOUT AN ARMED SECURITY GUARD!
JINKIES!
WHAT IN THE WORLD COULD BE SO HUSH-HUSH, BART?
DON'T ASK ME, BOSS LADY! I GET THE FEELING THAT GUY WOULD SHOOT ME IF I TRIED TO FIND OUT!
I'LL SEE YOU TOMORROW?
I WOULDN'T BE THE LEAST BIT SURPRISED! G'NIGHT, BART!
Hmm... NOW, WHAT SECRETS ARE HIDDEN INSIDE THE WORLD OF...
...TRUSTAR! THAT HAS TO BE IT! THERE'S NOTHING ELSE LODGE INDUSTRIES HOLDS THAT MIRTH ENTERPRISES CAN'T MATCH!
AND SINCE ARCHIE AND VERONICA BLOCKED THE PLANS I HAD WITH FRED FOR THE MEMORY LANE DEVELOPMENT--
--I CAN SEE HOW TRUSTAR'S LATEST DEVELOPMENTS WOULD PROVE USEFUL!
OF COURSE, I CAN'T LET ON THAT I KNOW MIRTH IS BEHIND THE TAKEOVER! AS LONG AS HE THINKS I'M IN THE DARK, HE'LL KEEP GOING...
...HOPEFULLY, RIGHT INTO OUR TRAP!
NEXT--
WHO'S TRAPPING WHOM?

"THE SEARCH FOR HIS DAUGHTER WAS DISTRACTING HIM,"

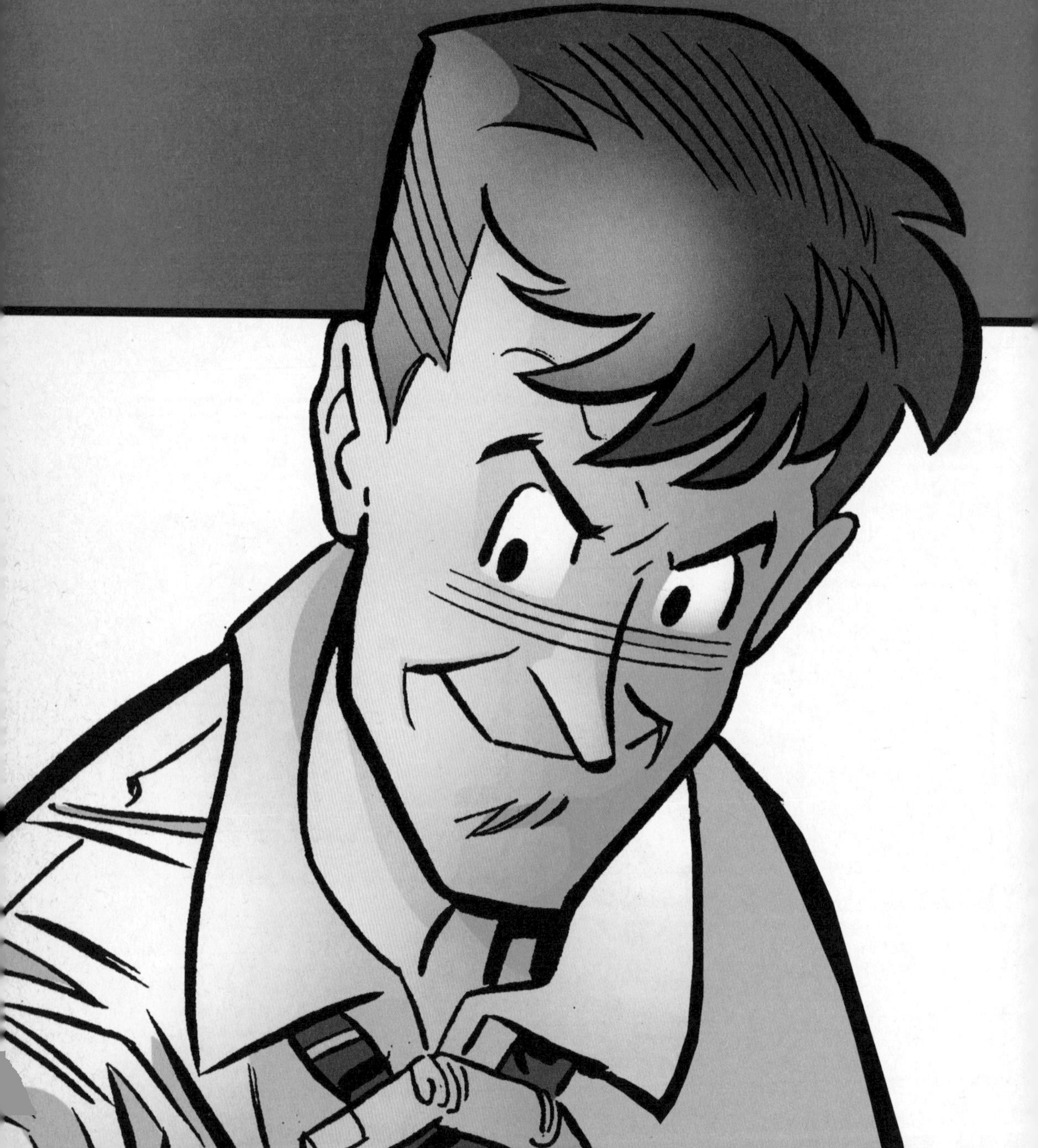

"BUT I SUPPOSE EVEN THE MOST *OPTIMISTIC* FATHER GIVES UP HOPE... ***EVENTUALLY!***"

- *FRED MIRTH*

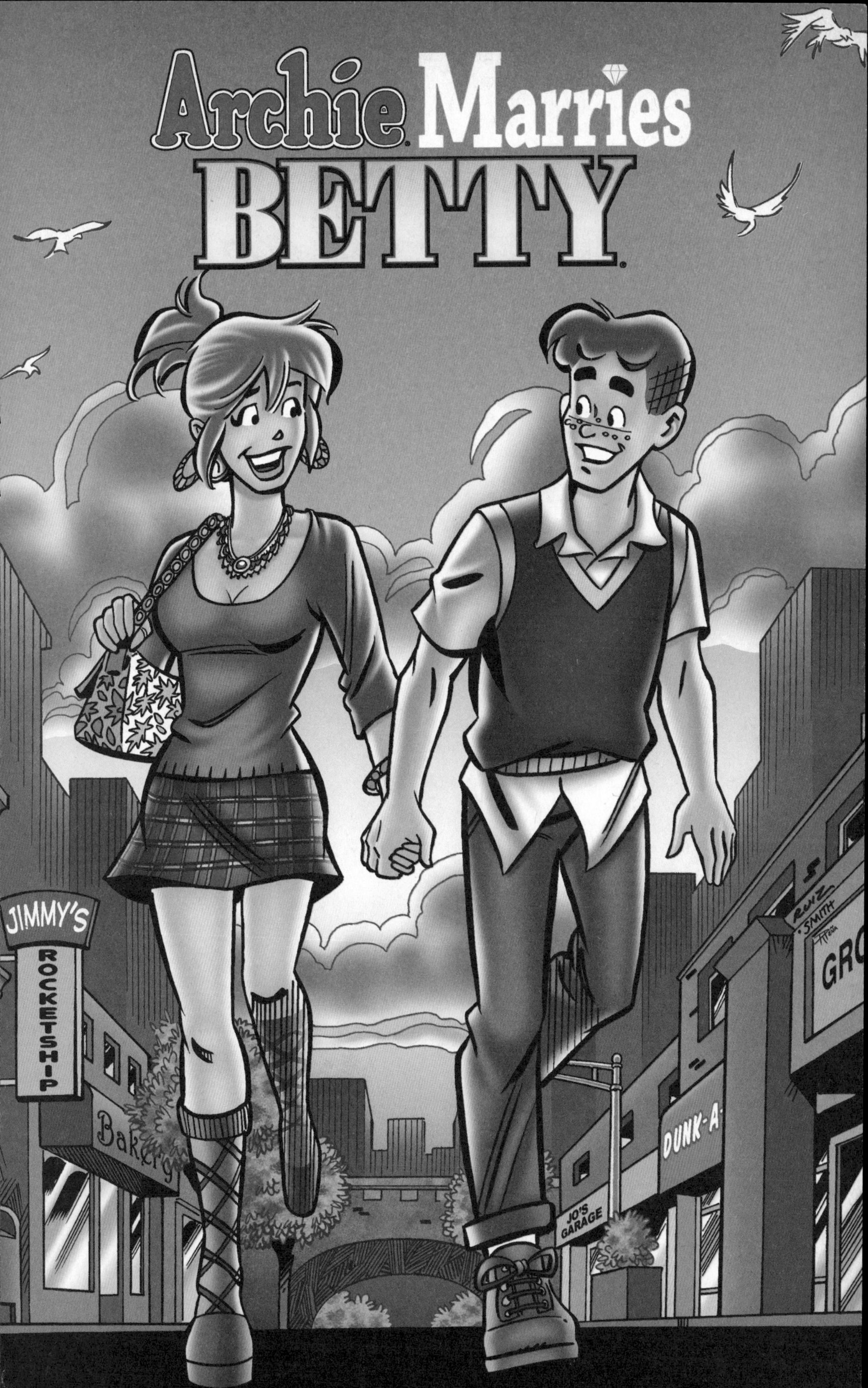

Archie Marries
BETTY
JIMMY'S
ROCKETSHIP
Bakery
DUNK-A-
JO'S GARAGE
GRO

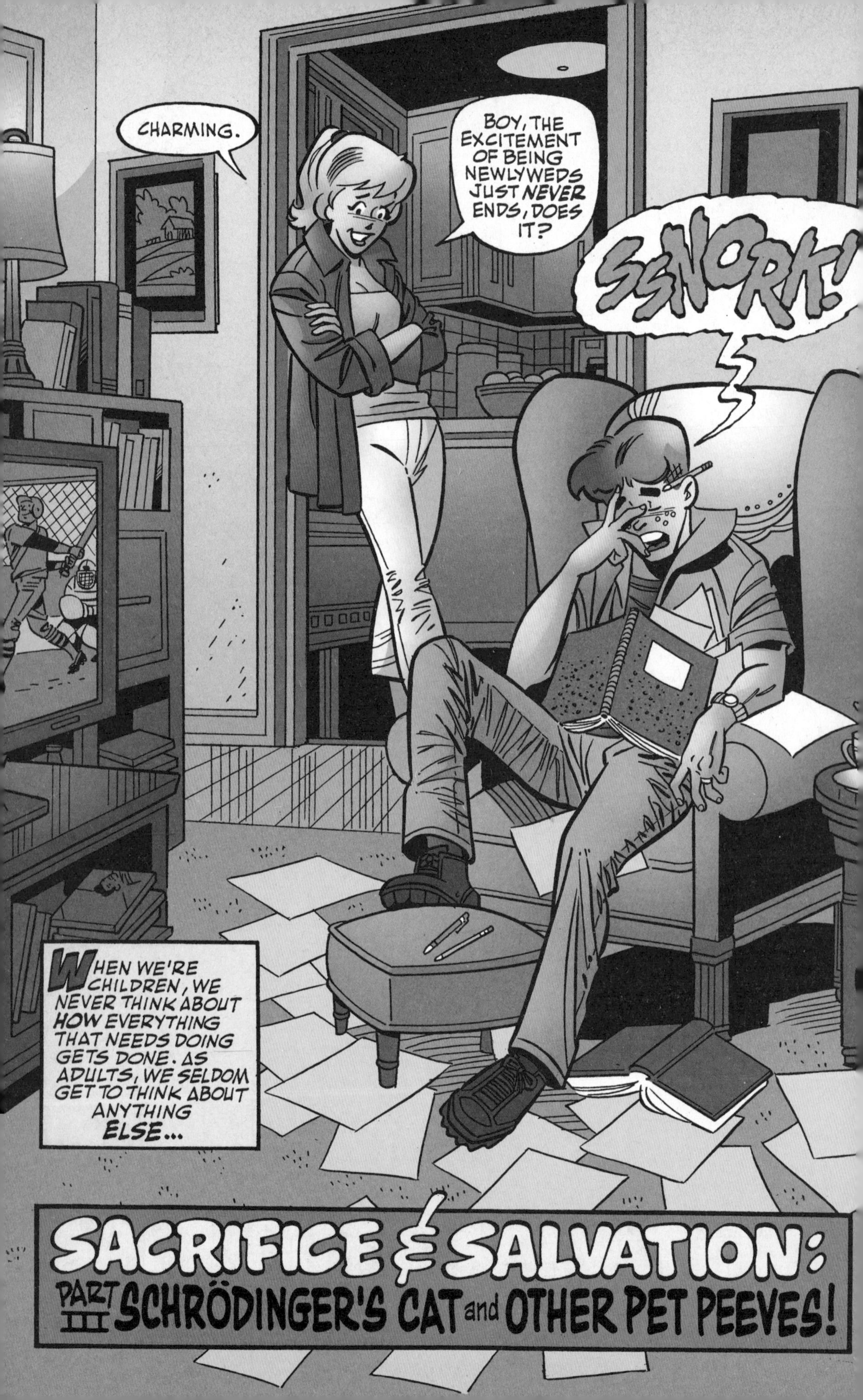
CHARMING.
BOY, THE EXCITEMENT OF BEING NEWLYWEDS JUST NEVER ENDS, DOES IT?
SSNORK!
WHEN WE'RE CHILDREN, WE NEVER THINK ABOUT HOW EVERYTHING THAT NEEDS DOING GETS DONE. AS ADULTS, WE SELDOM GET TO THINK ABOUT ANYTHING ELSE...
SACRIFICE & SALVATION:
PART III SCHRÖDINGER'S CAT and OTHER PET PEEVES!

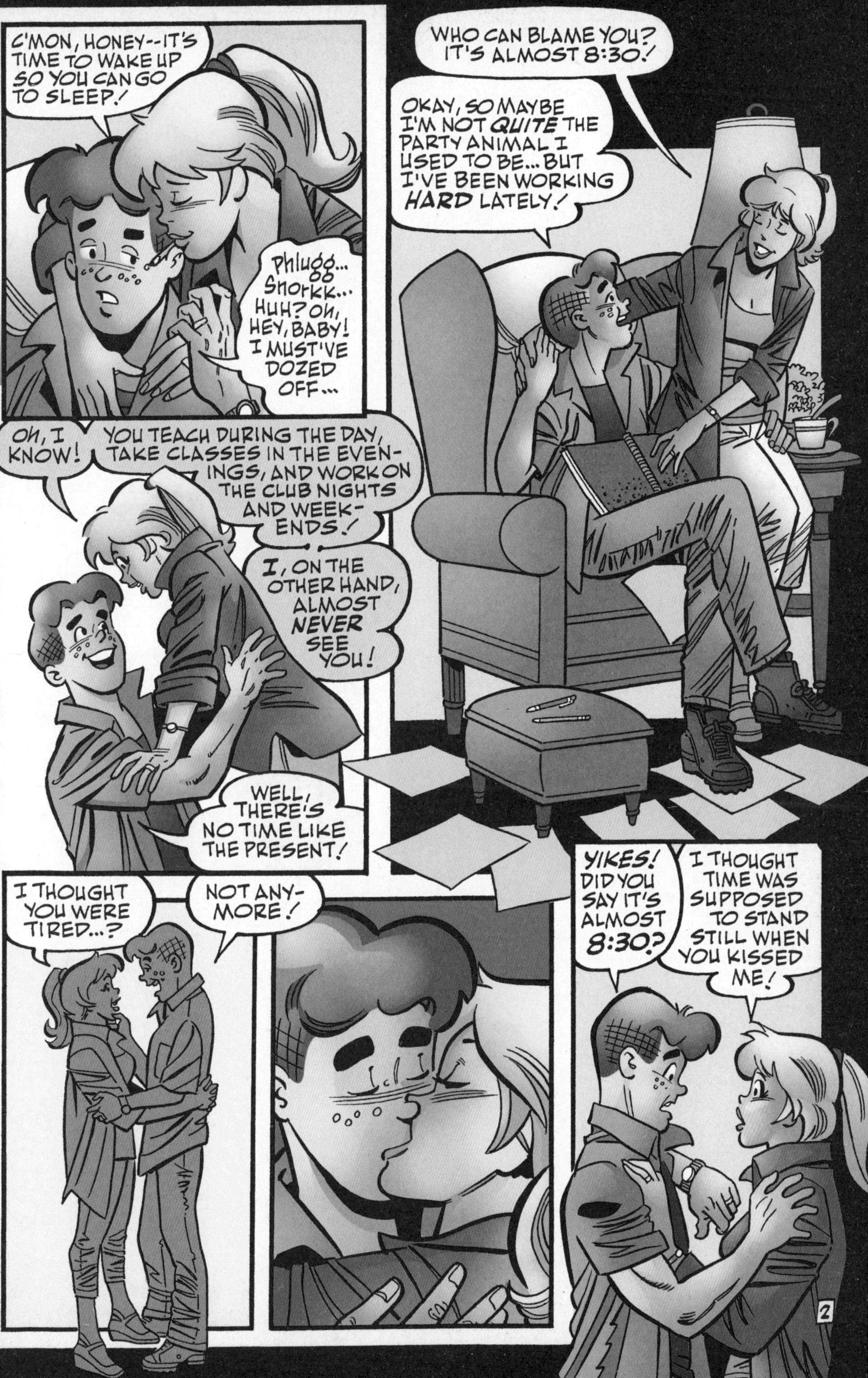
C'MON, HONEY--IT'S TIME TO WAKE UP SO YOU CAN GO TO SLEEP!
Phlugg... Snorkk... HUH? OH, HEY, BABY! I MUST'VE DOZED OFF...
WHO CAN BLAME YOU? IT'S ALMOST 8:30!
OKAY, SO MAYBE I'M NOT QUITE THE PARTY ANIMAL I USED TO BE... BUT I'VE BEEN WORKING HARD LATELY!
OH, I KNOW!
YOU TEACH DURING THE DAY, TAKE CLASSES IN THE EVENINGS, AND WORK ON THE CLUB NIGHTS AND WEEKENDS!
I, ON THE OTHER HAND, ALMOST NEVER SEE YOU!
WELL, THERE'S NO TIME LIKE THE PRESENT!
I THOUGHT YOU WERE TIRED...?
NOT ANYMORE!
YIKES! DID YOU SAY IT'S ALMOST 8:30?
I THOUGHT TIME WAS SUPPOSED TO STAND STILL WHEN YOU KISSED ME!
2

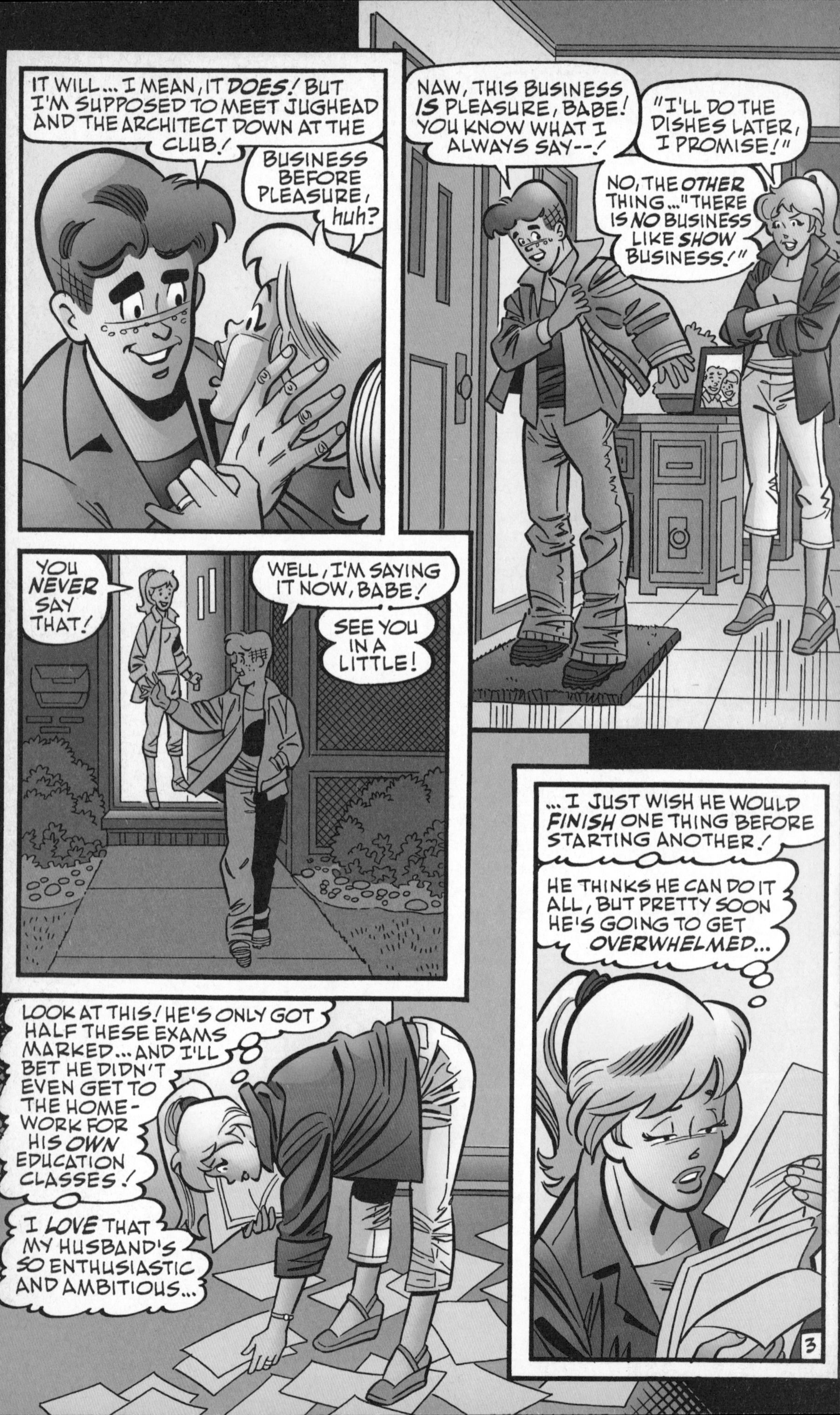
IT WILL... I MEAN, IT DOES! BUT I'M SUPPOSED TO MEET JUGHEAD AND THE ARCHITECT DOWN AT THE CLUB!
BUSINESS BEFORE PLEASURE, huh?
NAW, THIS BUSINESS IS PLEASURE, BABE! YOU KNOW WHAT I ALWAYS SAY--!
"I'LL DO THE DISHES LATER, I PROMISE!"
NO, THE OTHER THING..."THERE IS NO BUSINESS LIKE SHOW BUSINESS!"
YOU NEVER SAY THAT!
WELL, I'M SAYING IT NOW, BABE!
SEE YOU IN A LITTLE!
...I JUST WISH HE WOULD FINISH ONE THING BEFORE STARTING ANOTHER!
HE THINKS HE CAN DO IT ALL, BUT PRETTY SOON HE'S GOING TO GET OVERWHELMED...
LOOK AT THIS! HE'S ONLY GOT HALF THESE EXAMS MARKED... AND I'LL BET HE DIDN'T EVEN GET TO THE HOME-WORK FOR HIS OWN EDUCATION CLASSES!
I LOVE THAT MY HUSBAND'S SO ENTHUSIASTIC AND AMBITIOUS...
3

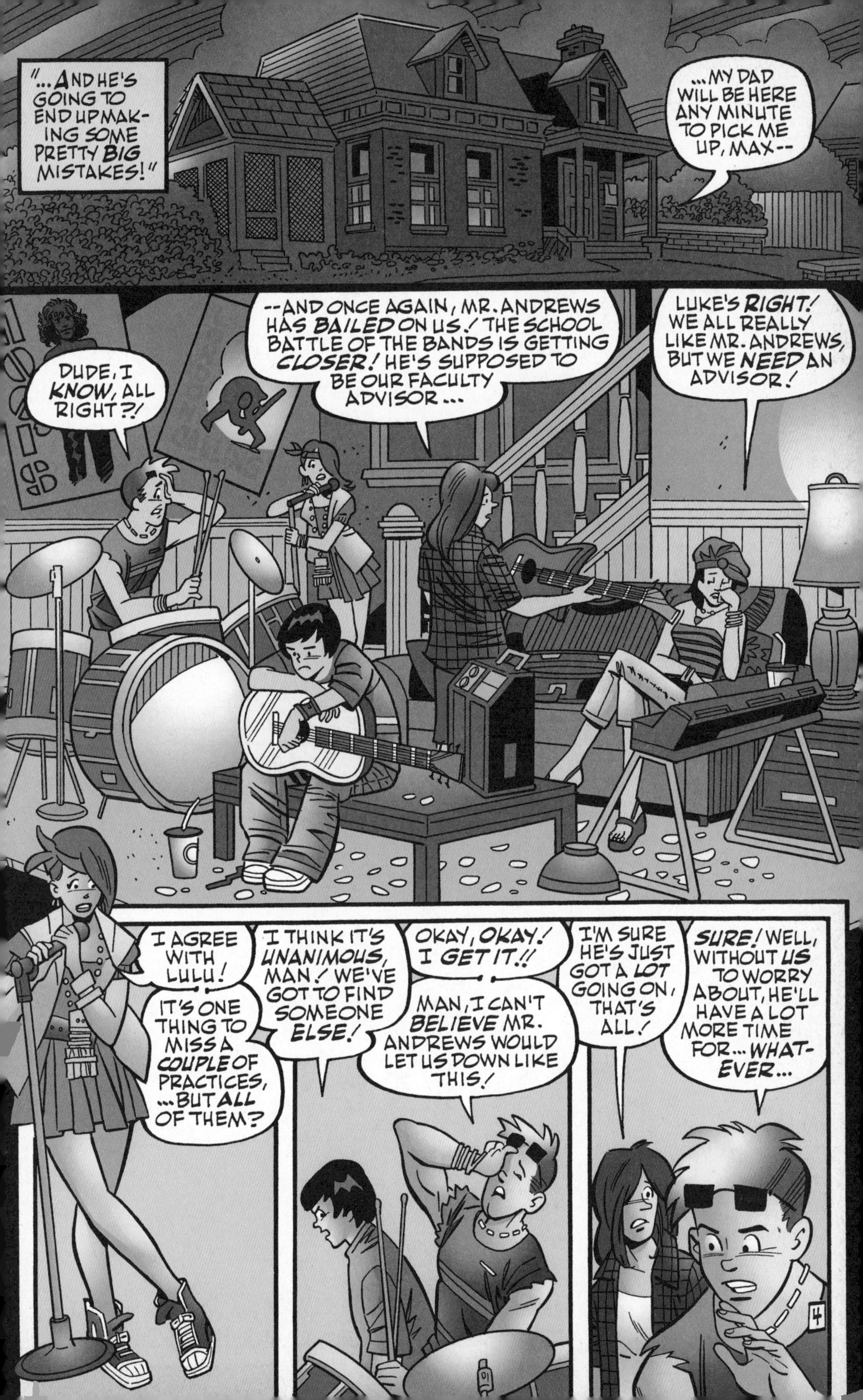
"...AND HE'S GOING TO END UP MAKING SOME PRETTY BIG MISTAKES!"
...MY DAD WILL BE HERE ANY MINUTE TO PICK ME UP, MAX--
DUDE, I KNOW, ALL RIGHT?!
--AND ONCE AGAIN, MR. ANDREWS HAS BAILED ON US! THE SCHOOL BATTLE OF THE BANDS IS GETTING CLOSER! HE'S SUPPOSED TO BE OUR FACULTY ADVISOR...
LUKE'S RIGHT! WE ALL REALLY LIKE MR. ANDREWS, BUT WE NEED AN ADVISOR!
I AGREE WITH LULU!
IT'S ONE THING TO MISS A COUPLE OF PRACTICES, ...BUT ALL OF THEM?
I THINK IT'S UNANIMOUS, MAN! WE'VE GOT TO FIND SOMEONE ELSE!
OKAY, OKAY! I GET IT!!
MAN, I CAN'T BELIEVE MR. ANDREWS WOULD LET US DOWN LIKE THIS!
I'M SURE HE'S JUST GOT A LOT GOING ON, THAT'S ALL!
SURE! WELL, WITHOUT US TO WORRY ABOUT, HE'LL HAVE A LOT MORE TIME FOR...WHATEVER...
4

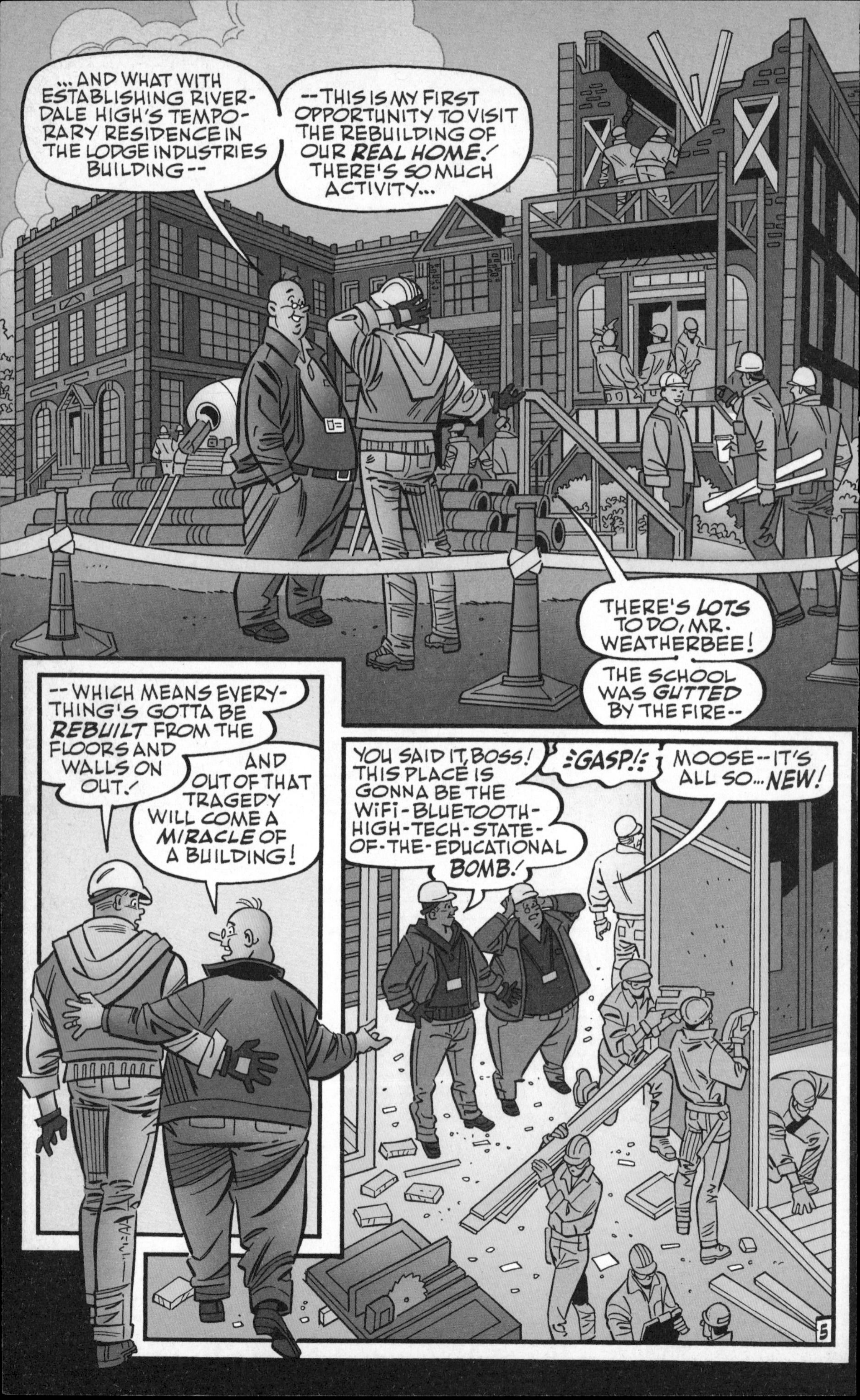
...AND WHAT WITH ESTABLISHING RIVERDALE HIGH'S TEMPORARY RESIDENCE IN THE LODGE INDUSTRIES BUILDING--
--THIS IS MY FIRST OPPORTUNITY TO VISIT THE REBUILDING OF OUR REAL HOME! THERE'S SO MUCH ACTIVITY...
THERE'S LOTS TO DO, MR. WEATHERBEE!
THE SCHOOL WAS GUTTED BY THE FIRE--
--WHICH MEANS EVERYTHING'S GOTTA BE REBUILT FROM THE FLOORS AND WALLS ON OUT!
AND OUT OF THAT TRAGEDY WILL COME A MIRACLE OF A BUILDING!
YOU SAID IT, BOSS! THIS PLACE IS GONNA BE THE WiFi-BLUETOOTH-HIGH-TECH-STATE-OF-THE-EDUCATIONAL BOMB!
GASP!
MOOSE--IT'S ALL SO...NEW!
5

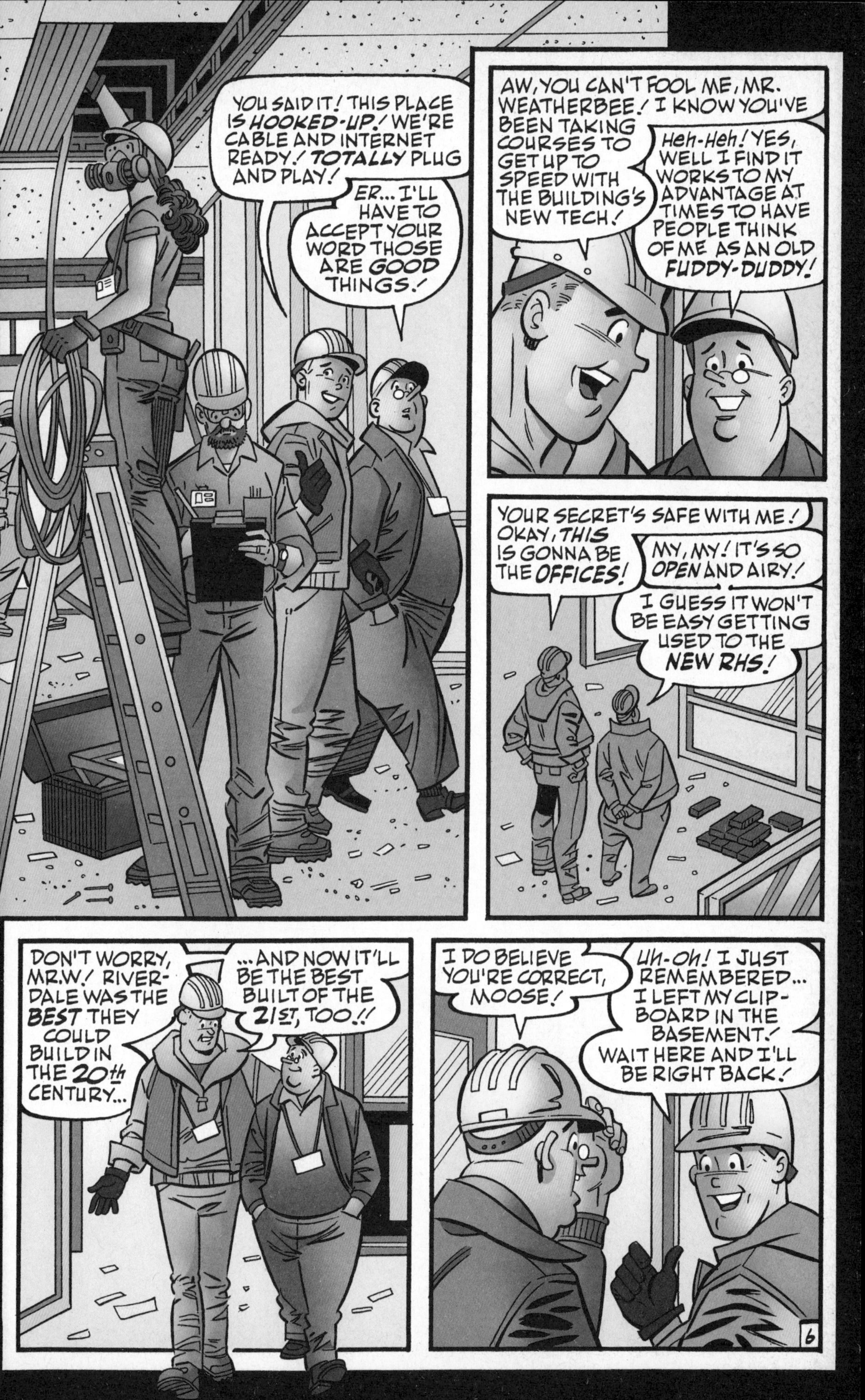
YOU SAID IT! THIS PLACE IS HOOKED-UP! WE'RE CABLE AND INTERNET READY! TOTALLY PLUG AND PLAY!
ER... I'LL HAVE TO ACCEPT YOUR WORD THOSE ARE GOOD THINGS!
AW, YOU CAN'T FOOL ME, MR. WEATHERBEE! I KNOW YOU'VE BEEN TAKING COURSES TO GET UP TO SPEED WITH THE BUILDING'S NEW TECH!
Heh-Heh! YES, WELL I FIND IT WORKS TO MY ADVANTAGE AT TIMES TO HAVE PEOPLE THINK OF ME AS AN OLD FUDDY-DUDDY!
YOUR SECRET'S SAFE WITH ME! OKAY, THIS IS GONNA BE THE OFFICES!
MY, MY! IT'S SO OPEN AND AIRY!
I GUESS IT WON'T BE EASY GETTING USED TO THE NEW RHS!
DON'T WORRY, MR.W! RIVERDALE WAS THE BEST THEY COULD BUILD IN THE 20th CENTURY...
...AND NOW IT'LL BE THE BEST BUILT OF THE 21ST, TOO!!
I DO BELIEVE YOU'RE CORRECT, MOOSE!
UH-OH! I JUST REMEMBERED... I LEFT MY CLIPBOARD IN THE BASEMENT! WAIT HERE AND I'LL BE RIGHT BACK!
6

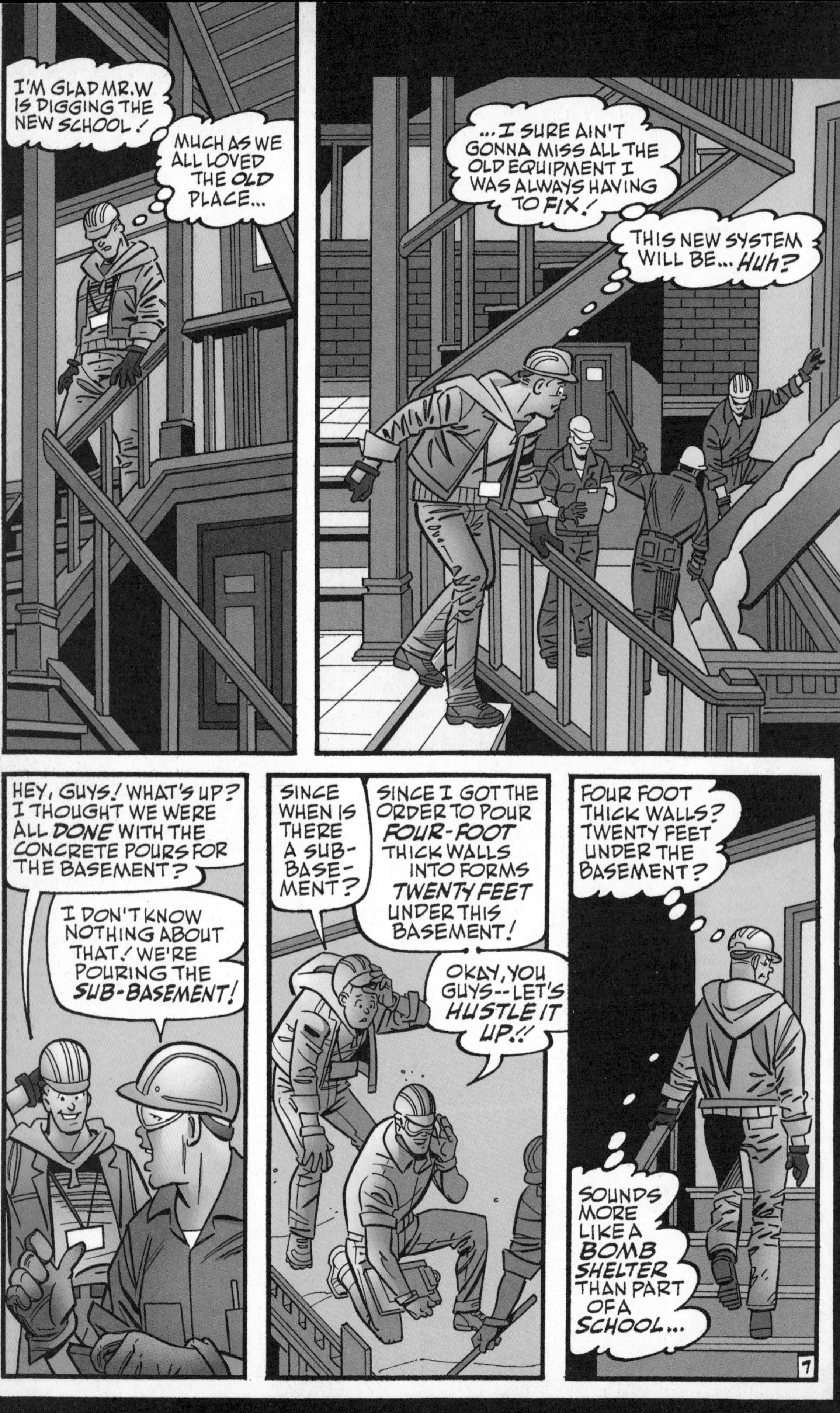
I'M GLAD MR.W IS DIGGING THE NEW SCHOOL!
MUCH AS WE ALL LOVED THE OLD PLACE...
...I SURE AIN'T GONNA MISS ALL THE OLD EQUIPMENT I WAS ALWAYS HAVING TO FIX!
THIS NEW SYSTEM WILL BE... Huh?
HEY, GUYS! WHAT'S UP? I THOUGHT WE WERE ALL DONE WITH THE CONCRETE POURS FOR THE BASEMENT?
I DON'T KNOW NOTHING ABOUT THAT! WE'RE POURING THE SUB-BASEMENT!
SINCE WHEN IS THERE A SUB-BASEMENT?
SINCE I GOT THE ORDER TO POUR FOUR-FOOT THICK WALLS INTO FORMS TWENTY FEET UNDER THIS BASEMENT!
OKAY, YOU GUYS--LET'S HUSTLE IT UP!!
FOUR FOOT THICK WALLS? TWENTY FEET UNDER THE BASEMENT?
SOUNDS MORE LIKE A BOMB SHELTER THAN PART OF A SCHOOL...

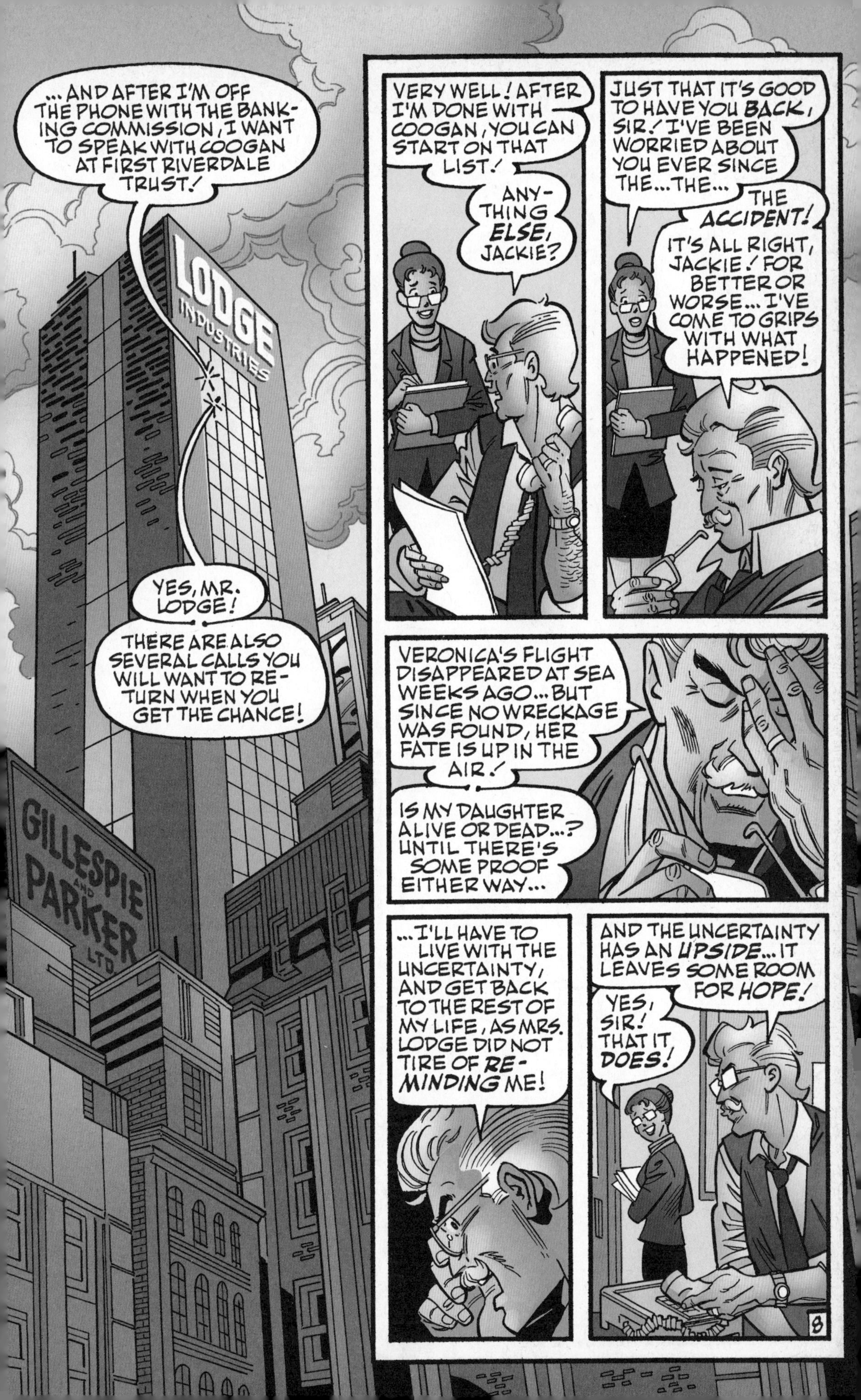
...AND AFTER I'M OFF THE PHONE WITH THE BANKING COMMISSION, I WANT TO SPEAK WITH COOGAN AT FIRST RIVERDALE TRUST!
LODGE INDUSTRIES
YES, MR. LODGE!
THERE ARE ALSO SEVERAL CALLS YOU WILL WANT TO RETURN WHEN YOU GET THE CHANCE!
GILLESPIE AND PARKER LTD.
VERY WELL! AFTER I'M DONE WITH COOGAN, YOU CAN START ON THAT LIST!
ANYTHING ELSE, JACKIE?
JUST THAT IT'S GOOD TO HAVE YOU BACK, SIR! I'VE BEEN WORRIED ABOUT YOU EVER SINCE THE...THE...
THE ACCIDENT!
IT'S ALL RIGHT, JACKIE! FOR BETTER OR WORSE... I'VE COME TO GRIPS WITH WHAT HAPPENED!
VERONICA'S FLIGHT DISAPPEARED AT SEA WEEKS AGO... BUT SINCE NO WRECKAGE WAS FOUND, HER FATE IS UP IN THE AIR!
IS MY DAUGHTER ALIVE OR DEAD...? UNTIL THERE'S SOME PROOF EITHER WAY...
...I'LL HAVE TO LIVE WITH THE UNCERTAINTY, AND GET BACK TO THE REST OF MY LIFE, AS MRS. LODGE DID NOT TIRE OF REMINDING ME!
AND THE UNCERTAINTY HAS AN UPSIDE... IT LEAVES SOME ROOM FOR HOPE!
YES, SIR! THAT IT DOES!
8

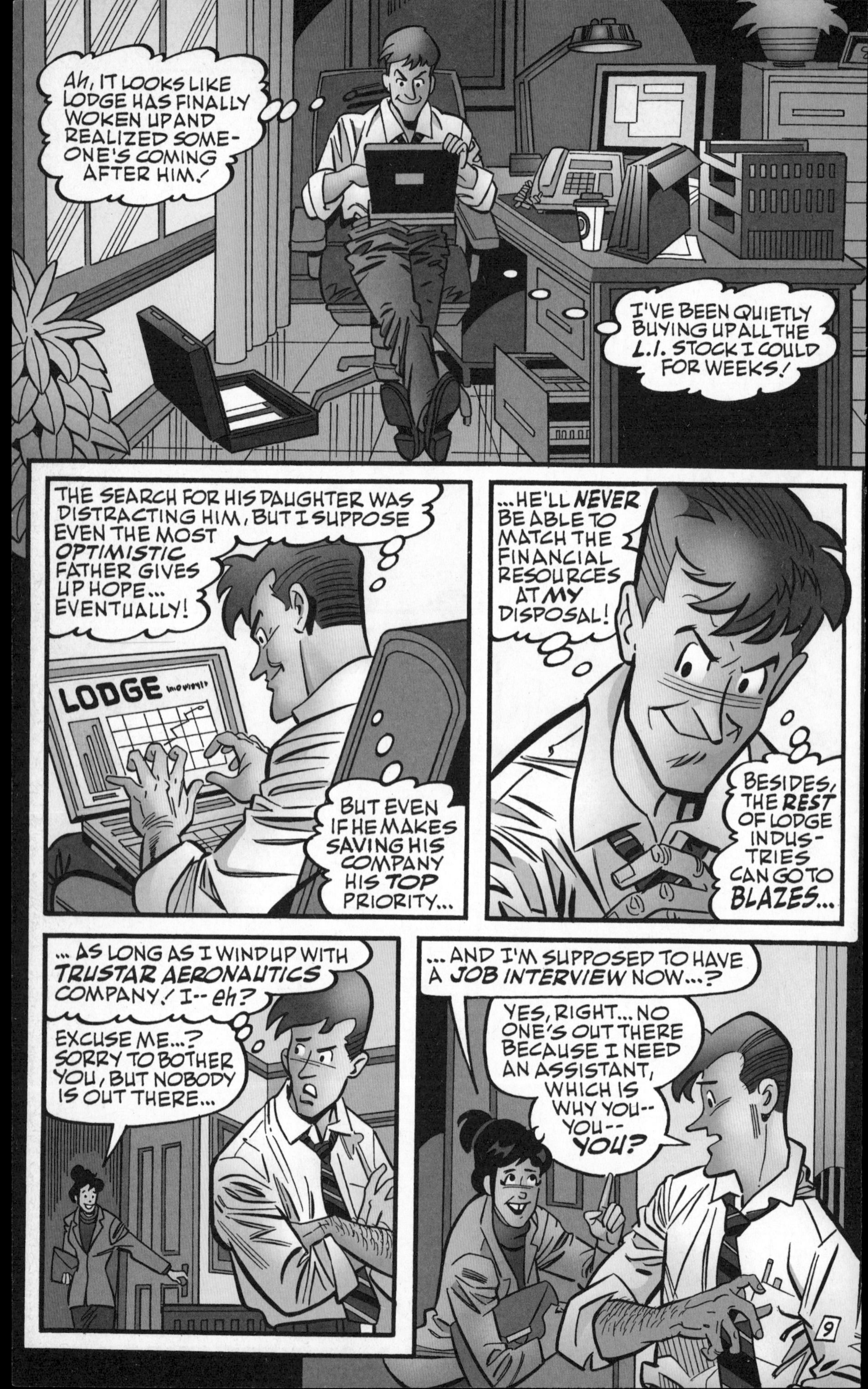

AH, IT LOOKS LIKE LODGE HAS FINALLY WOKEN UP AND REALIZED SOME-ONE'S COMING AFTER HIM!
I'VE BEEN QUIETLY BUYING UP ALL THE L.I. STOCK I COULD FOR WEEKS!
THE SEARCH FOR HIS DAUGHTER WAS DISTRACTING HIM, BUT I SUPPOSE EVEN THE MOST OPTIMISTIC FATHER GIVES UP HOPE... EVENTUALLY!
LODGE
BUT EVEN IF HE MAKES SAVING HIS COMPANY HIS TOP PRIORITY...
...HE'LL NEVER BE ABLE TO MATCH THE FINANCIAL RESOURCES AT MY DISPOSAL!
BESIDES, THE REST OF LODGE INDUS-TRIES CAN GO TO BLAZES...
... AS LONG AS I WIND UP WITH TRUSTAR AERONAUTICS COMPANY! I-- EH?
EXCUSE ME...? SORRY TO BOTHER YOU, BUT NOBODY IS OUT THERE...
... AND I'M SUPPOSED TO HAVE A JOB INTERVIEW NOW...?
YES, RIGHT... NO ONE'S OUT THERE BECAUSE I NEED AN ASSISTANT, WHICH IS WHY YOU-- YOU-- YOU-- YOU?

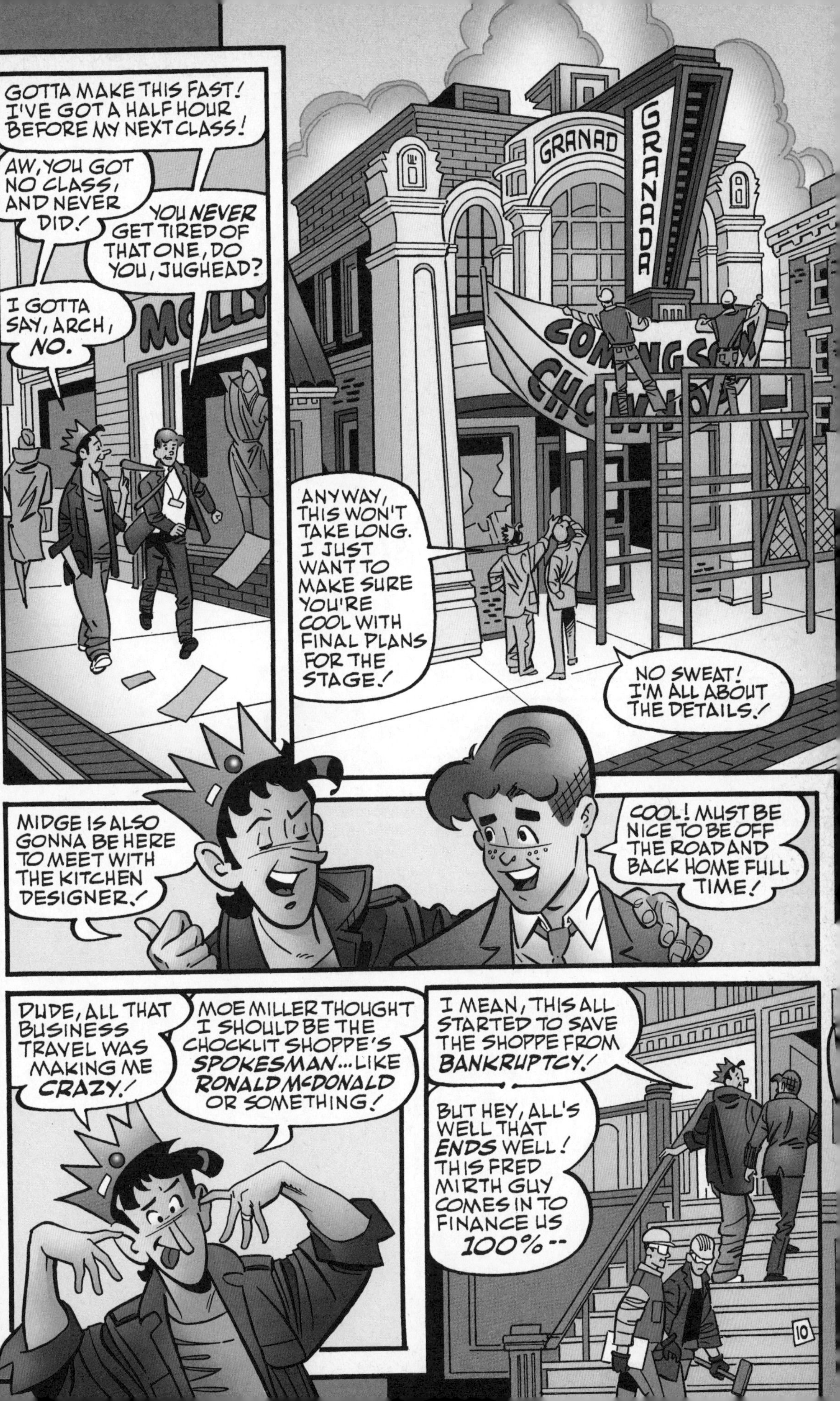
GOTTA MAKE THIS FAST! I'VE GOT A HALF HOUR BEFORE MY NEXT CLASS!
AW, YOU GOT NO CLASS, AND NEVER DID!
YOU NEVER GET TIRED OF THAT ONE, DO YOU, JUGHEAD?
I GOTTA SAY, ARCH, NO.
MOLLY
GRANAD
GRANADA
ANYWAY, THIS WON'T TAKE LONG. I JUST WANT TO MAKE SURE YOU'RE COOL WITH FINAL PLANS FOR THE STAGE!
NO SWEAT! I'M ALL ABOUT THE DETAILS!
MIDGE IS ALSO GONNA BE HERE TO MEET WITH THE KITCHEN DESIGNER!
COOL! MUST BE NICE TO BE OFF THE ROAD AND BACK HOME FULL TIME!
DUDE, ALL THAT BUSINESS TRAVEL WAS MAKING ME CRAZY!
MOE MILLER THOUGHT I SHOULD BE THE CHOCKLIT SHOPPE'S SPOKESMAN... LIKE RONALD McDONALD OR SOMETHING!
I MEAN, THIS ALL STARTED TO SAVE THE SHOPPE FROM BANKRUPTCY!
BUT HEY, ALL'S WELL THAT ENDS WELL! THIS FRED MIRTH GUY COMES IN TO FINANCE US 100% --

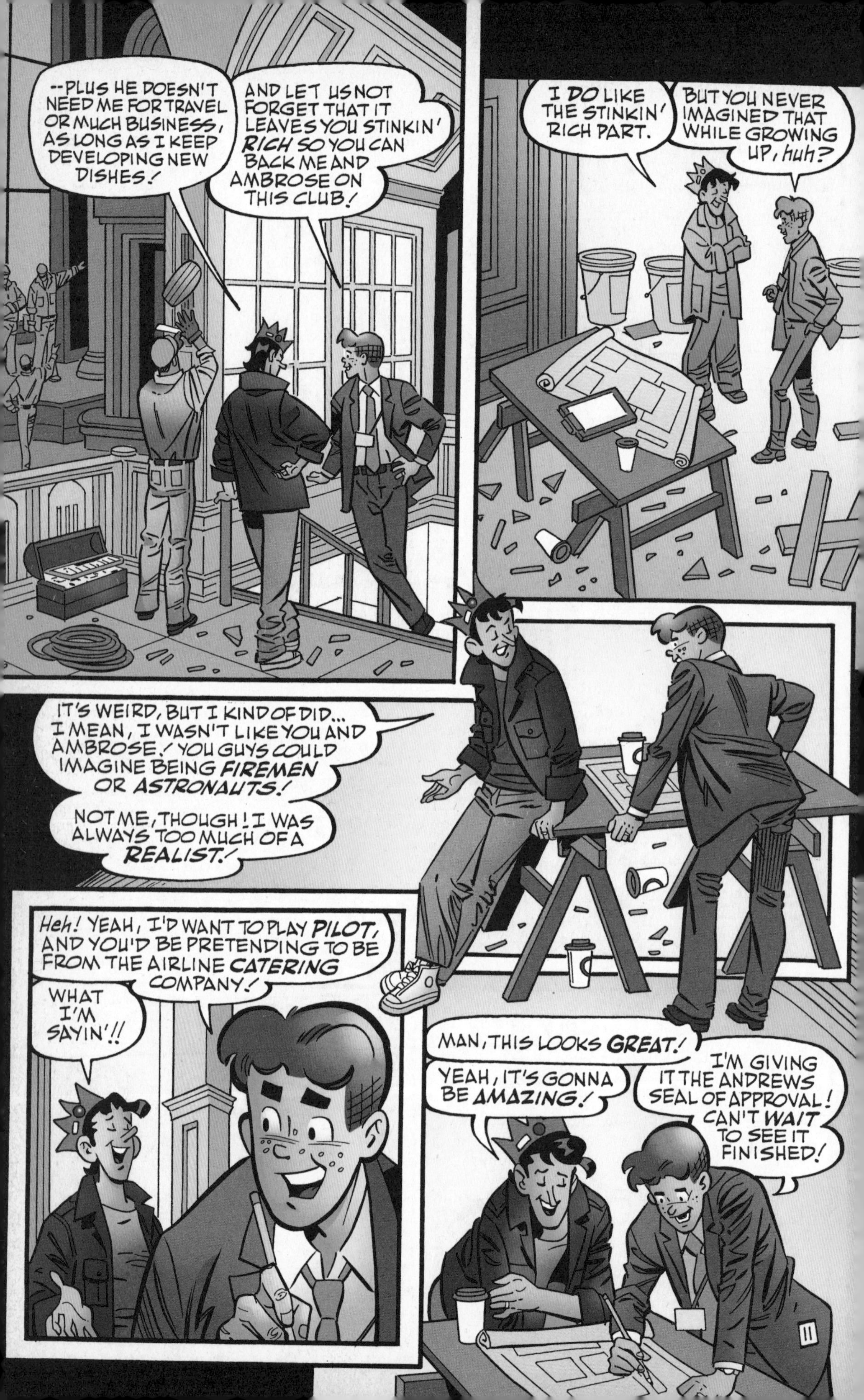
--PLUS HE DOESN'T NEED ME FOR TRAVEL OR MUCH BUSINESS, AS LONG AS I KEEP DEVELOPING NEW DISHES!
AND LET US NOT FORGET THAT IT LEAVES YOU STINKIN' RICH SO YOU CAN BACK ME AND AMBROSE ON THIS CLUB!
I DO LIKE THE STINKIN' RICH PART.
BUT YOU NEVER IMAGINED THAT WHILE GROWING UP, huh?
IT'S WEIRD, BUT I KIND OF DID... I MEAN, I WASN'T LIKE YOU AND AMBROSE! YOU GUYS COULD IMAGINE BEING FIREMEN OR ASTRONAUTS!
NOT ME, THOUGH! I WAS ALWAYS TOO MUCH OF A REALIST!
Heh! YEAH, I'D WANT TO PLAY PILOT, AND YOU'D BE PRETENDING TO BE FROM THE AIRLINE CATERING COMPANY!
WHAT I'M SAYIN'!!
MAN, THIS LOOKS GREAT!
YEAH, IT'S GONNA BE AMAZING!
I'M GIVING IT THE ANDREWS SEAL OF APPROVAL! CAN'T WAIT TO SEE IT FINISHED!
11

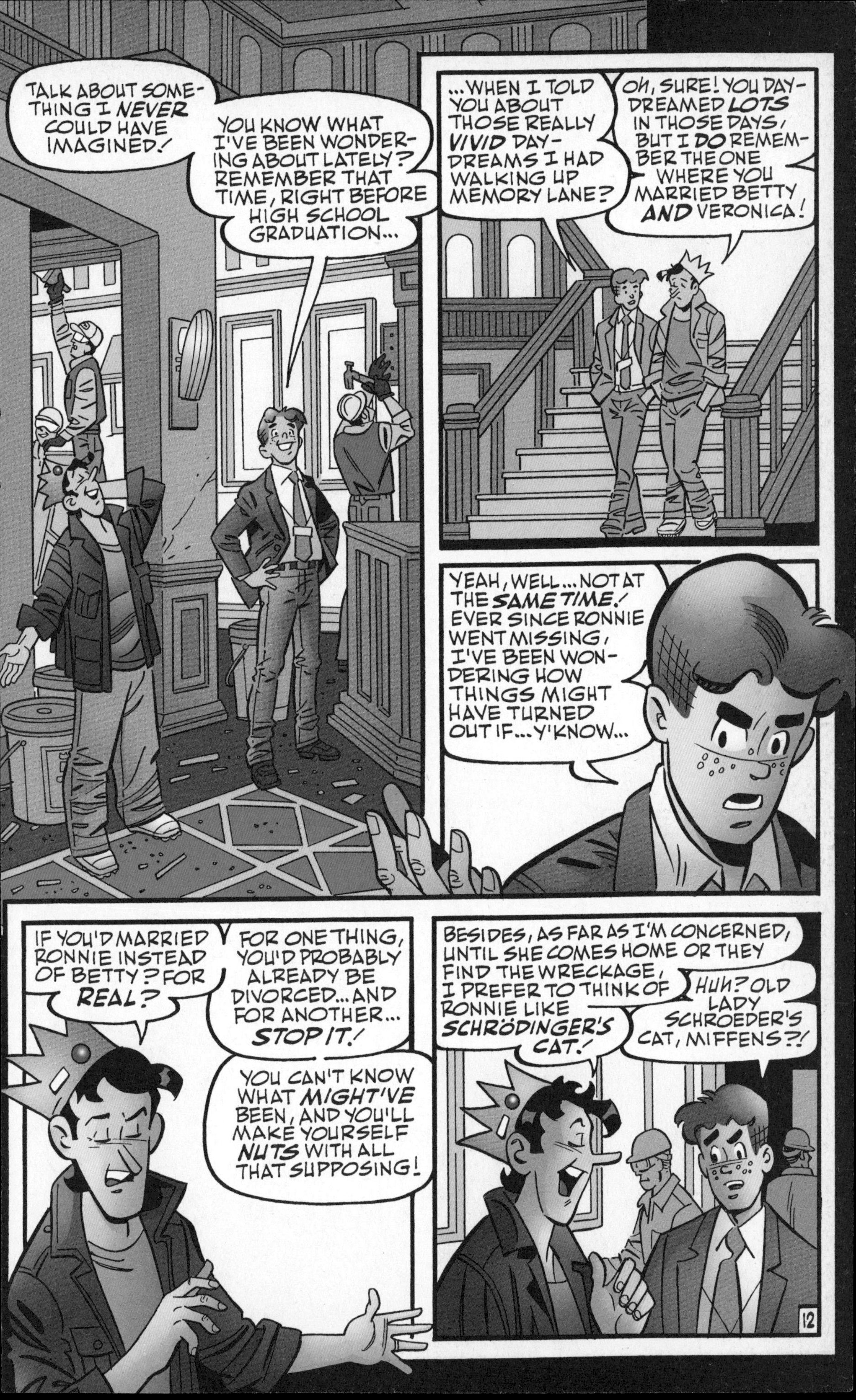
TALK ABOUT SOMETHING I NEVER COULD HAVE IMAGINED!
YOU KNOW WHAT I'VE BEEN WONDERING ABOUT LATELY? REMEMBER THAT TIME, RIGHT BEFORE HIGH SCHOOL GRADUATION...
...WHEN I TOLD YOU ABOUT THOSE REALLY VIVID DAYDREAMS I HAD WALKING UP MEMORY LANE?
OH, SURE! YOU DAYDREAMED LOTS IN THOSE DAYS, BUT I DO REMEMBER THE ONE WHERE YOU MARRIED BETTY AND VERONICA!
YEAH, WELL... NOT AT THE SAME TIME! EVER SINCE RONNIE WENT MISSING, I'VE BEEN WONDERING HOW THINGS MIGHT HAVE TURNED OUT IF... Y'KNOW...
IF YOU'D MARRIED RONNIE INSTEAD OF BETTY? FOR REAL?
FOR ONE THING, YOU'D PROBABLY ALREADY BE DIVORCED... AND FOR ANOTHER... STOP IT!
YOU CAN'T KNOW WHAT MIGHT'VE BEEN, AND YOU'LL MAKE YOURSELF NUTS WITH ALL THAT SUPPOSING!
BESIDES, AS FAR AS I'M CONCERNED, UNTIL SHE COMES HOME OR THEY FIND THE WRECKAGE, I PREFER TO THINK OF RONNIE LIKE SCHRÖDINGER'S CAT!
HUH? OLD LADY SCHROEDER'S CAT, MIFFENS?!
12

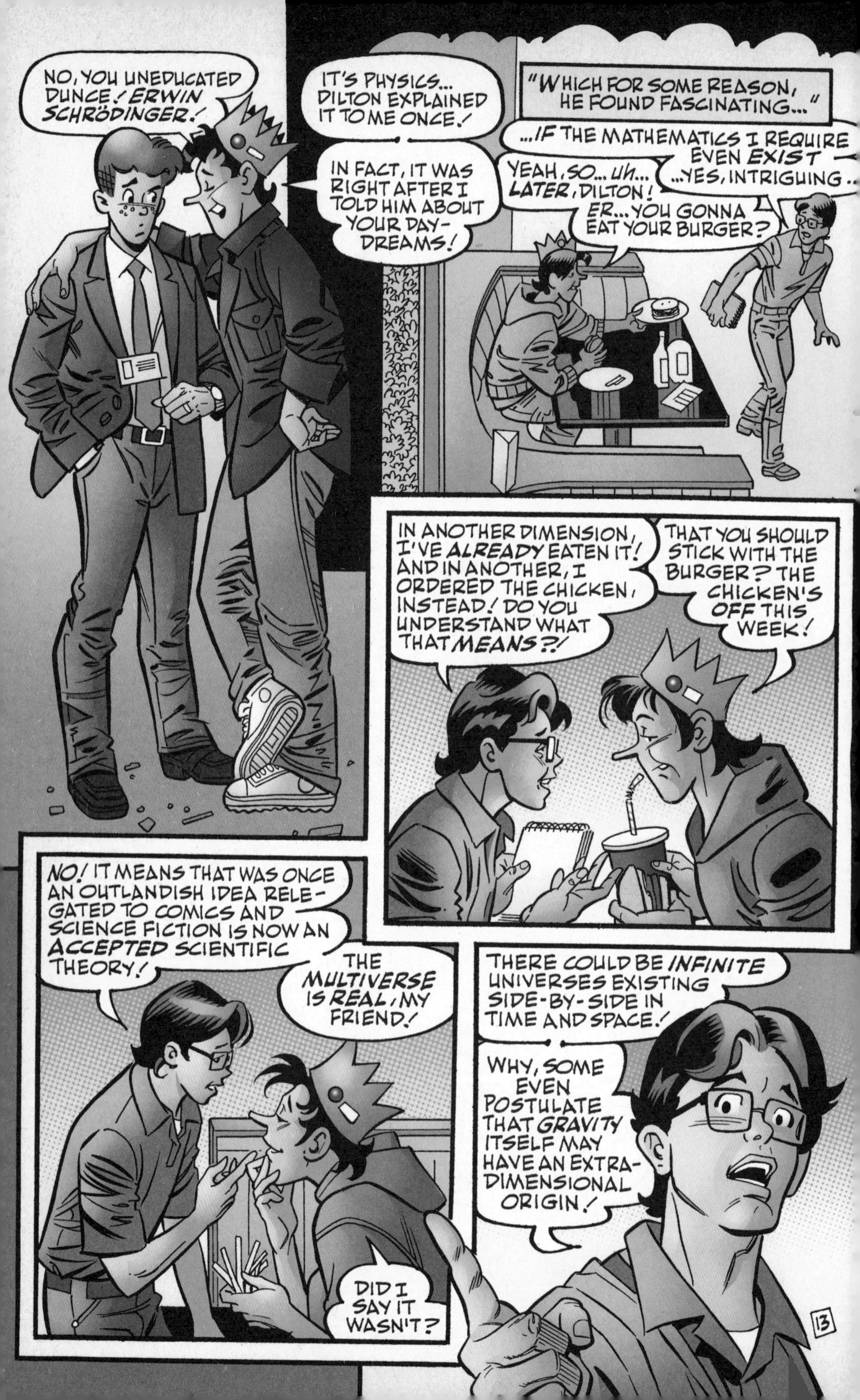
NO, YOU UNEDUCATED DUNCE! ERWIN SCHRÖDINGER!
IT'S PHYSICS... DILTON EXPLAINED IT TO ME ONCE!
IN FACT, IT WAS RIGHT AFTER I TOLD HIM ABOUT YOUR DAY-DREAMS!
"WHICH FOR SOME REASON, HE FOUND FASCINATING..."
...IF THE MATHEMATICS I REQUIRE EVEN EXIST ...YES, INTRIGUING...
YEAH, SO... uh... LATER, DILTON!
ER... YOU GONNA EAT YOUR BURGER?
IN ANOTHER DIMENSION, I'VE ALREADY EATEN IT! AND IN ANOTHER, I ORDERED THE CHICKEN, INSTEAD! DO YOU UNDERSTAND WHAT THAT MEANS?!
THAT YOU SHOULD STICK WITH THE BURGER? THE CHICKEN'S OFF THIS WEEK!
NO! IT MEANS THAT WAS ONCE AN OUTLANDISH IDEA RELEGATED TO COMICS AND SCIENCE FICTION IS NOW AN ACCEPTED SCIENTIFIC THEORY!
THE MULTIVERSE IS REAL, MY FRIEND!
DID I SAY IT WASN'T?
THERE COULD BE INFINITE UNIVERSES EXISTING SIDE-BY-SIDE IN TIME AND SPACE!
WHY, SOME EVEN POSTULATE THAT GRAVITY ITSELF MAY HAVE AN EXTRA-DIMENSIONAL ORIGIN!
13

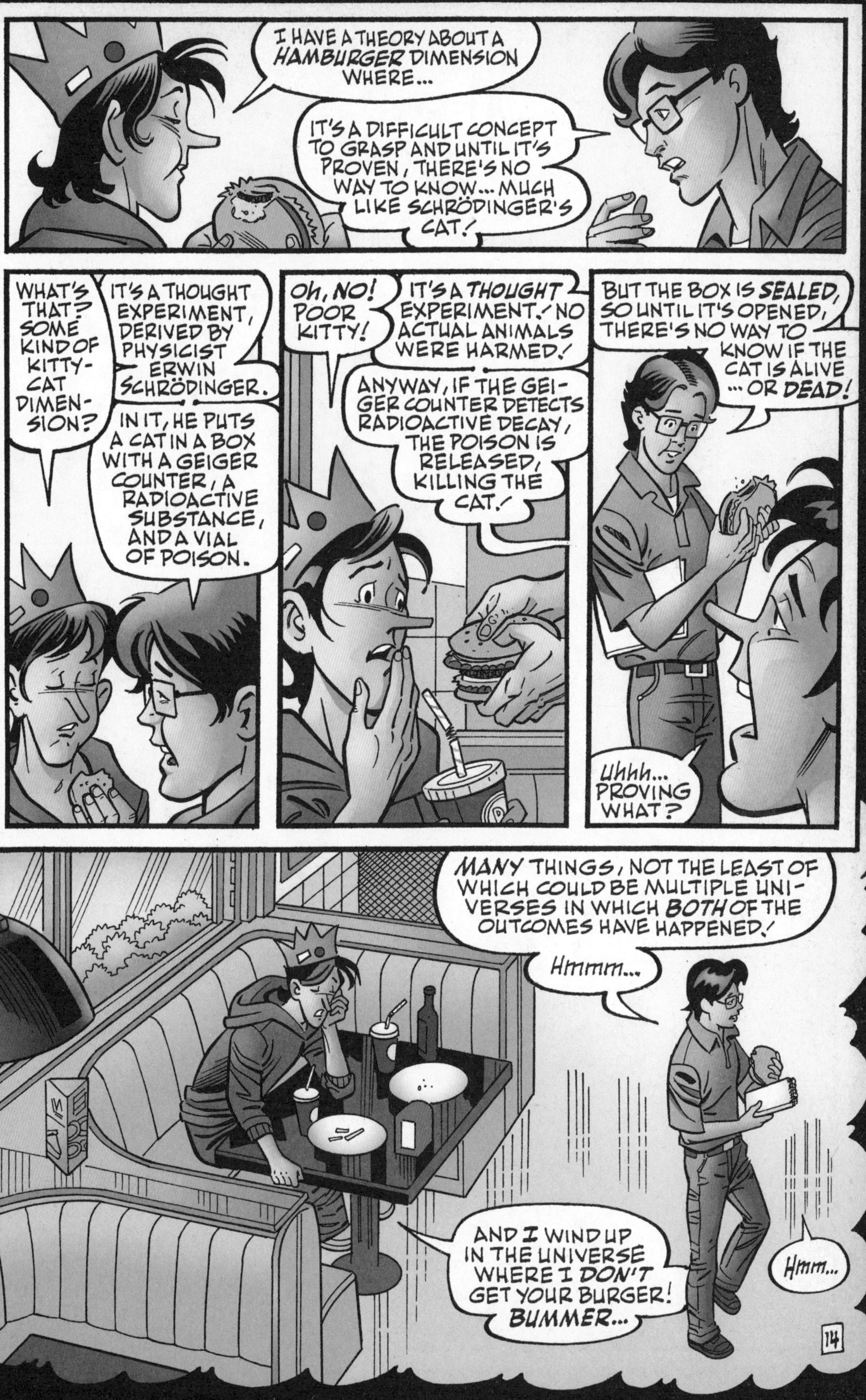

I HAVE A THEORY ABOUT A HAMBURGER DIMENSION WHERE...
IT'S A DIFFICULT CONCEPT TO GRASP AND UNTIL IT'S PROVEN, THERE'S NO WAY TO KNOW... MUCH LIKE SCHRÖDINGER'S CAT!
WHAT'S THAT? SOME KIND OF KITTY-CAT DIMENSION?
IT'S A THOUGHT EXPERIMENT, DERIVED BY PHYSICIST ERWIN SCHRÖDINGER.
IN IT, HE PUTS A CAT IN A BOX WITH A GEIGER COUNTER, A RADIOACTIVE SUBSTANCE, AND A VIAL OF POISON.
Oh, NO! POOR KITTY!
IT'S A THOUGHT EXPERIMENT! NO ACTUAL ANIMALS WERE HARMED!
ANYWAY, IF THE GEIGER COUNTER DETECTS RADIOACTIVE DECAY, THE POISON IS RELEASED, KILLING THE CAT!
BUT THE BOX IS SEALED, SO UNTIL IT'S OPENED, THERE'S NO WAY TO KNOW IF THE CAT IS ALIVE ...OR DEAD!
Uhhh... PROVING WHAT?
MANY THINGS, NOT THE LEAST OF WHICH COULD BE MULTIPLE UNIVERSES IN WHICH BOTH OF THE OUTCOMES HAVE HAPPENED!
Hmmm...
AND I WIND UP IN THE UNIVERSE WHERE I DON'T GET YOUR BURGER! BUMMER...
Hmm...

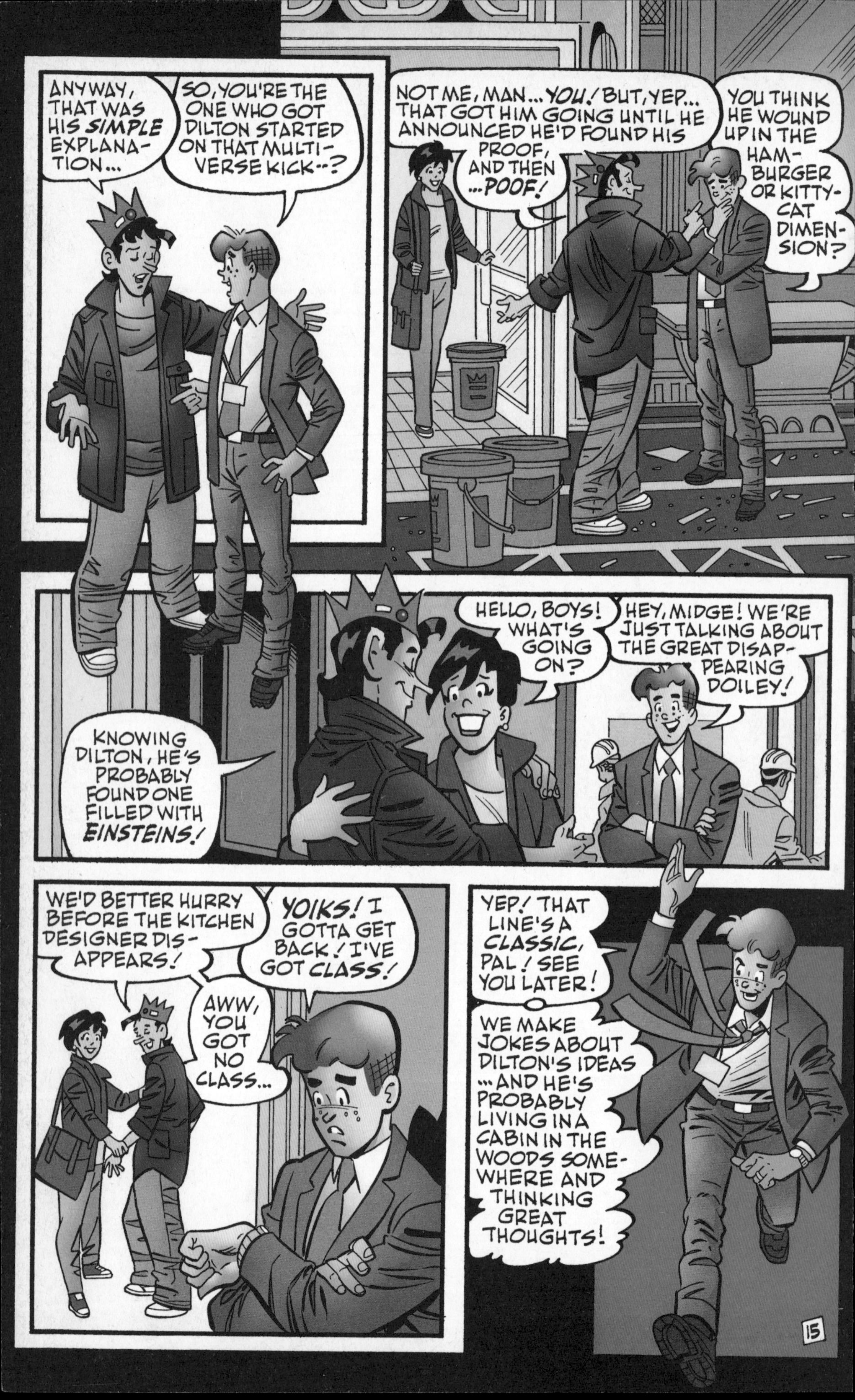
ANYWAY, THAT WAS HIS *SIMPLE* EXPLANATION...
SO, YOU'RE THE ONE WHO GOT DILTON STARTED ON THAT MULTI-VERSE KICK--?
NOT ME, MAN... *YOU!* BUT, YEP... THAT GOT HIM GOING UNTIL HE ANNOUNCED HE'D FOUND HIS PROOF, AND THEN ...*POOF!*
YOU THINK HE WOUND UP IN THE HAMBURGER OR KITTY-CAT DIMENSION?
HELLO, BOYS! WHAT'S GOING ON?
HEY, MIDGE! WE'RE JUST TALKING ABOUT THE GREAT DISAPPEARING DOILEY!
KNOWING DILTON, HE'S PROBABLY FOUND ONE FILLED WITH *EINSTEINS!*
WE'D BETTER HURRY BEFORE THE KITCHEN DESIGNER DISAPPEARS!
YOIKS! I GOTTA GET BACK! I'VE GOT *CLASS!*
AWW, YOU GOT NO CLASS...
YEP! THAT LINE'S A *CLASSIC,* PAL! SEE YOU LATER!
WE MAKE JOKES ABOUT DILTON'S IDEAS ...AND HE'S PROBABLY LIVING IN A CABIN IN THE WOODS SOMEWHERE AND THINKING GREAT THOUGHTS!
15

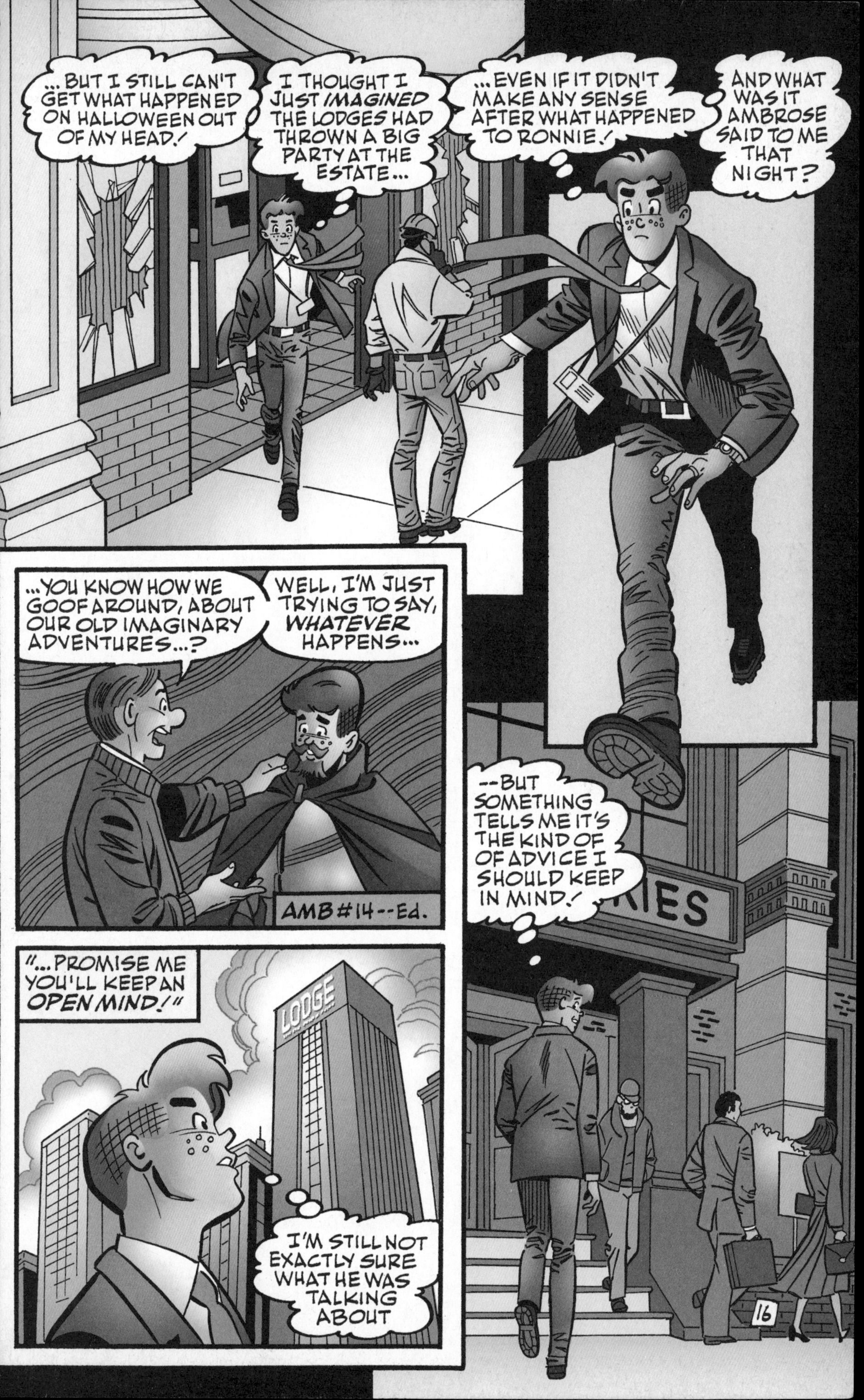
...BUT I STILL CAN'T GET WHAT HAPPENED ON HALLOWEEN OUT OF MY HEAD!
I THOUGHT I JUST *IMAGINED* THE LODGES HAD THROWN A BIG PARTY AT THE ESTATE...
...EVEN IF IT DIDN'T MAKE ANY SENSE AFTER WHAT HAPPENED TO RONNIE!
AND WHAT WAS IT AMBROSE SAID TO ME THAT NIGHT?
...YOU KNOW HOW WE GOOF AROUND, ABOUT OUR OLD IMAGINARY ADVENTURES...?
WELL, I'M JUST TRYING TO SAY, *WHATEVER* HAPPENS...
AMB #14--Ed.
"...PROMISE ME YOU'LL KEEP AN *OPEN MIND!*"
LODGE
I'M STILL NOT EXACTLY SURE WHAT HE WAS TALKING ABOUT
--BUT SOMETHING TELLS ME IT'S THE KIND OF OF ADVICE I SHOULD KEEP IN MIND!
RIES
16

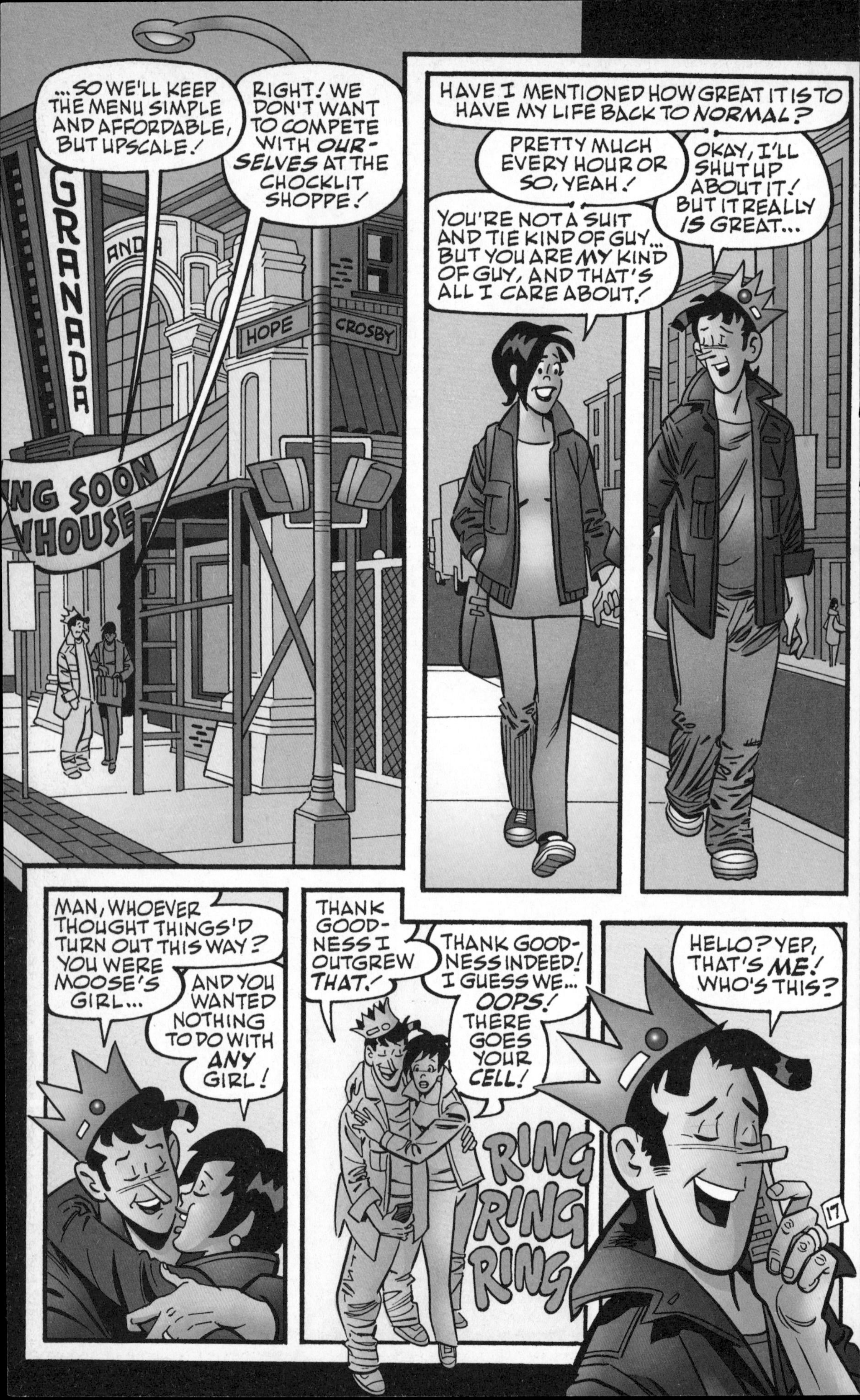
...SO WE'LL KEEP THE MENU SIMPLE AND AFFORDABLE, BUT UPSCALE!
RIGHT! WE DON'T WANT TO COMPETE WITH OURSELVES AT THE CHOCKLIT SHOPPE!
GRANADA
HOPE
CROSBY
NG SOON
HOUSE
HAVE I MENTIONED HOW GREAT IT IS TO HAVE MY LIFE BACK TO NORMAL?
PRETTY MUCH EVERY HOUR OR SO, YEAH!
YOU'RE NOT A SUIT AND TIE KIND OF GUY... BUT YOU ARE MY KIND OF GUY, AND THAT'S ALL I CARE ABOUT!
OKAY, I'LL SHUT UP ABOUT IT! BUT IT REALLY IS GREAT...
MAN, WHOEVER THOUGHT THINGS'D TURN OUT THIS WAY? YOU WERE MOOSE'S GIRL...
AND YOU WANTED NOTHING TO DO WITH ANY GIRL!
THANK GOODNESS I OUTGREW THAT!
THANK GOODNESS INDEED! I GUESS WE... OOPS! THERE GOES YOUR CELL!
RING RING RING
HELLO? YEP, THAT'S ME! WHO'S THIS?
17

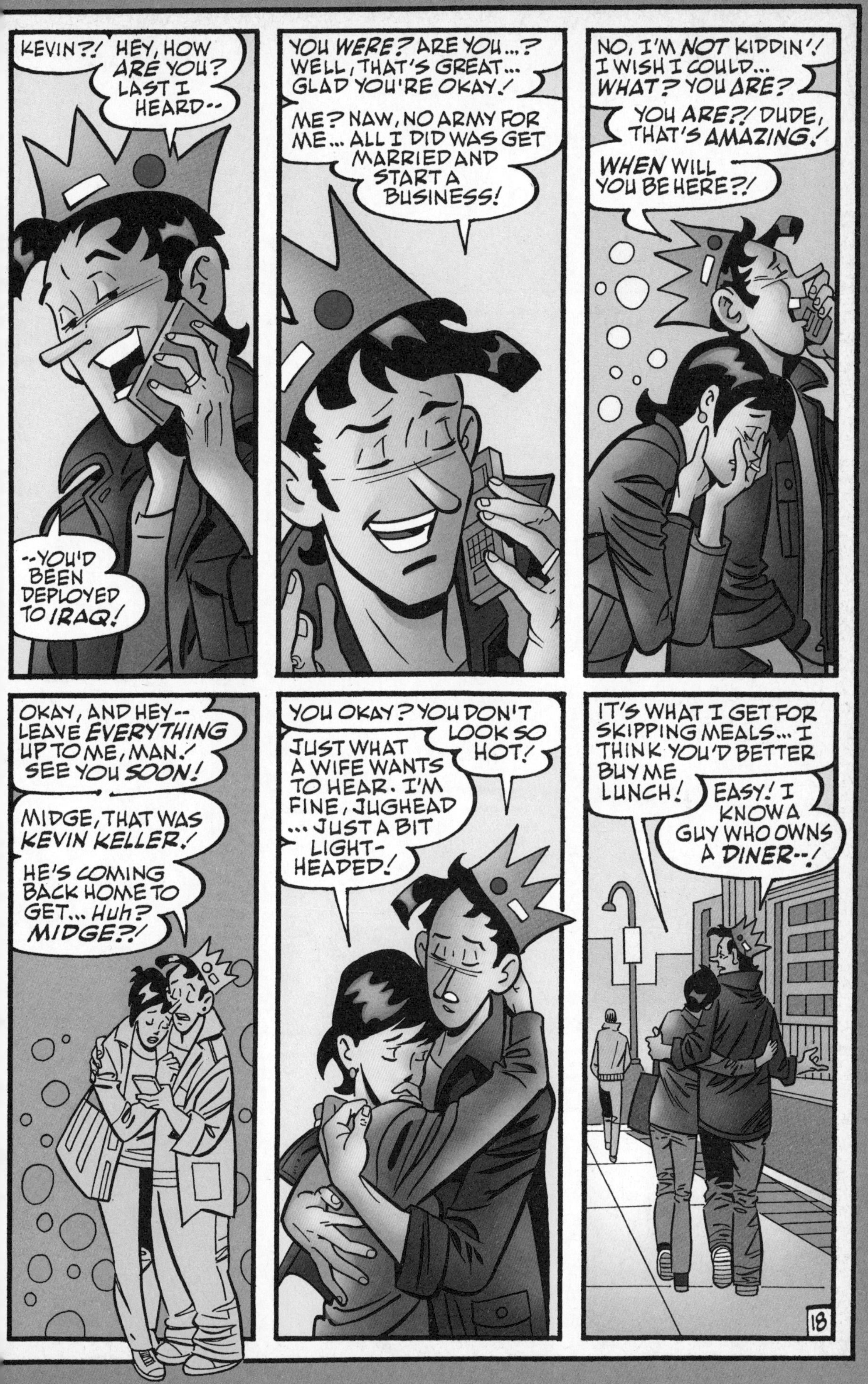
KEVIN?!
HEY, HOW ARE YOU? LAST I HEARD--
--YOU'D BEEN DEPLOYED TO IRAQ!
YOU WERE? ARE YOU...? WELL, THAT'S GREAT... GLAD YOU'RE OKAY!
ME? NAW, NO ARMY FOR ME... ALL I DID WAS GET MARRIED AND START A BUSINESS!
NO, I'M NOT KIDDIN'! I WISH I COULD... WHAT? YOU ARE?
YOU ARE?! DUDE, THAT'S AMAZING!
WHEN WILL YOU BE HERE?!
OKAY, AND HEY-- LEAVE EVERYTHING UP TO ME, MAN! SEE YOU SOON!
MIDGE, THAT WAS KEVIN KELLER!
HE'S COMING BACK HOME TO GET... Huh? MIDGE?!
YOU OKAY? YOU DON'T LOOK SO HOT!
JUST WHAT A WIFE WANTS TO HEAR. I'M FINE, JUGHEAD ...JUST A BIT LIGHT-HEADED!
IT'S WHAT I GET FOR SKIPPING MEALS... I THINK YOU'D BETTER BUY ME LUNCH!
EASY! I KNOW A GUY WHO OWNS A DINER--!
18

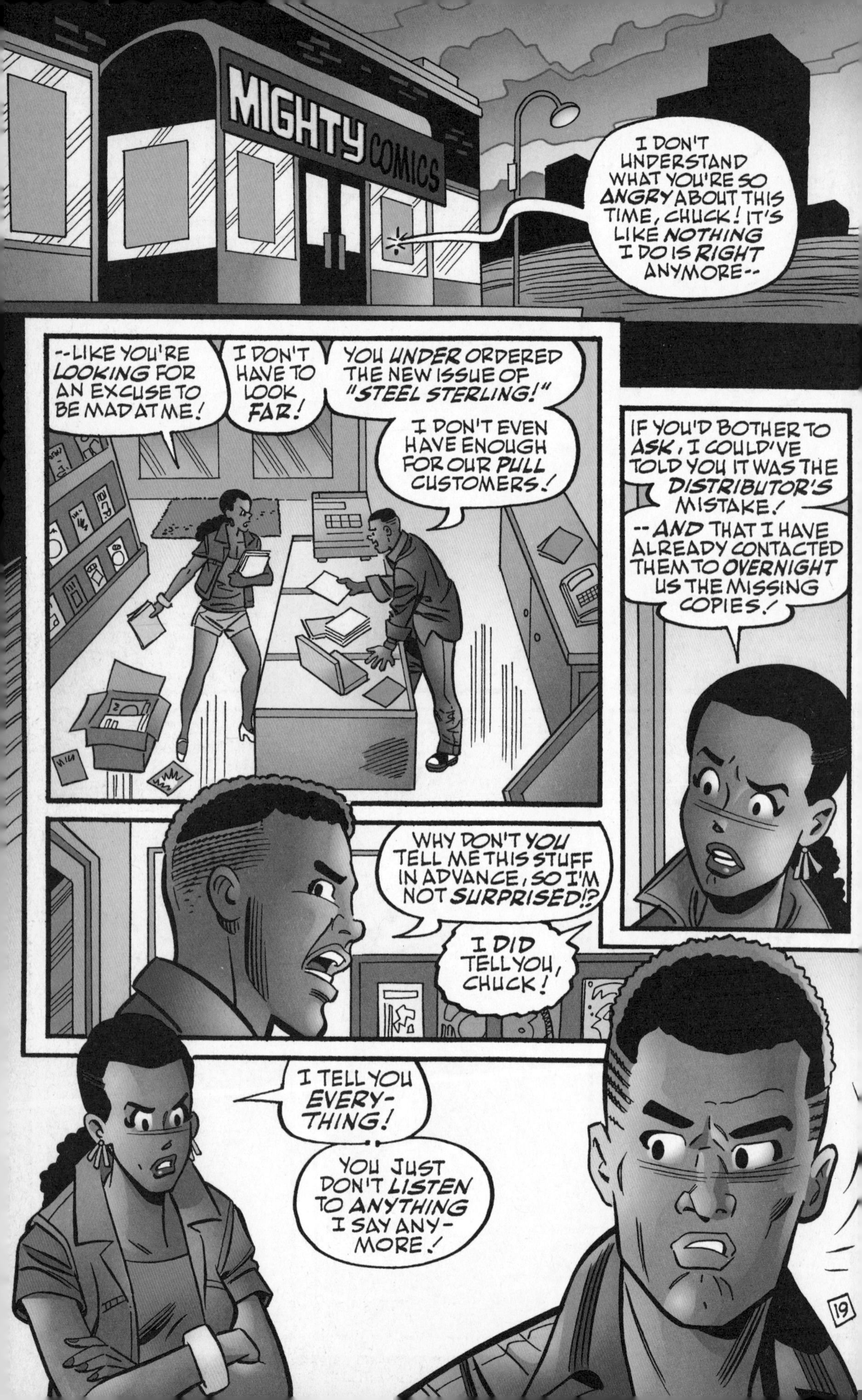
MIGHTY COMICS
I DON'T UNDERSTAND WHAT YOU'RE SO ANGRY ABOUT THIS TIME, CHUCK! IT'S LIKE NOTHING I DO IS RIGHT ANYMORE--
--LIKE YOU'RE LOOKING FOR AN EXCUSE TO BE MAD AT ME!
I DON'T HAVE TO LOOK FAR!
YOU UNDER ORDERED THE NEW ISSUE OF "STEEL STERLING!"
I DON'T EVEN HAVE ENOUGH FOR OUR PULL CUSTOMERS!
IF YOU'D BOTHER TO ASK, I COULD'VE TOLD YOU IT WAS THE DISTRIBUTOR'S MISTAKE!
--AND THAT I HAVE ALREADY CONTACTED THEM TO OVERNIGHT US THE MISSING COPIES!
WHY DON'T YOU TELL ME THIS STUFF IN ADVANCE, SO I'M NOT SURPRISED!?
I DID TELL YOU, CHUCK!
I TELL YOU EVERY-THING!
YOU JUST DON'T LISTEN TO ANYTHING I SAY ANY-MORE!

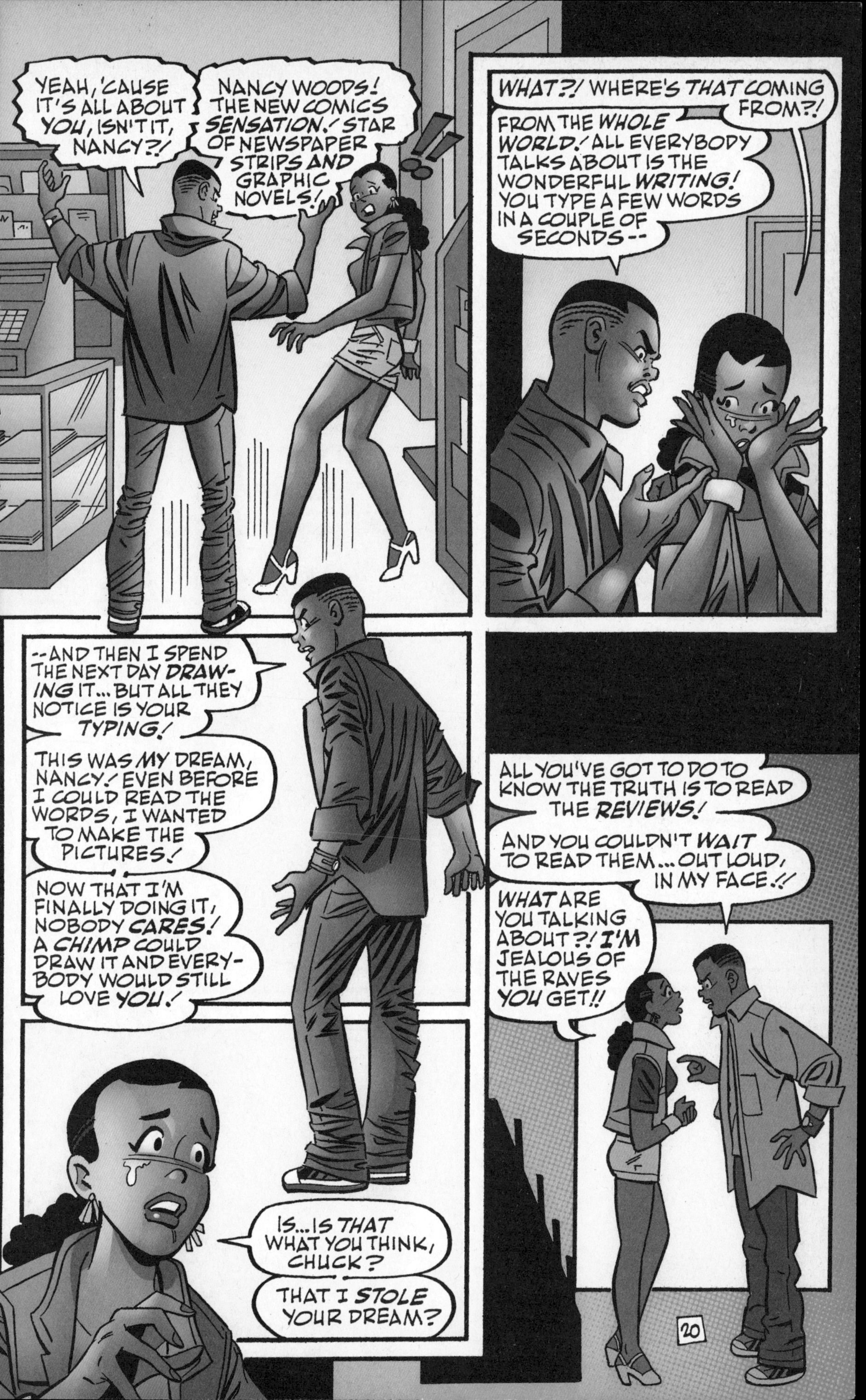
YEAH, 'CAUSE IT'S ALL ABOUT YOU, ISN'T IT, NANCY?!
NANCY WOODS! THE NEW COMICS SENSATION! STAR OF NEWSPAPER STRIPS AND GRAPHIC NOVELS!
WHAT?! WHERE'S THAT COMING FROM?!
FROM THE WHOLE WORLD! ALL EVERYBODY TALKS ABOUT IS THE WONDERFUL WRITING! YOU TYPE A FEW WORDS IN A COUPLE OF SECONDS --
--AND THEN I SPEND THE NEXT DAY DRAWING IT... BUT ALL THEY NOTICE IS YOUR TYPING!
THIS WAS MY DREAM, NANCY! EVEN BEFORE I COULD READ THE WORDS, I WANTED TO MAKE THE PICTURES!
NOW THAT I'M FINALLY DOING IT, NOBODY CARES! A CHIMP COULD DRAW IT AND EVERYBODY WOULD STILL LOVE YOU!
IS... IS THAT WHAT YOU THINK, CHUCK?
THAT I STOLE YOUR DREAM?
ALL YOU'VE GOT TO DO TO KNOW THE TRUTH IS TO READ THE REVIEWS!
AND YOU COULDN'T WAIT TO READ THEM... OUT LOUD, IN MY FACE!!
WHAT ARE YOU TALKING ABOUT?! I'M JEALOUS OF THE RAVES YOU GET!!

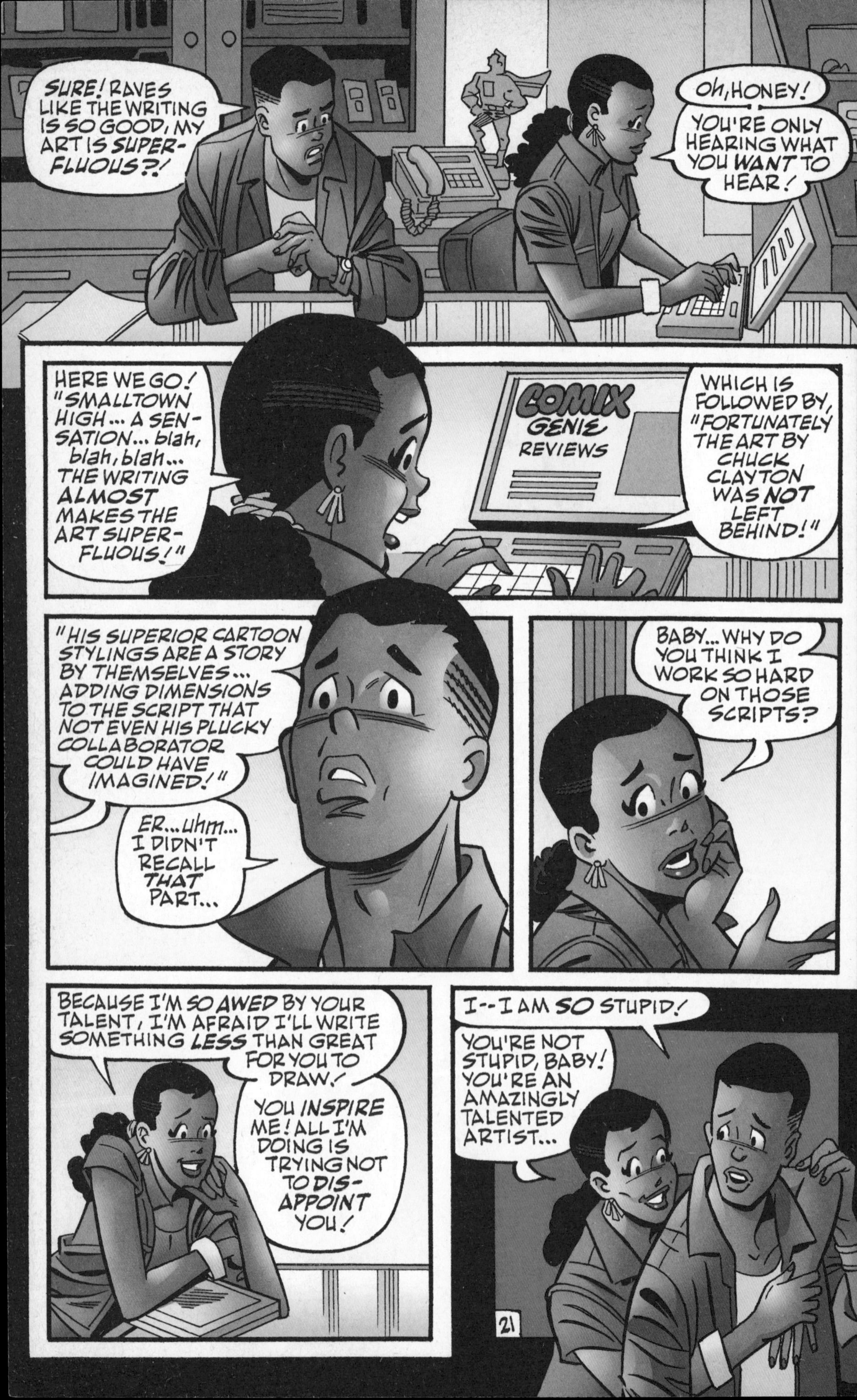
SURE! RAVES LIKE THE WRITING IS SO GOOD, MY ART IS SUPER-FLUOUS?!
Oh, HONEY!
YOU'RE ONLY HEARING WHAT YOU WANT TO HEAR!
HERE WE GO! "SMALLTOWN HIGH... A SEN-SATION... blah, blah, blah... THE WRITING ALMOST MAKES THE ART SUPER-FLUOUS!"
COMIX GENIE REVIEWS
WHICH IS FOLLOWED BY, "FORTUNATELY THE ART BY CHUCK CLAYTON WAS NOT LEFT BEHIND!"
"HIS SUPERIOR CARTOON STYLINGS ARE A STORY BY THEMSELVES... ADDING DIMENSIONS TO THE SCRIPT THAT NOT EVEN HIS PLUCKY COLLABORATOR COULD HAVE IMAGINED!"
ER... uhm... I DIDN'T RECALL THAT PART...
BABY... WHY DO YOU THINK I WORK SO HARD ON THOSE SCRIPTS?
BECAUSE I'M SO AWED BY YOUR TALENT, I'M AFRAID I'LL WRITE SOMETHING LESS THAN GREAT FOR YOU TO DRAW!
YOU INSPIRE ME! ALL I'M DOING IS TRYING NOT TO DIS-APPOINT YOU!
I--I AM SO STUPID!
YOU'RE NOT STUPID, BABY! YOU'RE AN AMAZINGLY TALENTED ARTIST...

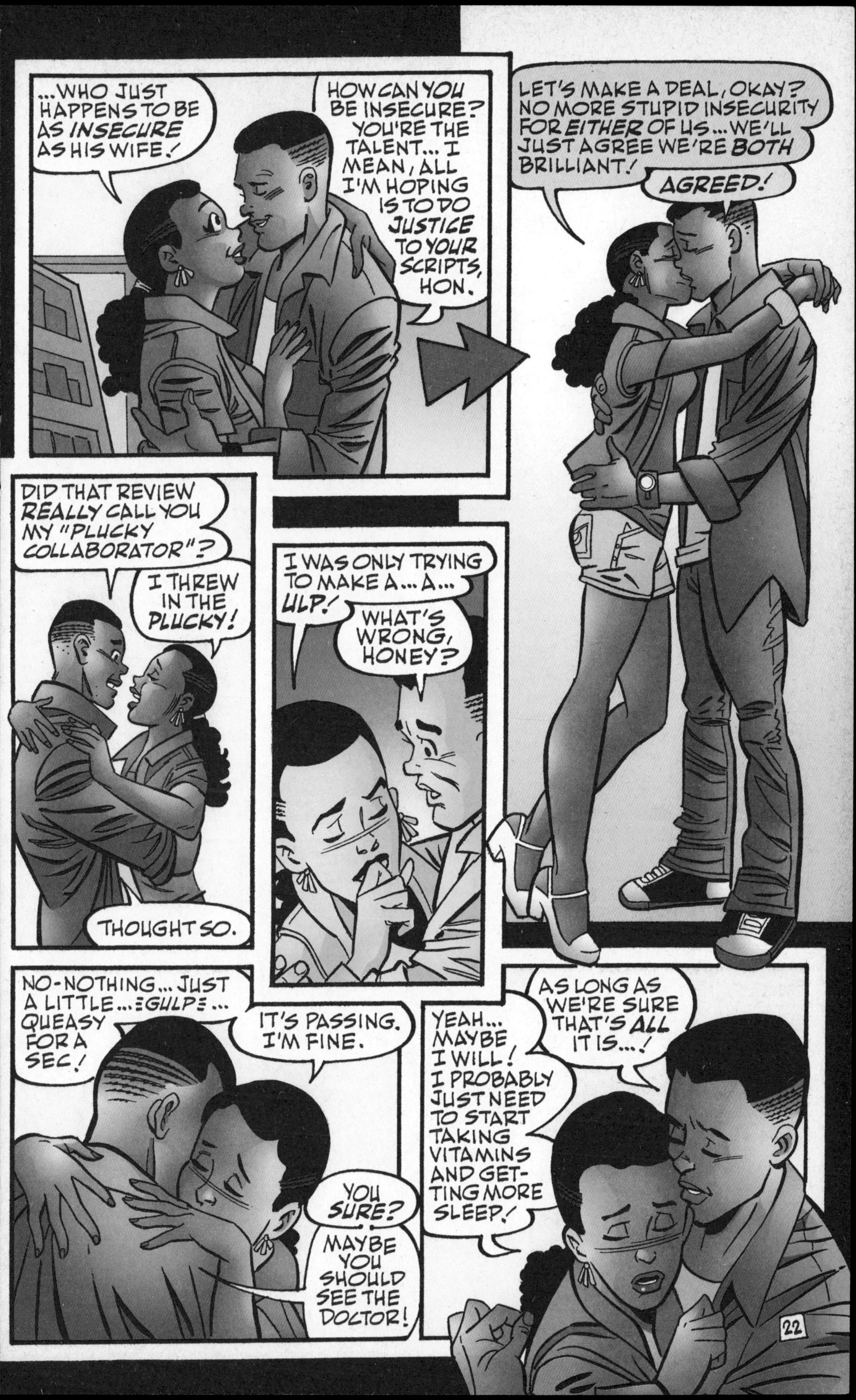
...WHO JUST HAPPENS TO BE AS INSECURE AS HIS WIFE!
HOW CAN YOU BE INSECURE? YOU'RE THE TALENT... I MEAN, ALL I'M HOPING IS TO DO JUSTICE TO YOUR SCRIPTS, HON.
LET'S MAKE A DEAL, OKAY? NO MORE STUPID INSECURITY FOR EITHER OF US... WE'LL JUST AGREE WE'RE BOTH BRILLIANT!
AGREED!
DID THAT REVIEW REALLY CALL YOU MY "PLUCKY COLLABORATOR"?
I THREW IN THE PLUCKY!
THOUGHT SO.
I WAS ONLY TRYING TO MAKE A... A... ULP!
WHAT'S WRONG, HONEY?
NO-NOTHING... JUST A LITTLE... GULP... QUEASY FOR A SEC!
IT'S PASSING. I'M FINE.
YOU SURE?
MAYBE YOU SHOULD SEE THE DOCTOR!
YEAH... MAYBE I WILL! I PROBABLY JUST NEED TO START TAKING VITAMINS AND GETTING MORE SLEEP!
AS LONG AS WE'RE SURE THAT'S ALL IT IS...!
22

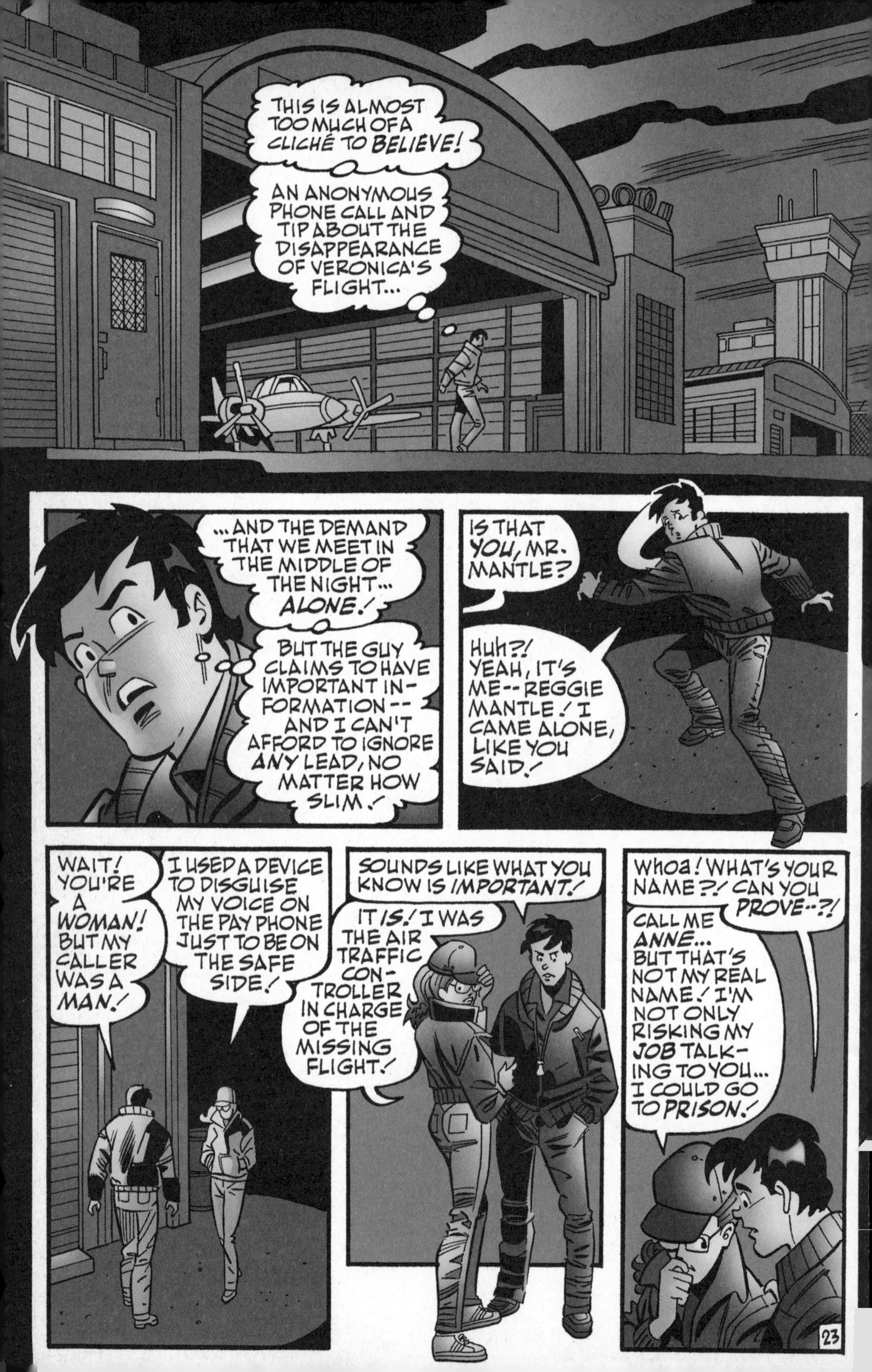

THIS IS ALMOST TOO MUCH OF A CLICHÉ TO BELIEVE!
AN ANONYMOUS PHONE CALL AND TIP ABOUT THE DISAPPEARANCE OF VERONICA'S FLIGHT...
...AND THE DEMAND THAT WE MEET IN THE MIDDLE OF THE NIGHT... ALONE!
BUT THE GUY CLAIMS TO HAVE IMPORTANT INFORMATION -- AND I CAN'T AFFORD TO IGNORE ANY LEAD, NO MATTER HOW SLIM!
IS THAT YOU, MR. MANTLE?
Huh?! YEAH, IT'S ME-- REGGIE MANTLE! I CAME ALONE, LIKE YOU SAID!
WAIT! YOU'RE A WOMAN! BUT MY CALLER WAS A MAN!
I USED A DEVICE TO DISGUISE MY VOICE ON THE PAY PHONE JUST TO BE ON THE SAFE SIDE!
SOUNDS LIKE WHAT YOU KNOW IS IMPORTANT!
IT IS! I WAS THE AIR TRAFFIC CONTROLLER IN CHARGE OF THE MISSING FLIGHT!
Whoa! WHAT'S YOUR NAME?! CAN YOU PROVE--?!
CALL ME ANNE... BUT THAT'S NOT MY REAL NAME! I'M NOT ONLY RISKING MY JOB TALKING TO YOU... I COULD GO TO PRISON!

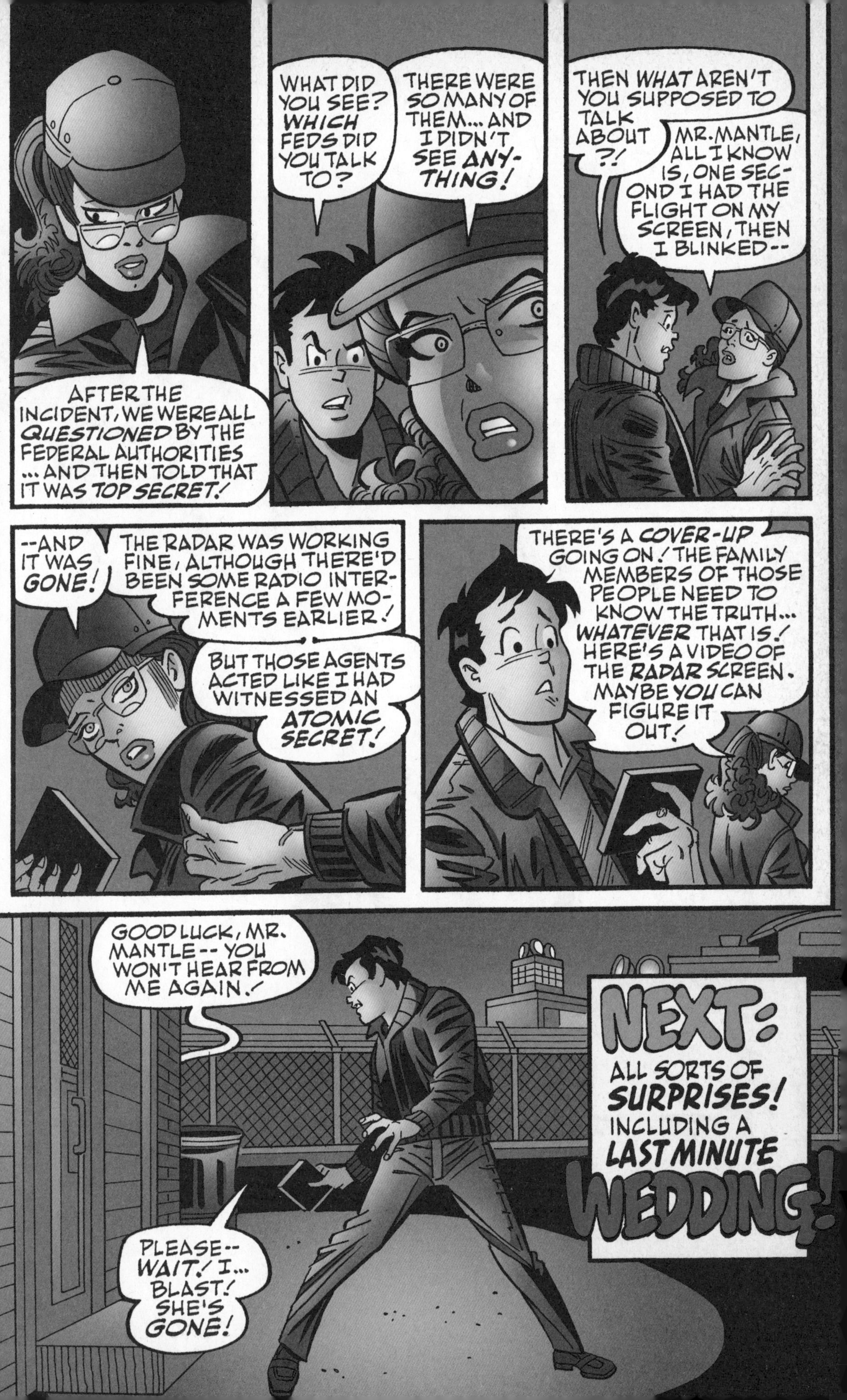
AFTER THE INCIDENT, WE WERE ALL QUESTIONED BY THE FEDERAL AUTHORITIES ... AND THEN TOLD THAT IT WAS TOP SECRET!
WHAT DID YOU SEE? WHICH FEDS DID YOU TALK TO?
THERE WERE SO MANY OF THEM... AND I DIDN'T SEE ANYTHING!
THEN WHAT AREN'T YOU SUPPOSED TO TALK ABOUT ?!
MR. MANTLE, ALL I KNOW IS, ONE SECOND I HAD THE FLIGHT ON MY SCREEN, THEN I BLINKED--
--AND IT WAS GONE!
THE RADAR WAS WORKING FINE, ALTHOUGH THERE'D BEEN SOME RADIO INTERFERENCE A FEW MOMENTS EARLIER!
BUT THOSE AGENTS ACTED LIKE I HAD WITNESSED AN ATOMIC SECRET!
THERE'S A COVER-UP GOING ON! THE FAMILY MEMBERS OF THOSE PEOPLE NEED TO KNOW THE TRUTH... WHATEVER THAT IS! HERE'S A VIDEO OF THE RADAR SCREEN. MAYBE YOU CAN FIGURE IT OUT!
GOOD LUCK, MR. MANTLE -- YOU WON'T HEAR FROM ME AGAIN.!
PLEASE-- WAIT! I... BLAST! SHE'S GONE!
NEXT:
ALL SORTS OF SURPRISES! INCLUDING A LAST MINUTE WEDDING!

"MARRIAGE DOESN'T PROVE YOU LOVE SOMEONE!"

"IT PROVES YOU'VE DECIDED THAT YOU NEVER NEED TO LOVE ANYONE ELSE!"

- ETHEL MUGGS

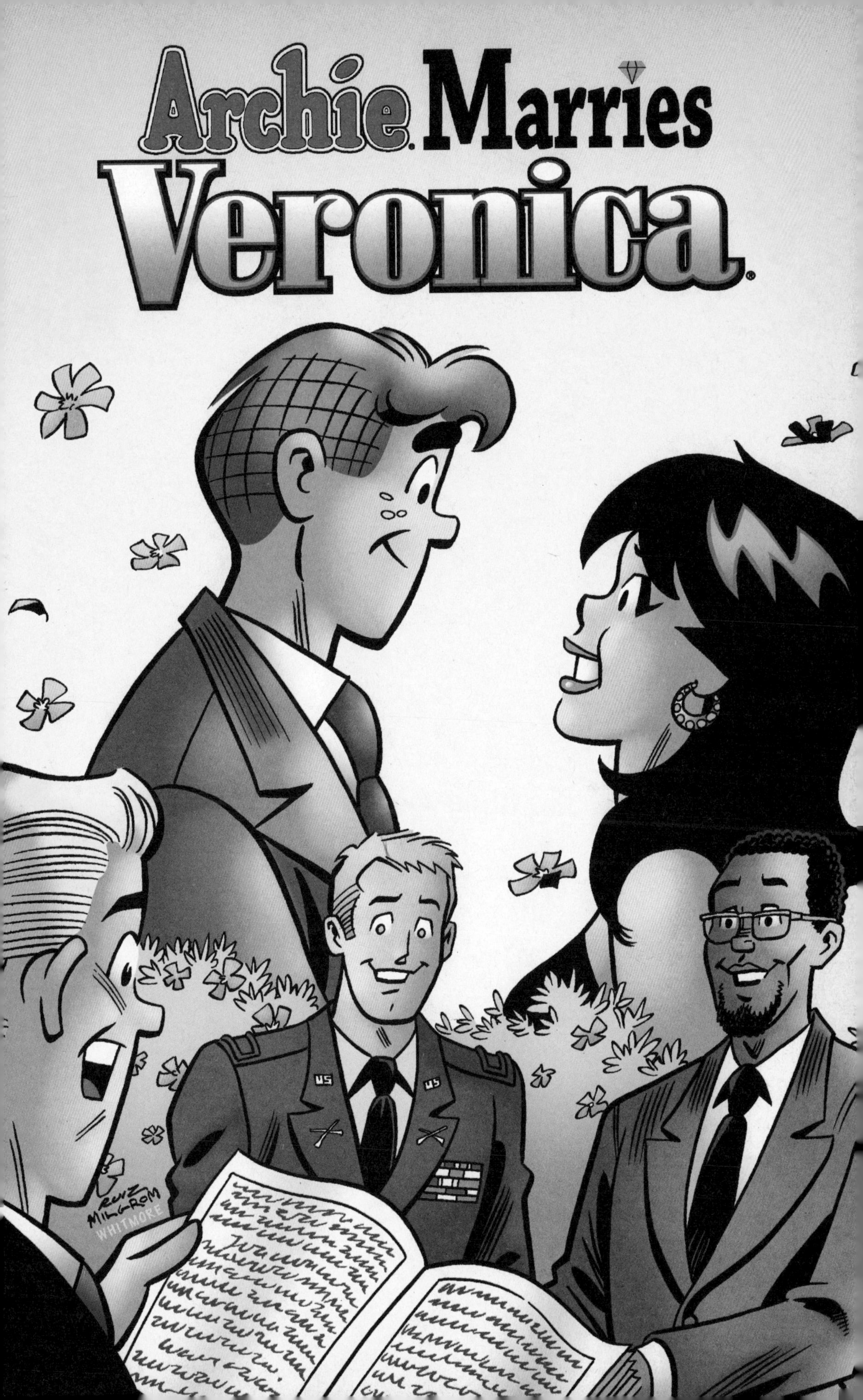
Archie Marries
Veronica
RUIZ
MILGROM
WHITMORE
US
US

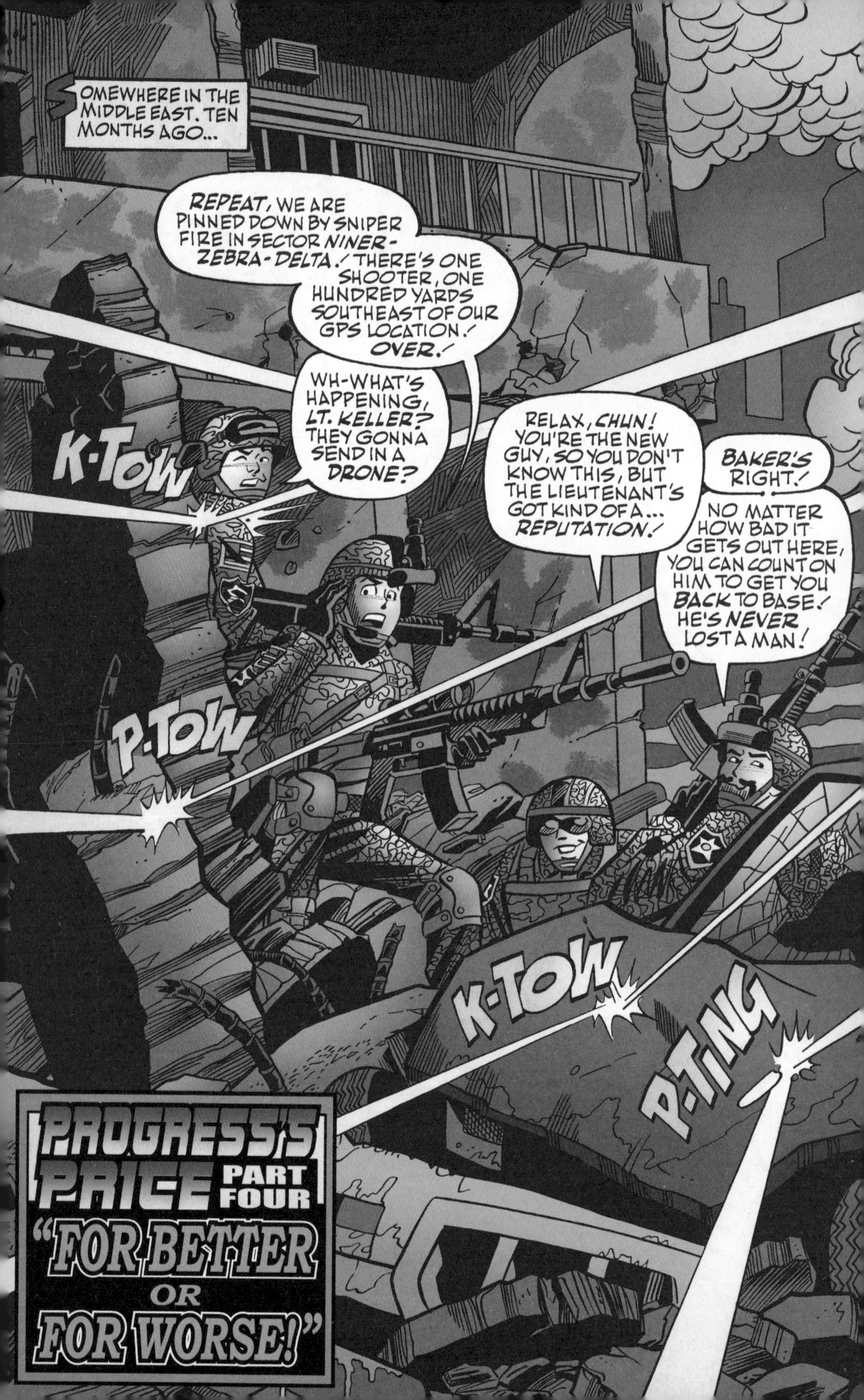
SOMEWHERE IN THE MIDDLE EAST. TEN MONTHS AGO...
REPEAT, WE ARE PINNED DOWN BY SNIPER FIRE IN SECTOR NINER-ZEBRA-DELTA! THERE'S ONE SHOOTER, ONE HUNDRED YARDS SOUTHEAST OF OUR GPS LOCATION! OVER!
WH-WHAT'S HAPPENING, LT. KELLER? THEY GONNA SEND IN A DRONE?
K-TOW
RELAX, CHUN! YOU'RE THE NEW GUY, SO YOU DON'T KNOW THIS, BUT THE LIEUTENANT'S GOT KIND OF A... REPUTATION!
BAKER'S RIGHT!
NO MATTER HOW BAD IT GETS OUT HERE, YOU CAN COUNT ON HIM TO GET YOU BACK TO BASE! HE'S NEVER LOST A MAN!
P-TOW
K-TOW
P-TING
PROGRESS'S PRICE PART FOUR
"FOR BETTER OR FOR WORSE!"

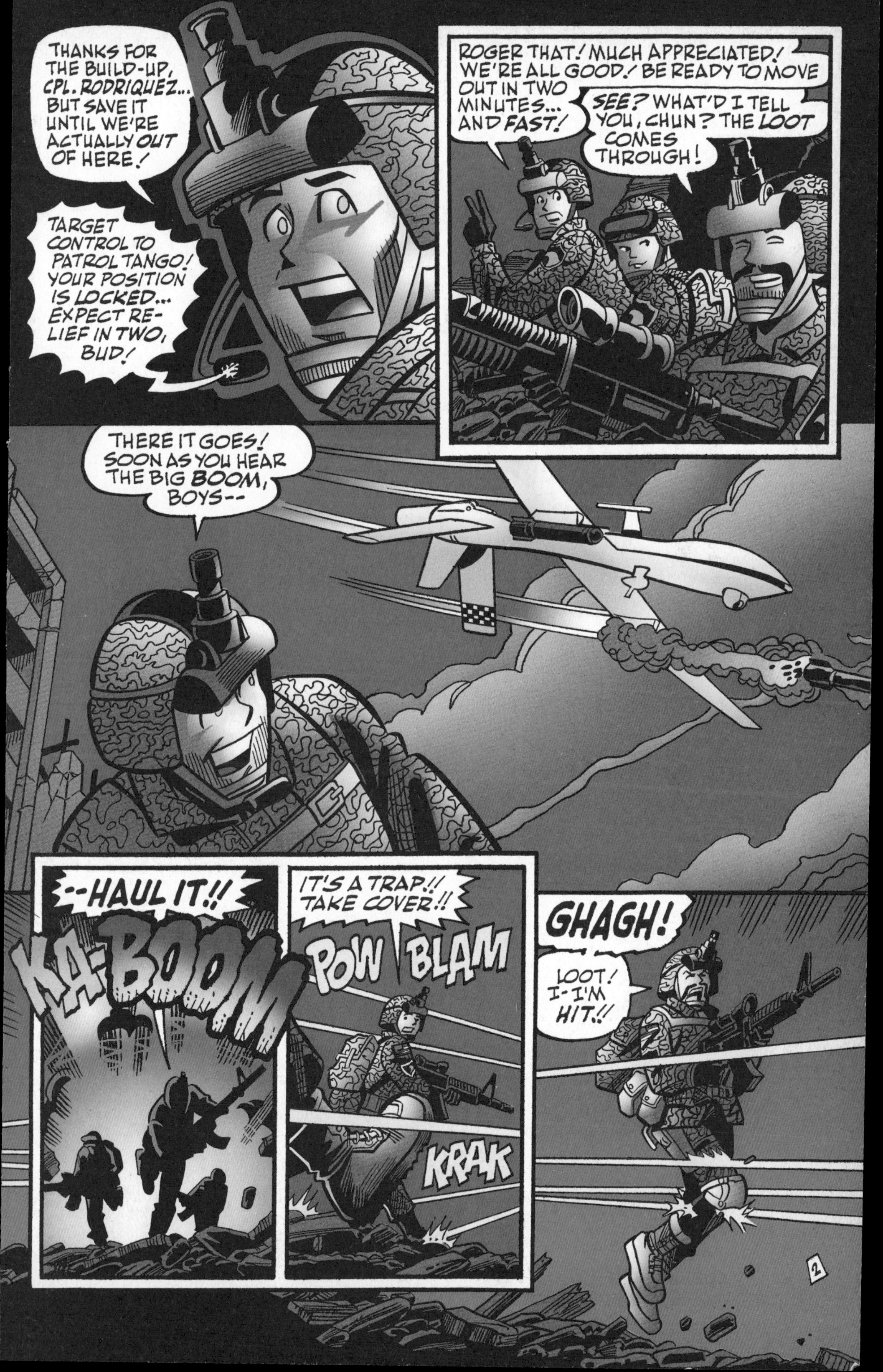
THANKS FOR THE BUILD-UP, CPL. RODRIQUEZ... BUT SAVE IT UNTIL WE'RE ACTUALLY OUT OF HERE!
TARGET CONTROL TO PATROL TANGO! YOUR POSITION IS LOCKED... EXPECT RE-LIEF IN TWO, BUD!
ROGER THAT! MUCH APPRECIATED! WE'RE ALL GOOD! BE READY TO MOVE OUT IN TWO MINUTES... AND FAST!
SEE? WHAT'D I TELL YOU, CHUN? THE LOOT COMES THROUGH!
THERE IT GOES! SOON AS YOU HEAR THE BIG BOOM, BOYS--
--HAUL IT!!
KA-BOOM
IT'S A TRAP!! TAKE COVER!!
POW
BLAM
KRAK
GHAGH!
LOOT! I-I'M HIT!!
2

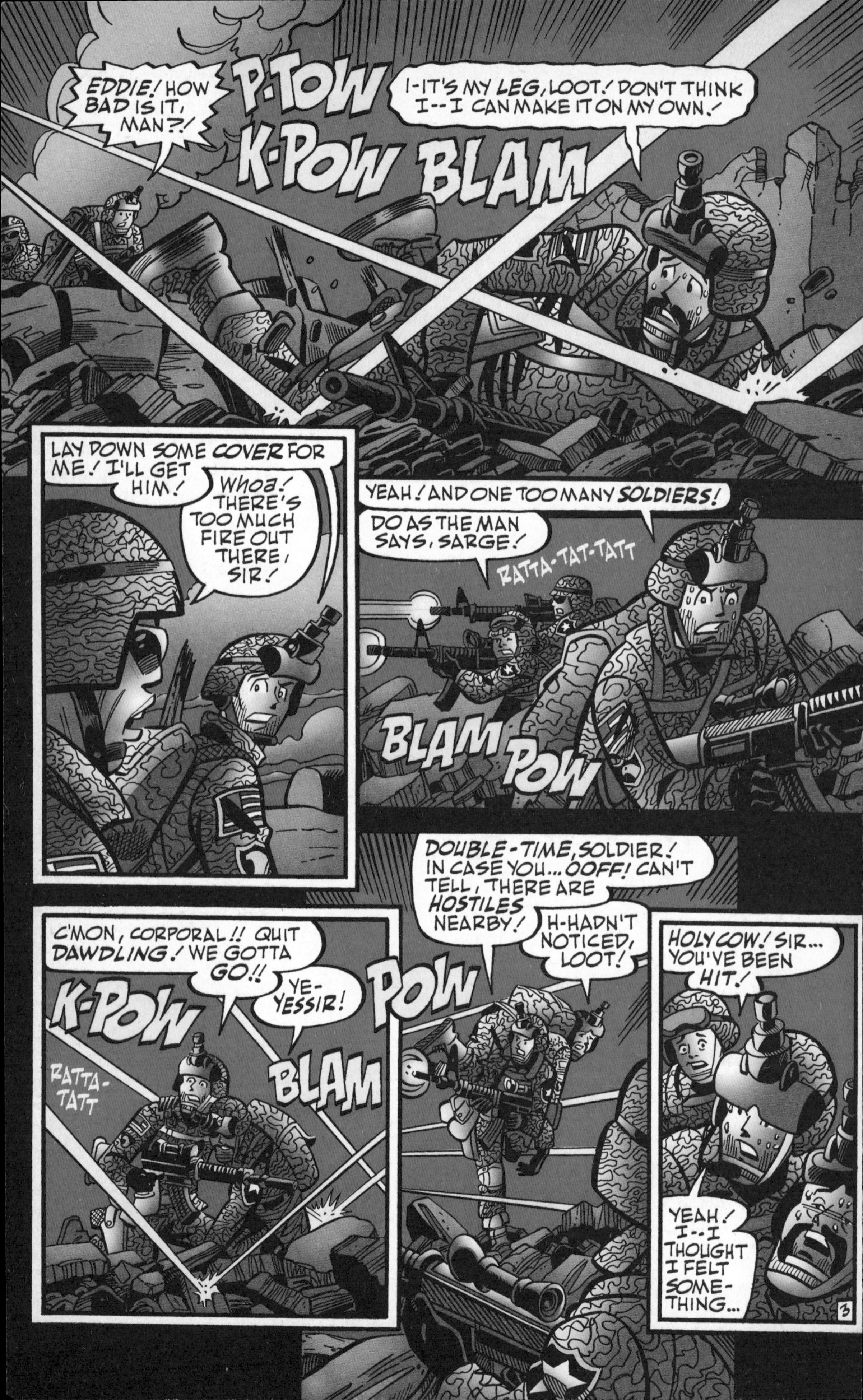
EDDIE! HOW BAD IS IT, MAN?!
P-TOW
K-POW
I-IT'S MY LEG, LOOT! DON'T THINK I--I CAN MAKE IT ON MY OWN!
BLAM
LAY DOWN SOME COVER FOR ME! I'LL GET HIM!
WHOA! THERE'S TOO MUCH FIRE OUT THERE, SIR!
YEAH! AND ONE TOO MANY SOLDIERS!
DO AS THE MAN SAYS, SARGE!
RATTA-TAT-TATT
BLAM
POW
C'MON, CORPORAL!! QUIT DAWDLING! WE GOTTA GO!!
YE-YESSIR!
K-POW
RATTA-TATT
BLAM
POW
DOUBLE-TIME, SOLDIER! IN CASE YOU... OOFF! CAN'T TELL, THERE ARE HOSTILES NEARBY!
H-HADN'T NOTICED, LOOT!
HOLY COW! SIR... YOU'VE BEEN HIT!
YEAH! I--I THOUGHT I FELT SOME-THING...
3

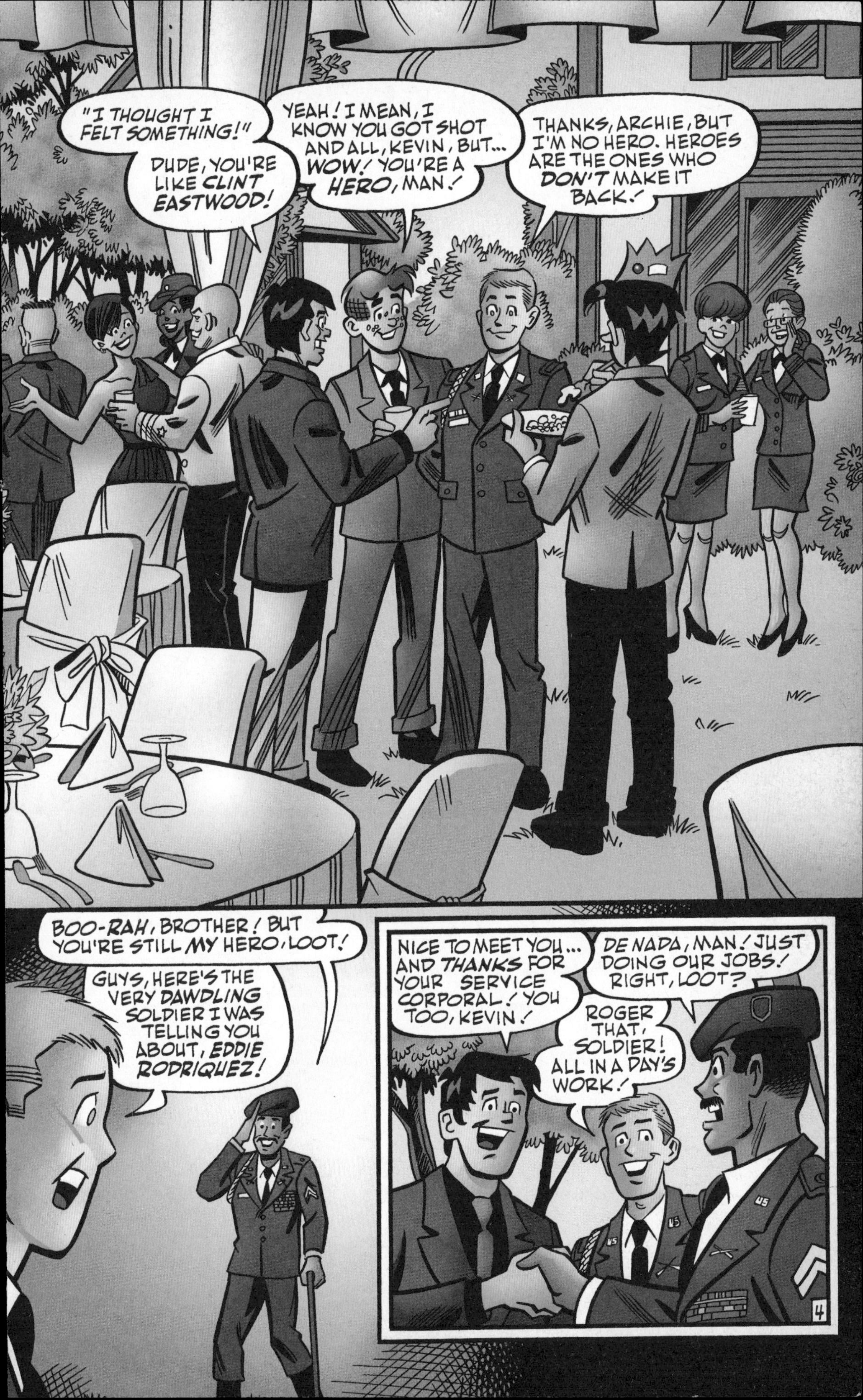
"I THOUGHT I FELT SOMETHING!"
DUDE, YOU'RE LIKE CLINT EASTWOOD!
YEAH! I MEAN, I KNOW YOU GOT SHOT AND ALL, KEVIN, BUT... WOW! YOU'RE A HERO, MAN!
THANKS, ARCHIE, BUT I'M NO HERO. HEROES ARE THE ONES WHO DON'T MAKE IT BACK!
BOO-RAH, BROTHER! BUT YOU'RE STILL MY HERO, LOOT!
GUYS, HERE'S THE VERY DAWDLING SOLDIER I WAS TELLING YOU ABOUT, EDDIE RODRIQUEZ!
NICE TO MEET YOU... AND THANKS FOR YOUR SERVICE CORPORAL! YOU TOO, KEVIN!
DE NADA, MAN! JUST DOING OUR JOBS! RIGHT, LOOT?
ROGER THAT, SOLDIER! ALL IN A DAY'S WORK!
4

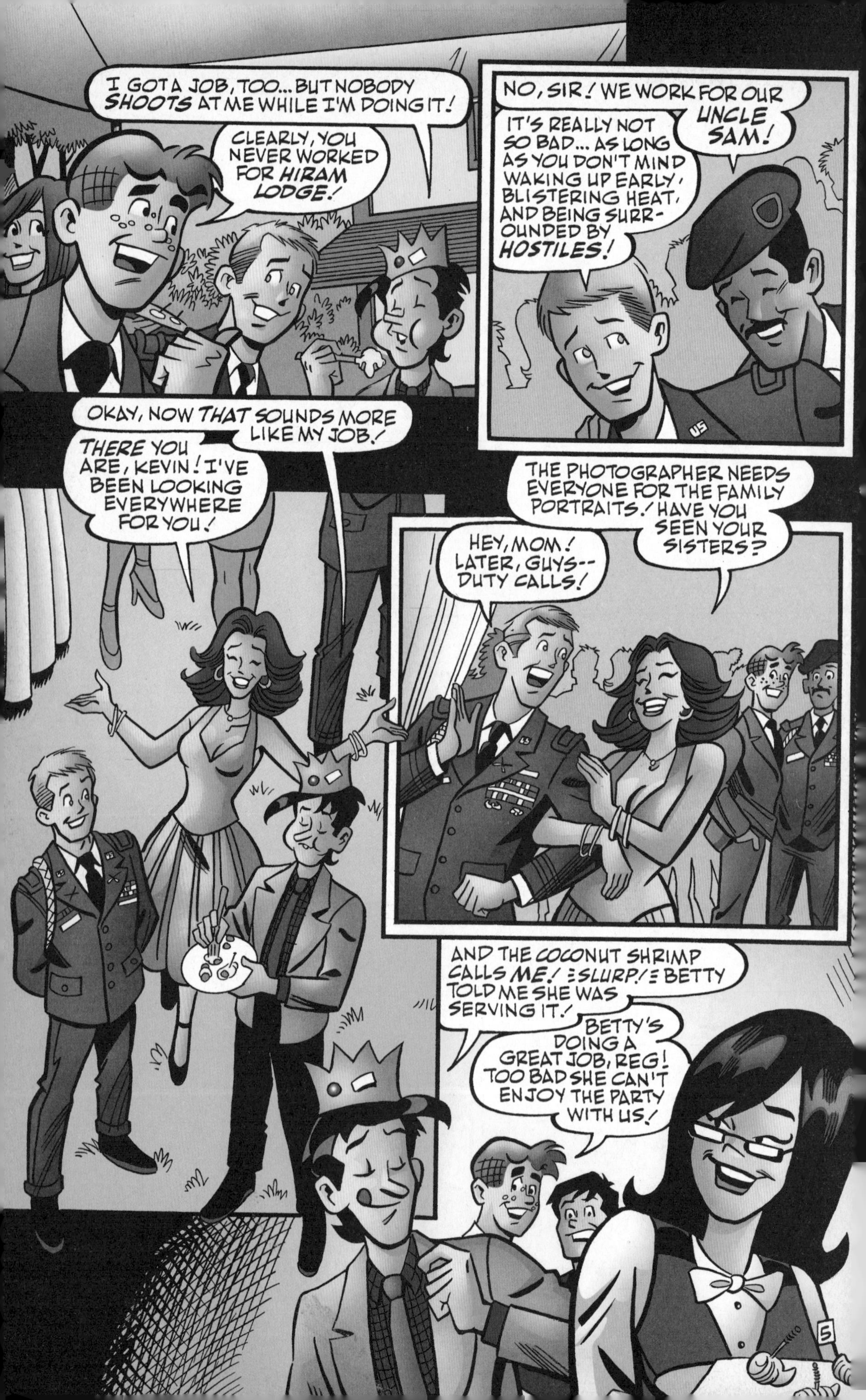
I GOT A JOB, TOO... BUT NOBODY SHOOTS AT ME WHILE I'M DOING IT!
CLEARLY, YOU NEVER WORKED FOR HIRAM LODGE!
NO, SIR! WE WORK FOR OUR UNCLE SAM!
IT'S REALLY NOT SO BAD... AS LONG AS YOU DON'T MIND WAKING UP EARLY, BLISTERING HEAT, AND BEING SURR-OUNDED BY HOSTILES!
OKAY, NOW THAT SOUNDS MORE LIKE MY JOB!
THERE YOU ARE, KEVIN! I'VE BEEN LOOKING EVERYWHERE FOR YOU!
THE PHOTOGRAPHER NEEDS EVERYONE FOR THE FAMILY PORTRAITS! HAVE YOU SEEN YOUR SISTERS?
HEY, MOM! LATER, GUYS-- DUTY CALLS!
AND THE COCONUT SHRIMP CALLS ME! SLURP! BETTY TOLD ME SHE WAS SERVING IT!
BETTY'S DOING A GREAT JOB, REG! TOO BAD SHE CAN'T ENJOY THE PARTY WITH US!
5

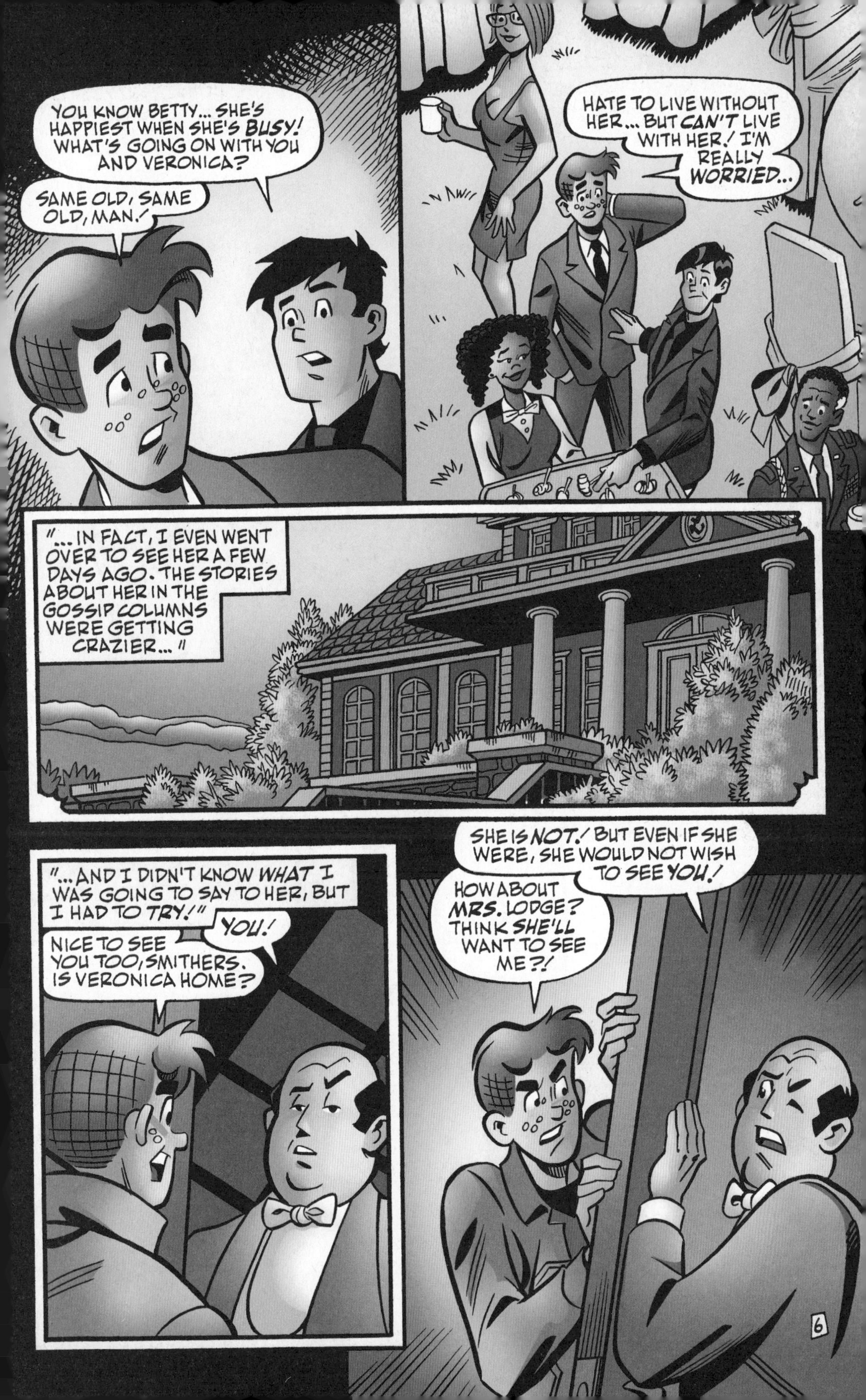
YOU KNOW BETTY... SHE'S HAPPIEST WHEN SHE'S BUSY! WHAT'S GOING ON WITH YOU AND VERONICA?
SAME OLD, SAME OLD, MAN!
HATE TO LIVE WITHOUT HER... BUT CAN'T LIVE WITH HER! I'M REALLY WORRIED...
"...IN FACT, I EVEN WENT OVER TO SEE HER A FEW DAYS AGO. THE STORIES ABOUT HER IN THE GOSSIP COLUMNS WERE GETTING CRAZIER..."
"...AND I DIDN'T KNOW WHAT I WAS GOING TO SAY TO HER, BUT I HAD TO TRY!"
YOU!
NICE TO SEE YOU TOO, SMITHERS. IS VERONICA HOME?
SHE IS NOT! BUT EVEN IF SHE WERE, SHE WOULD NOT WISH TO SEE YOU!
HOW ABOUT MRS. LODGE? THINK SHE'LL WANT TO SEE ME?!
6

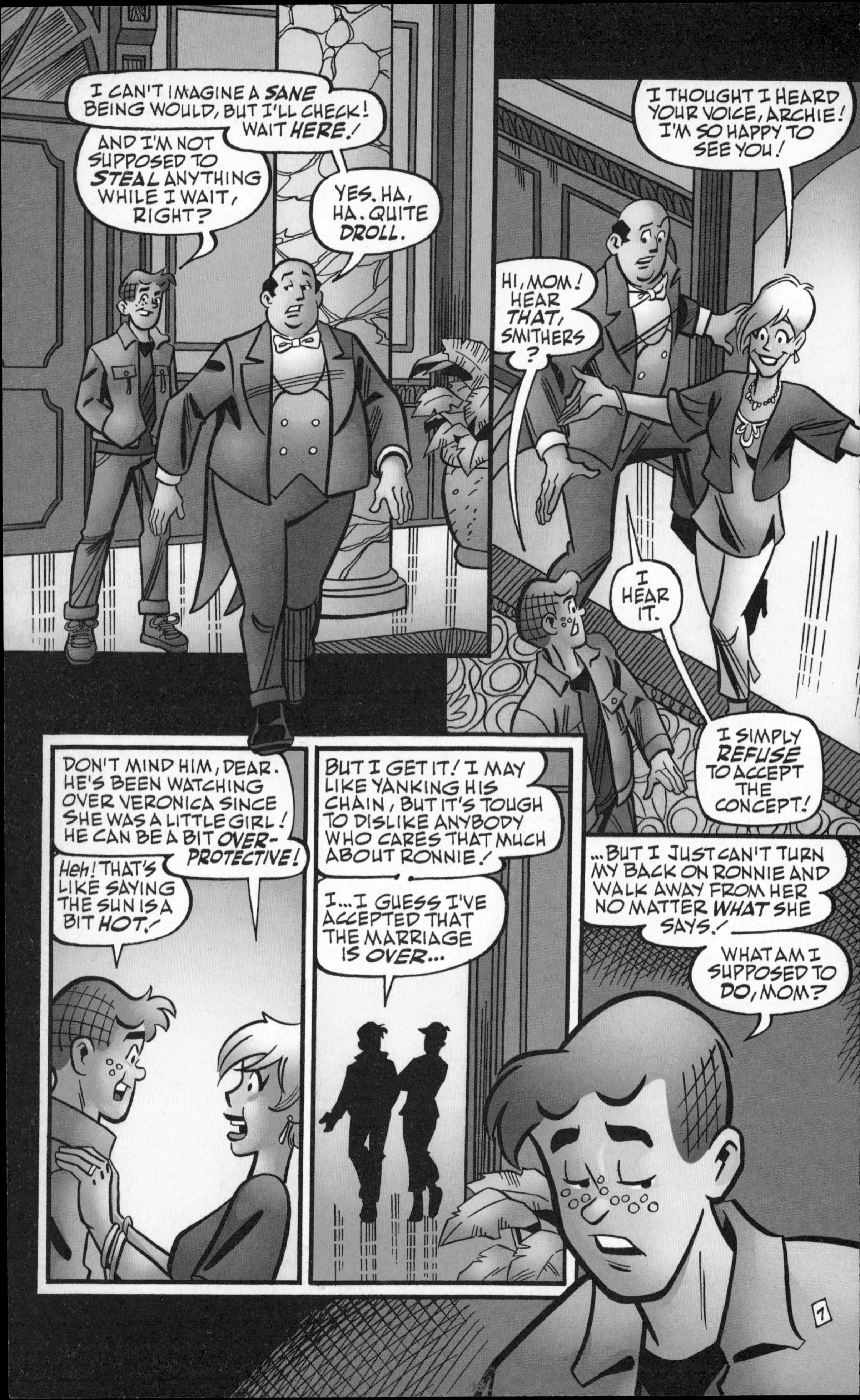

I CAN'T IMAGINE A SANE BEING WOULD, BUT I'LL CHECK! WAIT HERE!
AND I'M NOT SUPPOSED TO STEAL ANYTHING WHILE I WAIT, RIGHT?
YES. HA, HA. QUITE DROLL.
I THOUGHT I HEARD YOUR VOICE, ARCHIE! I'M SO HAPPY TO SEE YOU!
HI, MOM! HEAR THAT, SMITHERS?
I HEAR IT.
I SIMPLY REFUSE TO ACCEPT THE CONCEPT!
DON'T MIND HIM, DEAR. HE'S BEEN WATCHING OVER VERONICA SINCE SHE WAS A LITTLE GIRL! HE CAN BE A BIT OVER-PROTECTIVE!
Heh! THAT'S LIKE SAYING THE SUN IS A BIT HOT!
BUT I GET IT! I MAY LIKE YANKING HIS CHAIN, BUT IT'S TOUGH TO DISLIKE ANYBODY WHO CARES THAT MUCH ABOUT RONNIE!
I... I GUESS I'VE ACCEPTED THAT THE MARRIAGE IS OVER...
...BUT I JUST CAN'T TURN MY BACK ON RONNIE AND WALK AWAY FROM HER NO MATTER WHAT SHE SAYS!
WHAT AM I SUPPOSED TO DO, MOM?

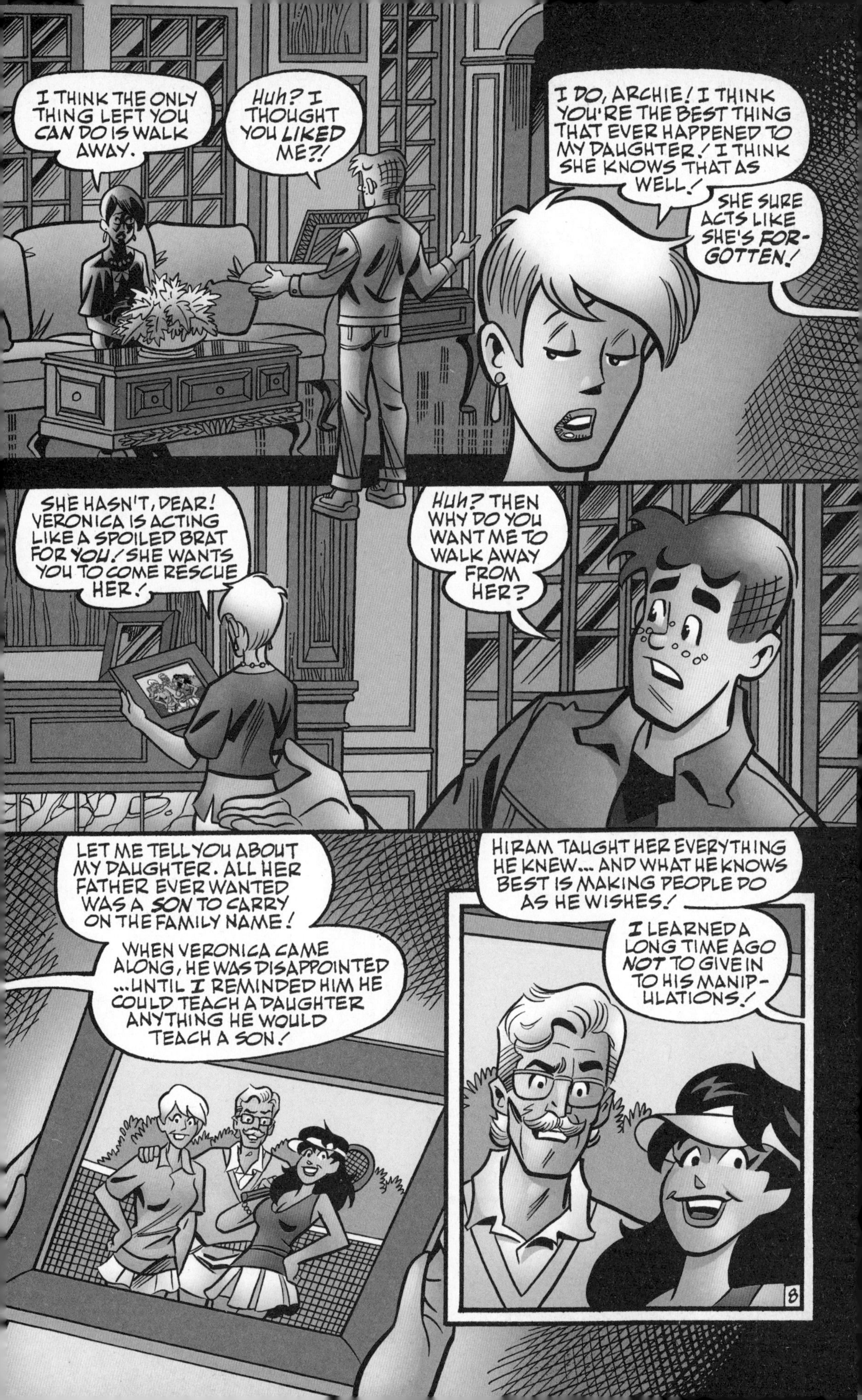
I THINK THE ONLY THING LEFT YOU CAN DO IS WALK AWAY.
HUH? I THOUGHT YOU LIKED ME?!
I DO, ARCHIE! I THINK YOU'RE THE BEST THING THAT EVER HAPPENED TO MY DAUGHTER! I THINK SHE KNOWS THAT AS WELL!
SHE SURE ACTS LIKE SHE'S FORGOTTEN!
SHE HASN'T, DEAR! VERONICA IS ACTING LIKE A SPOILED BRAT FOR YOU! SHE WANTS YOU TO COME RESCUE HER!
HUH? THEN WHY DO YOU WANT ME TO WALK AWAY FROM HER?
LET ME TELL YOU ABOUT MY DAUGHTER. ALL HER FATHER EVER WANTED WAS A SON TO CARRY ON THE FAMILY NAME!
WHEN VERONICA CAME ALONG, HE WAS DISAPPOINTED ...UNTIL I REMINDED HIM HE COULD TEACH A DAUGHTER ANYTHING HE WOULD TEACH A SON!
HIRAM TAUGHT HER EVERYTHING HE KNEW... AND WHAT HE KNOWS BEST IS MAKING PEOPLE DO AS HE WISHES!
I LEARNED A LONG TIME AGO NOT TO GIVE IN TO HIS MANIPULATIONS!
8

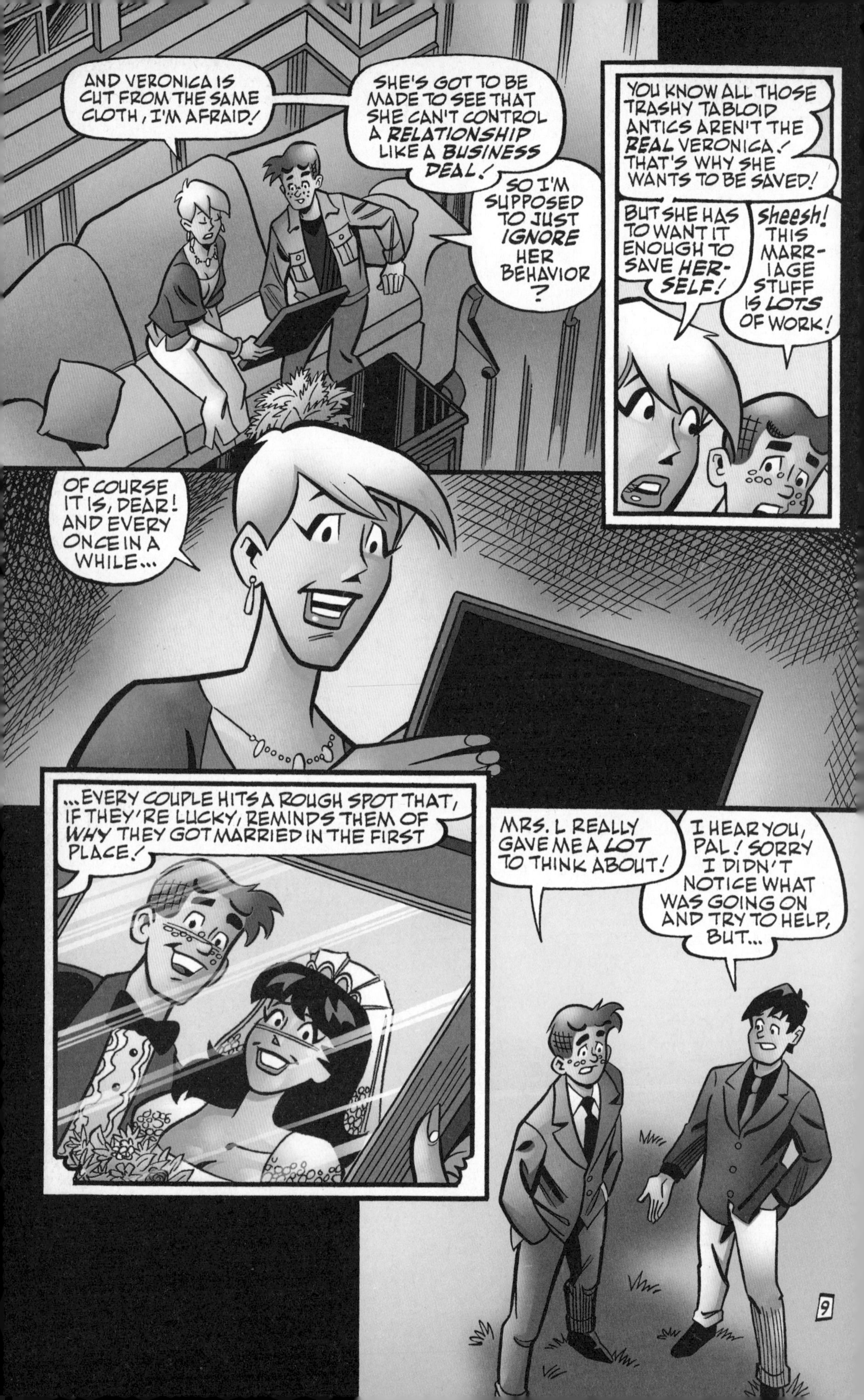

AND VERONICA IS CUT FROM THE SAME CLOTH, I'M AFRAID!
SHE'S GOT TO BE MADE TO SEE THAT SHE CAN'T CONTROL A RELATIONSHIP LIKE A BUSINESS DEAL!
SO I'M SUPPOSED TO JUST IGNORE HER BEHAVIOR?
YOU KNOW ALL THOSE TRASHY TABLOID ANTICS AREN'T THE REAL VERONICA! THAT'S WHY SHE WANTS TO BE SAVED!
BUT SHE HAS TO WANT IT ENOUGH TO SAVE HER-SELF!
Sheesh! THIS MARR-IAGE STUFF IS LOTS OF WORK!
OF COURSE IT IS, DEAR! AND EVERY ONCE IN A WHILE...
...EVERY COUPLE HITS A ROUGH SPOT THAT, IF THEY'RE LUCKY, REMINDS THEM OF WHY THEY GOT MARRIED IN THE FIRST PLACE!
MRS. L REALLY GAVE ME A LOT TO THINK ABOUT!
I HEAR YOU, PAL! SORRY I DIDN'T NOTICE WHAT WAS GOING ON AND TRY TO HELP, BUT...

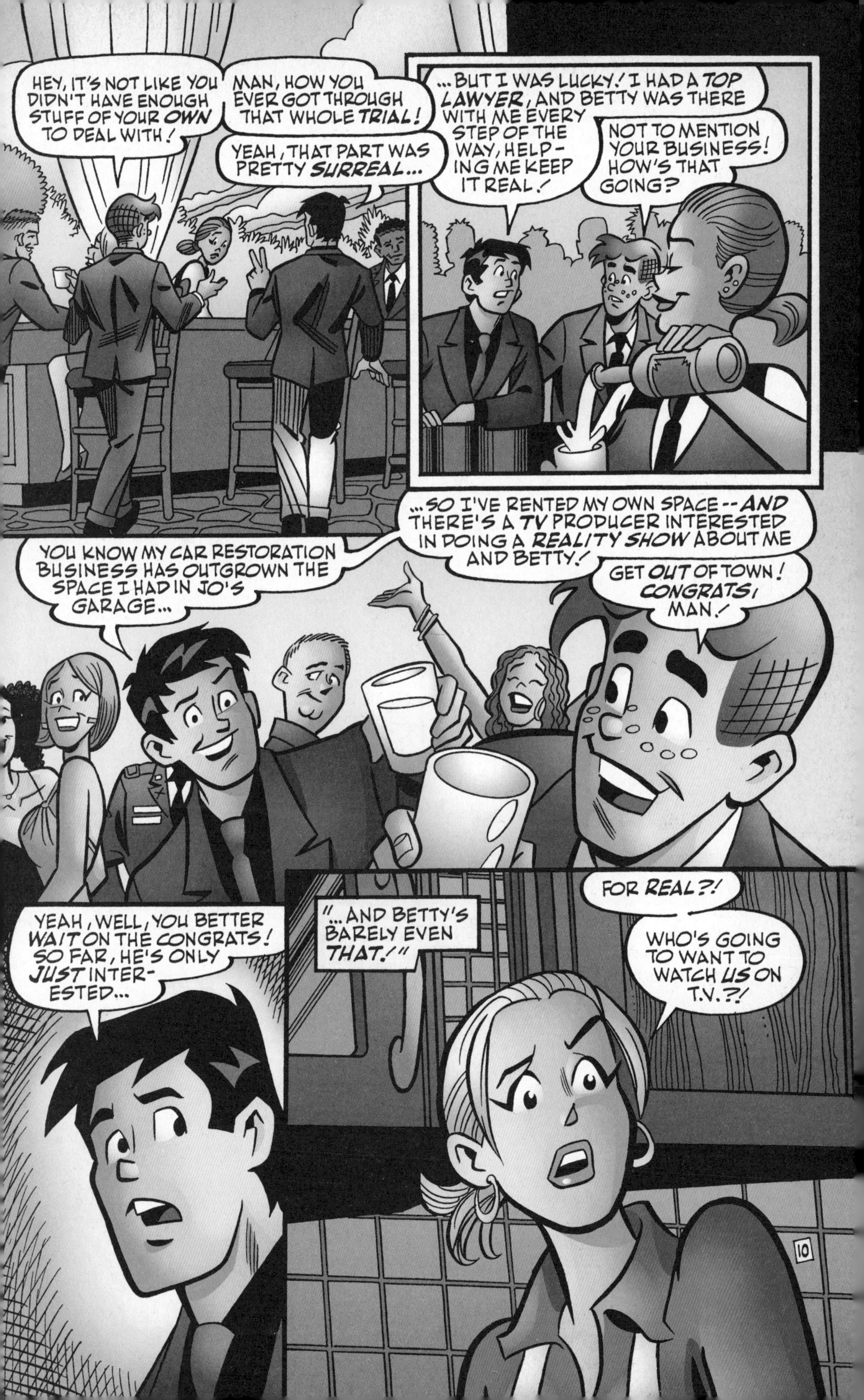

HEY, IT'S NOT LIKE YOU DIDN'T HAVE ENOUGH STUFF OF YOUR OWN TO DEAL WITH!
MAN, HOW YOU EVER GOT THROUGH THAT WHOLE TRIAL!
YEAH, THAT PART WAS PRETTY SURREAL...
...BUT I WAS LUCKY! I HAD A TOP LAWYER, AND BETTY WAS THERE WITH ME EVERY STEP OF THE WAY, HELPING ME KEEP IT REAL!
NOT TO MENTION YOUR BUSINESS! HOW'S THAT GOING?
YOU KNOW MY CAR RESTORATION BUSINESS HAS OUTGROWN THE SPACE I HAD IN JO'S GARAGE...
...SO I'VE RENTED MY OWN SPACE--AND THERE'S A TV PRODUCER INTERESTED IN DOING A REALITY SHOW ABOUT ME AND BETTY!
GET OUT OF TOWN! CONGRATS, MAN!
YEAH, WELL, YOU BETTER WAIT ON THE CONGRATS! SO FAR, HE'S ONLY JUST INTERESTED...
"...AND BETTY'S BARELY EVEN THAT!"
FOR REAL?!
WHO'S GOING TO WANT TO WATCH US ON T.V.?!
10

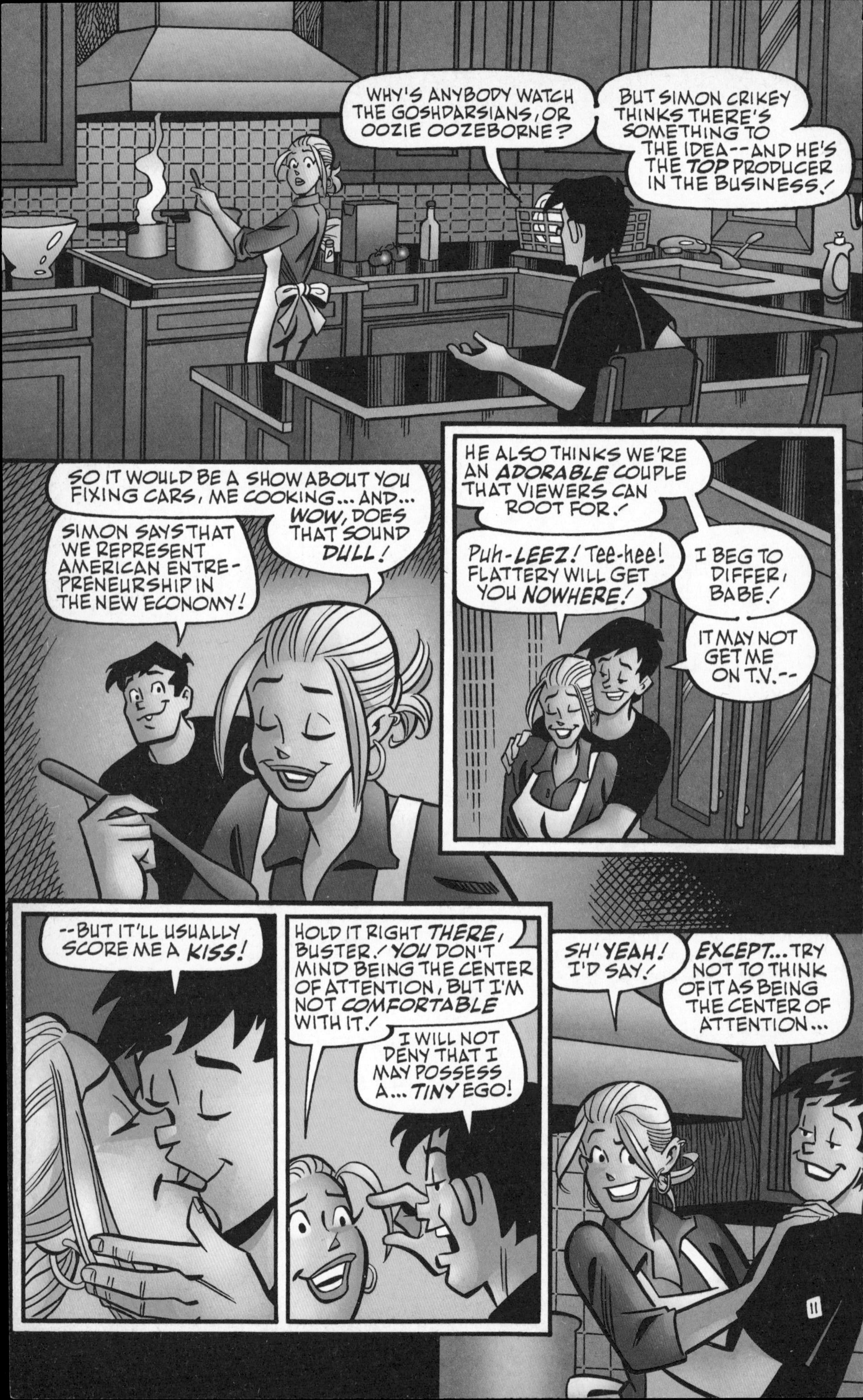
WHY'S ANYBODY WATCH THE GOSHDARSIANS, OR OOZIE OOZEBORNE?
BUT SIMON CRIKEY THINKS THERE'S SOMETHING TO THE IDEA--AND HE'S THE TOP PRODUCER IN THE BUSINESS!
SO IT WOULD BE A SHOW ABOUT YOU FIXING CARS, ME COOKING... AND... WOW, DOES THAT SOUND DULL!
SIMON SAYS THAT WE REPRESENT AMERICAN ENTRE-PRENEURSHIP IN THE NEW ECONOMY!
HE ALSO THINKS WE'RE AN ADORABLE COUPLE THAT VIEWERS CAN ROOT FOR!
Puh-LEEZ! Tee-hee! FLATTERY WILL GET YOU NOWHERE!
I BEG TO DIFFER, BABE!
IT MAY NOT GET ME ON T.V.--
--BUT IT'LL USUALLY SCORE ME A KISS!
HOLD IT RIGHT THERE, BUSTER! YOU DON'T MIND BEING THE CENTER OF ATTENTION, BUT I'M NOT COMFORTABLE WITH IT!
I WILL NOT DENY THAT I MAY POSSESS A... TINY EGO!
SH' YEAH! I'D SAY!
EXCEPT... TRY NOT TO THINK OF IT AS BEING THE CENTER OF ATTENTION...
11

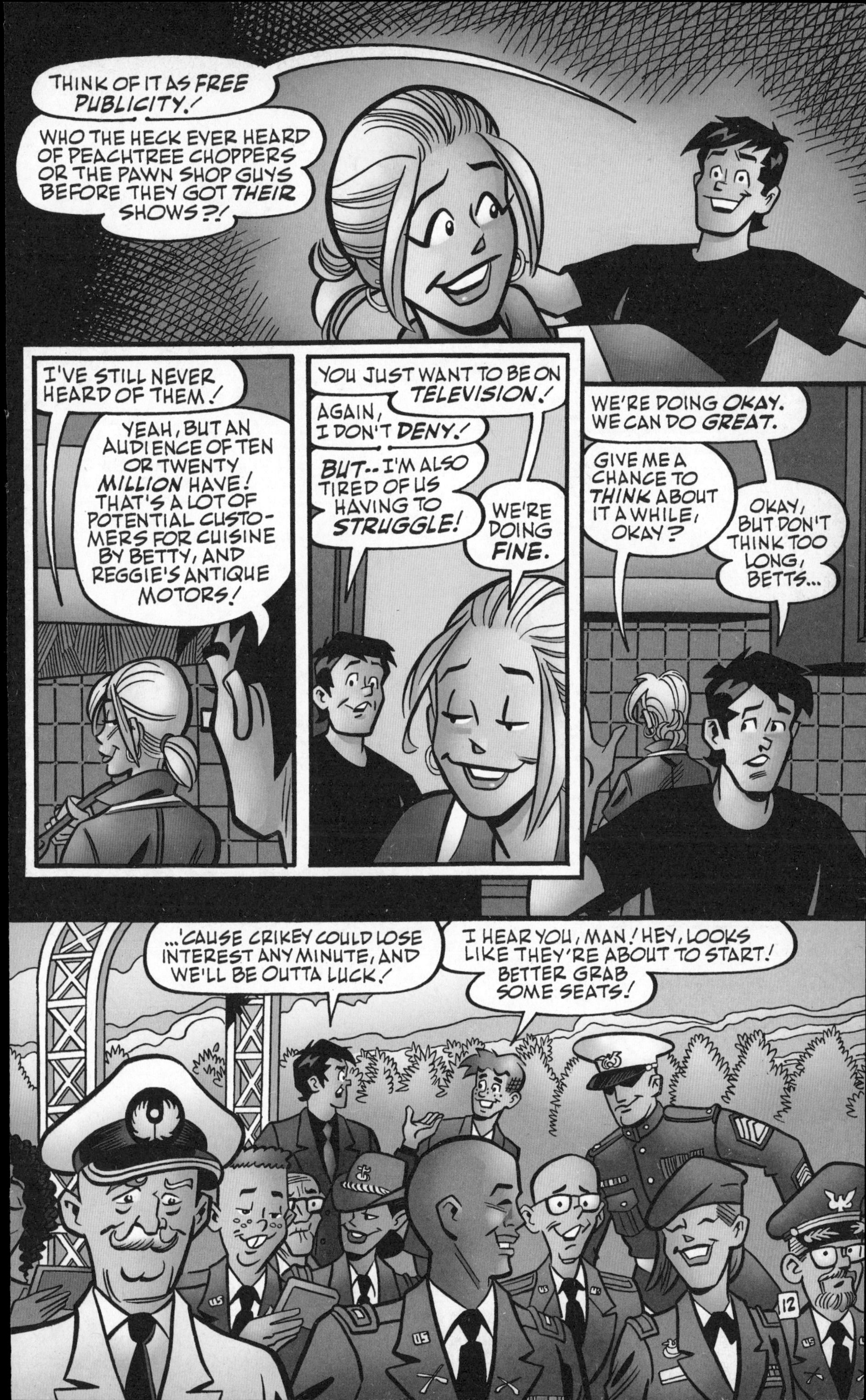
THINK OF IT AS FREE PUBLICITY!
WHO THE HECK EVER HEARD OF PEACHTREE CHOPPERS OR THE PAWN SHOP GUYS BEFORE THEY GOT THEIR SHOWS?!
I'VE STILL NEVER HEARD OF THEM!
YEAH, BUT AN AUDIENCE OF TEN OR TWENTY MILLION HAVE! THAT'S A LOT OF POTENTIAL CUSTO-MERS FOR CUISINE BY BETTY, AND REGGIE'S ANTIQUE MOTORS!
YOU JUST WANT TO BE ON TELEVISION!
AGAIN, I DON'T DENY!
BUT-- I'M ALSO TIRED OF US HAVING TO STRUGGLE!
WE'RE DOING FINE.
WE'RE DOING OKAY. WE CAN DO GREAT.
GIVE ME A CHANCE TO THINK ABOUT IT A WHILE, OKAY?
OKAY, BUT DON'T THINK TOO LONG, BETTS...
...'CAUSE CRIKEY COULD LOSE INTEREST ANY MINUTE, AND WE'LL BE OUTTA LUCK!
I HEAR YOU, MAN! HEY, LOOKS LIKE THEY'RE ABOUT TO START! BETTER GRAB SOME SEATS!
12

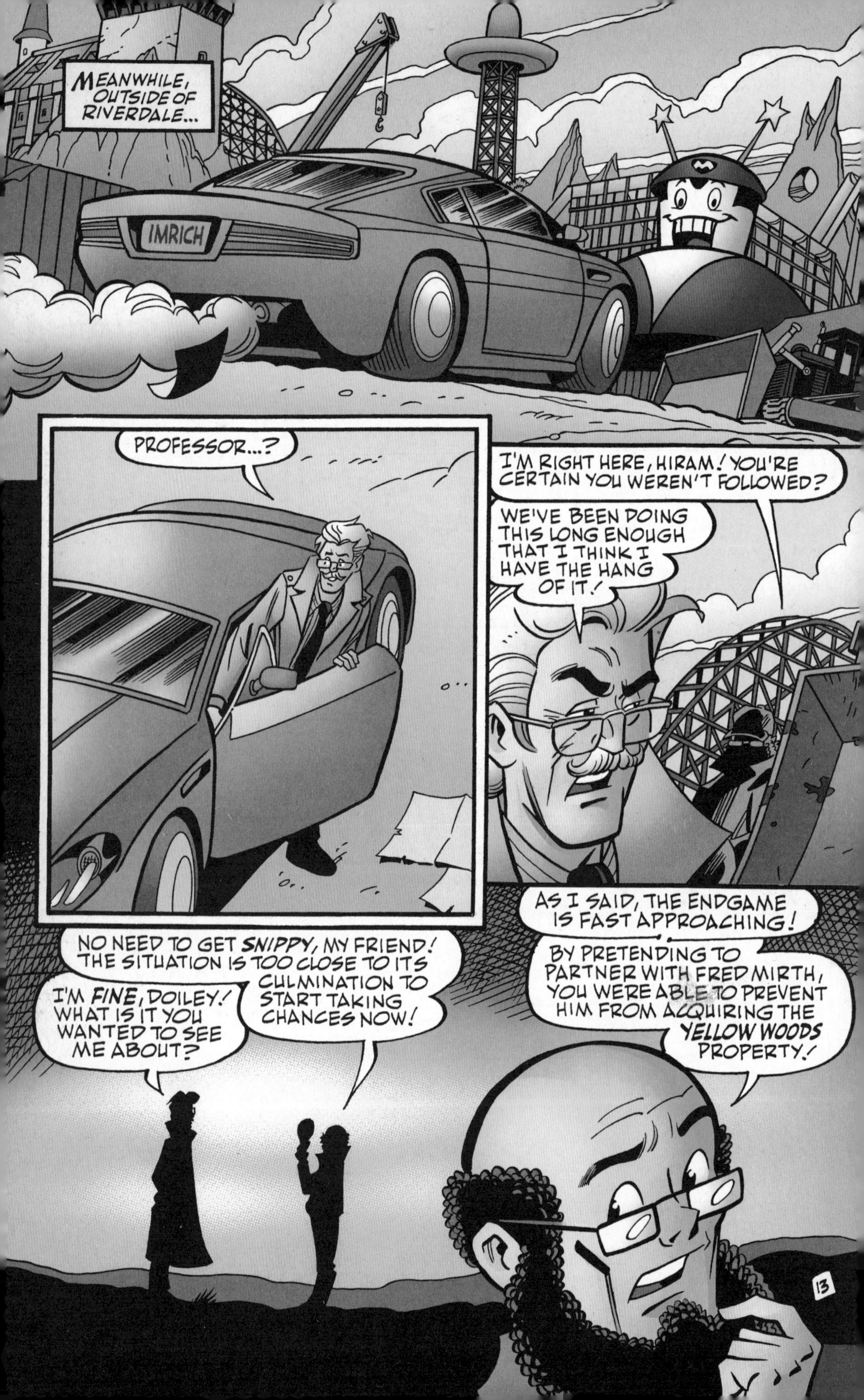
MEANWHILE, OUTSIDE OF RIVERDALE...
IMRICH
PROFESSOR...?
I'M RIGHT HERE, HIRAM! YOU'RE CERTAIN YOU WEREN'T FOLLOWED?
WE'VE BEEN DOING THIS LONG ENOUGH THAT I THINK I HAVE THE HANG OF IT!
NO NEED TO GET SNIPPY, MY FRIEND! THE SITUATION IS TOO CLOSE TO ITS CULMINATION TO START TAKING CHANCES NOW!
I'M FINE, DOILEY! WHAT IS IT YOU WANTED TO SEE ME ABOUT?
AS I SAID, THE ENDGAME IS FAST APPROACHING!
BY PRETENDING TO PARTNER WITH FRED MIRTH, YOU WERE ABLE TO PREVENT HIM FROM ACQUIRING THE YELLOW WOODS PROPERTY!
13

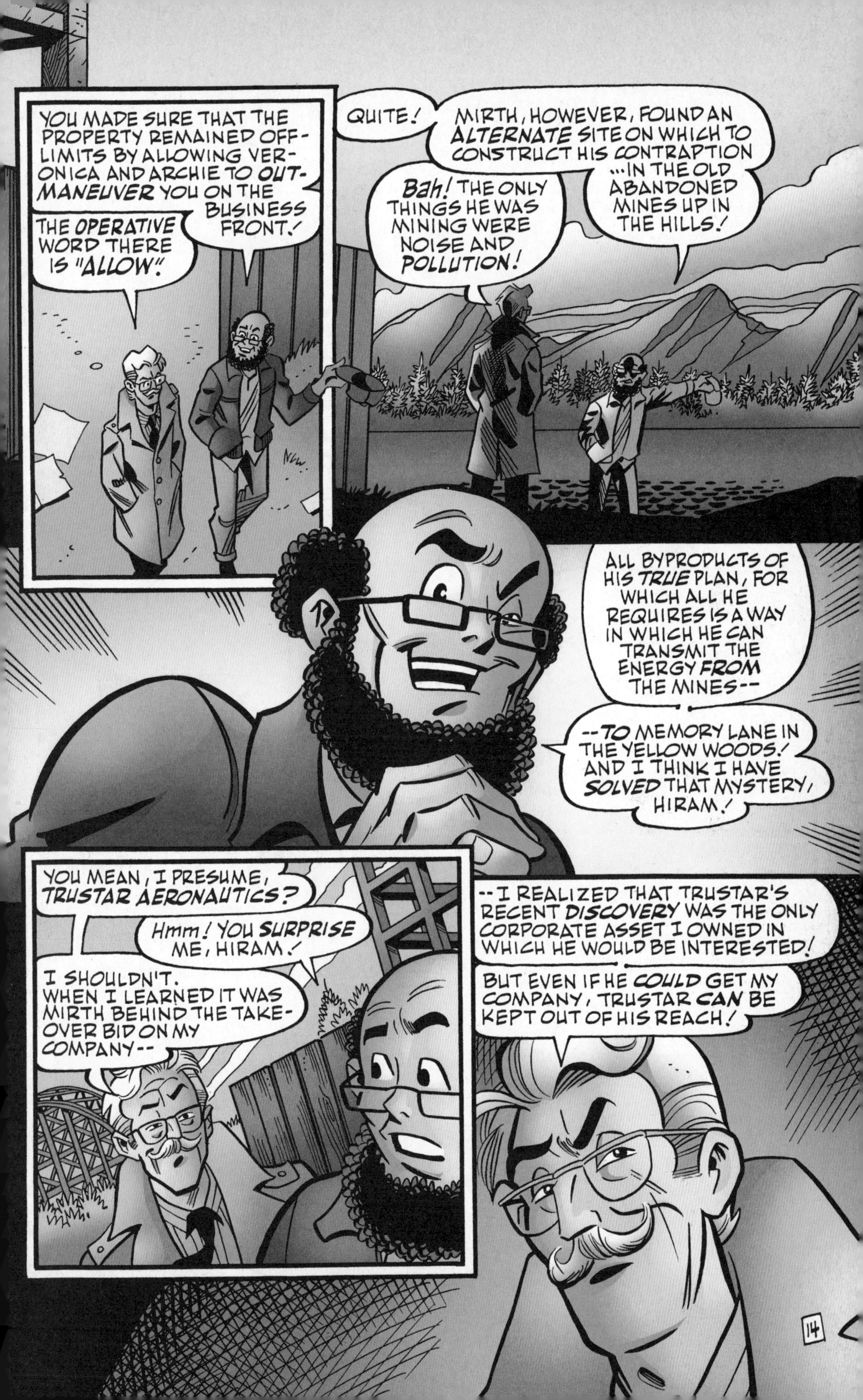
YOU MADE SURE THAT THE PROPERTY REMAINED OFF-LIMITS BY ALLOWING VERONICA AND ARCHIE TO OUT-MANEUVER YOU ON THE BUSINESS FRONT!
THE OPERATIVE WORD THERE IS "ALLOW"!
QUITE!
MIRTH, HOWEVER, FOUND AN ALTERNATE SITE ON WHICH TO CONSTRUCT HIS CONTRAPTION
...IN THE OLD ABANDONED MINES UP IN THE HILLS!
Bah! THE ONLY THINGS HE WAS MINING WERE NOISE AND POLLUTION!
ALL BYPRODUCTS OF HIS TRUE PLAN, FOR WHICH ALL HE REQUIRES IS A WAY IN WHICH HE CAN TRANSMIT THE ENERGY FROM THE MINES--
--TO MEMORY LANE IN THE YELLOW WOODS! AND I THINK I HAVE SOLVED THAT MYSTERY, HIRAM!
YOU MEAN, I PRESUME, TRUSTAR AERONAUTICS?
Hmm! YOU SURPRISE ME, HIRAM!
I SHOULDN'T. WHEN I LEARNED IT WAS MIRTH BEHIND THE TAKE-OVER BID ON MY COMPANY--
--I REALIZED THAT TRUSTAR'S RECENT DISCOVERY WAS THE ONLY CORPORATE ASSET I OWNED IN WHICH HE WOULD BE INTERESTED!
BUT EVEN IF HE COULD GET MY COMPANY, TRUSTAR CAN BE KEPT OUT OF HIS REACH!
14

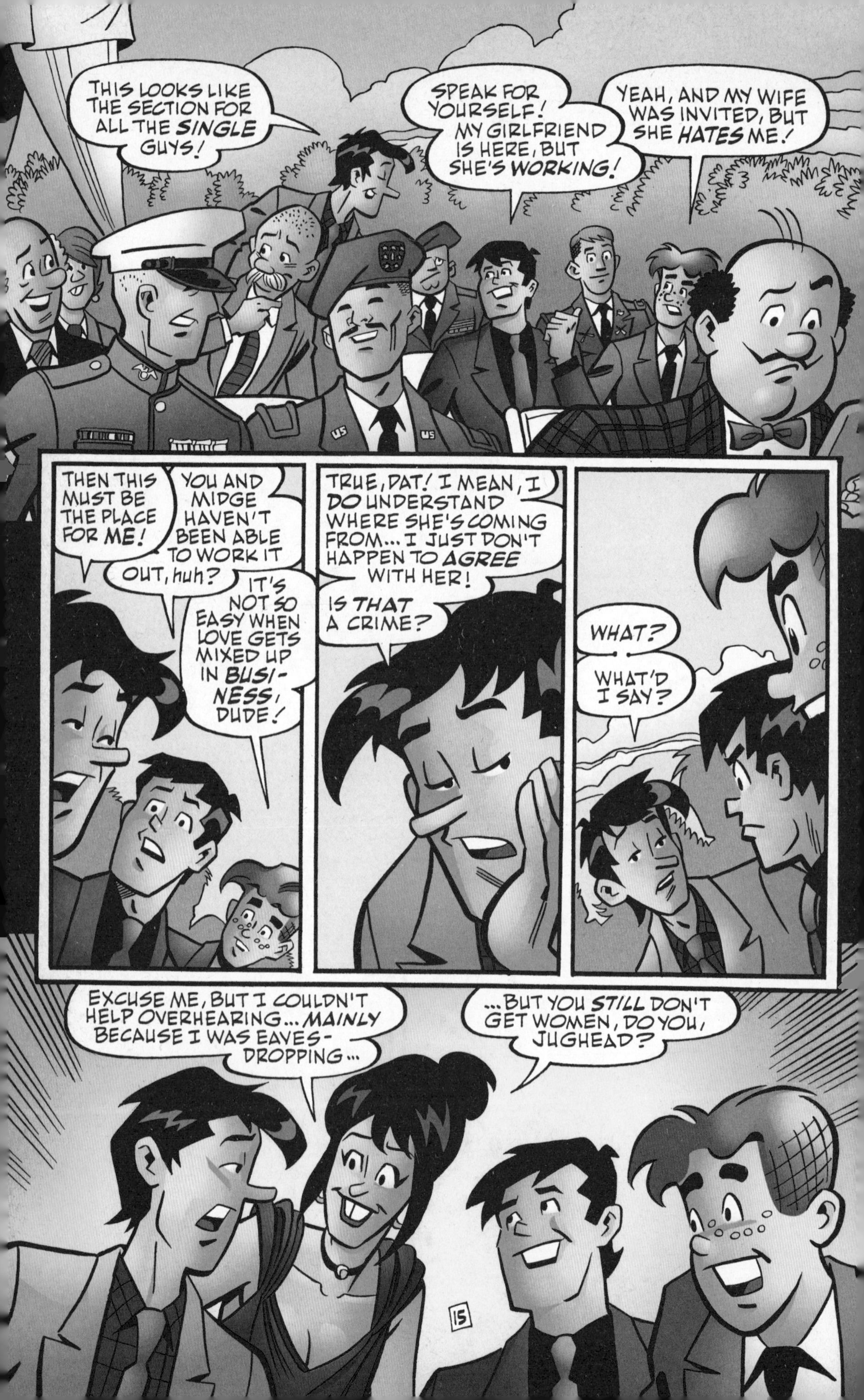
THIS LOOKS LIKE THE SECTION FOR ALL THE SINGLE GUYS!
SPEAK FOR YOURSELF! MY GIRLFRIEND IS HERE, BUT SHE'S WORKING!
YEAH, AND MY WIFE WAS INVITED, BUT SHE HATES ME!
THEN THIS MUST BE THE PLACE FOR ME!
YOU AND MIDGE HAVEN'T BEEN ABLE TO WORK IT OUT, huh?
IT'S NOT SO EASY WHEN LOVE GETS MIXED UP IN BUSI-NESS, DUDE!
TRUE, DAT! I MEAN, I DO UNDERSTAND WHERE SHE'S COMING FROM... I JUST DON'T HAPPEN TO AGREE WITH HER!
IS THAT A CRIME?
WHAT?
WHAT'D I SAY?
EXCUSE ME, BUT I COULDN'T HELP OVERHEARING... MAINLY BECAUSE I WAS EAVES-DROPPING...
...BUT YOU STILL DON'T GET WOMEN, DO YOU, JUGHEAD?

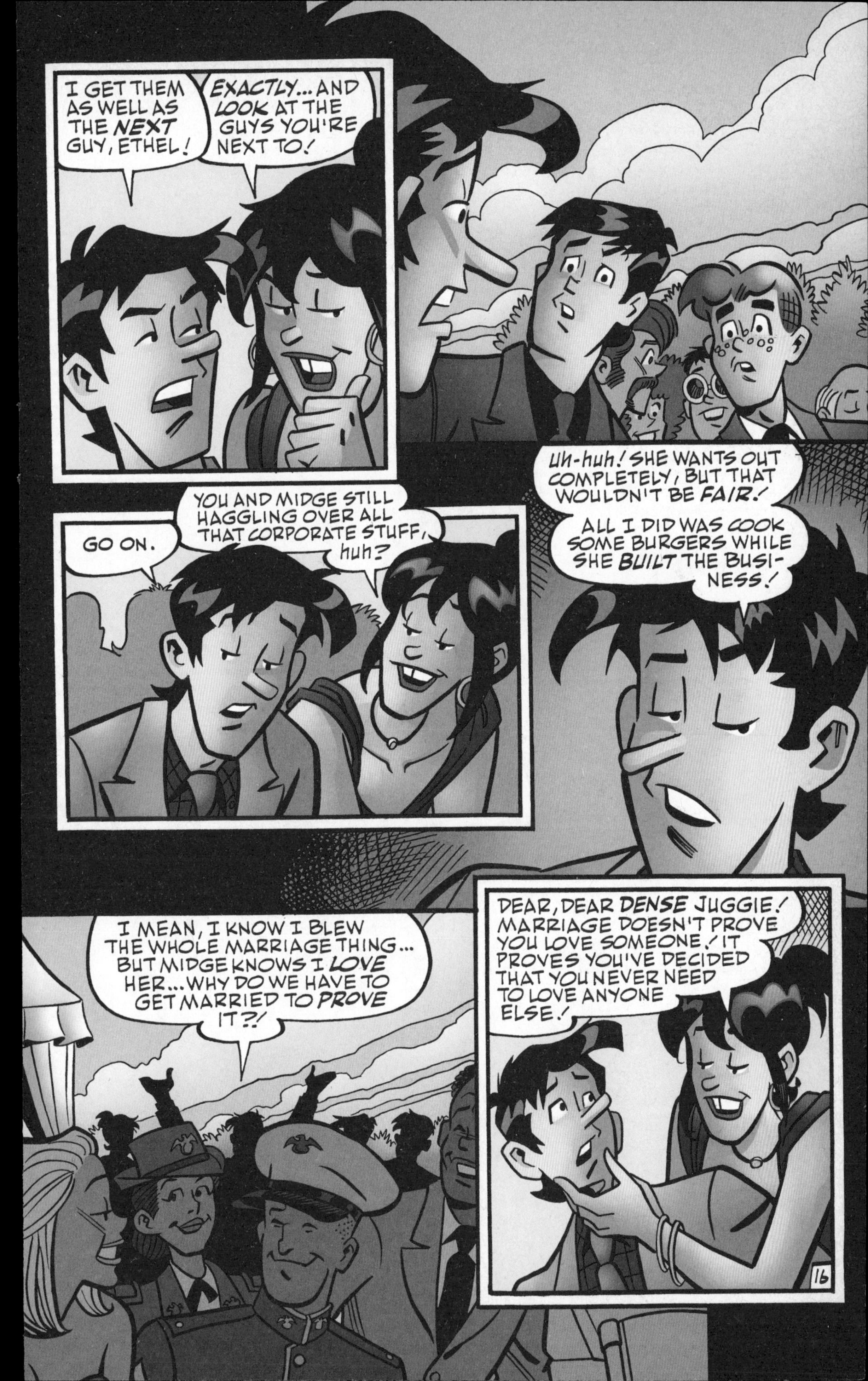
I GET THEM AS WELL AS THE NEXT GUY, ETHEL!
EXACTLY... AND LOOK AT THE GUYS YOU'RE NEXT TO!
GO ON.
YOU AND MIDGE STILL HAGGLING OVER ALL THAT CORPORATE STUFF, huh?
uh-huh! SHE WANTS OUT COMPLETELY, BUT THAT WOULDN'T BE FAIR!
ALL I DID WAS COOK SOME BURGERS WHILE SHE BUILT THE BUSINESS!
I MEAN, I KNOW I BLEW THE WHOLE MARRIAGE THING... BUT MIDGE KNOWS I LOVE HER... WHY DO WE HAVE TO GET MARRIED TO PROVE IT?!
DEAR, DEAR DENSE JUGGIE! MARRIAGE DOESN'T PROVE YOU LOVE SOMEONE! IT PROVES YOU'VE DECIDED THAT YOU NEVER NEED TO LOVE ANYONE ELSE!
16

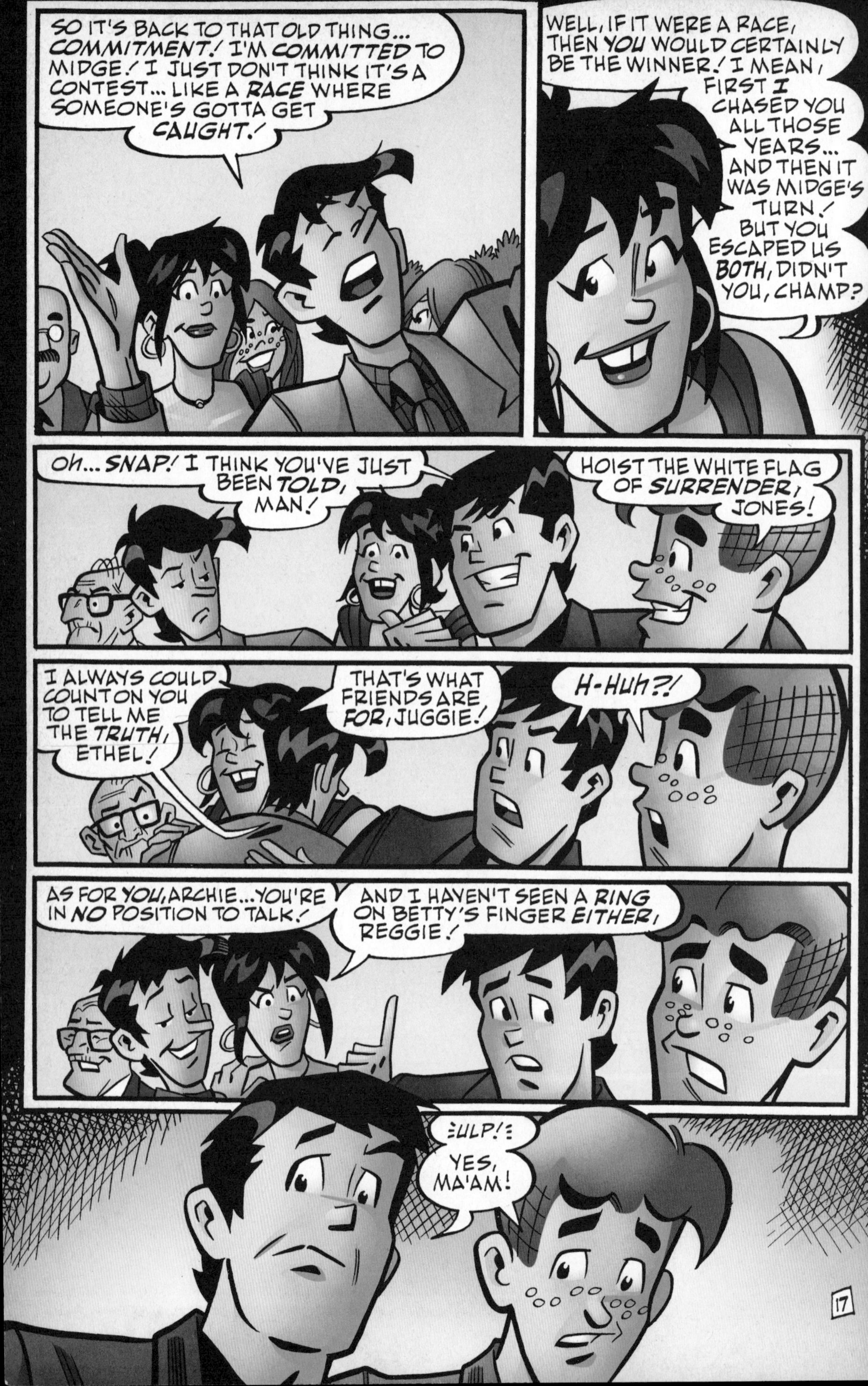
SO IT'S BACK TO THAT OLD THING... COMMITMENT! I'M COMMITTED TO MIDGE! I JUST DON'T THINK IT'S A CONTEST... LIKE A RACE WHERE SOMEONE'S GOTTA GET CAUGHT!
WELL, IF IT WERE A RACE, THEN YOU WOULD CERTAINLY BE THE WINNER! I MEAN, FIRST I CHASED YOU ALL THOSE YEARS... AND THEN IT WAS MIDGE'S TURN! BUT YOU ESCAPED US BOTH, DIDN'T YOU, CHAMP?
Oh... SNAP! I THINK YOU'VE JUST BEEN TOLD, MAN!
HOIST THE WHITE FLAG OF SURRENDER, JONES!
I ALWAYS COULD COUNT ON YOU TO TELL ME THE TRUTH, ETHEL!
THAT'S WHAT FRIENDS ARE FOR, JUGGIE!
H-Huh?!
AS FOR YOU, ARCHIE... YOU'RE IN NO POSITION TO TALK!
AND I HAVEN'T SEEN A RING ON BETTY'S FINGER EITHER, REGGIE!
ULP!
YES, MA'AM!
17

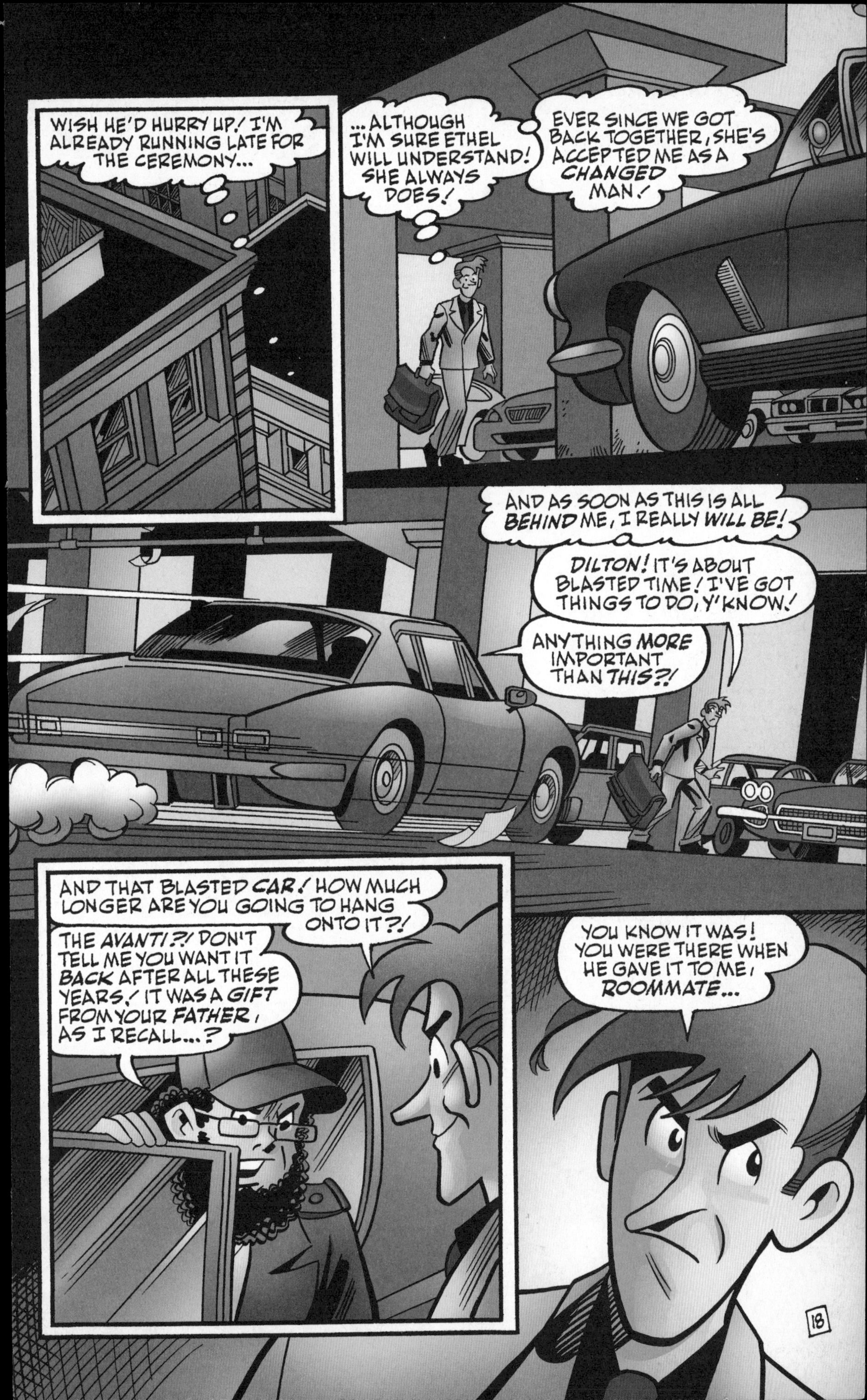
WISH HE'D HURRY UP! I'M ALREADY RUNNING LATE FOR THE CEREMONY...
...ALTHOUGH I'M SURE ETHEL WILL UNDERSTAND! SHE ALWAYS DOES!
EVER SINCE WE GOT BACK TOGETHER, SHE'S ACCEPTED ME AS A CHANGED MAN!
AND AS SOON AS THIS IS ALL BEHIND ME, I REALLY WILL BE!
DILTON! IT'S ABOUT BLASTED TIME! I'VE GOT THINGS TO DO, Y'KNOW!
ANYTHING MORE IMPORTANT THAN THIS?!
AND THAT BLASTED CAR! HOW MUCH LONGER ARE YOU GOING TO HANG ONTO IT?!
THE AVANTI?! DON'T TELL ME YOU WANT IT BACK AFTER ALL THESE YEARS! IT WAS A GIFT FROM YOUR FATHER, AS I RECALL...?
YOU KNOW IT WAS! YOU WERE THERE WHEN HE GAVE IT TO ME, ROOMMATE...
18

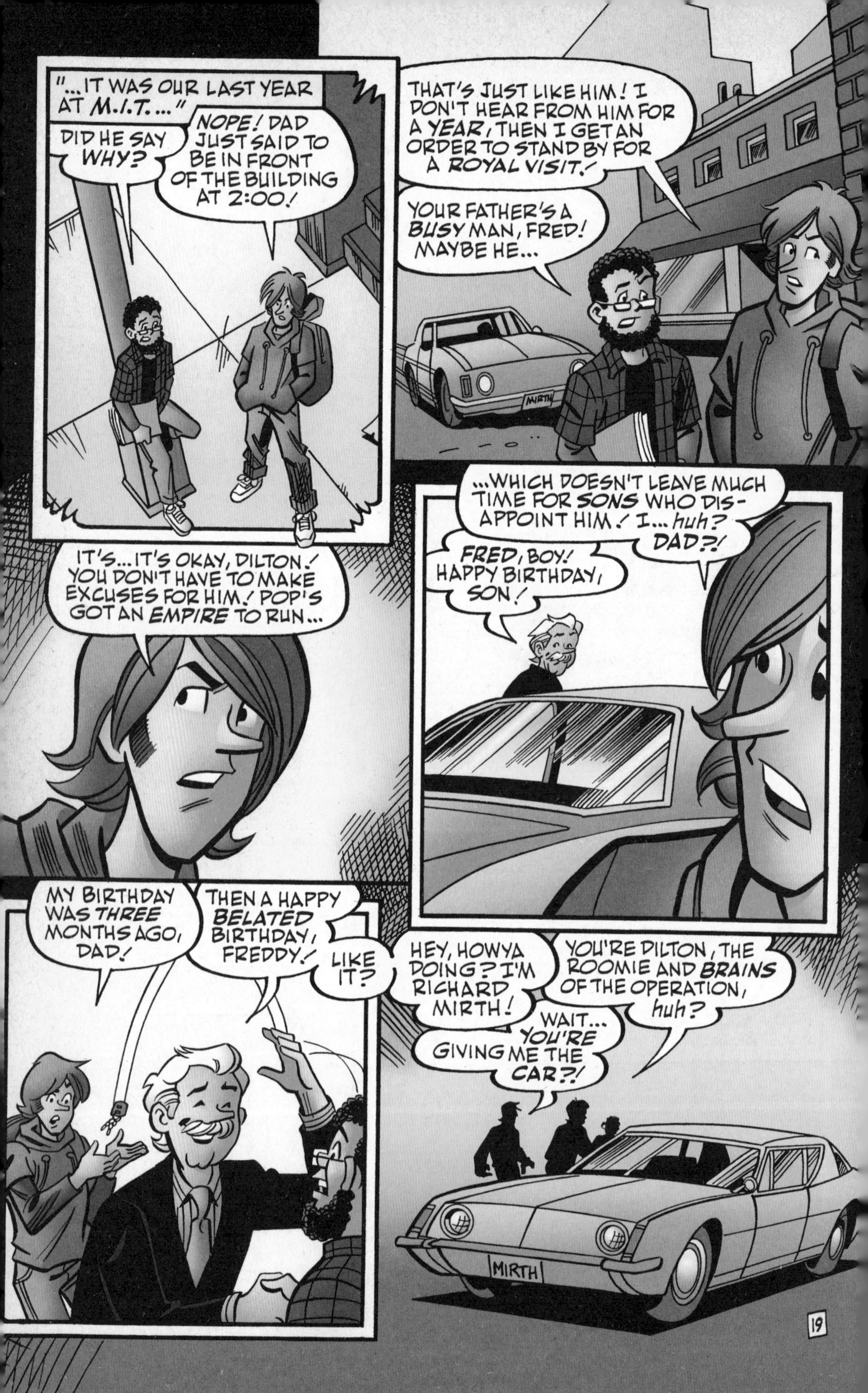
"...IT WAS OUR LAST YEAR AT M.I.T. ..."
DID HE SAY WHY?
NOPE! DAD JUST SAID TO BE IN FRONT OF THE BUILDING AT 2:00!
THAT'S JUST LIKE HIM! I DON'T HEAR FROM HIM FOR A YEAR, THEN I GET AN ORDER TO STAND BY FOR A ROYAL VISIT!
YOUR FATHER'S A BUSY MAN, FRED! MAYBE HE...
MIRTH
IT'S...IT'S OKAY, DILTON! YOU DON'T HAVE TO MAKE EXCUSES FOR HIM! POP'S GOT AN EMPIRE TO RUN...
...WHICH DOESN'T LEAVE MUCH TIME FOR SONS WHO DIS-APPOINT HIM! I... huh? DAD?!
FRED, BOY! HAPPY BIRTHDAY, SON!
MY BIRTHDAY WAS THREE MONTHS AGO, DAD!
THEN A HAPPY BELATED BIRTHDAY, FREDDY!
LIKE IT?
HEY, HOWYA DOING? I'M RICHARD MIRTH!
YOU'RE DILTON, THE ROOMIE AND BRAINS OF THE OPERATION, huh?
WAIT... YOU'RE GIVING ME THE CAR?!
MIRTH

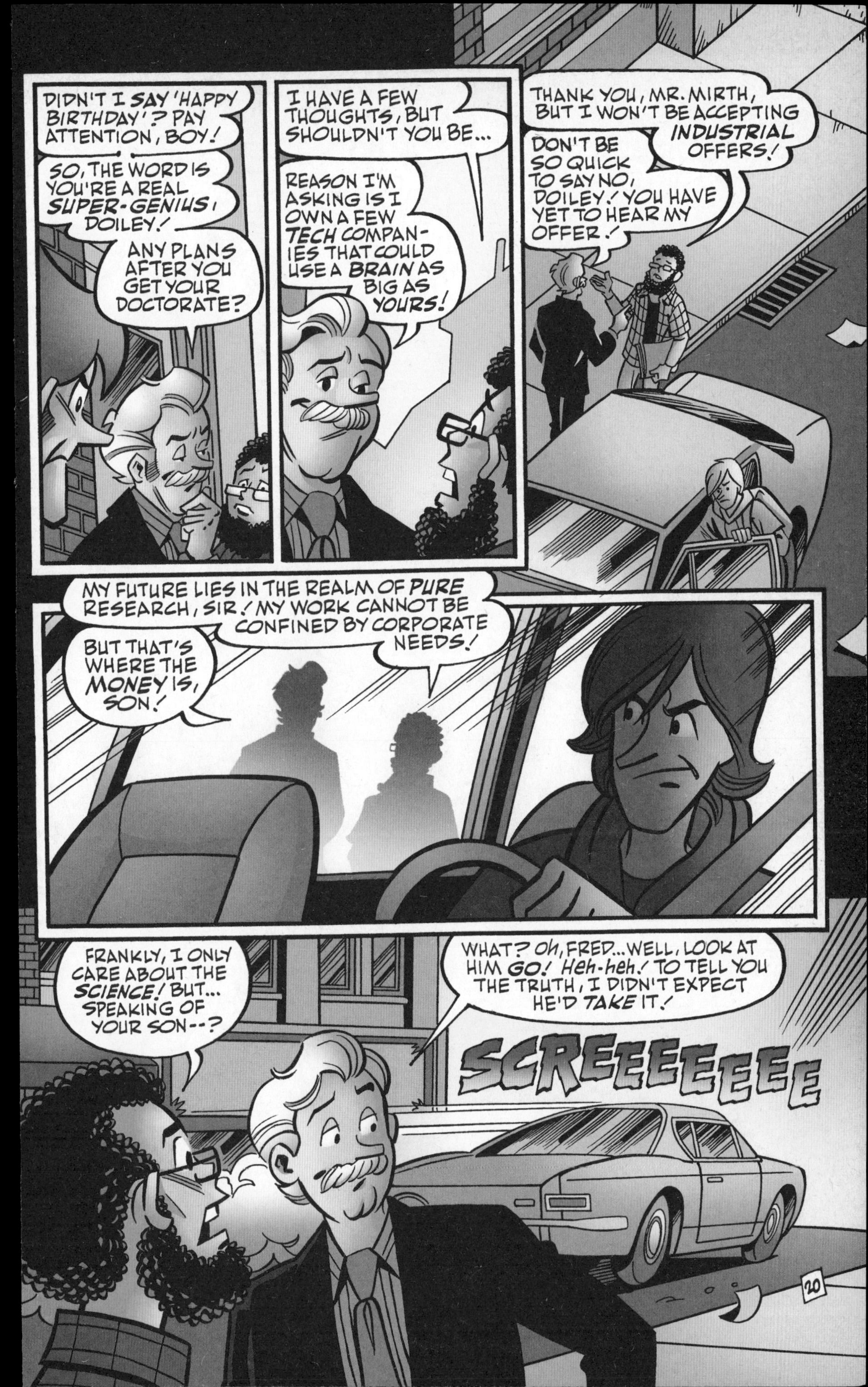
DIDN'T I SAY 'HAPPY BIRTHDAY'? PAY ATTENTION, BOY!
SO, THE WORD IS YOU'RE A REAL SUPER-GENIUS, DOILEY!
ANY PLANS AFTER YOU GET YOUR DOCTORATE?
I HAVE A FEW THOUGHTS, BUT SHOULDN'T YOU BE...
REASON I'M ASKING IS I OWN A FEW TECH COMPANIES THAT COULD USE A BRAIN AS BIG AS YOURS!
THANK YOU, MR. MIRTH, BUT I WON'T BE ACCEPTING INDUSTRIAL OFFERS!
DON'T BE SO QUICK TO SAY NO, DOILEY! YOU HAVE YET TO HEAR MY OFFER!
MY FUTURE LIES IN THE REALM OF PURE RESEARCH, SIR! MY WORK CANNOT BE CONFINED BY CORPORATE NEEDS!
BUT THAT'S WHERE THE MONEY IS, SON!
FRANKLY, I ONLY CARE ABOUT THE SCIENCE! BUT... SPEAKING OF YOUR SON--?
WHAT? OH, FRED... WELL, LOOK AT HIM GO! Heh-heh! TO TELL YOU THE TRUTH, I DIDN'T EXPECT HE'D TAKE IT!
SCREEEEEEEE
20

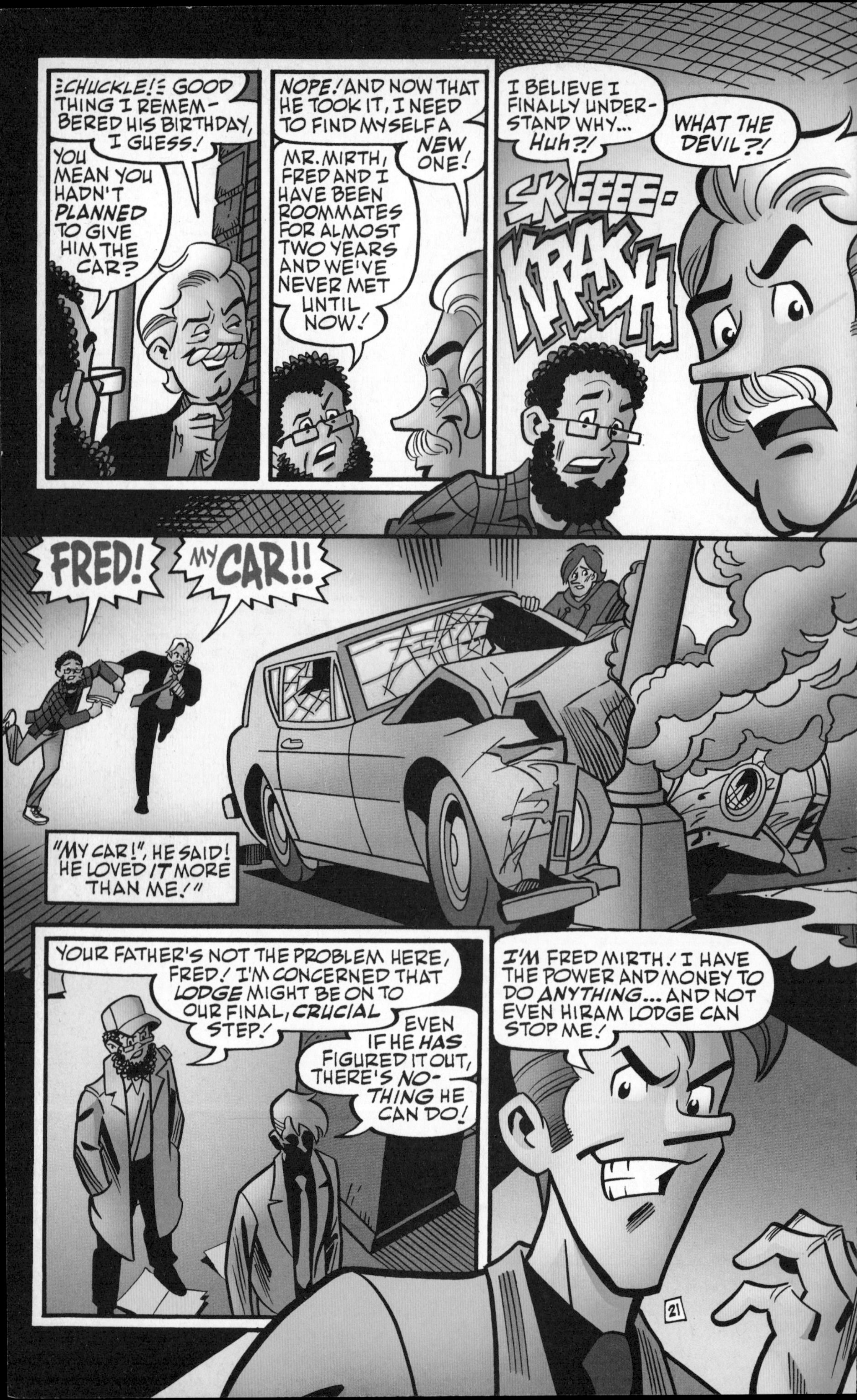

:CHUCKLE!: GOOD THING I REMEMBERED HIS BIRTHDAY, I GUESS!
YOU MEAN YOU HADN'T PLANNED TO GIVE HIM THE CAR?
NOPE! AND NOW THAT HE TOOK IT, I NEED TO FIND MYSELF A NEW ONE!
MR. MIRTH, FRED AND I HAVE BEEN ROOMMATES FOR ALMOST TWO YEARS AND WE'VE NEVER MET UNTIL NOW!
I BELIEVE I FINALLY UNDERSTAND WHY... Huh?!
WHAT THE DEVIL?!
SKEEEE-KRASH
FRED!
MY CAR!!
"MY CAR!", HE SAID! HE LOVED IT MORE THAN ME!"
YOUR FATHER'S NOT THE PROBLEM HERE, FRED! I'M CONCERNED THAT LODGE MIGHT BE ON TO OUR FINAL, CRUCIAL STEP!
EVEN IF HE HAS FIGURED IT OUT, THERE'S NOTHING HE CAN DO!
I'M FRED MIRTH! I HAVE THE POWER AND MONEY TO DO ANYTHING... AND NOT EVEN HIRAM LODGE CAN STOP ME!
21

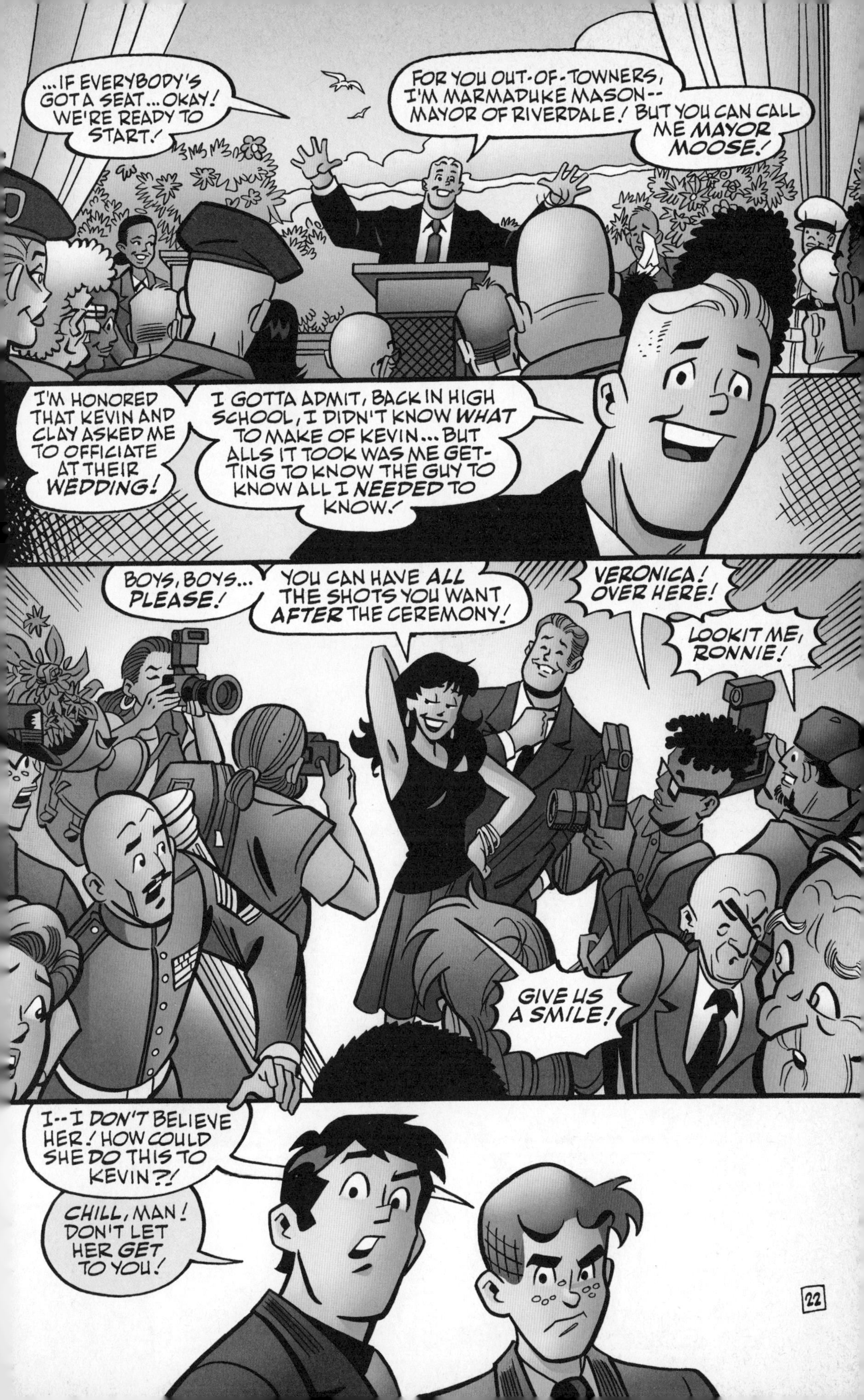
...IF EVERYBODY'S GOT A SEAT...OKAY! WE'RE READY TO START!
FOR YOU OUT-OF-TOWNERS, I'M MARMADUKE MASON-- MAYOR OF RIVERDALE! BUT YOU CAN CALL ME MAYOR MOOSE!
I'M HONORED THAT KEVIN AND CLAY ASKED ME TO OFFICIATE AT THEIR WEDDING!
I GOTTA ADMIT, BACK IN HIGH SCHOOL, I DIDN'T KNOW WHAT TO MAKE OF KEVIN... BUT ALLS IT TOOK WAS ME GETTING TO KNOW THE GUY TO KNOW ALL I NEEDED TO KNOW!
BOYS, BOYS... PLEASE!
YOU CAN HAVE ALL THE SHOTS YOU WANT AFTER THE CEREMONY!
VERONICA! OVER HERE!
LOOKIT ME, RONNIE!
GIVE US A SMILE!
I--I DON'T BELIEVE HER! HOW COULD SHE DO THIS TO KEVIN?!
CHILL, MAN! DON'T LET HER GET TO YOU!

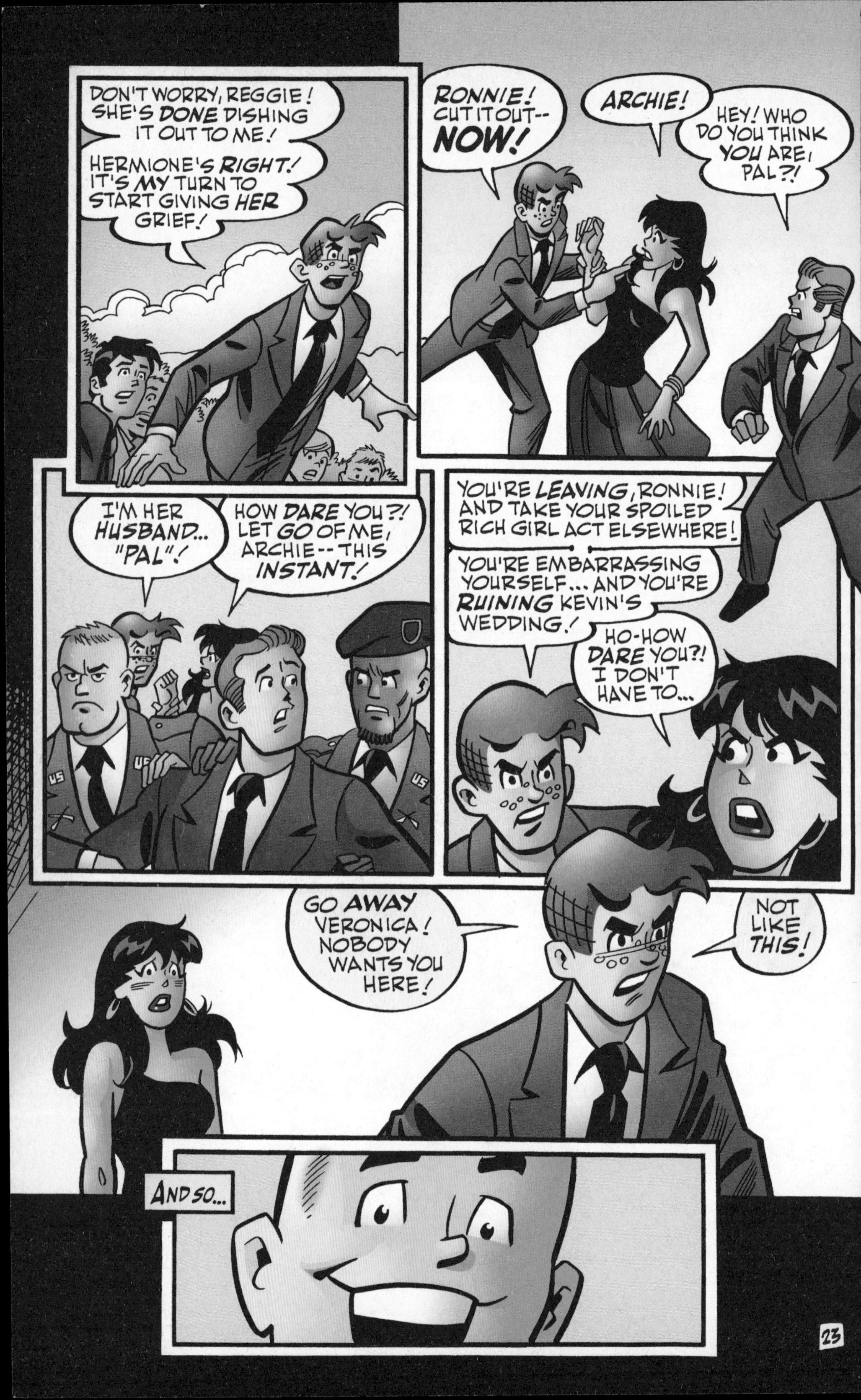
DON'T WORRY, REGGIE! SHE'S DONE DISHING IT OUT TO ME!
HERMIONE'S RIGHT! IT'S MY TURN TO START GIVING HER GRIEF!
RONNIE! CUT IT OUT-- NOW!
ARCHIE!
HEY! WHO DO YOU THINK YOU ARE, PAL?!
I'M HER HUSBAND... "PAL"!
HOW DARE YOU?! LET GO OF ME, ARCHIE-- THIS INSTANT!
YOU'RE LEAVING, RONNIE! AND TAKE YOUR SPOILED RICH GIRL ACT ELSEWHERE!
YOU'RE EMBARRASSING YOURSELF... AND YOU'RE RUINING KEVIN'S WEDDING!
HO-HOW DARE YOU?! I DON'T HAVE TO...
GO AWAY VERONICA! NOBODY WANTS YOU HERE!
NOT LIKE THIS!
AND SO...

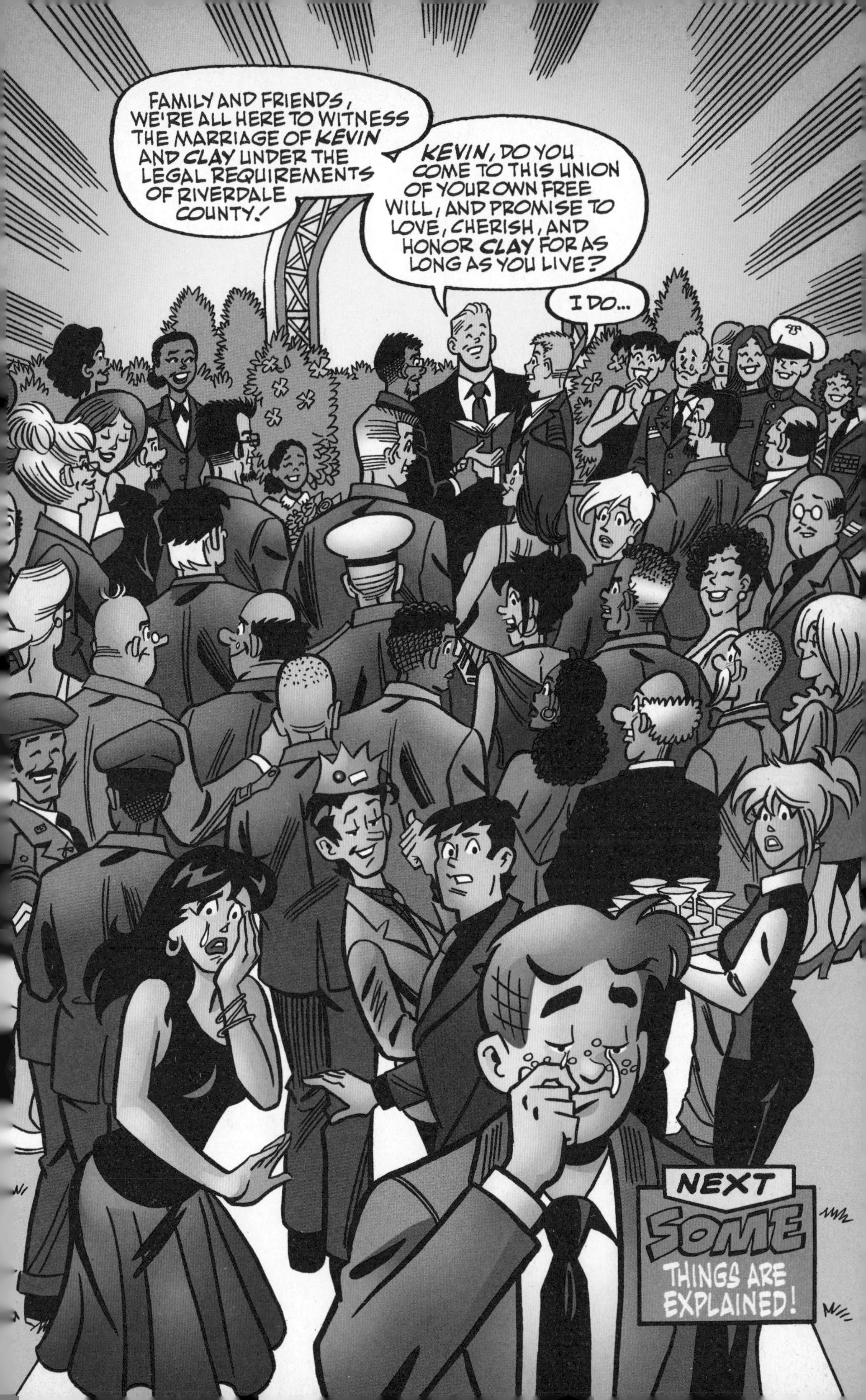
FAMILY AND FRIENDS, WE'RE ALL HERE TO WITNESS THE MARRIAGE OF KEVIN AND CLAY UNDER THE LEGAL REQUIREMENTS OF RIVERDALE COUNTY!
KEVIN, DO YOU COME TO THIS UNION OF YOUR OWN FREE WILL, AND PROMISE TO LOVE, CHERISH, AND HONOR CLAY FOR AS LONG AS YOU LIVE?
I DO...
NEXT
SOME THINGS ARE EXPLAINED!

"...*YOU'RE* RESPONSIBLE FOR THOSE KIDS, AND YOU LET THEM DOWN!"

"IT'S TIME TO STEP UP AND BE THE GROWN-UP, ARCHIE!"

- *COACH CLAYTON*

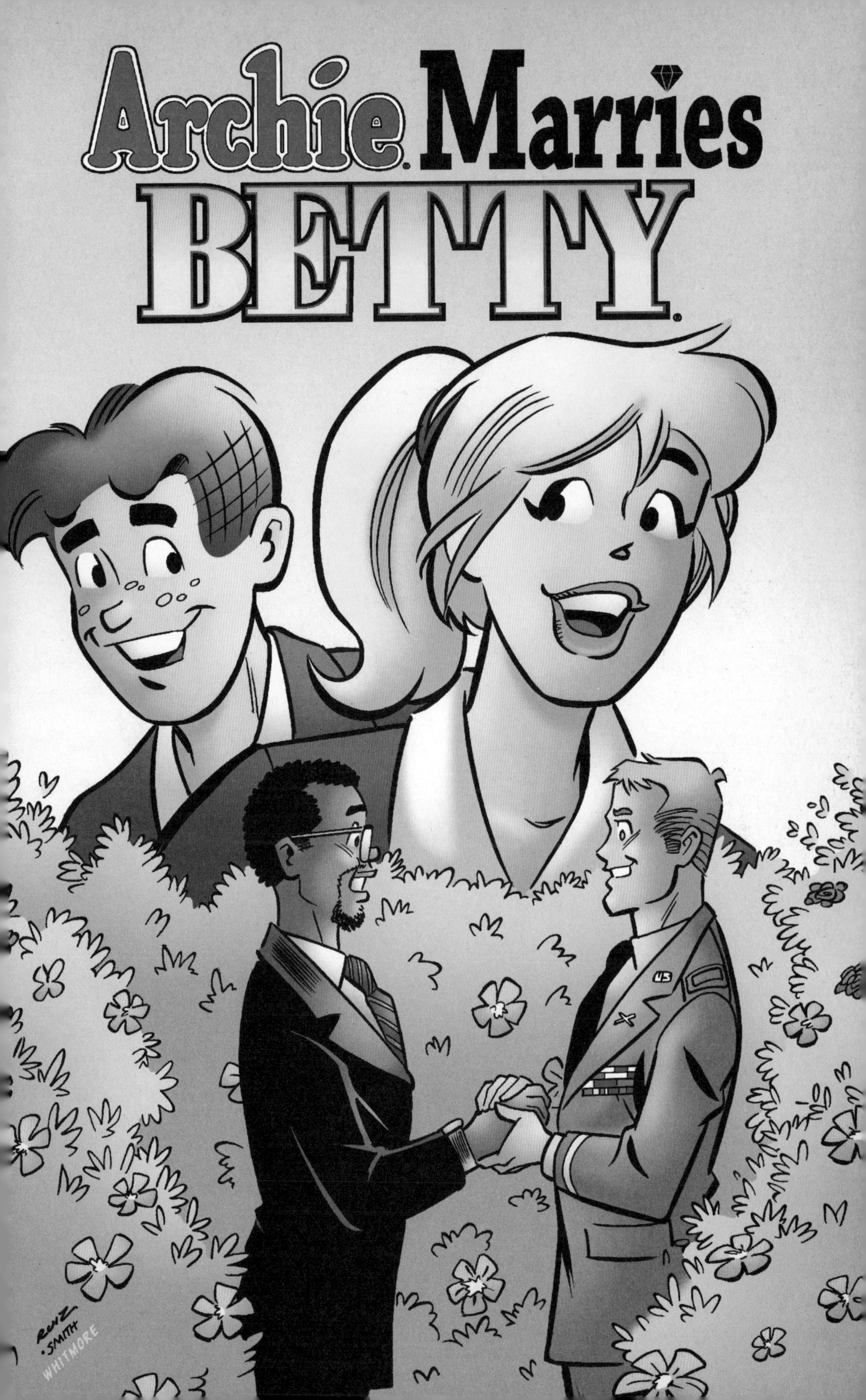
Archie Marries
BETTY

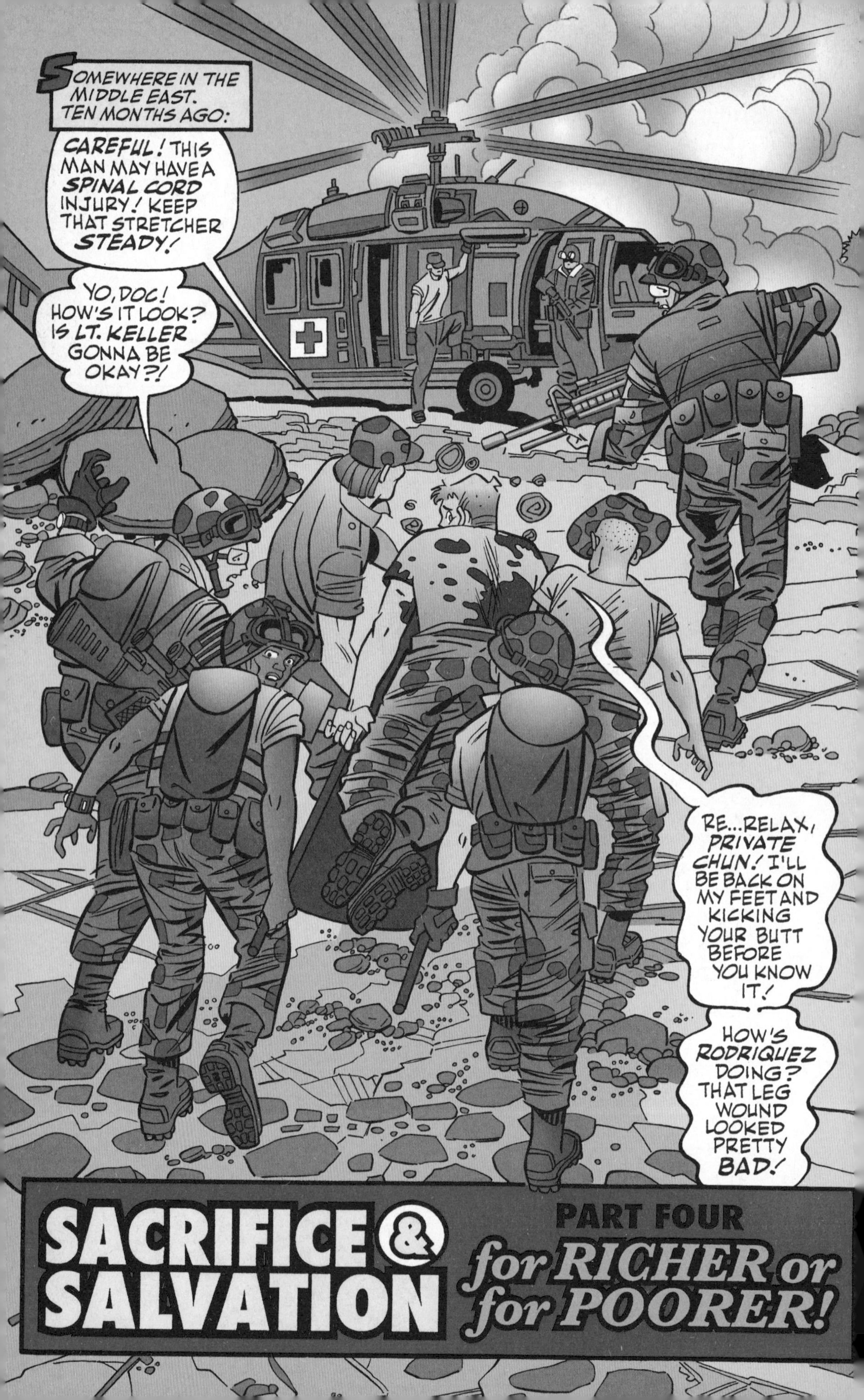
SOMEWHERE IN THE MIDDLE EAST. TEN MONTHS AGO:
CAREFUL! THIS MAN MAY HAVE A SPINAL CORD INJURY! KEEP THAT STRETCHER STEADY!
YO, DOC! HOW'S IT LOOK? IS LT. KELLER GONNA BE OKAY?!
RE...RELAX, PRIVATE CHUN! I'LL BE BACK ON MY FEET AND KICKING YOUR BUTT BEFORE YOU KNOW IT!
HOW'S RODRIQUEZ DOING? THAT LEG WOUND LOOKED PRETTY BAD!
SACRIFICE & SALVATION
PART FOUR
for RICHER or for POORER!

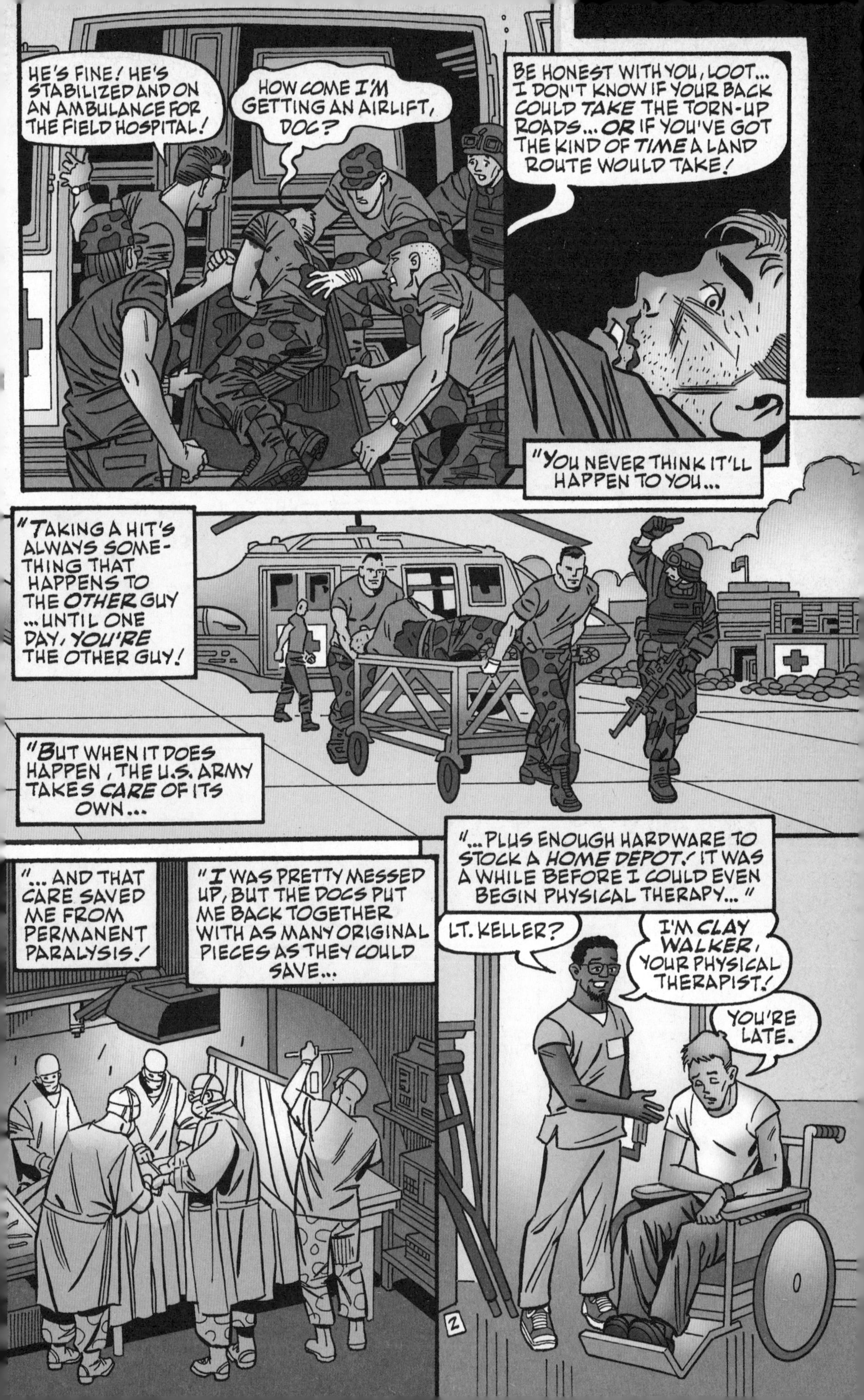
HE'S FINE! HE'S STABILIZED AND ON AN AMBULANCE FOR THE FIELD HOSPITAL!
HOW COME I'M GETTING AN AIRLIFT, DOC?
BE HONEST WITH YOU, LOOT... I DON'T KNOW IF YOUR BACK COULD TAKE THE TORN-UP ROADS... OR IF YOU'VE GOT THE KIND OF TIME A LAND ROUTE WOULD TAKE!
"YOU NEVER THINK IT'LL HAPPEN TO YOU...
"TAKING A HIT'S ALWAYS SOMETHING THAT HAPPENS TO THE OTHER GUY ...UNTIL ONE DAY, YOU'RE THE OTHER GUY!
"BUT WHEN IT DOES HAPPEN, THE U.S. ARMY TAKES CARE OF ITS OWN...
"... AND THAT CARE SAVED ME FROM PERMANENT PARALYSIS!
"I WAS PRETTY MESSED UP, BUT THE DOCS PUT ME BACK TOGETHER WITH AS MANY ORIGINAL PIECES AS THEY COULD SAVE...
"... PLUS ENOUGH HARDWARE TO STOCK A HOME DEPOT! IT WAS A WHILE BEFORE I COULD EVEN BEGIN PHYSICAL THERAPY..."
LT. KELLER?
I'M CLAY WALKER, YOUR PHYSICAL THERAPIST!
YOU'RE LATE.
2

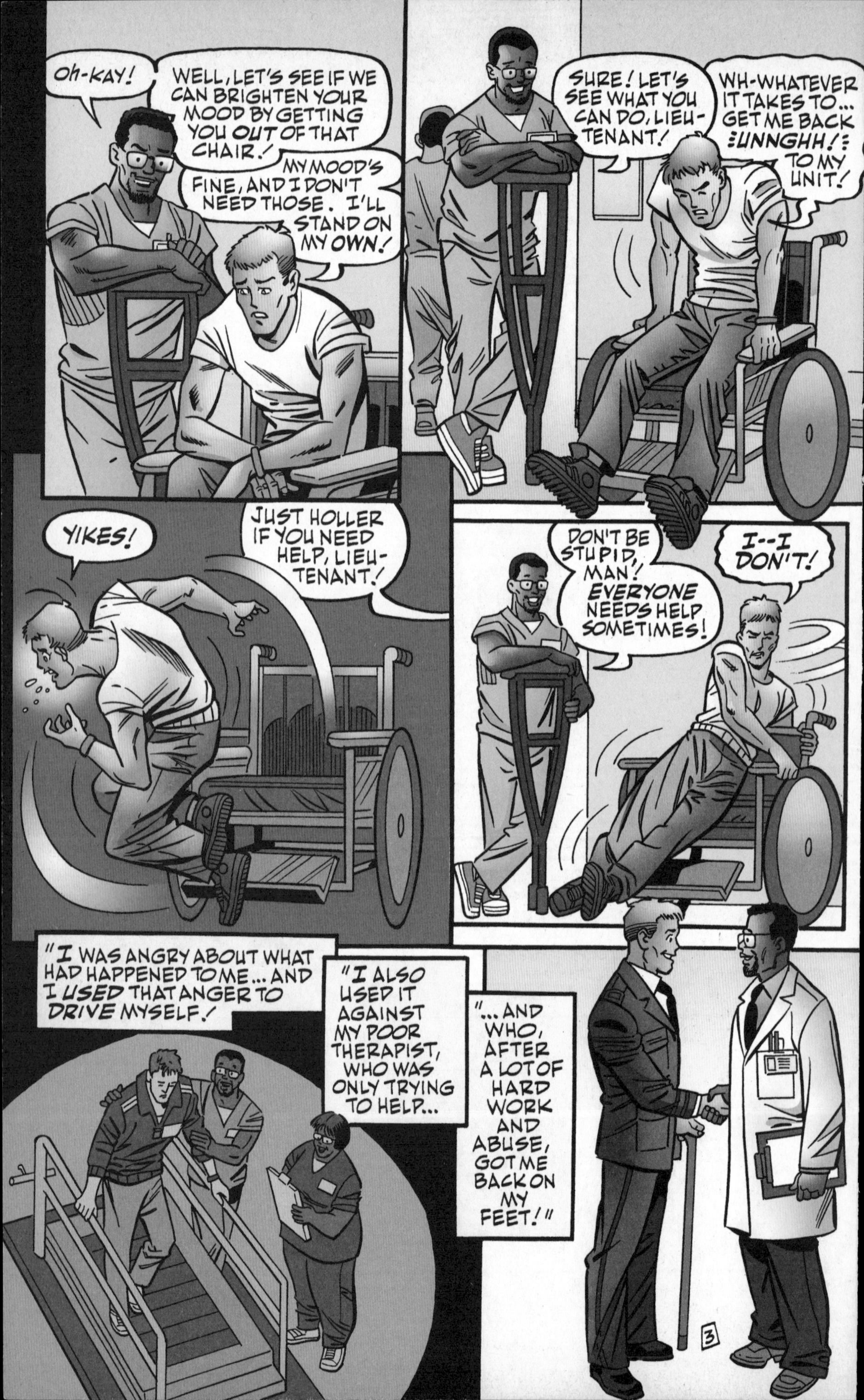

Oh-KAY!
WELL, LET'S SEE IF WE CAN BRIGHTEN YOUR MOOD BY GETTING YOU OUT OF THAT CHAIR.!
MY MOOD'S FINE, AND I DON'T NEED THOSE. I'LL STAND ON MY OWN!
SURE! LET'S SEE WHAT YOU CAN DO, LIEU-TENANT!
WH-WHATEVER IT TAKES TO... GET ME BACK UNNGHH!! TO MY UNIT!
YIKES!
JUST HOLLER IF YOU NEED HELP, LIEU-TENANT!
DON'T BE STUPID, MAN! EVERYONE NEEDS HELP SOMETIMES!
I--I DON'T!
"I WAS ANGRY ABOUT WHAT HAD HAPPENED TO ME... AND I USED THAT ANGER TO DRIVE MYSELF!
"I ALSO USED IT AGAINST MY POOR THERAPIST, WHO WAS ONLY TRYING TO HELP...
"...AND WHO, AFTER A LOT OF HARD WORK AND ABUSE, GOT ME BACK ON MY FEET!"

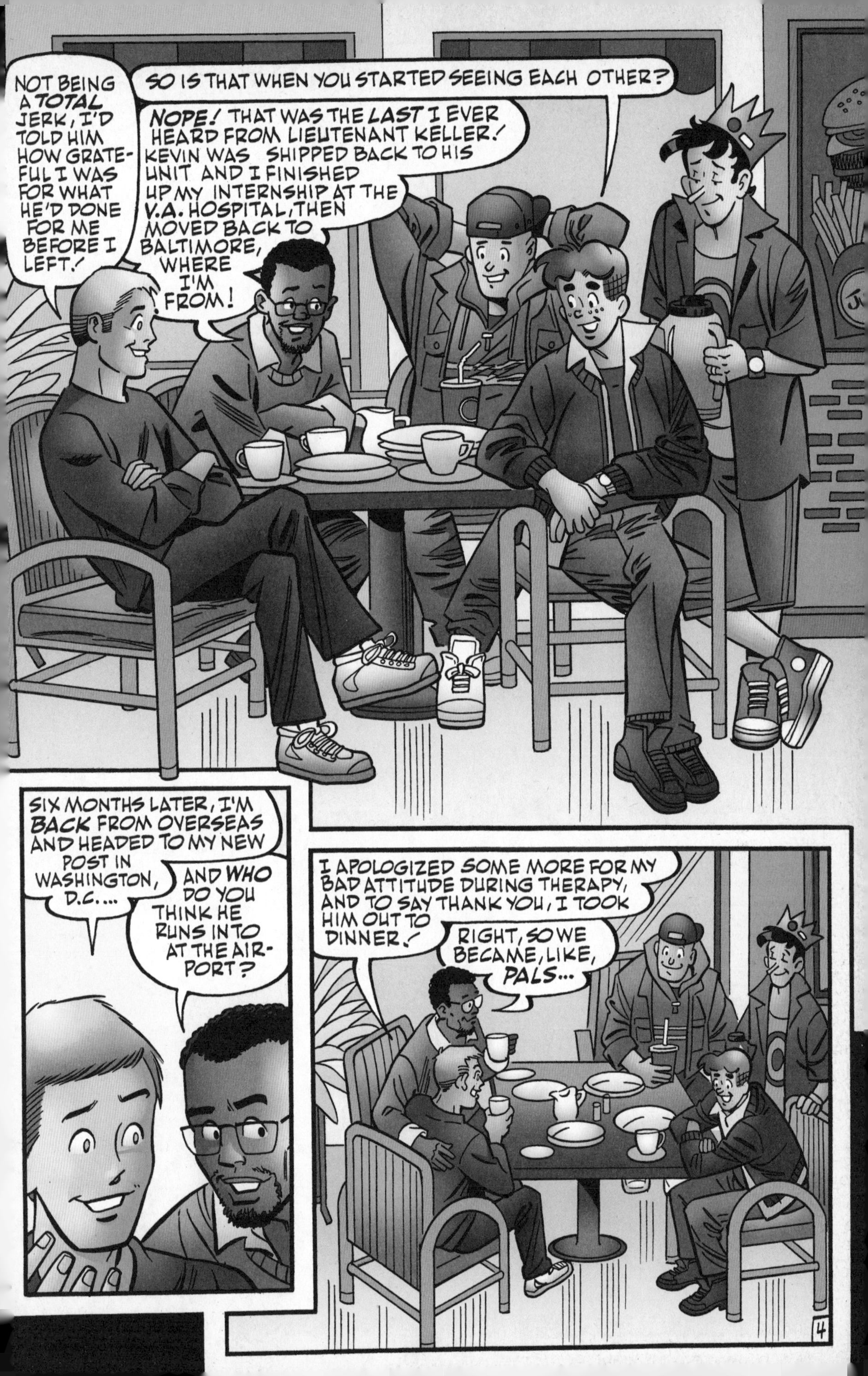

NOT BEING A TOTAL JERK, I'D TOLD HIM HOW GRATEFUL I WAS FOR WHAT HE'D DONE FOR ME BEFORE I LEFT!
SO IS THAT WHEN YOU STARTED SEEING EACH OTHER?
NOPE! THAT WAS THE LAST I EVER HEARD FROM LIEUTENANT KELLER! KEVIN WAS SHIPPED BACK TO HIS UNIT AND I FINISHED UP MY INTERNSHIP AT THE V.A. HOSPITAL, THEN MOVED BACK TO BALTIMORE, WHERE I'M FROM!
SIX MONTHS LATER, I'M BACK FROM OVERSEAS AND HEADED TO MY NEW POST IN WASHINGTON, D.C....
AND WHO DO YOU THINK HE RUNS INTO AT THE AIRPORT?
I APOLOGIZED SOME MORE FOR MY BAD ATTITUDE DURING THERAPY, AND TO SAY THANK YOU, I TOOK HIM OUT TO DINNER!
RIGHT, SO WE BECAME, LIKE, PALS...
4

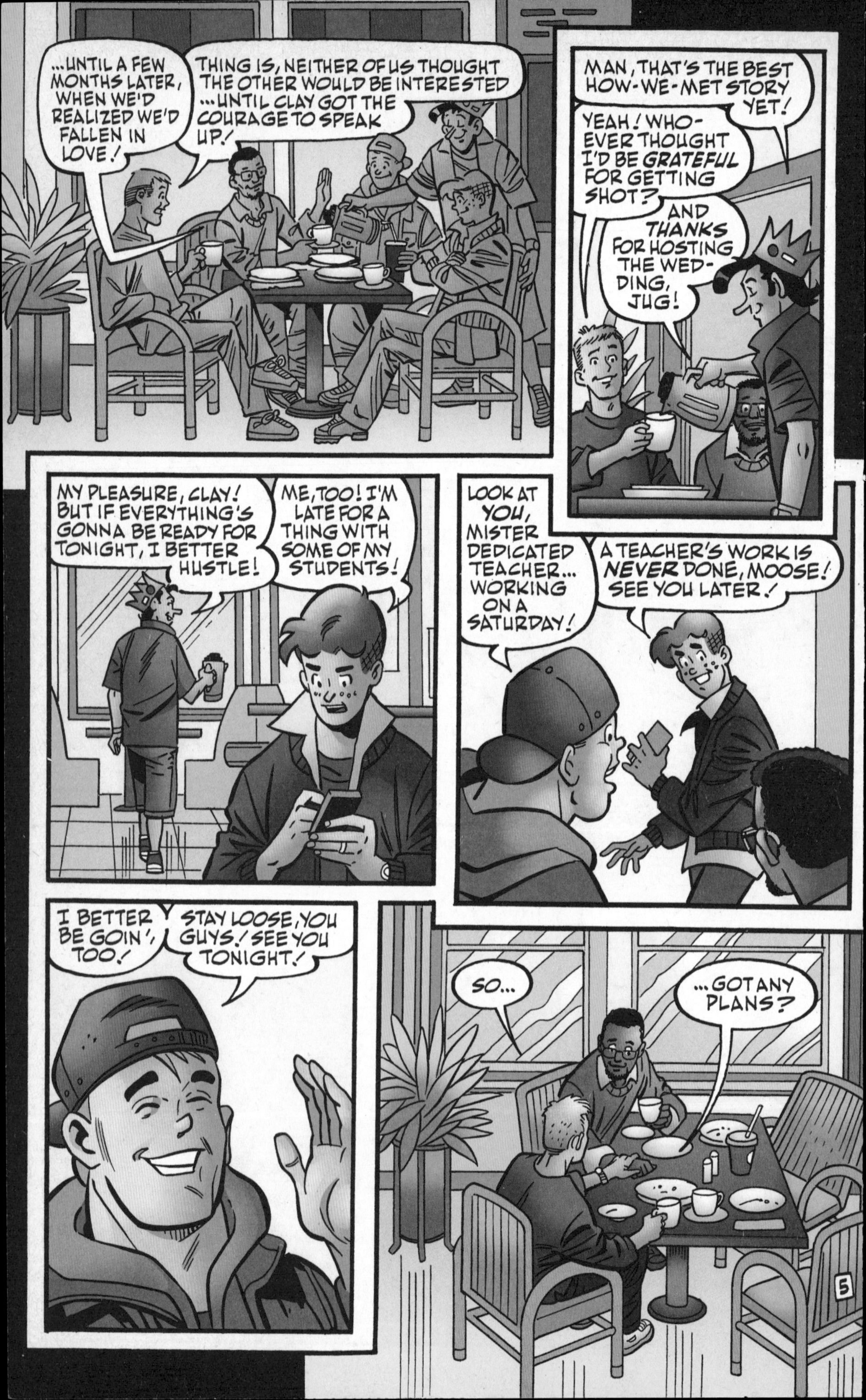
...UNTIL A FEW MONTHS LATER, WHEN WE'D REALIZED WE'D FALLEN IN LOVE!
THING IS, NEITHER OF US THOUGHT THE OTHER WOULD BE INTERESTED ...UNTIL CLAY GOT THE COURAGE TO SPEAK UP!
MAN, THAT'S THE BEST HOW-WE-MET STORY YET!
YEAH! WHO-EVER THOUGHT I'D BE GRATEFUL FOR GETTING SHOT?
AND THANKS FOR HOSTING THE WED-DING, JUG!
MY PLEASURE, CLAY! BUT IF EVERYTHING'S GONNA BE READY FOR TONIGHT, I BETTER HUSTLE!
ME, TOO! I'M LATE FOR A THING WITH SOME OF MY STUDENTS!
LOOK AT YOU, MISTER DEDICATED TEACHER... WORKING ON A SATURDAY!
A TEACHER'S WORK IS NEVER DONE, MOOSE! SEE YOU LATER!
I BETTER BE GOIN', TOO!
STAY LOOSE, YOU GUYS! SEE YOU TONIGHT!
SO...
...GOT ANY PLANS?
5

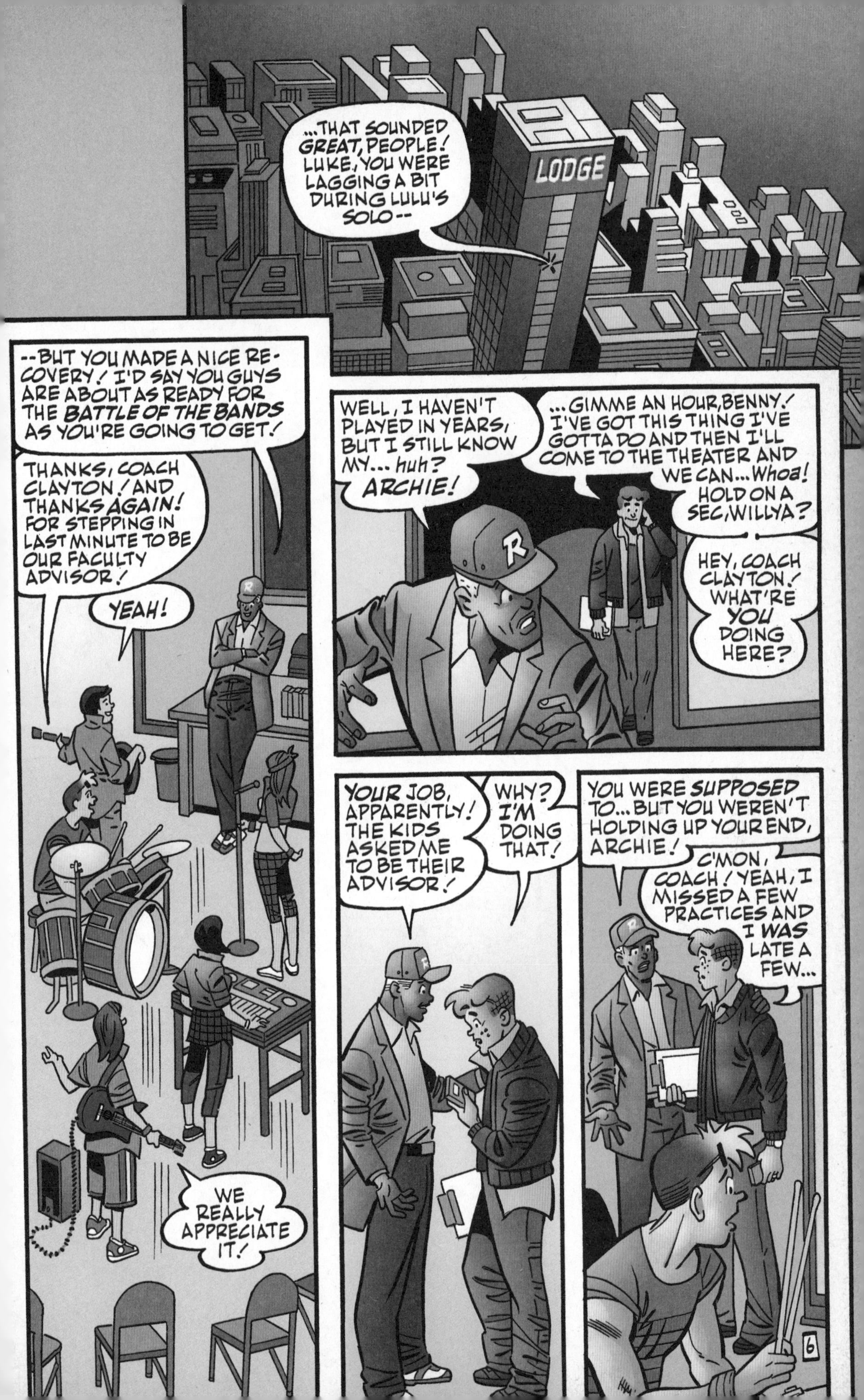
...THAT SOUNDED GREAT, PEOPLE! LUKE, YOU WERE LAGGING A BIT DURING LULU'S SOLO--
LODGE
--BUT YOU MADE A NICE RE-COVERY! I'D SAY YOU GUYS ARE ABOUT AS READY FOR THE BATTLE OF THE BANDS AS YOU'RE GOING TO GET!
THANKS, COACH CLAYTON! AND THANKS AGAIN! FOR STEPPING IN LAST MINUTE TO BE OUR FACULTY ADVISOR!
YEAH!
WE REALLY APPRECIATE IT!
WELL, I HAVEN'T PLAYED IN YEARS, BUT I STILL KNOW MY... huh? ARCHIE!
...GIMME AN HOUR, BENNY! I'VE GOT THIS THING I'VE GOTTA DO AND THEN I'LL COME TO THE THEATER AND WE CAN... Whoa! HOLD ON A SEC, WILLYA?
HEY, COACH CLAYTON! WHAT'RE YOU DOING HERE?
YOUR JOB, APPARENTLY! THE KIDS ASKED ME TO BE THEIR ADVISOR!
WHY? I'M DOING THAT!
YOU WERE SUPPOSED TO... BUT YOU WEREN'T HOLDING UP YOUR END, ARCHIE!
C'MON, COACH! YEAH, I MISSED A FEW PRACTICES AND I WAS LATE A FEW...
6

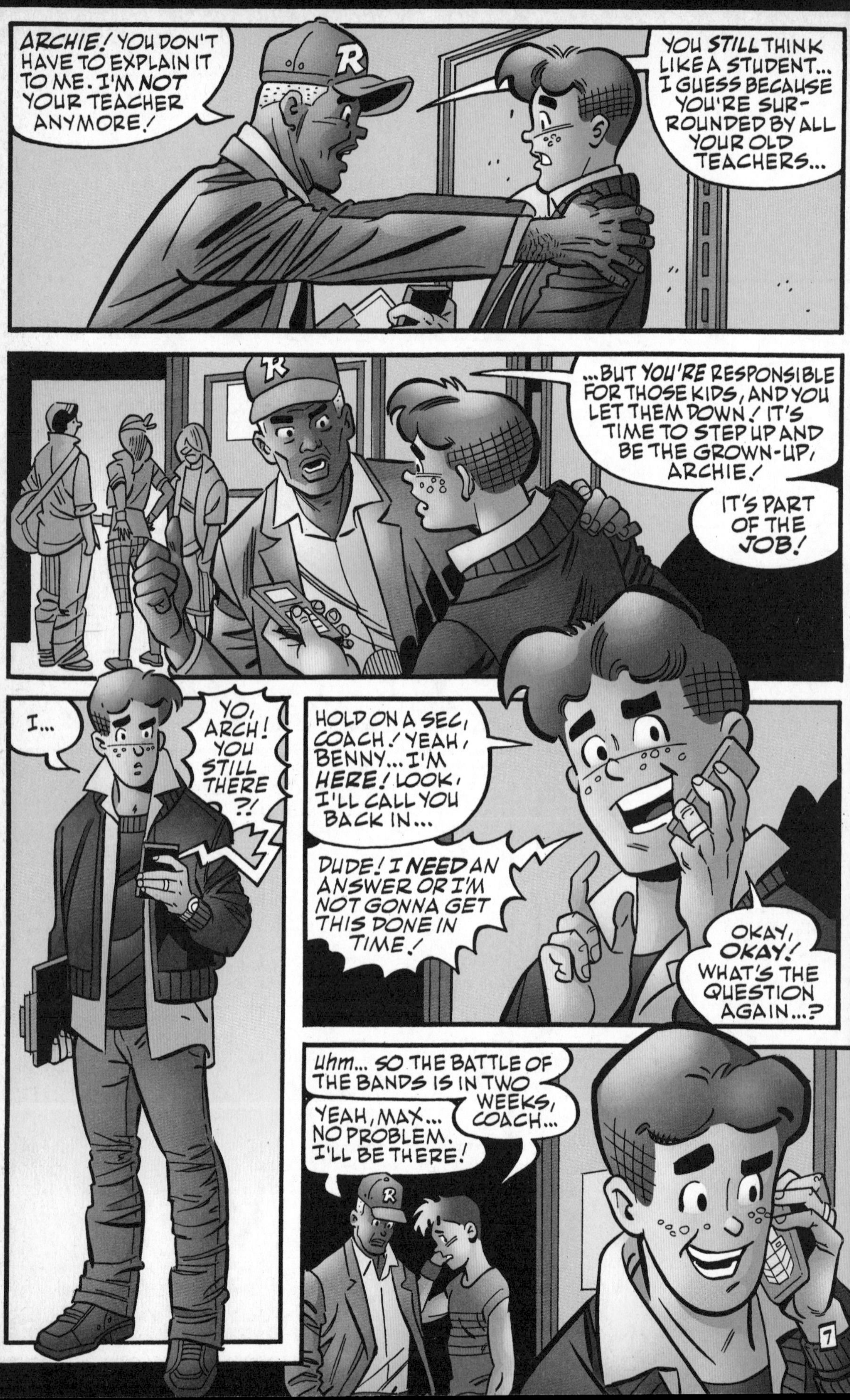
ARCHIE! YOU DON'T HAVE TO EXPLAIN IT TO ME. I'M NOT YOUR TEACHER ANYMORE!
YOU STILL THINK LIKE A STUDENT... I GUESS BECAUSE YOU'RE SUR-ROUNDED BY ALL YOUR OLD TEACHERS...
...BUT YOU'RE RESPONSIBLE FOR THOSE KIDS, AND YOU LET THEM DOWN! IT'S TIME TO STEP UP AND BE THE GROWN-UP, ARCHIE!
IT'S PART OF THE JOB!
I...
YO, ARCH! YOU STILL THERE?!
HOLD ON A SEC, COACH! YEAH, BENNY... I'M HERE! LOOK, I'LL CALL YOU BACK IN...
DUDE! I NEED AN ANSWER OR I'M NOT GONNA GET THIS DONE IN TIME!
OKAY, OKAY! WHAT'S THE QUESTION AGAIN...?
UHM... SO THE BATTLE OF THE BANDS IS IN TWO WEEKS, COACH...
YEAH, MAX... NO PROBLEM. I'LL BE THERE!
7

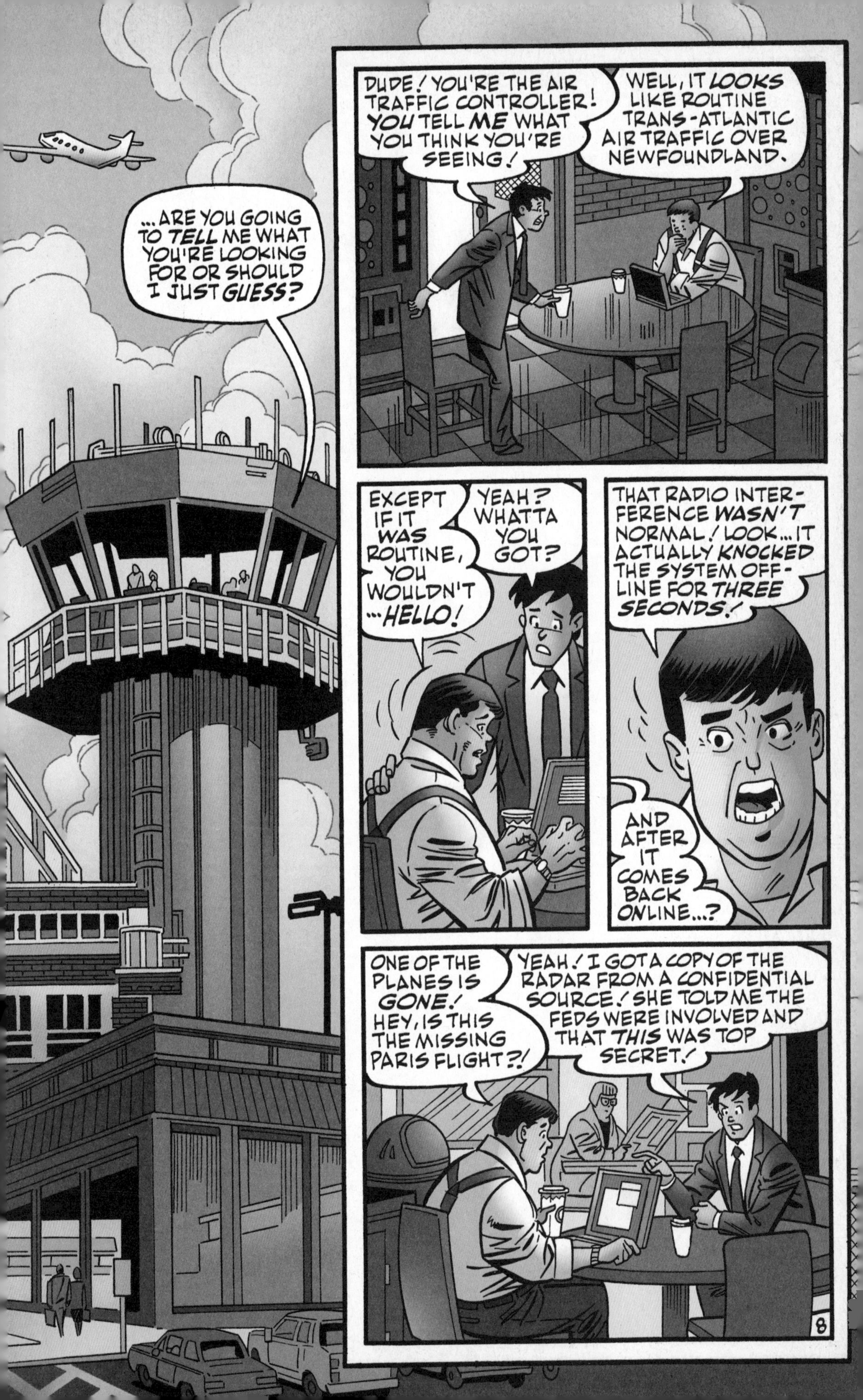

...ARE YOU GOING TO TELL ME WHAT YOU'RE LOOKING FOR OR SHOULD I JUST GUESS?
DUDE! YOU'RE THE AIR TRAFFIC CONTROLLER! YOU TELL ME WHAT YOU THINK YOU'RE SEEING!
WELL, IT LOOKS LIKE ROUTINE TRANS-ATLANTIC AIR TRAFFIC OVER NEWFOUNDLAND.
EXCEPT IF IT WAS ROUTINE, YOU WOULDN'T ...HELLO!
YEAH? WHATTA YOU GOT?
THAT RADIO INTERFERENCE WASN'T NORMAL! LOOK...IT ACTUALLY KNOCKED THE SYSTEM OFF-LINE FOR THREE SECONDS!
AND AFTER IT COMES BACK ONLINE...?
ONE OF THE PLANES IS GONE! HEY, IS THIS THE MISSING PARIS FLIGHT?!
YEAH! I GOT A COPY OF THE RADAR FROM A CONFIDENTIAL SOURCE! SHE TOLD ME THE FEDS WERE INVOLVED AND THAT THIS WAS TOP SECRET!

I COULD GET FIRED JUST FOR *LOOKING* AT THIS! I...I CAN'T HELP YOU...

YOU'VE *GOT TO*, JACKSON! MY GIRLFRIEND WAS *ON* THAT PLANE, MAN...

...ALONG WITH MORE THAN 260 *OTHER* GIRLFRIENDS, WIVES, HUSBANDS AND PARENTS!

THEY'RE COVERING UP WHAT HAPPENED TO OUR LOVED ONES!

EXCEPT THEY *FORGOT* ABOUT THINGS LIKE DETERMINED BOYFRIENDS, HONEST AIR TRAFFIC CONTROLLERS, AND A *FREE PRESS!*

:Sigh!: OKAY, REGGIE. I'LL LOOK AROUND.

fizz

THANKS, JACKSON! I OWE YOU, MAN!

I'M NOT PROMISING ANYTHING, BUT SOMETHING IS DEFINITELY *WRONG*...

...AND I THINK I HAVE A *RIGHT* TO KNOW *HOW* YOU'RE DOING THIS, HIRAM!

AS LONG AS WE HAVE THE RESOURCES TO BUY BACK OUR OWN STOCK, BILL...

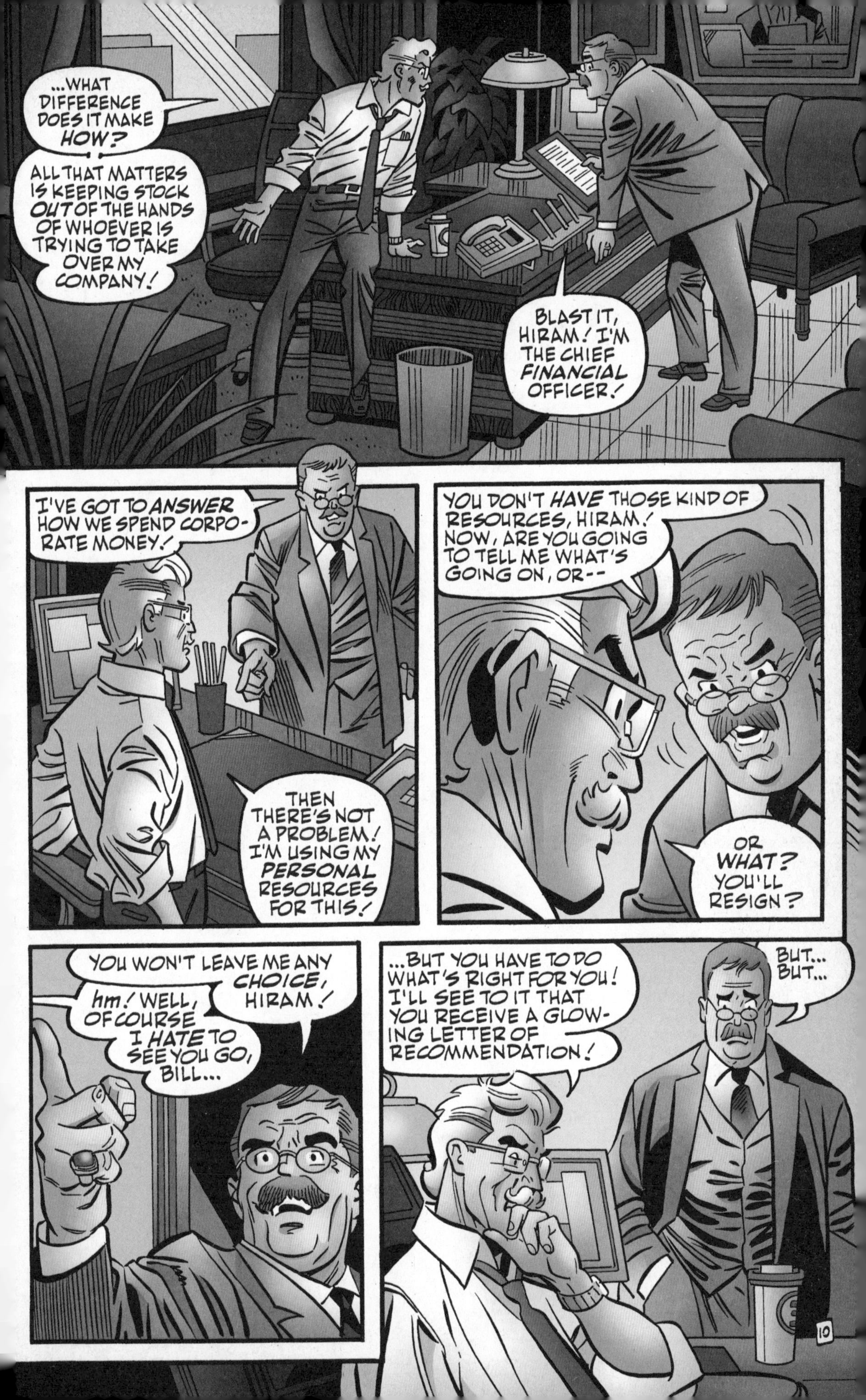
...WHAT DIFFERENCE DOES IT MAKE HOW?
ALL THAT MATTERS IS KEEPING STOCK OUT OF THE HANDS OF WHOEVER IS TRYING TO TAKE OVER MY COMPANY!
BLAST IT, HIRAM! I'M THE CHIEF FINANCIAL OFFICER!
I'VE GOT TO ANSWER HOW WE SPEND CORPORATE MONEY!
THEN THERE'S NOT A PROBLEM! I'M USING MY PERSONAL RESOURCES FOR THIS!
YOU DON'T HAVE THOSE KIND OF RESOURCES, HIRAM! NOW, ARE YOU GOING TO TELL ME WHAT'S GOING ON, OR--
OR WHAT? YOU'LL RESIGN?
YOU WON'T LEAVE ME ANY CHOICE, HIRAM!
hm! WELL, OF COURSE I HATE TO SEE YOU GO, BILL...
...BUT YOU HAVE TO DO WHAT'S RIGHT FOR YOU! I'LL SEE TO IT THAT YOU RECEIVE A GLOWING LETTER OF RECOMMENDATION!
BUT... BUT...
10

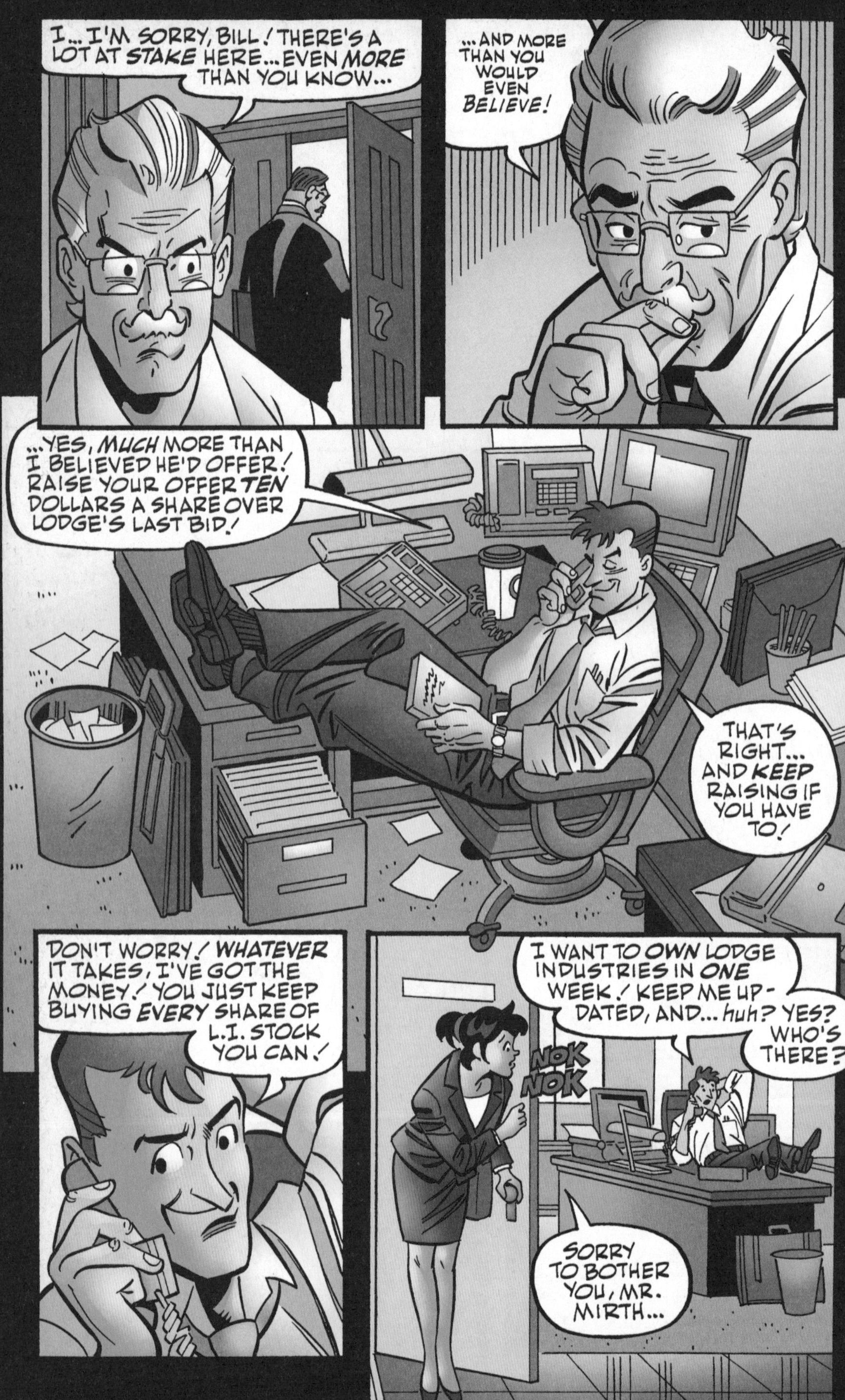
I... I'M SORRY, BILL! THERE'S A LOT AT STAKE HERE... EVEN MORE THAN YOU KNOW...
...AND MORE THAN YOU WOULD EVEN BELIEVE!
...YES, MUCH MORE THAN I BELIEVED HE'D OFFER! RAISE YOUR OFFER TEN DOLLARS A SHARE OVER LODGE'S LAST BID!
THAT'S RIGHT... AND KEEP RAISING IF YOU HAVE TO!
DON'T WORRY! WHATEVER IT TAKES, I'VE GOT THE MONEY! YOU JUST KEEP BUYING EVERY SHARE OF L.I. STOCK YOU CAN!
I WANT TO OWN LODGE INDUSTRIES IN ONE WEEK! KEEP ME UP-DATED, AND... huh? YES? WHO'S THERE?
NOK NOK
SORRY TO BOTHER YOU, MR. MIRTH...

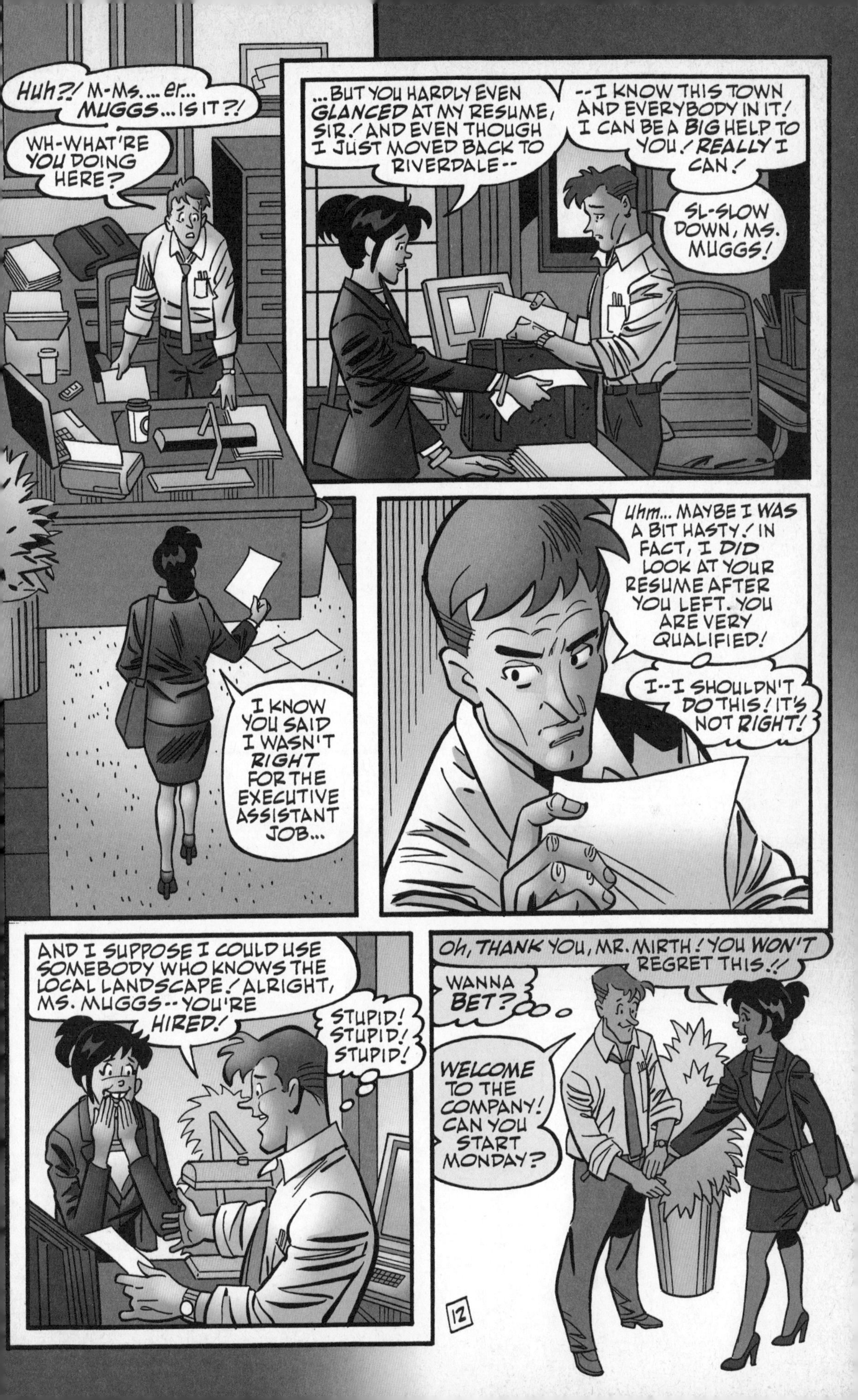
Huh?! M-Ms.... er... MUGGS... IS IT?!
WH-WHAT'RE YOU DOING HERE?
...BUT YOU HARDLY EVEN GLANCED AT MY RESUME, SIR! AND EVEN THOUGH I JUST MOVED BACK TO RIVERDALE--
--I KNOW THIS TOWN AND EVERYBODY IN IT! I CAN BE A BIG HELP TO YOU! REALLY I CAN!
SL-SLOW DOWN, MS. MUGGS!
I KNOW YOU SAID I WASN'T RIGHT FOR THE EXECUTIVE ASSISTANT JOB...
Uhm... MAYBE I WAS A BIT HASTY! IN FACT, I DID LOOK AT YOUR RESUME AFTER YOU LEFT. YOU ARE VERY QUALIFIED!
I--I SHOULDN'T DO THIS! IT'S NOT RIGHT!
AND I SUPPOSE I COULD USE SOMEBODY WHO KNOWS THE LOCAL LANDSCAPE! ALRIGHT, MS. MUGGS--YOU'RE HIRED!
STUPID! STUPID! STUPID!
Oh, THANK YOU, MR. MIRTH! YOU WON'T REGRET THIS!!
WANNA BET?
WELCOME TO THE COMPANY! CAN YOU START MONDAY?
12

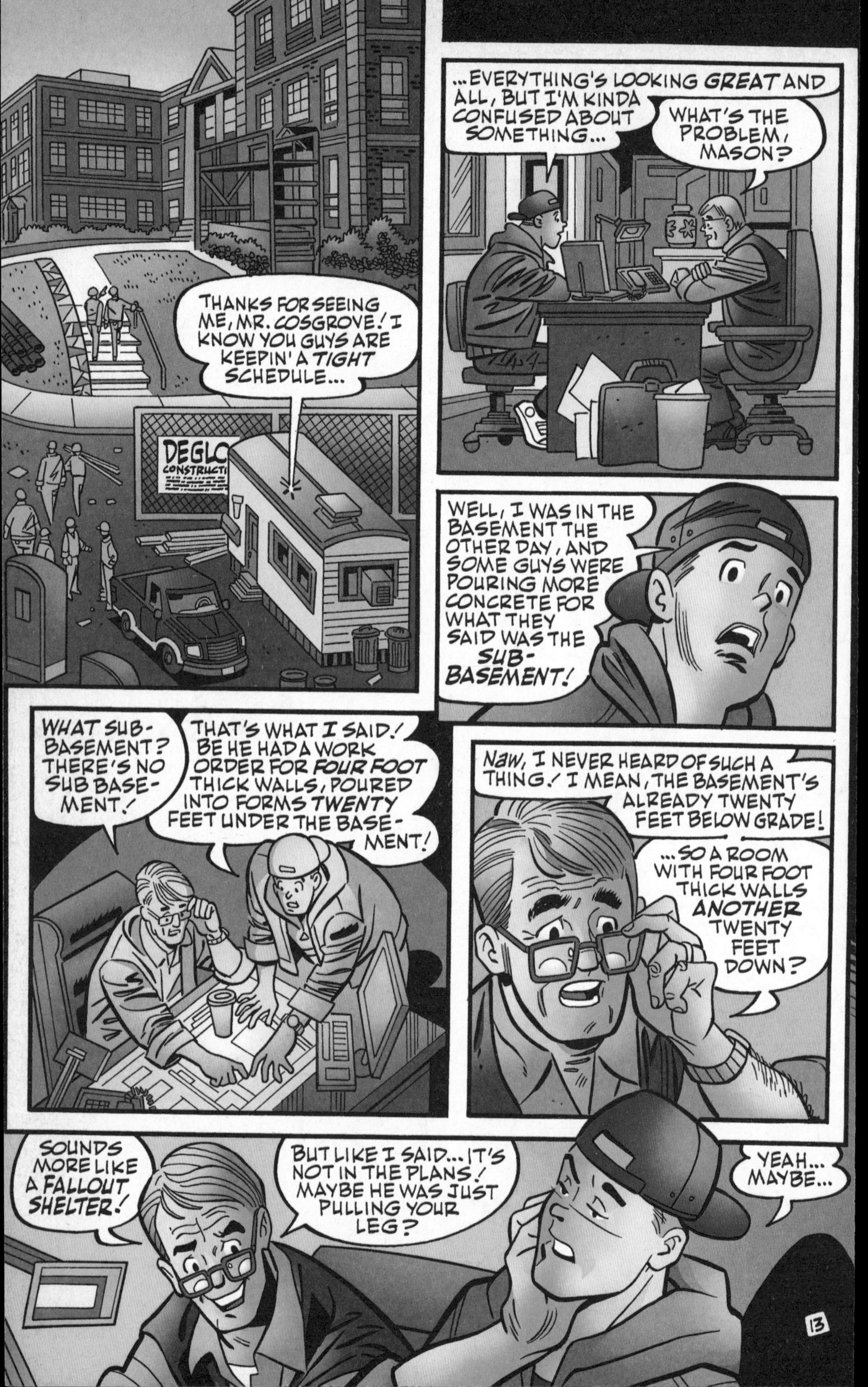
THANKS FOR SEEING ME, MR. COSGROVE! I KNOW YOU GUYS ARE KEEPIN' A TIGHT SCHEDULE...
...EVERYTHING'S LOOKING GREAT AND ALL, BUT I'M KINDA CONFUSED ABOUT SOMETHING...
WHAT'S THE PROBLEM, MASON?
WELL, I WAS IN THE BASEMENT THE OTHER DAY, AND SOME GUYS WERE POURING MORE CONCRETE FOR WHAT THEY SAID WAS THE SUB-BASEMENT!
WHAT SUB-BASEMENT? THERE'S NO SUB BASEMENT!
THAT'S WHAT I SAID! BE HE HAD A WORK ORDER FOR FOUR FOOT THICK WALLS, POURED INTO FORMS TWENTY FEET UNDER THE BASEMENT!
NAW, I NEVER HEARD OF SUCH A THING! I MEAN, THE BASEMENT'S ALREADY TWENTY FEET BELOW GRADE!
...SO A ROOM WITH FOUR FOOT THICK WALLS ANOTHER TWENTY FEET DOWN?
SOUNDS MORE LIKE A FALLOUT SHELTER!
BUT LIKE I SAID... IT'S NOT IN THE PLANS! MAYBE HE WAS JUST PULLING YOUR LEG?
YEAH... MAYBE...
DEGLO CONSTRUCTI

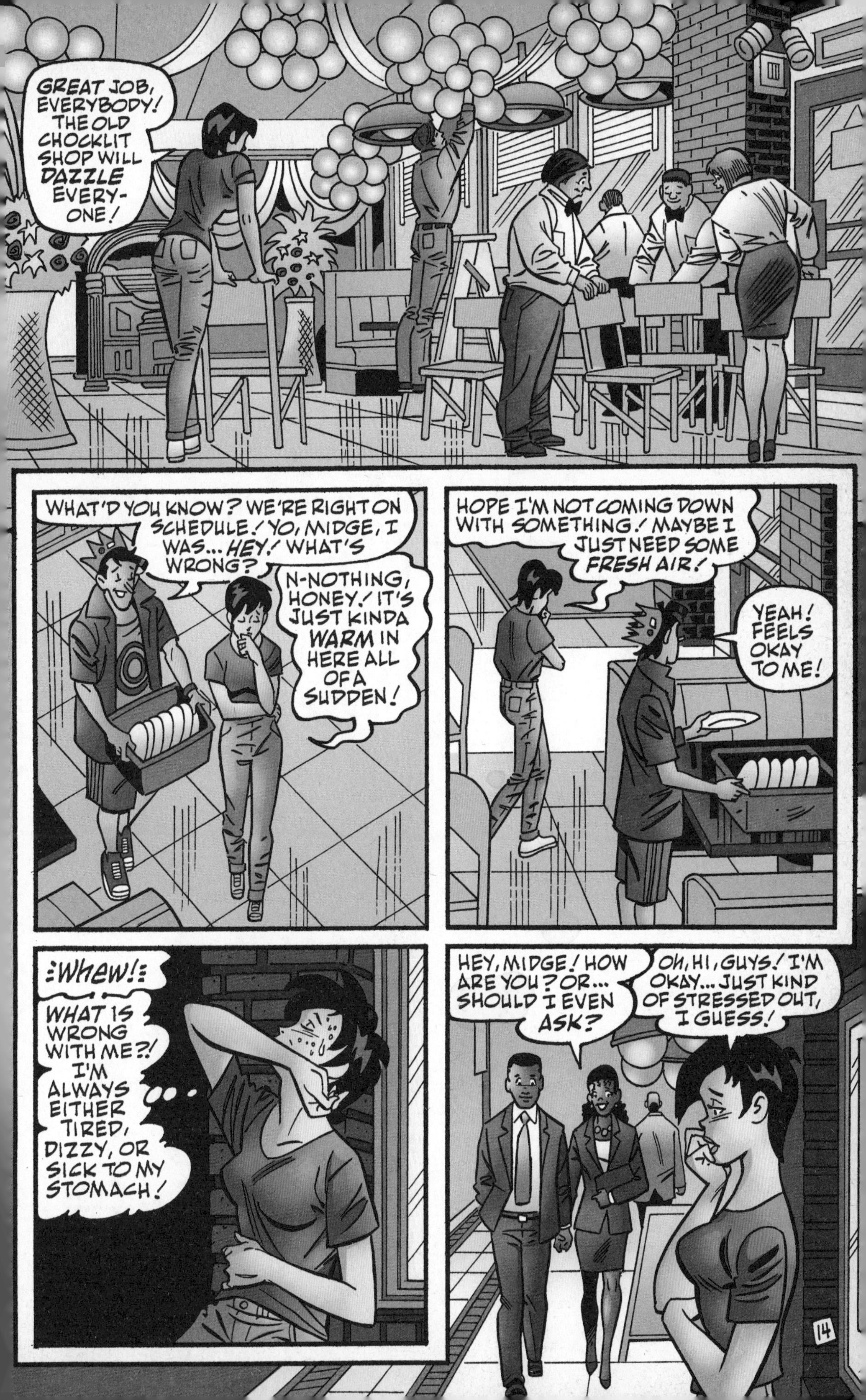
GREAT JOB, EVERYBODY! THE OLD CHOCKLIT SHOP WILL DAZZLE EVERY-ONE!
WHAT'D YOU KNOW? WE'RE RIGHT ON SCHEDULE! YO, MIDGE, I WAS... HEY! WHAT'S WRONG?
N-NOTHING, HONEY! IT'S JUST KINDA WARM IN HERE ALL OF A SUDDEN!
HOPE I'M NOT COMING DOWN WITH SOMETHING! MAYBE I JUST NEED SOME FRESH AIR!
YEAH! FEELS OKAY TO ME!
WHEW!
WHAT IS WRONG WITH ME?! I'M ALWAYS EITHER TIRED, DIZZY, OR SICK TO MY STOMACH!
HEY, MIDGE! HOW ARE YOU? OR... SHOULD I EVEN ASK?
OH, HI, GUYS! I'M OKAY... JUST KIND OF STRESSED OUT, I GUESS!
14

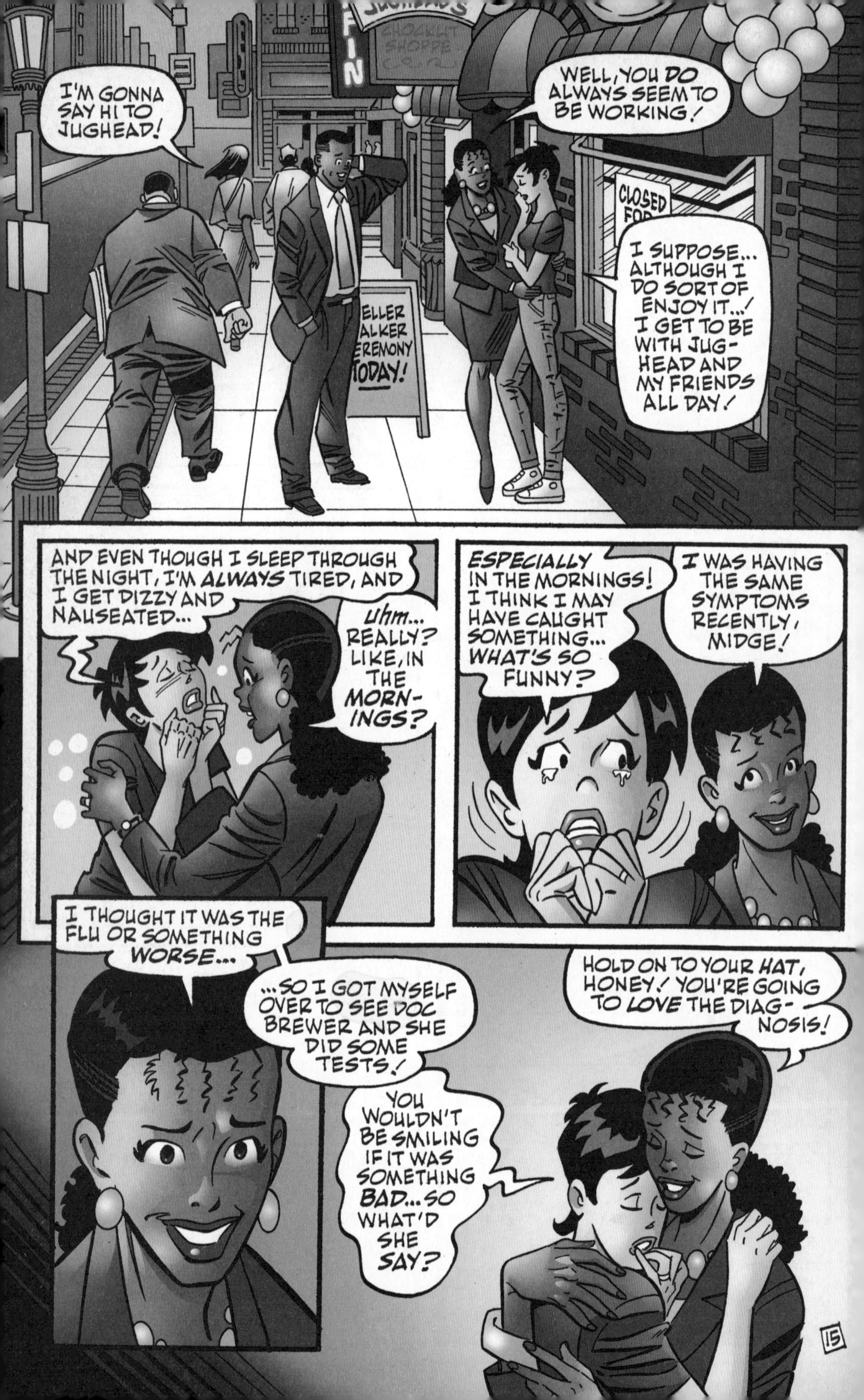
JUGHEAD'S
CHOCKLIT SHOPPE
I'M GONNA SAY HI TO JUGHEAD!
WELL, YOU DO ALWAYS SEEM TO BE WORKING!
CLOSED
I SUPPOSE... ALTHOUGH I DO SORT OF ENJOY IT...! I GET TO BE WITH JUGHEAD AND MY FRIENDS ALL DAY!
TODAY!
AND EVEN THOUGH I SLEEP THROUGH THE NIGHT, I'M ALWAYS TIRED, AND I GET DIZZY AND NAUSEATED...
uhm... REALLY? LIKE, IN THE MORNINGS?
ESPECIALLY IN THE MORNINGS! I THINK I MAY HAVE CAUGHT SOMETHING... WHAT'S SO FUNNY?
I WAS HAVING THE SAME SYMPTOMS RECENTLY, MIDGE!
I THOUGHT IT WAS THE FLU OR SOMETHING WORSE...
...SO I GOT MYSELF OVER TO SEE DOC BREWER AND SHE DID SOME TESTS!
YOU WOULDN'T BE SMILING IF IT WAS SOMETHING BAD... SO WHAT'D SHE SAY?
HOLD ON TO YOUR HAT, HONEY! YOU'RE GOING TO LOVE THE DIAGNOSIS!

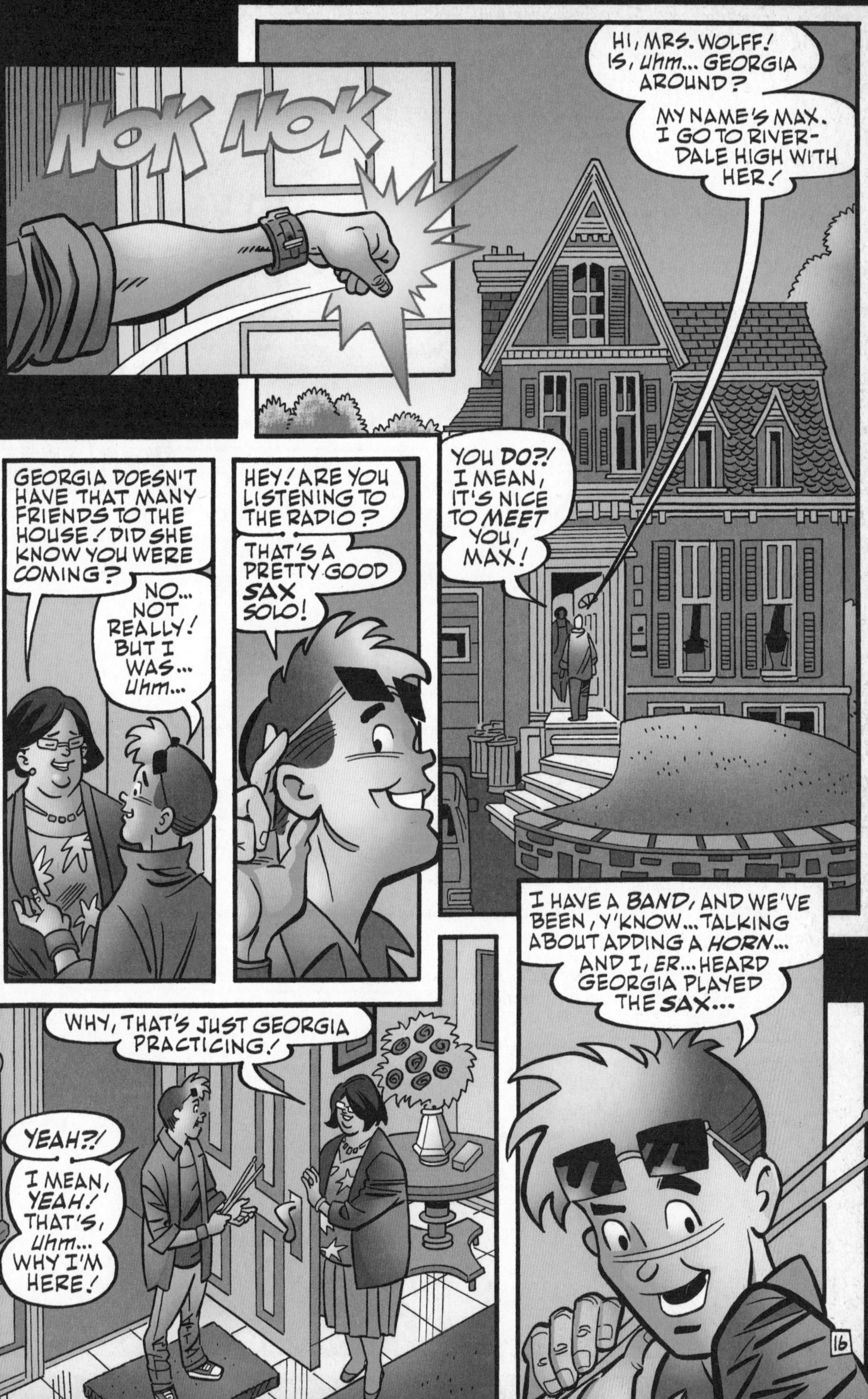
NOK NOK
HI, MRS. WOLFF! IS, UHM... GEORGIA AROUND?
MY NAME'S MAX. I GO TO RIVER-DALE HIGH WITH HER!
YOU DO?! I MEAN, IT'S NICE TO MEET YOU, MAX!
GEORGIA DOESN'T HAVE THAT MANY FRIENDS TO THE HOUSE! DID SHE KNOW YOU WERE COMING?
NO... NOT REALLY! BUT I WAS... UHM...
HEY! ARE YOU LISTENING TO THE RADIO?
THAT'S A PRETTY GOOD SAX SOLO!
WHY, THAT'S JUST GEORGIA PRACTICING!
YEAH?!
I MEAN, YEAH! THAT'S, UHM... WHY I'M HERE!
I HAVE A BAND, AND WE'VE BEEN, Y'KNOW... TALKING ABOUT ADDING A HORN... AND I, ER... HEARD GEORGIA PLAYED THE SAX...
16

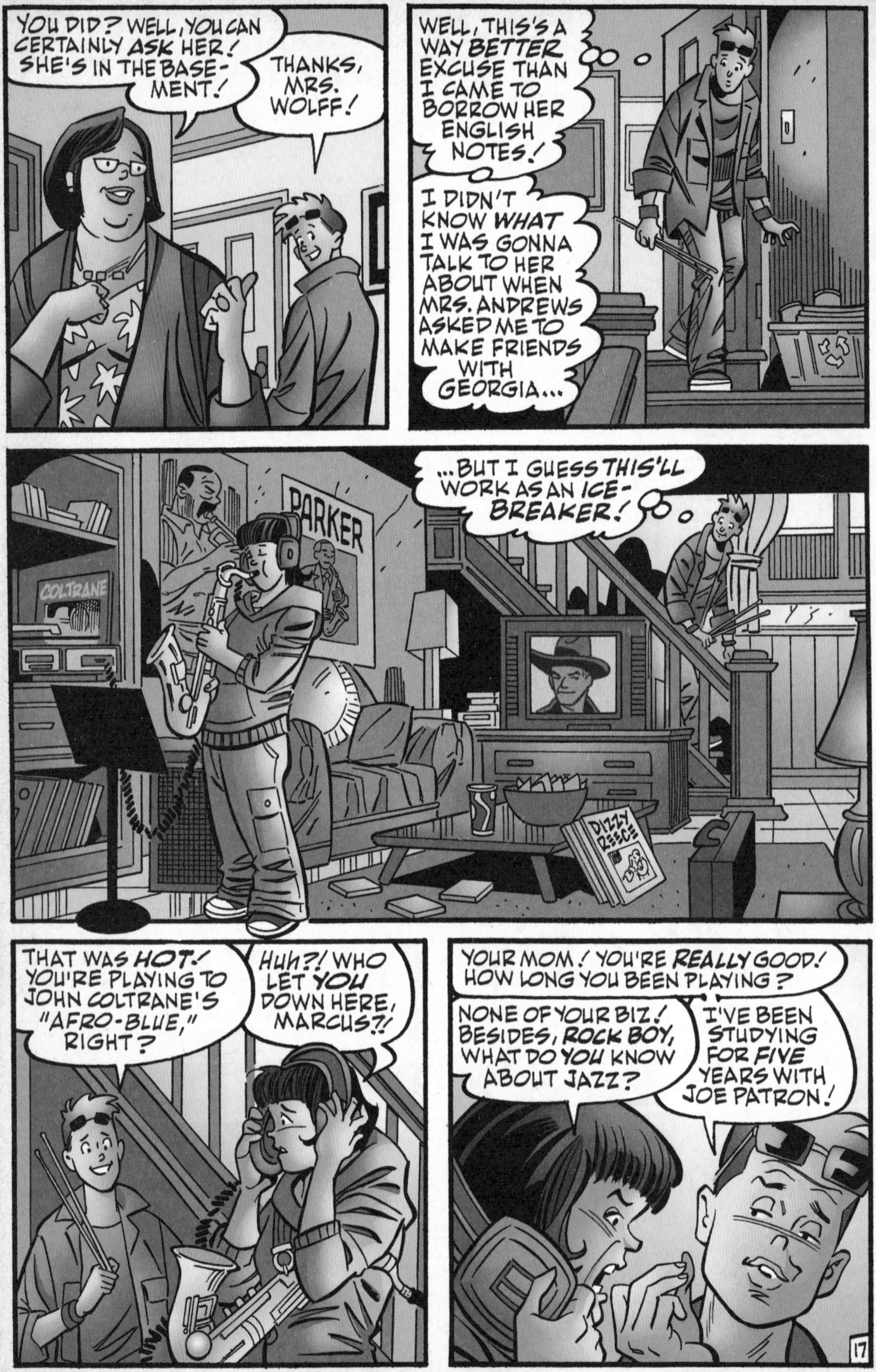

YOU DID? WELL, YOU CAN CERTAINLY ASK HER! SHE'S IN THE BASEMENT!
THANKS, MRS. WOLFF!
WELL, THIS'S A WAY BETTER EXCUSE THAN I CAME TO BORROW HER ENGLISH NOTES!
I DIDN'T KNOW WHAT I WAS GONNA TALK TO HER ABOUT WHEN MRS. ANDREWS ASKED ME TO MAKE FRIENDS WITH GEORGIA...
COLTRANE
PARKER
...BUT I GUESS THIS'LL WORK AS AN ICE-BREAKER!
DIZZY REECE
THAT WAS HOT! YOU'RE PLAYING TO JOHN COLTRANE'S "AFRO-BLUE," RIGHT?
HUH?! WHO LET YOU DOWN HERE, MARCUS?!
YOUR MOM! YOU'RE REALLY GOOD! HOW LONG YOU BEEN PLAYING?
NONE OF YOUR BIZ! BESIDES, ROCK BOY, WHAT DO YOU KNOW ABOUT JAZZ?
I'VE BEEN STUDYING FOR FIVE YEARS WITH JOE PATRON!

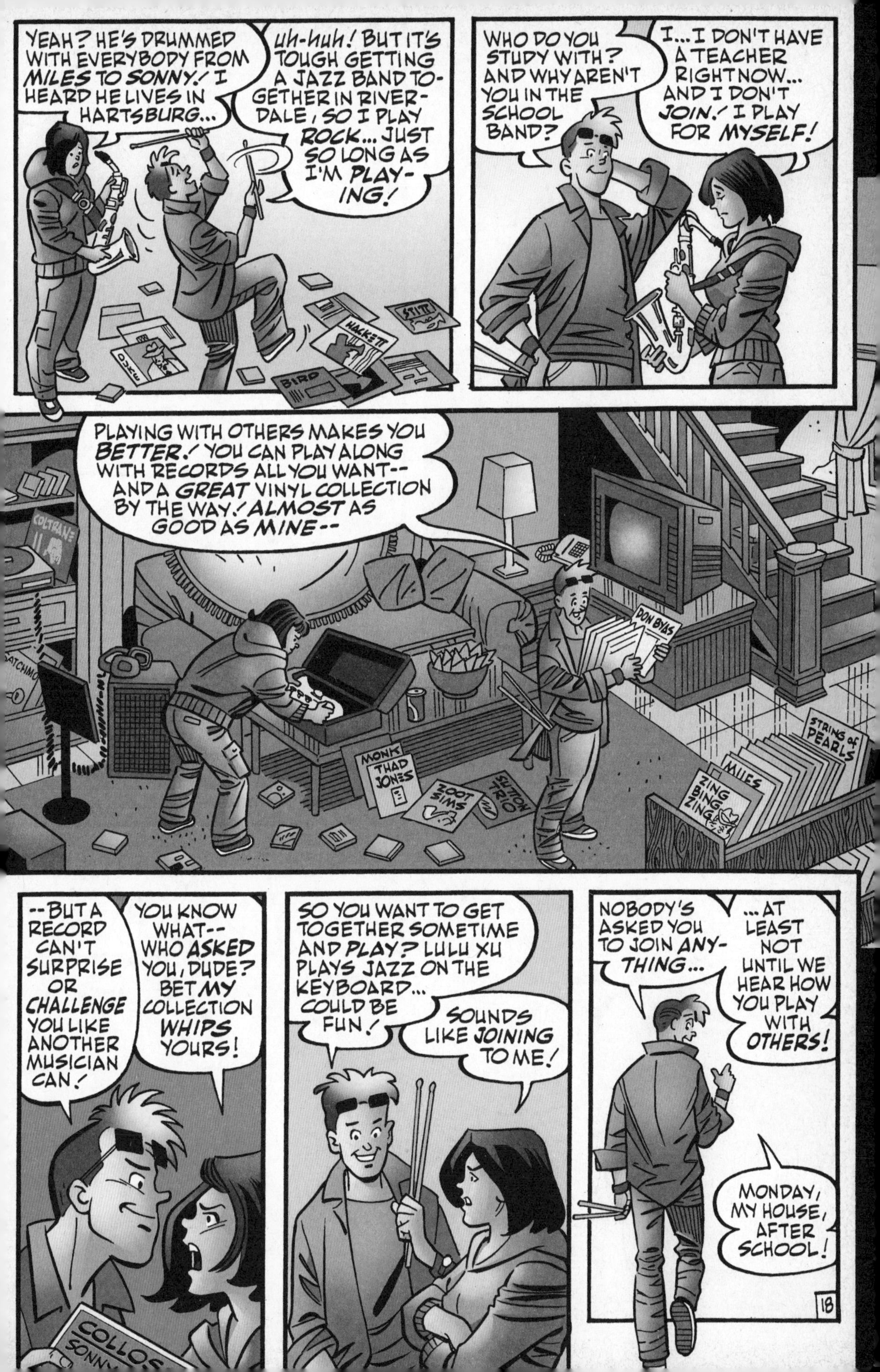
YEAH? HE'S DRUMMED WITH EVERYBODY FROM MILES TO SONNY! I HEARD HE LIVES IN HARTSBURG...
UH-HUH! BUT IT'S TOUGH GETTING A JAZZ BAND TOGETHER IN RIVERDALE, SO I PLAY ROCK... JUST SO LONG AS I'M PLAYING!
STITT
HACKETT
BIRD
WHO DO YOU STUDY WITH? AND WHY AREN'T YOU IN THE SCHOOL BAND?
I...I DON'T HAVE A TEACHER RIGHT NOW... AND I DON'T JOIN! I PLAY FOR MYSELF!
PLAYING WITH OTHERS MAKES YOU BETTER! YOU CAN PLAY ALONG WITH RECORDS ALL YOU WANT-- AND A GREAT VINYL COLLECTION BY THE WAY! ALMOST AS GOOD AS MINE--
COLTRANE
SATCHMO
DON BYAS
MONK
THAD JONES
ZOOT SIMS
SUTTON TRIO
MILES
STRING of PEARLS
ZING BING ZING
--BUT A RECORD CAN'T SURPRISE OR CHALLENGE YOU LIKE ANOTHER MUSICIAN CAN!
YOU KNOW WHAT-- WHO ASKED YOU, DUDE? BET MY COLLECTION WHIPS YOURS!
COLLOS
SONNY
SO YOU WANT TO GET TOGETHER SOMETIME AND PLAY? LULU XU PLAYS JAZZ ON THE KEYBOARD... COULD BE FUN!
SOUNDS LIKE JOINING TO ME!
NOBODY'S ASKED YOU TO JOIN ANYTHING...
...AT LEAST NOT UNTIL WE HEAR HOW YOU PLAY WITH OTHERS!
MONDAY, MY HOUSE, AFTER SCHOOL!

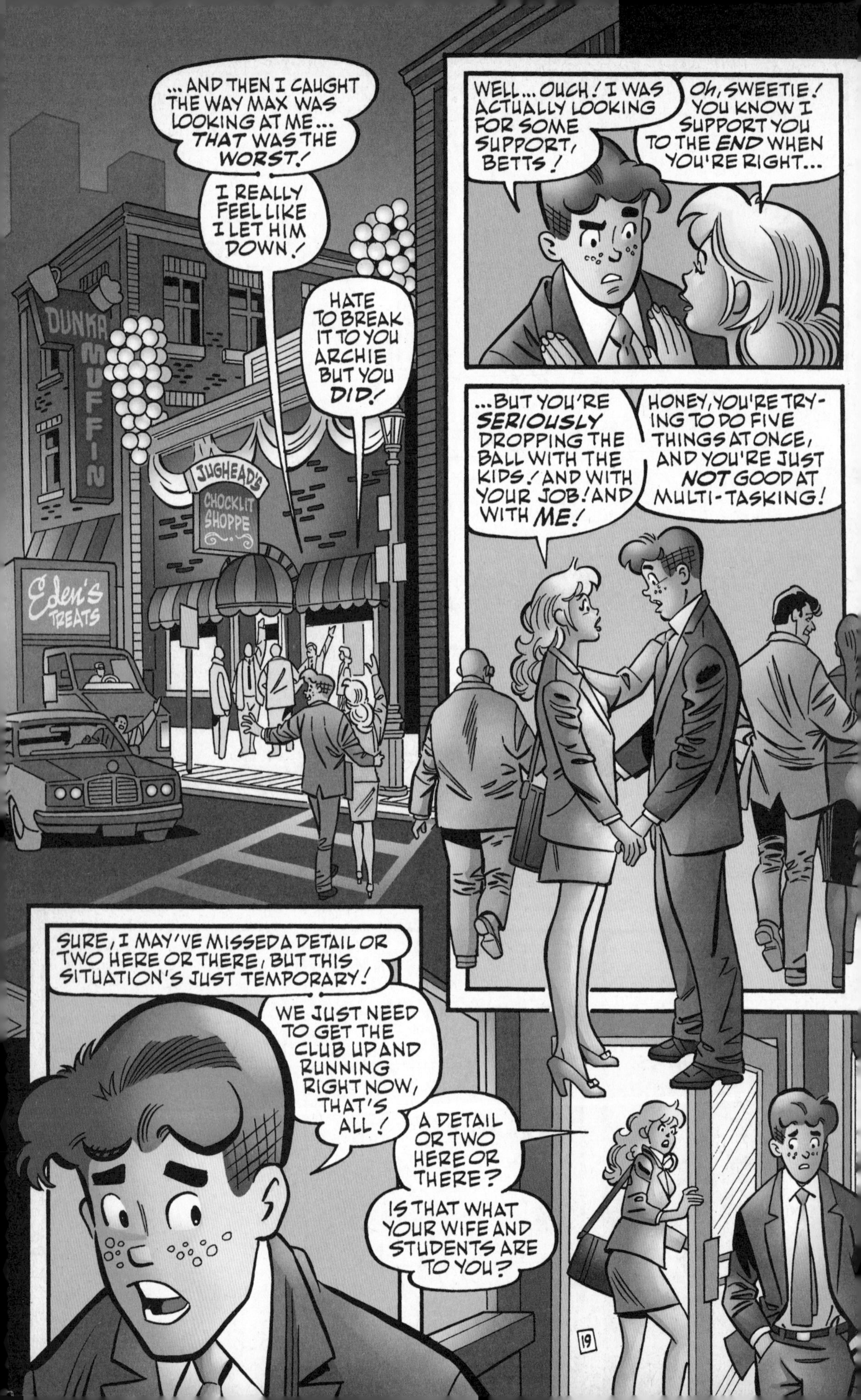
...AND THEN I CAUGHT THE WAY MAX WAS LOOKING AT ME... THAT WAS THE WORST!
I REALLY FEEL LIKE I LET HIM DOWN!
HATE TO BREAK IT TO YOU ARCHIE BUT YOU DID!
DUNKA MUFFIN
JUGHEAD'S CHOCKLIT SHOPPE
Eden's TREATS
WELL... OUCH! I WAS ACTUALLY LOOKING FOR SOME SUPPORT, BETTS!
Oh, SWEETIE! YOU KNOW I SUPPORT YOU TO THE END WHEN YOU'RE RIGHT...
...BUT YOU'RE SERIOUSLY DROPPING THE BALL WITH THE KIDS! AND WITH YOUR JOB! AND WITH ME!
HONEY, YOU'RE TRYING TO DO FIVE THINGS AT ONCE, AND YOU'RE JUST NOT GOOD AT MULTI-TASKING!
SURE, I MAY'VE MISSED A DETAIL OR TWO HERE OR THERE, BUT THIS SITUATION'S JUST TEMPORARY!
WE JUST NEED TO GET THE CLUB UP AND RUNNING RIGHT NOW, THAT'S ALL!
A DETAIL OR TWO HERE OR THERE?
IS THAT WHAT YOUR WIFE AND STUDENTS ARE TO YOU?

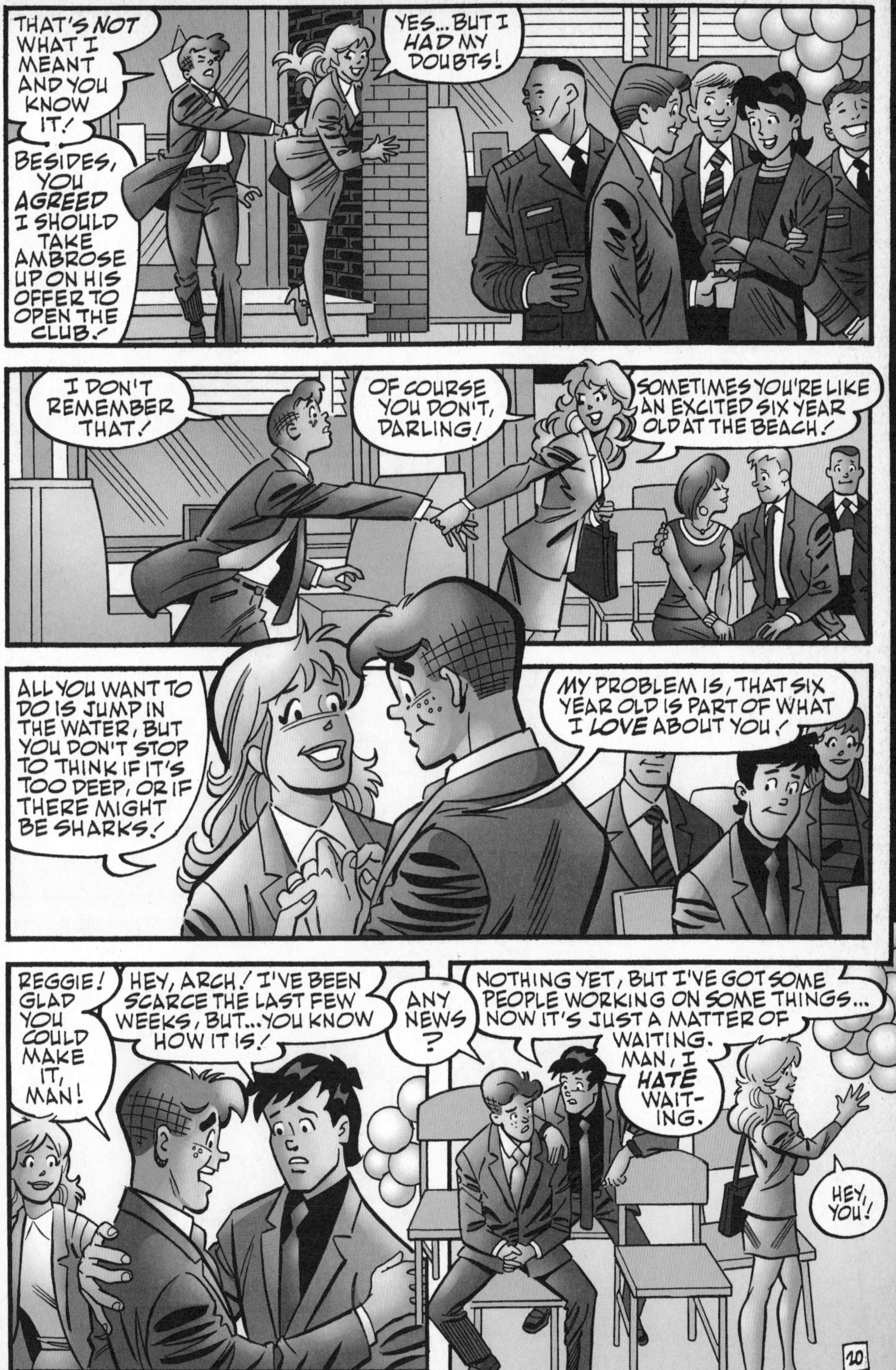
THAT'S NOT WHAT I MEANT AND YOU KNOW IT!
BESIDES, YOU AGREED I SHOULD TAKE AMBROSE UP ON HIS OFFER TO OPEN THE CLUB!
YES... BUT I HAD MY DOUBTS!
I DON'T REMEMBER THAT!
OF COURSE YOU DON'T, DARLING!
SOMETIMES YOU'RE LIKE AN EXCITED SIX YEAR OLD AT THE BEACH!
ALL YOU WANT TO DO IS JUMP IN THE WATER, BUT YOU DON'T STOP TO THINK IF IT'S TOO DEEP, OR IF THERE MIGHT BE SHARKS!
MY PROBLEM IS, THAT SIX YEAR OLD IS PART OF WHAT I LOVE ABOUT YOU!
REGGIE! GLAD YOU COULD MAKE IT, MAN!
HEY, ARCH! I'VE BEEN SCARCE THE LAST FEW WEEKS, BUT... YOU KNOW HOW IT IS!
ANY NEWS?
NOTHING YET, BUT I'VE GOT SOME PEOPLE WORKING ON SOME THINGS... NOW IT'S JUST A MATTER OF WAITING.
MAN, I HATE WAIT-ING.
HEY, YOU!
20

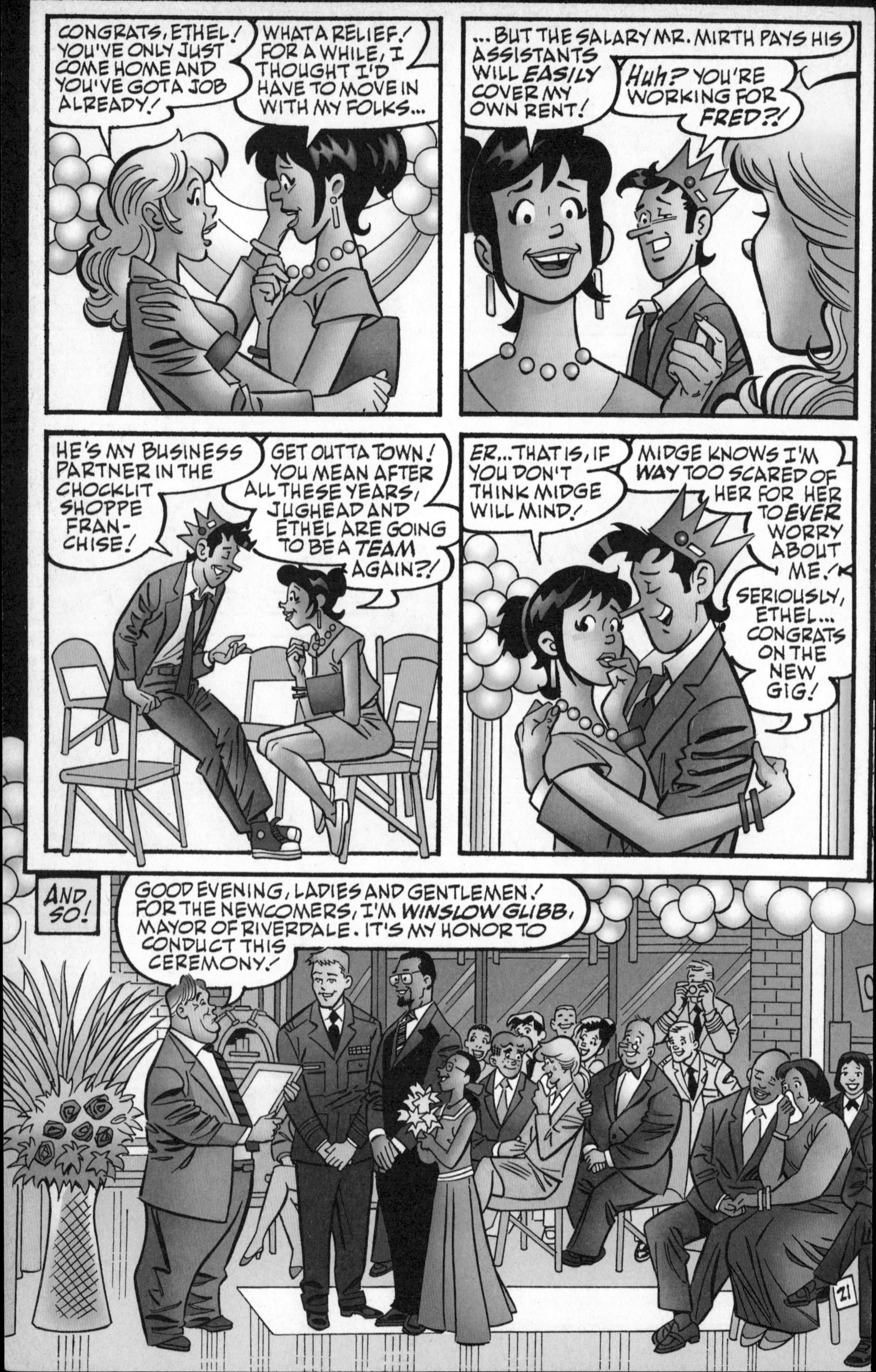
CONGRATS, ETHEL! YOU'VE ONLY JUST COME HOME AND YOU'VE GOT A JOB ALREADY!
WHAT A RELIEF! FOR A WHILE, I THOUGHT I'D HAVE TO MOVE IN WITH MY FOLKS...
...BUT THE SALARY MR. MIRTH PAYS HIS ASSISTANTS WILL EASILY COVER MY OWN RENT!
Huh? YOU'RE WORKING FOR FRED?!
HE'S MY BUSINESS PARTNER IN THE CHOCKLIT SHOPPE FRAN-CHISE!
GET OUTTA TOWN! YOU MEAN AFTER ALL THESE YEARS, JUGHEAD AND ETHEL ARE GOING TO BE A TEAM AGAIN?!
ER...THAT IS, IF YOU DON'T THINK MIDGE WILL MIND!
MIDGE KNOWS I'M WAY TOO SCARED OF HER FOR HER TO EVER WORRY ABOUT ME!
SERIOUSLY, ETHEL... CONGRATS ON THE NEW GIG!
AND SO!
GOOD EVENING, LADIES AND GENTLEMEN! FOR THE NEWCOMERS, I'M WINSLOW GLIBB, MAYOR OF RIVERDALE. IT'S MY HONOR TO CONDUCT THIS CEREMONY!
21

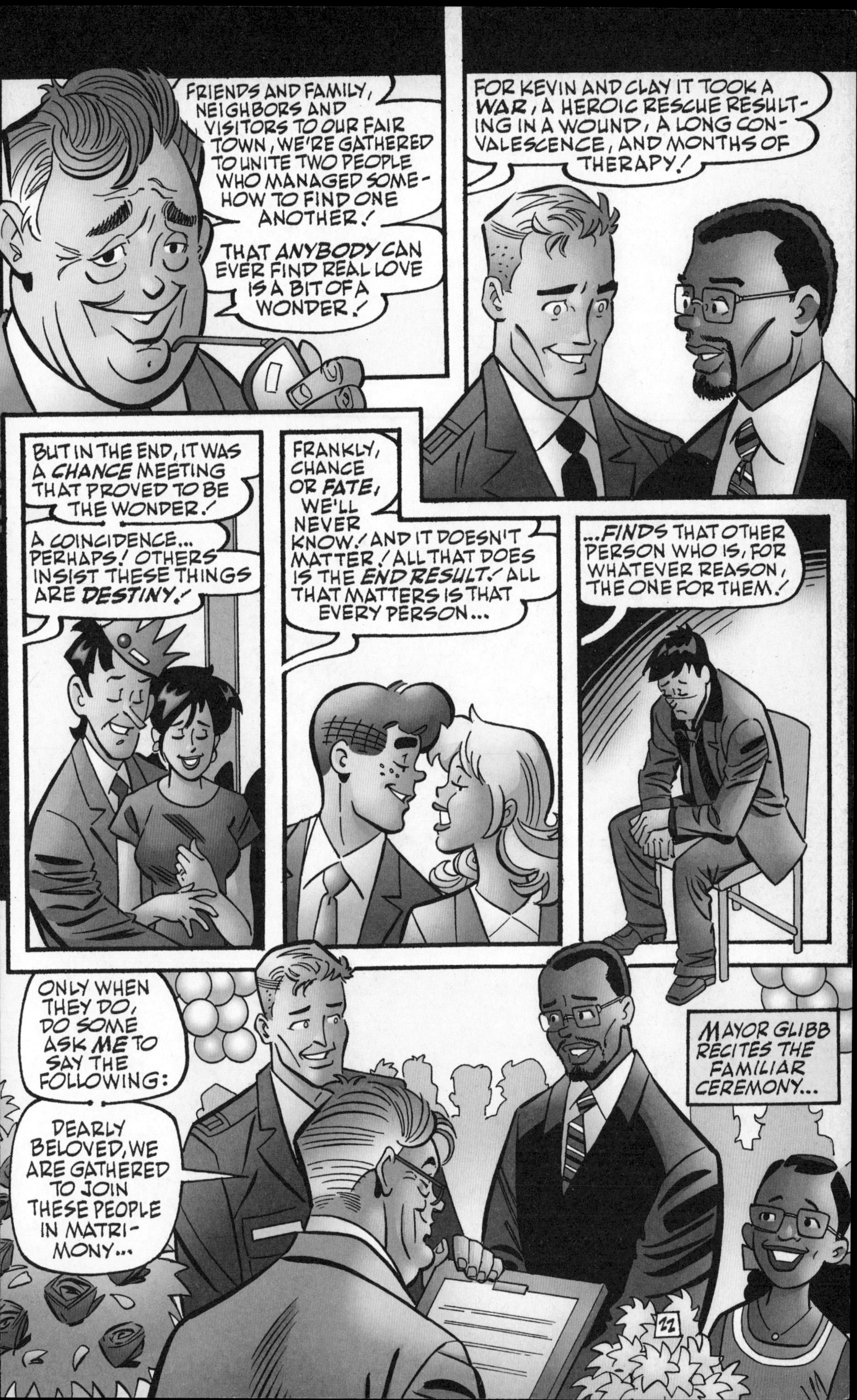
FRIENDS AND FAMILY, NEIGHBORS AND VISITORS TO OUR FAIR TOWN, WE'RE GATHERED TO UNITE TWO PEOPLE WHO MANAGED SOME-HOW TO FIND ONE ANOTHER!
THAT ANYBODY CAN EVER FIND REAL LOVE IS A BIT OF A WONDER!
FOR KEVIN AND CLAY IT TOOK A WAR, A HEROIC RESCUE RESULT-ING IN A WOUND, A LONG CON-VALESCENCE, AND MONTHS OF THERAPY!
BUT IN THE END, IT WAS A CHANCE MEETING THAT PROVED TO BE THE WONDER!
A COINCIDENCE... PERHAPS! OTHERS INSIST THESE THINGS ARE DESTINY!
FRANKLY, CHANCE OR FATE, WE'LL NEVER KNOW! AND IT DOESN'T MATTER! ALL THAT DOES IS THE END RESULT! ALL THAT MATTERS IS THAT EVERY PERSON...
...FINDS THAT OTHER PERSON WHO IS, FOR WHATEVER REASON, THE ONE FOR THEM!
ONLY WHEN THEY DO, DO SOME ASK ME TO SAY THE FOLLOWING:
DEARLY BELOVED, WE ARE GATHERED TO JOIN THESE PEOPLE IN MATRI-MONY...
MAYOR GLIBB RECITES THE FAMILIAR CEREMONY...
22

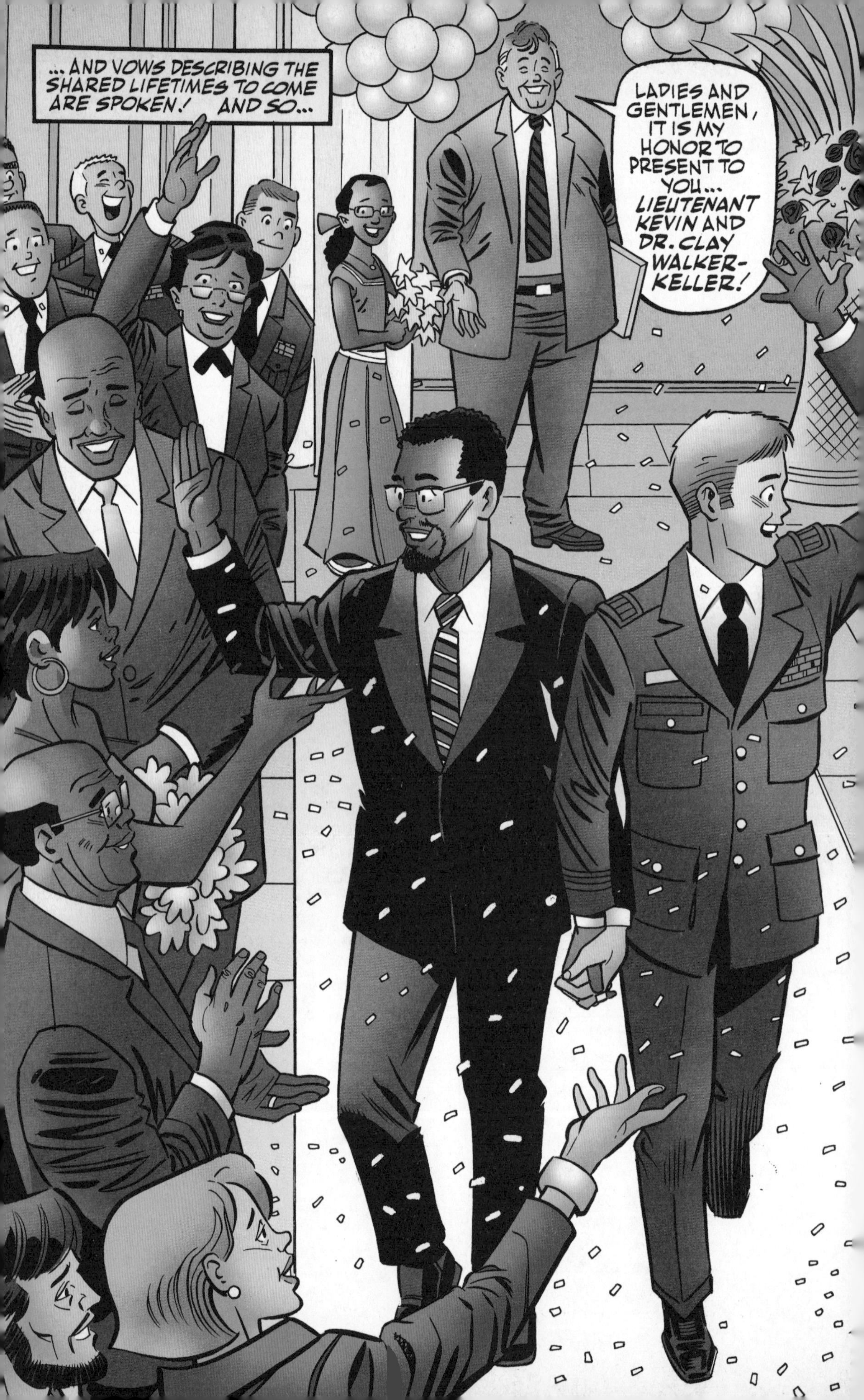
...AND VOWS DESCRIBING THE SHARED LIFETIMES TO COME ARE SPOKEN! AND SO...
LADIES AND GENTLEMEN, IT IS MY HONOR TO PRESENT TO YOU... LIEUTENANT KEVIN AND DR. CLAY WALKER-KELLER!

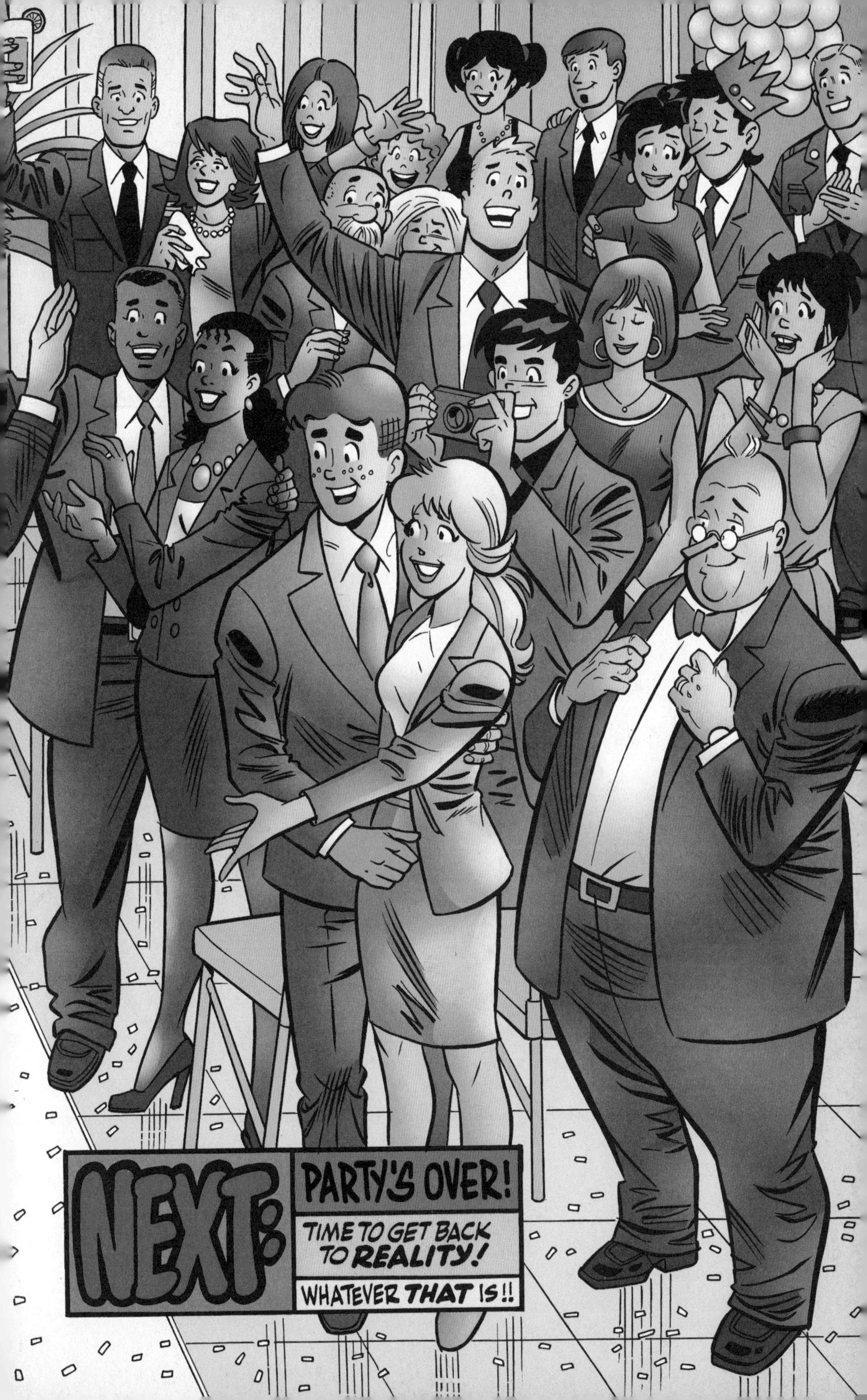
NEXT:
PARTY'S OVER!
TIME TO GET BACK TO REALITY!
WHATEVER THAT IS!!

"AS MUCH AS IT SURPRISES ME TO ADMIT IT..."

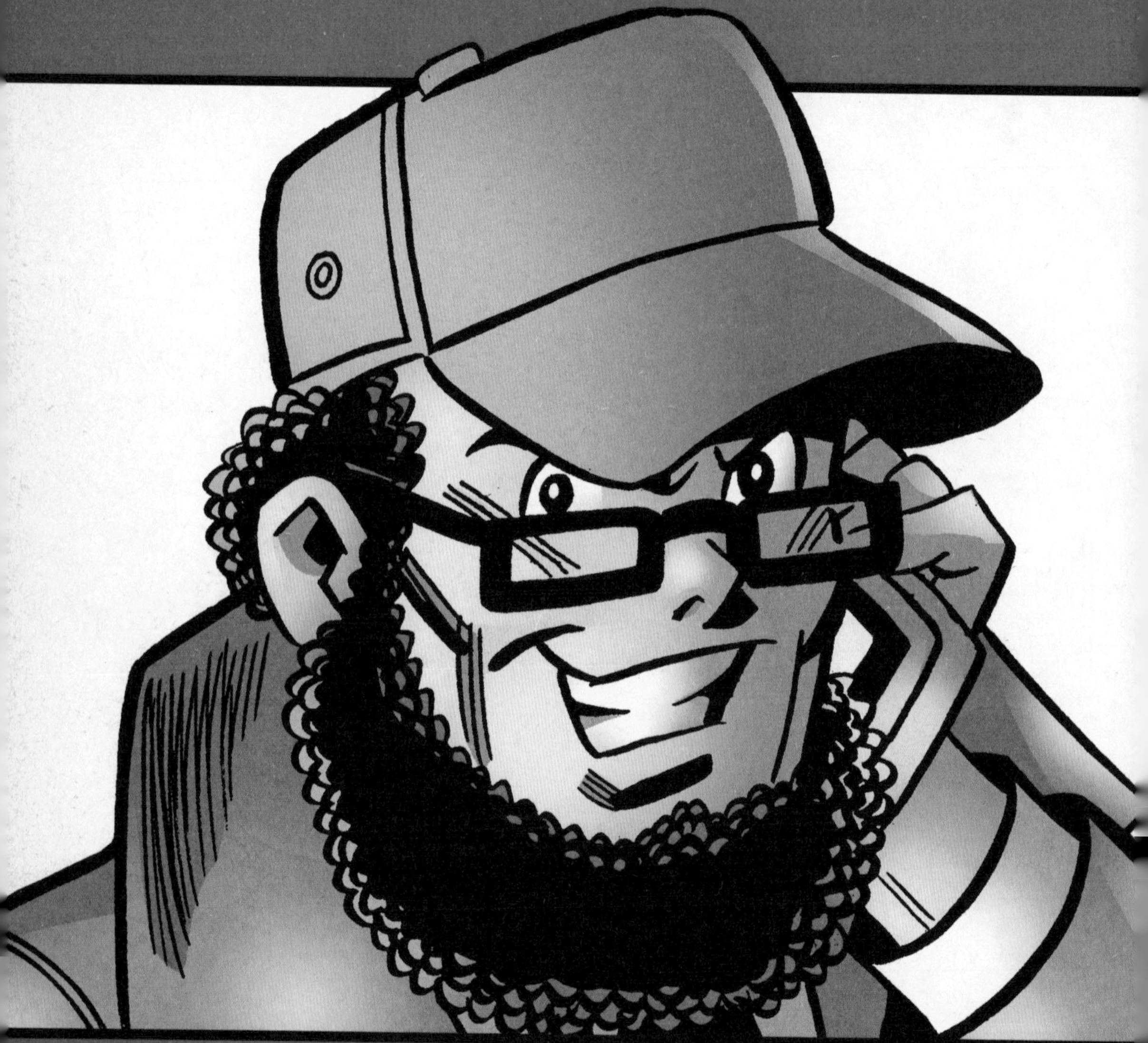

"...I'M *TIRED* OF HIDING!"

- DILTON DOILEY

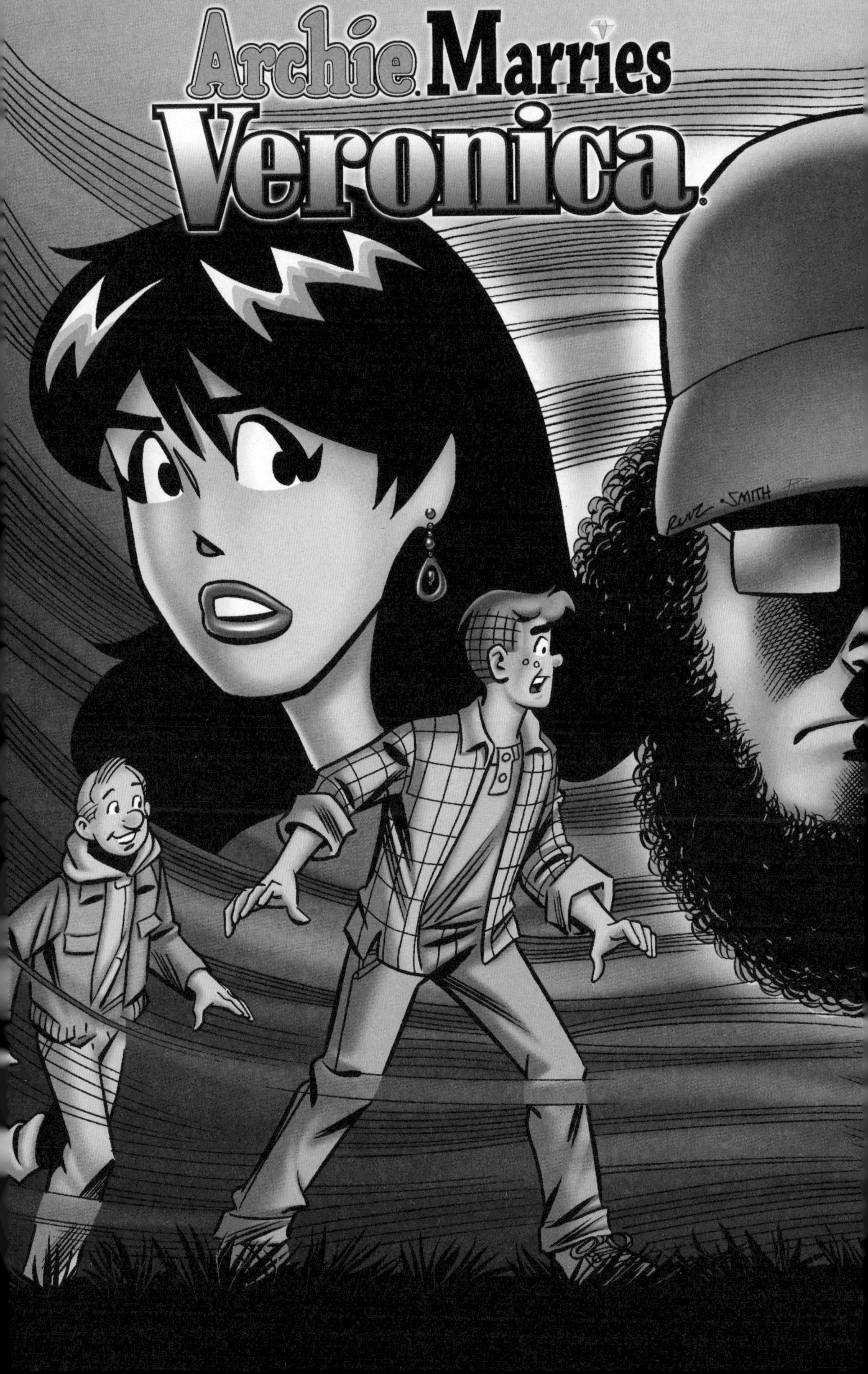

Archie Marries
Veronica
RUIZ · SMITH

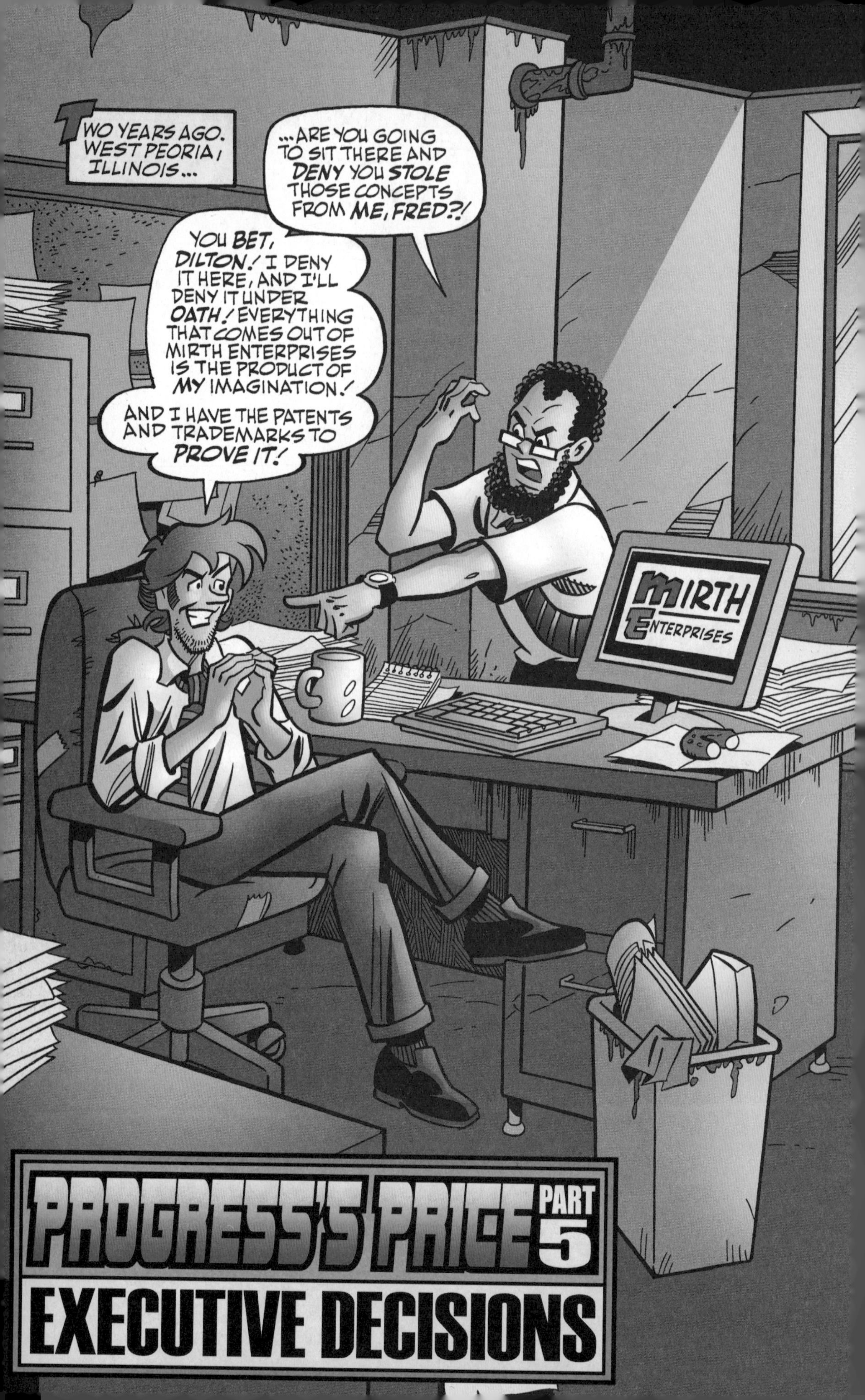
TWO YEARS AGO. WEST PEORIA, ILLINOIS...
...ARE YOU GOING TO SIT THERE AND DENY YOU STOLE THOSE CONCEPTS FROM ME, FRED?!
YOU BET, DILTON! I DENY IT HERE, AND I'LL DENY IT UNDER OATH! EVERYTHING THAT COMES OUT OF MIRTH ENTERPRISES IS THE PRODUCT OF MY IMAGINATION!
AND I HAVE THE PATENTS AND TRADEMARKS TO PROVE IT!
MIRTH ENTERPRISES
PROGRESS'S PRICE PART 5
EXECUTIVE DECISIONS

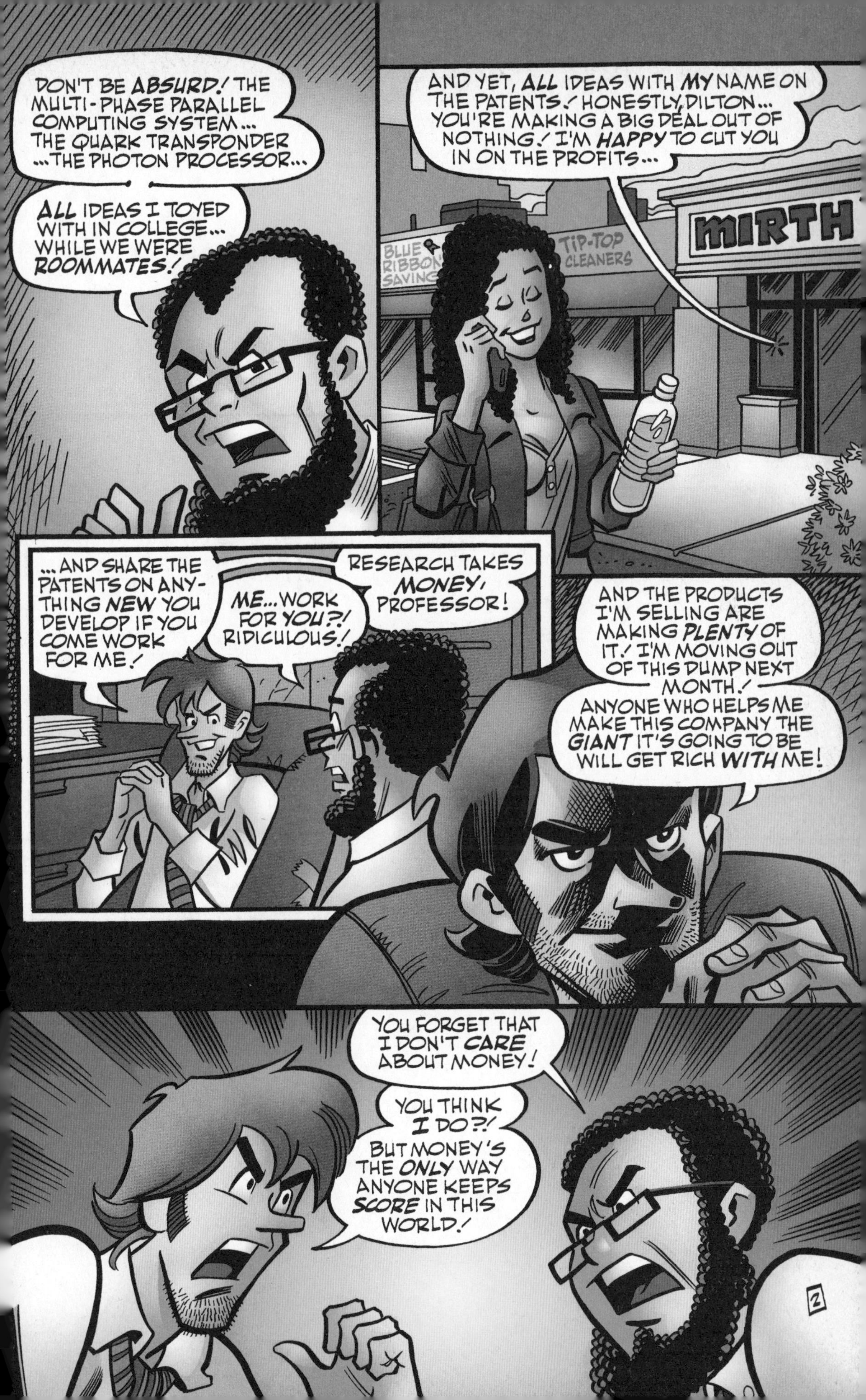
DON'T BE ABSURD! THE MULTI-PHASE PARALLEL COMPUTING SYSTEM... THE QUARK TRANSPONDER ...THE PHOTON PROCESSOR...
ALL IDEAS I TOYED WITH IN COLLEGE... WHILE WE WERE ROOMMATES!
AND YET, ALL IDEAS WITH MY NAME ON THE PATENTS! HONESTLY, DILTON... YOU'RE MAKING A BIG DEAL OUT OF NOTHING! I'M HAPPY TO CUT YOU IN ON THE PROFITS...
MIRTH
BLUE RIBBON SAVING
TIP-TOP CLEANERS
...AND SHARE THE PATENTS ON ANYTHING NEW YOU DEVELOP IF YOU COME WORK FOR ME!
ME...WORK FOR YOU?! RIDICULOUS!
RESEARCH TAKES MONEY, PROFESSOR!
AND THE PRODUCTS I'M SELLING ARE MAKING PLENTY OF IT! I'M MOVING OUT OF THIS DUMP NEXT MONTH!
ANYONE WHO HELPS ME MAKE THIS COMPANY THE GIANT IT'S GOING TO BE WILL GET RICH WITH ME!
YOU FORGET THAT I DON'T CARE ABOUT MONEY!
YOU THINK I DO?!
BUT MONEY'S THE ONLY WAY ANYONE KEEPS SCORE IN THIS WORLD!
2

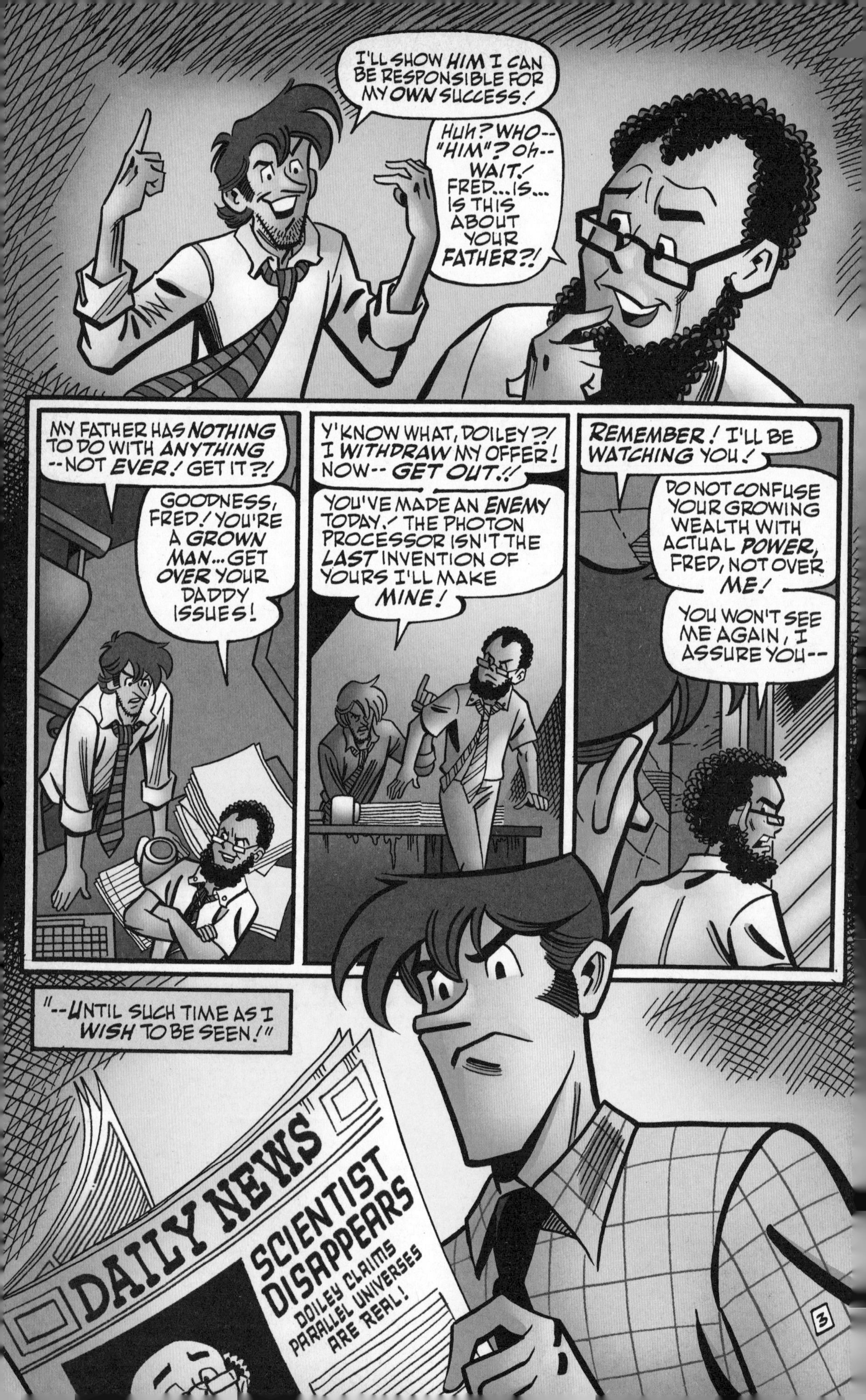
I'LL SHOW HIM I CAN BE RESPONSIBLE FOR MY OWN SUCCESS!
HUH? WHO-- "HIM"? OH-- WAIT! FRED...IS... IS THIS ABOUT YOUR FATHER?!
MY FATHER HAS NOTHING TO DO WITH ANYTHING --NOT EVER! GET IT?!
GOODNESS, FRED! YOU'RE A GROWN MAN...GET OVER YOUR DADDY ISSUES!
Y'KNOW WHAT, DOILEY?! I WITHDRAW MY OFFER! NOW-- GET OUT!!
YOU'VE MADE AN ENEMY TODAY! THE PHOTON PROCESSOR ISN'T THE LAST INVENTION OF YOURS I'LL MAKE MINE!
REMEMBER! I'LL BE WATCHING YOU!
DO NOT CONFUSE YOUR GROWING WEALTH WITH ACTUAL POWER, FRED, NOT OVER ME!
YOU WON'T SEE ME AGAIN, I ASSURE YOU--
"--UNTIL SUCH TIME AS I WISH TO BE SEEN!"
DAILY NEWS
SCIENTIST DISAPPEARS
DOILEY CLAIMS PARALLEL UNIVERSES ARE REAL!
3

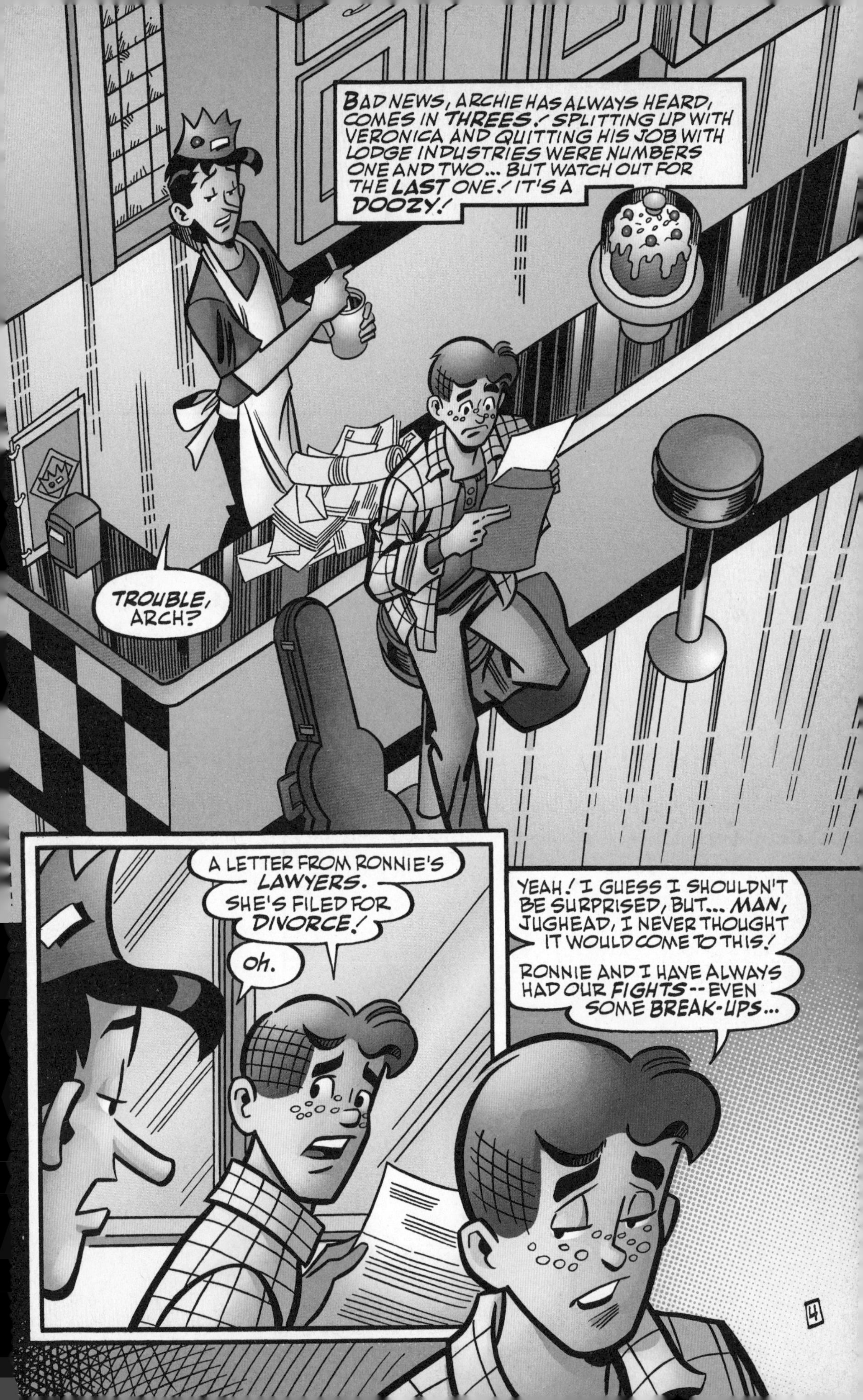
BAD NEWS, ARCHIE HAS ALWAYS HEARD, COMES IN THREES! SPLITTING UP WITH VERONICA AND QUITTING HIS JOB WITH LODGE INDUSTRIES WERE NUMBERS ONE AND TWO... BUT WATCH OUT FOR THE LAST ONE! IT'S A DOOZY!
TROUBLE, ARCH?
A LETTER FROM RONNIE'S LAWYERS. SHE'S FILED FOR DIVORCE!
oh.
YEAH! I GUESS I SHOULDN'T BE SURPRISED, BUT... MAN, JUGHEAD, I NEVER THOUGHT IT WOULD COME TO THIS!
RONNIE AND I HAVE ALWAYS HAD OUR FIGHTS -- EVEN SOME BREAK-UPS...
4

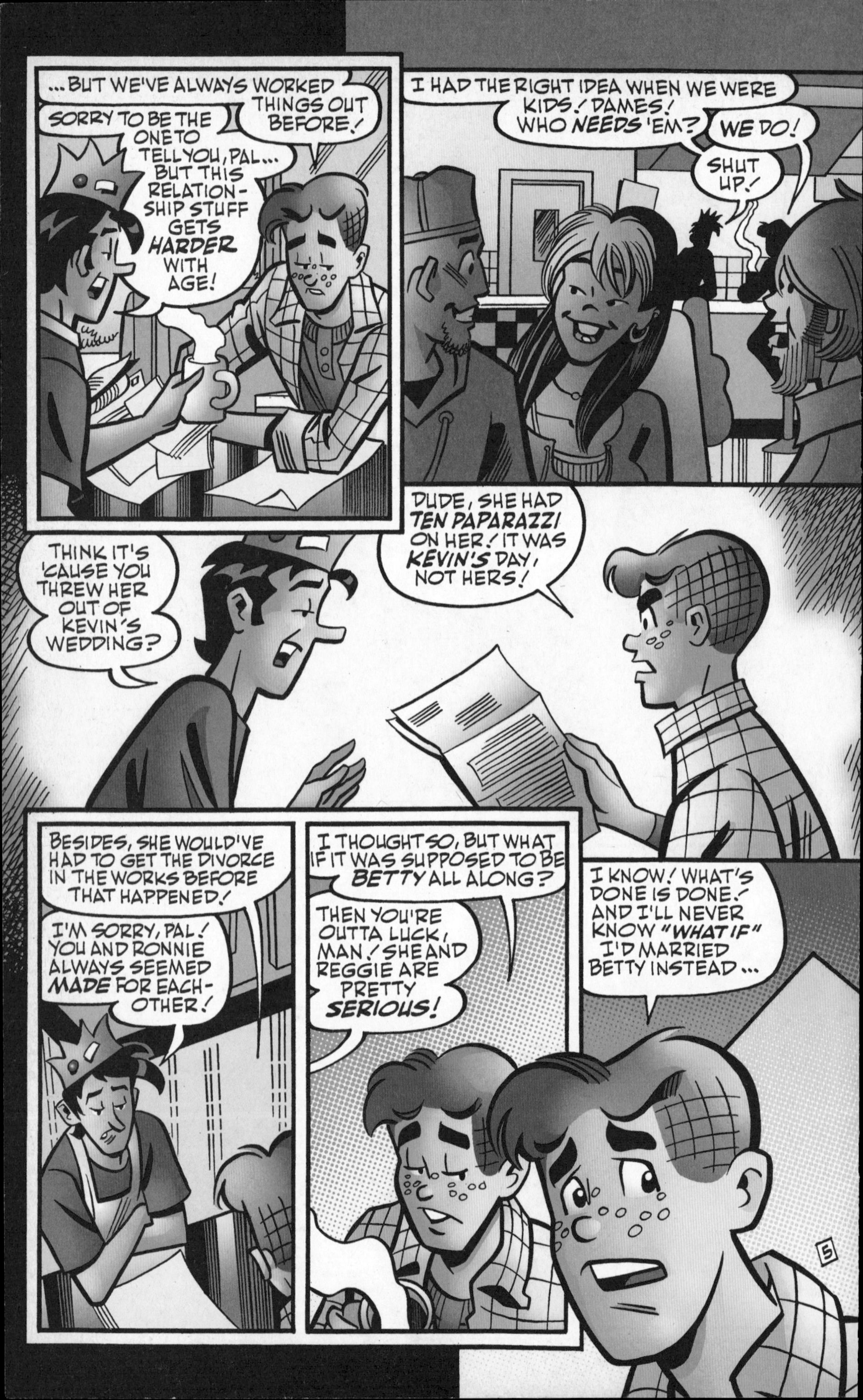

... BUT WE'VE ALWAYS WORKED THINGS OUT BEFORE!
SORRY TO BE THE ONE TO TELL YOU, PAL... BUT THIS RELATIONSHIP STUFF GETS HARDER WITH AGE!
I HAD THE RIGHT IDEA WHEN WE WERE KIDS! DAMES! WHO NEEDS 'EM?
WE DO!
SHUT UP!
THINK IT'S 'CAUSE YOU THREW HER OUT OF KEVIN'S WEDDING?
DUDE, SHE HAD TEN PAPARAZZI ON HER! IT WAS KEVIN'S DAY, NOT HERS!
BESIDES, SHE WOULD'VE HAD TO GET THE DIVORCE IN THE WORKS BEFORE THAT HAPPENED!
I'M SORRY, PAL! YOU AND RONNIE ALWAYS SEEMED MADE FOR EACH-OTHER!
I THOUGHT SO, BUT WHAT IF IT WAS SUPPOSED TO BE BETTY ALL ALONG?
THEN YOU'RE OUTTA LUCK, MAN! SHE AND REGGIE ARE PRETTY SERIOUS!
I KNOW! WHAT'S DONE IS DONE! AND I'LL NEVER KNOW "WHAT IF" I'D MARRIED BETTY INSTEAD...
5

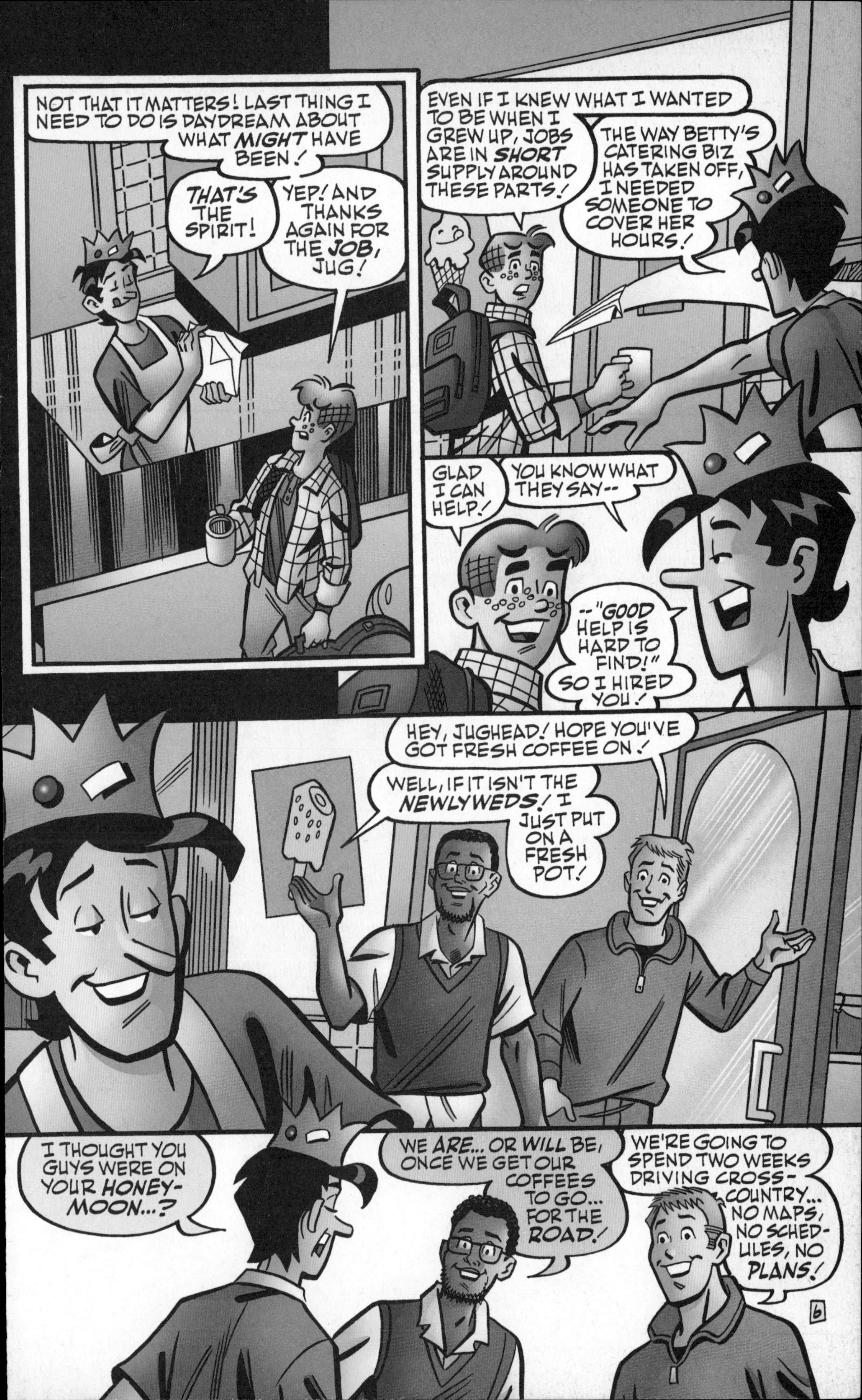
NOT THAT IT MATTERS! LAST THING I NEED TO DO IS DAYDREAM ABOUT WHAT MIGHT HAVE BEEN!
THAT'S THE SPIRIT!
YEP! AND THANKS AGAIN FOR THE JOB, JUG!
EVEN IF I KNEW WHAT I WANTED TO BE WHEN I GREW UP, JOBS ARE IN SHORT SUPPLY AROUND THESE PARTS!
THE WAY BETTY'S CATERING BIZ HAS TAKEN OFF, I NEEDED SOMEONE TO COVER HER HOURS!
GLAD I CAN HELP!
YOU KNOW WHAT THEY SAY--
--"GOOD HELP IS HARD TO FIND!" SO I HIRED YOU!
HEY, JUGHEAD! HOPE YOU'VE GOT FRESH COFFEE ON!
WELL, IF IT ISN'T THE NEWLYWEDS! I JUST PUT ON A FRESH POT!
I THOUGHT YOU GUYS WERE ON YOUR HONEY-MOON...?
WE ARE... OR WILL BE, ONCE WE GET OUR COFFEES TO GO... FOR THE ROAD!
WE'RE GOING TO SPEND TWO WEEKS DRIVING CROSS-COUNTRY... NO MAPS, NO SCHED-ULES, NO PLANS!
6

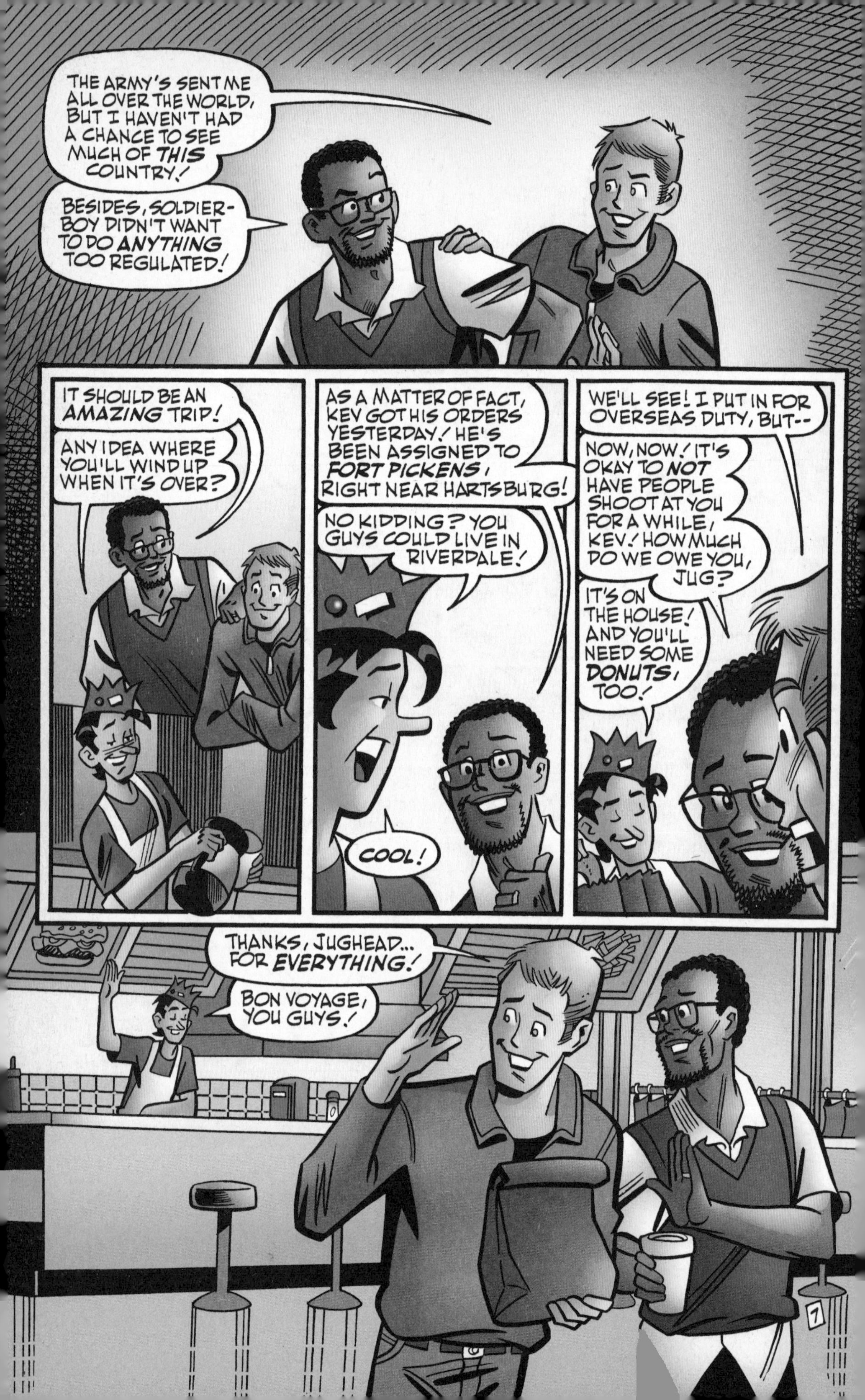
THE ARMY'S SENT ME ALL OVER THE WORLD, BUT I HAVEN'T HAD A CHANCE TO SEE MUCH OF THIS COUNTRY!
BESIDES, SOLDIER-BOY DIDN'T WANT TO DO ANYTHING TOO REGULATED!
IT SHOULD BE AN AMAZING TRIP!
ANY IDEA WHERE YOU'LL WIND UP WHEN IT'S OVER?
AS A MATTER OF FACT, KEV GOT HIS ORDERS YESTERDAY! HE'S BEEN ASSIGNED TO FORT PICKENS, RIGHT NEAR HARTSBURG!
NO KIDDING? YOU GUYS COULD LIVE IN RIVERDALE!
COOL!
WE'LL SEE! I PUT IN FOR OVERSEAS DUTY, BUT--
NOW, NOW! IT'S OKAY TO NOT HAVE PEOPLE SHOOT AT YOU FOR A WHILE, KEV! HOW MUCH DO WE OWE YOU, JUG?
IT'S ON THE HOUSE! AND YOU'LL NEED SOME DONUTS, TOO!
THANKS, JUGHEAD... FOR EVERYTHING!
BON VOYAGE, YOU GUYS!
7

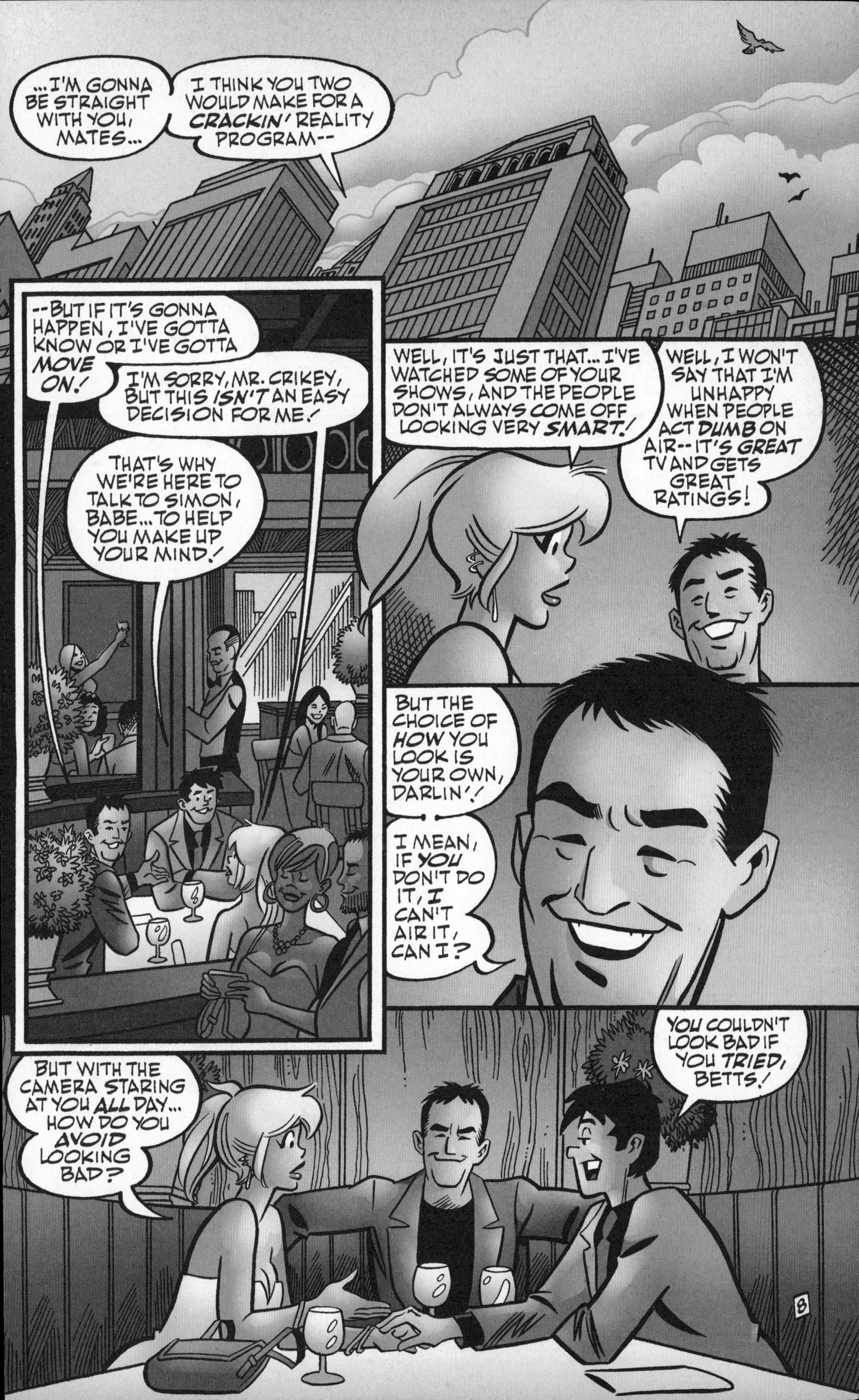
...I'M GONNA BE STRAIGHT WITH YOU, MATES...
I THINK YOU TWO WOULD MAKE FOR A CRACKIN' REALITY PROGRAM--
--BUT IF IT'S GONNA HAPPEN, I'VE GOTTA KNOW OR I'VE GOTTA MOVE ON!
I'M SORRY, MR. CRIKEY, BUT THIS ISN'T AN EASY DECISION FOR ME!
THAT'S WHY WE'RE HERE TO TALK TO SIMON, BABE... TO HELP YOU MAKE UP YOUR MIND!
WELL, IT'S JUST THAT... I'VE WATCHED SOME OF YOUR SHOWS, AND THE PEOPLE DON'T ALWAYS COME OFF LOOKING VERY SMART!
WELL, I WON'T SAY THAT I'M UNHAPPY WHEN PEOPLE ACT DUMB ON AIR-- IT'S GREAT TV AND GETS GREAT RATINGS!
BUT THE CHOICE OF HOW YOU LOOK IS YOUR OWN, DARLIN'!
I MEAN, IF YOU DON'T DO IT, I CAN'T AIR IT, CAN I?
BUT WITH THE CAMERA STARING AT YOU ALL DAY... HOW DO YOU AVOID LOOKING BAD?
YOU COULDN'T LOOK BAD IF YOU TRIED, BETTS!
8

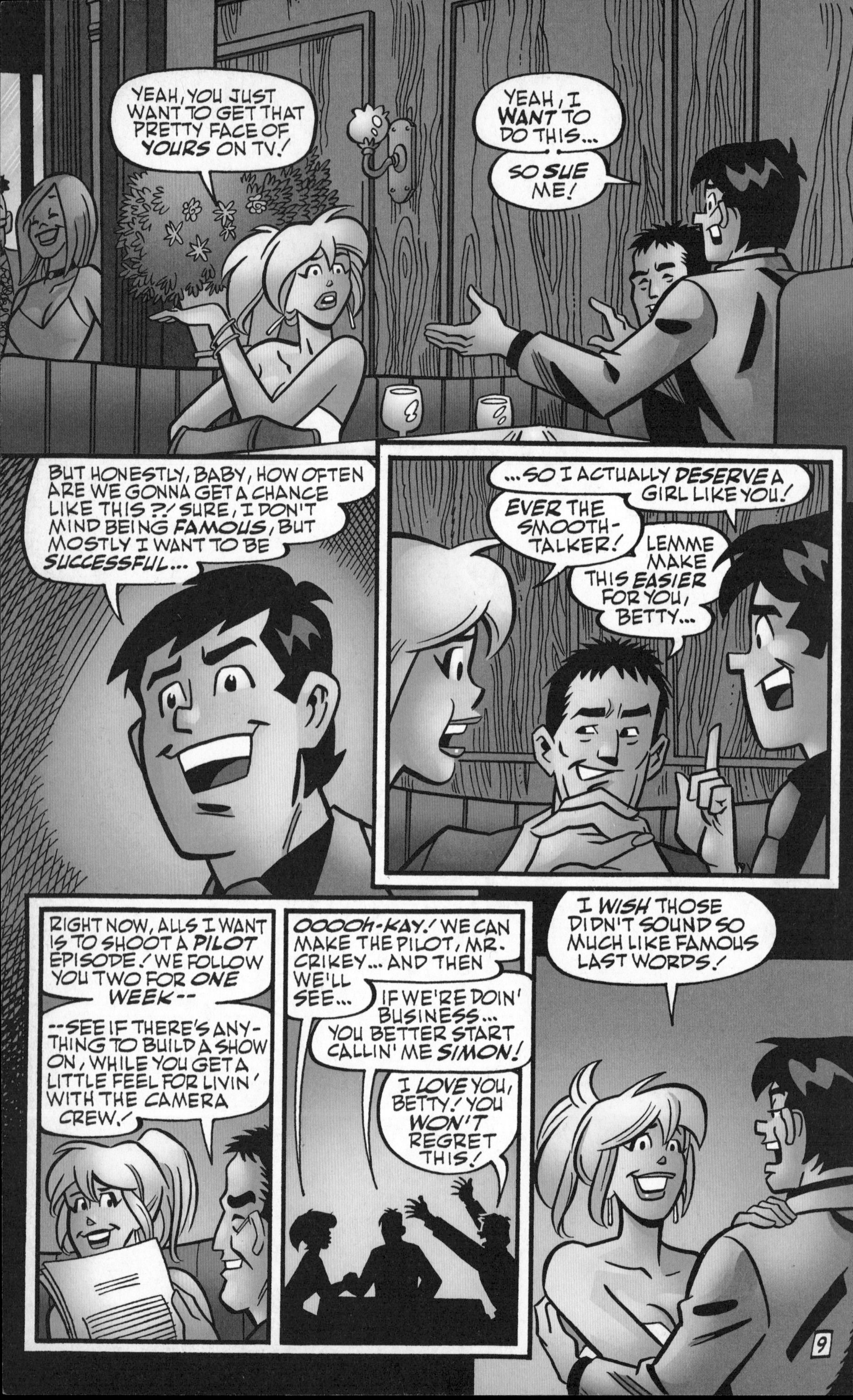
YEAH, YOU JUST WANT TO GET THAT PRETTY FACE OF YOURS ON TV!
YEAH, I WANT TO DO THIS...
SO SUE ME!
BUT HONESTLY, BABY, HOW OFTEN ARE WE GONNA GET A CHANCE LIKE THIS?! SURE, I DON'T MIND BEING FAMOUS, BUT MOSTLY I WANT TO BE SUCCESSFUL...
...SO I ACTUALLY DESERVE A GIRL LIKE YOU!
EVER THE SMOOTH-TALKER!
LEMME MAKE THIS EASIER FOR YOU, BETTY...
RIGHT NOW, ALLS I WANT IS TO SHOOT A PILOT EPISODE! WE FOLLOW YOU TWO FOR ONE WEEK--
--SEE IF THERE'S ANY-THING TO BUILD A SHOW ON, WHILE YOU GET A LITTLE FEEL FOR LIVIN' WITH THE CAMERA CREW!
OOOOOh-KAY! WE CAN MAKE THE PILOT, MR. CRIKEY... AND THEN WE'LL SEE...
IF WE'RE DOIN' BUSINESS... YOU BETTER START CALLIN' ME SIMON!
I LOVE YOU, BETTY! YOU WON'T REGRET THIS!
I WISH THOSE DIDN'T SOUND SO MUCH LIKE FAMOUS LAST WORDS!

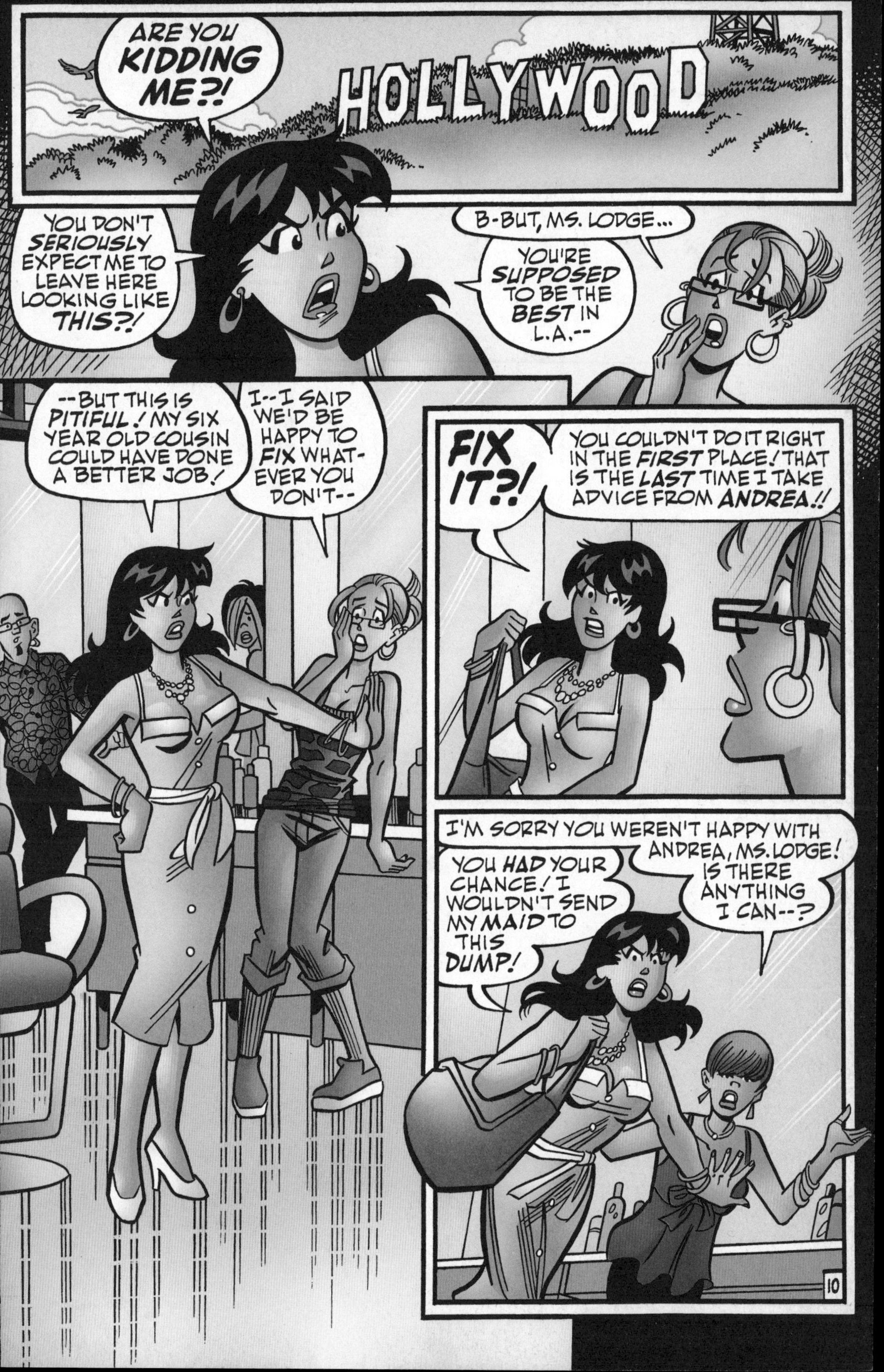

ARE YOU KIDDING ME?!
HOLLYWOOD
YOU DON'T SERIOUSLY EXPECT ME TO LEAVE HERE LOOKING LIKE THIS?!
B-BUT, MS. LODGE...
YOU'RE SUPPOSED TO BE THE BEST IN L.A.--
--BUT THIS IS PITIFUL! MY SIX YEAR OLD COUSIN COULD HAVE DONE A BETTER JOB!
I--I SAID WE'D BE HAPPY TO FIX WHAT-EVER YOU DON'T--
FIX IT?!
YOU COULDN'T DO IT RIGHT IN THE FIRST PLACE! THAT IS THE LAST TIME I TAKE ADVICE FROM ANDREA!!
I'M SORRY YOU WEREN'T HAPPY WITH ANDREA, MS. LODGE! IS THERE ANYTHING I CAN--?
YOU HAD YOUR CHANCE! I WOULDN'T SEND MY MAID TO THIS DUMP!
10

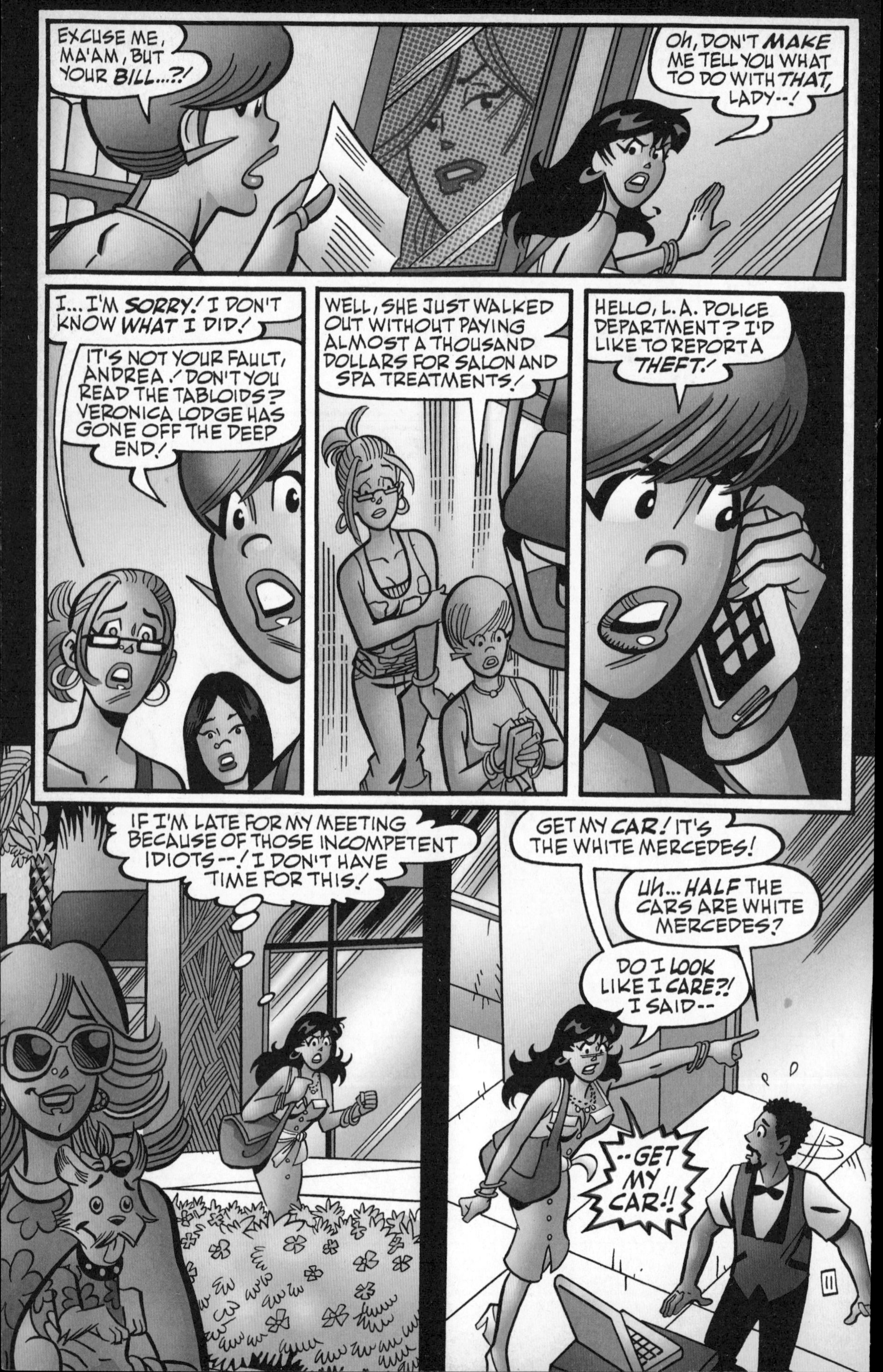
EXCUSE ME, MA'AM, BUT YOUR BILL...?!
OH, DON'T MAKE ME TELL YOU WHAT TO DO WITH THAT, LADY--!
I... I'M SORRY! I DON'T KNOW WHAT I DID!
IT'S NOT YOUR FAULT, ANDREA! DON'T YOU READ THE TABLOIDS? VERONICA LODGE HAS GONE OFF THE DEEP END!
WELL, SHE JUST WALKED OUT WITHOUT PAYING ALMOST A THOUSAND DOLLARS FOR SALON AND SPA TREATMENTS!
HELLO, L.A. POLICE DEPARTMENT? I'D LIKE TO REPORT A THEFT!
IF I'M LATE FOR MY MEETING BECAUSE OF THOSE INCOMPETENT IDIOTS--! I DON'T HAVE TIME FOR THIS!
GET MY CAR! IT'S THE WHITE MERCEDES!
UH... HALF THE CARS ARE WHITE MERCEDES?
DO I LOOK LIKE I CARE?! I SAID--
--GET MY CAR!!
11

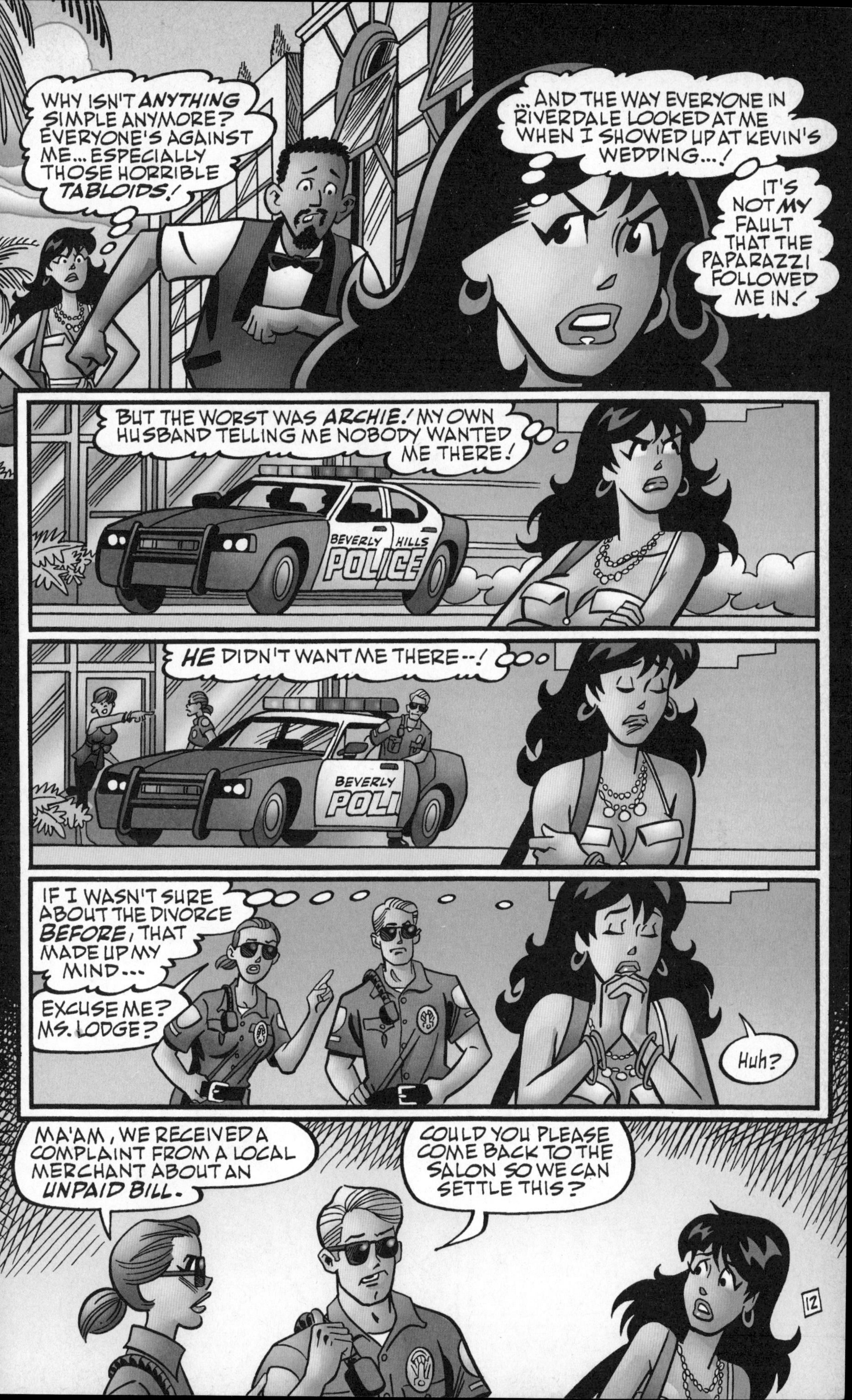
WHY ISN'T ANYTHING SIMPLE ANYMORE? EVERYONE'S AGAINST ME... ESPECIALLY THOSE HORRIBLE TABLOIDS!
...AND THE WAY EVERYONE IN RIVERDALE LOOKED AT ME WHEN I SHOWED UP AT KEVIN'S WEDDING...!
IT'S NOT MY FAULT THAT THE PAPARAZZI FOLLOWED ME IN!
BUT THE WORST WAS ARCHIE! MY OWN HUSBAND TELLING ME NOBODY WANTED ME THERE!
BEVERLY HILLS POLICE
HE DIDN'T WANT ME THERE--!
BEVERLY POLI
IF I WASN'T SURE ABOUT THE DIVORCE BEFORE, THAT MADE UP MY MIND...
EXCUSE ME? MS. LODGE?
Huh?
MA'AM, WE RECEIVED A COMPLAINT FROM A LOCAL MERCHANT ABOUT AN UNPAID BILL.
COULD YOU PLEASE COME BACK TO THE SALON SO WE CAN SETTLE THIS?
12

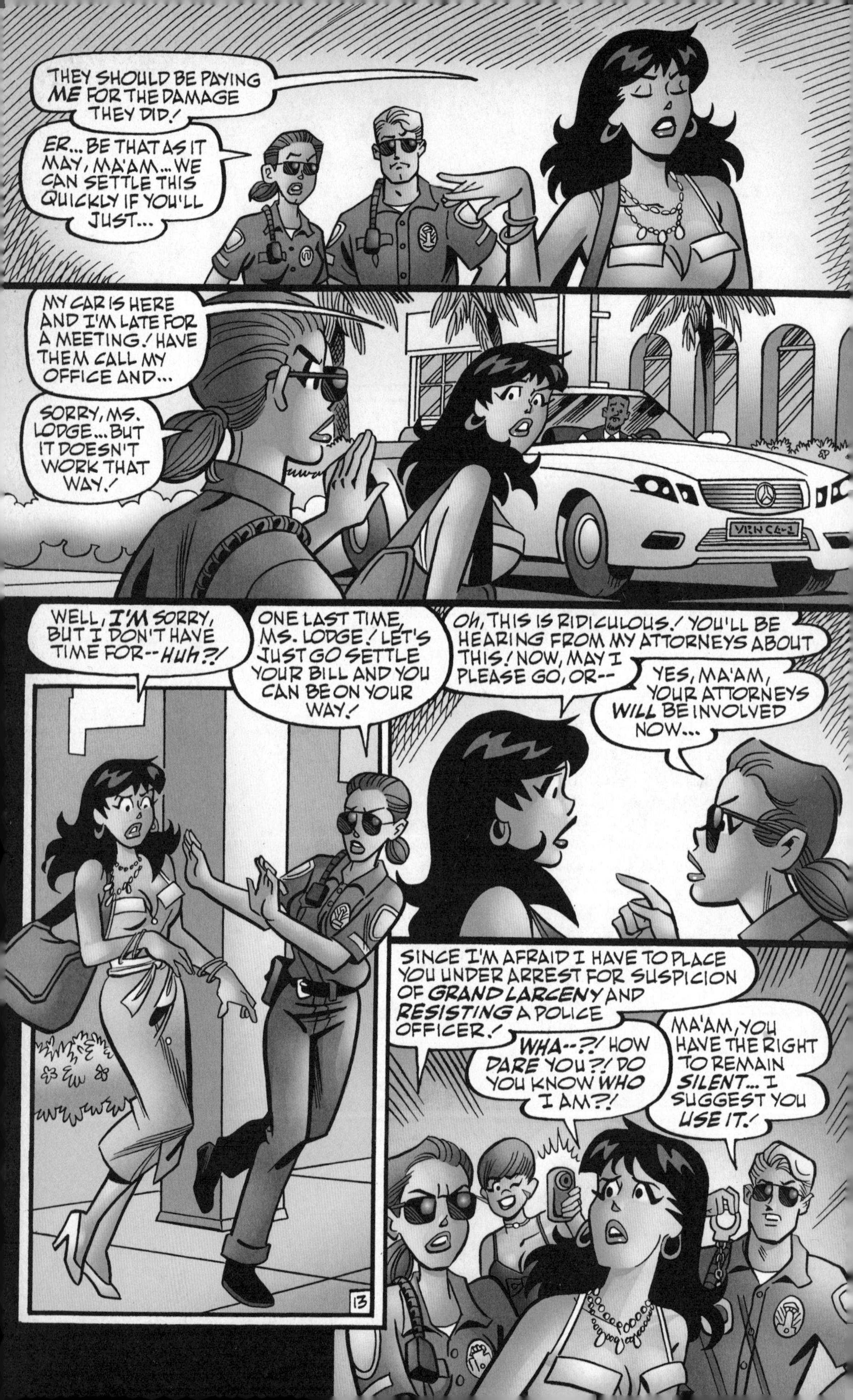

THEY SHOULD BE PAYING ME FOR THE DAMAGE THEY DID!
ER... BE THAT AS IT MAY, MA'AM... WE CAN SETTLE THIS QUICKLY IF YOU'LL JUST...
MY CAR IS HERE AND I'M LATE FOR A MEETING! HAVE THEM CALL MY OFFICE AND...
SORRY, MS. LODGE... BUT IT DOESN'T WORK THAT WAY!
VRN CA-1
WELL, I'M SORRY, BUT I DON'T HAVE TIME FOR-- HUH?!
ONE LAST TIME, MS. LODGE! LET'S JUST GO SETTLE YOUR BILL AND YOU CAN BE ON YOUR WAY!
OH, THIS IS RIDICULOUS! YOU'LL BE HEARING FROM MY ATTORNEYS ABOUT THIS! NOW, MAY I PLEASE GO, OR--
YES, MA'AM, YOUR ATTORNEYS WILL BE INVOLVED NOW...
SINCE I'M AFRAID I HAVE TO PLACE YOU UNDER ARREST FOR SUSPICION OF GRAND LARCENY AND RESISTING A POLICE OFFICER!
WHA--?! HOW DARE YOU?! DO YOU KNOW WHO I AM?!
MA'AM, YOU HAVE THE RIGHT TO REMAIN SILENT... I SUGGEST YOU USE IT!
13

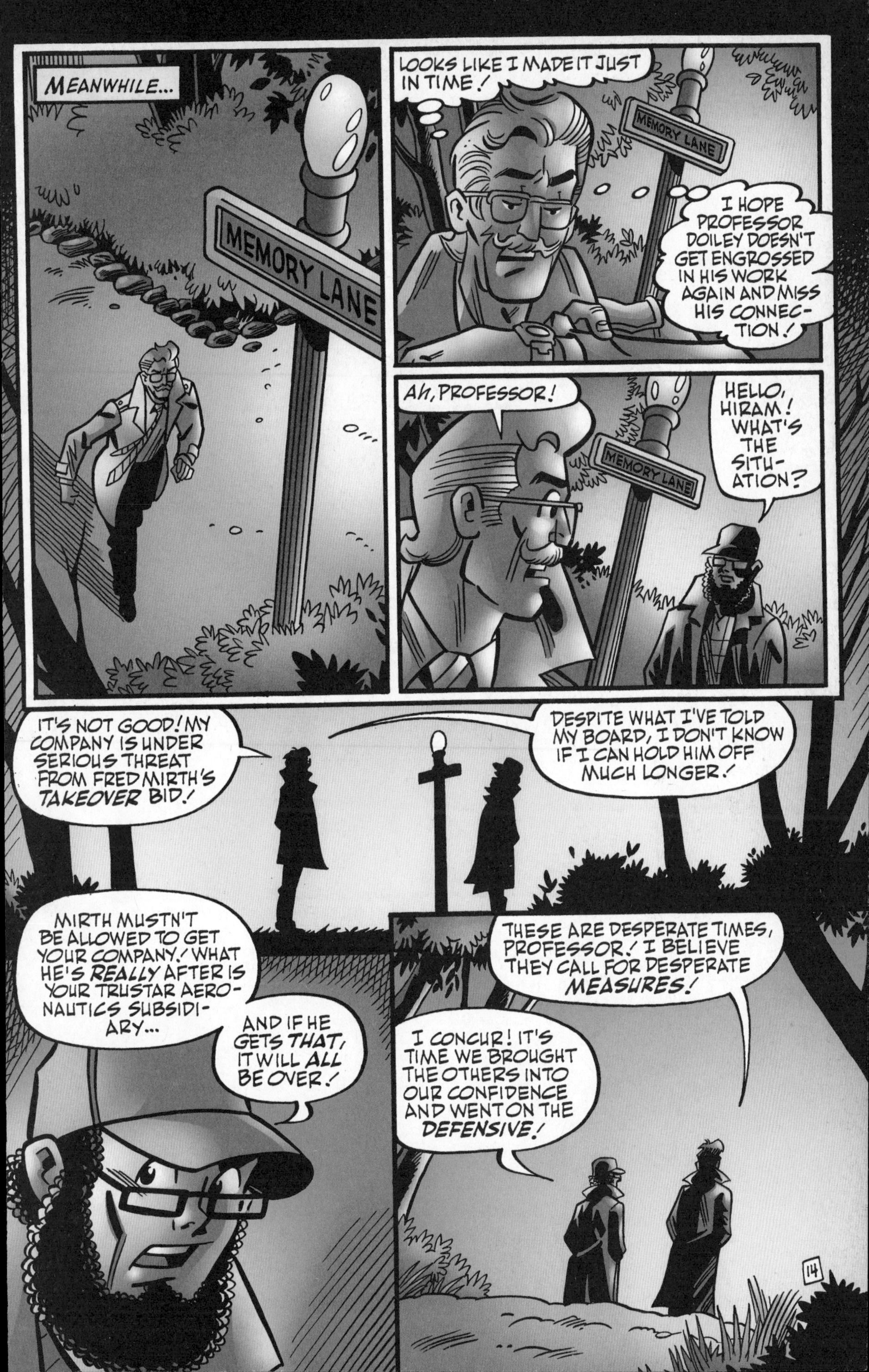
MEANWHILE...
MEMORY LANE
LOOKS LIKE I MADE IT JUST IN TIME!
MEMORY LANE
I HOPE PROFESSOR DOILEY DOESN'T GET ENGROSSED IN HIS WORK AGAIN AND MISS HIS CONNEC-TION!
AH, PROFESSOR!
MEMORY LANE
HELLO, HIRAM! WHAT'S THE SITU-ATION?
IT'S NOT GOOD! MY COMPANY IS UNDER SERIOUS THREAT FROM FRED MIRTH'S TAKEOVER BID!
DESPITE WHAT I'VE TOLD MY BOARD, I DON'T KNOW IF I CAN HOLD HIM OFF MUCH LONGER!
MIRTH MUSTN'T BE ALLOWED TO GET YOUR COMPANY! WHAT HE'S REALLY AFTER IS YOUR TRUSTAR AERO-NAUTICS SUBSIDI-ARY...
AND IF HE GETS THAT, IT WILL ALL BE OVER!
THESE ARE DESPERATE TIMES, PROFESSOR! I BELIEVE THEY CALL FOR DESPERATE MEASURES!
I CONCUR! IT'S TIME WE BROUGHT THE OTHERS INTO OUR CONFIDENCE AND WENT ON THE DEFENSIVE!
14

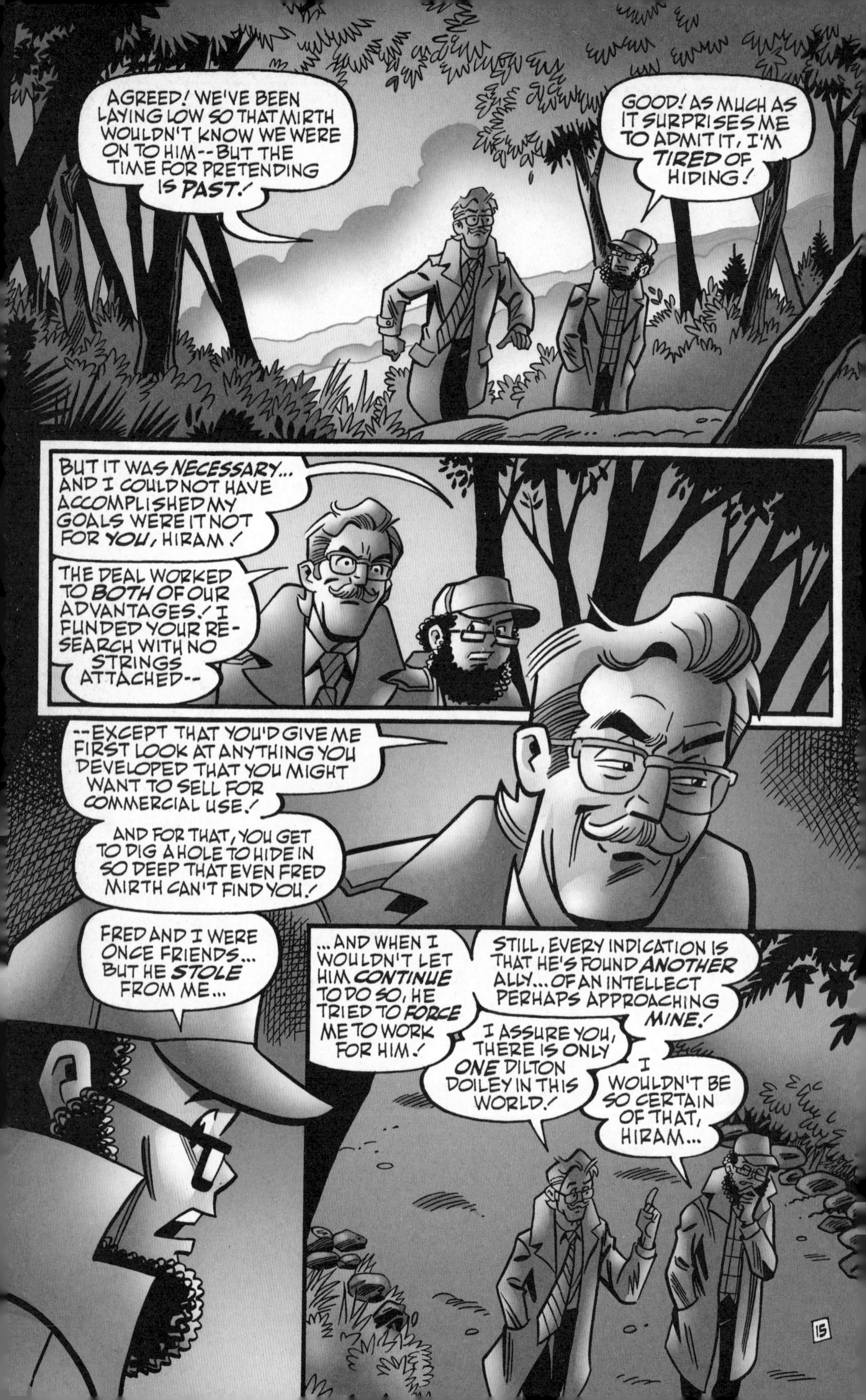

AGREED! WE'VE BEEN LAYING LOW SO THAT MIRTH WOULDN'T KNOW WE WERE ON TO HIM--BUT THE TIME FOR PRETENDING IS PAST!
GOOD! AS MUCH AS IT SURPRISES ME TO ADMIT IT, I'M TIRED OF HIDING!
BUT IT WAS NECESSARY... AND I COULD NOT HAVE ACCOMPLISHED MY GOALS WERE IT NOT FOR YOU, HIRAM!
THE DEAL WORKED TO BOTH OF OUR ADVANTAGES! I FUNDED YOUR RE-SEARCH WITH NO STRINGS ATTACHED--
--EXCEPT THAT YOU'D GIVE ME FIRST LOOK AT ANYTHING YOU DEVELOPED THAT YOU MIGHT WANT TO SELL FOR COMMERCIAL USE!
AND FOR THAT, YOU GET TO DIG A HOLE TO HIDE IN SO DEEP THAT EVEN FRED MIRTH CAN'T FIND YOU!
FRED AND I WERE ONCE FRIENDS... BUT HE STOLE FROM ME...
...AND WHEN I WOULDN'T LET HIM CONTINUE TO DO SO, HE TRIED TO FORCE ME TO WORK FOR HIM!
STILL, EVERY INDICATION IS THAT HE'S FOUND ANOTHER ALLY... OF AN INTELLECT PERHAPS APPROACHING MINE!
I ASSURE YOU, THERE IS ONLY ONE DILTON DOILEY IN THIS WORLD!
I WOULDN'T BE SO CERTAIN OF THAT, HIRAM...
15

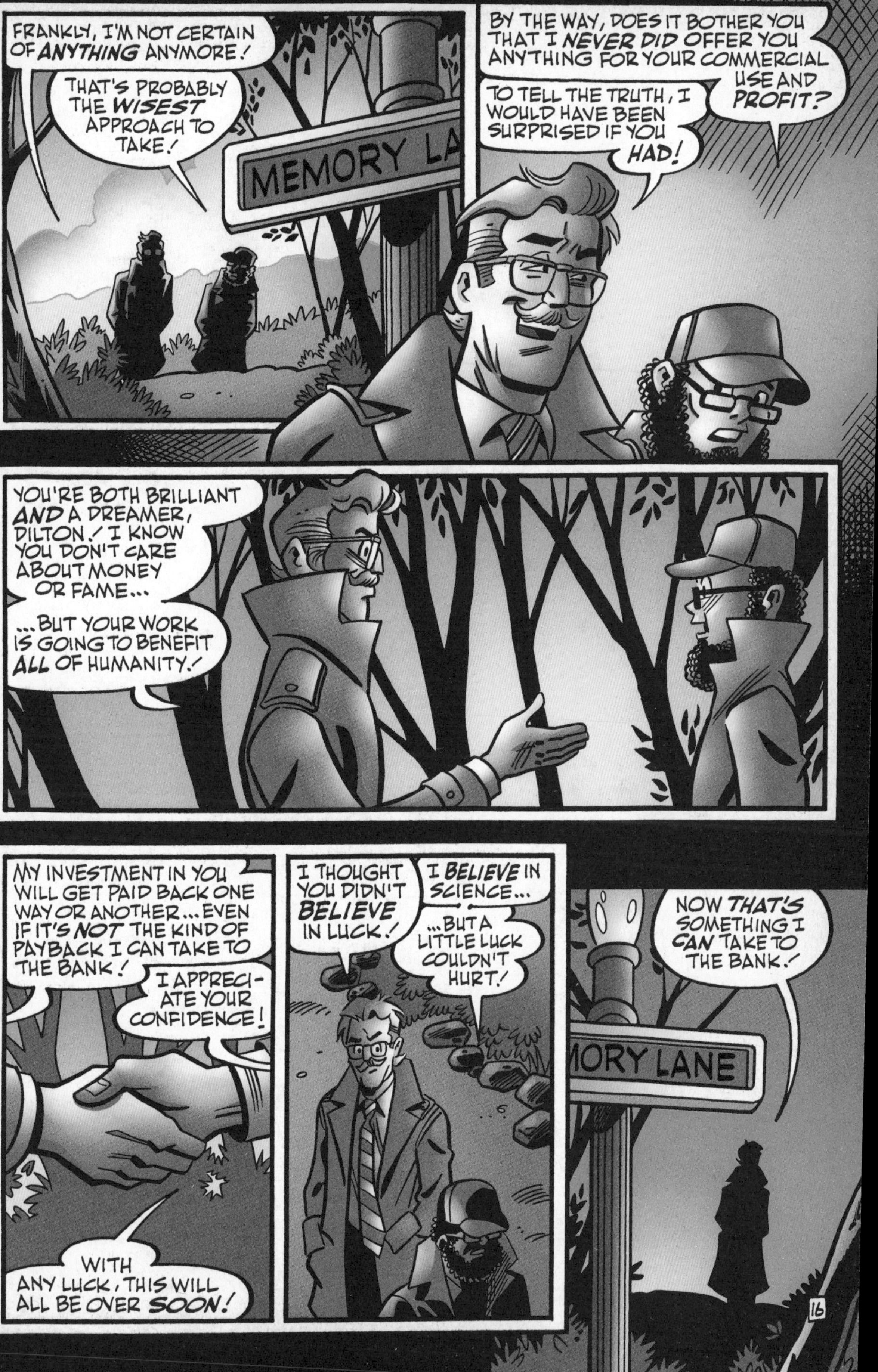
FRANKLY, I'M NOT CERTAIN OF ANYTHING ANYMORE!
THAT'S PROBABLY THE WISEST APPROACH TO TAKE!
MEMORY LA
BY THE WAY, DOES IT BOTHER YOU THAT I NEVER DID OFFER YOU ANYTHING FOR YOUR COMMERCIAL USE AND PROFIT?
TO TELL THE TRUTH, I WOULD HAVE BEEN SURPRISED IF YOU HAD!
YOU'RE BOTH BRILLIANT AND A DREAMER, DILTON! I KNOW YOU DON'T CARE ABOUT MONEY OR FAME...
...BUT YOUR WORK IS GOING TO BENEFIT ALL OF HUMANITY!
MY INVESTMENT IN YOU WILL GET PAID BACK ONE WAY OR ANOTHER... EVEN IF IT'S NOT THE KIND OF PAYBACK I CAN TAKE TO THE BANK!
I APPRECI-ATE YOUR CONFIDENCE!
WITH ANY LUCK, THIS WILL ALL BE OVER SOON!
I THOUGHT YOU DIDN'T BELIEVE IN LUCK!
I BELIEVE IN SCIENCE...
...BUT A LITTLE LUCK COULDN'T HURT!
NOW THAT'S SOMETHING I CAN TAKE TO THE BANK!
ORY LANE
16

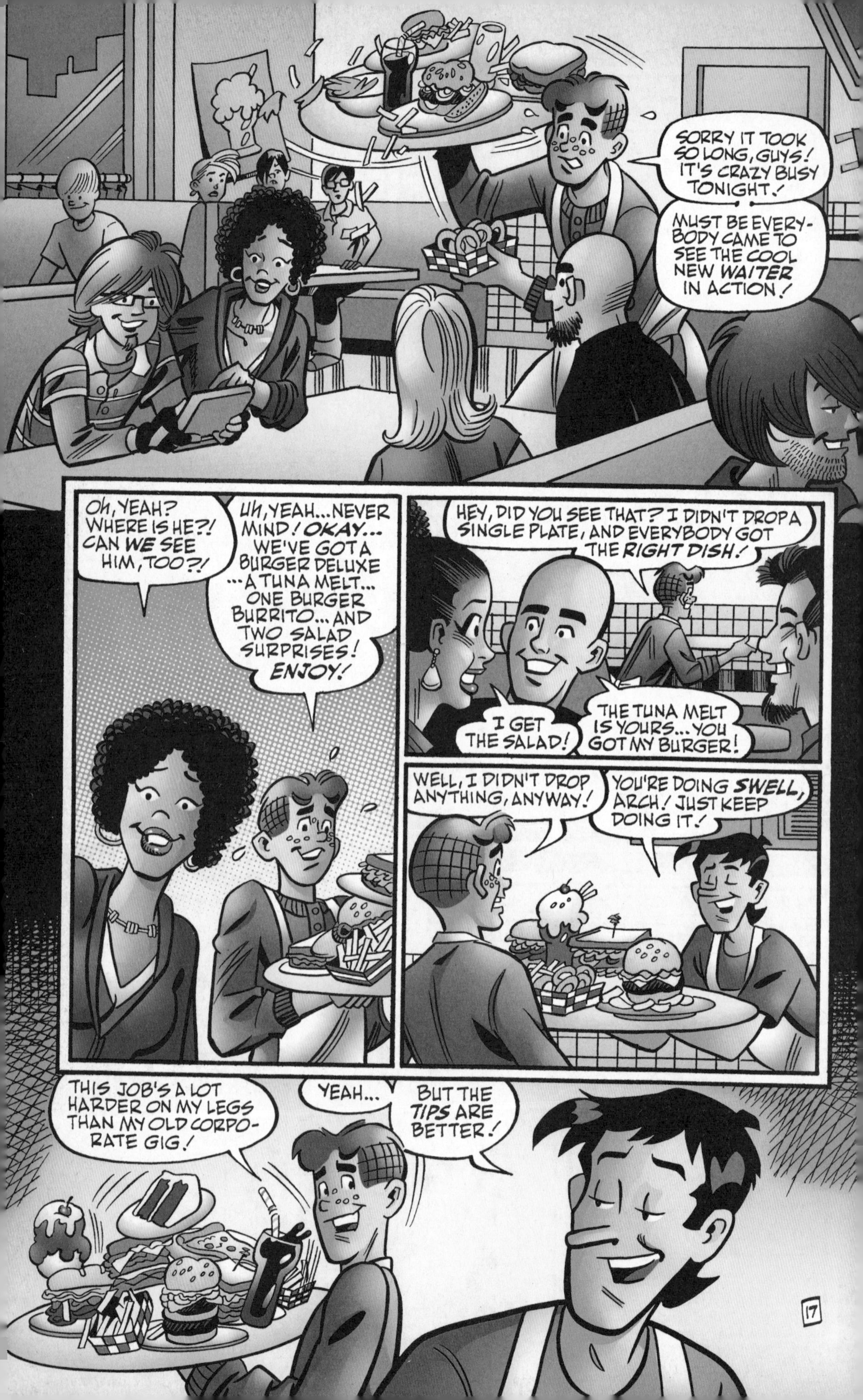
SORRY IT TOOK SO LONG, GUYS! IT'S CRAZY BUSY TONIGHT!
MUST BE EVERYBODY CAME TO SEE THE COOL NEW WAITER IN ACTION!
OH, YEAH? WHERE IS HE?! CAN WE SEE HIM, TOO?!
UH, YEAH... NEVER MIND! OKAY... WE'VE GOT A BURGER DELUXE ... A TUNA MELT... ONE BURGER BURRITO... AND TWO SALAD SURPRISES! ENJOY!
HEY, DID YOU SEE THAT? I DIDN'T DROP A SINGLE PLATE, AND EVERYBODY GOT THE RIGHT DISH!
I GET THE SALAD!
THE TUNA MELT IS YOURS... YOU GOT MY BURGER!
WELL, I DIDN'T DROP ANYTHING, ANYWAY!
YOU'RE DOING SWELL, ARCH! JUST KEEP DOING IT!
THIS JOB'S A LOT HARDER ON MY LEGS THAN MY OLD CORPORATE GIG!
YEAH...
BUT THE TIPS ARE BETTER!

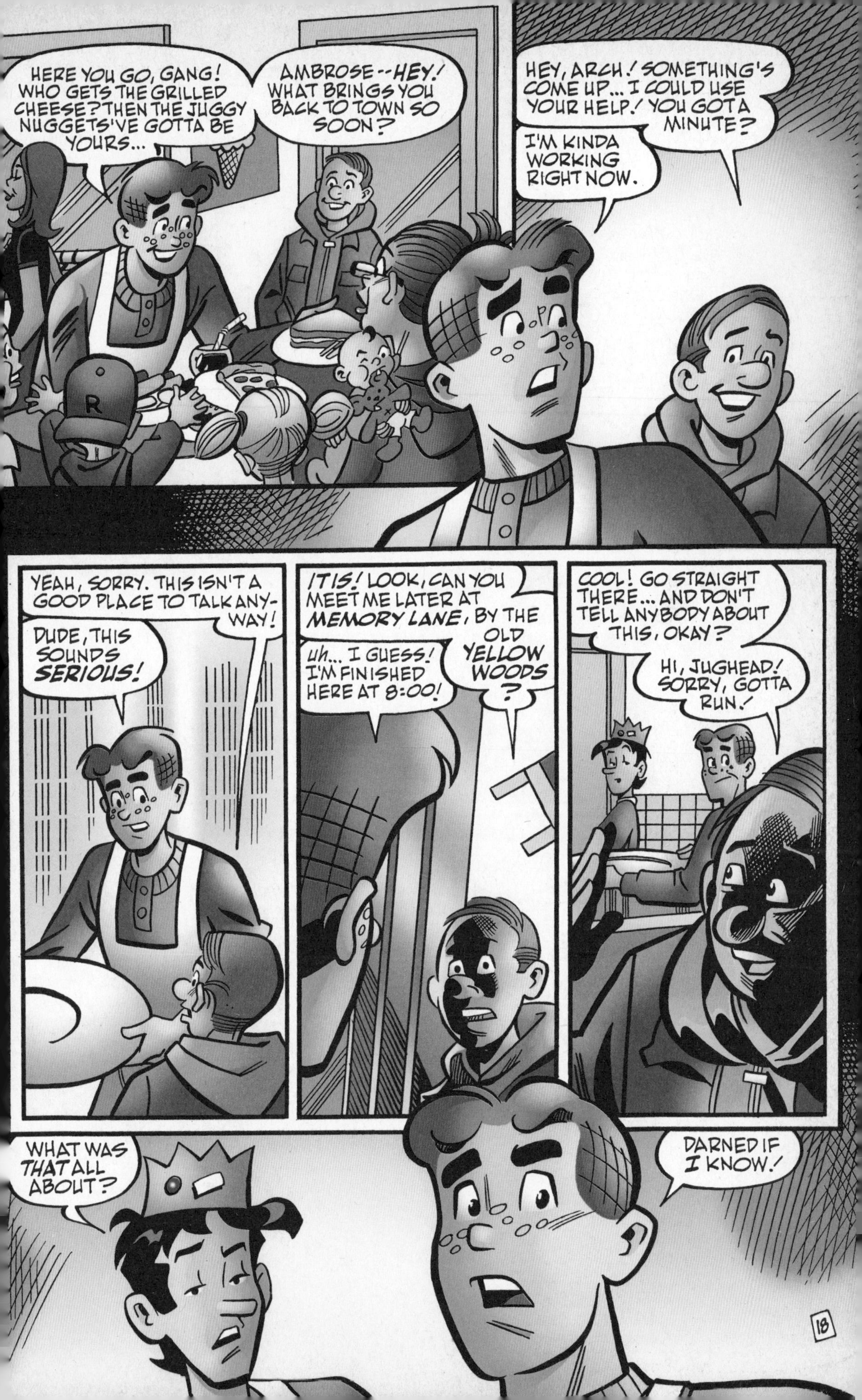
HERE YOU GO, GANG! WHO GETS THE GRILLED CHEESE? THEN THE JUGGY NUGGETS'VE GOTTA BE YOURS...
AMBROSE--HEY! WHAT BRINGS YOU BACK TO TOWN SO SOON?
HEY, ARCH! SOMETHING'S COME UP... I COULD USE YOUR HELP! YOU GOT A MINUTE?
I'M KINDA WORKING RIGHT NOW.
YEAH, SORRY. THIS ISN'T A GOOD PLACE TO TALK ANYWAY!
DUDE, THIS SOUNDS SERIOUS!
IT IS! LOOK, CAN YOU MEET ME LATER AT MEMORY LANE, BY THE OLD YELLOW WOODS?
UH... I GUESS! I'M FINISHED HERE AT 8:00!
COOL! GO STRAIGHT THERE... AND DON'T TELL ANYBODY ABOUT THIS, OKAY?
HI, JUGHEAD! SORRY, GOTTA RUN!
WHAT WAS THAT ALL ABOUT?
DARNED IF I KNOW!

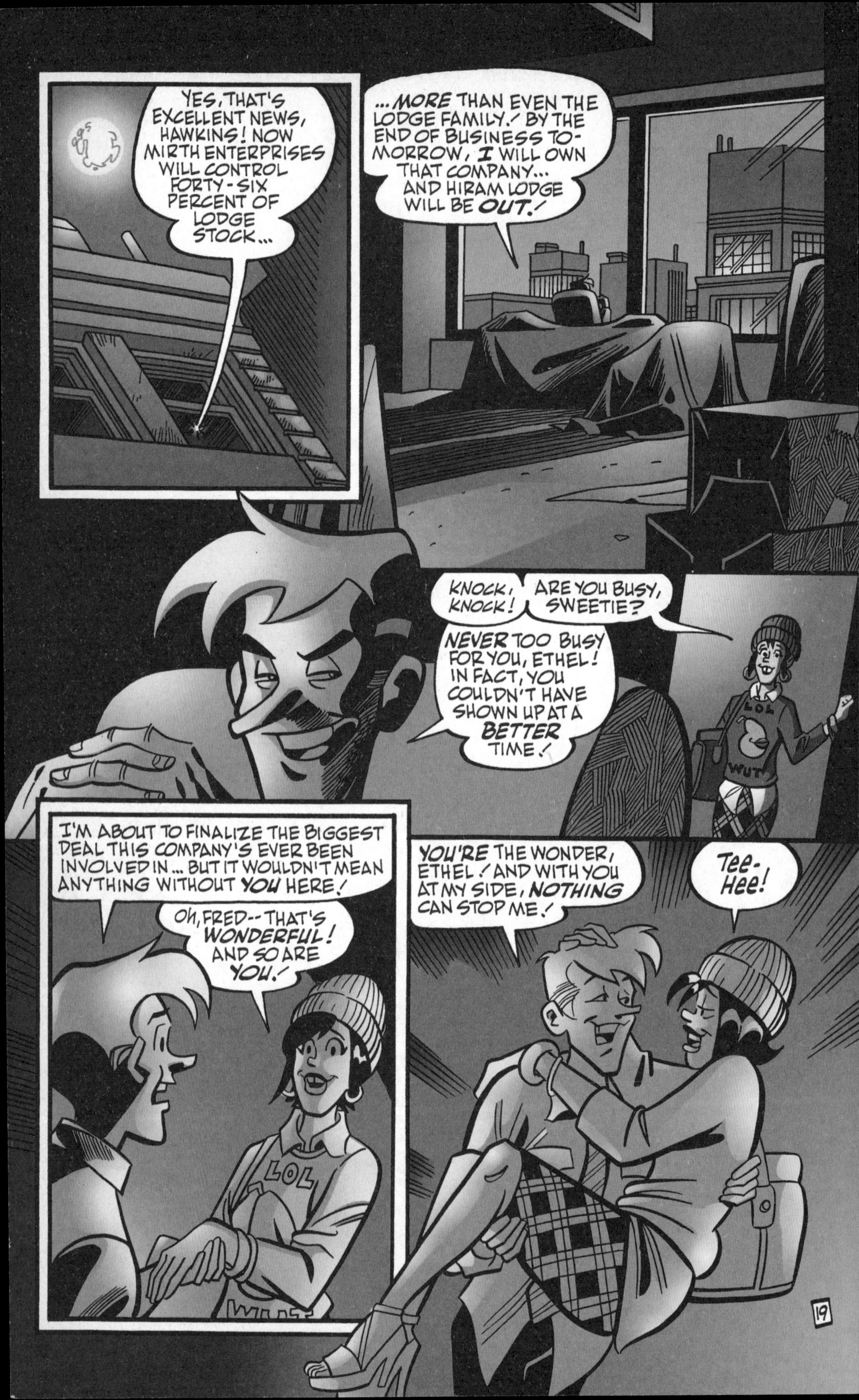
YES, THAT'S EXCELLENT NEWS, HAWKINS! NOW MIRTH ENTERPRISES WILL CONTROL FORTY-SIX PERCENT OF LODGE STOCK...
...MORE THAN EVEN THE LODGE FAMILY! BY THE END OF BUSINESS TO-MORROW, I WILL OWN THAT COMPANY... AND HIRAM LODGE WILL BE OUT!
KNOCK, KNOCK!
ARE YOU BUSY, SWEETIE?
NEVER TOO BUSY FOR YOU, ETHEL! IN FACT, YOU COULDN'T HAVE SHOWN UP AT A BETTER TIME!
LOL
WUT
I'M ABOUT TO FINALIZE THE BIGGEST DEAL THIS COMPANY'S EVER BEEN INVOLVED IN... BUT IT WOULDN'T MEAN ANYTHING WITHOUT YOU HERE!
OH, FRED-- THAT'S WONDERFUL! AND SO ARE YOU!
YOU'RE THE WONDER, ETHEL! AND WITH YOU AT MY SIDE, NOTHING CAN STOP ME!
Tee-Hee!

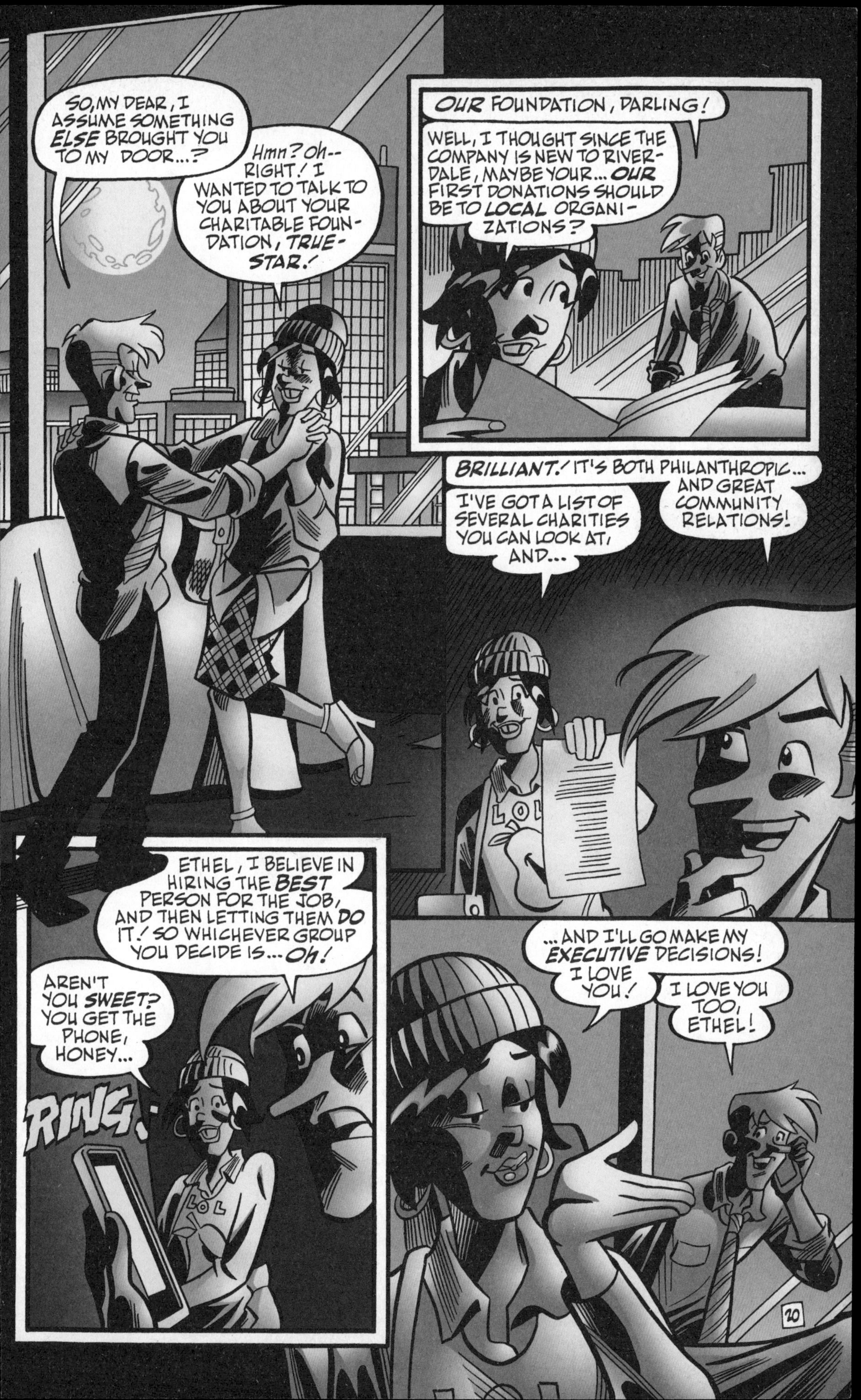
SO, MY DEAR, I ASSUME SOMETHING ELSE BROUGHT YOU TO MY DOOR...?
Hmn? Oh-- RIGHT! I WANTED TO TALK TO YOU ABOUT YOUR CHARITABLE FOUNDATION, TRUE-STAR!
OUR FOUNDATION, DARLING!
WELL, I THOUGHT SINCE THE COMPANY IS NEW TO RIVERDALE, MAYBE YOUR... OUR FIRST DONATIONS SHOULD BE TO LOCAL ORGANIZATIONS?
BRILLIANT! IT'S BOTH PHILANTHROPIC... AND GREAT COMMUNITY RELATIONS!
I'VE GOT A LIST OF SEVERAL CHARITIES YOU CAN LOOK AT, AND...
LOL
ETHEL, I BELIEVE IN HIRING THE BEST PERSON FOR THE JOB, AND THEN LETTING THEM DO IT! SO WHICHEVER GROUP YOU DECIDE IS... Oh!
AREN'T YOU SWEET? YOU GET THE PHONE, HONEY...
RING!
LOL
...AND I'LL GO MAKE MY EXECUTIVE DECISIONS! I LOVE YOU!
I LOVE YOU TOO, ETHEL!
20

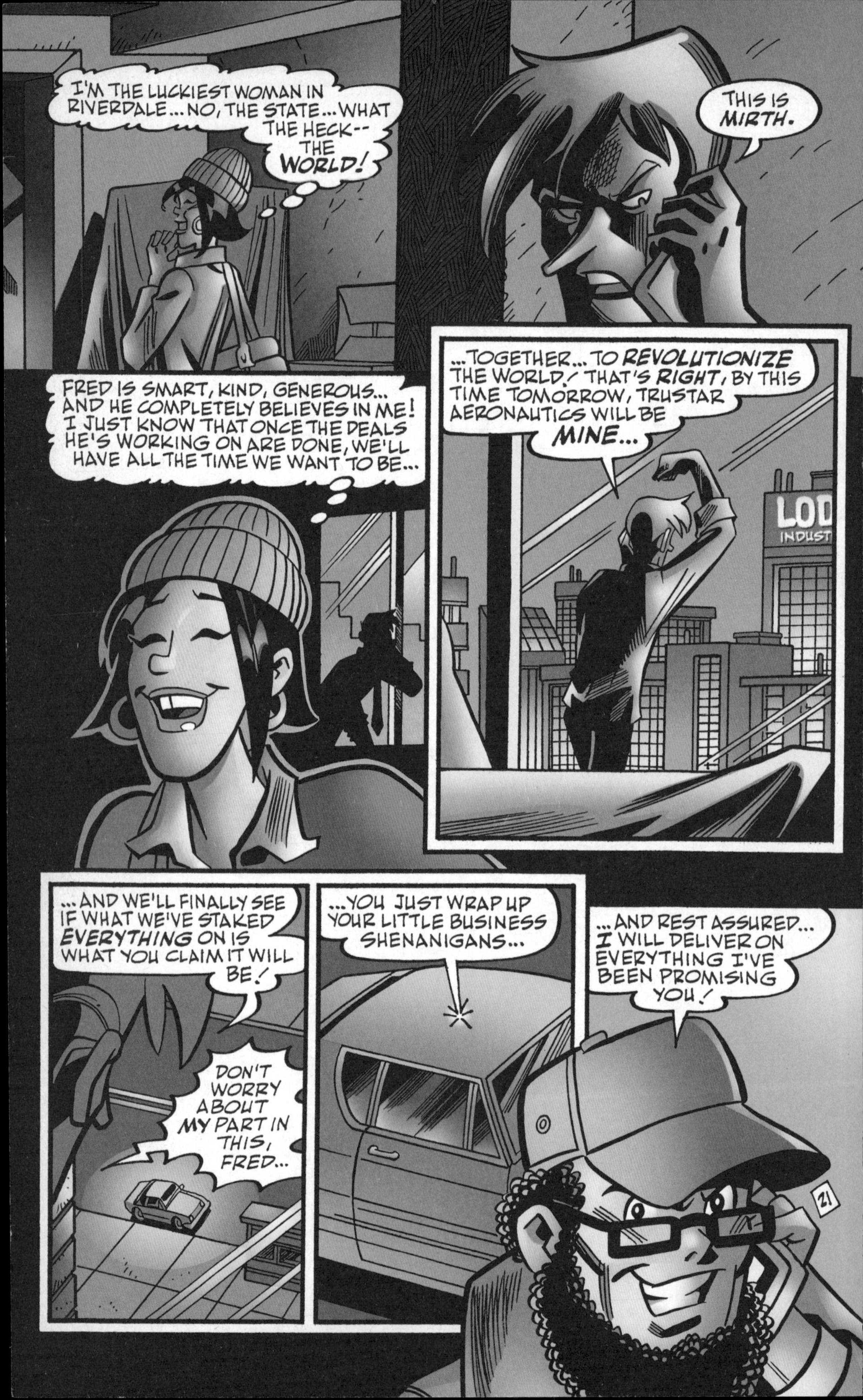

I'M THE LUCKIEST WOMAN IN RIVERDALE... NO, THE STATE... WHAT THE HECK-- THE WORLD!
THIS IS MIRTH.
FRED IS SMART, KIND, GENEROUS... AND HE COMPLETELY BELIEVES IN ME! I JUST KNOW THAT ONCE THE DEALS HE'S WORKING ON ARE DONE, WE'LL HAVE ALL THE TIME WE WANT TO BE...
...TOGETHER... TO REVOLUTIONIZE THE WORLD! THAT'S RIGHT, BY THIS TIME TOMORROW, TRUSTAR AERONAUTICS WILL BE MINE...
LOD
INDUST
...AND WE'LL FINALLY SEE IF WHAT WE'VE STAKED EVERYTHING ON IS WHAT YOU CLAIM IT WILL BE!
DON'T WORRY ABOUT MY PART IN THIS, FRED...
...YOU JUST WRAP UP YOUR LITTLE BUSINESS SHENANIGANS...
...AND REST ASSURED... I WILL DELIVER ON EVERYTHING I'VE BEEN PROMISING YOU!

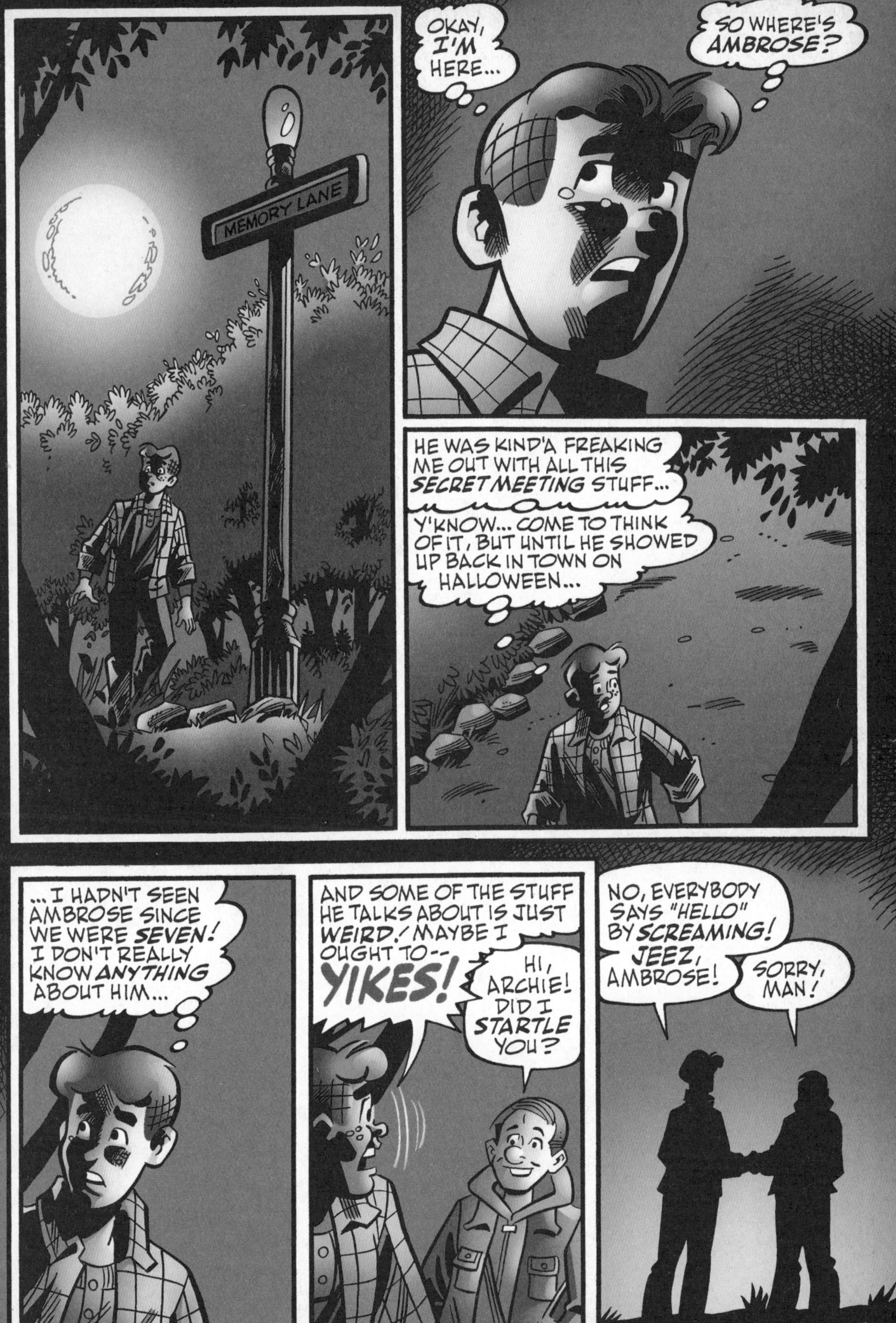
MEMORY LANE
OKAY, I'M HERE...
SO WHERE'S AMBROSE?
HE WAS KIND'A FREAKING ME OUT WITH ALL THIS SECRET MEETING STUFF...
Y'KNOW... COME TO THINK OF IT, BUT UNTIL HE SHOWED UP BACK IN TOWN ON HALLOWEEN...
... I HADN'T SEEN AMBROSE SINCE WE WERE SEVEN! I DON'T REALLY KNOW ANYTHING ABOUT HIM...
AND SOME OF THE STUFF HE TALKS ABOUT IS JUST WEIRD! MAYBE I OUGHT TO--
YIKES!
HI, ARCHIE! DID I STARTLE YOU?
NO, EVERYBODY SAYS "HELLO" BY SCREAMING! JEEZ, AMBROSE!
SORRY, MAN!
22

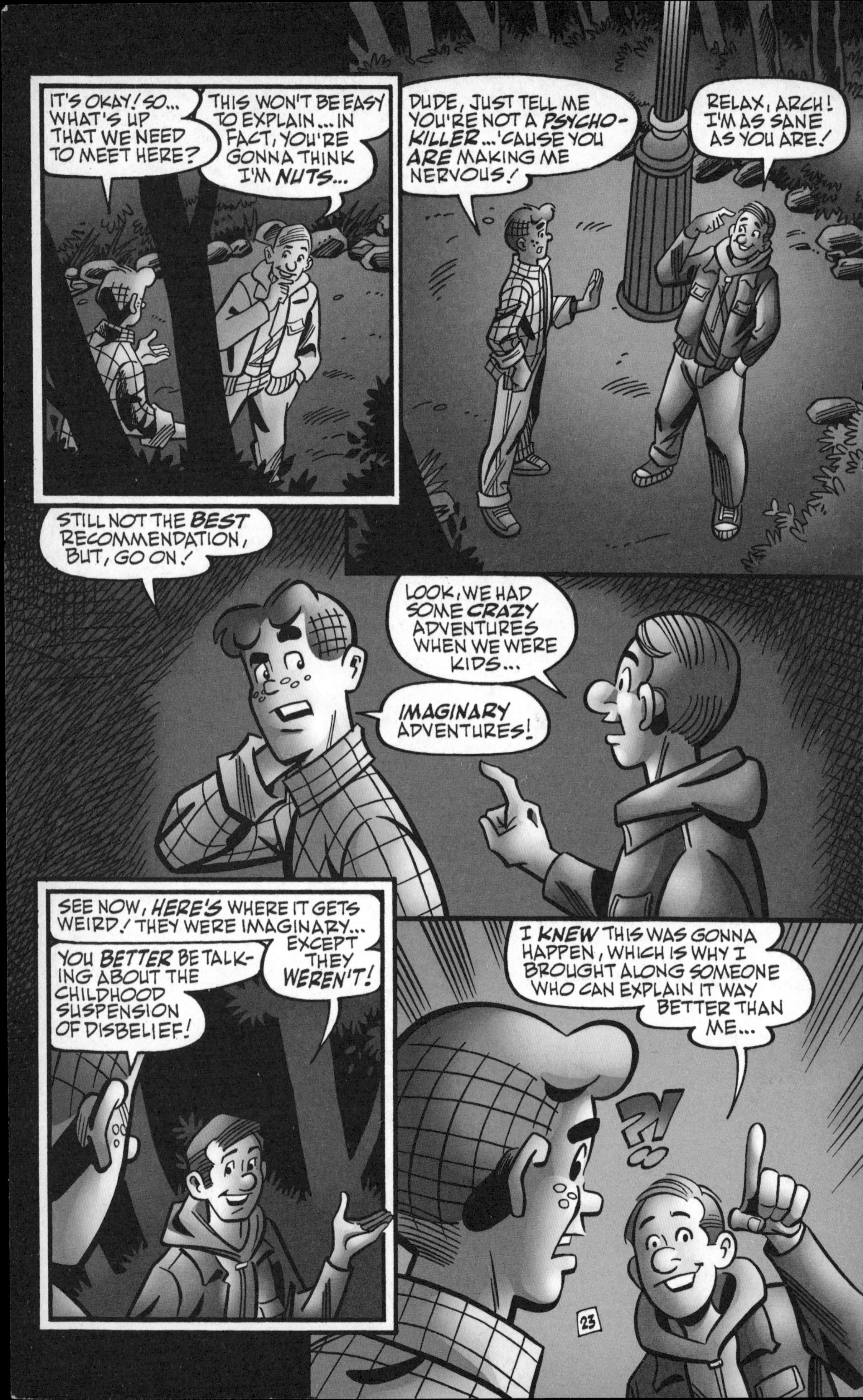
IT'S OKAY! SO... WHAT'S UP THAT WE NEED TO MEET HERE?
THIS WON'T BE EASY TO EXPLAIN... IN FACT, YOU'RE GONNA THINK I'M NUTS...
DUDE, JUST TELL ME YOU'RE NOT A PSYCHO-KILLER... 'CAUSE YOU ARE MAKING ME NERVOUS!
RELAX, ARCH! I'M AS SANE AS YOU ARE!
STILL NOT THE BEST RECOMMENDATION, BUT, GO ON!
LOOK, WE HAD SOME CRAZY ADVENTURES WHEN WE WERE KIDS...
IMAGINARY ADVENTURES!
SEE NOW, HERE'S WHERE IT GETS WEIRD! THEY WERE IMAGINARY... EXCEPT THEY WEREN'T!
YOU BETTER BE TALKING ABOUT THE CHILDHOOD SUSPENSION OF DISBELIEF!
I KNEW THIS WAS GONNA HAPPEN, WHICH IS WHY I BROUGHT ALONG SOMEONE WHO CAN EXPLAIN IT WAY BETTER THAN ME...
?!

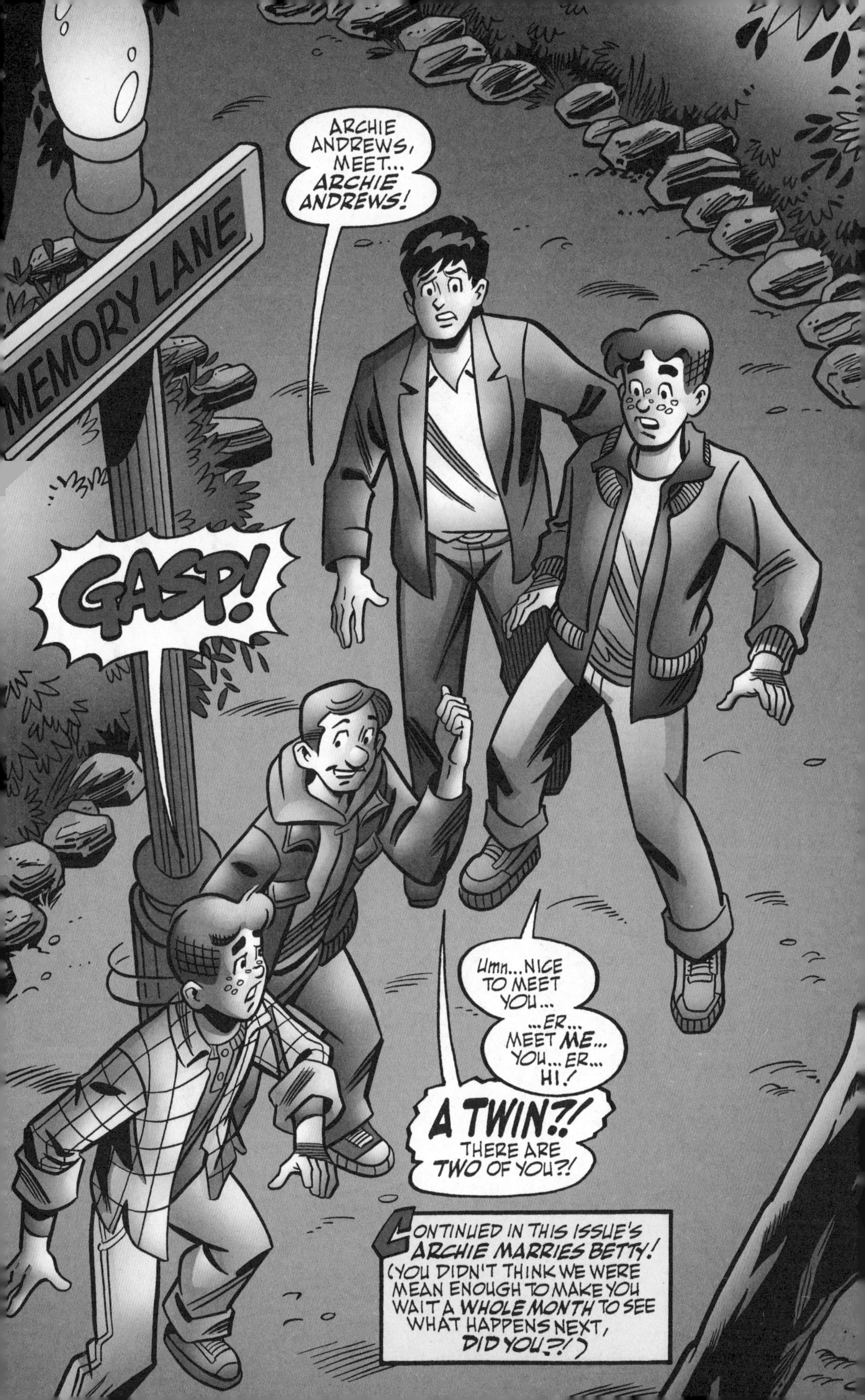
MEMORY LANE
ARCHIE ANDREWS, MEET... ARCHIE ANDREWS!
GASP!
UMN... NICE TO MEET YOU...
...ER... MEET ME... YOU... ER... HI!
A TWIN?! THERE ARE TWO OF YOU?!
CONTINUED IN THIS ISSUE'S ARCHIE MARRIES BETTY! (YOU DIDN'T THINK WE WERE MEAN ENOUGH TO MAKE YOU WAIT A WHOLE MONTH TO SEE WHAT HAPPENS NEXT, DID YOU?!)

"YOU WANT ME TO ANSWER *YOUR* QUESTIONS..."

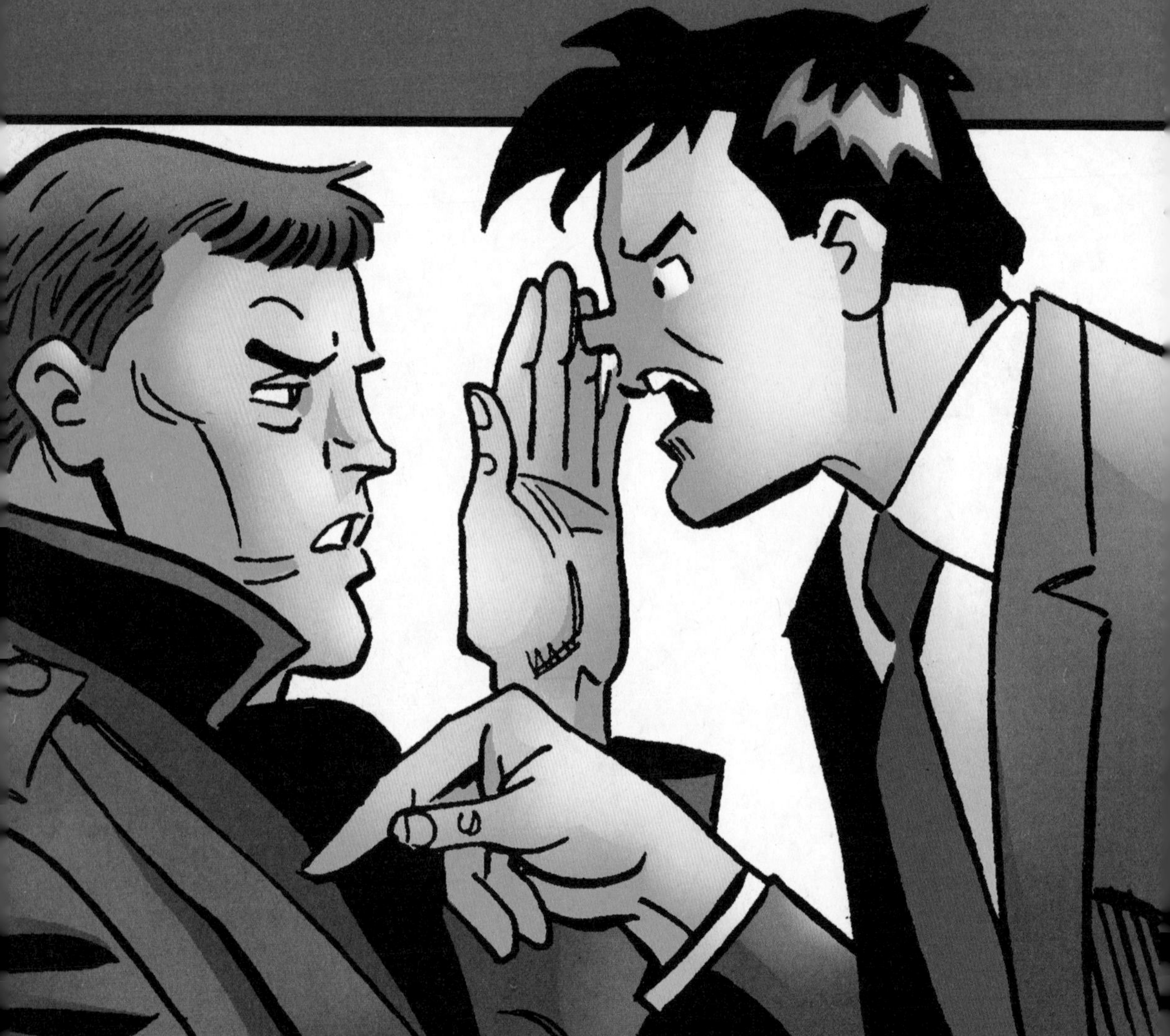

"HOW ABOUT ANSWERING *ONE* OF *MINE?*"

- REGGIE MANTLE

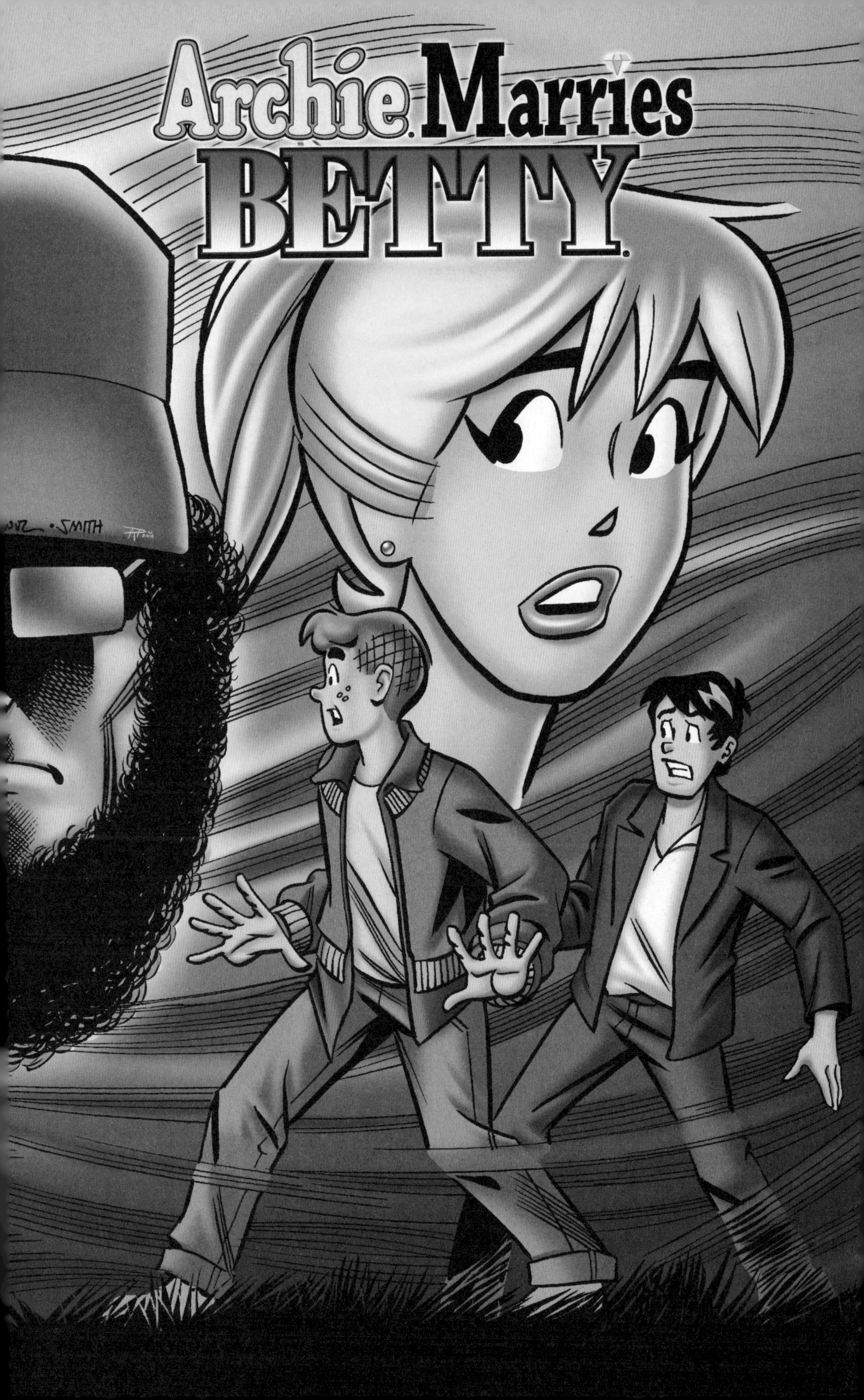
Archie Marries
BETTY
SMITH

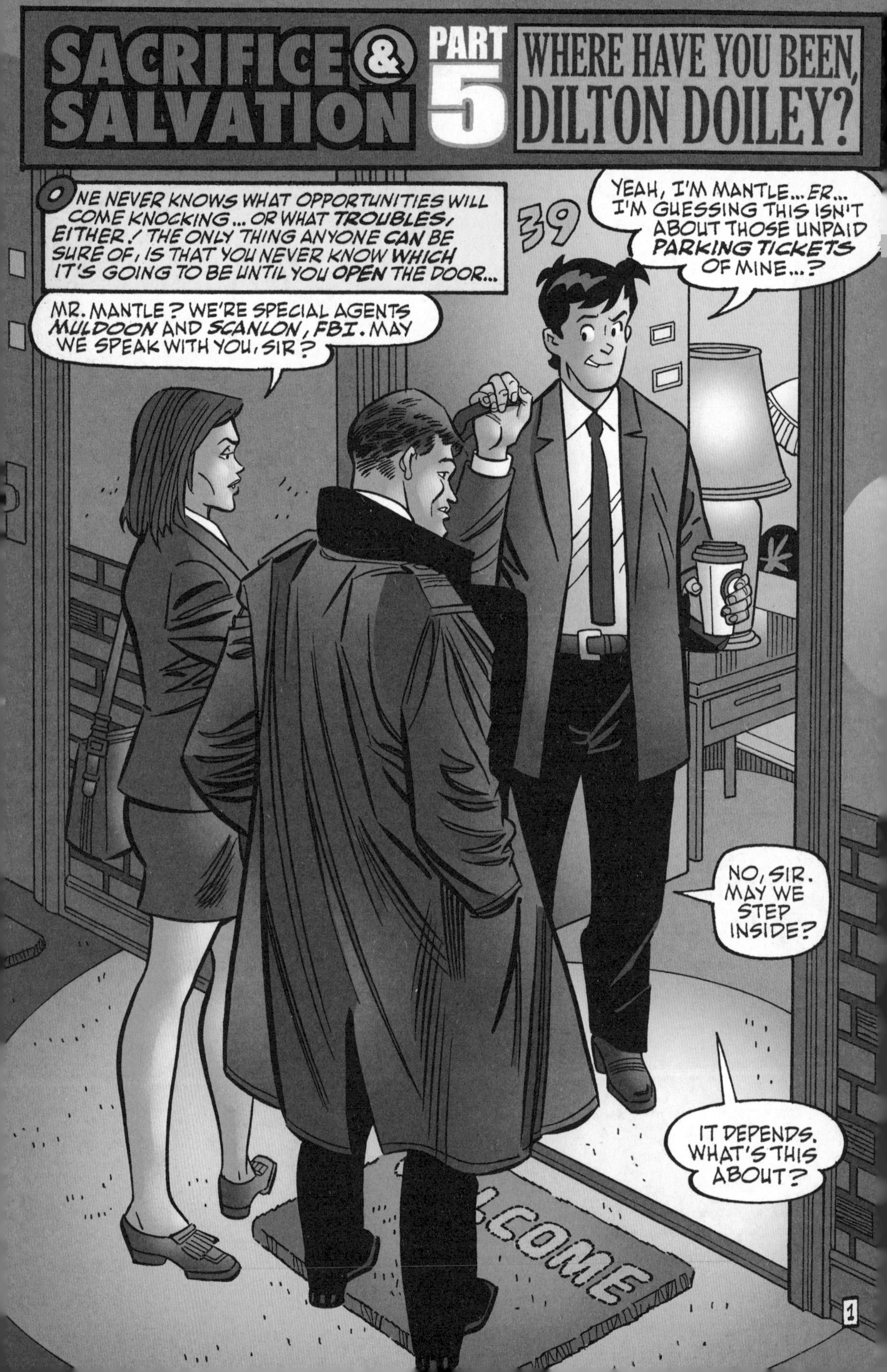
SACRIFICE & SALVATION
PART 5
WHERE HAVE YOU BEEN, DILTON DOILEY?
ONE NEVER KNOWS WHAT OPPORTUNITIES WILL COME KNOCKING... OR WHAT TROUBLES, EITHER! THE ONLY THING ANYONE CAN BE SURE OF, IS THAT YOU NEVER KNOW WHICH IT'S GOING TO BE UNTIL YOU OPEN THE DOOR...
39
MR. MANTLE? WE'RE SPECIAL AGENTS MULDOON AND SCANLON, FBI. MAY WE SPEAK WITH YOU, SIR?
YEAH, I'M MANTLE... ER... I'M GUESSING THIS ISN'T ABOUT THOSE UNPAID PARKING TICKETS OF MINE...?
NO, SIR. MAY WE STEP INSIDE?
IT DEPENDS. WHAT'S THIS ABOUT?
1

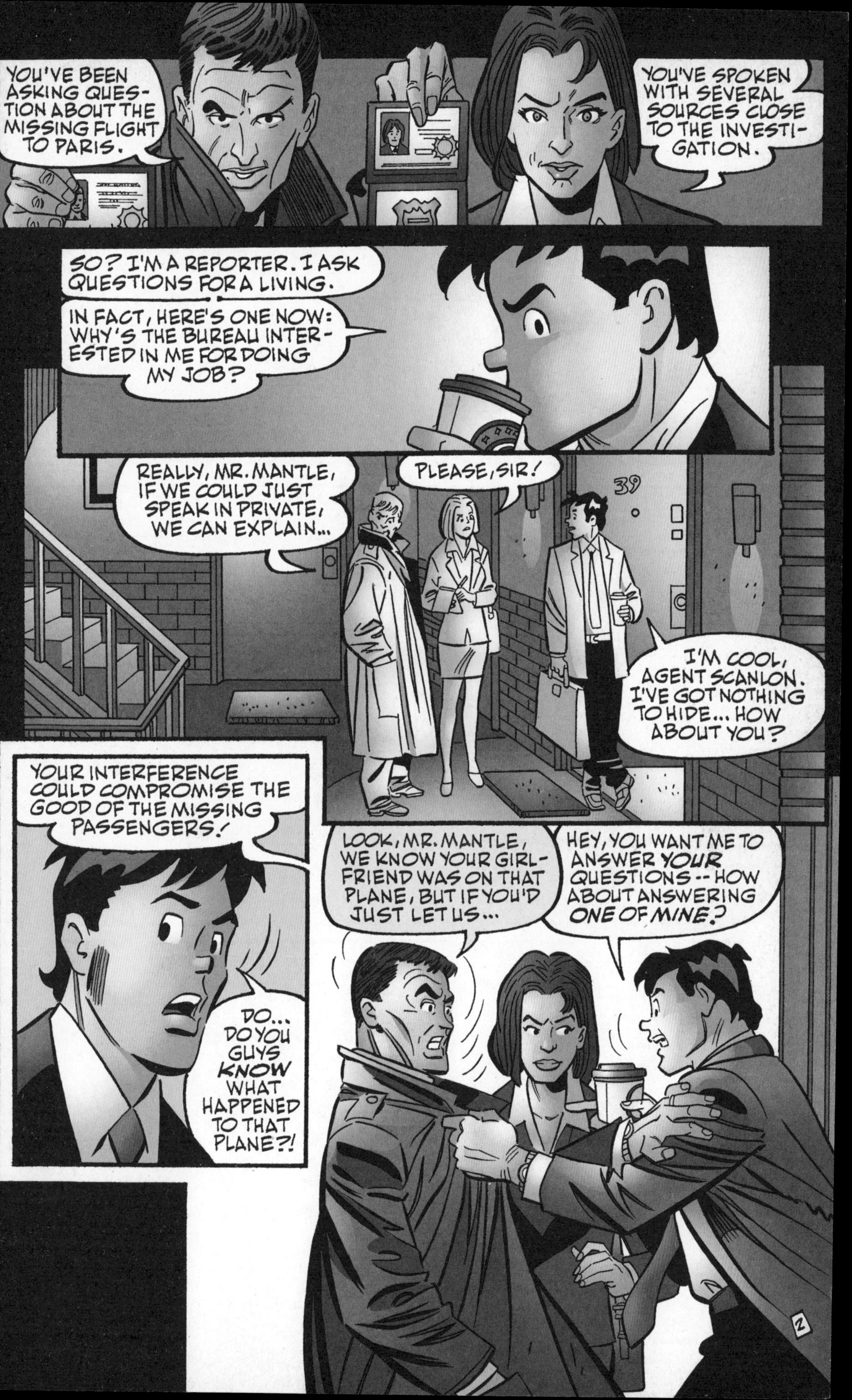
YOU'VE BEEN ASKING QUESTION ABOUT THE MISSING FLIGHT TO PARIS.
YOU'VE SPOKEN WITH SEVERAL SOURCES CLOSE TO THE INVESTIGATION.
SO? I'M A REPORTER. I ASK QUESTIONS FOR A LIVING.
IN FACT, HERE'S ONE NOW: WHY'S THE BUREAU INTERESTED IN ME FOR DOING MY JOB?
REALLY, MR. MANTLE, IF WE COULD JUST SPEAK IN PRIVATE, WE CAN EXPLAIN...
PLEASE, SIR!
39
I'M COOL, AGENT SCANLON. I'VE GOT NOTHING TO HIDE... HOW ABOUT YOU?
YOUR INTERFERENCE COULD COMPROMISE THE GOOD OF THE MISSING PASSENGERS!
DO... DO YOU GUYS KNOW WHAT HAPPENED TO THAT PLANE?!
LOOK, MR. MANTLE, WE KNOW YOUR GIRLFRIEND WAS ON THAT PLANE, BUT IF YOU'D JUST LET US...
HEY, YOU WANT ME TO ANSWER YOUR QUESTIONS -- HOW ABOUT ANSWERING ONE OF MINE?
2

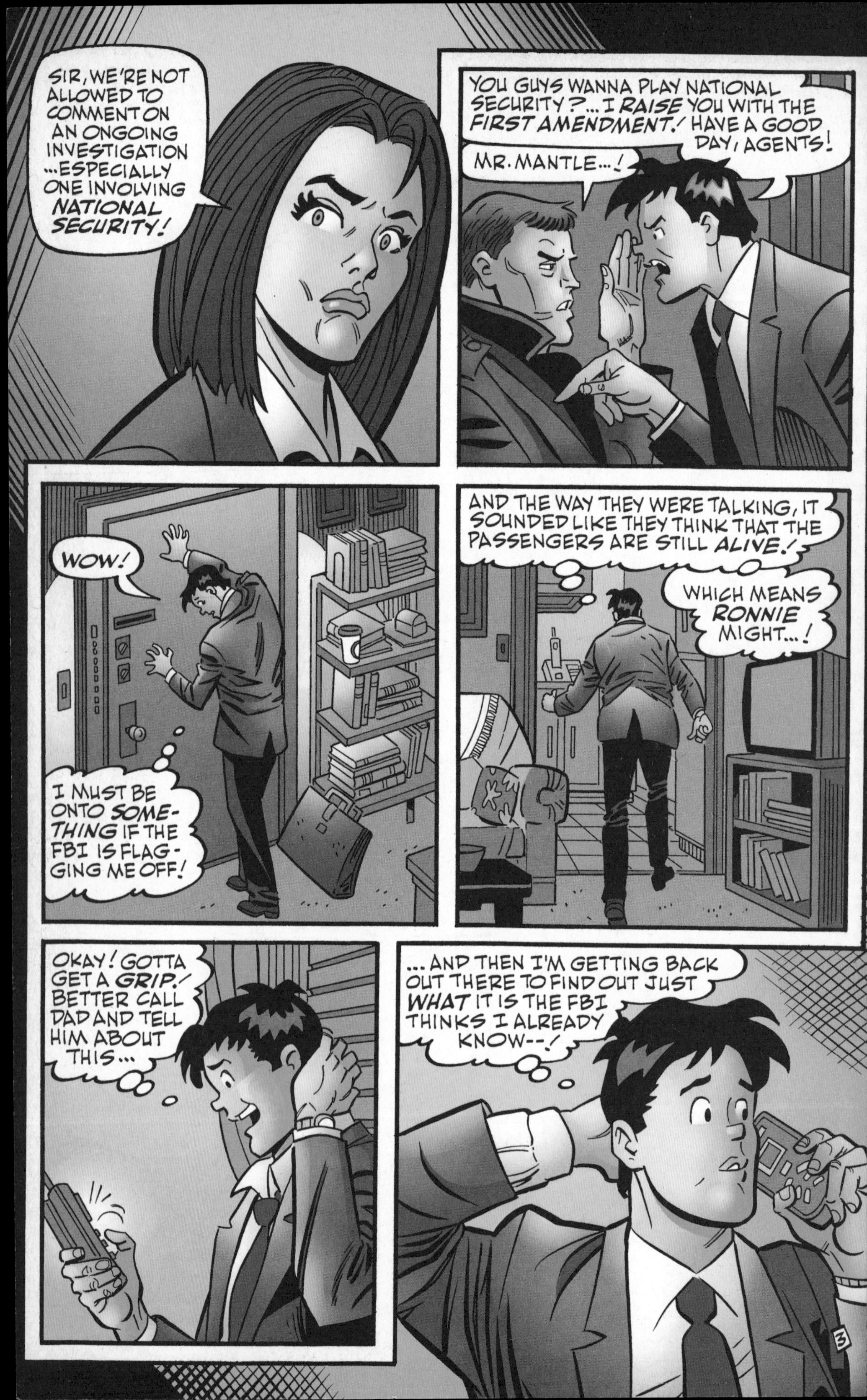
SIR, WE'RE NOT ALLOWED TO COMMENT ON AN ONGOING INVESTIGATION ...ESPECIALLY ONE INVOLVING NATIONAL SECURITY!
YOU GUYS WANNA PLAY NATIONAL SECURITY?... I RAISE YOU WITH THE FIRST AMENDMENT! HAVE A GOOD DAY, AGENTS!
MR. MANTLE...!
WOW!
I MUST BE ONTO SOMETHING IF THE FBI IS FLAGGING ME OFF!
AND THE WAY THEY WERE TALKING, IT SOUNDED LIKE THEY THINK THAT THE PASSENGERS ARE STILL ALIVE!
WHICH MEANS RONNIE MIGHT...!
OKAY! GOTTA GET A GRIP! BETTER CALL DAD AND TELL HIM ABOUT THIS...
...AND THEN I'M GETTING BACK OUT THERE TO FIND OUT JUST WHAT IT IS THE FBI THINKS I ALREADY KNOW--!
3

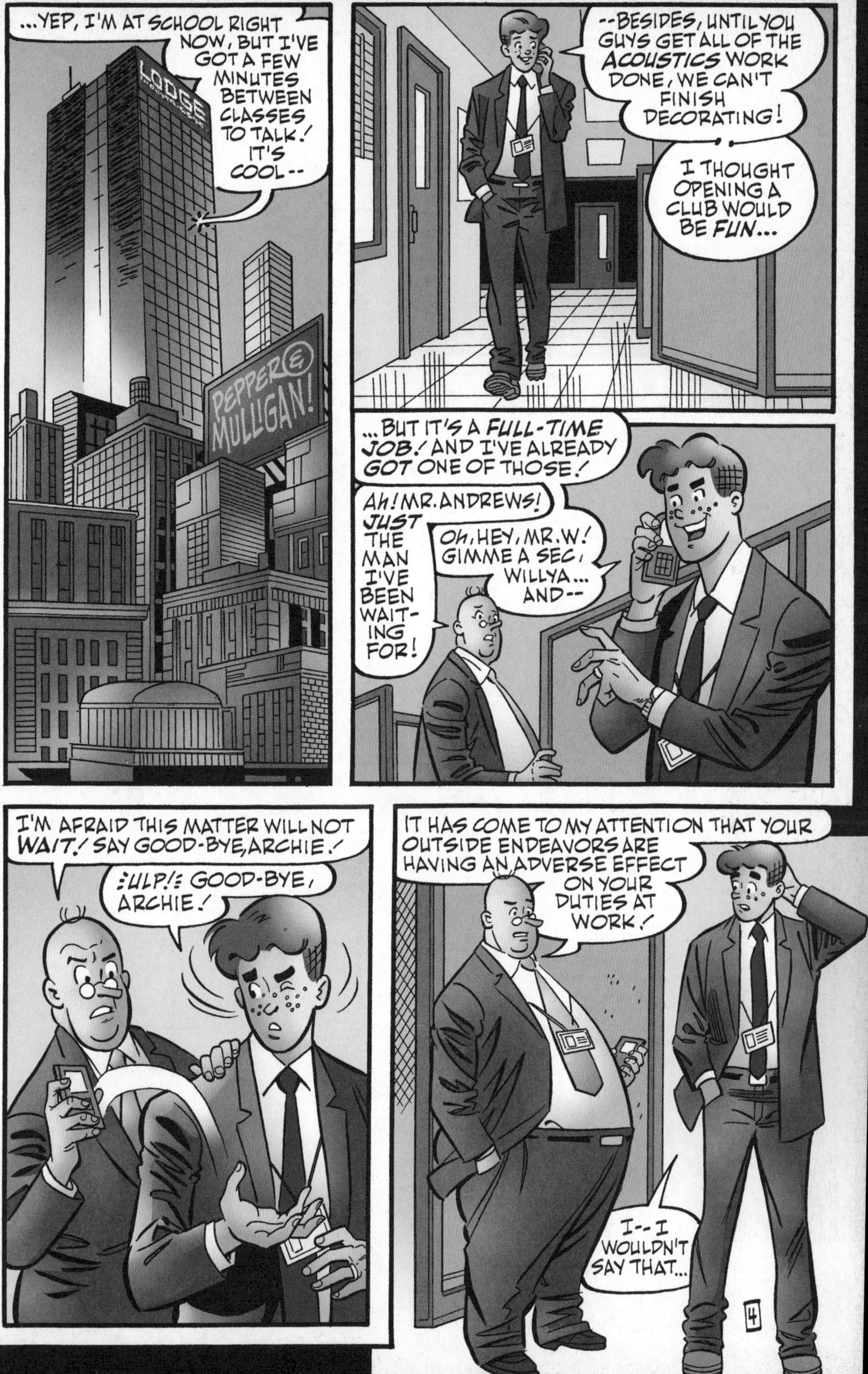
...YEP, I'M AT SCHOOL RIGHT NOW, BUT I'VE GOT A FEW MINUTES BETWEEN CLASSES TO TALK! IT'S COOL--
LODGE
PEPPER & MULLIGAN!
--BESIDES, UNTIL YOU GUYS GET ALL OF THE ACOUSTICS WORK DONE, WE CAN'T FINISH DECORATING!
I THOUGHT OPENING A CLUB WOULD BE FUN...
...BUT IT'S A FULL-TIME JOB! AND I'VE ALREADY GOT ONE OF THOSE!
Ah! MR. ANDREWS! JUST THE MAN I'VE BEEN WAIT-ING FOR!
Oh, HEY, MR. W! GIMME A SEC, WILLYA... AND--
I'M AFRAID THIS MATTER WILL NOT WAIT! SAY GOOD-BYE, ARCHIE!
:ULP!: GOOD-BYE, ARCHIE!
IT HAS COME TO MY ATTENTION THAT YOUR OUTSIDE ENDEAVORS ARE HAVING AN ADVERSE EFFECT ON YOUR DUTIES AT WORK!
I-- I WOULDN'T SAY THAT...
4

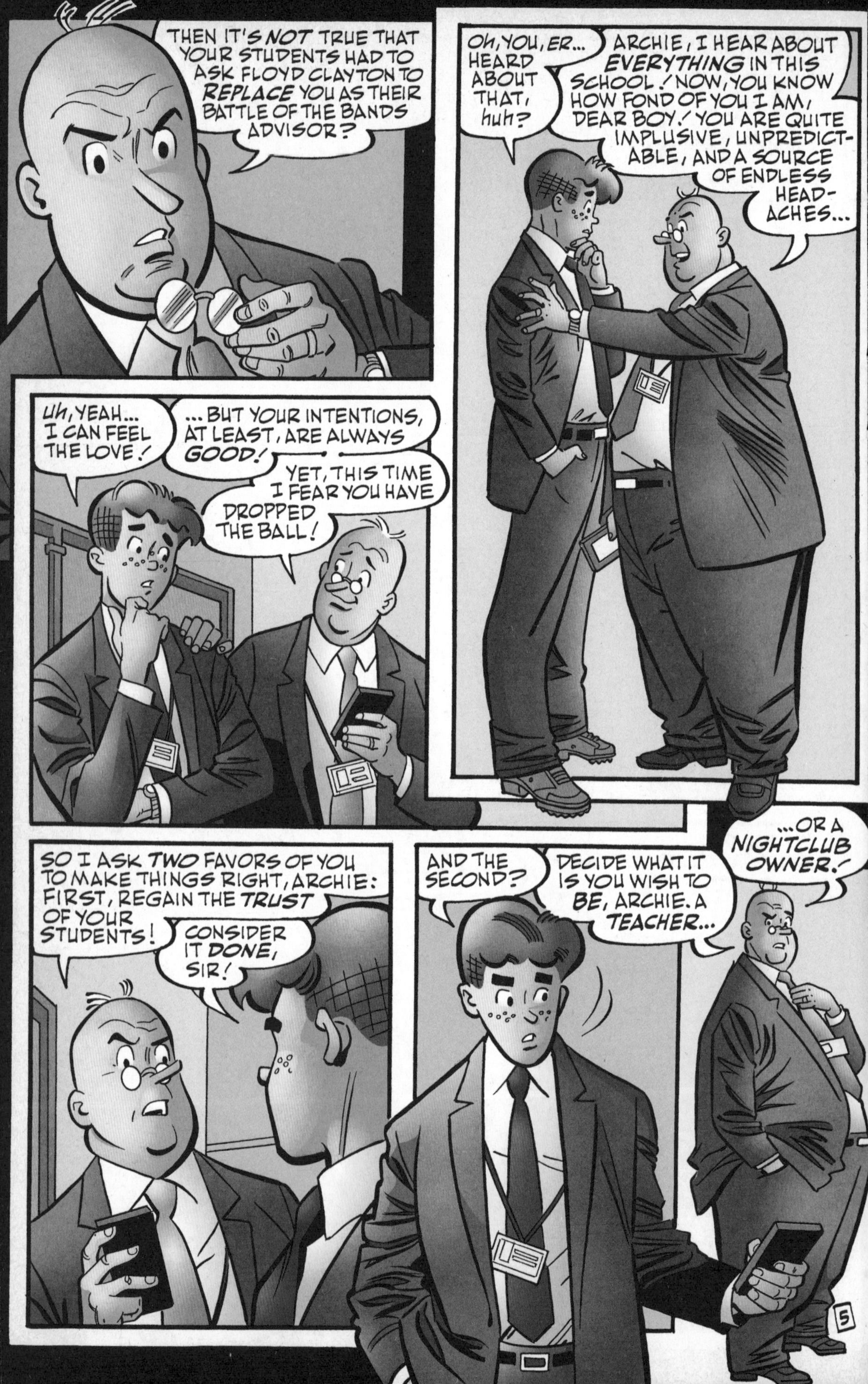
THEN IT'S NOT TRUE THAT YOUR STUDENTS HAD TO ASK FLOYD CLAYTON TO REPLACE YOU AS THEIR BATTLE OF THE BANDS ADVISOR?
Oh, YOU, ER... HEARD ABOUT THAT, huh?
ARCHIE, I HEAR ABOUT EVERYTHING IN THIS SCHOOL! NOW, YOU KNOW HOW FOND OF YOU I AM, DEAR BOY! YOU ARE QUITE IMPLUSIVE, UNPREDICTABLE, AND A SOURCE OF ENDLESS HEADACHES...
Uh, YEAH... I CAN FEEL THE LOVE!
...BUT YOUR INTENTIONS, AT LEAST, ARE ALWAYS GOOD!
YET, THIS TIME I FEAR YOU HAVE DROPPED THE BALL!
SO I ASK TWO FAVORS OF YOU TO MAKE THINGS RIGHT, ARCHIE: FIRST, REGAIN THE TRUST OF YOUR STUDENTS!
CONSIDER IT DONE, SIR!
AND THE SECOND?
DECIDE WHAT IT IS YOU WISH TO BE, ARCHIE. A TEACHER...
...OR A NIGHTCLUB OWNER!

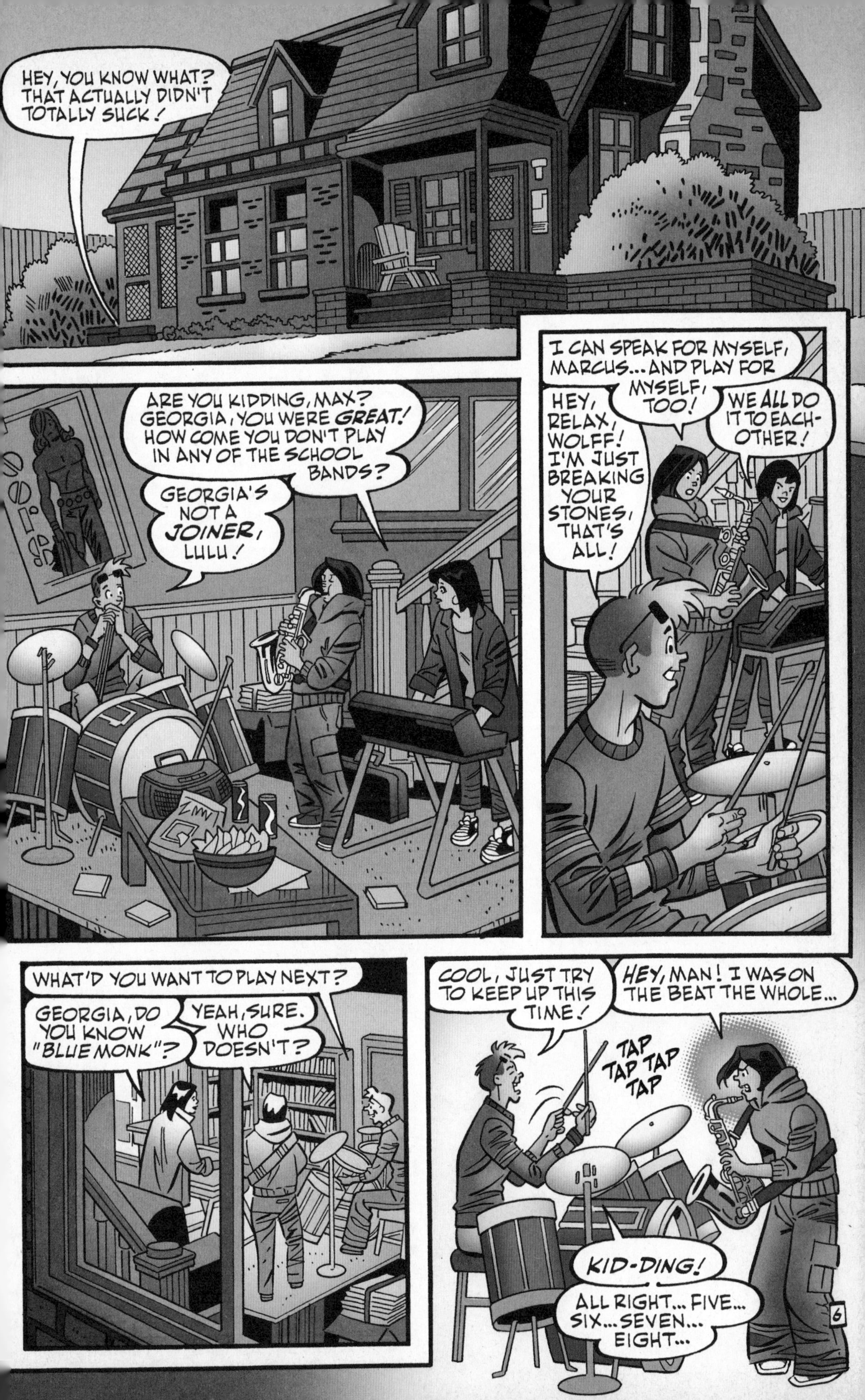
HEY, YOU KNOW WHAT? THAT ACTUALLY DIDN'T TOTALLY SUCK!
ARE YOU KIDDING, MAX? GEORGIA, YOU WERE GREAT! HOW COME YOU DON'T PLAY IN ANY OF THE SCHOOL BANDS?
GEORGIA'S NOT A JOINER, LULU!
I CAN SPEAK FOR MYSELF, MARCUS... AND PLAY FOR MYSELF, TOO!
HEY, RELAX, WOLFF! I'M JUST BREAKING YOUR STONES, THAT'S ALL!
WE ALL DO IT TO EACH-OTHER!
WHAT'D YOU WANT TO PLAY NEXT?
GEORGIA, DO YOU KNOW "BLUE MONK"?
YEAH, SURE. WHO DOESN'T?
COOL, JUST TRY TO KEEP UP THIS TIME!
HEY, MAN! I WAS ON THE BEAT THE WHOLE...
TAP TAP TAP TAP
KID-DING!
ALL RIGHT... FIVE... SIX... SEVEN... EIGHT...
6

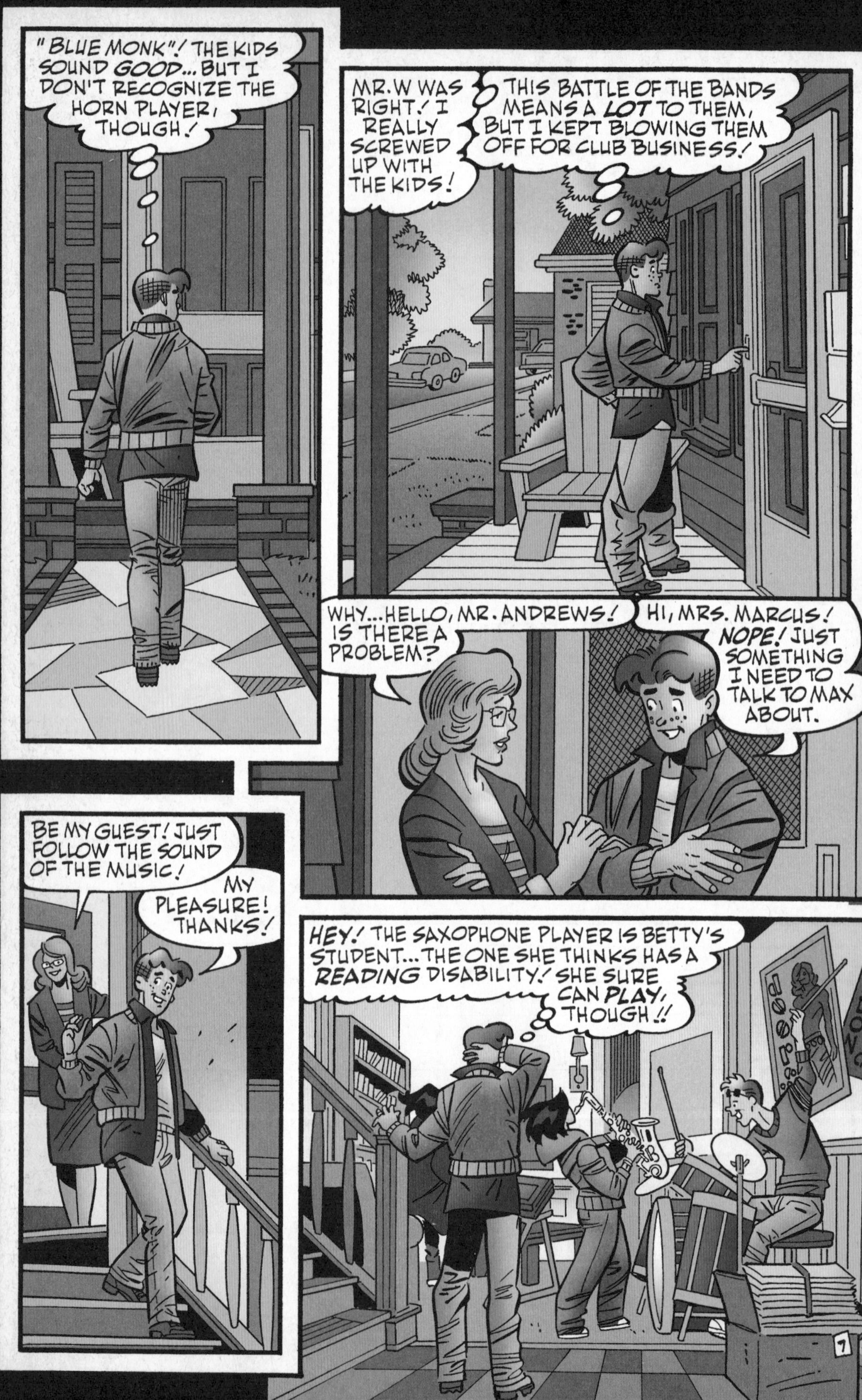
"BLUE MONK"! THE KIDS SOUND GOOD... BUT I DON'T RECOGNIZE THE HORN PLAYER, THOUGH!
MR. W WAS RIGHT! I REALLY SCREWED UP WITH THE KIDS!
THIS BATTLE OF THE BANDS MEANS A LOT TO THEM, BUT I KEPT BLOWING THEM OFF FOR CLUB BUSINESS!
WHY... HELLO, MR. ANDREWS! IS THERE A PROBLEM?
HI, MRS. MARCUS! NOPE! JUST SOMETHING I NEED TO TALK TO MAX ABOUT.
BE MY GUEST! JUST FOLLOW THE SOUND OF THE MUSIC!
MY PLEASURE! THANKS!
HEY! THE SAXOPHONE PLAYER IS BETTY'S STUDENT... THE ONE SHE THINKS HAS A READING DISABILITY! SHE SURE CAN PLAY, THOUGH!!

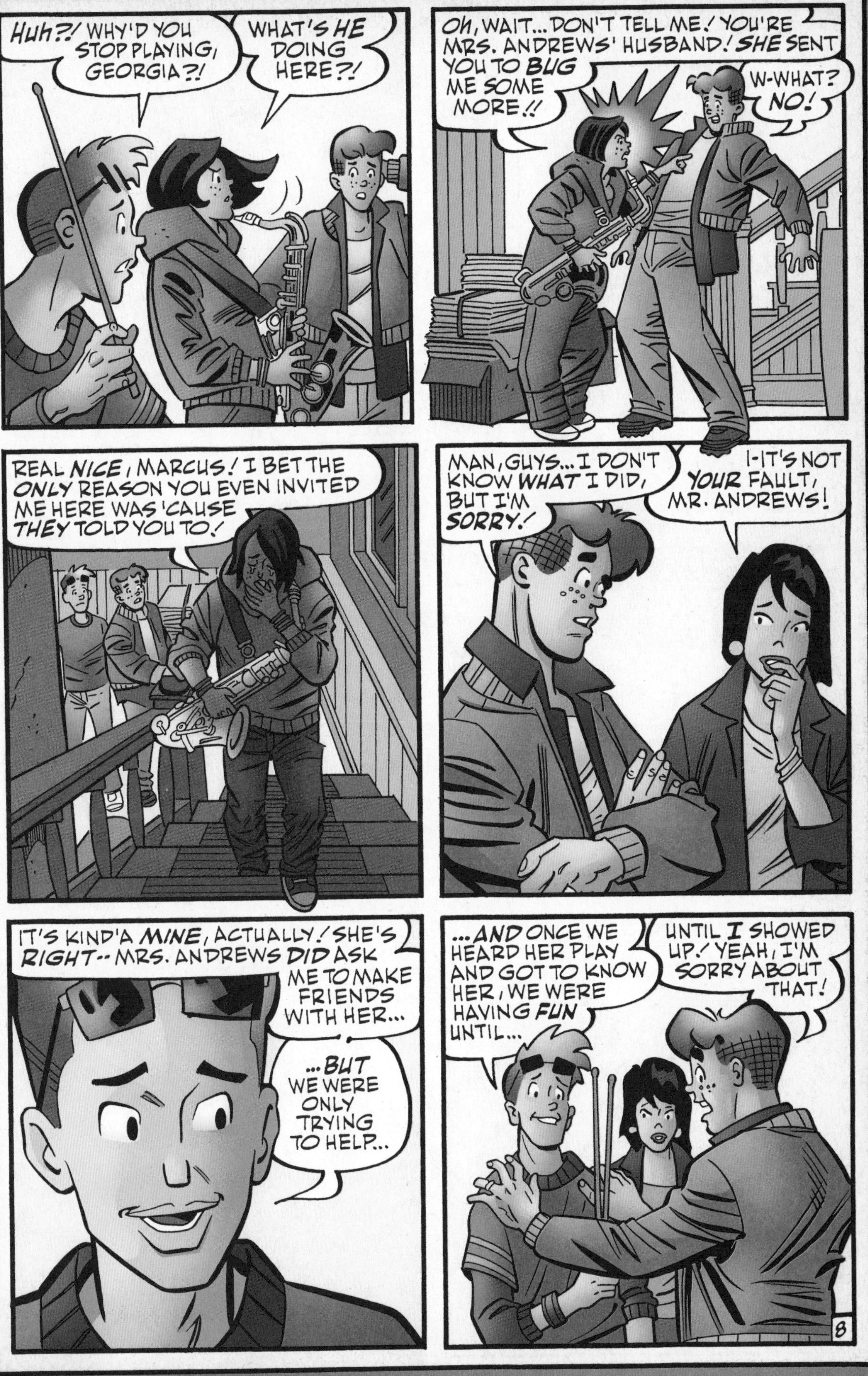

HUH?! WHY'D YOU STOP PLAYING, GEORGIA?!
WHAT'S HE DOING HERE?!
OH, WAIT... DON'T TELL ME! YOU'RE MRS. ANDREWS' HUSBAND! SHE SENT YOU TO BUG ME SOME MORE!!
W-WHAT? NO!
REAL NICE, MARCUS! I BET THE ONLY REASON YOU EVEN INVITED ME HERE WAS 'CAUSE THEY TOLD YOU TO!
MAN, GUYS... I DON'T KNOW WHAT I DID, BUT I'M SORRY!
I-IT'S NOT YOUR FAULT, MR. ANDREWS!
IT'S KIND'A MINE, ACTUALLY! SHE'S RIGHT-- MRS. ANDREWS DID ASK ME TO MAKE FRIENDS WITH HER...
...BUT WE WERE ONLY TRYING TO HELP...
...AND ONCE WE HEARD HER PLAY AND GOT TO KNOW HER, WE WERE HAVING FUN UNTIL...
UNTIL I SHOWED UP! YEAH, I'M SORRY ABOUT THAT!
8

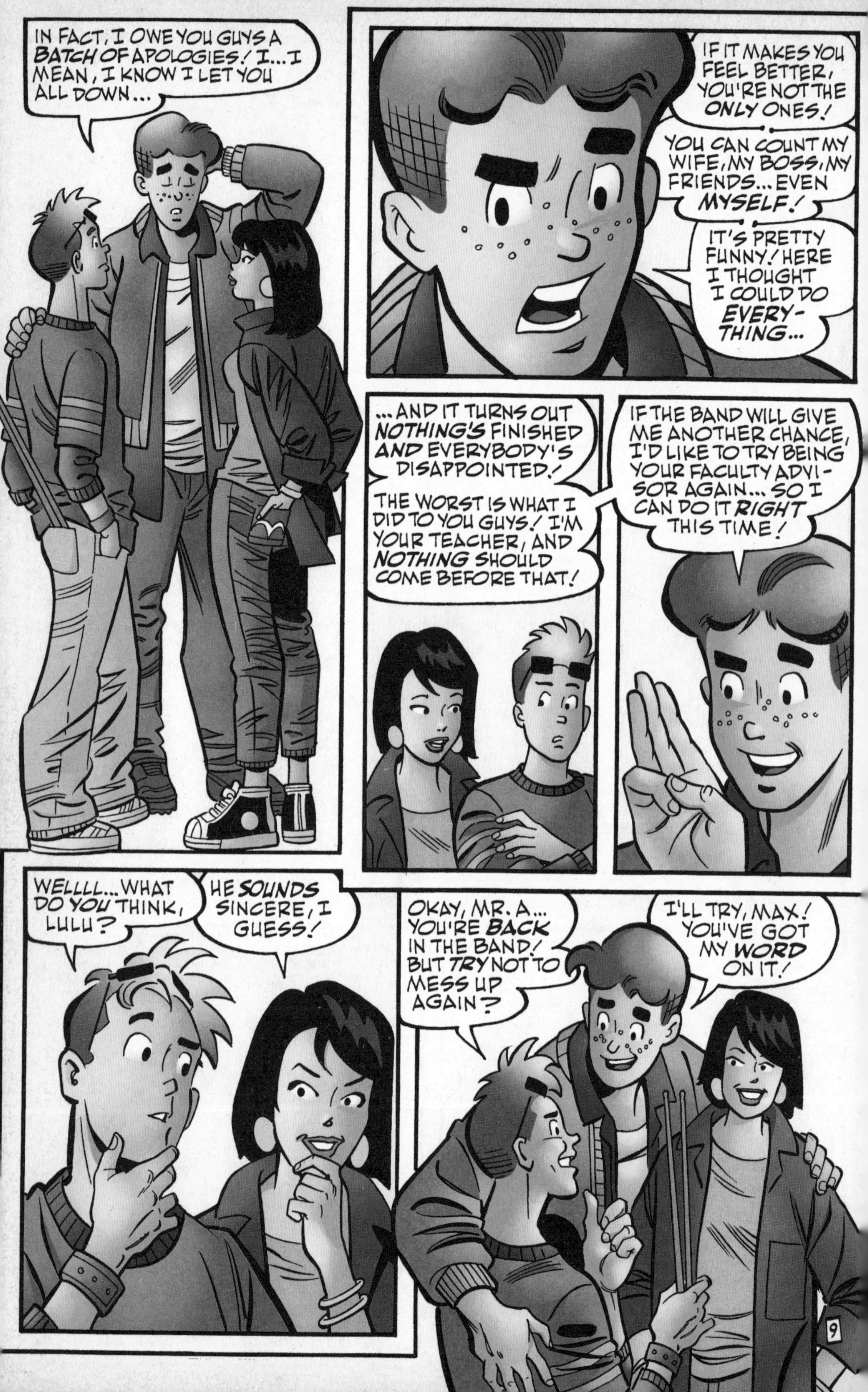
IN FACT, I OWE YOU GUYS A BATCH OF APOLOGIES! I... I MEAN, I KNOW I LET YOU ALL DOWN...
IF IT MAKES YOU FEEL BETTER, YOU'RE NOT THE ONLY ONES!
YOU CAN COUNT MY WIFE, MY BOSS, MY FRIENDS... EVEN MYSELF!
IT'S PRETTY FUNNY! HERE I THOUGHT I COULD DO EVERY-THING...
...AND IT TURNS OUT NOTHING'S FINISHED AND EVERYBODY'S DISAPPOINTED!
THE WORST IS WHAT I DID TO YOU GUYS! I'M YOUR TEACHER, AND NOTHING SHOULD COME BEFORE THAT!
IF THE BAND WILL GIVE ME ANOTHER CHANCE, I'D LIKE TO TRY BEING YOUR FACULTY ADVI-SOR AGAIN... SO I CAN DO IT RIGHT THIS TIME!
WELLLL... WHAT DO YOU THINK, LULU?
HE SOUNDS SINCERE, I GUESS!
OKAY, MR. A... YOU'RE BACK IN THE BAND! BUT TRY NOT TO MESS UP AGAIN?
I'LL TRY, MAX! YOU'VE GOT MY WORD ON IT!

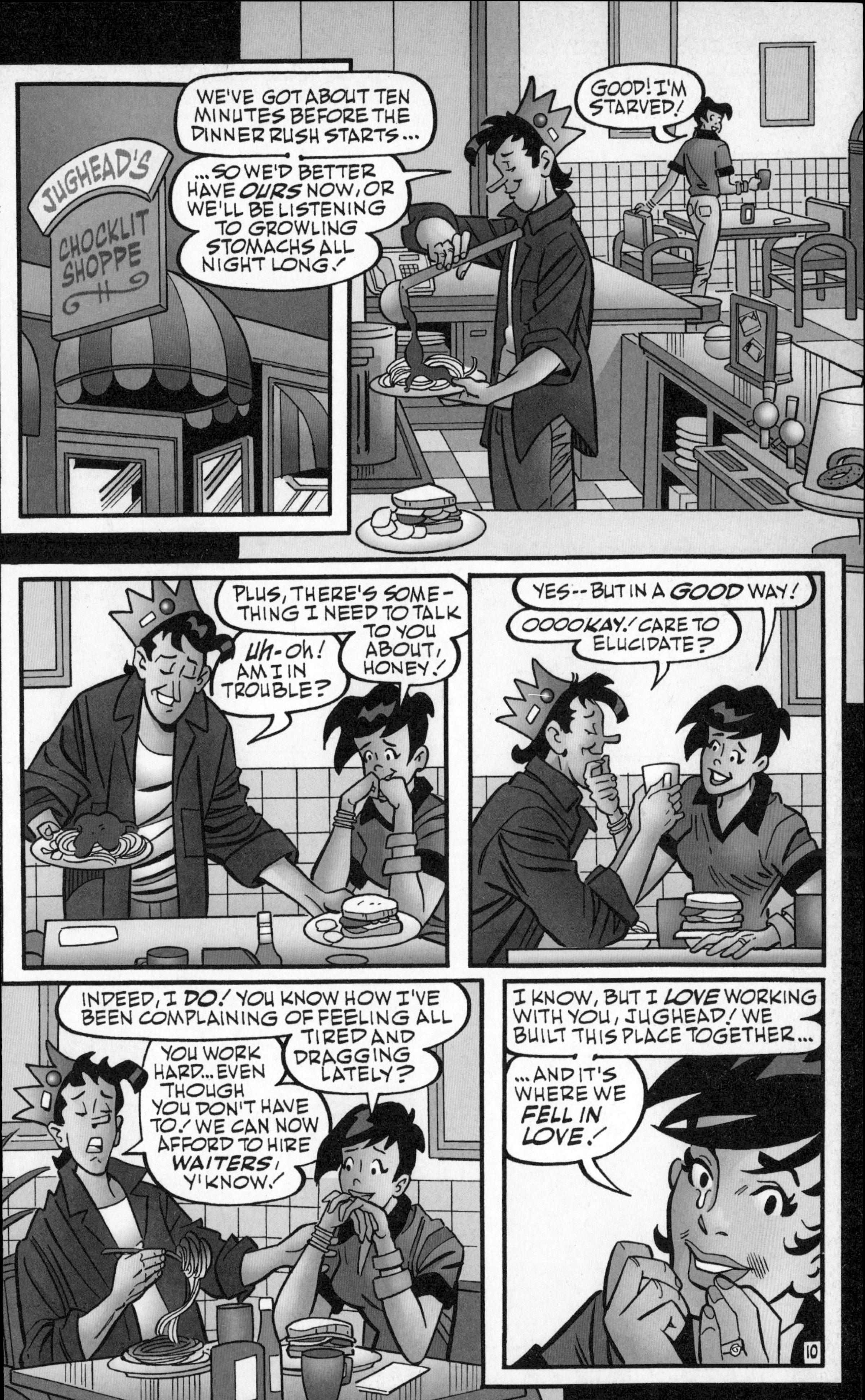
JUGHEAD'S CHOCKLIT SHOPPE
WE'VE GOT ABOUT TEN MINUTES BEFORE THE DINNER RUSH STARTS...
...SO WE'D BETTER HAVE OURS NOW, OR WE'LL BE LISTENING TO GROWLING STOMACHS ALL NIGHT LONG!
GOOD! I'M STARVED!
PLUS, THERE'S SOMETHING I NEED TO TALK TO YOU ABOUT, HONEY!
UH-OH! AM I IN TROUBLE?
YES--BUT IN A GOOD WAY!
OOOOKAY! CARE TO ELUCIDATE?
INDEED, I DO! YOU KNOW HOW I'VE BEEN COMPLAINING OF FEELING ALL TIRED AND DRAGGING LATELY?
YOU WORK HARD... EVEN THOUGH YOU DON'T HAVE TO! WE CAN NOW AFFORD TO HIRE WAITERS, Y'KNOW!
I KNOW, BUT I LOVE WORKING WITH YOU, JUGHEAD! WE BUILT THIS PLACE TOGETHER...
...AND IT'S WHERE WE FELL IN LOVE!

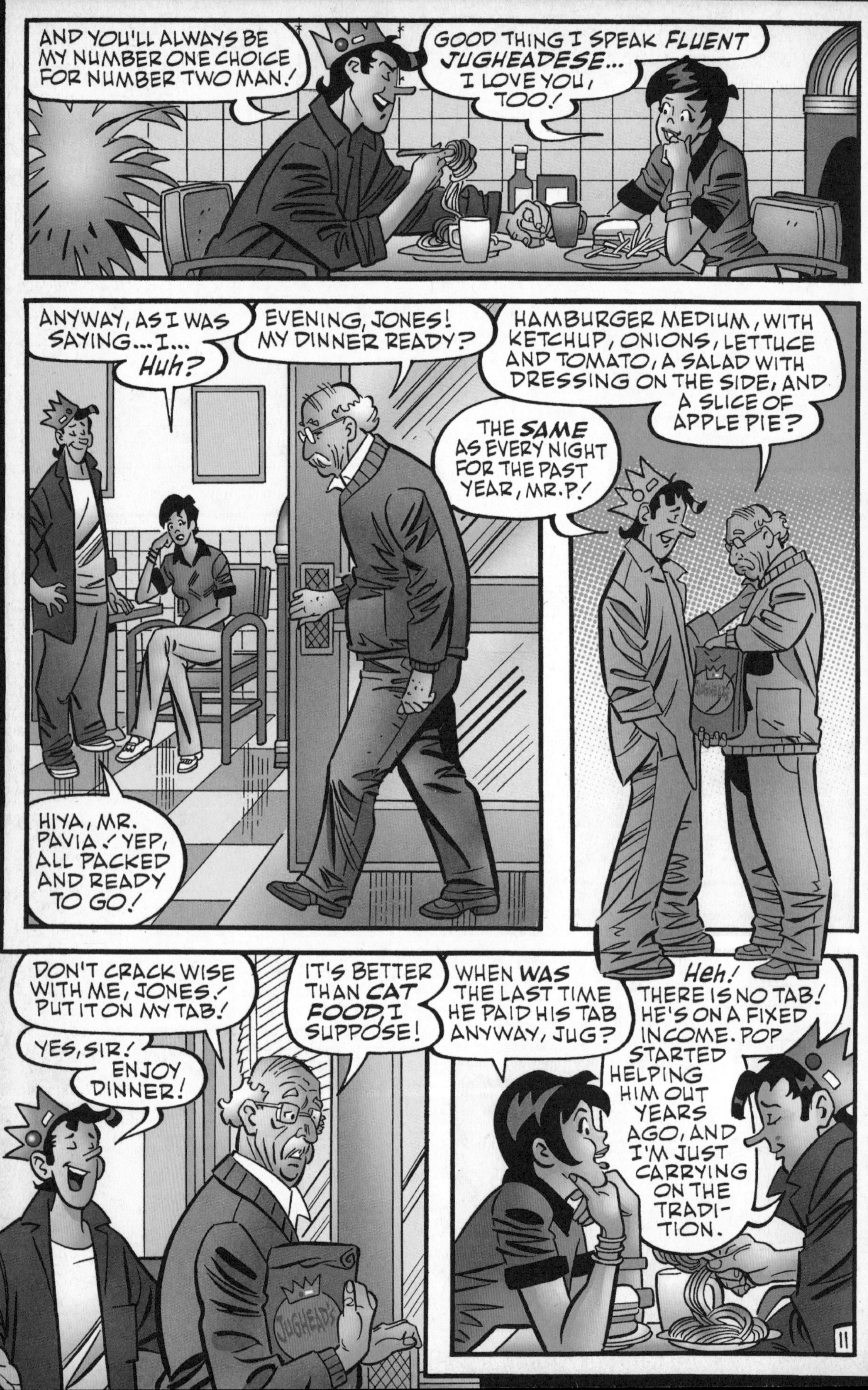

AND YOU'LL ALWAYS BE MY NUMBER ONE CHOICE FOR NUMBER TWO MAN!
GOOD THING I SPEAK FLUENT JUGHEADESE... I LOVE YOU, TOO!
ANYWAY, AS I WAS SAYING... I... Huh?
EVENING, JONES! MY DINNER READY?
HIYA, MR. PAVIA! YEP, ALL PACKED AND READY TO GO!
HAMBURGER MEDIUM, WITH KETCHUP, ONIONS, LETTUCE AND TOMATO, A SALAD WITH DRESSING ON THE SIDE, AND A SLICE OF APPLE PIE?
THE SAME AS EVERY NIGHT FOR THE PAST YEAR, MR. P!
DON'T CRACK WISE WITH ME, JONES! PUT IT ON MY TAB!
YES, SIR! ENJOY DINNER!
IT'S BETTER THAN CAT FOOD, I SUPPOSE!
JUGHEAD'S
WHEN WAS THE LAST TIME HE PAID HIS TAB ANYWAY, JUG?
Heh! THERE IS NO TAB! HE'S ON A FIXED INCOME. POP STARTED HELPING HIM OUT YEARS AGO, AND I'M JUST CARRYING ON THE TRADITION.

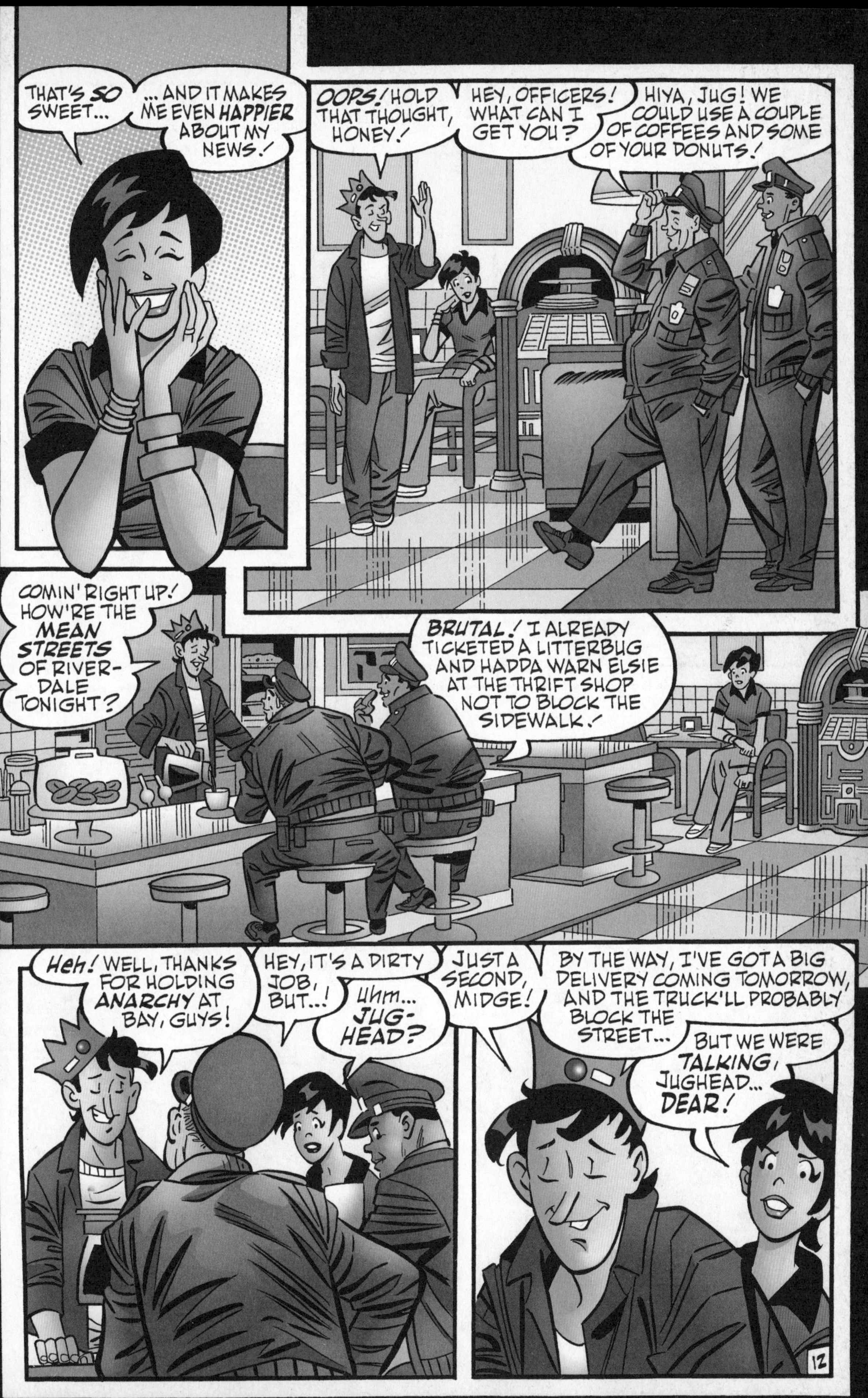
THAT'S SO SWEET...
...AND IT MAKES ME EVEN HAPPIER ABOUT MY NEWS!
OOPS! HOLD THAT THOUGHT, HONEY!
HEY, OFFICERS! WHAT CAN I GET YOU?
HIYA, JUG! WE COULD USE A COUPLE OF COFFEES AND SOME OF YOUR DONUTS!
COMIN' RIGHT UP! HOW'RE THE MEAN STREETS OF RIVER-DALE TONIGHT?
BRUTAL! I ALREADY TICKETED A LITTERBUG AND HADDA WARN ELSIE AT THE THRIFT SHOP NOT TO BLOCK THE SIDEWALK!
Heh! WELL, THANKS FOR HOLDING ANARCHY AT BAY, GUYS!
HEY, IT'S A DIRTY JOB, BUT...!
Uhm... JUG-HEAD?
JUST A SECOND, MIDGE!
BY THE WAY, I'VE GOT A BIG DELIVERY COMING TOMORROW, AND THE TRUCK'LL PROBABLY BLOCK THE STREET...
BUT WE WERE TALKING, JUGHEAD... DEAR!
12

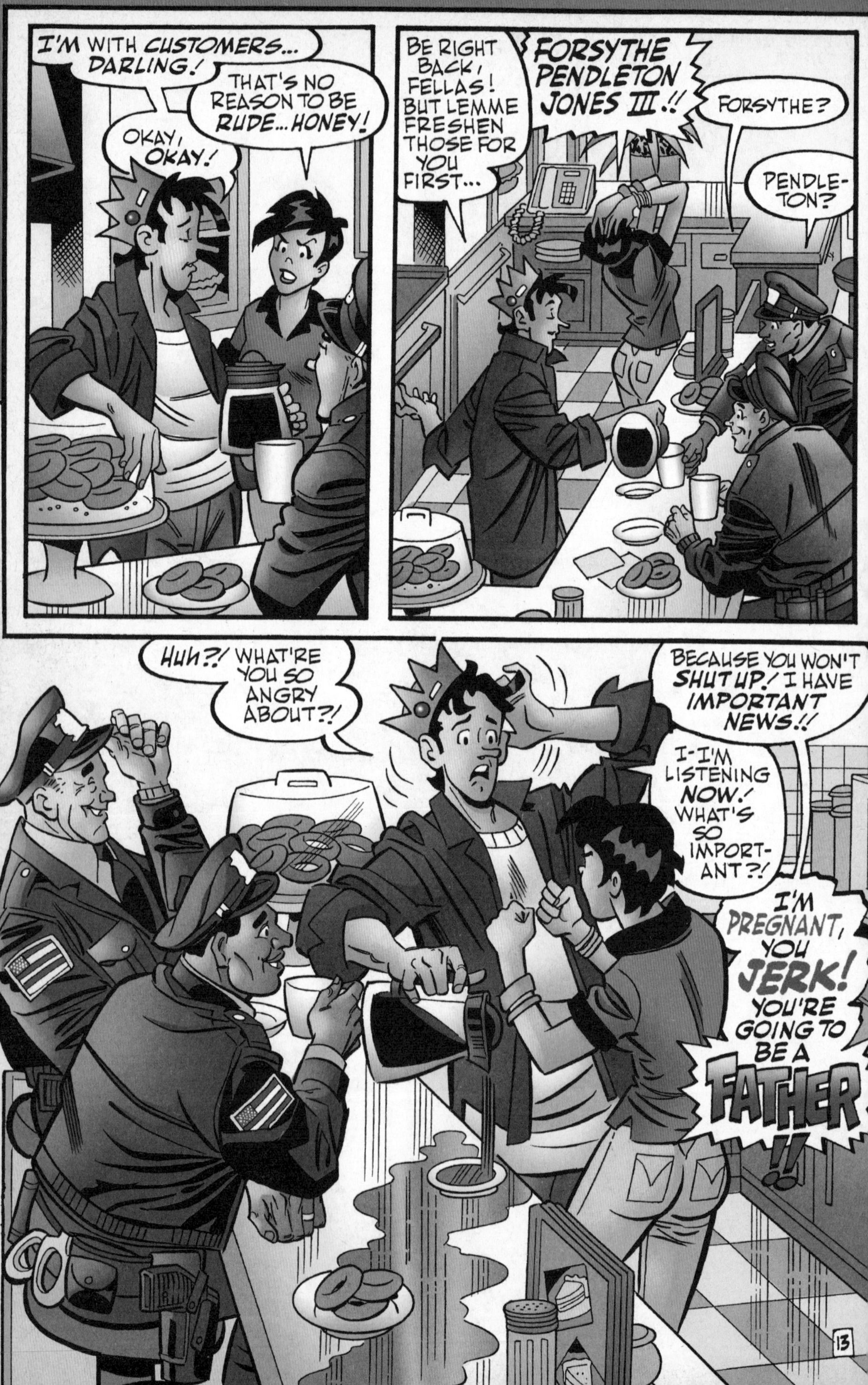
I'M WITH CUSTOMERS... DARLING!
THAT'S NO REASON TO BE RUDE... HONEY!
OKAY, OKAY!
BE RIGHT BACK, FELLAS! BUT LEMME FRESHEN THOSE FOR YOU FIRST...
FORSYTHE PENDLETON JONES III!!
FORSYTHE?
PENDLE-TON?
HUH?! WHAT'RE YOU SO ANGRY ABOUT?!
BECAUSE YOU WON'T SHUT UP! I HAVE IMPORTANT NEWS!!
I-I'M LISTENING NOW! WHAT'S SO IMPORT-ANT?!
I'M PREGNANT, YOU JERK! YOU'RE GOING TO BE A FATHER!!
13

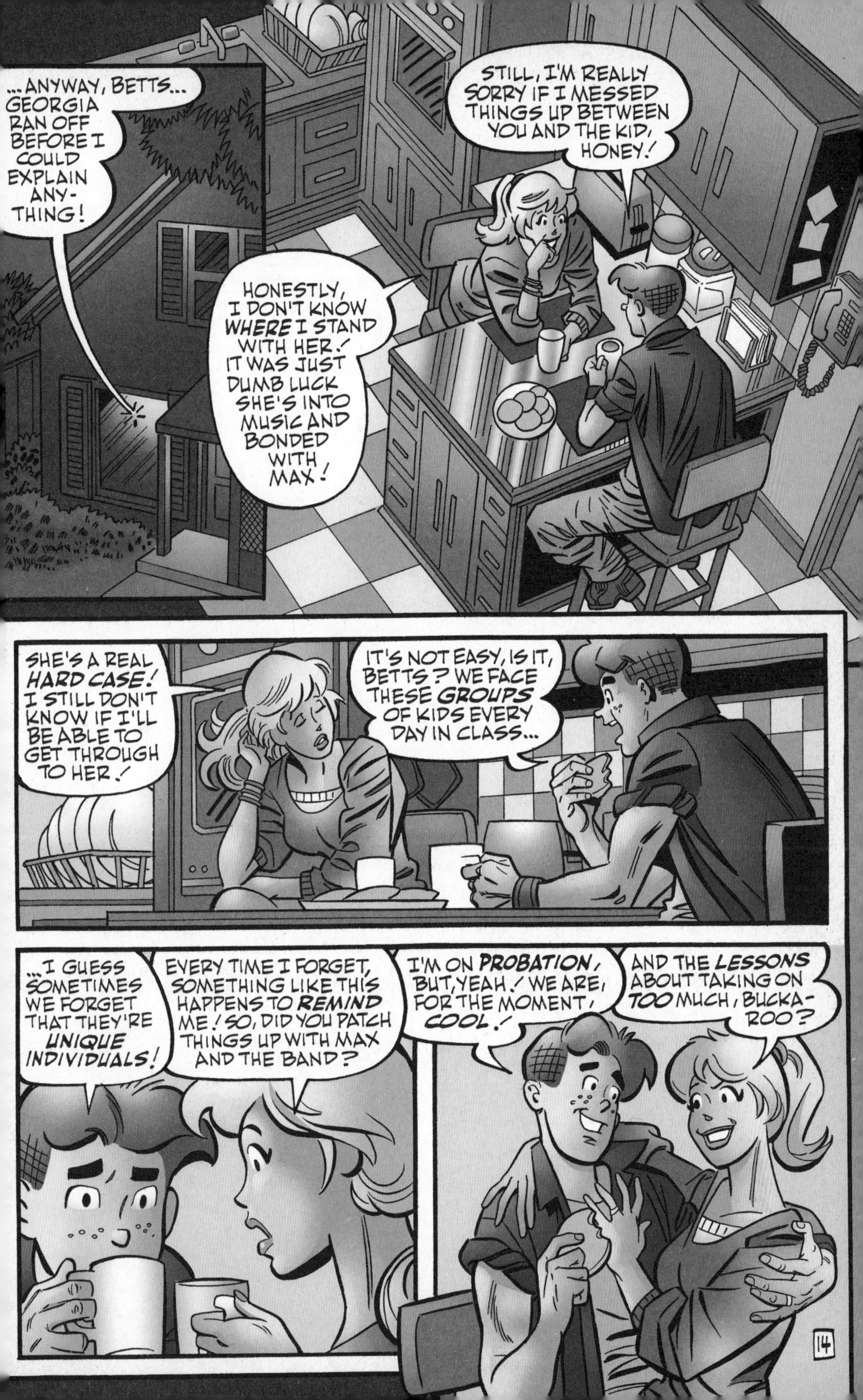
...ANYWAY, BETTS... GEORGIA RAN OFF BEFORE I COULD EXPLAIN ANY-THING!
STILL, I'M REALLY SORRY IF I MESSED THINGS UP BETWEEN YOU AND THE KID, HONEY!
HONESTLY, I DON'T KNOW WHERE I STAND WITH HER! IT WAS JUST DUMB LUCK SHE'S INTO MUSIC AND BONDED WITH MAX!
SHE'S A REAL HARD CASE! I STILL DON'T KNOW IF I'LL BE ABLE TO GET THROUGH TO HER!
IT'S NOT EASY, IS IT, BETTS? WE FACE THESE GROUPS OF KIDS EVERY DAY IN CLASS...
...I GUESS SOMETIMES WE FORGET THAT THEY'RE UNIQUE INDIVIDUALS!
EVERY TIME I FORGET, SOMETHING LIKE THIS HAPPENS TO REMIND ME! SO, DID YOU PATCH THINGS UP WITH MAX AND THE BAND?
I'M ON PROBATION, BUT, YEAH! WE ARE, FOR THE MOMENT, COOL!
AND THE LESSONS ABOUT TAKING ON TOO MUCH, BUCKA-ROO?
14

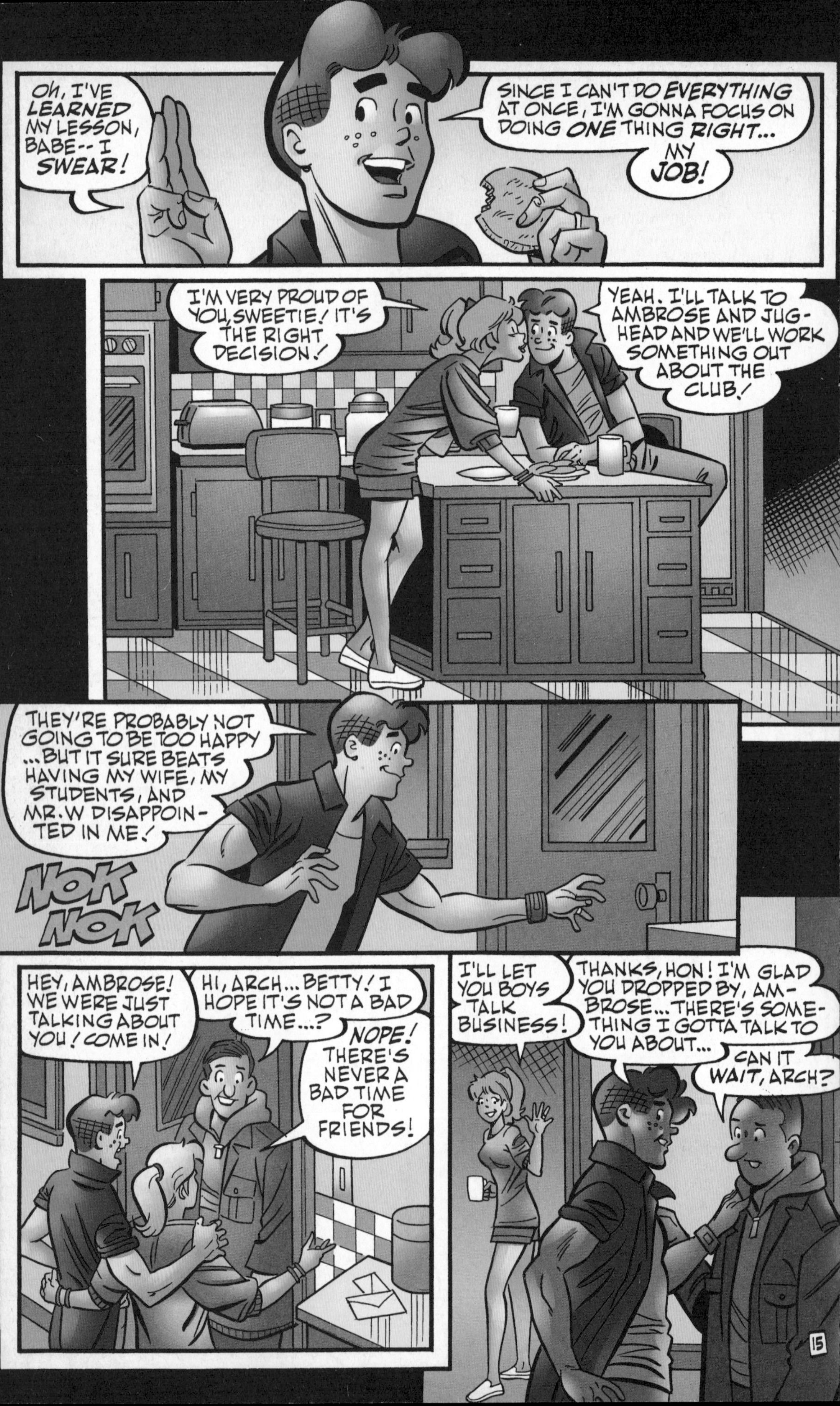
OH, I'VE LEARNED MY LESSON, BABE-- I SWEAR!
SINCE I CAN'T DO EVERYTHING AT ONCE, I'M GONNA FOCUS ON DOING ONE THING RIGHT... MY JOB!
I'M VERY PROUD OF YOU, SWEETIE! IT'S THE RIGHT DECISION!
YEAH. I'LL TALK TO AMBROSE AND JUG-HEAD AND WE'LL WORK SOMETHING OUT ABOUT THE CLUB!
THEY'RE PROBABLY NOT GOING TO BE TOO HAPPY ...BUT IT SURE BEATS HAVING MY WIFE, MY STUDENTS, AND MR. W DISAPPOINT-TED IN ME!
NOK NOK
HEY, AMBROSE! WE WERE JUST TALKING ABOUT YOU! COME IN!
HI, ARCH... BETTY! I HOPE IT'S NOT A BAD TIME...?
NOPE! THERE'S NEVER A BAD TIME FOR FRIENDS!
I'LL LET YOU BOYS TALK BUSINESS!
THANKS, HON! I'M GLAD YOU DROPPED BY, AM-BROSE... THERE'S SOME-THING I GOTTA TALK TO YOU ABOUT...
CAN IT WAIT, ARCH?
15

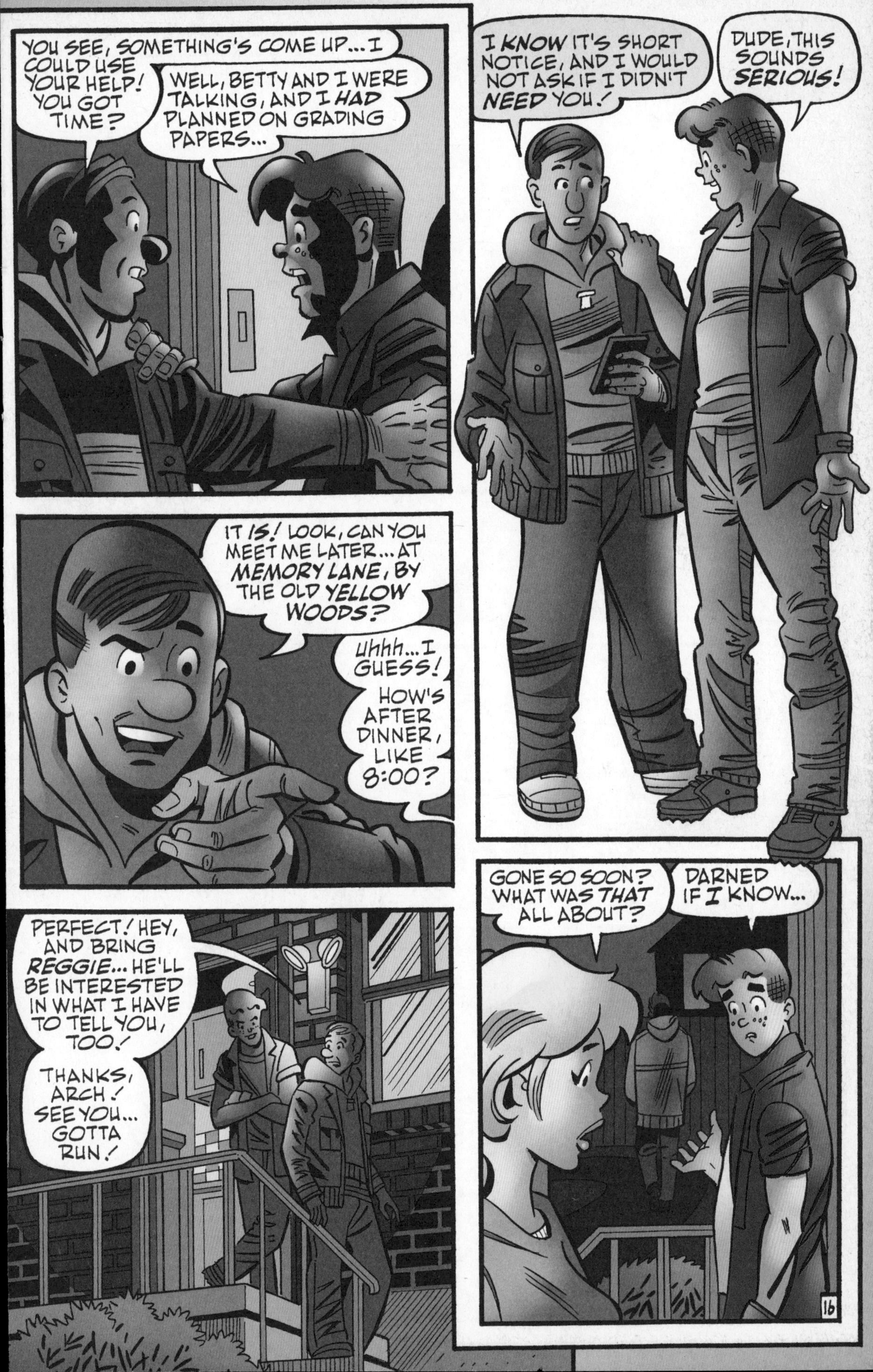
YOU SEE, SOMETHING'S COME UP... I COULD USE YOUR HELP! YOU GOT TIME?
WELL, BETTY AND I WERE TALKING, AND I HAD PLANNED ON GRADING PAPERS...
I KNOW IT'S SHORT NOTICE, AND I WOULD NOT ASK IF I DIDN'T NEED YOU!
DUDE, THIS SOUNDS SERIOUS!
IT IS! LOOK, CAN YOU MEET ME LATER... AT MEMORY LANE, BY THE OLD YELLOW WOODS?
UHHH... I GUESS!
HOW'S AFTER DINNER, LIKE 8:00?
PERFECT! HEY, AND BRING REGGIE... HE'LL BE INTERESTED IN WHAT I HAVE TO TELL YOU, TOO!
THANKS, ARCH! SEE YOU... GOTTA RUN!
GONE SO SOON? WHAT WAS THAT ALL ABOUT?
DARNED IF I KNOW...
16

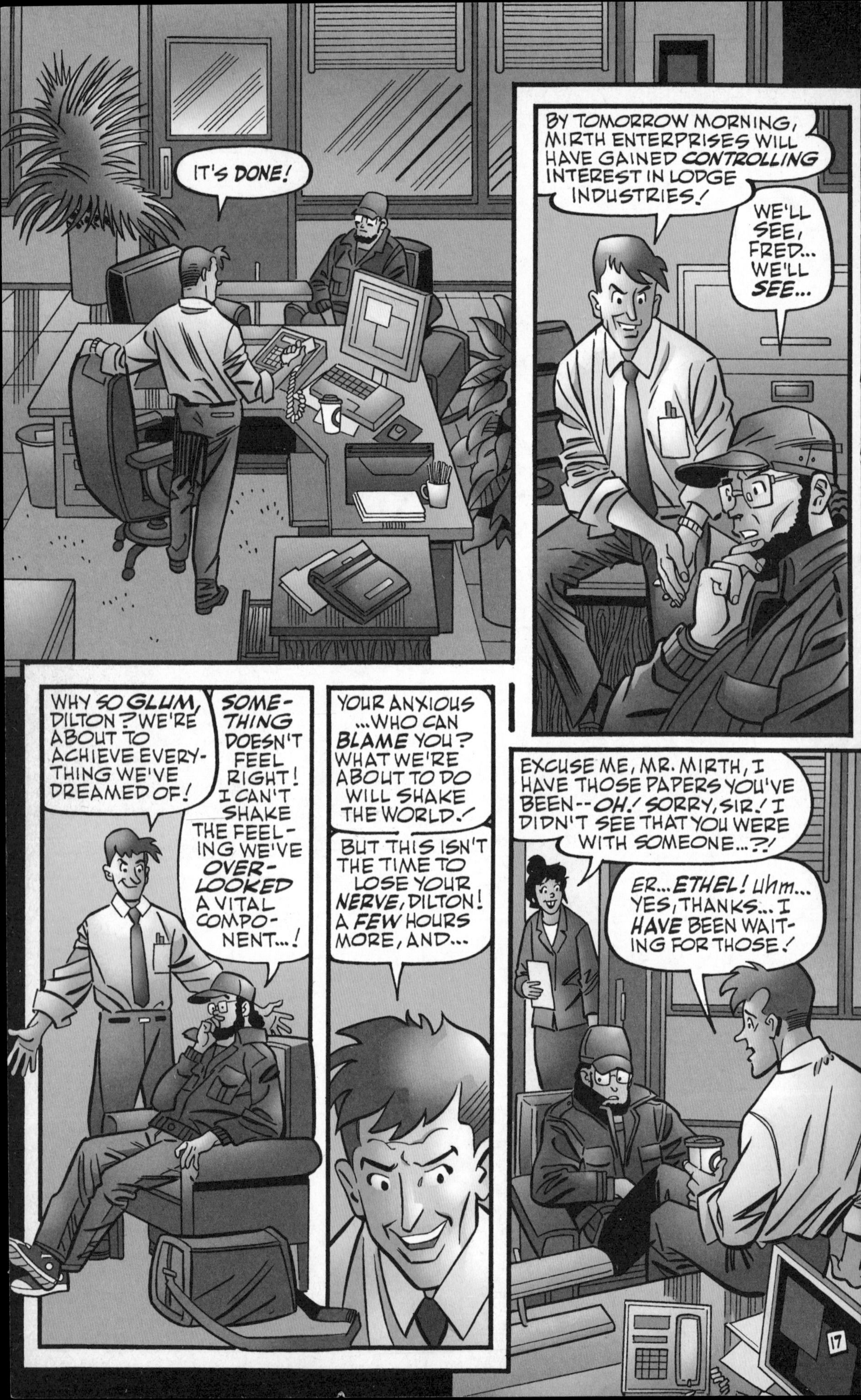
IT'S DONE!
BY TOMORROW MORNING, MIRTH ENTERPRISES WILL HAVE GAINED CONTROLLING INTEREST IN LODGE INDUSTRIES!
WE'LL SEE, FRED... WE'LL SEE...
WHY SO GLUM, DILTON? WE'RE ABOUT TO ACHIEVE EVERY-THING WE'VE DREAMED OF!
SOME-THING DOESN'T FEEL RIGHT! I CAN'T SHAKE THE FEEL-ING WE'VE OVER-LOOKED A VITAL COMPO-NENT...!
YOUR ANXIOUS ...WHO CAN BLAME YOU? WHAT WE'RE ABOUT TO DO WILL SHAKE THE WORLD!
BUT THIS ISN'T THE TIME TO LOSE YOUR NERVE, DILTON! A FEW HOURS MORE, AND...
EXCUSE ME, MR. MIRTH, I HAVE THOSE PAPERS YOU'VE BEEN--OH! SORRY, SIR! I DIDN'T SEE THAT YOU WERE WITH SOMEONE...?!
ER...ETHEL! UHM... YES, THANKS... I HAVE BEEN WAIT-ING FOR THOSE!
17

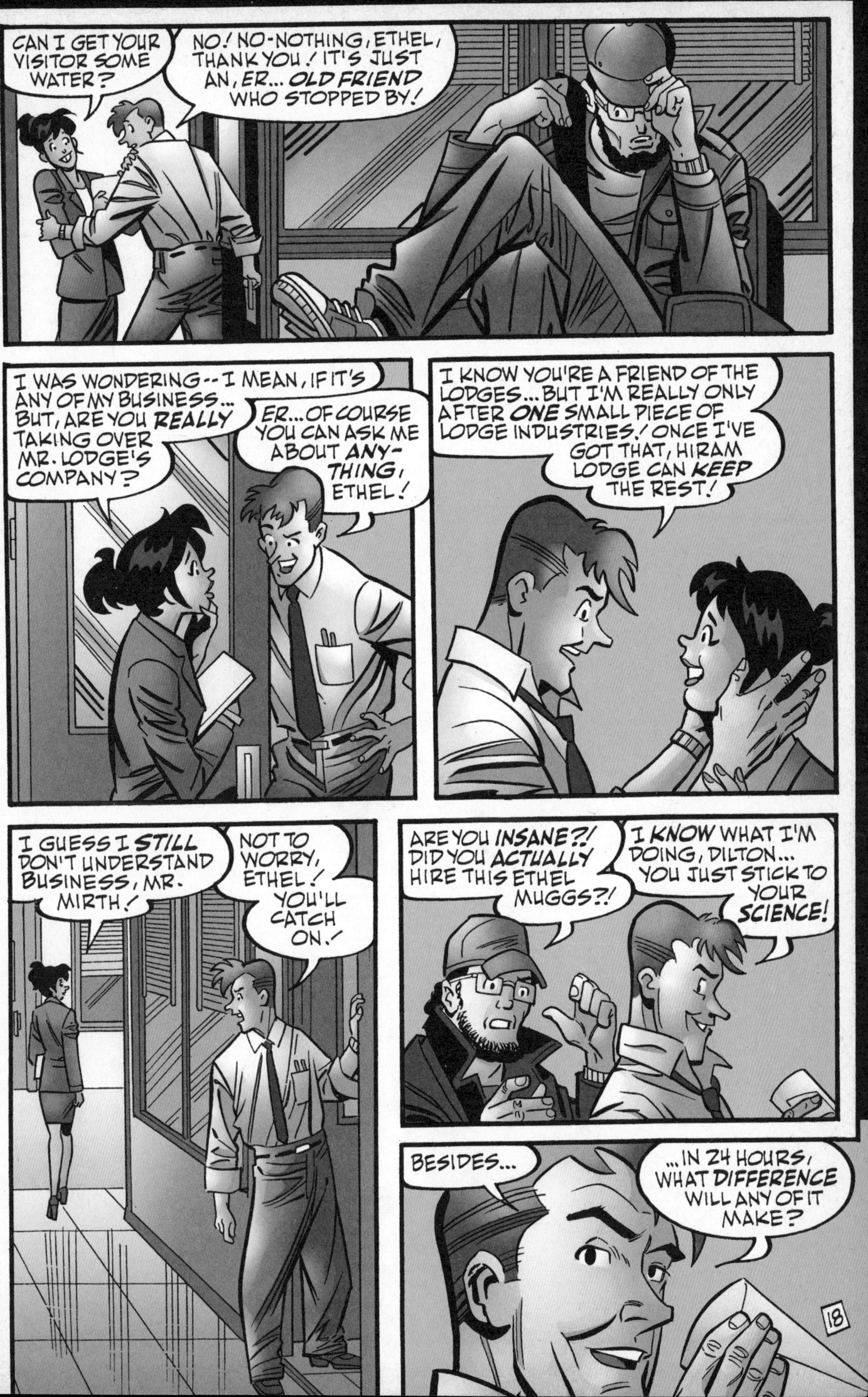
CAN I GET YOUR VISITOR SOME WATER?
NO! NO-NOTHING, ETHEL, THANK YOU! IT'S JUST AN, ER... OLD FRIEND WHO STOPPED BY!
I WAS WONDERING -- I MEAN, IF IT'S ANY OF MY BUSINESS... BUT, ARE YOU REALLY TAKING OVER MR. LODGE'S COMPANY?
ER... OF COURSE YOU CAN ASK ME ABOUT ANYTHING, ETHEL!
I KNOW YOU'RE A FRIEND OF THE LODGES... BUT I'M REALLY ONLY AFTER ONE SMALL PIECE OF LODGE INDUSTRIES! ONCE I'VE GOT THAT, HIRAM LODGE CAN KEEP THE REST!
I GUESS I STILL DON'T UNDERSTAND BUSINESS, MR. MIRTH!
NOT TO WORRY, ETHEL! YOU'LL CATCH ON!
ARE YOU INSANE?! DID YOU ACTUALLY HIRE THIS ETHEL MUGGS?!
I KNOW WHAT I'M DOING, DILTON... YOU JUST STICK TO YOUR SCIENCE!
BESIDES...
...IN 24 HOURS, WHAT DIFFERENCE WILL ANY OF IT MAKE?

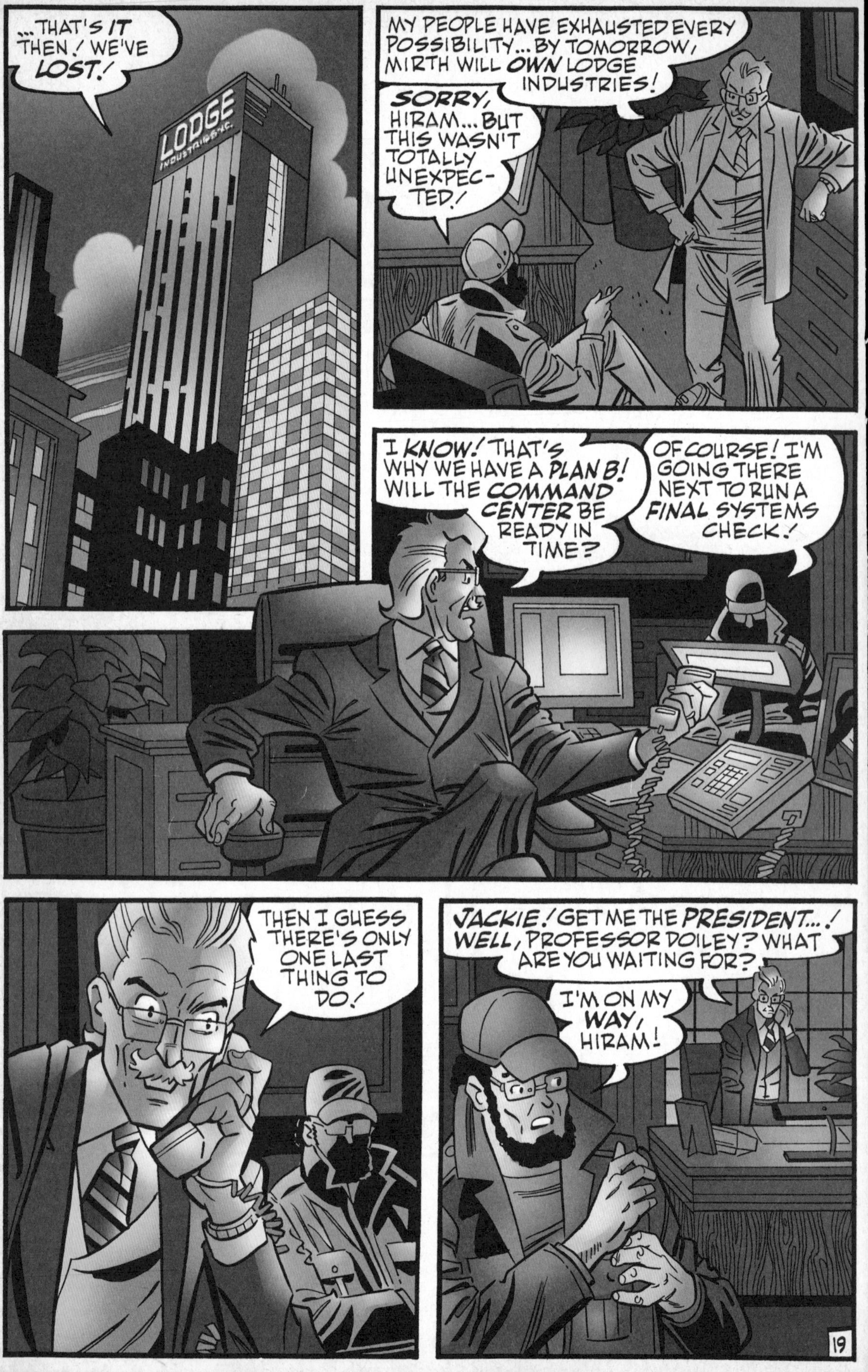
...THAT'S IT THEN! WE'VE LOST!
LODGE INDUSTRIES INC.
MY PEOPLE HAVE EXHAUSTED EVERY POSSIBILITY... BY TOMORROW, MIRTH WILL OWN LODGE INDUSTRIES!
SORRY, HIRAM... BUT THIS WASN'T TOTALLY UNEXPEC-TED!
I KNOW! THAT'S WHY WE HAVE A PLAN B! WILL THE COMMAND CENTER BE READY IN TIME?
OF COURSE! I'M GOING THERE NEXT TO RUN A FINAL SYSTEMS CHECK!
THEN I GUESS THERE'S ONLY ONE LAST THING TO DO!
JACKIE! GET ME THE PRESIDENT...! WELL, PROFESSOR DOILEY? WHAT ARE YOU WAITING FOR?
I'M ON MY WAY, HIRAM!

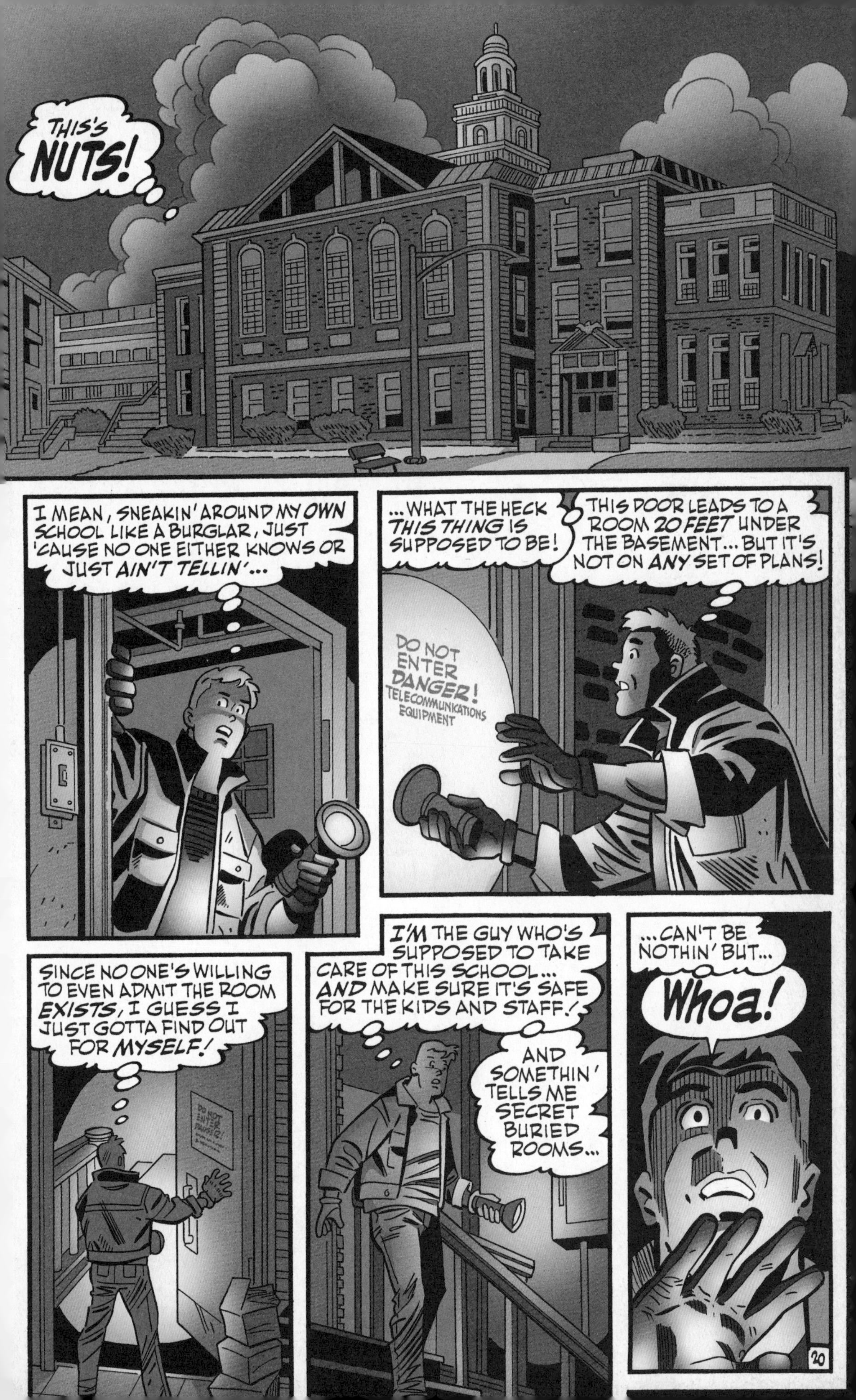
THIS'S NUTS!
I MEAN, SNEAKIN' AROUND MY OWN SCHOOL LIKE A BURGLAR, JUST 'CAUSE NO ONE EITHER KNOWS OR JUST AIN'T TELLIN'...
...WHAT THE HECK THIS THING IS SUPPOSED TO BE!
THIS DOOR LEADS TO A ROOM 20 FEET UNDER THE BASEMENT... BUT IT'S NOT ON ANY SET OF PLANS!
DO NOT ENTER DANGER! TELECOMMUNICATIONS EQUIPMENT
SINCE NO ONE'S WILLING TO EVEN ADMIT THE ROOM EXISTS, I GUESS I JUST GOTTA FIND OUT FOR MYSELF!
I'M THE GUY WHO'S SUPPOSED TO TAKE CARE OF THIS SCHOOL... AND MAKE SURE IT'S SAFE FOR THE KIDS AND STAFF!
AND SOMETHIN' TELLS ME SECRET BURIED ROOMS...
...CAN'T BE NOTHIN' BUT...
Whoa!
20

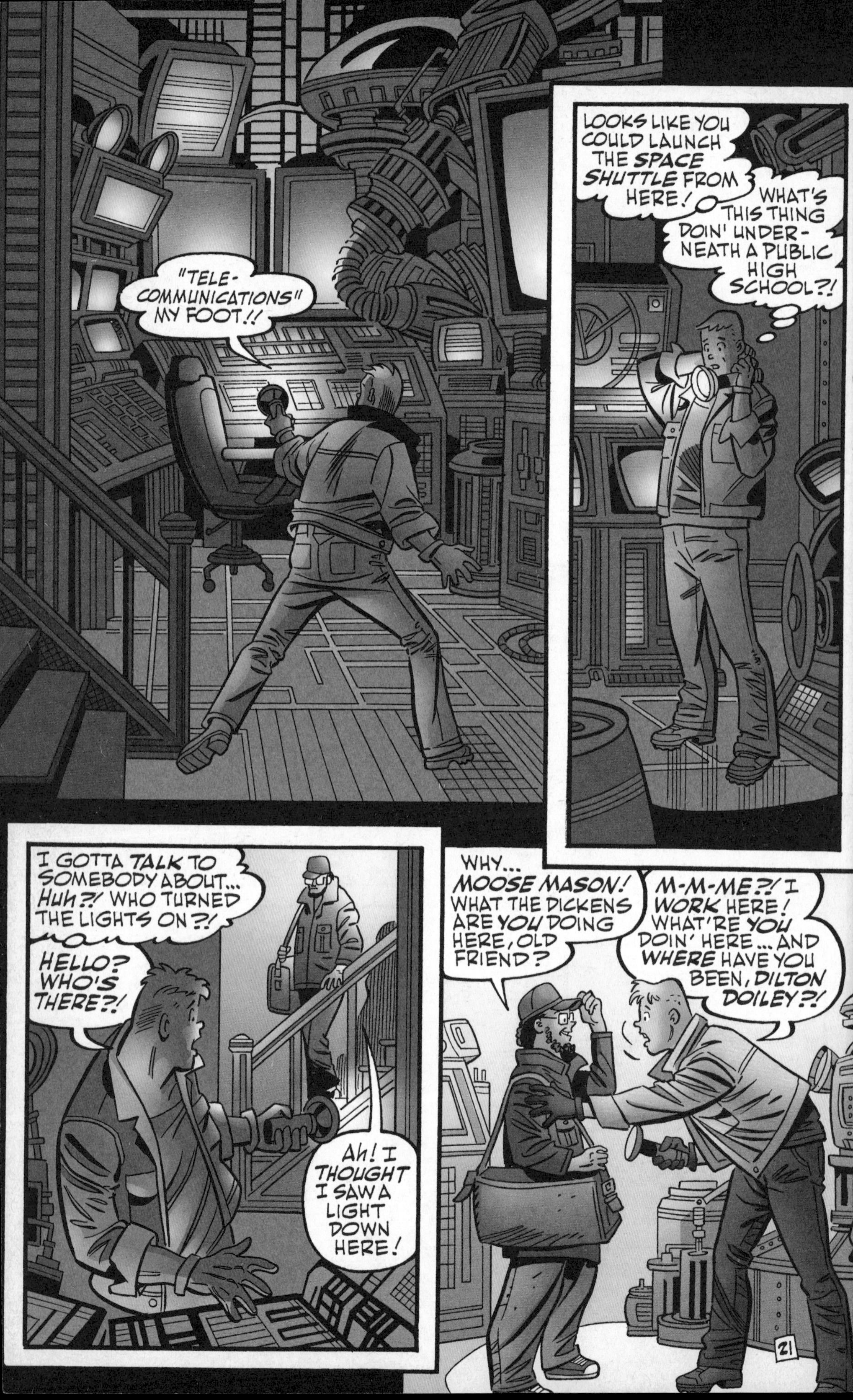
"TELE-COMMUNICATIONS" MY FOOT!!
LOOKS LIKE YOU COULD LAUNCH THE SPACE SHUTTLE FROM HERE!
WHAT'S THIS THING DOIN' UNDER-NEATH A PUBLIC HIGH SCHOOL?!
I GOTTA TALK TO SOMEBODY ABOUT... Huh?! WHO TURNED THE LIGHTS ON?!
HELLO? WHO'S THERE?!
Ah! I THOUGHT I SAW A LIGHT DOWN HERE!
WHY... MOOSE MASON! WHAT THE DICKENS ARE YOU DOING HERE, OLD FRIEND?
M-M-ME?! I WORK HERE! WHAT'RE YOU DOIN' HERE... AND WHERE HAVE YOU BEEN, DILTON DOILEY?!
21

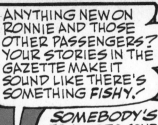

...I STILL DON'T GET WHY AMBROSE WANTS *ME* HERE!

WE WERE NEVER PALS!

MEMORY LANE

ANYTHING NEW ON RONNIE AND THOSE OTHER PASSENGERS? YOUR STORIES IN THE GAZETTE MAKE IT SOUND LIKE THERE'S SOMETHING *FISHY!*

SOMEBODY'S TRYING TO COVER *SOMETHING* UP...

...AND I THINK I'M GETTING *CLOSE* TO FINDING OUT WHAT!

WELL, IF THERE'S ANYTHING I CAN DO...

I DUNNO. HE'S BEEN ACTING PRETTY ODD... BUT THANKS FOR COMING, REGGIE!

HEY, GUYS! SORRY I'M LATE!

HUH?!

WHERE'D YOU COME FROM?

WHERE I CAME FROM IS PART OF WHAT I'VE GOT TO *EXPLAIN* TO YOU!

WHAT'S UP HERE?

FOLLOW ME!

YOU GUYS MAY WANT TO *CLOSE* YOUR EYES!

HEY!

CUT IT *OUT*, WILLYA?!

22

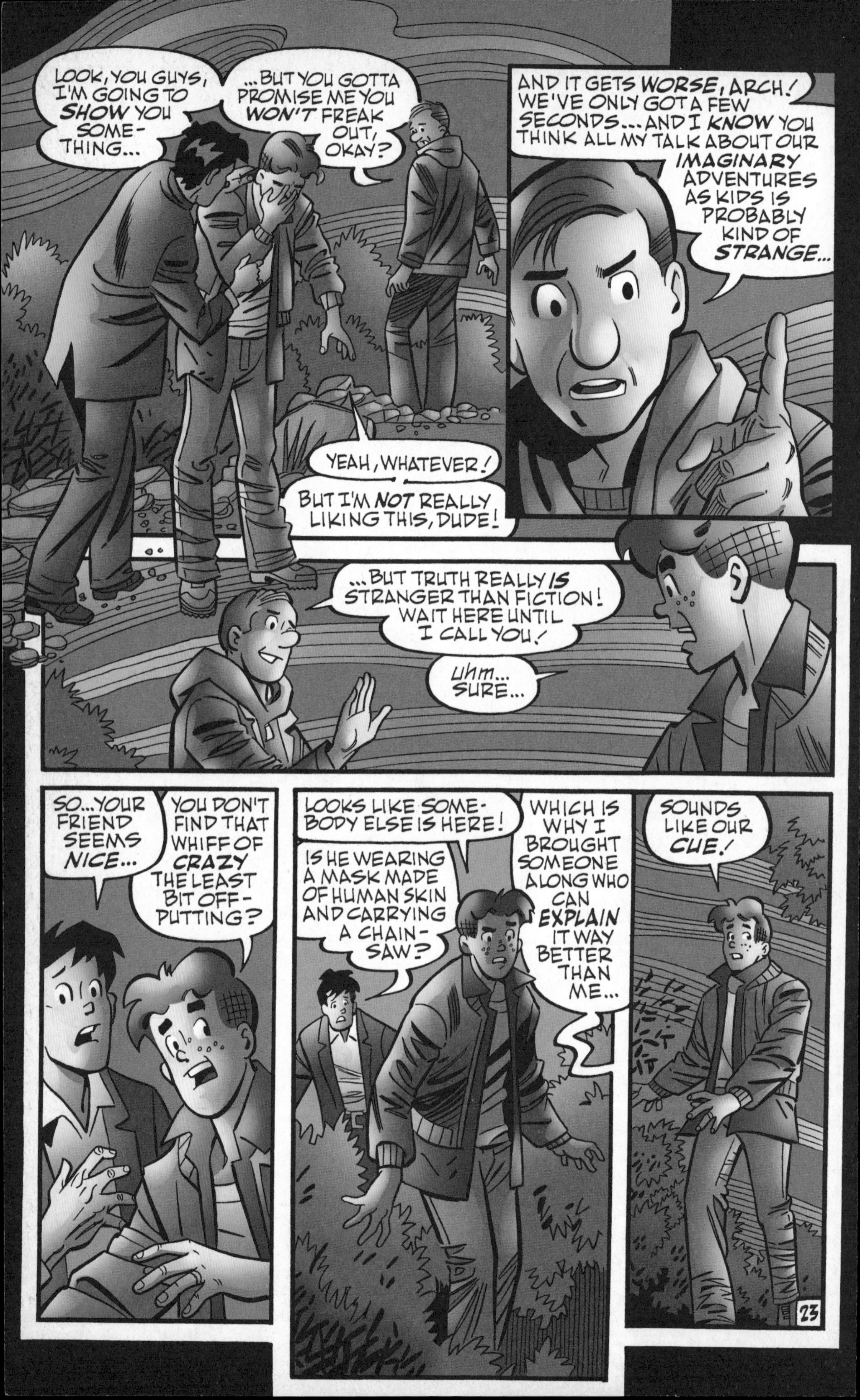
LOOK, YOU GUYS, I'M GOING TO SHOW YOU SOME-THING...
...BUT YOU GOTTA PROMISE ME YOU WON'T FREAK OUT, OKAY?
YEAH, WHATEVER!
BUT I'M NOT REALLY LIKING THIS, DUDE!
AND IT GETS WORSE, ARCH! WE'VE ONLY GOT A FEW SECONDS... AND I KNOW YOU THINK ALL MY TALK ABOUT OUR IMAGINARY ADVENTURES AS KIDS IS PROBABLY KIND OF STRANGE...
...BUT TRUTH REALLY IS STRANGER THAN FICTION! WAIT HERE UNTIL I CALL YOU!
UHM... SURE...
SO... YOUR FRIEND SEEMS NICE...
YOU DON'T FIND THAT WHIFF OF CRAZY THE LEAST BIT OFF-PUTTING?
LOOKS LIKE SOME-BODY ELSE IS HERE!
IS HE WEARING A MASK MADE OF HUMAN SKIN AND CARRYING A CHAIN-SAW?
WHICH IS WHY I BROUGHT SOMEONE ALONG WHO CAN EXPLAIN IT WAY BETTER THAN ME...
SOUNDS LIKE OUR CUE!
23

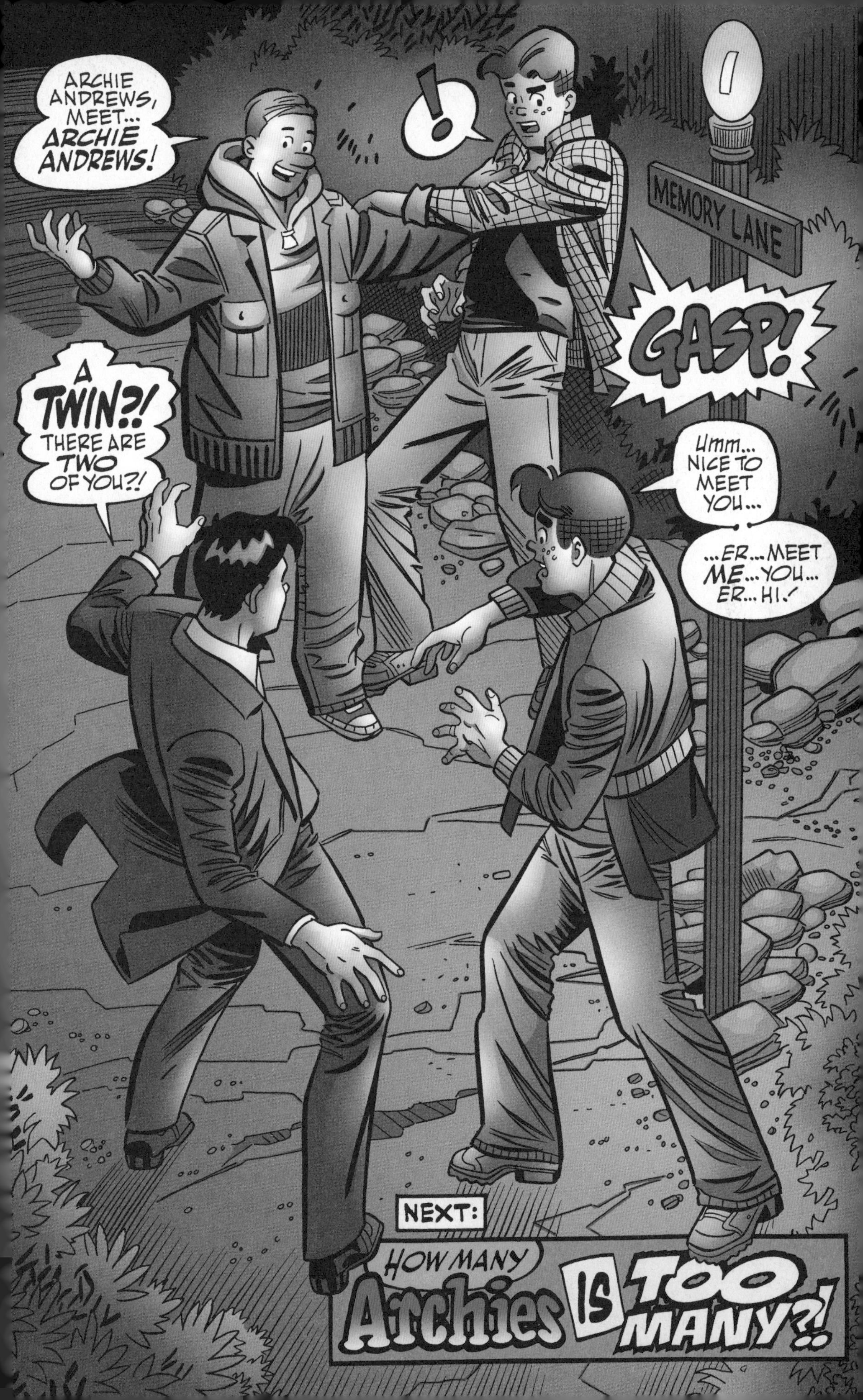
ARCHIE ANDREWS, MEET... ARCHIE ANDREWS!
!
MEMORY LANE
GASP!
A TWIN?! THERE ARE TWO OF YOU?!
Umm... NICE TO MEET YOU...
...ER...MEET ME...YOU... ER...HI.!
NEXT:
HOW MANY Archies IS TOO MANY?!

" WE'VE LEFT CRAZY FAR BEHIND!
I SUGGEST YOU START *BELIEVING*
YOUR EYES, 'CAUSE AS WEIRD AS
IT'S BEEN SO FAR..."

"...YOU AIN'T SEEN *NOTHIN'* YET!!"

- *AMBROSE PIPS*

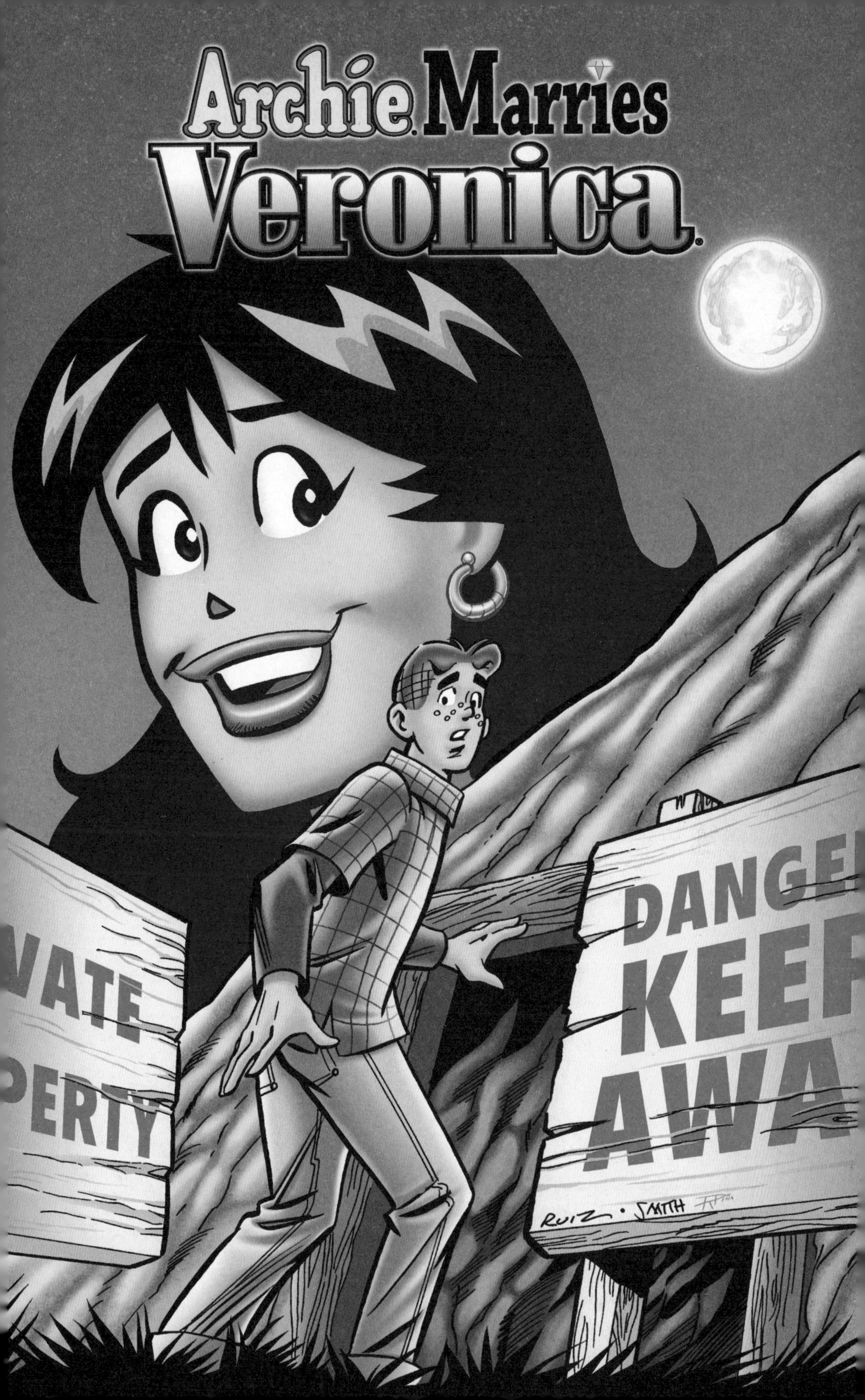
Archie Marries Veronica
VATE
PERTY
DANGE
KEE
AWA
RUIZ · SMITH

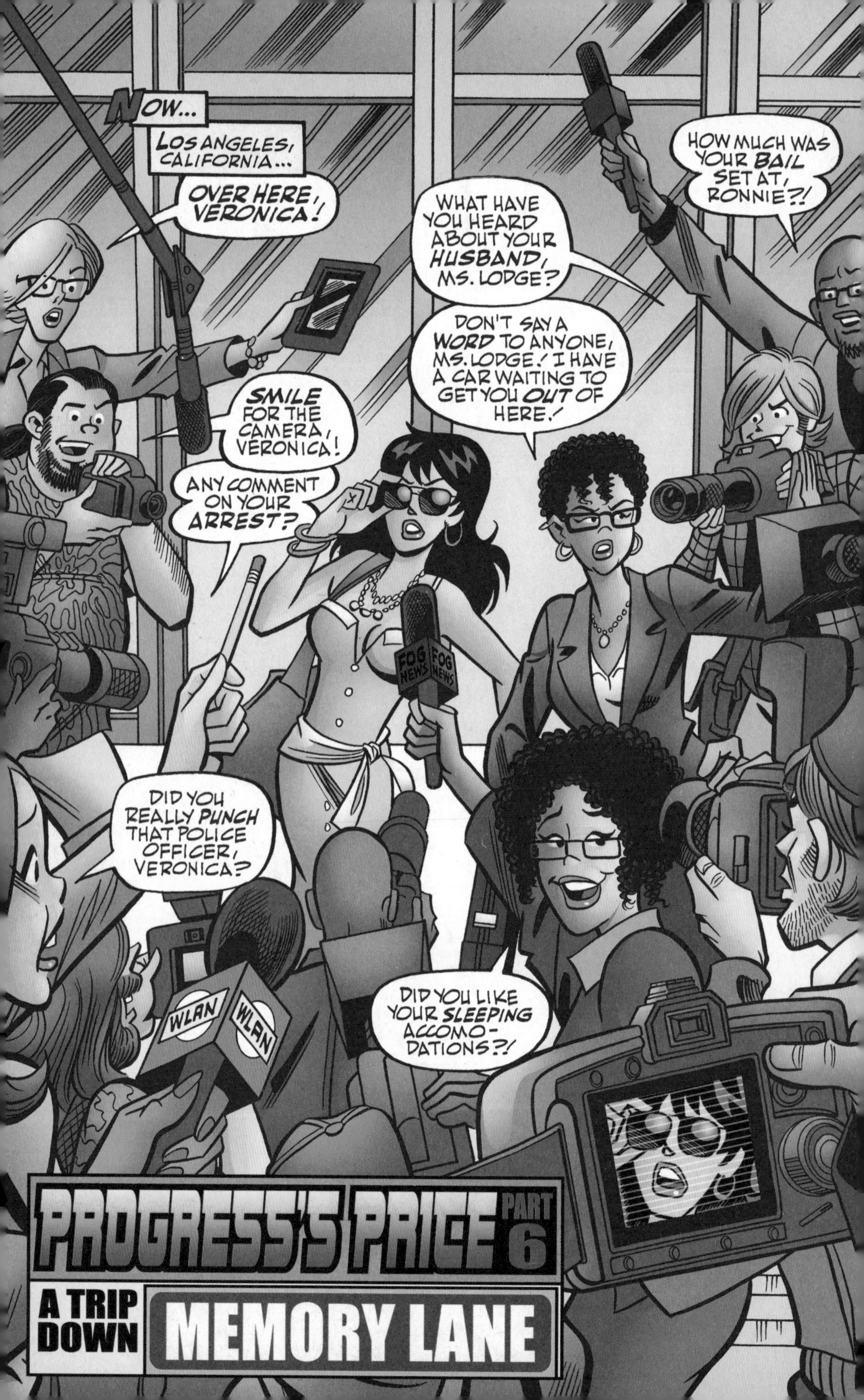
NOW...
LOS ANGELES, CALIFORNIA...
OVER HERE, VERONICA!
WHAT HAVE YOU HEARD ABOUT YOUR HUSBAND, MS. LODGE?
HOW MUCH WAS YOUR BAIL SET AT, RONNIE?!
DON'T SAY A WORD TO ANYONE, MS. LODGE! I HAVE A CAR WAITING TO GET YOU OUT OF HERE!
SMILE FOR THE CAMERA, VERONICA!
ANY COMMENT ON YOUR ARREST?
FOG NEWS
DID YOU REALLY PUNCH THAT POLICE OFFICER, VERONICA?
WLAN
DID YOU LIKE YOUR SLEEPING ACCOMO-DATIONS?!
PROGRESS'S PRICE PART 6
A TRIP DOWN MEMORY LANE

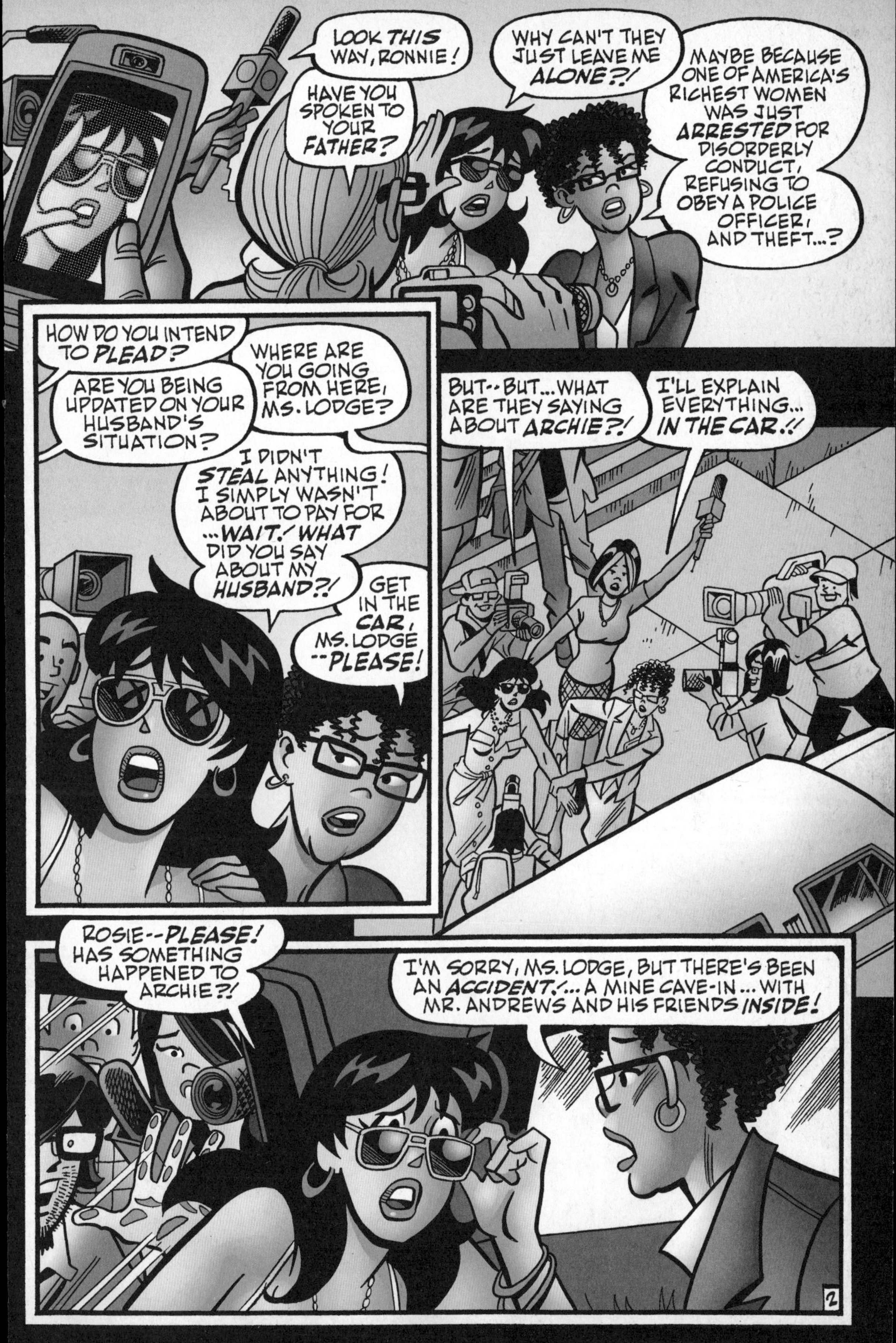
LOOK THIS WAY, RONNIE!
HAVE YOU SPOKEN TO YOUR FATHER?
WHY CAN'T THEY JUST LEAVE ME ALONE?!
MAYBE BECAUSE ONE OF AMERICA'S RICHEST WOMEN WAS JUST ARRESTED FOR DISORDERLY CONDUCT, REFUSING TO OBEY A POLICE OFFICER, AND THEFT...?
HOW DO YOU INTEND TO PLEAD?
WHERE ARE YOU GOING FROM HERE, MS. LODGE?
ARE YOU BEING UPDATED ON YOUR HUSBAND'S SITUATION?
I DIDN'T STEAL ANYTHING! I SIMPLY WASN'T ABOUT TO PAY FOR ...WAIT! WHAT DID YOU SAY ABOUT MY HUSBAND?!
GET IN THE CAR, MS. LODGE --PLEASE!
BUT--BUT...WHAT ARE THEY SAYING ABOUT ARCHIE?!
I'LL EXPLAIN EVERYTHING... IN THE CAR.!!
ROSIE--PLEASE! HAS SOMETHING HAPPENED TO ARCHIE?!
I'M SORRY, MS. LODGE, BUT THERE'S BEEN AN ACCIDENT!... A MINE CAVE-IN ... WITH MR. ANDREWS AND HIS FRIENDS INSIDE!

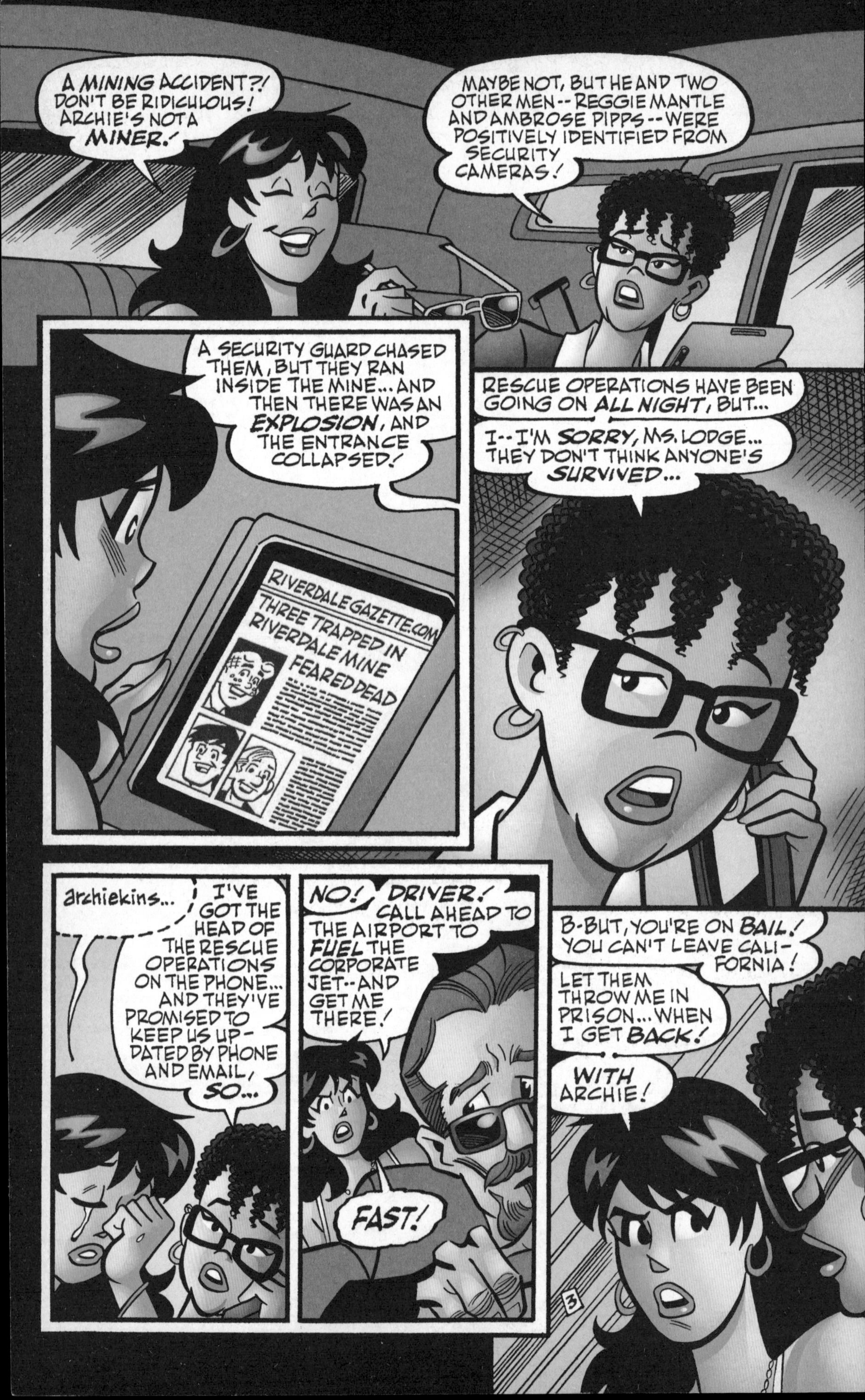

A MINING ACCIDENT?! DON'T BE RIDICULOUS! ARCHIE'S NOT A MINER!
MAYBE NOT, BUT HE AND TWO OTHER MEN -- REGGIE MANTLE AND AMBROSE PIPPS -- WERE POSITIVELY IDENTIFIED FROM SECURITY CAMERAS!
A SECURITY GUARD CHASED THEM, BUT THEY RAN INSIDE THE MINE... AND THEN THERE WAS AN EXPLOSION, AND THE ENTRANCE COLLAPSED!
RIVERDALEGAZETTE.COM
THREE TRAPPED IN RIVERDALE MINE FEARED DEAD
RESCUE OPERATIONS HAVE BEEN GOING ON ALL NIGHT, BUT...
I-- I'M SORRY, MS. LODGE... THEY DON'T THINK ANYONE'S SURVIVED...
archiekins...
I'VE GOT THE HEAD OF THE RESCUE OPERATIONS ON THE PHONE... AND THEY'VE PROMISED TO KEEP US UPDATED BY PHONE AND EMAIL, SO...
NO! DRIVER! CALL AHEAD TO THE AIRPORT TO FUEL THE CORPORATE JET -- AND GET ME THERE!
FAST!
B-BUT, YOU'RE ON BAIL! YOU CAN'T LEAVE CALIFORNIA!
LET THEM THROW ME IN PRISON... WHEN I GET BACK!
WITH ARCHIE!
3

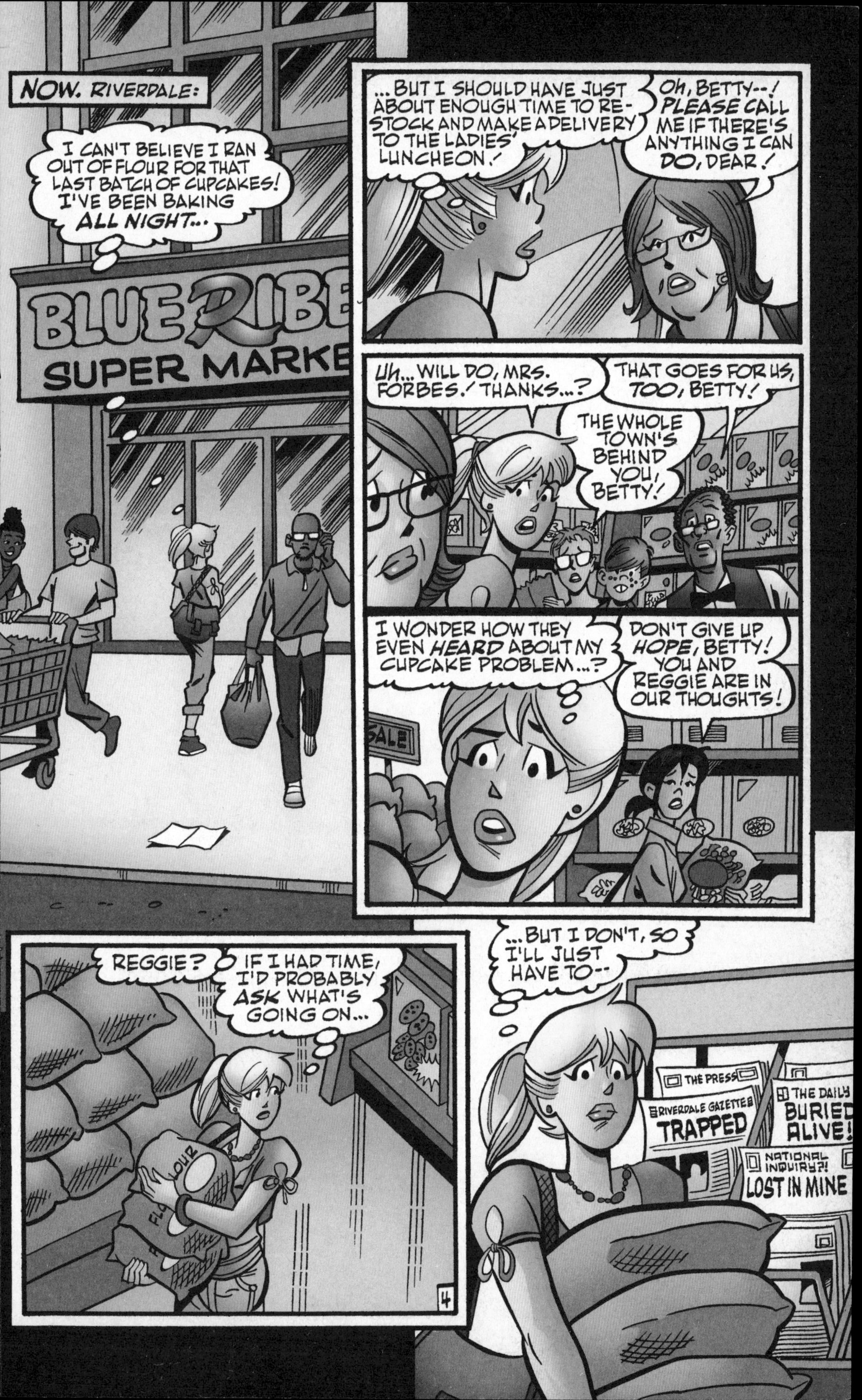
NOW. RIVERDALE:
I CAN'T BELIEVE I RAN OUT OF FLOUR FOR THAT LAST BATCH OF CUPCAKES! I'VE BEEN BAKING ALL NIGHT...
BLUE RIBB
SUPER MARKE
...BUT I SHOULD HAVE JUST ABOUT ENOUGH TIME TO RE-STOCK AND MAKE A DELIVERY TO THE LADIES' LUNCHEON!
Oh, BETTY--! PLEASE CALL ME IF THERE'S ANYTHING I CAN DO, DEAR!
Uh... WILL DO, MRS. FORBES! THANKS...?
THAT GOES FOR US, TOO, BETTY!
THE WHOLE TOWN'S BEHIND YOU, BETTY!
I WONDER HOW THEY EVEN HEARD ABOUT MY CUPCAKE PROBLEM...?
DON'T GIVE UP HOPE, BETTY! YOU AND REGGIE ARE IN OUR THOUGHTS!
SALE
REGGIE?
IF I HAD TIME, I'D PROBABLY ASK WHAT'S GOING ON...
FLOUR
...BUT I DON'T, SO I'LL JUST HAVE TO--
THE PRESS
RIVERDALE GAZETTE
TRAPPED
THE DAILY
BURIED ALIVE!
NATIONAL INQUIRY?!
LOST IN MINE

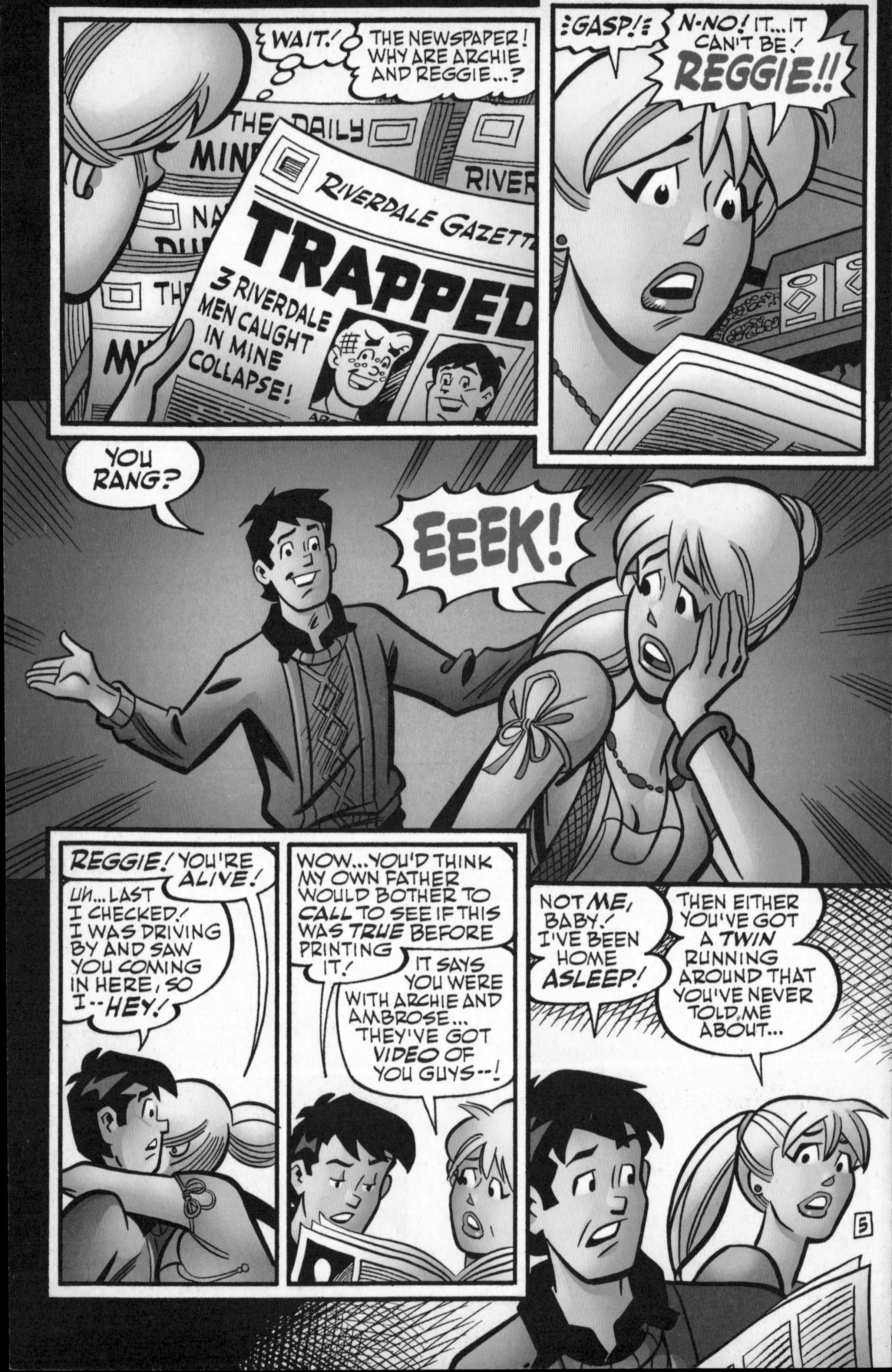
WAIT!
THE NEWSPAPER! WHY ARE ARCHIE AND REGGIE...?
THE DAILY
RIVERDALE GAZETTE
TRAPPED
3 RIVERDALE MEN CAUGHT IN MINE COLLAPSE!
GASP!
N-NO! IT...IT CAN'T BE! REGGIE!!
YOU RANG?
EEEK!
REGGIE! YOU'RE ALIVE!
UH...LAST I CHECKED! I WAS DRIVING BY AND SAW YOU COMING IN HERE, SO I--HEY!
WOW...YOU'D THINK MY OWN FATHER WOULD BOTHER TO CALL TO SEE IF THIS WAS TRUE BEFORE PRINTING IT!
IT SAYS YOU WERE WITH ARCHIE AND AMBROSE... THEY'VE GOT VIDEO OF YOU GUYS--!
NOT ME, BABY! I'VE BEEN HOME ASLEEP!
THEN EITHER YOU'VE GOT A TWIN RUNNING AROUND THAT YOU'VE NEVER TOLD ME ABOUT...
5

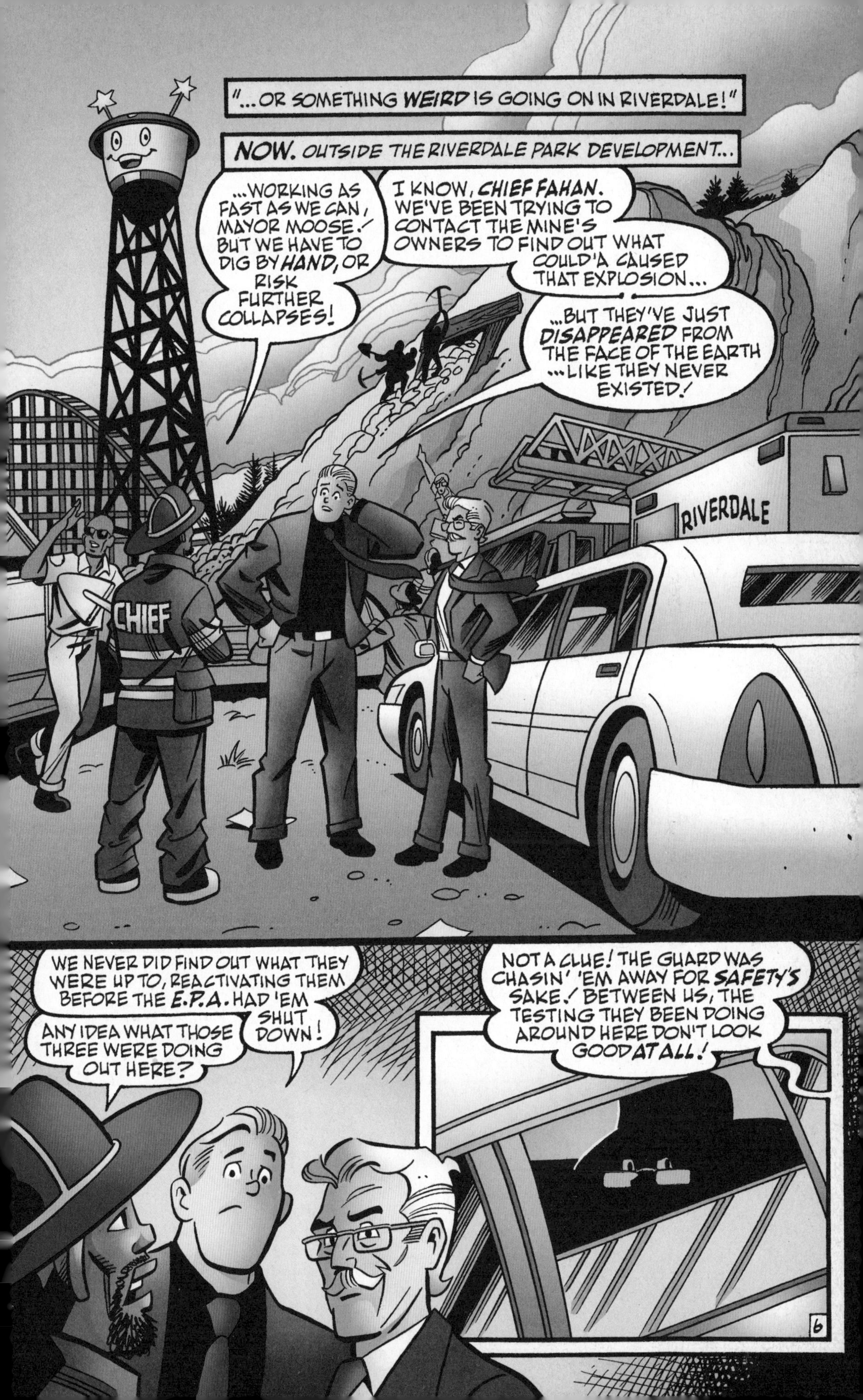
"...OR SOMETHING WEIRD IS GOING ON IN RIVERDALE!"
NOW. OUTSIDE THE RIVERDALE PARK DEVELOPMENT...
...WORKING AS FAST AS WE CAN, MAYOR MOOSE! BUT WE HAVE TO DIG BY HAND, OR RISK FURTHER COLLAPSES!
I KNOW, CHIEF FAHAN. WE'VE BEEN TRYING TO CONTACT THE MINE'S OWNERS TO FIND OUT WHAT COULD'A CAUSED THAT EXPLOSION...
...BUT THEY'VE JUST DISAPPEARED FROM THE FACE OF THE EARTH ...LIKE THEY NEVER EXISTED!
RIVERDALE
CHIEF
WE NEVER DID FIND OUT WHAT THEY WERE UP TO, REACTIVATING THEM BEFORE THE E.P.A. HAD 'EM SHUT DOWN!
ANY IDEA WHAT THOSE THREE WERE DOING OUT HERE?
NOT A CLUE! THE GUARD WAS CHASIN' 'EM AWAY FOR SAFETY'S SAKE! BETWEEN US, THE TESTING THEY BEEN DOING AROUND HERE DON'T LOOK GOOD AT ALL!

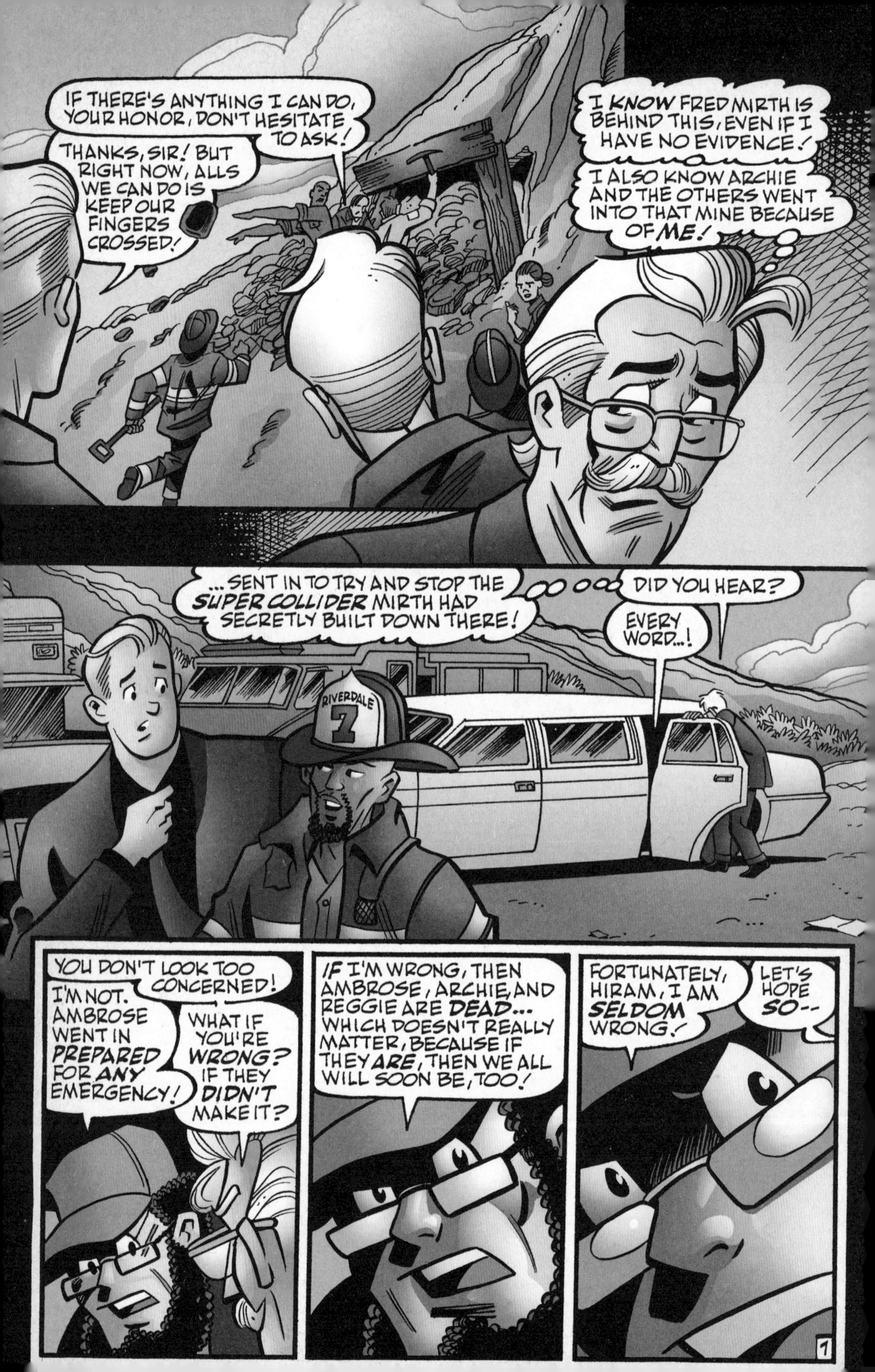
IF THERE'S ANYTHING I CAN DO, YOUR HONOR, DON'T HESITATE TO ASK!
THANKS, SIR! BUT RIGHT NOW, ALL'S WE CAN DO IS KEEP OUR FINGERS CROSSED!
I KNOW FRED MIRTH IS BEHIND THIS, EVEN IF I HAVE NO EVIDENCE!
I ALSO KNOW ARCHIE AND THE OTHERS WENT INTO THAT MINE BECAUSE OF ME!
... SENT IN TO TRY AND STOP THE SUPER COLLIDER MIRTH HAD SECRETLY BUILT DOWN THERE!
DID YOU HEAR?
EVERY WORD...!
RIVERDALE
7
YOU DON'T LOOK TOO CONCERNED!
I'M NOT. AMBROSE WENT IN PREPARED FOR ANY EMERGENCY!
WHAT IF YOU'RE WRONG? IF THEY DIDN'T MAKE IT?
IF I'M WRONG, THEN AMBROSE, ARCHIE, AND REGGIE ARE DEAD... WHICH DOESN'T REALLY MATTER, BECAUSE IF THEY ARE, THEN WE ALL WILL SOON BE, TOO!
FORTUNATELY, HIRAM, I AM SELDOM WRONG!
LET'S HOPE SO--

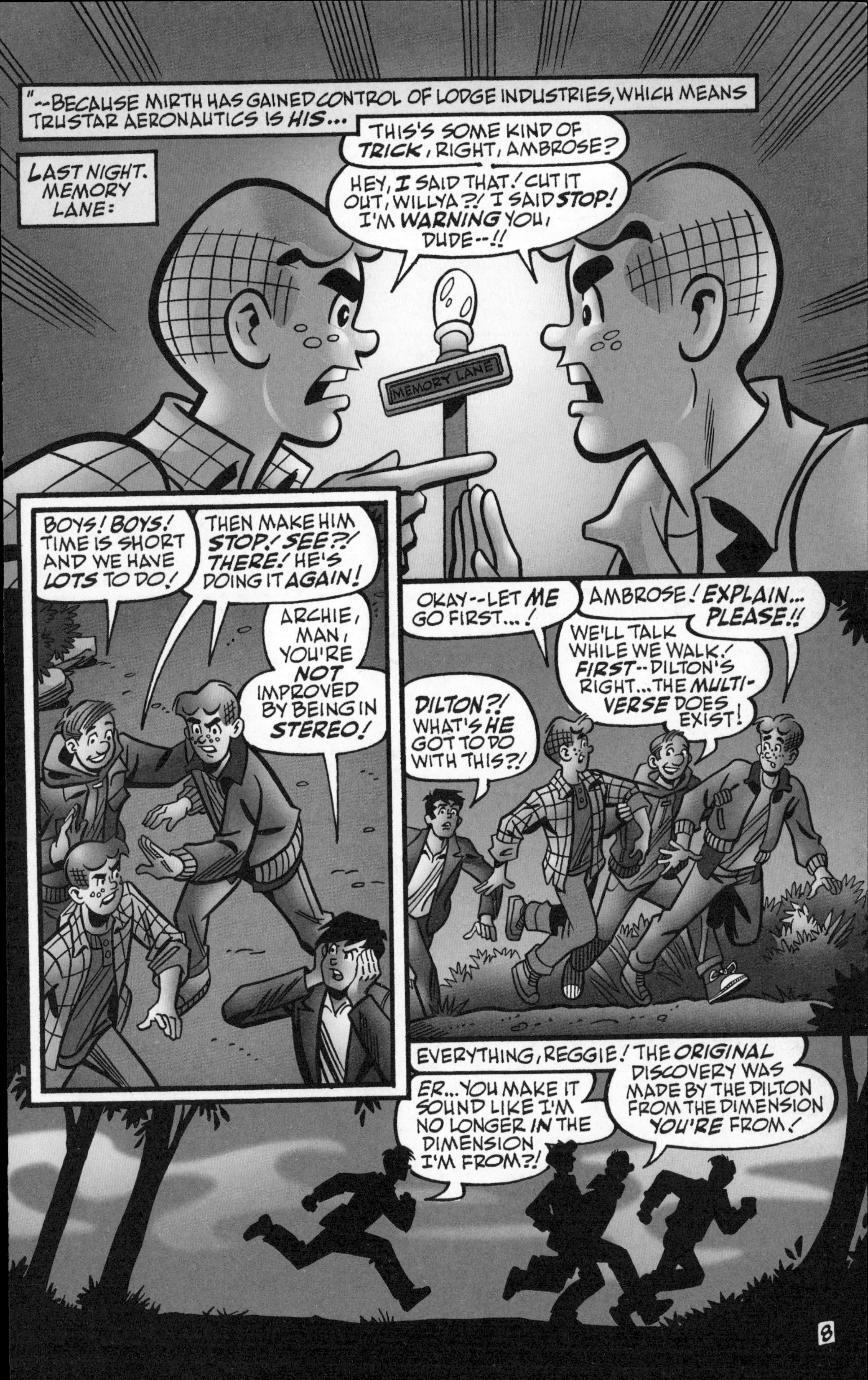
"--BECAUSE MIRTH HAS GAINED CONTROL OF LODGE INDUSTRIES, WHICH MEANS TRUSTAR AERONAUTICS IS HIS...
LAST NIGHT. MEMORY LANE:
THIS'S SOME KIND OF TRICK, RIGHT, AMBROSE?
HEY, I SAID THAT! CUT IT OUT, WILLYA?! I SAID STOP! I'M WARNING YOU, DUDE--!!
MEMORY LANE
BOYS! BOYS! TIME IS SHORT AND WE HAVE LOTS TO DO!
THEN MAKE HIM STOP! SEE?! THERE! HE'S DOING IT AGAIN!
ARCHIE, MAN, YOU'RE NOT IMPROVED BY BEING IN STEREO!
OKAY--LET ME GO FIRST...!
AMBROSE! EXPLAIN... PLEASE!!
WE'LL TALK WHILE WE WALK! FIRST--DILTON'S RIGHT...THE MULTI-VERSE DOES EXIST!
DILTON?! WHAT'S HE GOT TO DO WITH THIS?!
EVERYTHING, REGGIE! THE ORIGINAL DISCOVERY WAS MADE BY THE DILTON FROM THE DIMENSION YOU'RE FROM!
ER...YOU MAKE IT SOUND LIKE I'M NO LONGER IN THE DIMENSION I'M FROM?!

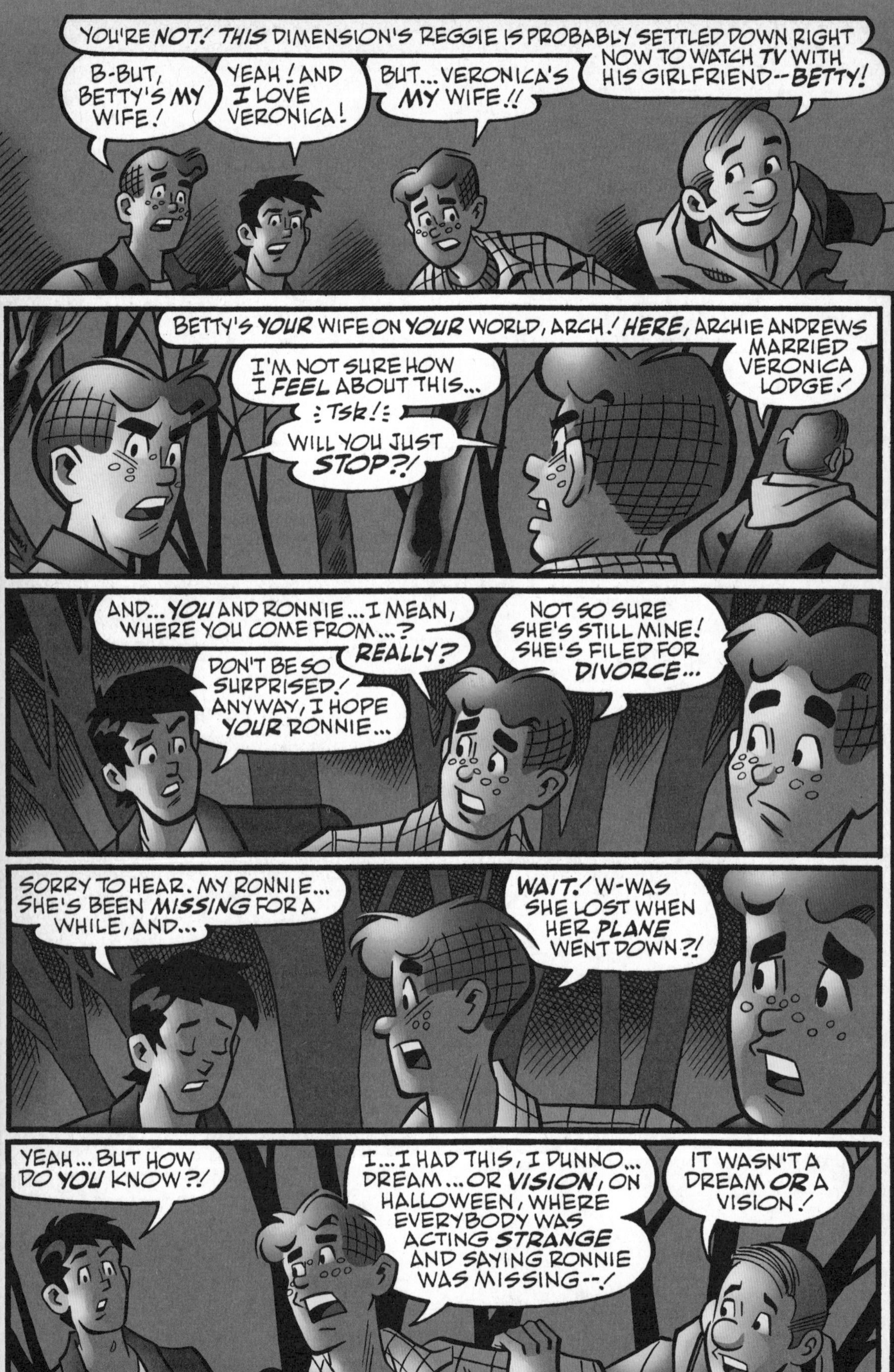
YOU'RE NOT! THIS DIMENSION'S REGGIE IS PROBABLY SETTLED DOWN RIGHT NOW TO WATCH TV WITH HIS GIRLFRIEND--BETTY!
B-BUT, BETTY'S MY WIFE!
YEAH! AND I LOVE VERONICA!
BUT... VERONICA'S MY WIFE!!
BETTY'S YOUR WIFE ON YOUR WORLD, ARCH! HERE, ARCHIE ANDREWS MARRIED VERONICA LODGE!
I'M NOT SURE HOW I FEEL ABOUT THIS...
Tsk!
WILL YOU JUST STOP?!
AND... YOU AND RONNIE... I MEAN, WHERE YOU COME FROM...? REALLY?
DON'T BE SO SURPRISED! ANYWAY, I HOPE YOUR RONNIE...
NOT SO SURE SHE'S STILL MINE! SHE'S FILED FOR DIVORCE...
SORRY TO HEAR. MY RONNIE... SHE'S BEEN MISSING FOR A WHILE, AND...
WAIT! W-WAS SHE LOST WHEN HER PLANE WENT DOWN?!
YEAH... BUT HOW DO YOU KNOW?!
I... I HAD THIS, I DUNNO... DREAM... OR VISION, ON HALLOWEEN, WHERE EVERYBODY WAS ACTING STRANGE AND SAYING RONNIE WAS MISSING--!
IT WASN'T A DREAM OR A VISION!
9

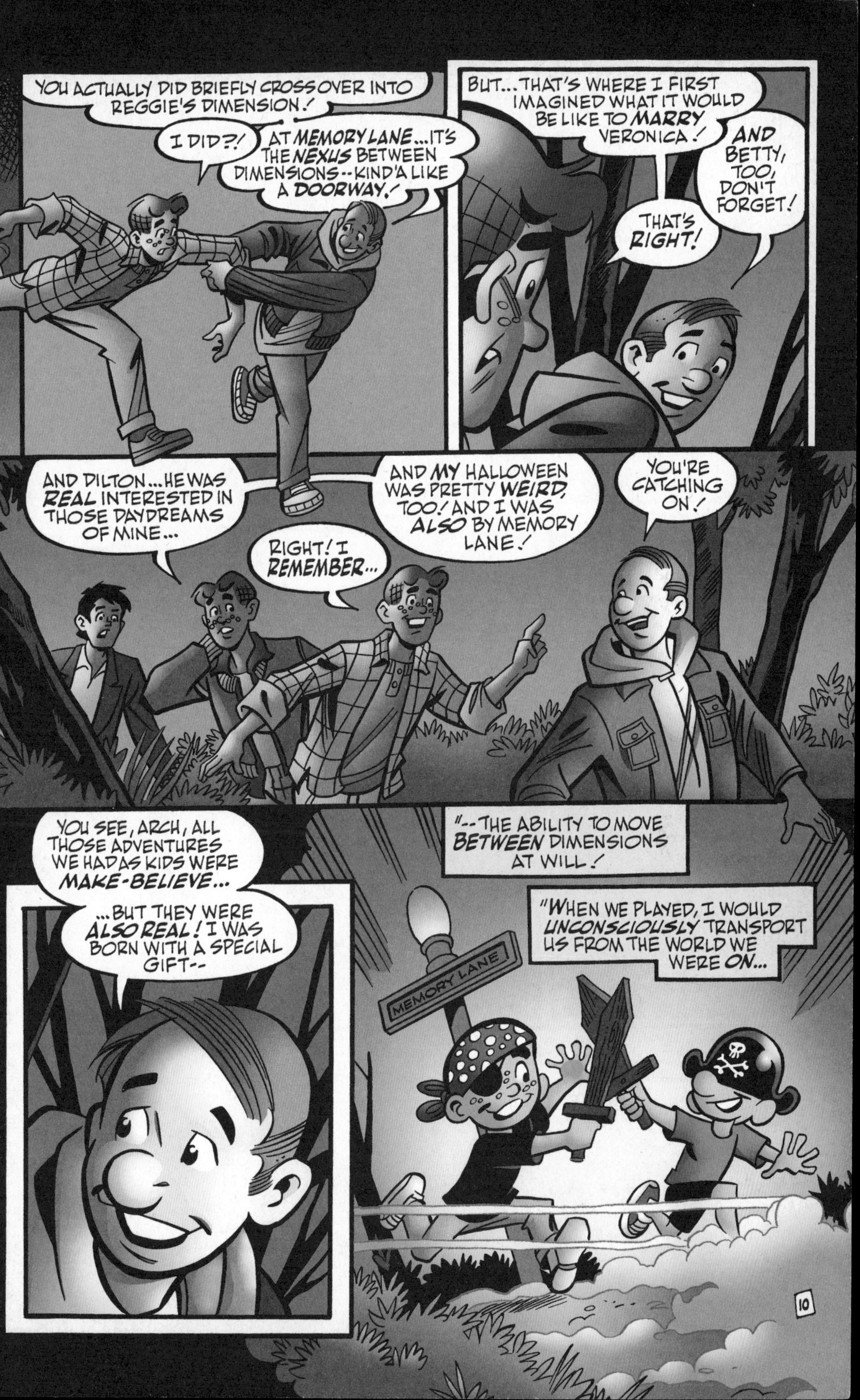

YOU ACTUALLY DID BRIEFLY CROSS OVER INTO REGGIE'S DIMENSION!
I DID?!
AT MEMORY LANE...IT'S THE NEXUS BETWEEN DIMENSIONS--KIND'A LIKE A DOORWAY!
BUT...THAT'S WHERE I FIRST IMAGINED WHAT IT WOULD BE LIKE TO MARRY VERONICA!
AND BETTY, TOO, DON'T FORGET!
THAT'S RIGHT!
AND DILTON...HE WAS REAL INTERESTED IN THOSE DAYDREAMS OF MINE...
AND MY HALLOWEEN WAS PRETTY WEIRD, TOO! AND I WAS ALSO BY MEMORY LANE!
RIGHT! I REMEMBER...
YOU'RE CATCHING ON!
YOU SEE, ARCH, ALL THOSE ADVENTURES WE HAD AS KIDS WERE MAKE-BELIEVE...
...BUT THEY WERE ALSO REAL! I WAS BORN WITH A SPECIAL GIFT--
"--THE ABILITY TO MOVE BETWEEN DIMENSIONS AT WILL!
"WHEN WE PLAYED, I WOULD UNCONSCIOUSLY TRANSPORT US FROM THE WORLD WE WERE ON...
MEMORY LANE
10

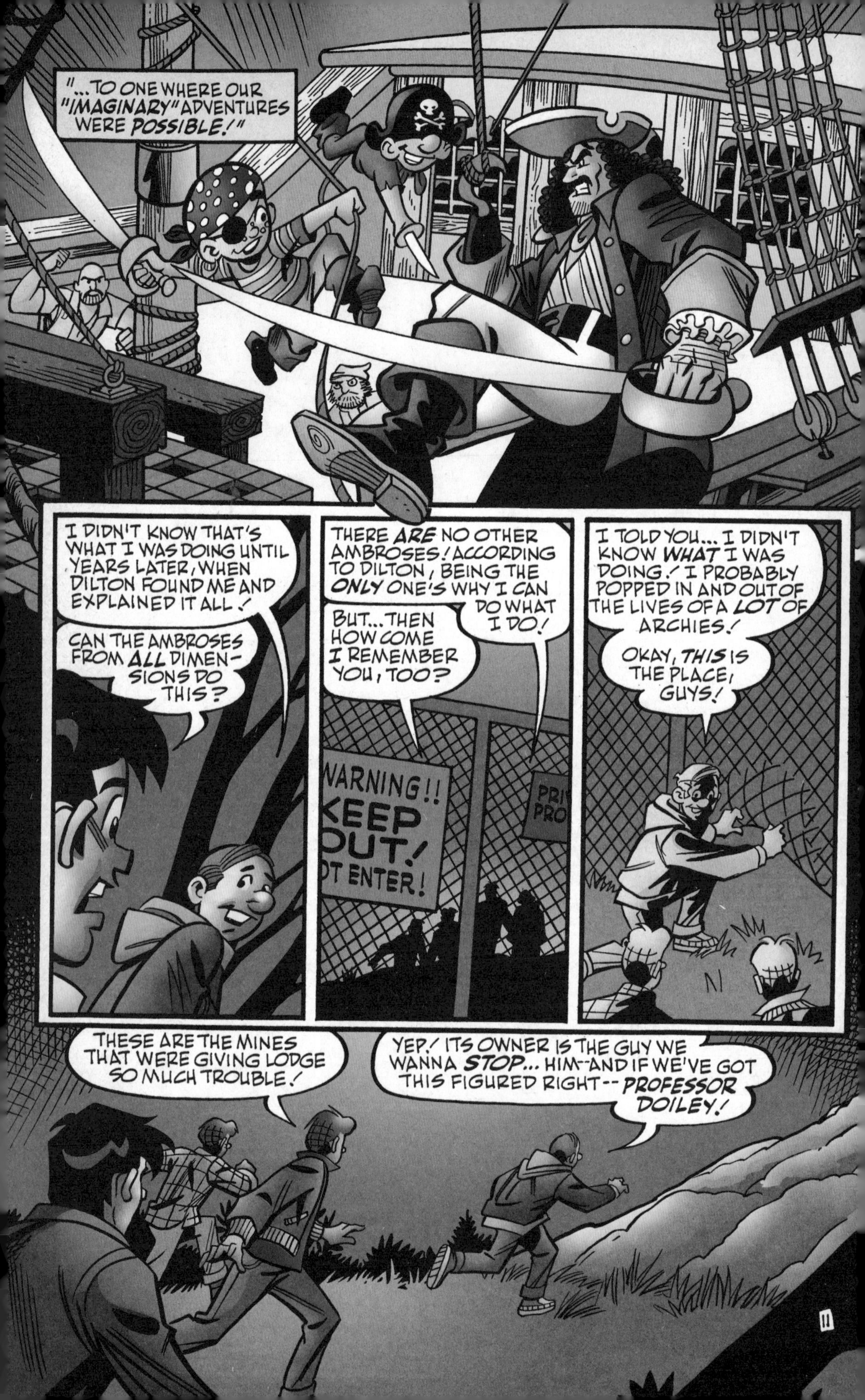
"...TO ONE WHERE OUR "IMAGINARY" ADVENTURES WERE POSSIBLE!"
I DIDN'T KNOW THAT'S WHAT I WAS DOING UNTIL YEARS LATER, WHEN DILTON FOUND ME AND EXPLAINED IT ALL!
CAN THE AMBROSES FROM ALL DIMENSIONS DO THIS?
THERE ARE NO OTHER AMBROSES! ACCORDING TO DILTON, BEING THE ONLY ONE'S WHY I CAN DO WHAT I DO!
BUT... THEN HOW COME I REMEMBER YOU, TOO?
WARNING!! KEEP OUT!
I TOLD YOU... I DIDN'T KNOW WHAT I WAS DOING! I PROBABLY POPPED IN AND OUT OF THE LIVES OF A LOT OF ARCHIES!
OKAY, THIS IS THE PLACE, GUYS!
THESE ARE THE MINES THAT WERE GIVING LODGE SO MUCH TROUBLE!
YEP! ITS OWNER IS THE GUY WE WANNA STOP... HIM--AND IF WE'VE GOT THIS FIGURED RIGHT--PROFESSOR DOILEY!

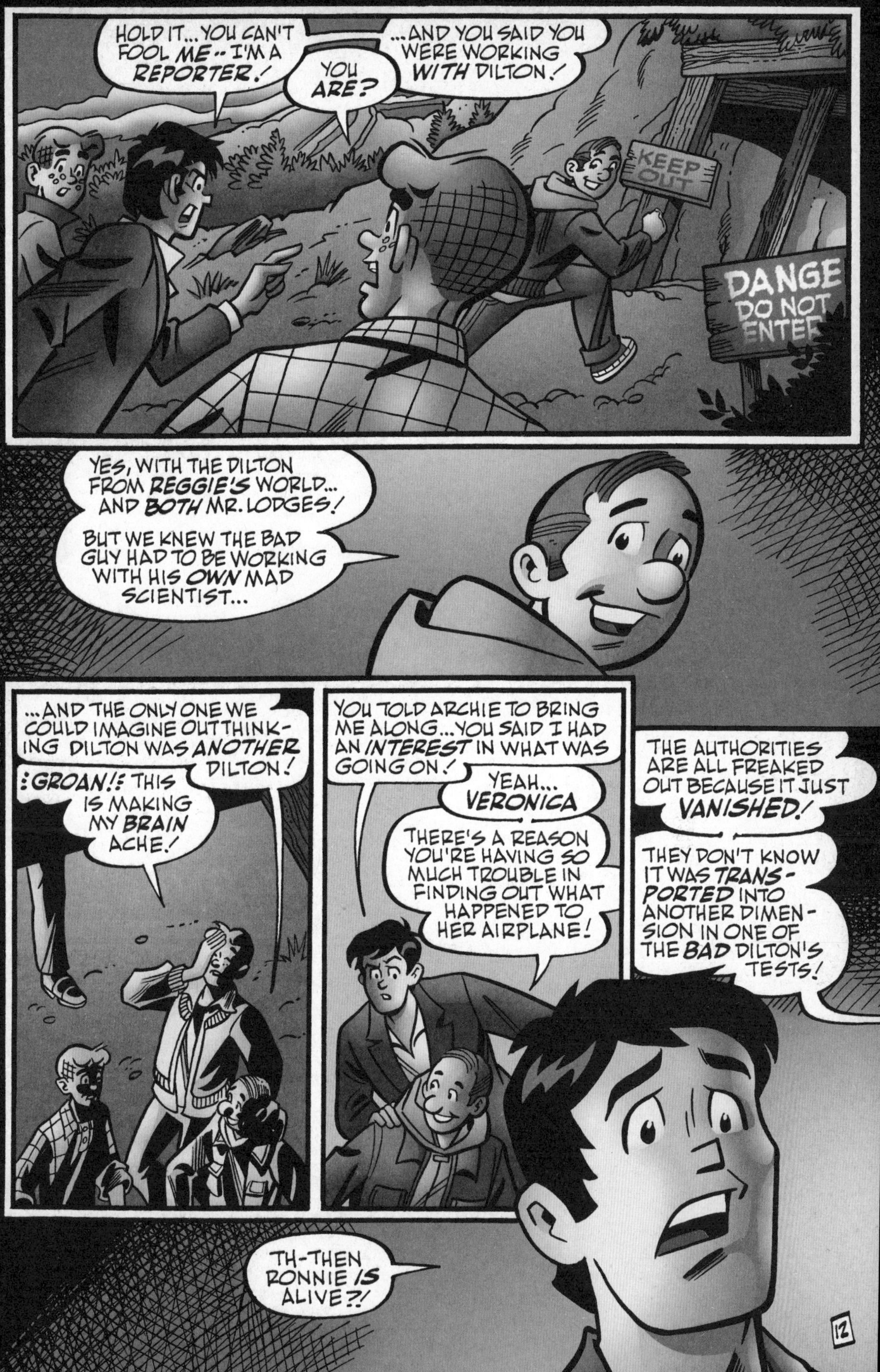
HOLD IT... YOU CAN'T FOOL ME -- I'M A REPORTER!
YOU ARE?
...AND YOU SAID YOU WERE WORKING WITH DILTON!
KEEP OUT
DANGE DO NOT ENTER
YES, WITH THE DILTON FROM REGGIE'S WORLD... AND BOTH MR. LODGES!
BUT WE KNEW THE BAD GUY HAD TO BE WORKING WITH HIS OWN MAD SCIENTIST...
...AND THE ONLY ONE WE COULD IMAGINE OUTTHINKING DILTON WAS ANOTHER DILTON!
:GROAN!: THIS IS MAKING MY BRAIN ACHE!
YOU TOLD ARCHIE TO BRING ME ALONG... YOU SAID I HAD AN INTEREST IN WHAT WAS GOING ON!
YEAH... VERONICA
THERE'S A REASON YOU'RE HAVING SO MUCH TROUBLE IN FINDING OUT WHAT HAPPENED TO HER AIRPLANE!
THE AUTHORITIES ARE ALL FREAKED OUT BECAUSE IT JUST VANISHED!
THEY DON'T KNOW IT WAS TRANSPORTED INTO ANOTHER DIMENSION IN ONE OF THE BAD DILTON'S TESTS!
TH-THEN RONNIE IS ALIVE?!
12

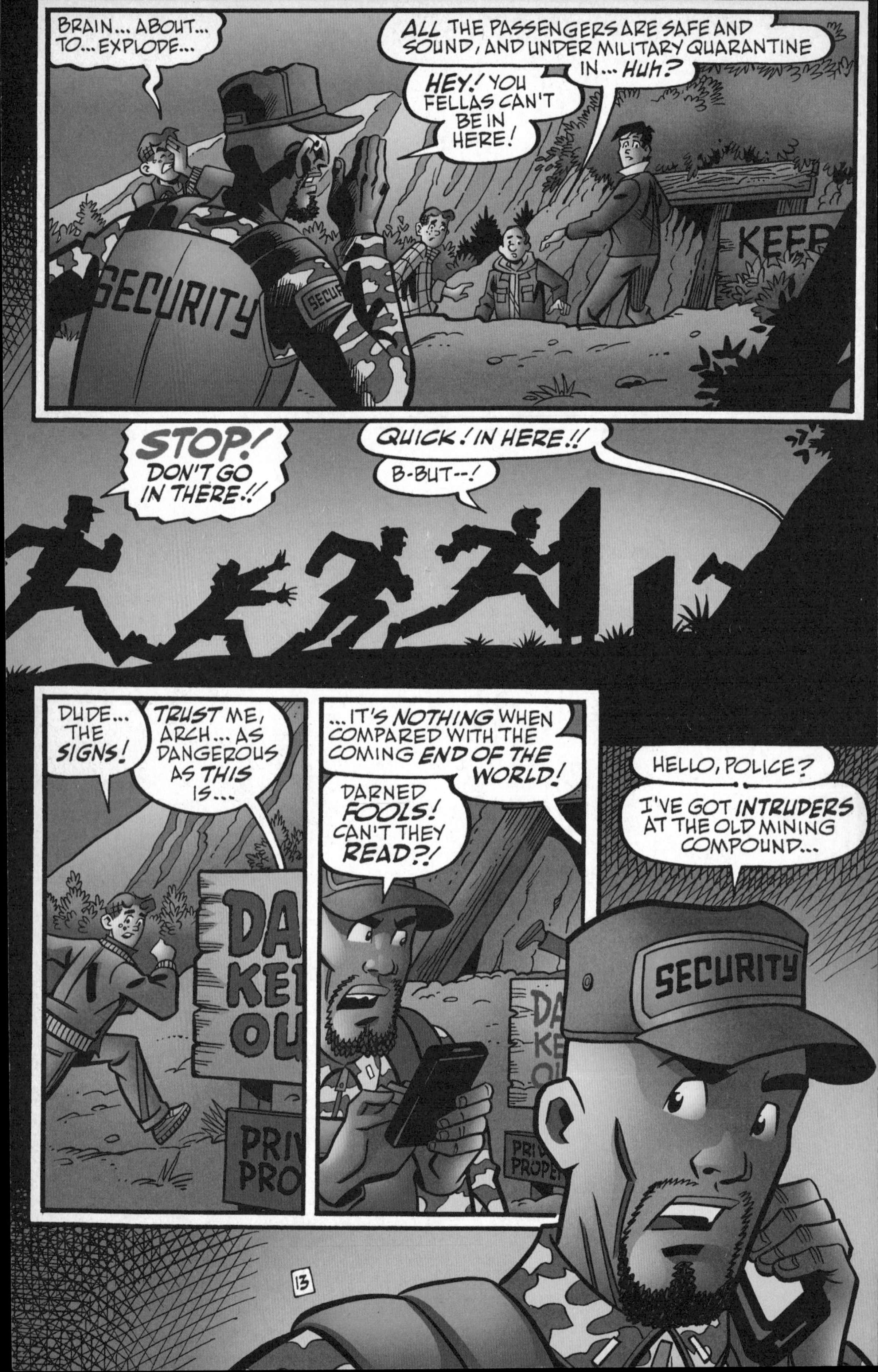
BRAIN... ABOUT... TO... EXPLODE...
ALL THE PASSENGERS ARE SAFE AND SOUND, AND UNDER MILITARY QUARANTINE IN... HUH?
HEY! YOU FELLAS CAN'T BE IN HERE!
SECURITY
KEEP
STOP! DON'T GO IN THERE!!
QUICK! IN HERE!!
B-BUT--!
DUDE... THE SIGNS!
TRUST ME, ARCH... AS DANGEROUS AS THIS IS...
...IT'S NOTHING WHEN COMPARED WITH THE COMING END OF THE WORLD!
DARNED FOOLS! CAN'T THEY READ?!
HELLO, POLICE?
I'VE GOT INTRUDERS AT THE OLD MINING COMPOUND...
SECURITY
13

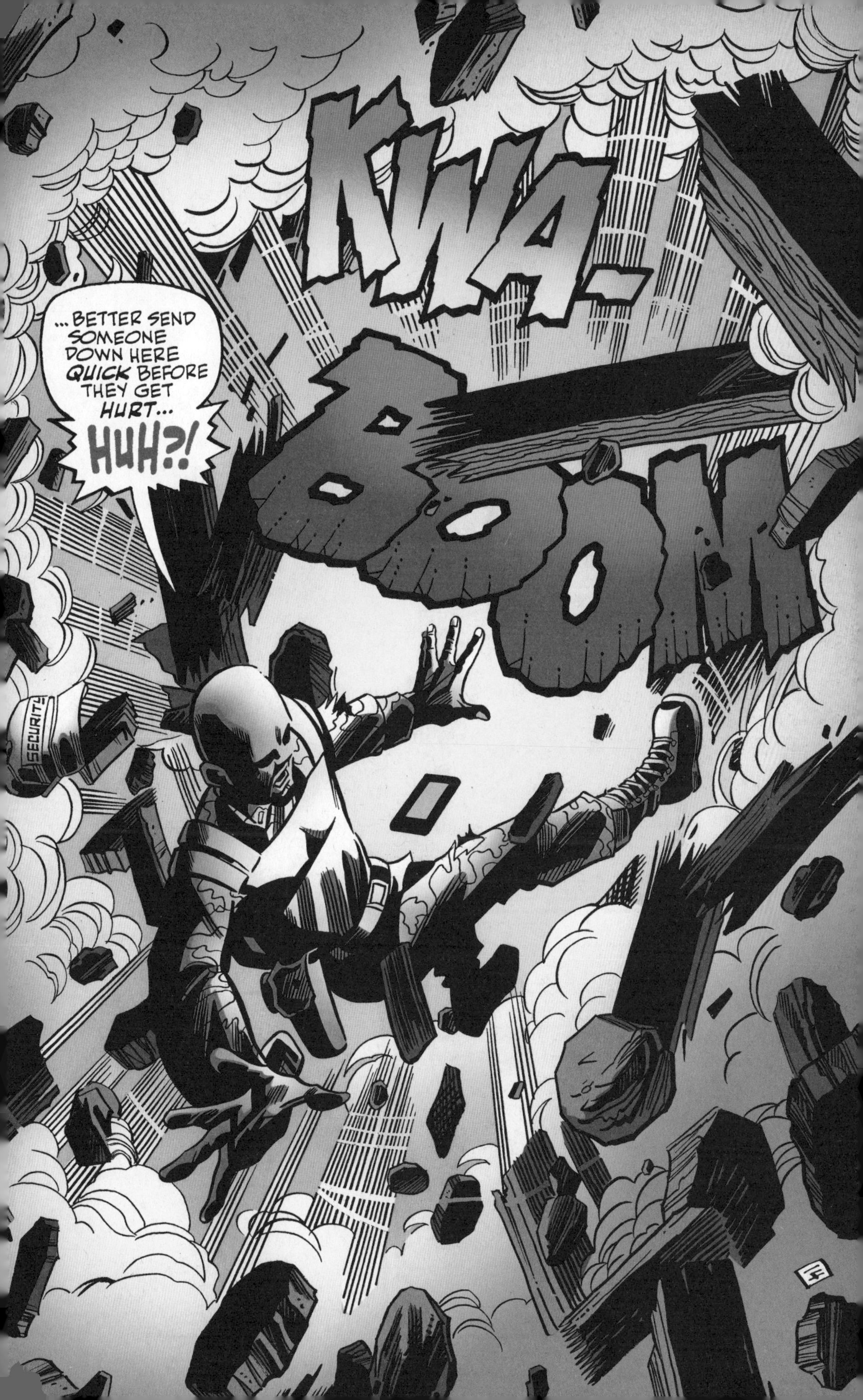
KWA-
BOOM
...BETTER SEND SOMEONE DOWN HERE QUICK BEFORE THEY GET HURT... HUH?!
SECURITY

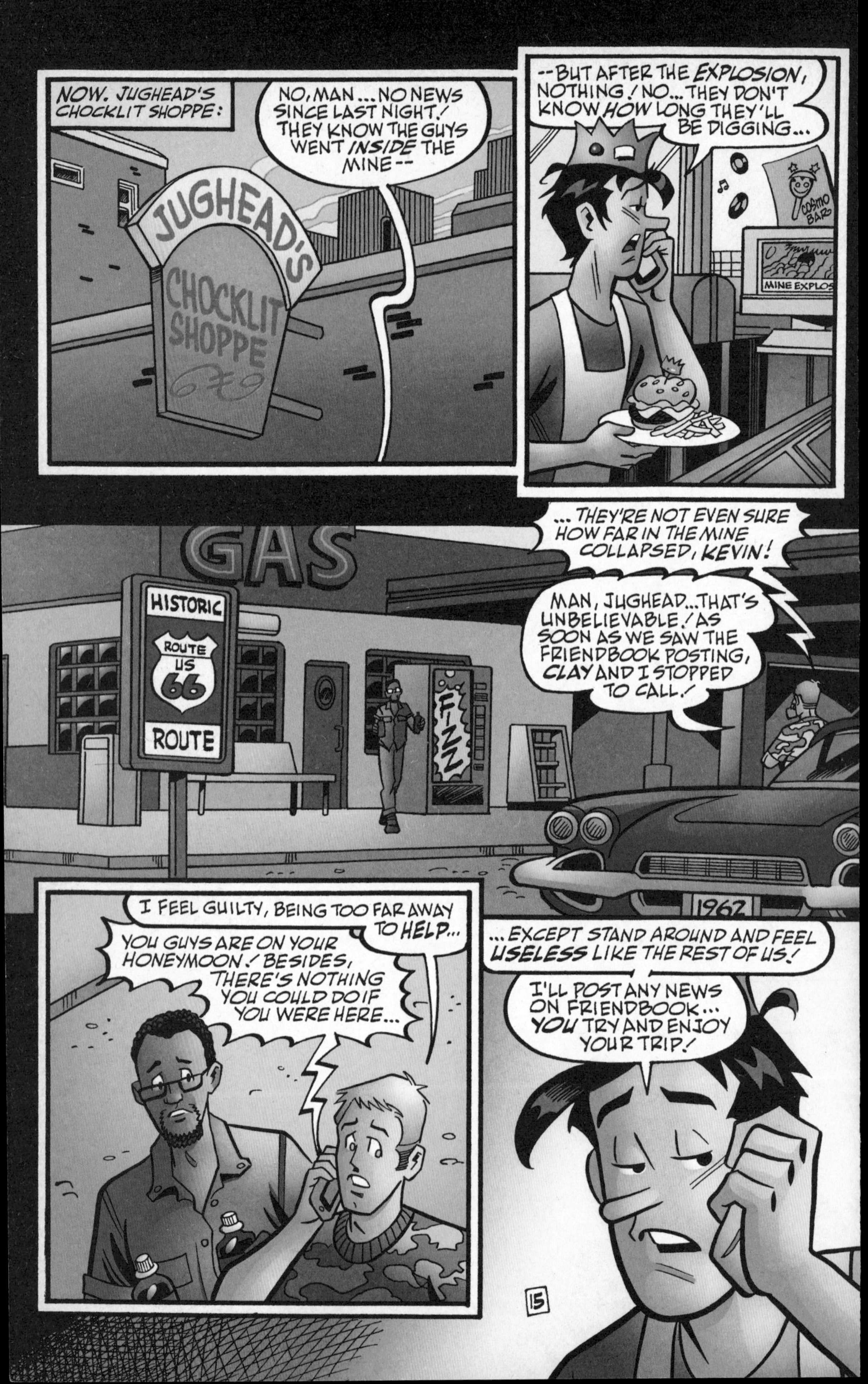
NOW. JUGHEAD'S CHOCKLIT SHOPPE:
NO, MAN ... NO NEWS SINCE LAST NIGHT! THEY KNOW THE GUYS WENT INSIDE THE MINE --
JUGHEAD'S CHOCKLIT SHOPPE
--BUT AFTER THE EXPLOSION, NOTHING! NO... THEY DON'T KNOW HOW LONG THEY'LL BE DIGGING...
COSMO BAR
MINE EXPLOS
GAS
HISTORIC ROUTE US 66 ROUTE
FIZZ
... THEY'RE NOT EVEN SURE HOW FAR IN THE MINE COLLAPSED, KEVIN!
MAN, JUGHEAD...THAT'S UNBELIEVABLE! AS SOON AS WE SAW THE FRIENDBOOK POSTING, CLAY AND I STOPPED TO CALL!
1962
I FEEL GUILTY, BEING TOO FAR AWAY TO HELP...
YOU GUYS ARE ON YOUR HONEYMOON! BESIDES, THERE'S NOTHING YOU COULD DO IF YOU WERE HERE...
... EXCEPT STAND AROUND AND FEEL USELESS LIKE THE REST OF US!
I'LL POST ANY NEWS ON FRIENDBOOK... YOU TRY AND ENJOY YOUR TRIP!
15

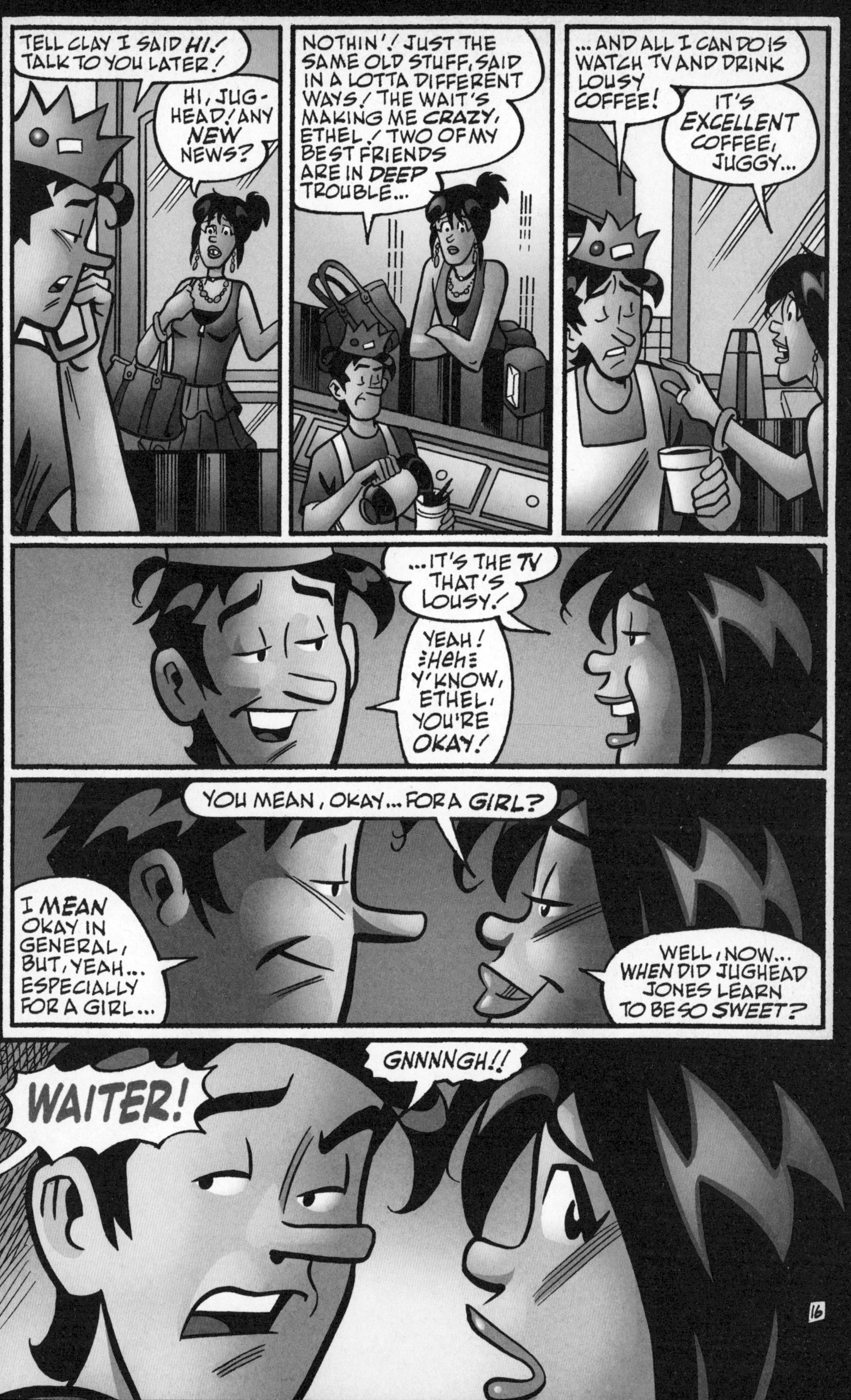
TELL CLAY I SAID HI! TALK TO YOU LATER!
HI, JUG-HEAD! ANY NEW NEWS?
NOTHIN'! JUST THE SAME OLD STUFF, SAID IN A LOTTA DIFFERENT WAYS! THE WAIT'S MAKING ME CRAZY, ETHEL! TWO OF MY BEST FRIENDS ARE IN DEEP TROUBLE...
...AND ALL I CAN DO IS WATCH TV AND DRINK LOUSY COFFEE!
IT'S EXCELLENT COFFEE, JUGGY...
...IT'S THE TV THAT'S LOUSY!
YEAH! HEH Y'KNOW, ETHEL, YOU'RE OKAY!
YOU MEAN, OKAY... FOR A GIRL?
I MEAN OKAY IN GENERAL, BUT, YEAH... ESPECIALLY FOR A GIRL...
WELL, NOW... WHEN DID JUGHEAD JONES LEARN TO BE SO SWEET?
GNNNNGH!!
WAITER!

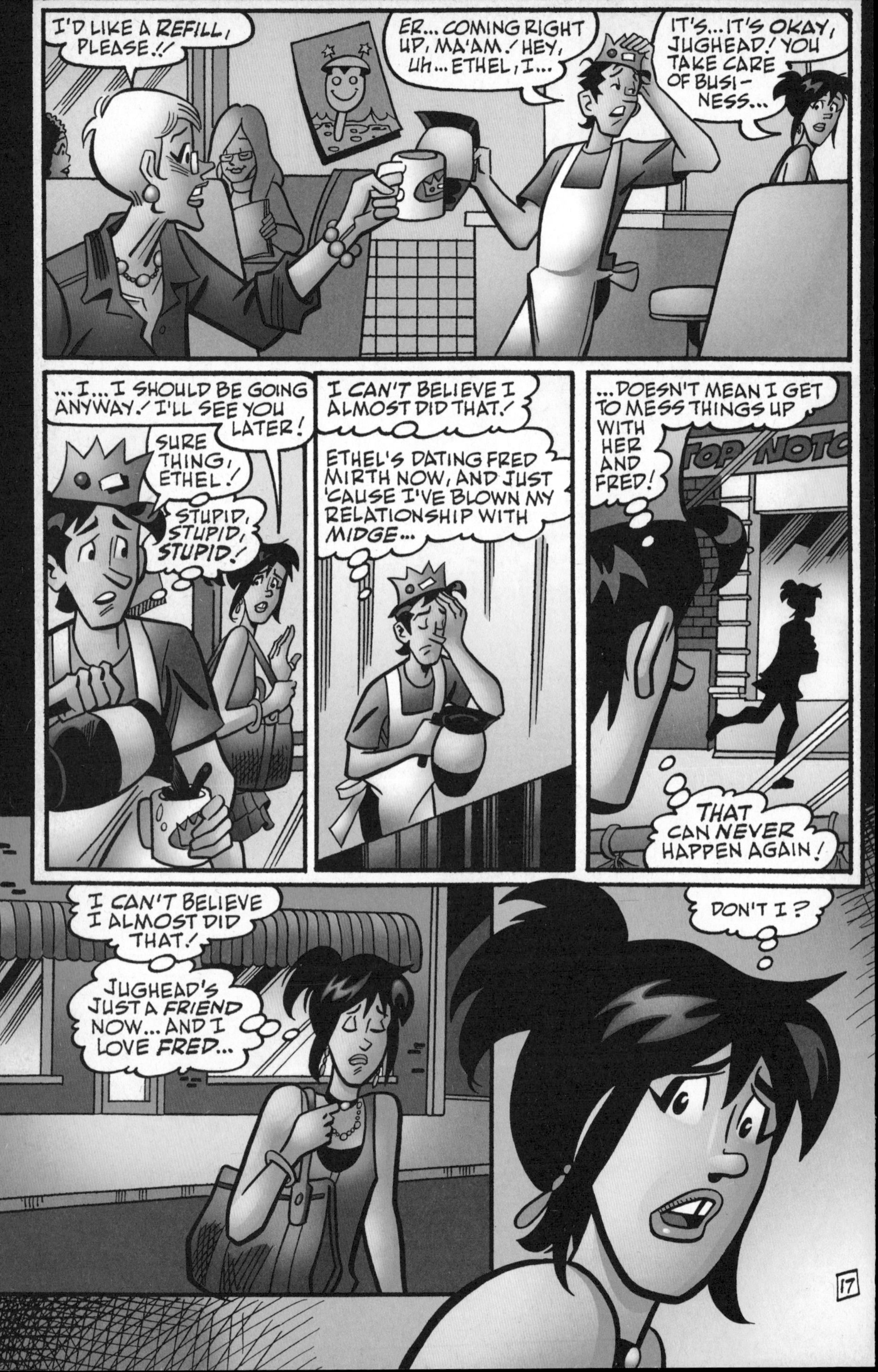
I'D LIKE A REFILL, PLEASE!!
ER... COMING RIGHT UP, MA'AM! HEY, UH... ETHEL, I...
IT'S... IT'S OKAY, JUGHEAD! YOU TAKE CARE OF BUSI- NESS...
...I... I SHOULD BE GOING ANYWAY! I'LL SEE YOU LATER!
SURE THING, ETHEL!
STUPID, STUPID, STUPID!
I CAN'T BELIEVE I ALMOST DID THAT!
ETHEL'S DATING FRED MIRTH NOW, AND JUST 'CAUSE I'VE BLOWN MY RELATIONSHIP WITH MIDGE...
...DOESN'T MEAN I GET TO MESS THINGS UP WITH HER AND FRED!
TOP NOTC
THAT CAN NEVER HAPPEN AGAIN!
I CAN'T BELIEVE I ALMOST DID THAT!
JUGHEAD'S JUST A FRIEND NOW... AND I LOVE FRED...
DON'T I?

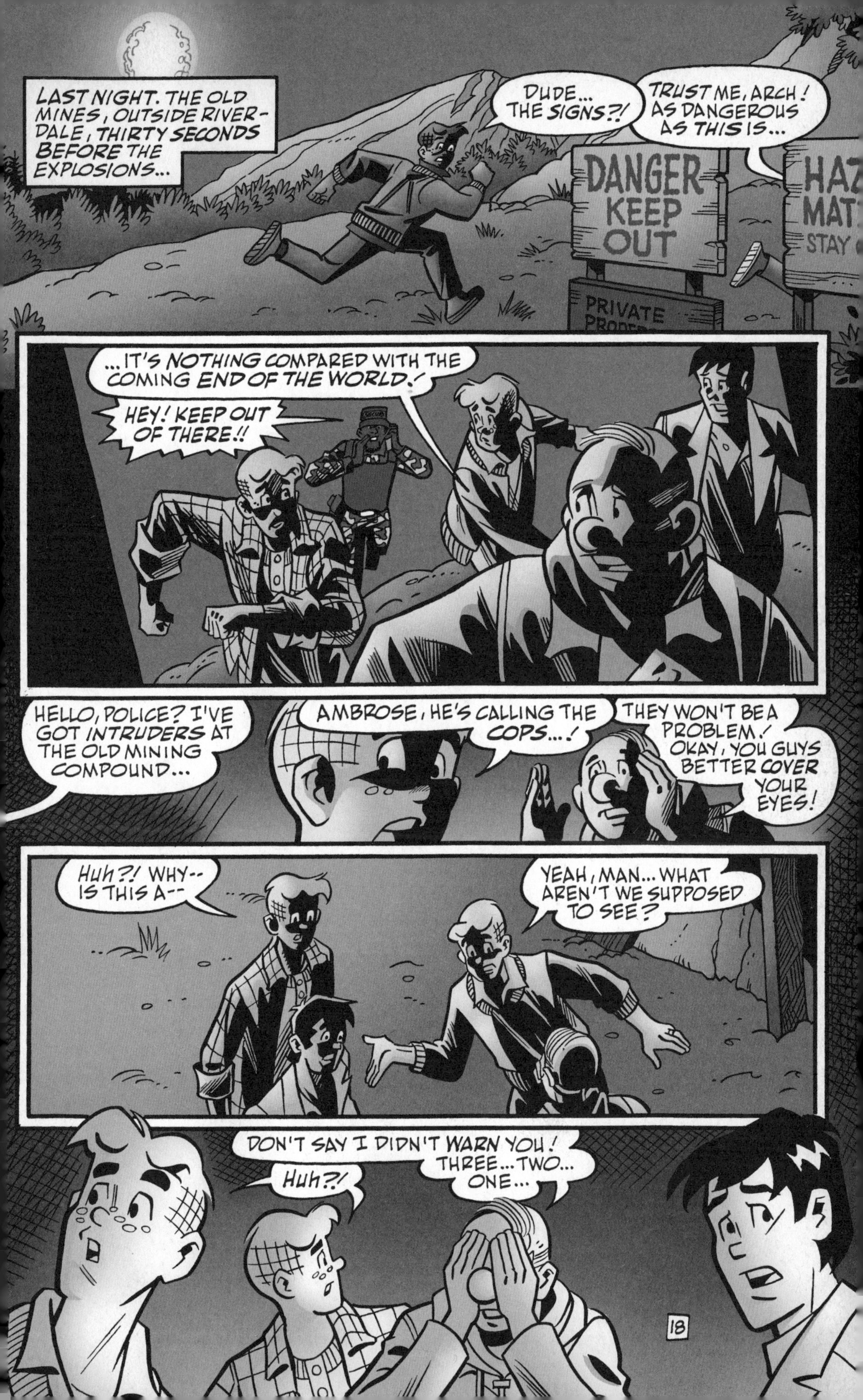
LAST NIGHT. THE OLD MINES, OUTSIDE RIVERDALE, THIRTY SECONDS BEFORE THE EXPLOSIONS...
DUDE... THE SIGNS?!
TRUST ME, ARCH! AS DANGEROUS AS THIS IS...
DANGER KEEP OUT
PRIVATE
...IT'S NOTHING COMPARED WITH THE COMING END OF THE WORLD!
HEY! KEEP OUT OF THERE!!
HELLO, POLICE? I'VE GOT INTRUDERS AT THE OLD MINING COMPOUND...
AMBROSE, HE'S CALLING THE COPS...!
THEY WON'T BE A PROBLEM! OKAY, YOU GUYS BETTER COVER YOUR EYES!
HUH?! WHY-- IS THIS A--
YEAH, MAN... WHAT AREN'T WE SUPPOSED TO SEE?
DON'T SAY I DIDN'T WARN YOU! THREE... TWO... ONE...
HUH?!
18

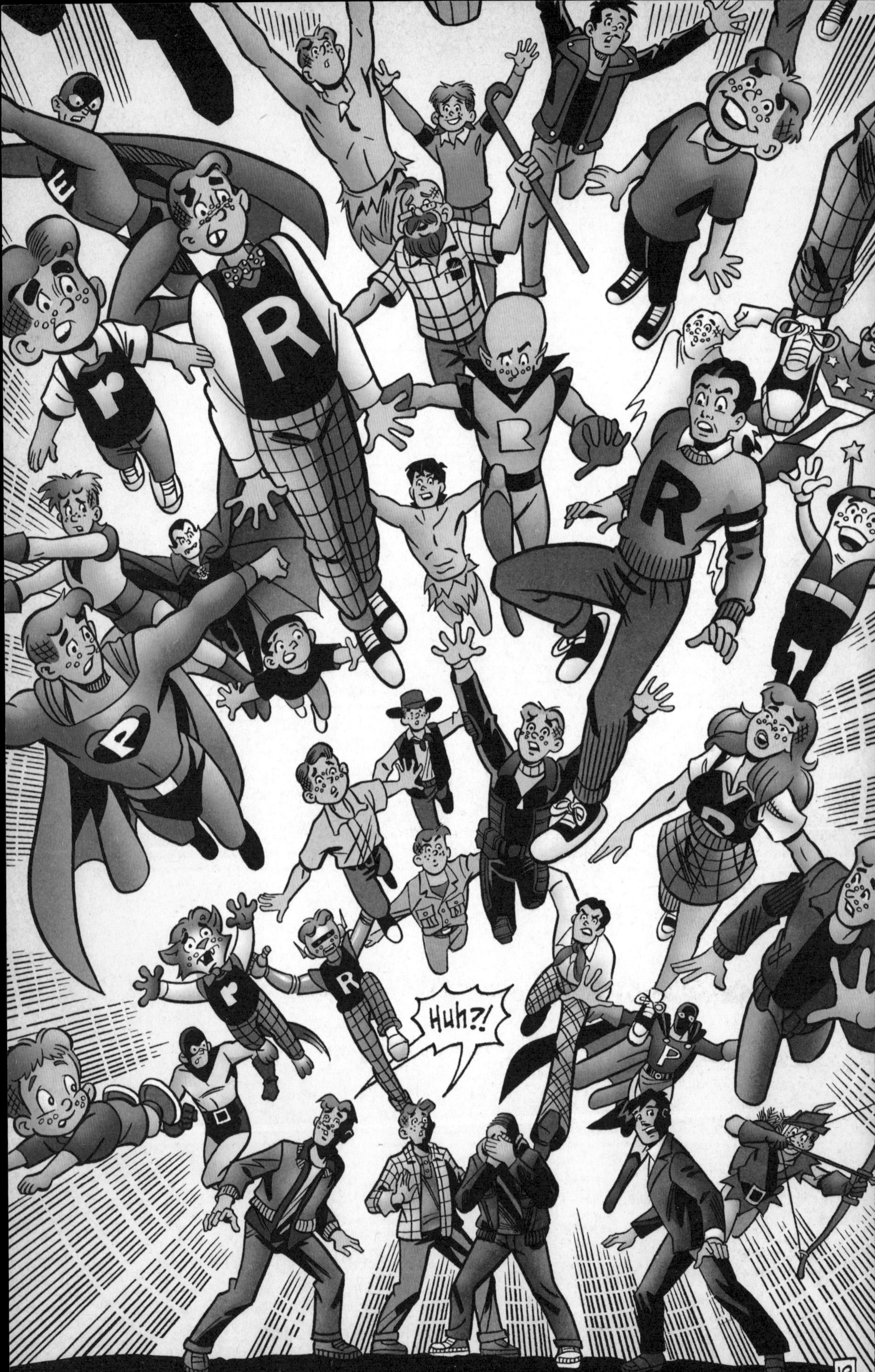
Huh?!

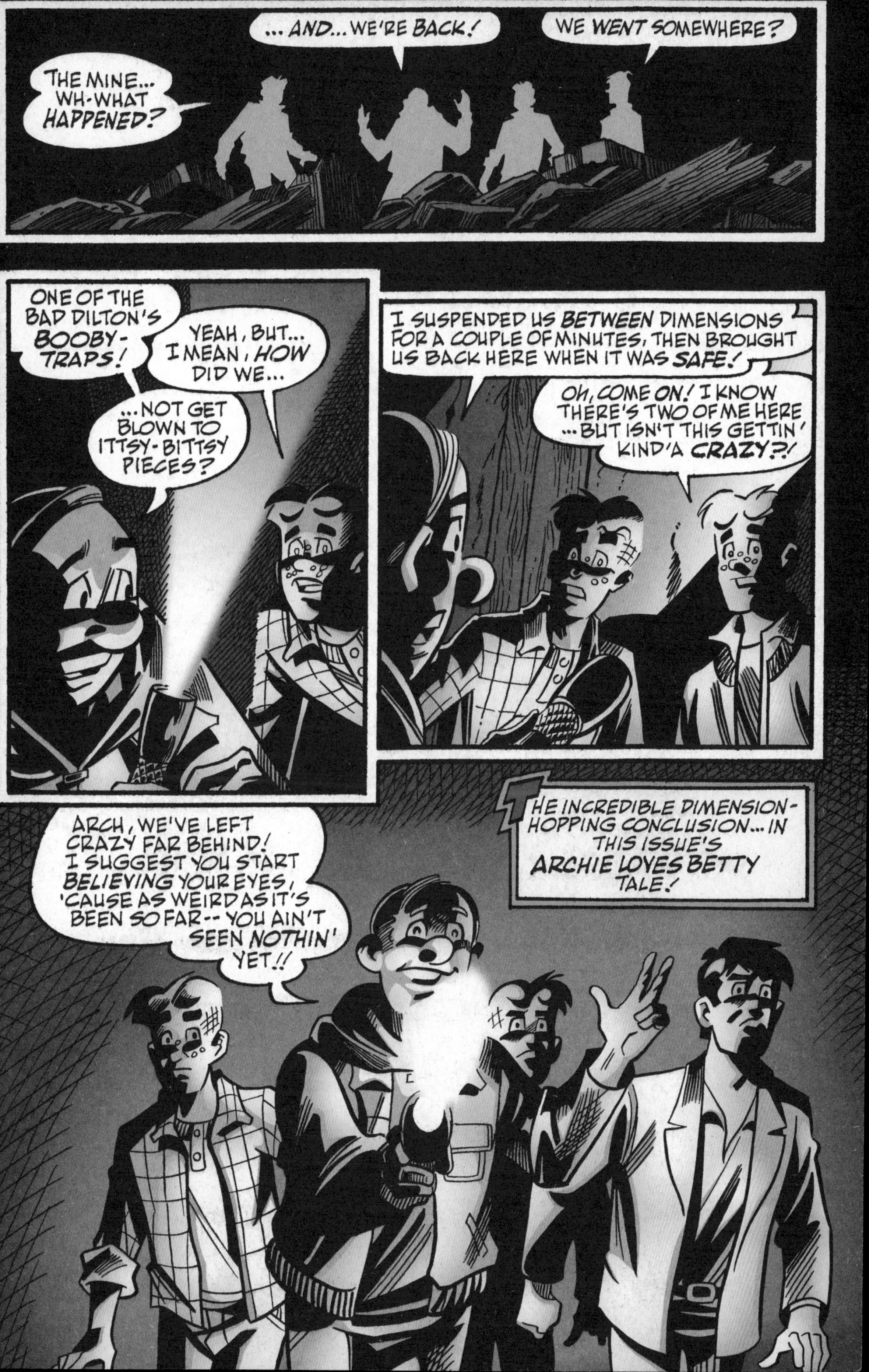
THE MINE... WH-WHAT HAPPENED?
...AND...WE'RE BACK!
WE WENT SOMEWHERE?
ONE OF THE BAD DILTON'S BOOBY-TRAPS!
YEAH, BUT... I MEAN, HOW DID WE...
...NOT GET BLOWN TO ITTSY-BITTSY PIECES?
I SUSPENDED US BETWEEN DIMENSIONS FOR A COUPLE OF MINUTES, THEN BROUGHT US BACK HERE WHEN IT WAS SAFE!
OH, COME ON! I KNOW THERE'S TWO OF ME HERE ...BUT ISN'T THIS GETTIN' KIND'A CRAZY?!
THE INCREDIBLE DIMENSION-HOPPING CONCLUSION... IN THIS ISSUE'S ARCHIE LOVES BETTY TALE!
ARCH, WE'VE LEFT CRAZY FAR BEHIND! I SUGGEST YOU START BELIEVING YOUR EYES, 'CAUSE AS WEIRD AS IT'S BEEN SO FAR -- YOU AIN'T SEEN NOTHIN' YET!!

"THERE'S *PLENTY* OF ARCHIES IN THE MULTIVERSE!"

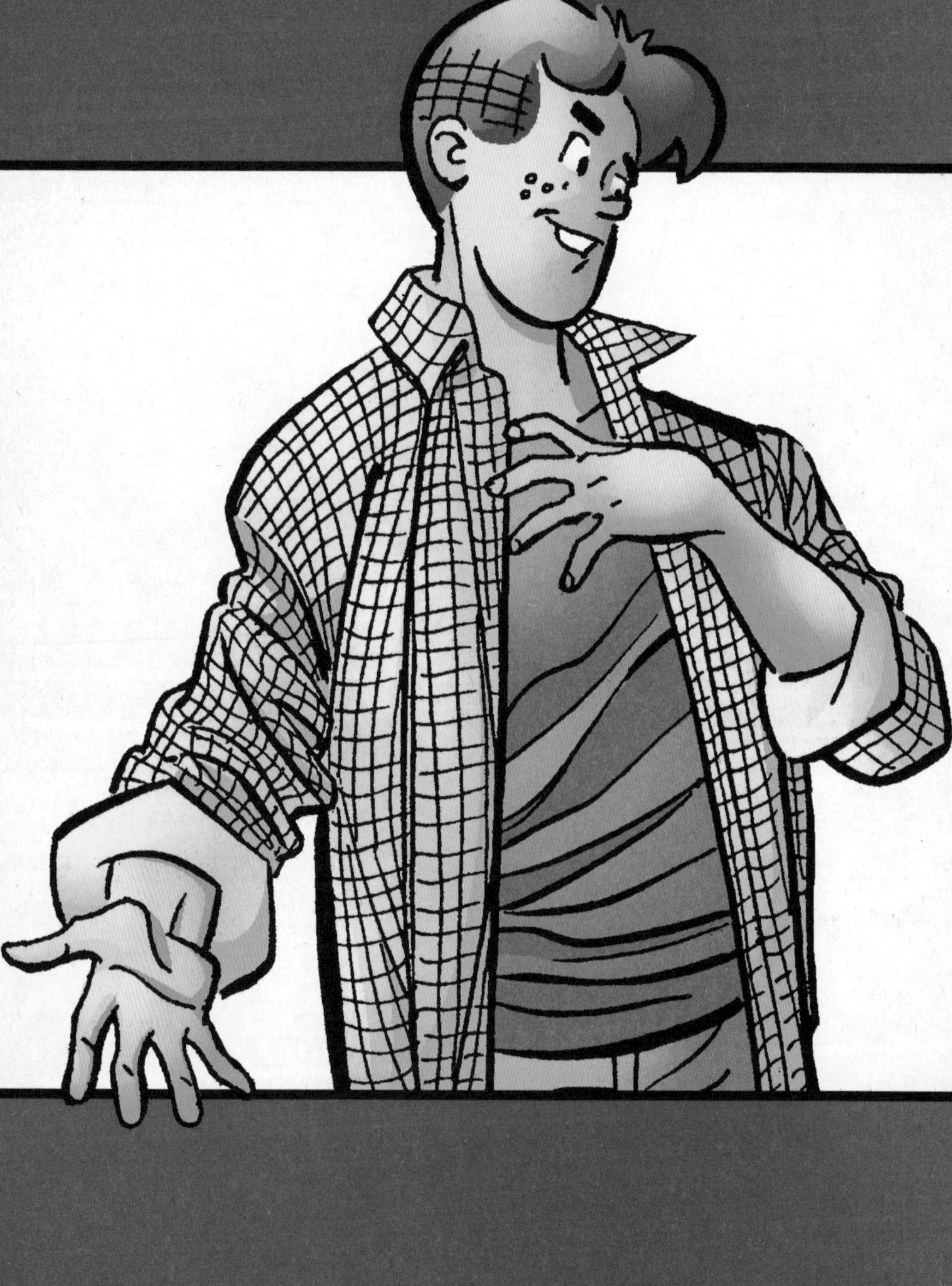

- ARCHIE ANDREWS

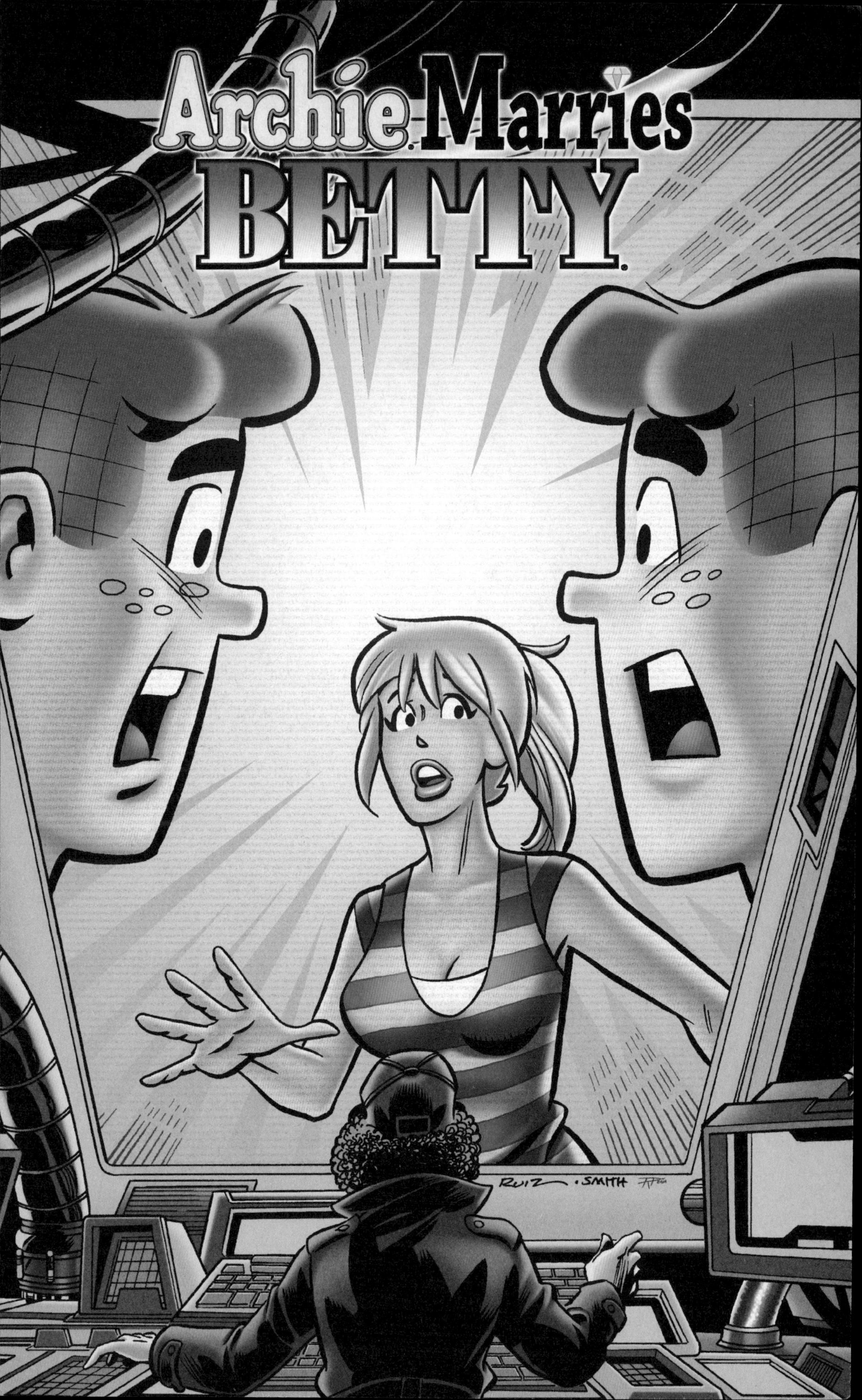
Archie Marries
BETTY
RUIZ · SMITH

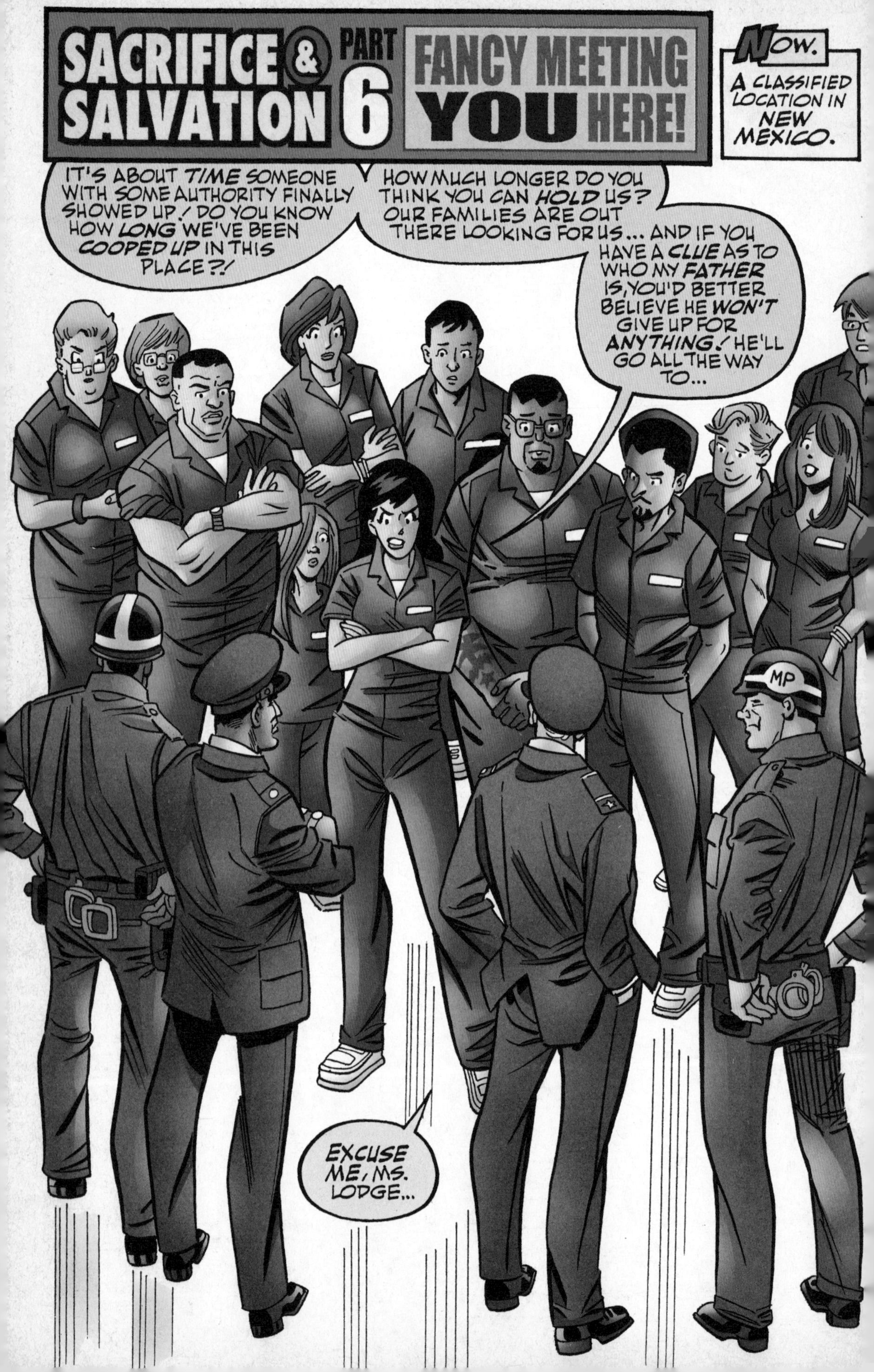
SACRIFICE & SALVATION PART 6
FANCY MEETING YOU HERE!
NOW. A CLASSIFIED LOCATION IN NEW MEXICO.
IT'S ABOUT TIME SOMEONE WITH SOME AUTHORITY FINALLY SHOWED UP! DO YOU KNOW HOW LONG WE'VE BEEN COOPED UP IN THIS PLACE?!
HOW MUCH LONGER DO YOU THINK YOU CAN HOLD US? OUR FAMILIES ARE OUT THERE LOOKING FOR US... AND IF YOU HAVE A CLUE AS TO WHO MY FATHER IS, YOU'D BETTER BELIEVE HE WON'T GIVE UP FOR ANYTHING! HE'LL GO ALL THE WAY TO...
MP
EXCUSE ME, MS. LODGE...

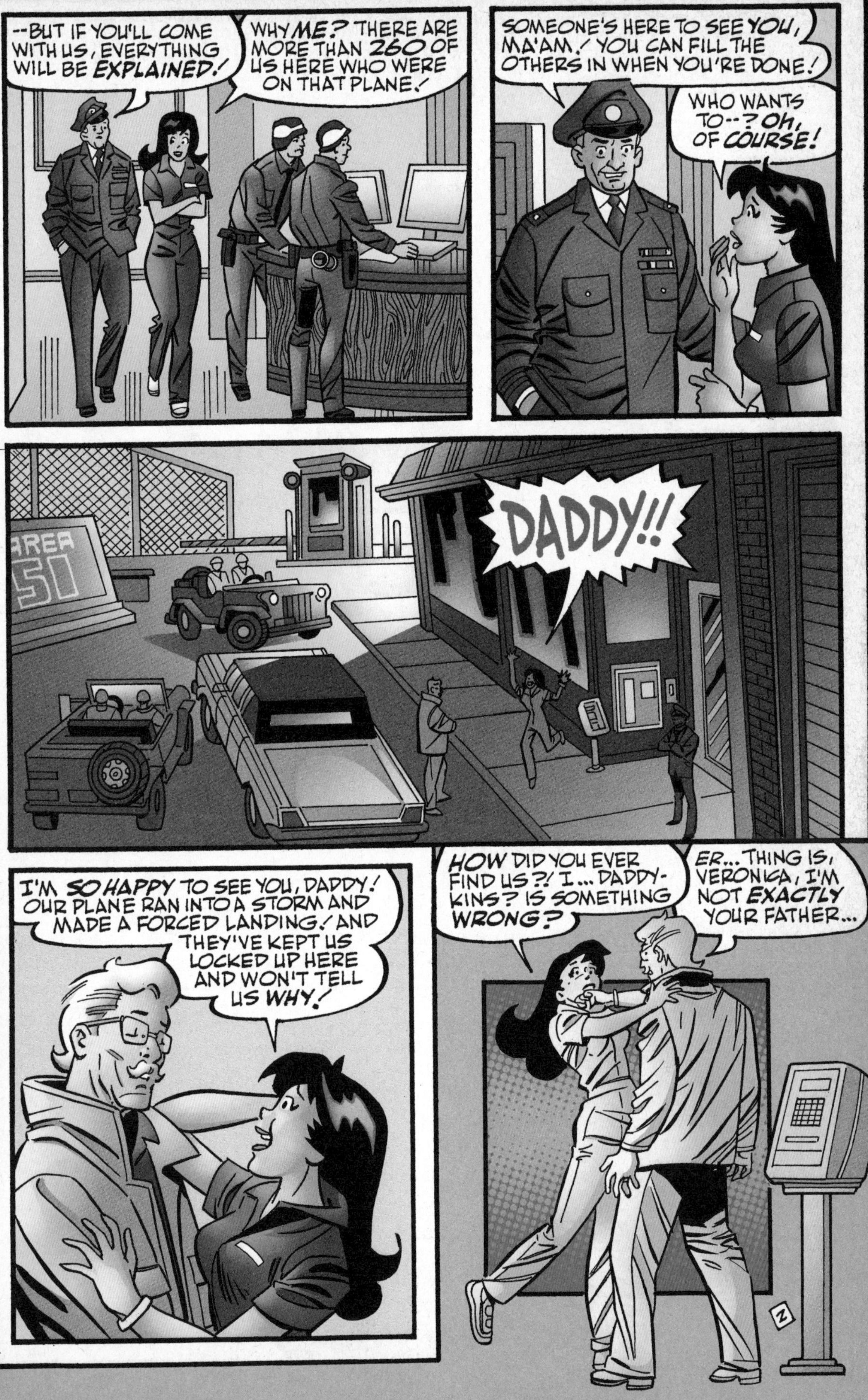
--BUT IF YOU'LL COME WITH US, EVERYTHING WILL BE EXPLAINED!
WHY ME? THERE ARE MORE THAN 260 OF US HERE WHO WERE ON THAT PLANE!
SOMEONE'S HERE TO SEE YOU, MA'AM! YOU CAN FILL THE OTHERS IN WHEN YOU'RE DONE!
WHO WANTS TO--? OH, OF COURSE!
AREA 51
DADDY!!
I'M SO HAPPY TO SEE YOU, DADDY! OUR PLANE RAN INTO A STORM AND MADE A FORCED LANDING! AND THEY'VE KEPT US LOCKED UP HERE AND WON'T TELL US WHY!
HOW DID YOU EVER FIND US?! I... DADDY-KINS? IS SOMETHING WRONG?
ER... THING IS, VERONICA, I'M NOT EXACTLY YOUR FATHER...
2

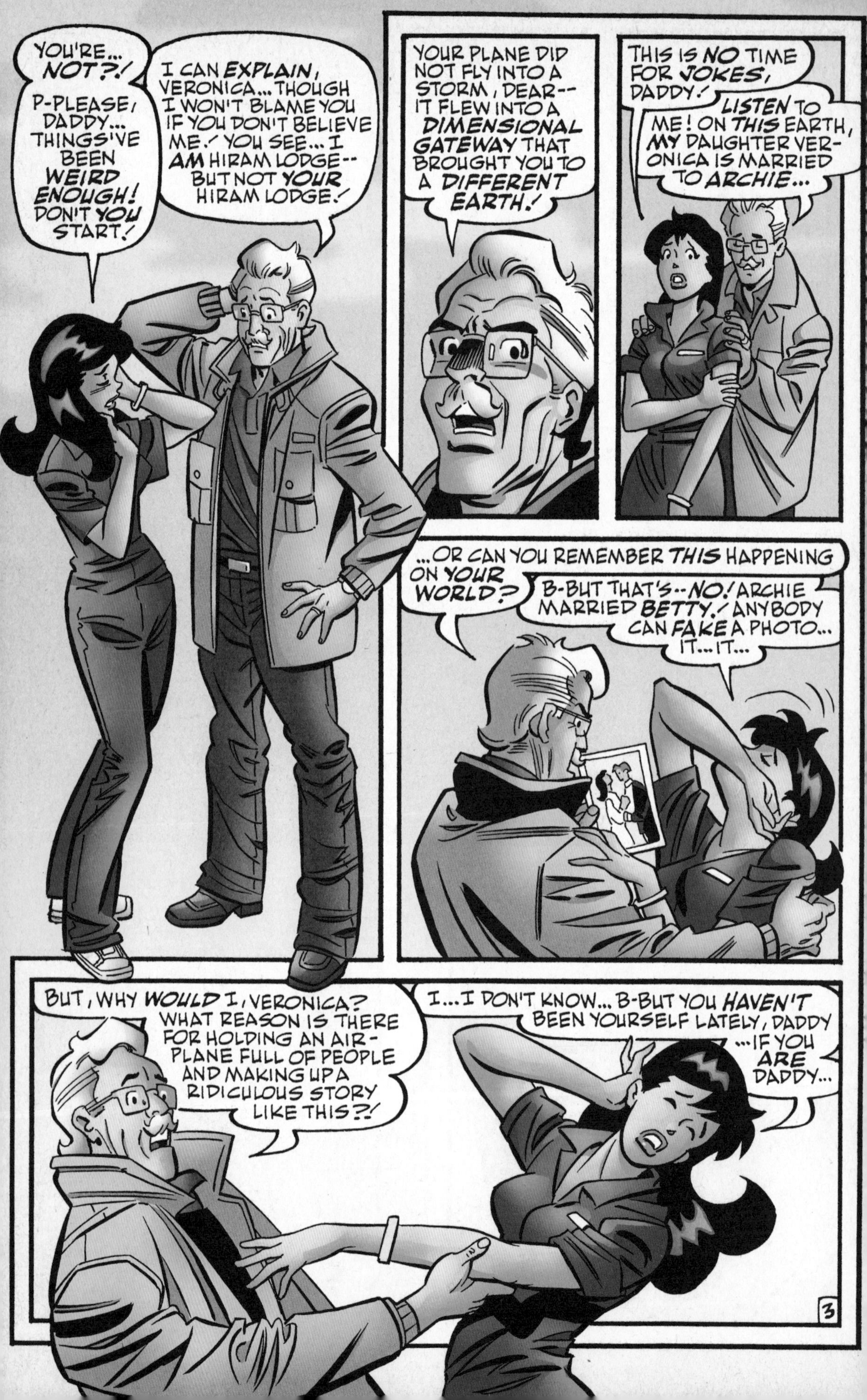
YOU'RE... NOT?!
P-PLEASE, DADDY... THINGS'VE BEEN WEIRD ENOUGH! DON'T YOU START!
I CAN EXPLAIN, VERONICA... THOUGH I WON'T BLAME YOU IF YOU DON'T BELIEVE ME! YOU SEE... I AM HIRAM LODGE-- BUT NOT YOUR HIRAM LODGE!
YOUR PLANE DID NOT FLY INTO A STORM, DEAR-- IT FLEW INTO A DIMENSIONAL GATEWAY THAT BROUGHT YOU TO A DIFFERENT EARTH!
THIS IS NO TIME FOR JOKES, DADDY!
LISTEN TO ME! ON THIS EARTH, MY DAUGHTER VERONICA IS MARRIED TO ARCHIE...
...OR CAN YOU REMEMBER THIS HAPPENING ON YOUR WORLD?
B-BUT THAT'S-- NO! ARCHIE MARRIED BETTY! ANYBODY CAN FAKE A PHOTO... IT... IT...
BUT, WHY WOULD I, VERONICA? WHAT REASON IS THERE FOR HOLDING AN AIRPLANE FULL OF PEOPLE AND MAKING UP A RIDICULOUS STORY LIKE THIS?!
I... I DON'T KNOW... B-BUT YOU HAVEN'T BEEN YOURSELF LATELY, DADDY ...IF YOU ARE DADDY...
3

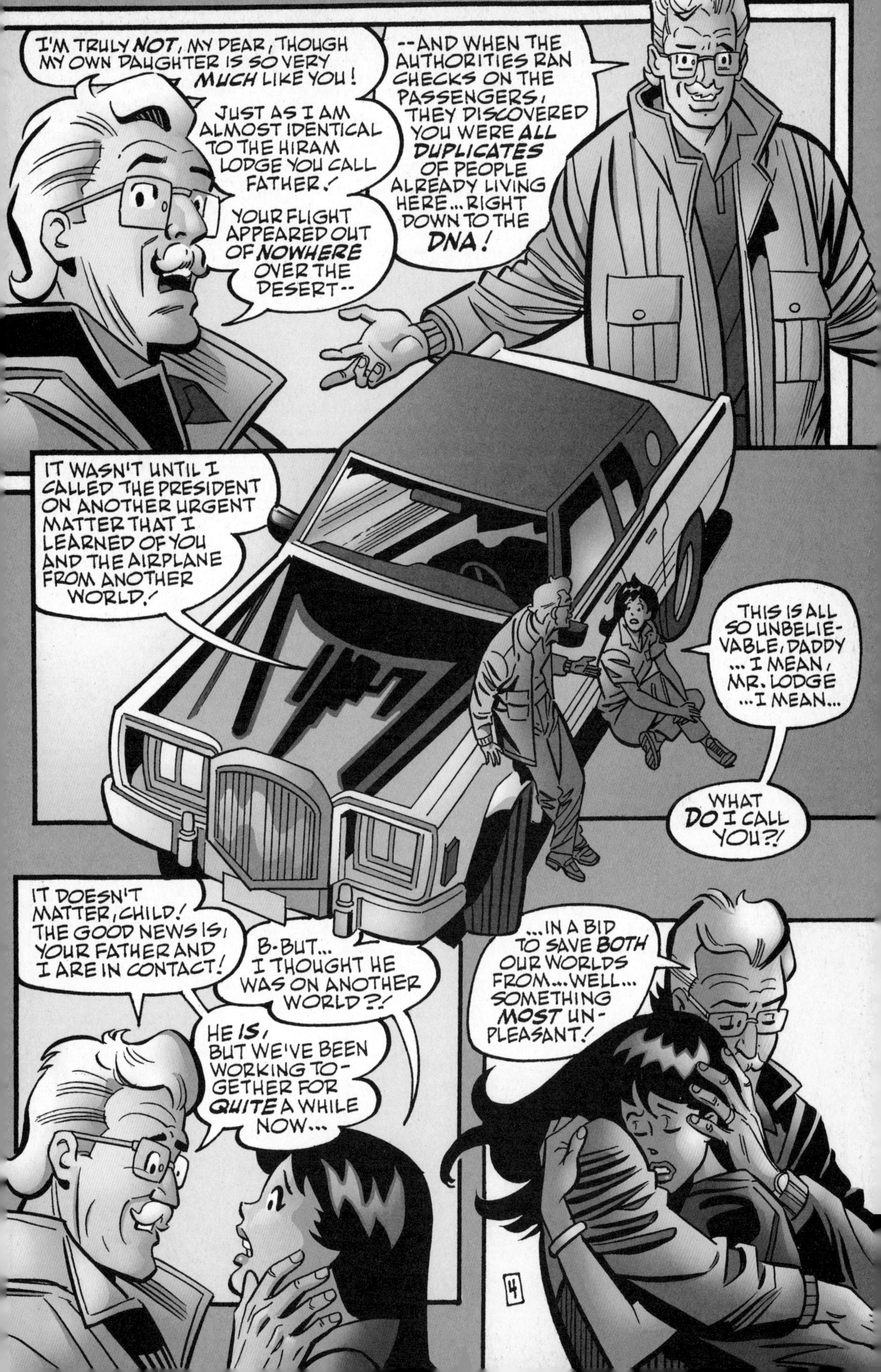

I'M TRULY NOT, MY DEAR, THOUGH MY OWN DAUGHTER IS SO VERY MUCH LIKE YOU!
JUST AS I AM ALMOST IDENTICAL TO THE HIRAM LODGE YOU CALL FATHER!
YOUR FLIGHT APPEARED OUT OF NOWHERE OVER THE DESERT--
--AND WHEN THE AUTHORITIES RAN CHECKS ON THE PASSENGERS, THEY DISCOVERED YOU WERE ALL DUPLICATES OF PEOPLE ALREADY LIVING HERE... RIGHT DOWN TO THE DNA!
IT WASN'T UNTIL I CALLED THE PRESIDENT ON ANOTHER URGENT MATTER THAT I LEARNED OF YOU AND THE AIRPLANE FROM ANOTHER WORLD!
THIS IS ALL SO UNBELIEVABLE, DADDY ... I MEAN, MR. LODGE ...I MEAN...
WHAT DO I CALL YOU?!
IT DOESN'T MATTER, CHILD! THE GOOD NEWS IS, YOUR FATHER AND I ARE IN CONTACT!
B-BUT... I THOUGHT HE WAS ON ANOTHER WORLD?!
HE IS, BUT WE'VE BEEN WORKING TOGETHER FOR QUITE A WHILE NOW...
...IN A BID TO SAVE BOTH OUR WORLDS FROM... WELL... SOMETHING MOST UNPLEASANT!
4

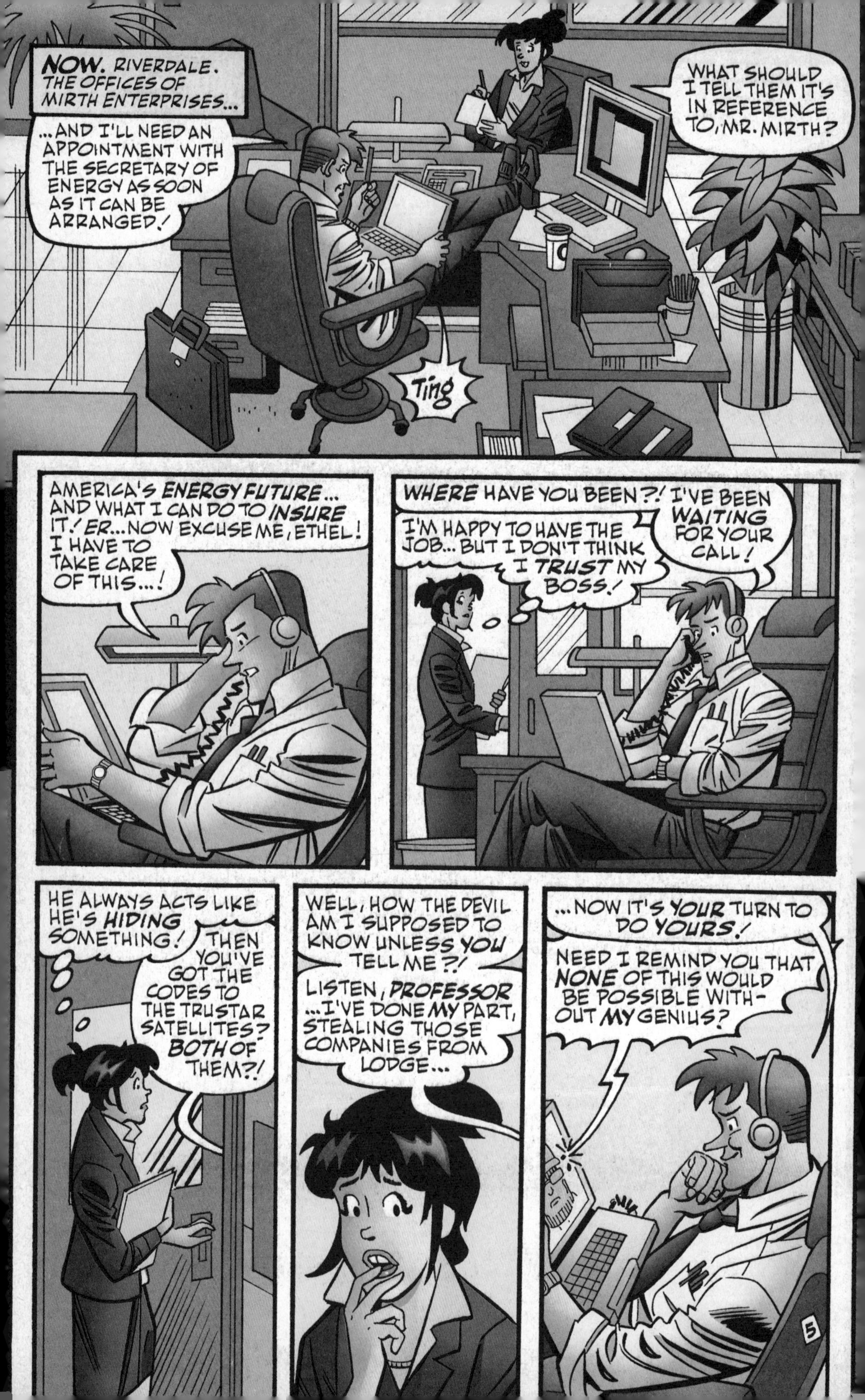

NOW. RIVERDALE. THE OFFICES OF MIRTH ENTERPRISES...
...AND I'LL NEED AN APPOINTMENT WITH THE SECRETARY OF ENERGY AS SOON AS IT CAN BE ARRANGED!
WHAT SHOULD I TELL THEM IT'S IN REFERENCE TO, MR. MIRTH?
Ting
AMERICA'S ENERGY FUTURE... AND WHAT I CAN DO TO INSURE IT! ER...NOW EXCUSE ME, ETHEL! I HAVE TO TAKE CARE OF THIS...!
WHERE HAVE YOU BEEN?! I'VE BEEN WAITING FOR YOUR CALL!
I'M HAPPY TO HAVE THE JOB... BUT I DON'T THINK I TRUST MY BOSS!
HE ALWAYS ACTS LIKE HE'S HIDING SOMETHING!
THEN YOU'VE GOT THE CODES TO THE TRUSTAR SATELLITES? BOTH OF THEM?!
WELL, HOW THE DEVIL AM I SUPPOSED TO KNOW UNLESS YOU TELL ME?!
LISTEN, PROFESSOR ...I'VE DONE MY PART, STEALING THOSE COMPANIES FROM LODGE...
...NOW IT'S YOUR TURN TO DO YOURS!
NEED I REMIND YOU THAT NONE OF THIS WOULD BE POSSIBLE WITHOUT MY GENIUS?
5

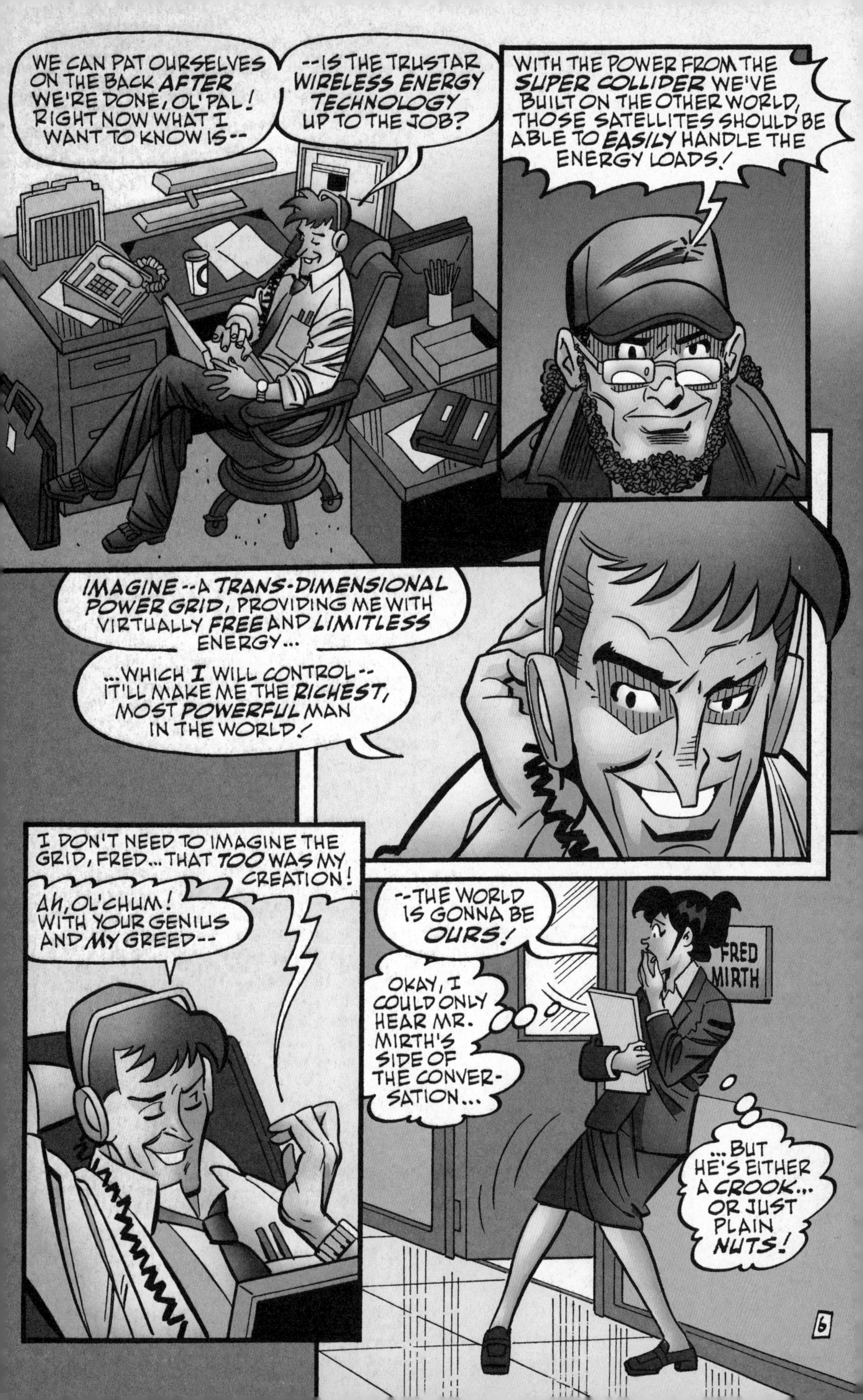

WE CAN PAT OURSELVES ON THE BACK AFTER WE'RE DONE, OL' PAL! RIGHT NOW WHAT I WANT TO KNOW IS--
--IS THE TRUSTAR WIRELESS ENERGY TECHNOLOGY UP TO THE JOB?
WITH THE POWER FROM THE SUPER COLLIDER WE'VE BUILT ON THE OTHER WORLD, THOSE SATELLITES SHOULD BE ABLE TO EASILY HANDLE THE ENERGY LOADS!
IMAGINE--A TRANS-DIMENSIONAL POWER GRID, PROVIDING ME WITH VIRTUALLY FREE AND LIMITLESS ENERGY...
...WHICH I WILL CONTROL--IT'LL MAKE ME THE RICHEST, MOST POWERFUL MAN IN THE WORLD!
I DON'T NEED TO IMAGINE THE GRID, FRED... THAT TOO WAS MY CREATION!
Ah, OL' CHUM! WITH YOUR GENIUS AND MY GREED--
--THE WORLD IS GONNA BE OURS!
FRED MIRTH
OKAY, I COULD ONLY HEAR MR. MIRTH'S SIDE OF THE CONVERSATION...
...BUT HE'S EITHER A CROOK... OR JUST PLAIN NUTS!
6

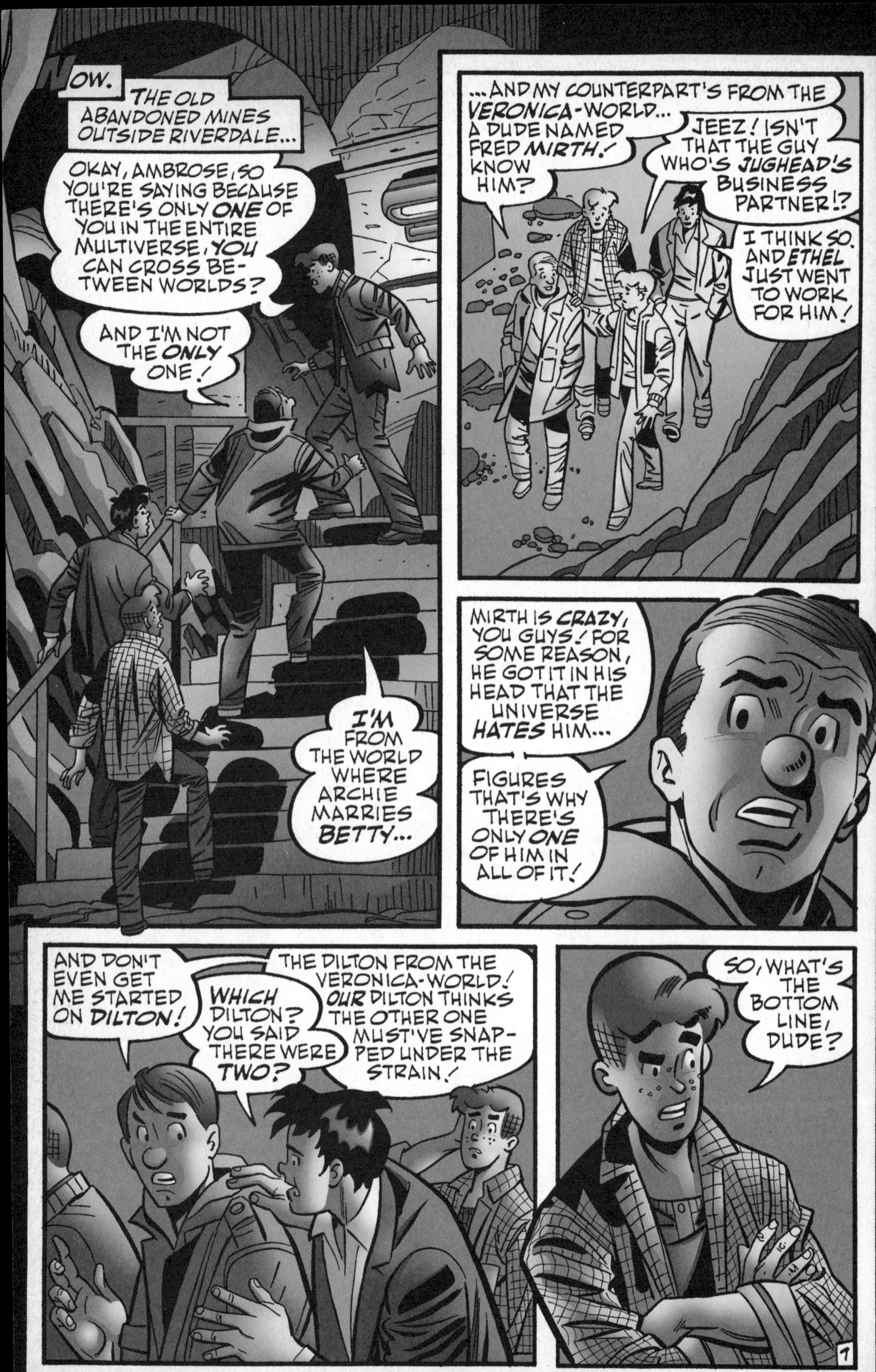
NOW.
THE OLD ABANDONED MINES OUTSIDE RIVERDALE...
OKAY, AMBROSE, SO YOU'RE SAYING BECAUSE THERE'S ONLY ONE OF YOU IN THE ENTIRE MULTIVERSE, YOU CAN CROSS BETWEEN WORLDS?
AND I'M NOT THE ONLY ONE!
I'M FROM THE WORLD WHERE ARCHIE MARRIES BETTY...
...AND MY COUNTERPART'S FROM THE VERONICA-WORLD... A DUDE NAMED FRED MIRTH! KNOW HIM?
JEEZ! ISN'T THAT THE GUY WHO'S JUGHEAD'S BUSINESS PARTNER!?
I THINK SO. AND ETHEL JUST WENT TO WORK FOR HIM!
MIRTH IS CRAZY, YOU GUYS! FOR SOME REASON, HE GOT IT IN HIS HEAD THAT THE UNIVERSE HATES HIM...
FIGURES THAT'S WHY THERE'S ONLY ONE OF HIM IN ALL OF IT!
AND DON'T EVEN GET ME STARTED ON DILTON!
WHICH DILTON? YOU SAID THERE WERE TWO?
THE DILTON FROM THE VERONICA-WORLD! OUR DILTON THINKS THE OTHER ONE MUST'VE SNAPPED UNDER THE STRAIN!
SO, WHAT'S THE BOTTOM LINE, DUDE?

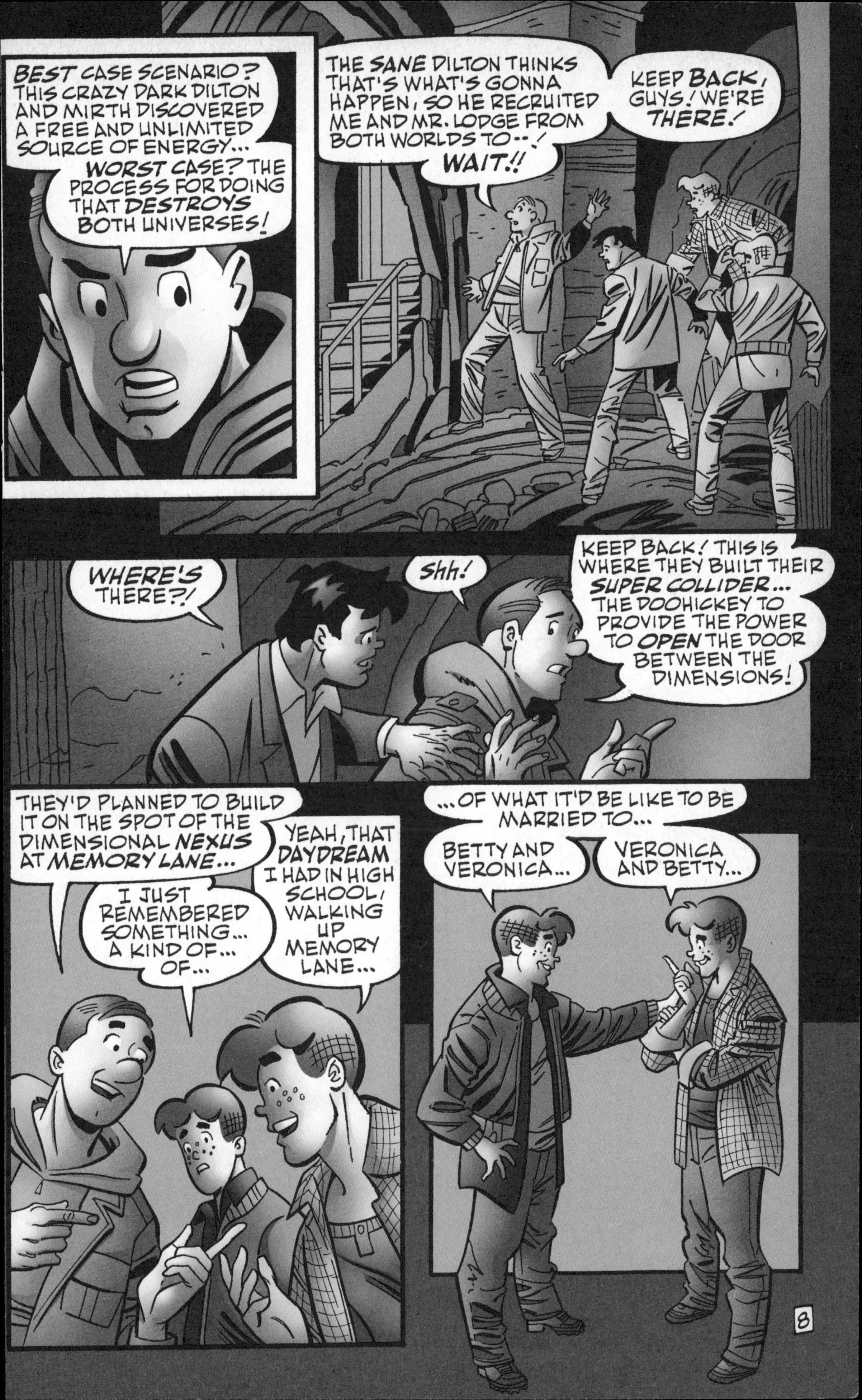
BEST CASE SCENARIO? THIS CRAZY DARK DILTON AND MIRTH DISCOVERED A FREE AND UNLIMITED SOURCE OF ENERGY...
WORST CASE? THE PROCESS FOR DOING THAT DESTROYS BOTH UNIVERSES!
THE SANE DILTON THINKS THAT'S WHAT'S GONNA HAPPEN, SO HE RECRUITED ME AND MR. LODGE FROM BOTH WORLDS TO--!
WAIT!!
KEEP BACK, GUYS! WE'RE THERE!
WHERE'S THERE?!
Shh!
KEEP BACK! THIS IS WHERE THEY BUILT THEIR SUPER COLLIDER... THE DOOHICKEY TO PROVIDE THE POWER TO OPEN THE DOOR BETWEEN THE DIMENSIONS!
THEY'D PLANNED TO BUILD IT ON THE SPOT OF THE DIMENSIONAL NEXUS AT MEMORY LANE...
I JUST REMEMBERED SOMETHING... A KIND OF... OF...
YEAH, THAT DAYDREAM I HAD IN HIGH SCHOOL, WALKING UP MEMORY LANE...
...OF WHAT IT'D BE LIKE TO BE MARRIED TO...
BETTY AND VERONICA...
VERONICA AND BETTY...

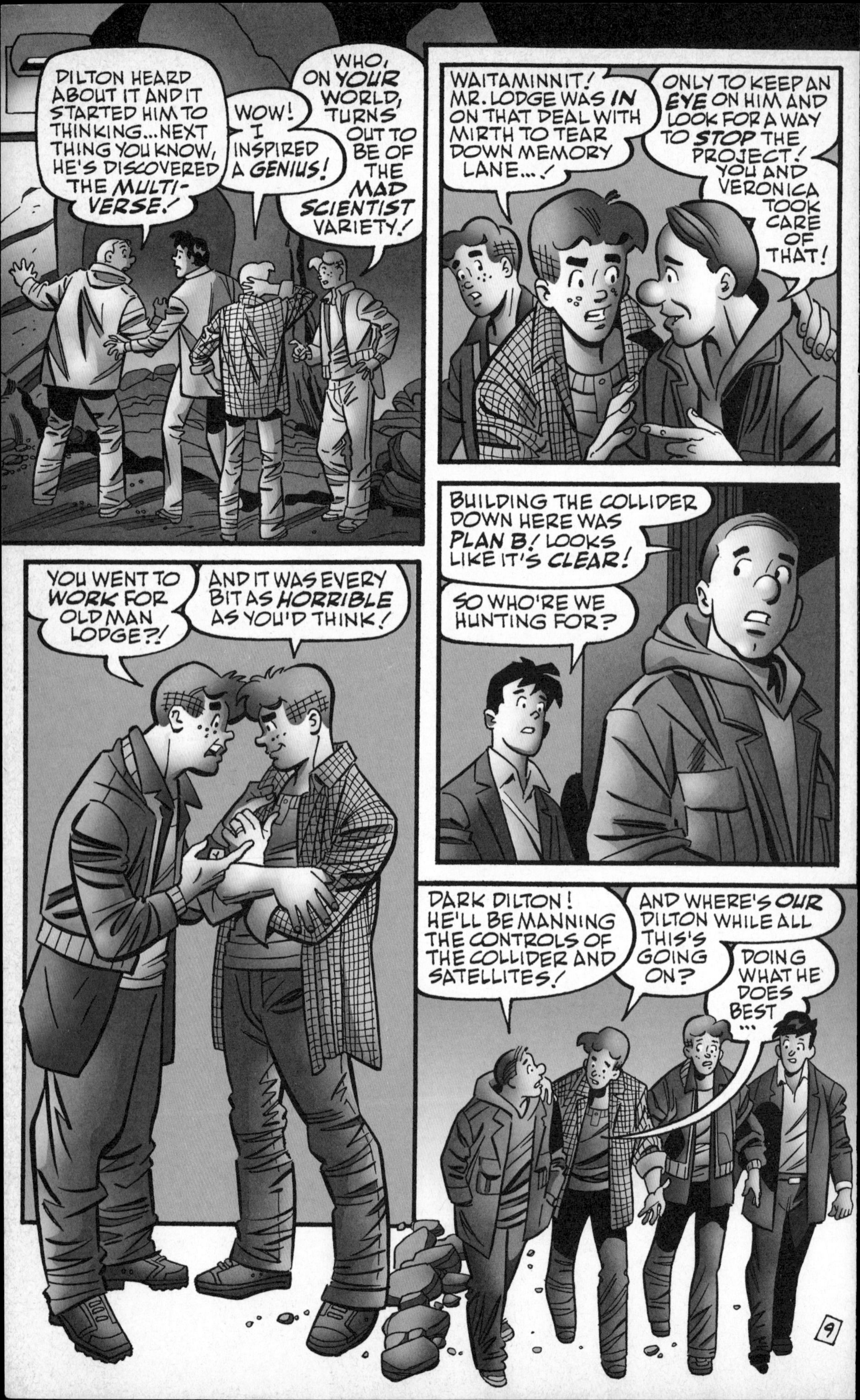
DILTON HEARD ABOUT IT AND IT STARTED HIM TO THINKING...NEXT THING YOU KNOW, HE'S DISCOVERED THE MULTI-VERSE!
WOW! I INSPIRED A GENIUS!
WHO, ON YOUR WORLD, TURNS OUT TO BE OF THE MAD SCIENTIST VARIETY!
WAITAMINNIT! MR. LODGE WAS IN ON THAT DEAL WITH MIRTH TO TEAR DOWN MEMORY LANE...!
ONLY TO KEEP AN EYE ON HIM AND LOOK FOR A WAY TO STOP THE PROJECT! YOU AND VERONICA TOOK CARE OF THAT!
YOU WENT TO WORK FOR OLD MAN LODGE?!
AND IT WAS EVERY BIT AS HORRIBLE AS YOU'D THINK!
BUILDING THE COLLIDER DOWN HERE WAS PLAN B! LOOKS LIKE IT'S CLEAR!
SO WHO'RE WE HUNTING FOR?
DARK DILTON! HE'LL BE MANNING THE CONTROLS OF THE COLLIDER AND SATELLITES!
AND WHERE'S OUR DILTON WHILE ALL THIS'S GOING ON?
DOING WHAT HE DOES BEST...
9

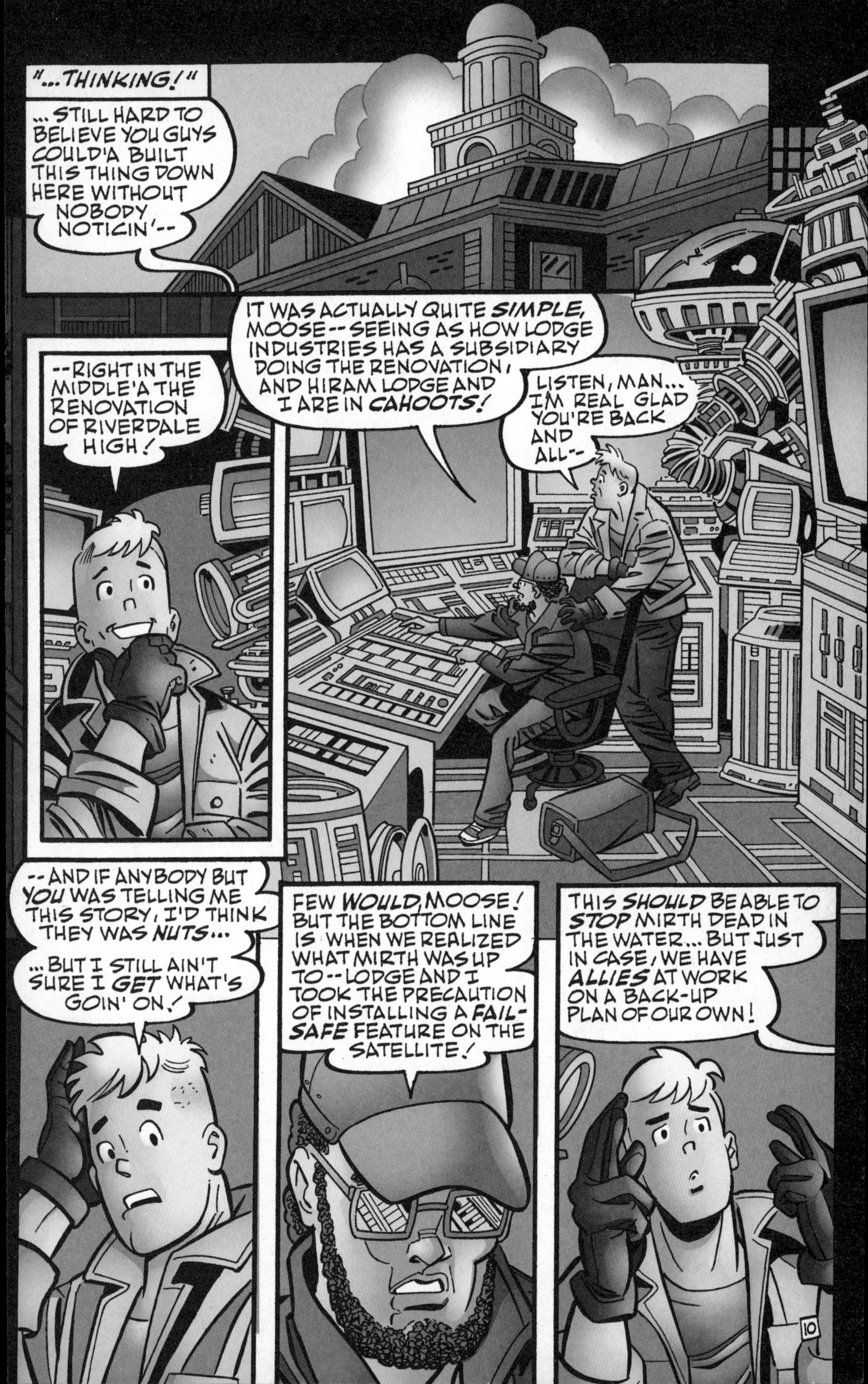
"...THINKING!"
... STILL HARD TO BELIEVE YOU GUYS COULD'A BUILT THIS THING DOWN HERE WITHOUT NOBODY NOTICIN'--
--RIGHT IN THE MIDDLE'A THE RENOVATION OF RIVERDALE HIGH!
IT WAS ACTUALLY QUITE SIMPLE, MOOSE-- SEEING AS HOW LODGE INDUSTRIES HAS A SUBSIDIARY DOING THE RENOVATION, AND HIRAM LODGE AND I ARE IN CAHOOTS!
LISTEN, MAN... I'M REAL GLAD YOU'RE BACK AND ALL--
--AND IF ANYBODY BUT YOU WAS TELLING ME THIS STORY, I'D THINK THEY WAS NUTS...
... BUT I STILL AIN'T SURE I GET WHAT'S GOIN' ON!
FEW WOULD, MOOSE! BUT THE BOTTOM LINE IS WHEN WE REALIZED WHAT MIRTH WAS UP TO-- LODGE AND I TOOK THE PRECAUTION OF INSTALLING A FAIL-SAFE FEATURE ON THE SATELLITE!
THIS SHOULD BE ABLE TO STOP MIRTH DEAD IN THE WATER... BUT JUST IN CASE, WE HAVE ALLIES AT WORK ON A BACK-UP PLAN OF OUR OWN!
10

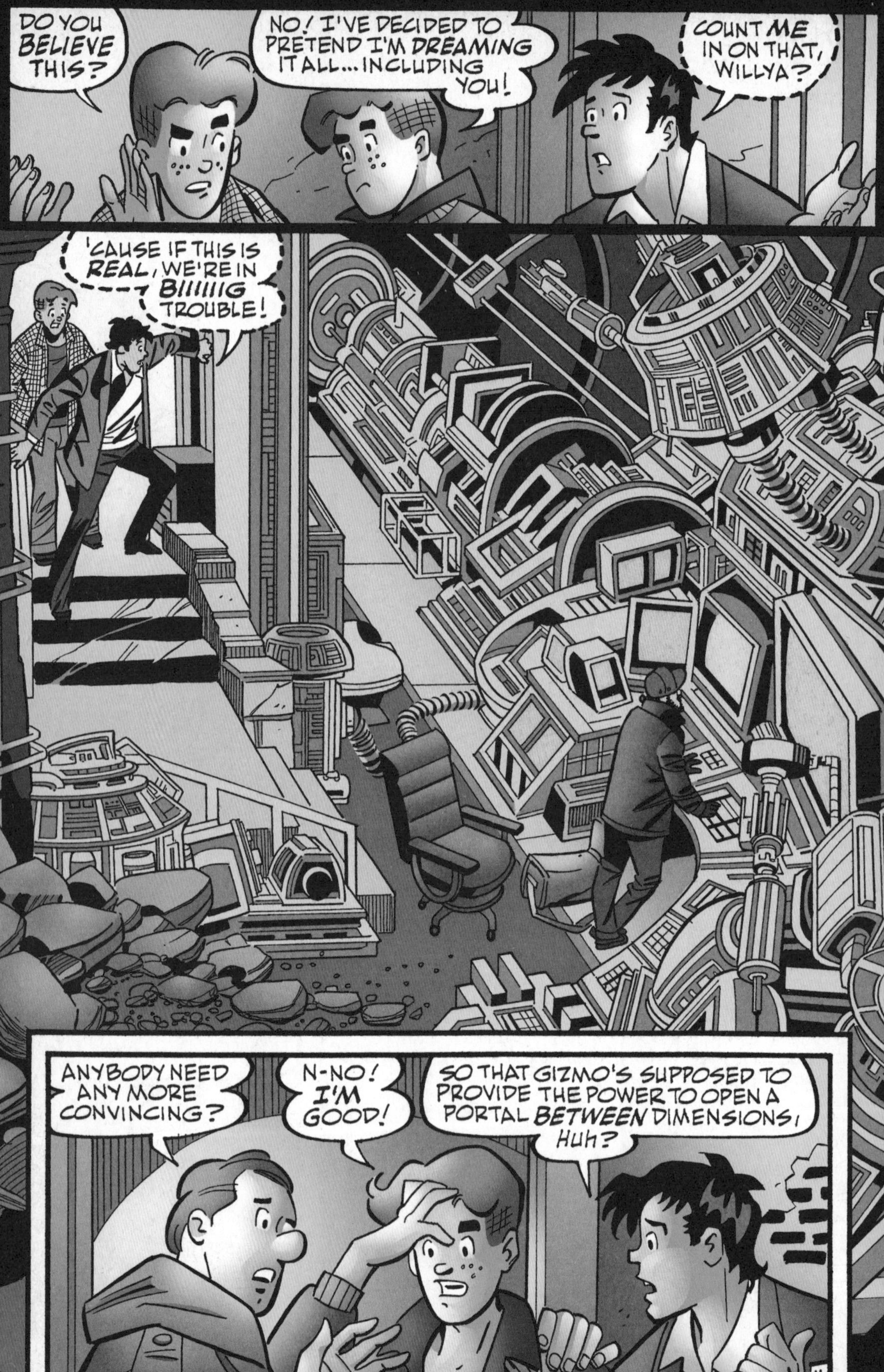
DO YOU BELIEVE THIS?
NO! I'VE DECIDED TO PRETEND I'M DREAMING IT ALL... INCLUDING YOU!
COUNT ME IN ON THAT, WILLYA?
'CAUSE IF THIS IS REAL, WE'RE IN BIIIIIIG TROUBLE!
ANYBODY NEED ANY MORE CONVINCING?
N-NO! I'M GOOD!
SO THAT GIZMO'S SUPPOSED TO PROVIDE THE POWER TO OPEN A PORTAL BETWEEN DIMENSIONS, HUH?
11

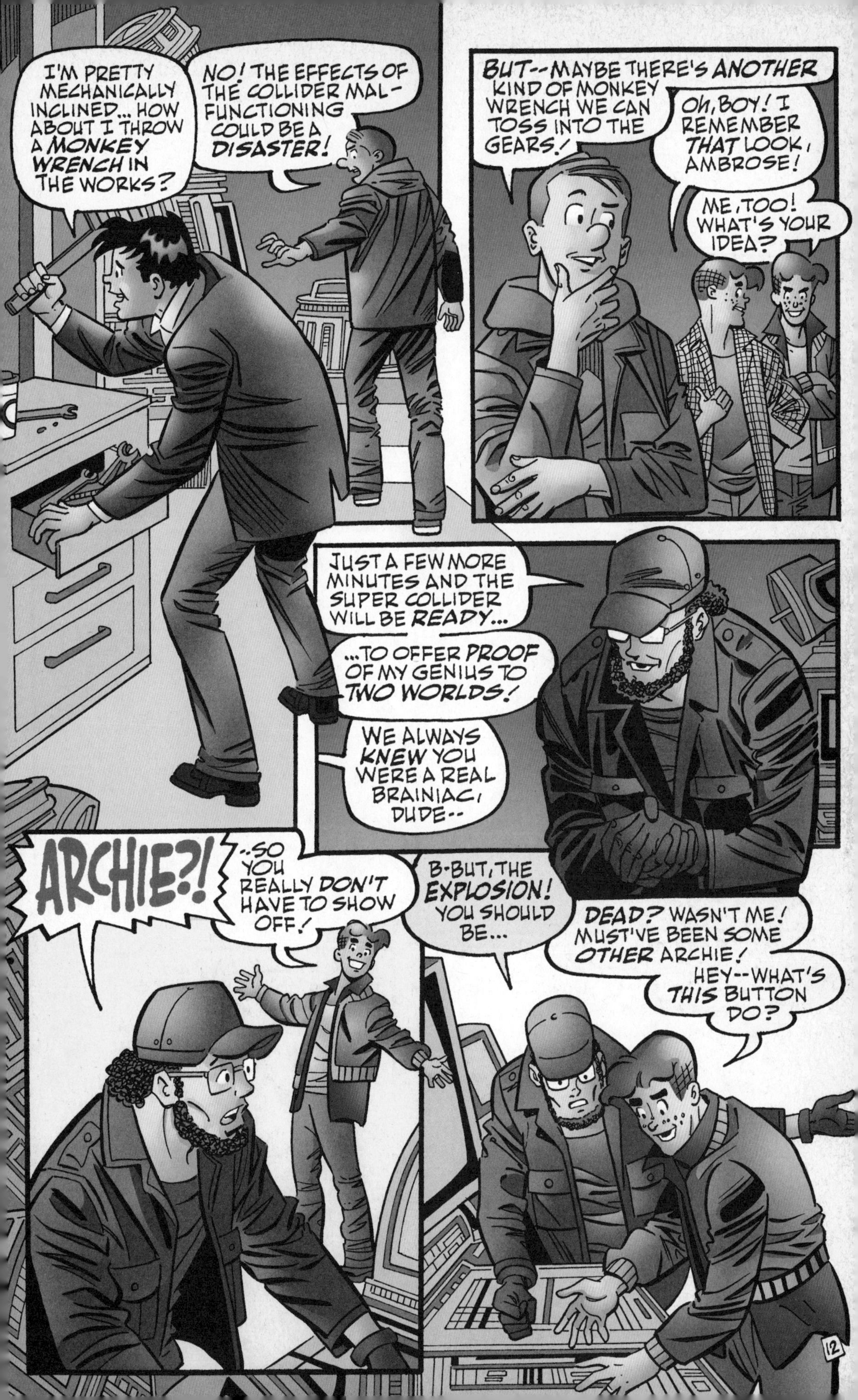
I'M PRETTY MECHANICALLY INCLINED... HOW ABOUT I THROW A MONKEY WRENCH IN THE WORKS?
NO! THE EFFECTS OF THE COLLIDER MAL-FUNCTIONING COULD BE A DISASTER!
BUT--MAYBE THERE'S ANOTHER KIND OF MONKEY WRENCH WE CAN TOSS INTO THE GEARS!
OH, BOY! I REMEMBER THAT LOOK, AMBROSE!
ME, TOO! WHAT'S YOUR IDEA?
JUST A FEW MORE MINUTES AND THE SUPER COLLIDER WILL BE READY...
...TO OFFER PROOF OF MY GENIUS TO TWO WORLDS!
WE ALWAYS KNEW YOU WERE A REAL BRAINIAC, DUDE--
ARCHIE?!
--SO YOU REALLY DON'T HAVE TO SHOW OFF!
B-BUT, THE EXPLOSION! YOU SHOULD BE...
DEAD? WASN'T ME! MUST'VE BEEN SOME OTHER ARCHIE!
HEY--WHAT'S THIS BUTTON DO?
12

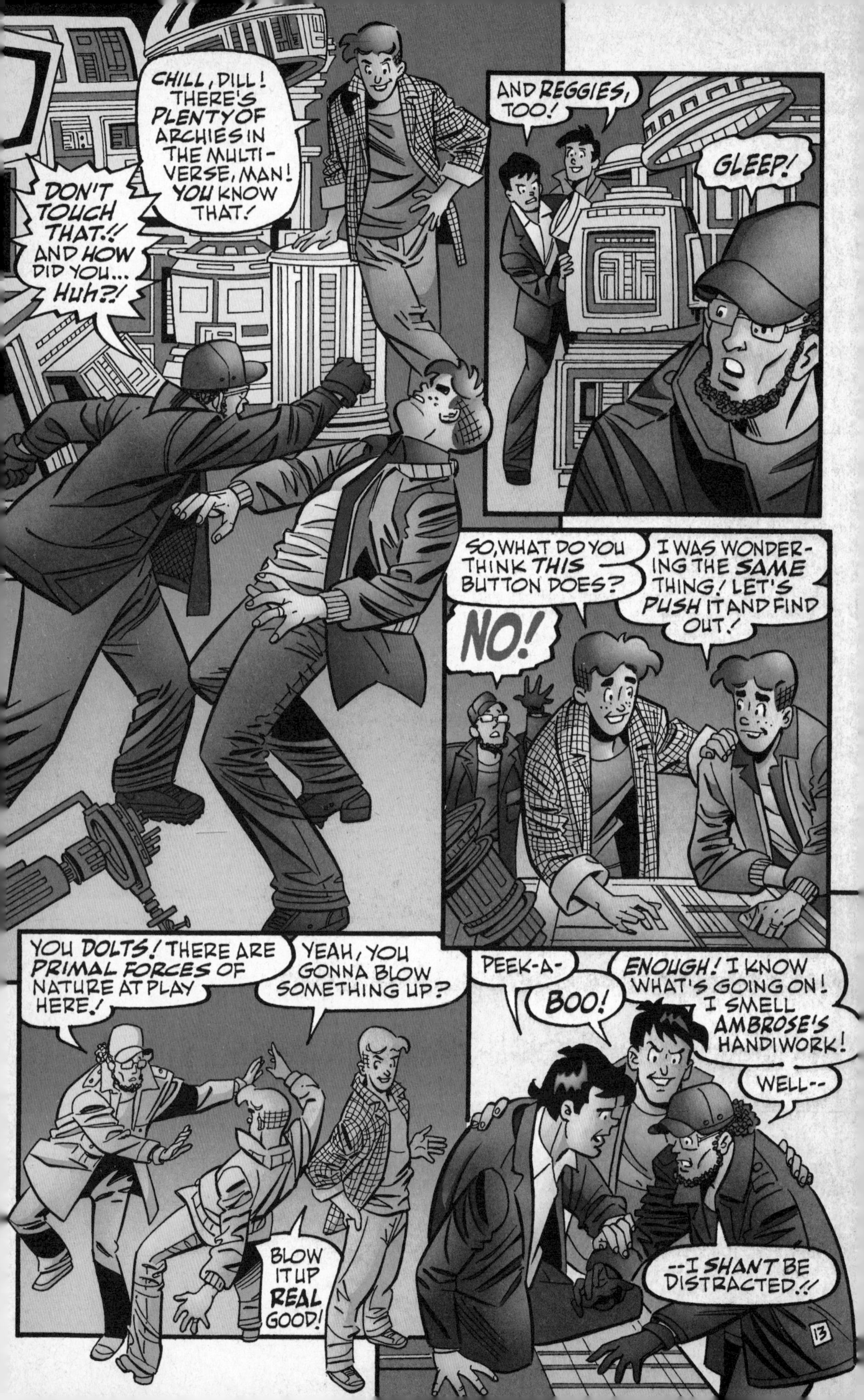
CHILL, DILL! THERE'S PLENTY OF ARCHIES IN THE MULTI-VERSE, MAN! YOU KNOW THAT!
DON'T TOUCH THAT!! AND HOW DID YOU... Huh?!
AND REGGIES, TOO!
GLEEP!
SO, WHAT DO YOU THINK THIS BUTTON DOES?
I WAS WONDER-ING THE SAME THING! LET'S PUSH IT AND FIND OUT!
NO!
YOU DOLTS! THERE ARE PRIMAL FORCES OF NATURE AT PLAY HERE!
YEAH, YOU GONNA BLOW SOMETHING UP?
BLOW IT UP REAL GOOD!
PEEK-A-
BOO!
ENOUGH! I KNOW WHAT'S GOING ON! I SMELL AMBROSE'S HANDIWORK!
WELL--
--I SHANT BE DISTRACTED!!
13

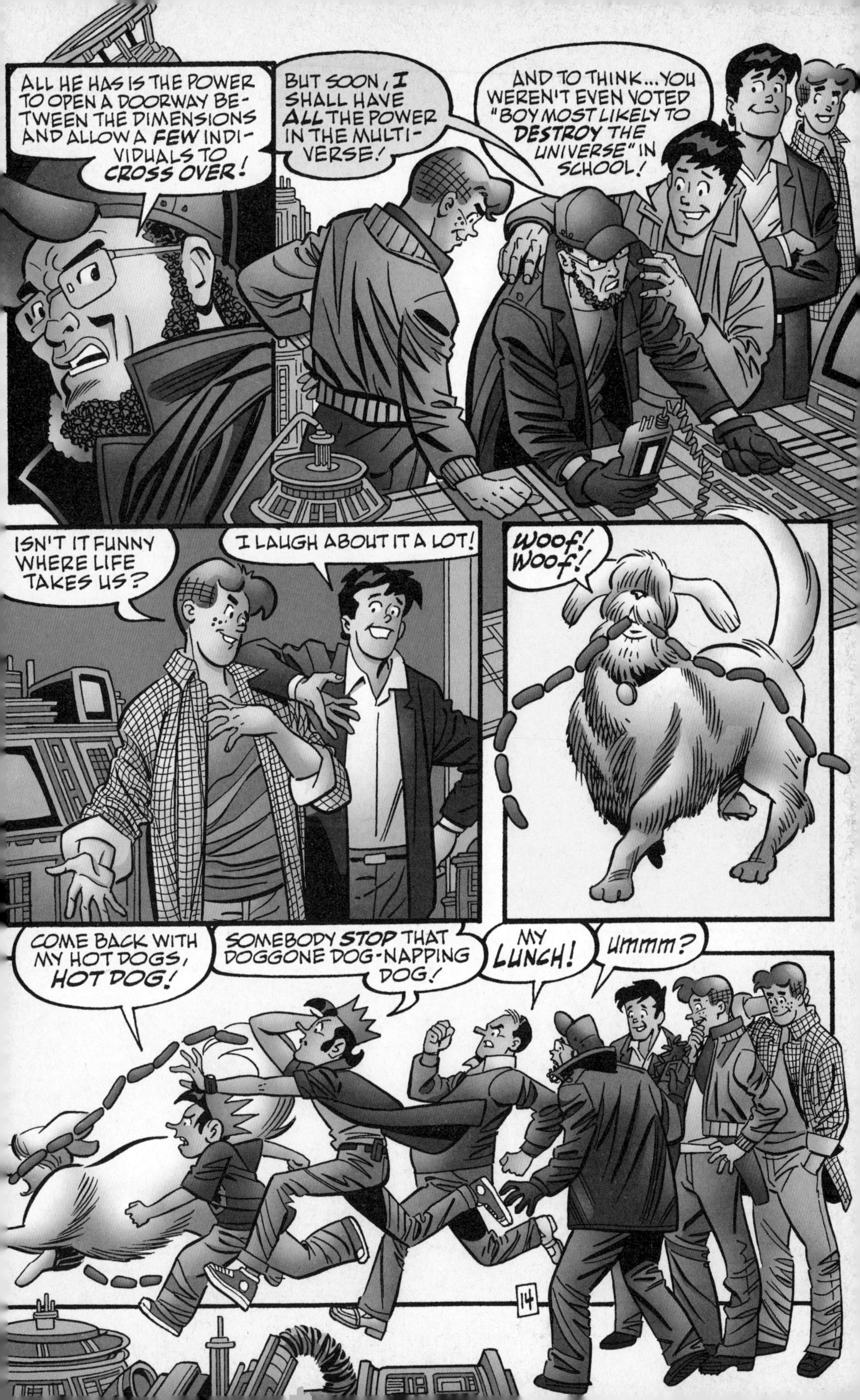
ALL HE HAS IS THE POWER TO OPEN A DOORWAY BETWEEN THE DIMENSIONS AND ALLOW A FEW INDIVIDUALS TO CROSS OVER!
BUT SOON, I SHALL HAVE ALL THE POWER IN THE MULTIVERSE!
AND TO THINK... YOU WEREN'T EVEN VOTED "BOY MOST LIKELY TO DESTROY THE UNIVERSE" IN SCHOOL!
ISN'T IT FUNNY WHERE LIFE TAKES US?
I LAUGH ABOUT IT A LOT!
Woof! Woof!
COME BACK WITH MY HOT DOGS, HOT DOG!
SOMEBODY STOP THAT DOGGONE DOG-NAPPING DOG!
MY LUNCH!
Ummm?
14

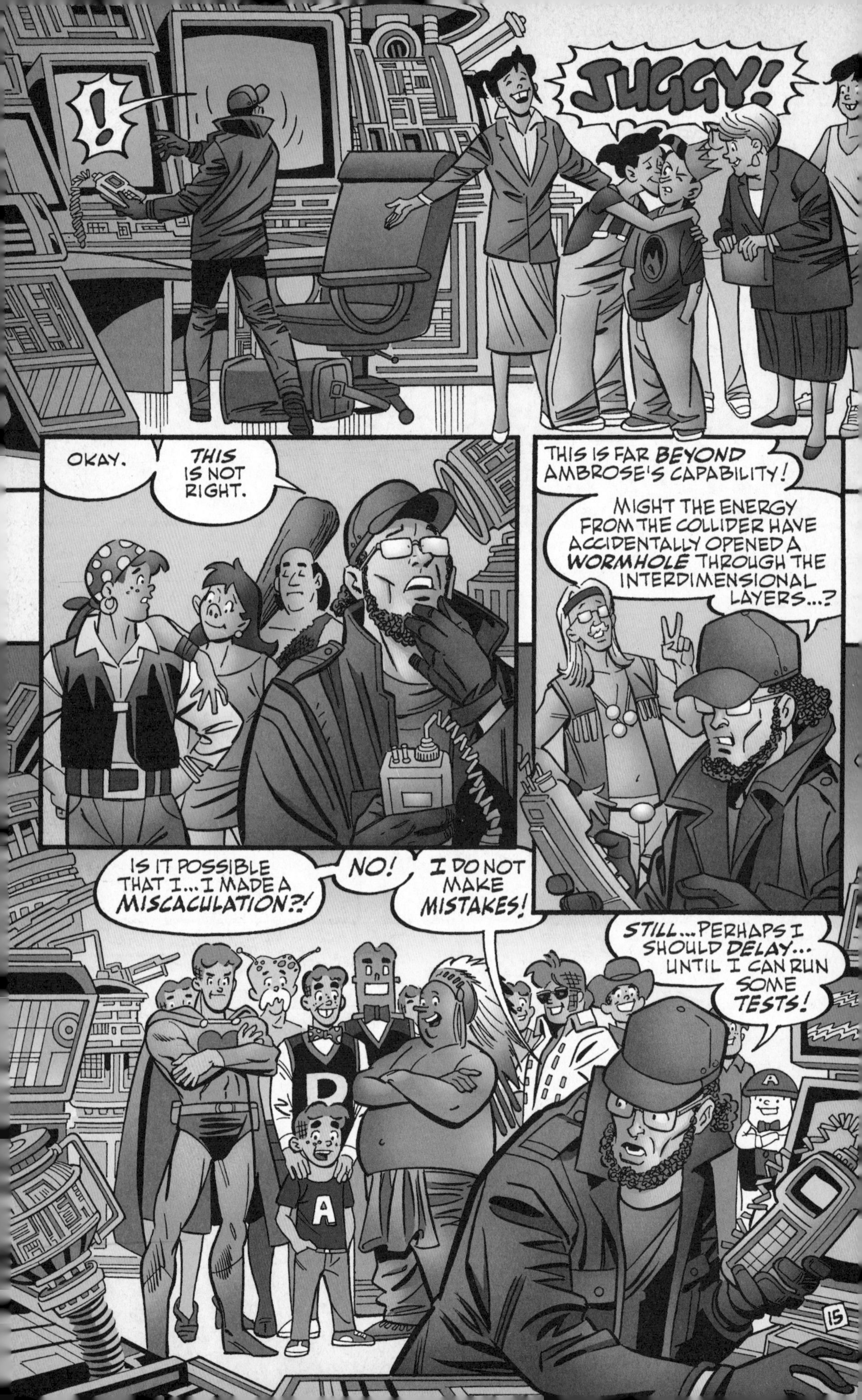
!
JUGGY!
OKAY.
THIS IS NOT RIGHT.
THIS IS FAR BEYOND AMBROSE'S CAPABILITY!
MIGHT THE ENERGY FROM THE COLLIDER HAVE ACCIDENTALLY OPENED A WORMHOLE THROUGH THE INTERDIMENSIONAL LAYERS...?
IS IT POSSIBLE THAT I... I MADE A MISCACULATION?!
NO!
I DO NOT MAKE MISTAKES!
STILL... PERHAPS I SHOULD DELAY... UNTIL I CAN RUN SOME TESTS!
15

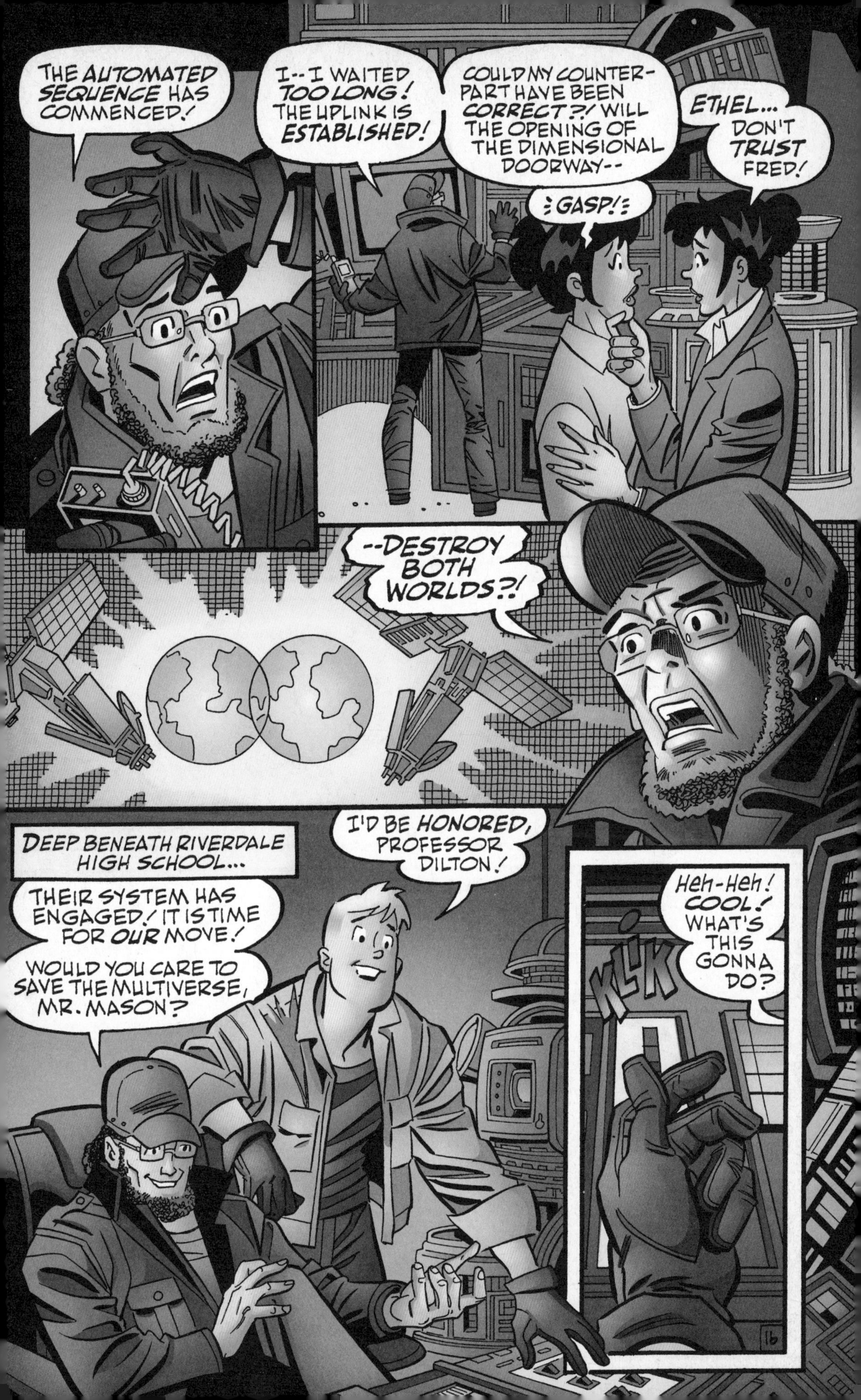

THE AUTOMATED SEQUENCE HAS COMMENCED!
I-- I WAITED TOO LONG! THE UPLINK IS ESTABLISHED!
COULD MY COUNTERPART HAVE BEEN CORRECT?! WILL THE OPENING OF THE DIMENSIONAL DOORWAY--
GASP!
ETHEL... DON'T TRUST FRED!
--DESTROY BOTH WORLDS?!
DEEP BENEATH RIVERDALE HIGH SCHOOL...
THEIR SYSTEM HAS ENGAGED! IT IS TIME FOR OUR MOVE!
WOULD YOU CARE TO SAVE THE MULTIVERSE, MR. MASON?
I'D BE HONORED, PROFESSOR DILTON!
KLIK
Heh-Heh! COOL! WHAT'S THIS GONNA DO?
16

"WELL, MOOSE... EVEN AS WE SPEAK, MY *DOPPELGÄNGER'S* DEVICE IS SENDING ITS ENERGY TO THE *SATELLITE* IN ORBIT OVER *HIS* EARTH...

"...WHICH IT WILL USE TO *BREACH* THE PORTAL BETWEEN OUR WORLDS...

"...SENDING IT TO A *DUPLICATE* SATELLITE OVER *OUR* EARTH, FROM WHICH HE THEORIZED IT CAN BE CONVERTED TO FREE, SAFE ENERGY!

"HE IS ONLY *HALF* CORRECT! IT *IS* FREE!

"WHAT WE HAVE DONE IS TO *TURN OFF* THE *RECEIVING* SATELLITE!

"THUS, THE TRANSMITTED ENERGY HAS NO RECEPTOR, AND *DESTROYS* THE SATELLITE INSTEAD..."

...CREATING FEED-BACK WHICH *SEALS* THE PORTAL BEFORE IT CAN DO ANY *PERMANENT* DAMAGE TO THE *MULTIVERSE!*

NICE WORK, MOOSE!

Y'MEAN... THAT'S *IT*?!

YES. THE UNIVERSE IS, AS IT *WERE,* SAVED!

WELL, *DANG!* IT'S *GOOD* T'SEE YOU AGAIN, DILTON!

GLEEP!

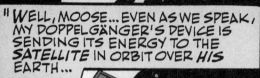

17

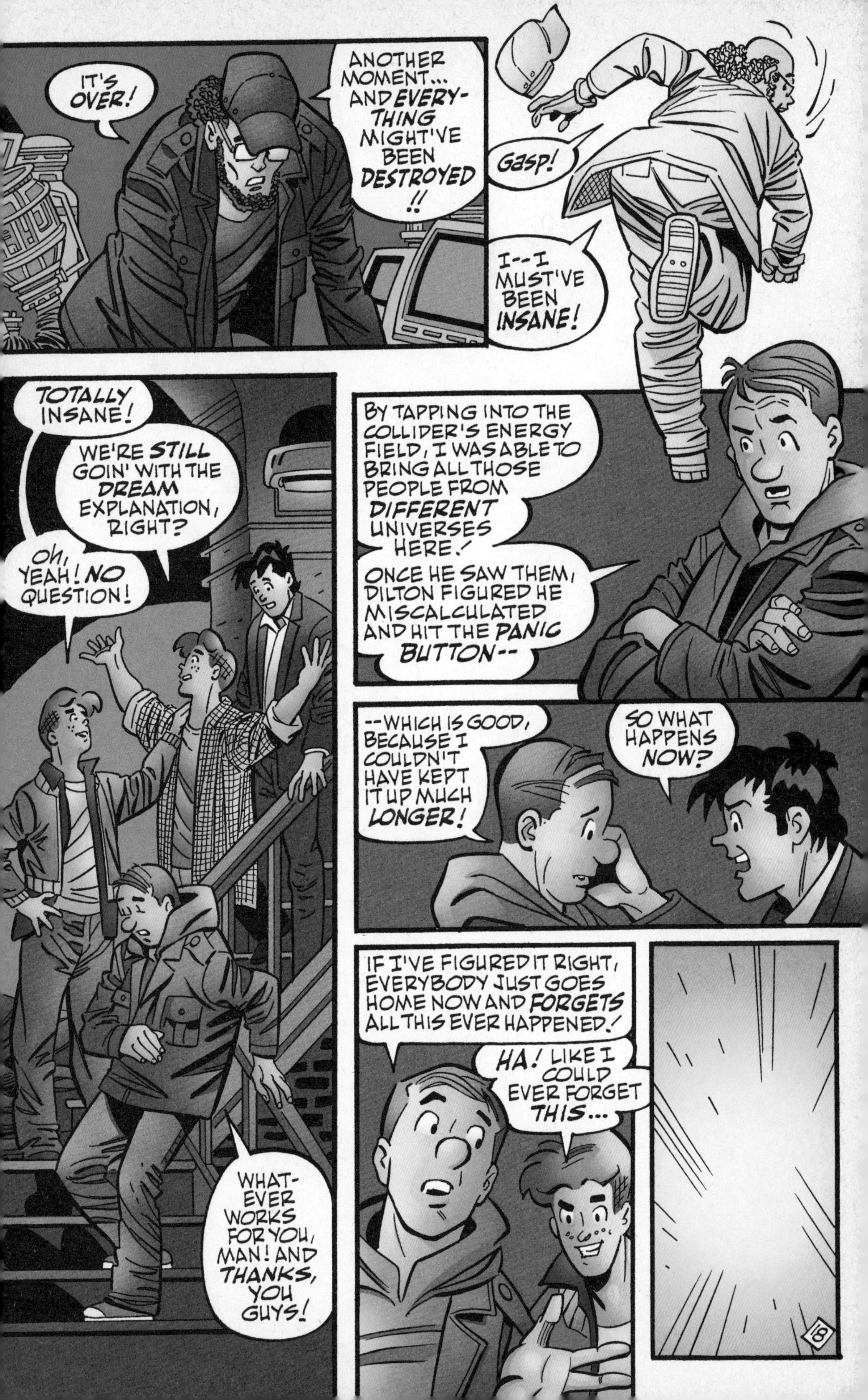
IT'S OVER!
ANOTHER MOMENT... AND EVERYTHING MIGHT'VE BEEN DESTROYED!!
Gasp!
I--I MUST'VE BEEN INSANE!
TOTALLY INSANE!
WE'RE STILL GOIN' WITH THE DREAM EXPLANATION, RIGHT?
Oh, YEAH! NO QUESTION!
WHAT-EVER WORKS FOR YOU, MAN! AND THANKS, YOU GUYS!
BY TAPPING INTO THE COLLIDER'S ENERGY FIELD, I WAS ABLE TO BRING ALL THOSE PEOPLE FROM DIFFERENT UNIVERSES HERE!
ONCE HE SAW THEM, DILTON FIGURED HE MISCALCULATED AND HIT THE PANIC BUTTON--
--WHICH IS GOOD, BECAUSE I COULDN'T HAVE KEPT IT UP MUCH LONGER!
SO WHAT HAPPENS NOW?
IF I'VE FIGURED IT RIGHT, EVERYBODY JUST GOES HOME NOW AND FORGETS ALL THIS EVER HAPPENED!
HA! LIKE I COULD EVER FORGET THIS...
18

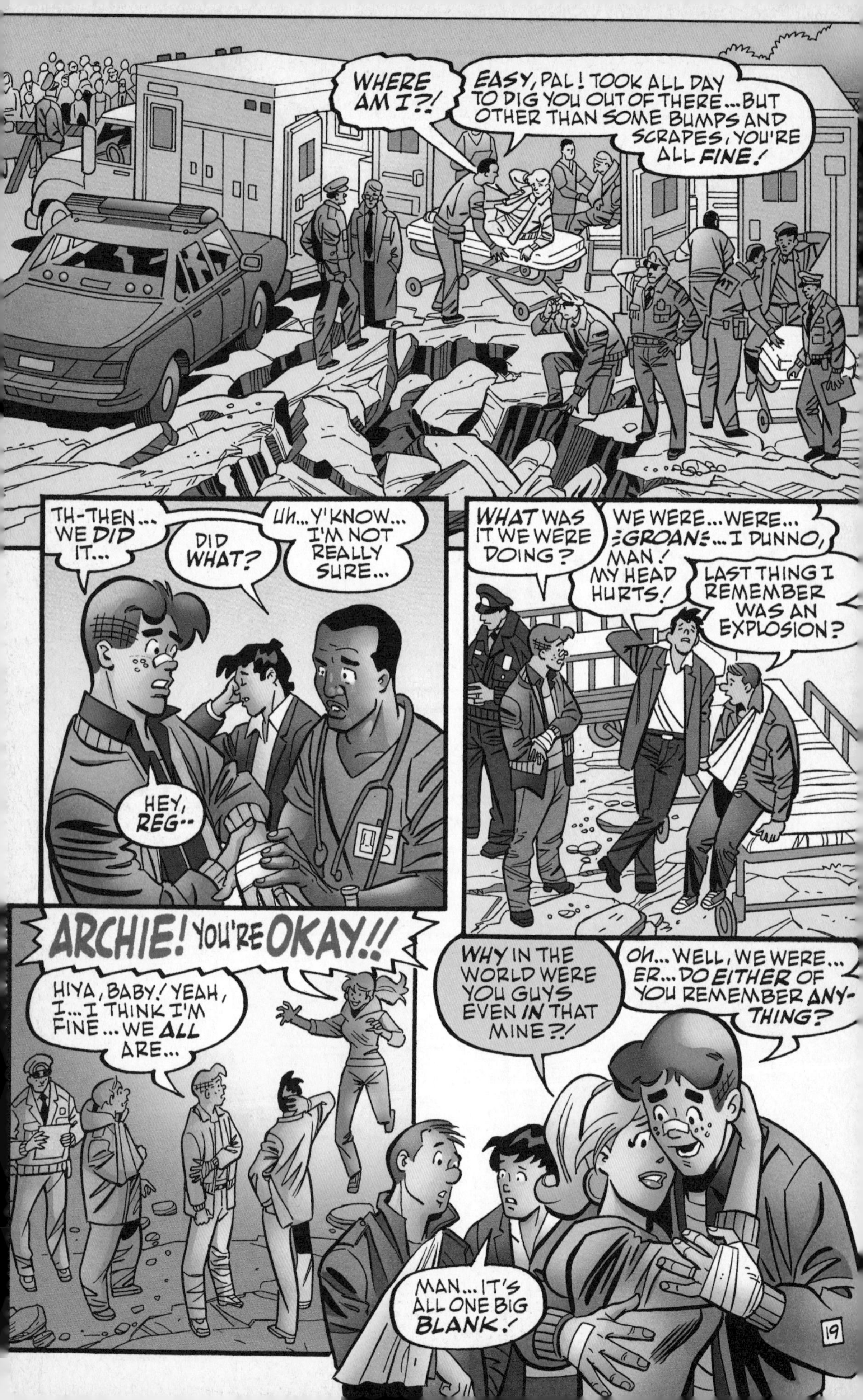

WHERE AM I?!
EASY, PAL! TOOK ALL DAY TO DIG YOU OUT OF THERE... BUT OTHER THAN SOME BUMPS AND SCRAPES, YOU'RE ALL FINE!
TH-THEN... WE DID IT...
DID WHAT?
UH... Y'KNOW... I'M NOT REALLY SURE...
HEY, REG--
WHAT WAS IT WE WERE DOING?
WE WERE... WERE... =GROAN=... I DUNNO, MAN!
MY HEAD HURTS!
LAST THING I REMEMBER WAS AN EXPLOSION?
ARCHIE! YOU'RE OKAY!!
HIYA, BABY! YEAH, I... I THINK I'M FINE... WE ALL ARE...
WHY IN THE WORLD WERE YOU GUYS EVEN IN THAT MINE?!
OH... WELL, WE WERE... ER... DO EITHER OF YOU REMEMBER ANY-THING?
MAN... IT'S ALL ONE BIG BLANK!
19

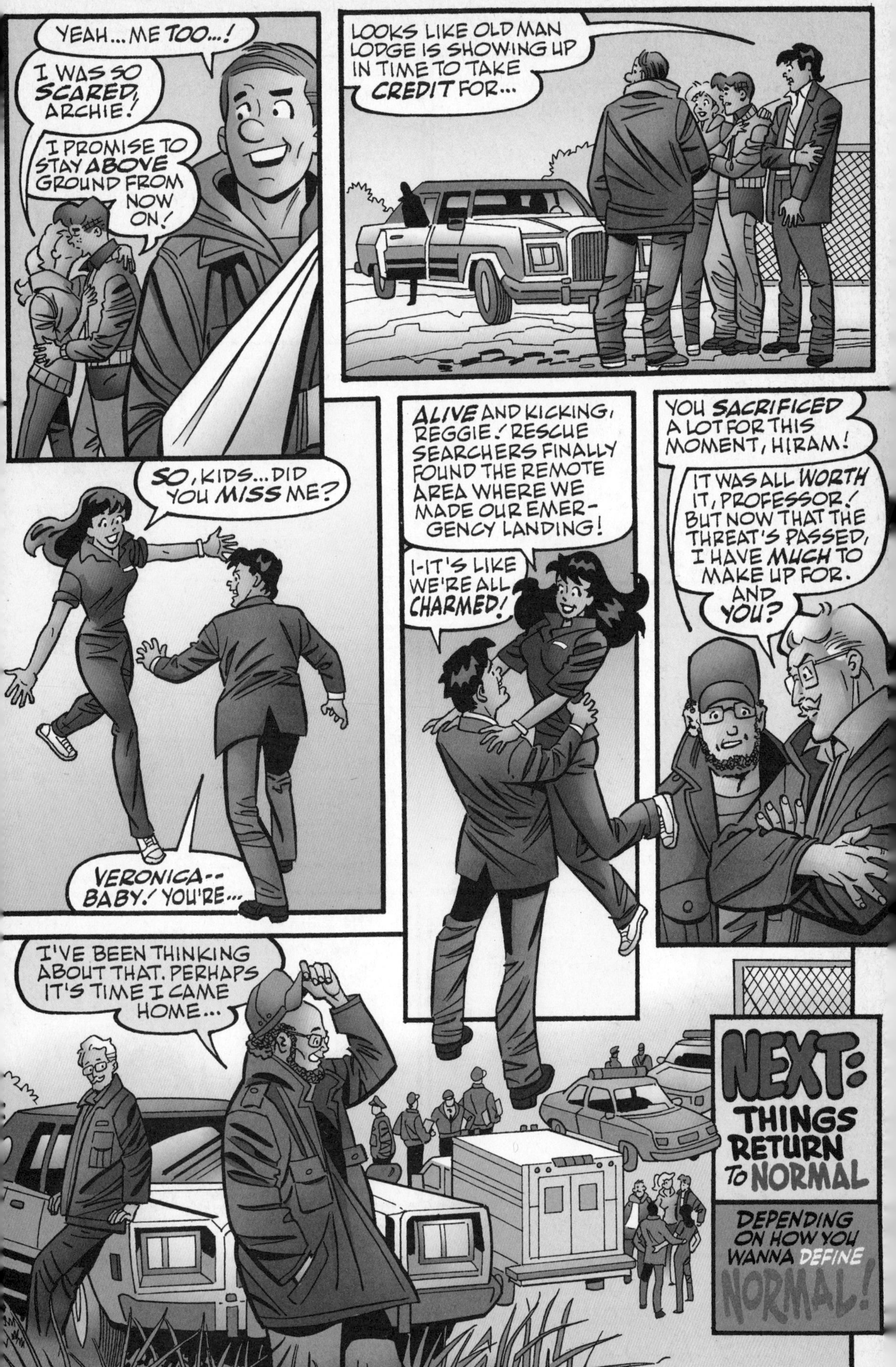
YEAH... ME TOO...!
I WAS SO SCARED, ARCHIE!
I PROMISE TO STAY ABOVE GROUND FROM NOW ON!
LOOKS LIKE OLD MAN LODGE IS SHOWING UP IN TIME TO TAKE CREDIT FOR...
SO, KIDS... DID YOU MISS ME?
VERONICA-- BABY! YOU'RE...
ALIVE AND KICKING, REGGIE! RESCUE SEARCHERS FINALLY FOUND THE REMOTE AREA WHERE WE MADE OUR EMERGENCY LANDING!
I-IT'S LIKE WE'RE ALL CHARMED!
YOU SACRIFICED A LOT FOR THIS MOMENT, HIRAM!
IT WAS ALL WORTH IT, PROFESSOR! BUT NOW THAT THE THREAT'S PASSED, I HAVE MUCH TO MAKE UP FOR. AND YOU?
I'VE BEEN THINKING ABOUT THAT. PERHAPS IT'S TIME I CAME HOME...
NEXT: THINGS RETURN TO NORMAL
DEPENDING ON HOW YOU WANNA DEFINE NORMAL!

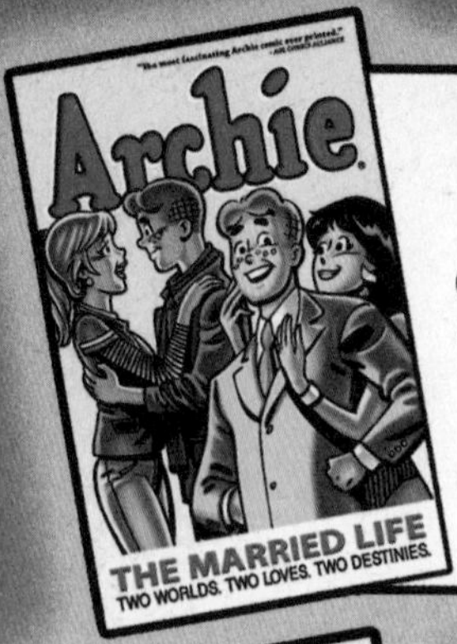
Archie
THE MARRIED LIFE
TWO WORLDS. TWO LOVES. TWO DESTINIES.

Archie: The Married Life Book One

Collecting the first 6 parts of the critically acclaimed Archie Marries... story.

ISBN:
978-1-936975-01-3

Archie: The Married Life Book Two

Collecting parts 7-12 of the critically acclaimed Archie Marries... story.

ISBN:
978-1-879794-99-3

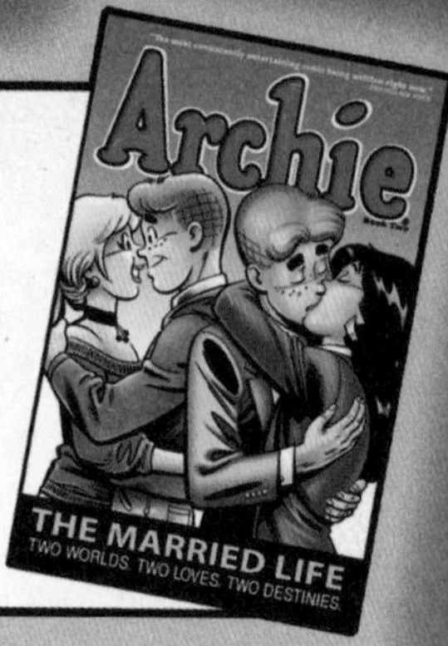
Archie
THE MARRIED LIFE
TWO WORLDS. TWO LOVES. TWO DESTINIES.

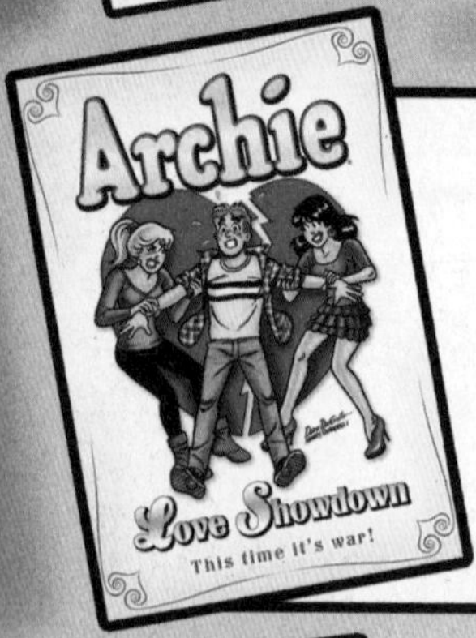
Archie
Love Showdown
This time it's war!

Archie: Love Showdown

The epic love triangle is challenged when a rival returns for Archie!

ISBN:
978-1-936975-21-1

The Archie Wedding: Will You Marry Me?

Archie has finally chosen! The winner is... BOTH OF THEM!

ISBN:
978-1-879794-51-1

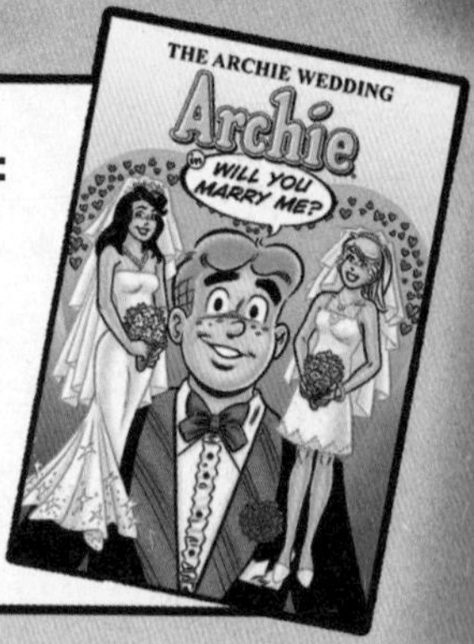
THE ARCHIE WEDDING
Archie
WILL YOU MARRY ME?

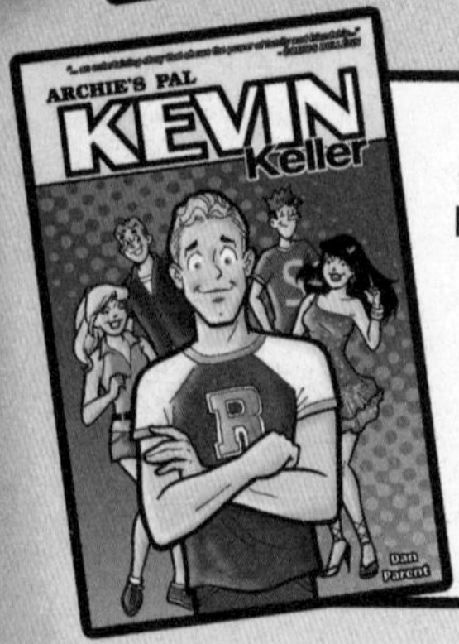
ARCHIE'S PAL
KEVIN
Keller
Dan Parent

Kevin Keller

Meet the newest addition to the little town of Riverdale! Kevin Keller will show the locals that he's more than just a pretty face!

ISBN:
978-1-879794-93-1

Archie Meets KISS

Two of the most iconic forces in history have finally teamed up for one awesome adventure!

Hardcover Collector's Edition:
978-1-879794-14-3

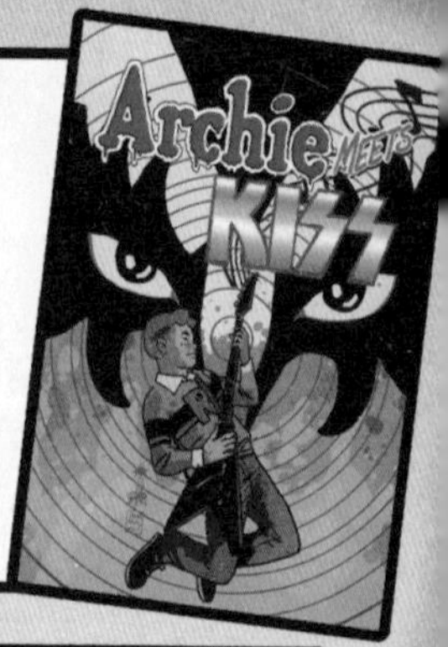
Archie MEETS KISS

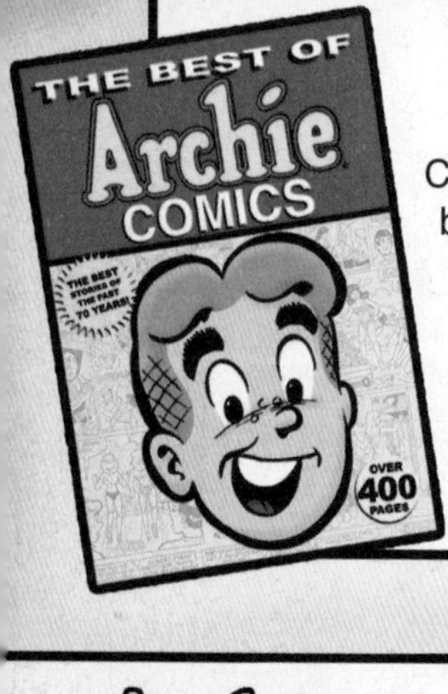
THE BEST OF
Archie
COMICS
OVER 400 PAGES

The Best of Archie Comics

Collecting some of the very best stories from the past 70 years!

ISBN:
978-1-879794-84-9

The Best of Archie Comics Book Two

Collecting some of the very best stories from the past 70 years!

ISBN:
978-1-936975-20-4

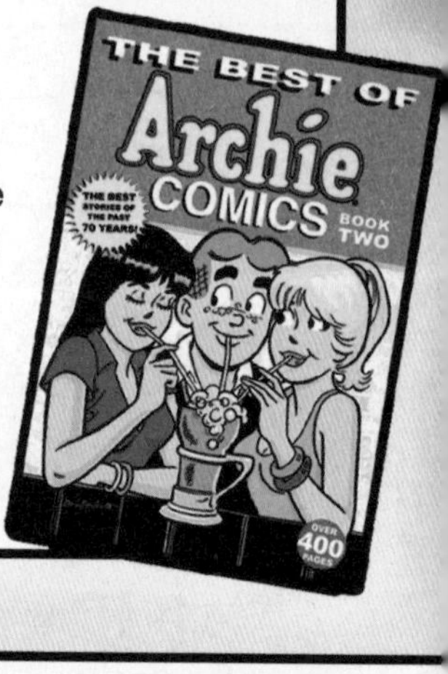
THE BEST OF
Archie
COMICS
BOOK TWO
OVER 400 PAGES

Archie COMICS
ARCHIECOMICS.COM

LOOK FOR THIS AND OTHER GRAPHIC NOVELS AT COMIC SHOPS AND BOOKSTORES EVERYWHERE!
ALSO AVAILABLE ONLINE AT ARCHIECOMICS.COM

HERE'S AN EXCLUSIVE SNEAK PEEK AT VOLUME FOUR OF THE MARRIED LIFE

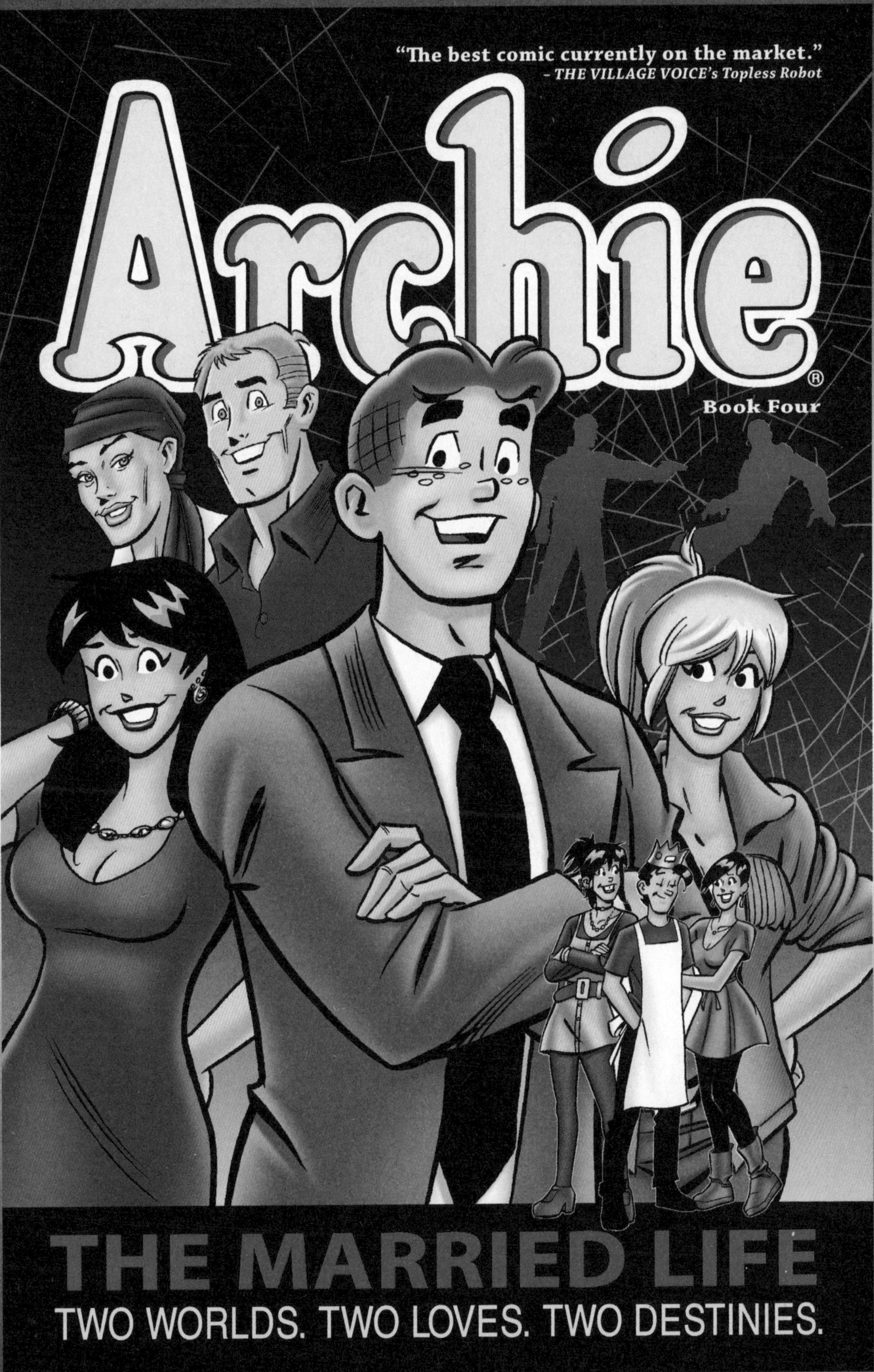
"The best comic currently on the market."
– THE VILLAGE VOICE's Topless Robot
Archie®
Book Four
THE MARRIED LIFE
TWO WORLDS. TWO LOVES. TWO DESTINIES.

ON SALE IN NOVEMBER 2013!

HERE'S AN EXCLUSIVE SNEAK PEEK AT VOLUME FOUR OF THE MARRIED LIFE

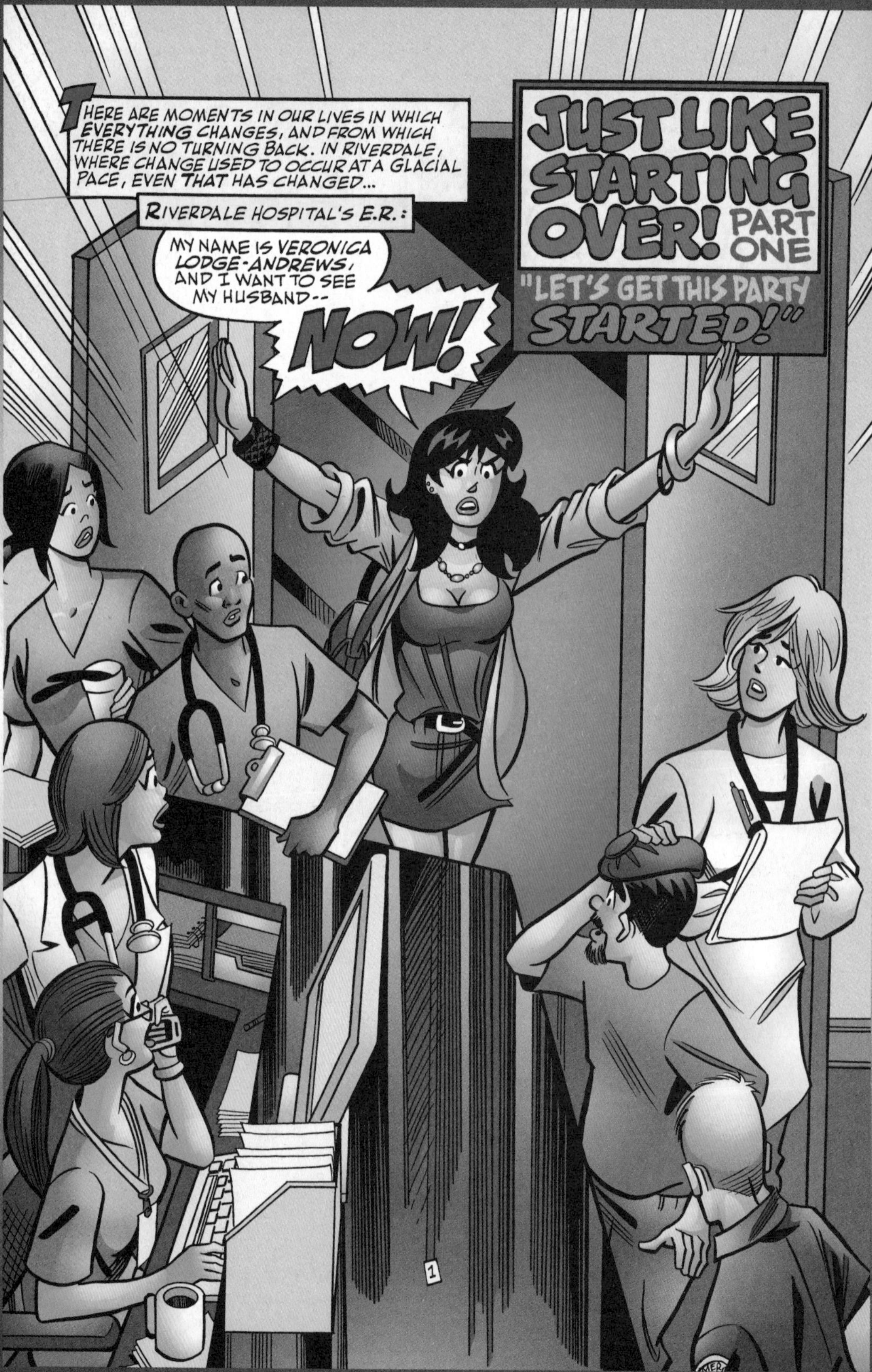
THERE ARE MOMENTS IN OUR LIVES IN WHICH EVERYTHING CHANGES, AND FROM WHICH THERE IS NO TURNING BACK. IN RIVERDALE, WHERE CHANGE USED TO OCCUR AT A GLACIAL PACE, EVEN THAT HAS CHANGED...
RIVERDALE HOSPITAL'S E.R.:
MY NAME IS VERONICA LODGE-ANDREWS, AND I WANT TO SEE MY HUSBAND--
NOW!
JUST LIKE STARTING OVER! PART ONE
"LET'S GET THIS PARTY STARTED!"
1

ON SALE IN NOVEMBER 2013!

HERE'S AN EXCLUSIVE SNEAK PEEK AT VOLUME FOUR OF THE MARRIED LIFE

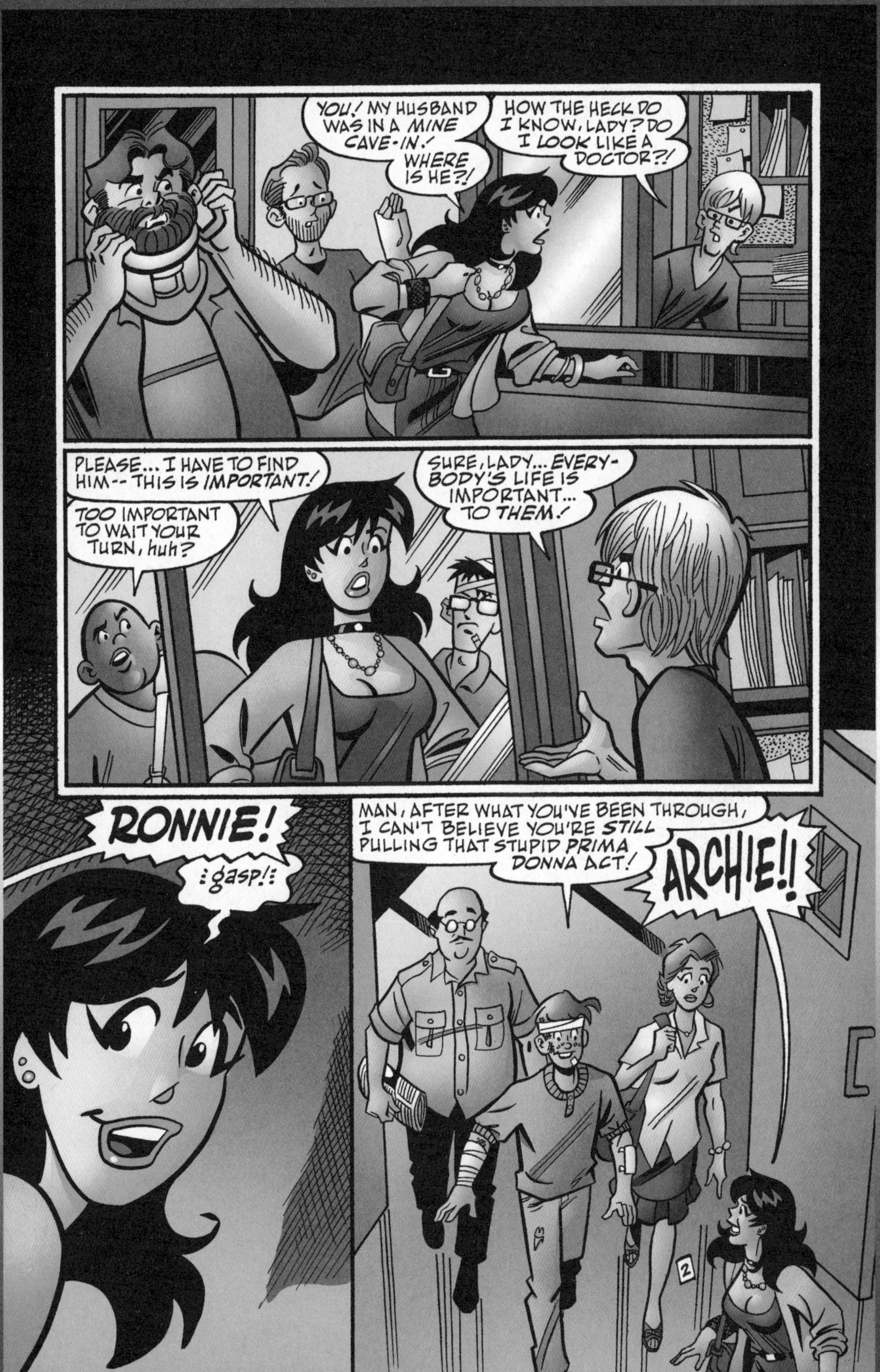
YOU! MY HUSBAND WAS IN A MINE CAVE-IN! WHERE IS HE?!
HOW THE HECK DO I KNOW, LADY? DO I LOOK LIKE A DOCTOR?!
PLEASE... I HAVE TO FIND HIM-- THIS IS IMPORTANT!
TOO IMPORTANT TO WAIT YOUR TURN, huh?
SURE, LADY... EVERYBODY'S LIFE IS IMPORTANT... TO THEM!
RONNIE!
gasp!
MAN, AFTER WHAT YOU'VE BEEN THROUGH, I CAN'T BELIEVE YOU'RE STILL PULLING THAT STUPID PRIMA DONNA ACT!
ARCHIE!!
2

ON SALE IN NOVEMBER 2013!

HERE'S AN EXCLUSIVE SNEAK PEEK AT VOLUME FOUR OF THE MARRIED LIFE

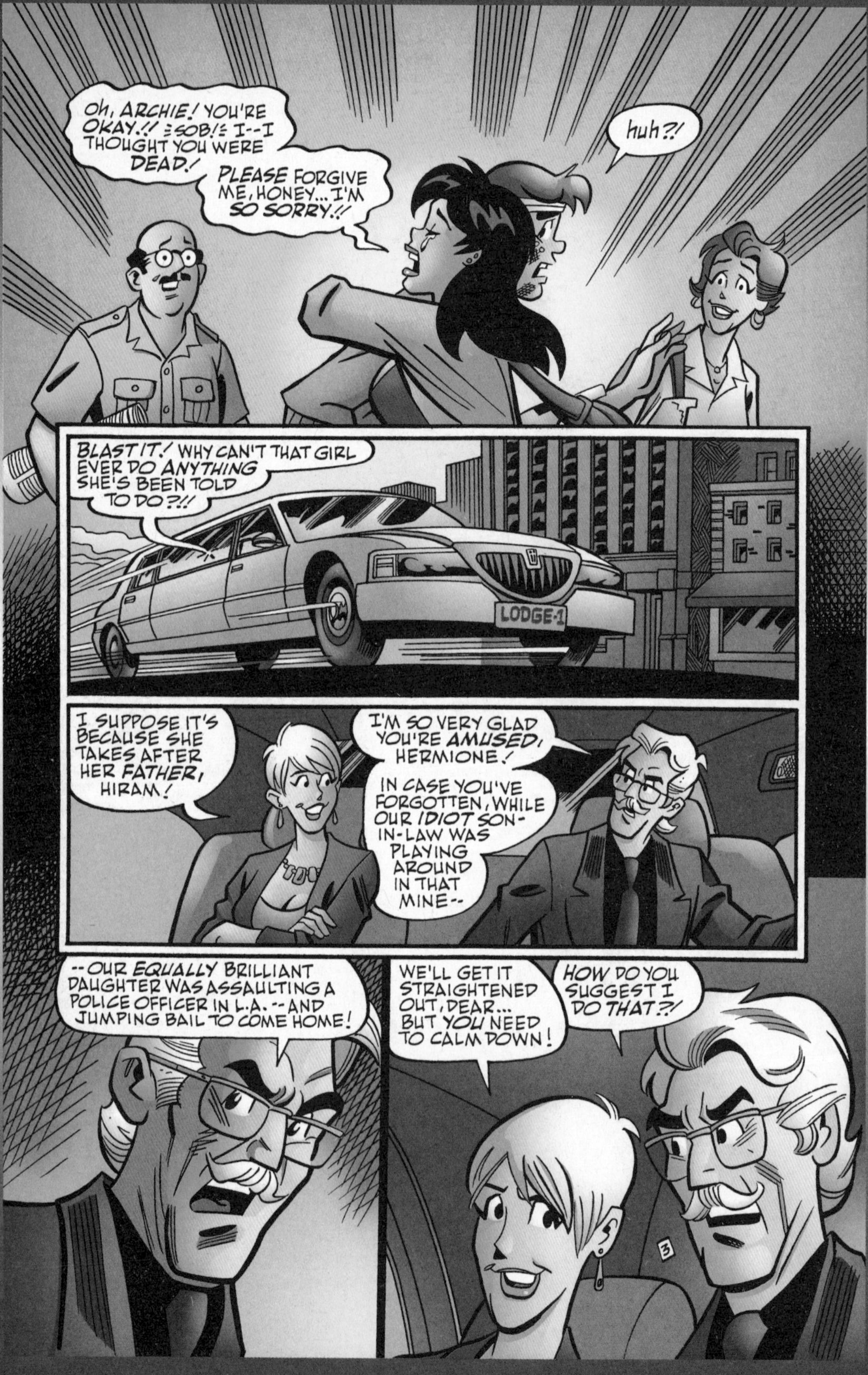

Oh, ARCHIE! YOU'RE OKAY.!! =SOB!= I--I THOUGHT YOU WERE DEAD!
PLEASE FORGIVE ME, HONEY... I'M SO SORRY.!!
huh?!
BLAST IT! WHY CAN'T THAT GIRL EVER DO ANYTHING SHE'S BEEN TOLD TO DO?!!
LODGE-1
I SUPPOSE IT'S BECAUSE SHE TAKES AFTER HER FATHER, HIRAM!
I'M SO VERY GLAD YOU'RE AMUSED, HERMIONE!
IN CASE YOU'VE FORGOTTEN, WHILE OUR IDIOT SON-IN-LAW WAS PLAYING AROUND IN THAT MINE--
--OUR EQUALLY BRILLIANT DAUGHTER WAS ASSAULTING A POLICE OFFICER IN L.A.--AND JUMPING BAIL TO COME HOME!
WE'LL GET IT STRAIGHTENED OUT, DEAR... BUT YOU NEED TO CALM DOWN!
HOW DO YOU SUGGEST I DO THAT?!
3

ON SALE IN NOVEMBER 2013!

HERE'S AN EXCLUSIVE SNEAK PEEK AT VOLUME FOUR OF THE MARRIED LIFE

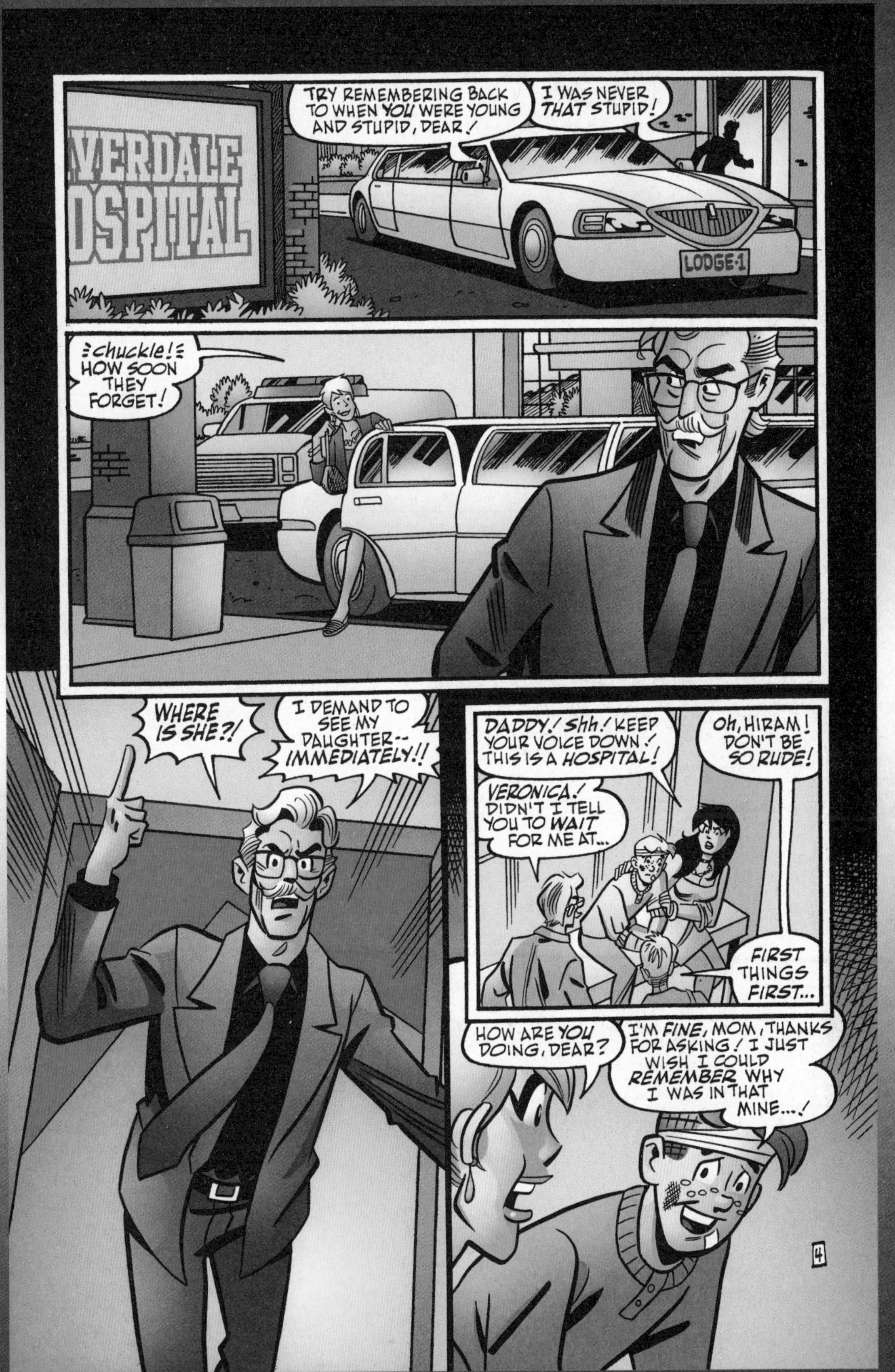
VERDALE
OSPITAL
TRY REMEMBERING BACK TO WHEN YOU WERE YOUNG AND STUPID, DEAR!
I WAS NEVER THAT STUPID!
LODGE-1
≶chuckle!≷ HOW SOON THEY FORGET!
WHERE IS SHE?!
I DEMAND TO SEE MY DAUGHTER-- IMMEDIATELY!!
DADDY! Shh! KEEP YOUR VOICE DOWN! THIS IS A HOSPITAL!
Oh, HIRAM! DON'T BE SO RUDE!
VERONICA! DIDN'T I TELL YOU TO WAIT FOR ME AT...
FIRST THINGS FIRST...
HOW ARE YOU DOING, DEAR?
I'M FINE, MOM, THANKS FOR ASKING! I JUST WISH I COULD REMEMBER WHY I WAS IN THAT MINE...!
4

ON SALE IN NOVEMBER 2013!

HERE'S AN EXCLUSIVE SNEAK PEEK AT VOLUME FOUR OF THE MARRIED LIFE

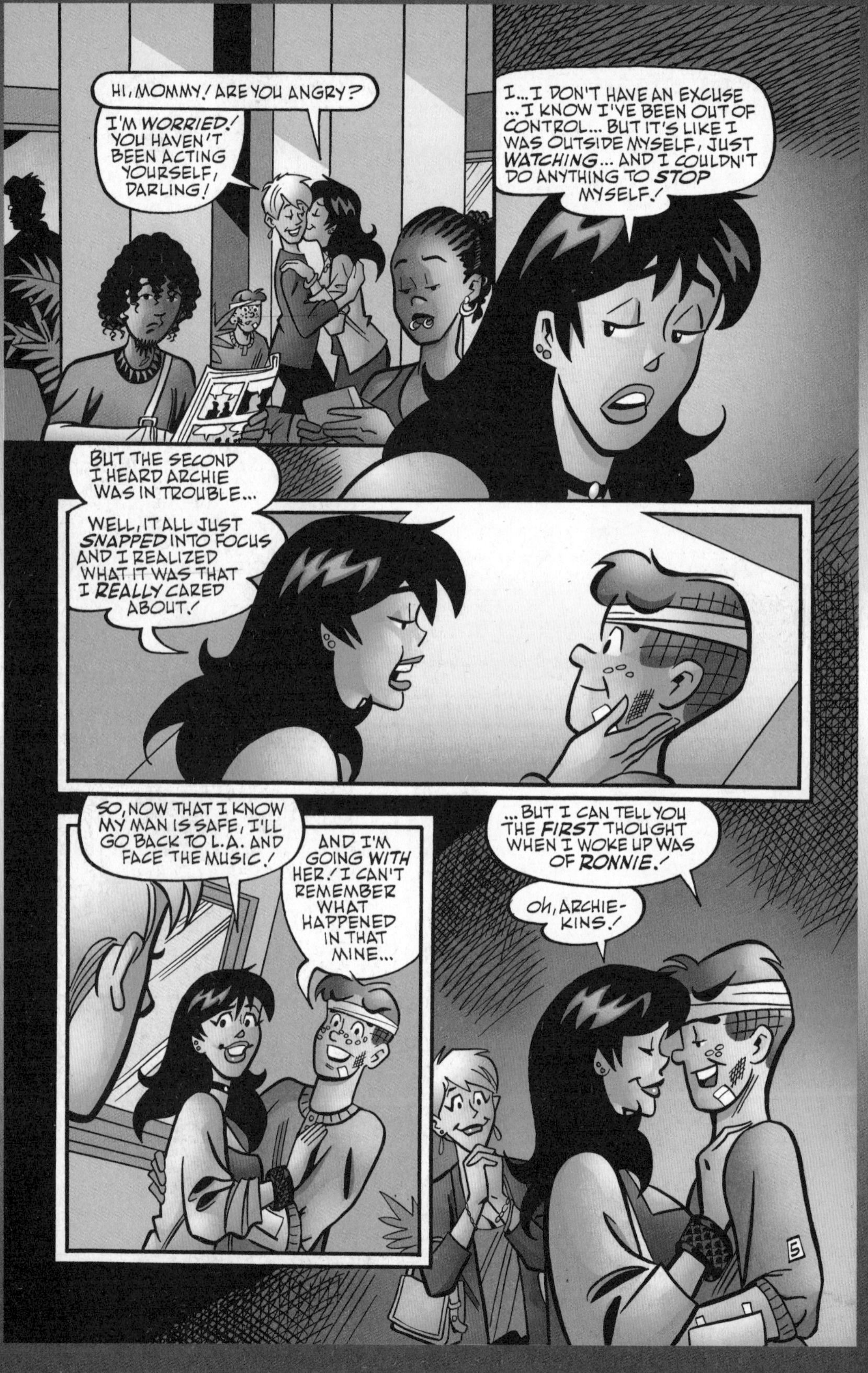
HI, MOMMY! ARE YOU ANGRY?
I'M WORRIED! YOU HAVEN'T BEEN ACTING YOURSELF, DARLING!
I... I DON'T HAVE AN EXCUSE ...I KNOW I'VE BEEN OUT OF CONTROL... BUT IT'S LIKE I WAS OUTSIDE MYSELF, JUST WATCHING... AND I COULDN'T DO ANYTHING TO STOP MYSELF!
BUT THE SECOND I HEARD ARCHIE WAS IN TROUBLE...
WELL, IT ALL JUST SNAPPED INTO FOCUS AND I REALIZED WHAT IT WAS THAT I REALLY CARED ABOUT!
SO, NOW THAT I KNOW MY MAN IS SAFE, I'LL GO BACK TO L.A. AND FACE THE MUSIC!
AND I'M GOING WITH HER! I CAN'T REMEMBER WHAT HAPPENED IN THAT MINE...
...BUT I CAN TELL YOU THE FIRST THOUGHT WHEN I WOKE UP WAS OF RONNIE!
Oh, ARCHIE-KINS!
5

ON SALE IN NOVEMBER 2013!

HERE'S AN EXCLUSIVE SNEAK PEEK AT VOLUME FOUR OF THE MARRIED LIFE

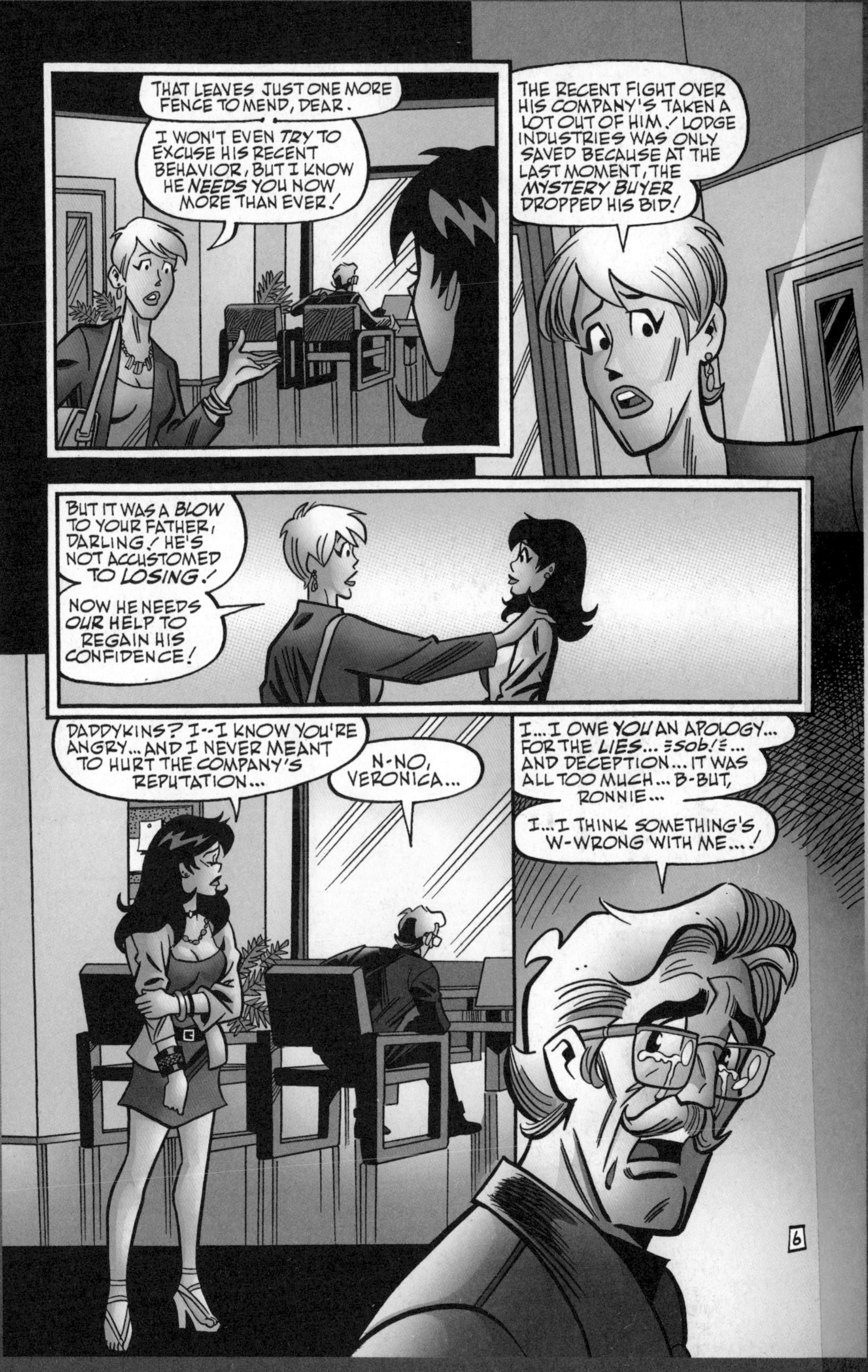
THAT LEAVES JUST ONE MORE FENCE TO MEND, DEAR.
I WON'T EVEN *TRY* TO EXCUSE HIS RECENT BEHAVIOR, BUT I KNOW HE *NEEDS* YOU NOW MORE THAN EVER!
THE RECENT FIGHT OVER HIS COMPANY'S TAKEN A LOT OUT OF HIM! LODGE INDUSTRIES WAS ONLY SAVED BECAUSE AT THE LAST MOMENT, THE *MYSTERY BUYER* DROPPED HIS BID!
BUT IT WAS A *BLOW* TO YOUR FATHER, DARLING! HE'S NOT ACCUSTOMED TO *LOSING*!
NOW HE NEEDS *OUR* HELP TO REGAIN HIS CONFIDENCE!
DADDYKINS? I--I KNOW YOU'RE ANGRY... AND I NEVER MEANT TO HURT THE COMPANY'S REPUTATION...
N-NO, VERONICA...
I... I OWE *YOU* AN APOLOGY... FOR THE *LIES*... *sob!*... AND DECEPTION... IT WAS ALL TOO MUCH... B-BUT, RONNIE...
I... I THINK SOMETHING'S W-WRONG WITH ME...!
6

ON SALE IN NOVEMBER 2013!

HERE'S AN EXCLUSIVE SNEAK PEEK AT VOLUME FOUR OF THE MARRIED LIFE

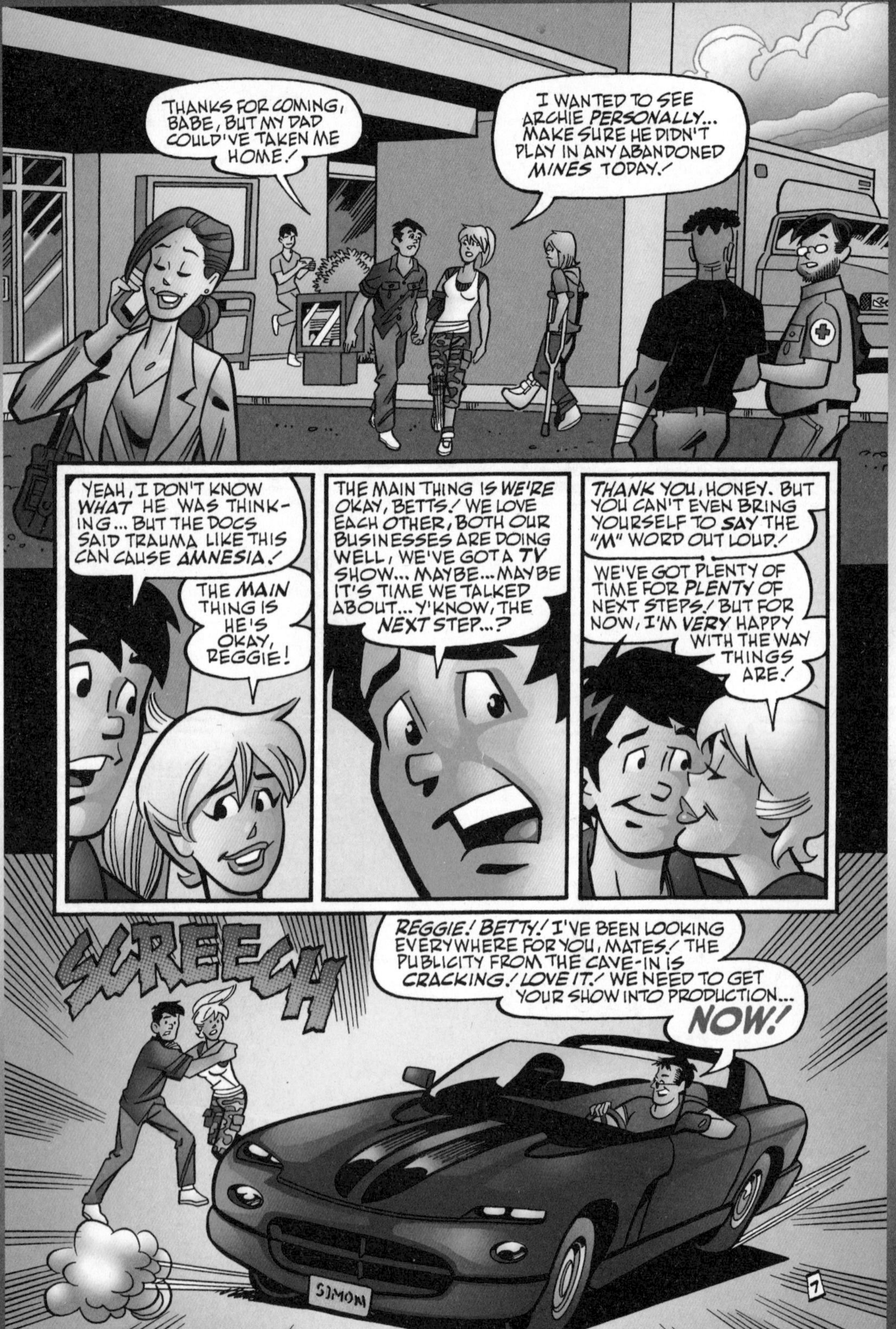
THANKS FOR COMING, BABE, BUT MY DAD COULD'VE TAKEN ME HOME!
I WANTED TO SEE ARCHIE PERSONALLY... MAKE SURE HE DIDN'T PLAY IN ANY ABANDONED MINES TODAY!
YEAH, I DON'T KNOW WHAT HE WAS THINKING... BUT THE DOCS SAID TRAUMA LIKE THIS CAN CAUSE AMNESIA!
THE MAIN THING IS HE'S OKAY, REGGIE!
THE MAIN THING IS WE'RE OKAY, BETTS! WE LOVE EACH OTHER, BOTH OUR BUSINESSES ARE DOING WELL, WE'VE GOT A TV SHOW... MAYBE... MAYBE IT'S TIME WE TALKED ABOUT... Y'KNOW, THE NEXT STEP...?
THANK YOU, HONEY. BUT YOU CAN'T EVEN BRING YOURSELF TO SAY THE "M" WORD OUT LOUD!
WE'VE GOT PLENTY OF TIME FOR PLENTY OF NEXT STEPS! BUT FOR NOW, I'M VERY HAPPY WITH THE WAY THINGS ARE!
SCREECH
REGGIE! BETTY! I'VE BEEN LOOKING EVERYWHERE FOR YOU, MATES! THE PUBLICITY FROM THE CAVE-IN IS CRACKING! LOVE IT! WE NEED TO GET YOUR SHOW INTO PRODUCTION... NOW!
SIMON
7

ON SALE IN NOVEMBER 2013!